A WHITE HOUSE DIARY

Book Seventeen
LOUANN ATKINS TEMPLE WOMEN & CULTURE SERIES

Books about women and families, and their changing role in society

A White House Diary

LADY BIRD JOHNSON

UNIVERSITY OF TEXAS PRESS Austin

The LBJ Library Foundation made a generous contribution to the
publication of this book.

*The Louann Atkins Temple Women & Culture Series is supported by
Allison, Doug, Taylor, and Andy Bacon; Margaret, Lawrence, Will,
John, and Annie Temple; Larry Temple; the Temple-Inland Foundation;
and the National Endowment for the Humanities.*

TO LYNDON, WITH LOVE

PREFACE

I began talking my White House diary into a tape recorder at our home, The Elms, two or three days after November 22, 1963. A little of it was recorded in hotel rooms on our trips, and in my bedroom at the LBJ Ranch, but the great bulk of it was done in a small room in the southwest corner of the second floor of the White House, which became a combination dressing room and office for me. I loved that room. I put my own furniture in it—my blue velvet sofa from The Elms (the back of it is faded from the sun that streamed in the southwest window), two comfortable French armchairs flanking the fireplace, and a desk that has followed me through all of my three Washington homes and now sits in the bay window in my "forever" bedroom at the Ranch. The walls were covered in the loveliest Chinese wallpaper I've ever seen. In winter, I often recorded sitting on the sofa looking at the fire burning merrily in the little corner fireplace. And in the summer I reversed one of the chairs and talked into my machine while I looked out over Andrew Jackson's magnolias to the Washington Monument—my favorite view in all of Washington, often outlined against the drama of sunset. Sometimes, I sat at the desk and looked right down into the Rose Garden and across to Lyndon's office. By all odds the best time to record was from about 7 in the evening till 9 or 10 or whatever late hour Lyndon came home to dinner. The day's activities were at an end, my staff had gone home, and this was "my time."

Why did I record it? I think for the following reasons: I realized shortly after November 22, that—amazed and timorously—I stood in a unique position, as wife of the President of the United States. Nobody else would live through the next months in quite the way that I would and see the events unroll from this vantage point. And this certain portion of time I wanted to preserve as it happened. I wanted to remember it, and I wanted my children and grandchildren to see it through my eyes. The second reason is a difficult one to describe—it has something to do with discipline. I wanted to see if I could keep up this arduous task. In a way, I made myself a dare. And somehow if you make yourself record what went on in the day, it makes you more organized, it makes you remember things better. My third reason for recording this White House diary was that I *like* writing—fearful labor though I sometimes find it—I like words. As time passed there began to emerge a fourth reason, dimly felt, something like this—I wanted to share life in this house, in these times. It was too great a thing to have alone.

I soon evolved the system of having a manila envelope for each day with a mimeographed sheet in it on which my secretary wrote the day's appointments. Then I would collect, or ask her to collect, two or three newspaper headlines of the day and stories that related to what Lyndon was doing, or I, or the children, speech cards if I made a speech, the schedule if I was on a trip. Or, if there was a White House entertainment, guest lists and menu and program. Then when I would record—and it might be the next day or two or three days later, or sometimes a week later—I would have the material at hand to put me back in the mood and the spirit of that day. The greatest help were the little shorthand notes I had jotted down in my daily schedule book. Gradually I, the most unmechanical of women, made friends with this little machine and learned how to thread it and change it, and hold it in abeyance while I thought of my next phrase.

A tape recorder makes for a far more verbose volume of work than a pencil in your hand. And so I left the White House in January of 1969 with a suitcase full of tapes, recorded over five full years and the brief six weeks or so of the year 1963, and the first twenty days of the year 1969, all in all a total, as well as I could estimate after it was transcribed, of about 1,750,000 words. During the last year and a half, I have re-read it all—and sometimes smiled wryly at my judgments and reactions of that time. I have tried to select from this mass of material days that would carry the narrative and convey the changing mood and feel and color of the times, hopefully significant days, but some quiet days. It has been a gargantuan job! Sometimes I have felt like William Faulkner, who is reported to have said to his editor when he was slashing out some of his favorite writing "You are killing my darlings!" The result is actually a "sampler" of my diary—a book of some 800 pages—using about one seventh of the material. But the full diary—many golden days that I loved living and writing about, and others that I'm afraid I made sound tedious and dull—will be in the Lyndon Baines Johnson Library and will in the future be available for scholars or historians to peruse, for whatever little crumbs of interest they may add to the story of our life and times.

Editing was not easy. I have tried as much as possible to use full days but could not avoid using sections from others. For the benefit of the reader I was told it was necessary to identify or give full names to people or events already familiar to me, thus intruding on the casual and sometimes intimate character of these recordings.

This diary is throughout completely personal and subjective. It is the way I saw and lived these events and knew these people. It is, if anything, the story of a family in a unique set of circumstances at a significant point in history.

I want to express my gratitude to everyone who has helped on this book, in editorial assistance, and research, and typing—to the wonderful staff, past and present—Charles Maguire, Harry Middleton, Walt Rostow, Mary Rather, Dorothy Nichols, Helene Lindow, Carole Bryant; to Dorothy Territo and her researchers; to the White House photographers—especially Yoichi Okamoto, Frank Wolfe, and Bob Knudsen; to Maggie Cousins and Liz Carpenter for their dedication to the task of helping to select which days and events should appear in the book; to Pace Barnes of Holt, Rinehart and Winston; to Arthur Krim who has shared so much; and to my family—Lyndon and Lynda Bird and Luci.

As I look back on those five years of turmoil and achievement, of triumph and pain, I feel amazement that it happened to me, and gratitude that I had the opportunity to live them, and strongest of all—out of all the trips that I made and all the people that I met—a deep, roaring faith in and love for this country.

Lady Bird Johnson

LBJ Ranch
August 15, 1970

BOOK ONE

1963-1964

Winter 1963–1964

DALLAS *Friday, November 22, 1963* It all began so beautifully. After a drizzle in the morning, the sun came out bright and clear. We were driving into Dallas. In the lead car were President and Mrs. Kennedy, John and Nellie Connally, a Secret Service car full of men, and then our car with Lyndon and me and Senator Ralph Yarborough.

The streets were lined with people—lots and lots of people —the children all smiling, placards, confetti, people waving from windows. One last happy moment I had was looking up and seeing Mary Griffith leaning out of a window waving at me. (Mary for many years had been in charge of altering the clothes which I purchased at Neiman-Marcus.)

Then, almost at the edge of town, on our way to the Trade Mart for the Presidential luncheon, we were rounding a curve, going down a hill, and suddenly there was a sharp, loud report. It sounded like a shot. The sound seemed to me to come from a building on the right above my shoulder. A moment passed, and then two more shots rang out in rapid succession.

3

There had been such a gala air about the day that I thought the noise must come from firecrackers—part of the celebration. Then the Secret Service men were suddenly down in the lead car. Over the car radio system, I heard "Let's get out of here!" and our Secret Service man, Rufus Youngblood, vaulted over the front seat on top of Lyndon, threw him to the floor, and said, "Get down."

Senator Yarborough and I ducked our heads. The car accelerated terrifically—faster and faster. Then, suddenly, the brakes were put on so hard that I wondered if we were going to make it as we wheeled left and went around the corner. We pulled up to a building. I looked up and saw a sign, "HOSPITAL." Only then did I believe that this might be what it was. Senator Yarborough kept saying in an excited voice, "Have they shot the President? Have they shot the President?" I said something like, "No, it can't be."

As we ground to a halt—we were still the third car—Secret Service men began to pull, lead, guide, and hustle us out. I cast one last look over my shoulder and saw in the President's car a bundle of pink, just like a drift of blossoms, lying on the back seat. It was Mrs. Kennedy lying over the President's body.

The Secret Service men rushed us to the right, then to the left, and then onward into a quiet room in the hospital—a very small room. It was lined with white sheets, I believe.

People came and went—Kenny O'Donnell, the President's top aide, Congressman Homer Thornberry, Congressman Jack Brooks. Always there was Rufe right there and other Secret Service agents—Emory Roberts, Jerry Kivett, Lem Johns, and Woody Taylor. People spoke of how widespread this might be. There was talk about where we would go—to the plane, to our house, back to Washington.

Through it all Lyndon was remarkably calm and quiet. He suggested that the Presidential plane ought to be moved to another part of the field. He spoke of going back out to the plane in unmarked black cars. Every face that came in, you searched for the answer. I think the face I kept seeing the answer on was the face of Kenny O'Donnell, who loved President Kennedy so much.

It was Lyndon who spoke of it first, although I knew I would not leave without doing it. He said, "You had better try to see Jackie and Nellie." We didn't know what had happened to John.

I asked the Secret Service if I could be taken to them. They began to lead me up one corridor and down another. Suddenly I found myself face to face with Jackie in a small hallway. I believe it was right outside the operating room. You always think of someone like her as being insulated, protected. She was quite alone. I don't think I ever saw anyone so much alone in my life. I went up to her, put my arms around her, and said something to her. I'm sure it was something like "God, help us all," because my feelings for her were too tumultuous to put into words.

And then I went to see Nellie. There it was different, because Nellie and I have gone through so many things together since 1938. I hugged her tight and we both cried and I said, "Nellie, John's going to be all right." And Nellie said, "Yes, John's going to be all right." Among her many other fine qualities, she is also strong.

I turned and went back to the small white room where Lyndon was. Mac Kilduff, the President's press man on this trip, and Kenny O'Donnell were coming and going. I think it was from Kenny's face that I first knew the truth and from Kenny's voice that I first heard the words "The President is dead." Mr. Kilduff entered and said to Lyndon, "Mr. President."

It was decided that we would go immediately to the airport. Hurried plans were made about how we should get to the cars and who was to ride in which car. Our departure from the hospital and approach to the cars was one of the swiftest walks I have ever made.

We got in. Lyndon told the agents to stop the sirens. We drove along as fast as we could. I looked up at a building and there, already, was a flag at half-mast. I think that was when the enormity of what had happened first struck me.

When we got to the field, we entered *Air Force One* for the first time. There was a TV set on and the commentator was saying, "Lyndon B. Johnson, now President of the United States." The news commentator was saying the President had been shot with a 30-30 rifle. The police had a suspect. They were not sure he was the assassin.

On the plane, all the shades were lowered. We heard that we were going to wait for Mrs. Kennedy and the coffin. There was a telephone call to Washington—I believe to the Attorney General. It was decided that Lyndon should be sworn in here as quickly as possible, because of national and world implications, and because we did not know how widespread this was as to intended victims. Judge Sarah Hughes, a Federal Judge in Dallas—and I am glad it was she—was called and asked to come in a hurry to administer the oath.

Mrs. Kennedy had arrived by this time, as had the coffin. There, in the very narrow confines of the plane—with Jackie standing by Lyndon, her hair falling in her face but very composed, with me beside him, Judge Hughes in front of him, and a cluster of Secret Service people, staff, and Congressmen we had known for a long time around him—Lyndon took the oath of office.

It's odd the little things that come to your mind at times of utmost stress, the flashes of deep compassion you feel for people who are really not at the center of the tragedy. I heard a Secret Service man say in the most desolate voice—and I hurt for him: "We never lost a President in the Service." Then, Police Chief Curry of Dallas came on the plane and said, "Mrs. Kennedy, believe me, we did everything we possibly could." That must have been an agonizing moment for him.

We all sat around the plane. The casket was in the corridor. I went in the small private room to see Mrs. Kennedy, and though it was a very hard thing to do, she made it as easy as possible. She said things like, "Oh, Lady Bird, we've liked you two so much. . . . Oh, what if I had not been there. I'm so glad I was there."

I looked at her. Mrs. Kennedy's dress was stained with blood. One leg was almost entirely covered with it and her right glove was caked, it was caked with blood—her husband's blood. Somehow that was one of the most poignant sights—that immaculate woman exquisitely dressed, and caked in blood.

I asked her if I couldn't get someone in to help her change and she said, "Oh, no. Perhaps later I'll ask Mary Gallagher but not right now." And then with almost an element of fierceness—if a person that gentle, that dignified, can be said to have such a quality—she said, "I want them to see what they have done to Jack."

I tried to express how we felt. I said, "Oh, Mrs. Kennedy, you know we never even wanted to be Vice President and now, dear God, it's come to this." I would have done anything to help her, but there was nothing I could do, so rather quickly I left and went back to the main part of the airplane where everyone was seated.

The flight to Washington was silent, each sitting with his own thoughts. One of mine was a recollection of what I had said about Lyndon a long time ago—he's a good man in a tight spot. I remembered one little thing he had said in that hospital room—"Tell the children to get a Secret Service man with them."

Finally we got to Washington, with a cluster of people waiting and many bright lights. The casket went off first, then Mrs. Kennedy, and then we followed. The family had come to join her. Lyndon made a very simple, very brief, and, I think, strong statement to the people there. Only about four sentences. We got in helicopters, dropped him off at the White House, and I came home in a car with Liz Carpenter.

Saturday, November 23

THE ELMS, WASHINGTON

Today the President lay in state in the White House. It was a gray day, suited to the occasion.

I went down to the Executive Office Building to meet Lyndon and we went over to the White House and met the Kennedy family in the Green Room. Lyndon walked slowly past the President's body in the East Room. The catafalque was in the center and on it the casket, draped with the American flag. At each corner there was a large candle and a very rigid military man, representing each one of the services. At one end was a Catholic image, I don't know quite what it was. It wasn't just a cross, but more elaborate. That was the first time in those three days that I was reminded, caught up in the thought, that the Catholic faith has a pattern for everything—a pattern for life, and a pattern for death.

Others were there besides the family of the President—the Cabinet, Congressional leaders, the Supreme Court, and White House staff. An air of quiet prevailed, an utter, complete quiet that seemed to grip—well, the whole country, I suppose—and certainly the surroundings where I spent the entire three days.

Part of the Cabinet had been called back from half way around the world. They were on a plane bound for Japan when they heard the news in mid-air and turned the plane around and returned. They were here now, standing shocked and sad-faced, filing past as all of us had filed past, like automatons. There was black crepe on the chandeliers.

After we left the White House we went to a brief service at St. John's Episcopal Church, right across Lafayette Square, a very "high church" —a stern, rigid church—but most fitting for the day. And then we went on —and what we did the rest of the day, I don't remember. I am sure Lyndon worked terribly hard. I collapsed with Luci.

I thought—I will have to sell our house, give up control of my business, see about getting Lynda Bird to come back and live in Washington with

7 / BOOK ONE: 1963–1964

us and go to school somewhere up here (and that will be a selling job!). There are all the million and one things to be done—just the simple things that are part of going on living, if one is among those who are going to go on living. Lyndon will be wrestling with the very big business of making the country go on living.

Sunday, November 24

This was the day that President Kennedy lay in state at the Capitol. It was a day I will never forget—nor will the people of America. In contrast to yesterday, it was a bright, clear day of sparkling sun. We began by going to St. Marks to church, with Luci and Congressman Thornberry. There was a haunting line in Bill Baxter's sermon—something about how every man who had fostered, or had permitted to be fostered around him, an atmosphere of hate had had his hand on the gun barrel that day.

After church we went to the White House and waited in the Green Room for the Kennedy family. After they came Mrs. Sargent Shriver turned to me and said, "I hear Oswald has been killed." It was the first news I had had about Oswald.

We were told by protocol officials that we would ride with Mrs. Kennedy and the Attorney General. Suddenly Mrs. Kennedy came in, leading John Jr. with one hand and Caroline with the other, the children looking small and so dear in little blue coats. Then I realized there would be six of us in the car and I wondered if the arrangement shouldn't be changed —if we shouldn't ride in another car. But it turned out that we all got into the same limousine—Mrs. Kennedy and Lyndon in the back seat, the Attorney General and I in the jump seats, Caroline next to her mother, and John-John, in a peripatetic mood, jumping from the back seat to his uncle's lap to the front seat and back again.

As soon as we emerged from the gates of the White House, I became aware of that sea of faces stretching away on every side—silent, watching faces. I wanted to cry for them and with them, but it was impossible to permit the catharsis of tears. I don't know quite why, except that perhaps continuity of strength demands restraint. Another reason was that the dignity of Mrs. Kennedy and the members of the family demanded it.

In front of us was a handsome, black, riderless horse, carrying reversed boots. I recognized this at once as the symbol of the fallen leader, but I didn't really know much about the tradition. I asked Lynda Bird later and she said the custom went long back into history, back to Genghis Khan, when the leader's horse was always sacrificed at the grave. A few centuries ago they abolished that part of the ritual.

In front of the horse was a caisson, drawn by six white horses; the caisson itself was draped with the flag. Soldiers were marching, and always there was the sound of muffled drums in the background. Flags flew at half-mast. But most vivid of all was the feeling of a sea of faces all around us and that curious sense of silence, broken only by an occasional sob. I kept on comparing it in my mind with the time Franklin Roosevelt died, but that was so different, because then everybody could be as emotional as they felt like being. The feeling persisted that I was moving, step by step, through a Greek tragedy. I remembered a definition from college days—that a Greek tragedy is concerned with a noble protagonist overtaken by an inevitable doom. There is a third ingredient but I can't remember it. Some time I must look it up.

We were a silent group as we rode along, each wrapped in his own thoughts. The only light moments came from John-John, who jumped from the back to his uncle's lap to the front, until finally Bobby Kennedy said, "John-John, be good, you be good, and we'll give you a flag afterward. You can march with Dave Powers."

The only time the Attorney General said anything else was when we passed a big building on the left, and he looked over and said (I think as though to himself, or perhaps to the children), "That was where it all began. That was where he ran for the Presidency." His face was grave, white, sorrowful, and there was a flinching of the jaw at that moment that almost made—well, it made your soul flinch for him.

After that interminable drive we reached the Capitol and entered the Rotunda. In the center, directly underneath the dome, stood the flag-draped coffin with the honor guard around it. One of them, I noticed, wore the green beret. There were eulogies by Chief Justice Earl Warren, by Speaker John McCormack, and by Senator Mansfield. I shall never forget Mike Mansfield's speech—he, that most precise and restrained of men, repeated over and over the phrase "and she took a ring from her finger and placed it on his hand."

Lyndon went forward and laid a wreath at the foot of the casket. Then Mrs. Kennedy went over and knelt. I remember how carefully she knelt and kissed the casket, and Caroline by her side simply put her little hand on the flag—sort of underneath the flag. John-John had disappeared. And then we left in separate cars.

To me, one of the saddest things in the whole tragedy was that Mrs. Kennedy achieved on this desperate day something she had never quite achieved in the years she'd been in the White House—a state of love, a state of rapport between herself and the people of this country. Her behavior from the moment of the shot until I last saw her was, to me, one of the most memorable things of all. Maybe it was a combination of great breeding, great discipline, great character. I only know it was great. Her composure is one of the things that keeps on coming back to me. Another is the contrast with the death of FDR, because this time there's something much worse about it. There is shame for the violence and hatred that has gripped our land. But there is also a determination to help wipe it out!

When we got home early in the afternoon, after that emotionally exhausting experience, I began to think of Lynda Bird, and I decided, difficult as it was for her to come up from Texas and go right back in a day or two, I was going to call and ask her to catch a plane and come for the President's funeral. In spite of the difference in age and eminence, Lynda Bird had never felt anything of a gulf between herself and President Kennedy, so I wanted her to be here. I called her and she said she could pack in ten or fifteen minutes. She arrived about 10:30 tonight.

Tuesday, November 26

Now the time has come to get the wheels of life rolling again—so Mr. J. B. West, Head Usher of the White House, came out to The Elms this morning and we talked about moving three suites of furniture to occupy the rooms that will soon be vacant—my bedroom suite to go into Mrs. Kennedy's room, Lynda Bird's probably into Caroline's, and Luci's into John-John's. We discussed what furniture could be stored at the White House and how much I would need to send to commercial or government warehouses. It was one of my first encounters with Mr. West, and I have the feeling that I will be seeing a lot more of him.

At 3 this afternoon came the most important event of the day. Mrs. Kennedy had asked me to come to the White House to discuss the housekeeping details, which any woman moving out would talk over with any woman moving in. A lovely tea table was spread, and we sat down together in the private sitting room—the family sitting room on the second floor called the West Hall.

She was orderly, composed, and radiating her particular sort of aliveness and charm and warmth. Mrs. Kennedy is like an indescribably fresh flower—so I won't try to describe her, except that there is an element of steel and stamina somewhere within her to keep her going on as she is. She told me that two people in the house that I could always depend on were Mr. West, who knew more about it than anybody else, and Mr. James Ketchum, the Curator.

She said, "Lady Bird, never tell a waiter if you don't like this particular type of cookie that you would rather have a macaroon, because you will not see that particular butler again for two weeks. He'll be gone on vacation or working in another part of the mansion. Just tell everything to Mr. West."

She told me she would like to ask a favor of me. The way she asked this, if it had been a request to chop off one's right hand one would have said, "Sure," just that minute. What she wanted was to let the school continue on the third floor where Caroline and about twenty of her young playmates in the kindergarten and the first grade go to school. They will make other plans after Christmas, but they thought it would not be a good idea to disrupt the school right now. It was an easy, most delightful thing to say "Yes" to.

She went on to say a lot of things, like "Don't be frightened of this house—some of the happiest years of my marriage have been spent here —you will be happy here." In fact, she repeated that over and over, as though she were trying to reassure me. Then we got up and walked around from room to room so that I could see how my furniture would fit into her bedroom. We went into her sitting room (or perhaps it should be called a dressing room)—one of the most exquisite rooms I have ever seen, with the closet doors covered with bright and beautiful trompe l'oeils —little pictures of *Profiles in Courage*, Caroline at two, a yacht at Hyannis Port—all the things that mean something to her—a stamp or trademark that will not be repeated by anybody for a long time. For me, so much work will have to come first that I expect the room will be turned into an office rather than a dressing room, and it will get short shrift, at least these first few months.

We talked about the staff. She said that the French chef, René Verdon, was "absolutely divine," although everything he did for them was "very rich." She used the words "Jack never likes those rich things that René does." Neither one of us noticed the present tense—or rather neither one of us showed that we had noticed it. She said René has absolutely no temperament, which is "divine in a Frenchman"—that I was fortunate to have him.

We walked through the hall and Jackie pointed out a bust by Houdon, circa 1795, of Joel Barlow, Chaplain in George Washington's Army. She told me of the incredible value that is put on this art object. It was an anonymous gift—anonymous, I hope, to everybody except the Internal Revenue Service! We went into the lovely Yellow Room where the Cézannes hang, and this room, obviously, is what Mrs. Kennedy likes best in the whole house—or so I gathered. There on the table were the black boots—the boots that were on the riderless horse in the funeral procession. There was also a folded flag.

Then we went into the two rooms that are now Caroline's and John-John's. And such exquisite gay little confections of rooms—Caroline's especially, delicate pink-and-white sprigged material on a canopy bed, with pictures, pictures, pictures everywhere—some of them crayons done by the children themselves, I think, and I believe one or two painted by Mrs. Kennedy. There were several Kennedy family members running in and out of doors as we wended our very businesslike way through the halls.

Finally, about 5, we went to the East Room, where Lyndon was meeting with the Alliance for Progress members to reassure them of our country's continued strength and interest in them. We took our seats very quietly behind him and listened to his speech. It is doubtful that anyone else is a star when Mrs. Kennedy is present—but all the more my heart went out to the bravery of Lyndon, who marches into this circumstance with so much determination and not all the preparation that one would have sought, if one could have foreseen one's destiny at sixteen.

In the evening I went home to dinner at The Elms and the companionship of a few close friends.

Monday, December 2

Lyndon presented the Enrico Fermi Award to Dr. Robert Oppenheimer in the Cabinet Room late this afternoon in an atmosphere charged with drama. The event was the climax of a story that has gone into its third decade, beginning in the 1940's when Dr. Oppenheimer was Director of Los Alamos Scientific Laboratory in New Mexico, where he helped produce the first atomic bomb. In the aftermath of the war, when so many were being questioned as to their association with Communists and he came under public suspicion, President Eisenhower ordered a blank wall placed between him and secret information—in other words, he took away Oppenheimer's security clearance. Now, in the sixties, the last act of the drama occurs. Oppenheimer, in receiving the Fermi Award, is having his name cleared and his reputation upheld before the American public once more as a great scientist who has served his country well.

I felt that I was in the front-row seat of a good Broadway production. Dr. Oppenheimer is a lean, pale, white-haired man who looks as if he has been seared in the fires of public suspicion and doubt. He is a living example of how somebody survives that, and it must be one of the cruelest ordeals a person can live through.

Dr. Oppenheimer's wife stood by him—a gentle-faced, happy, sensible-looking woman. She must have helped her husband keep his sanity when it was all going on. His children, Katherine and Peter, were there as well as a group of his friends; also the senior Democrats on the Atomic Energy Committee; Dr. Edward Teller, once his chief adversary on the question of whether to develop the hydrogen bomb; and Dr. Henry Smyth, the lone dissenter in the 4-to-1 Commission decision when Dr. Oppenheimer lost his security clearance. Notably absent were the ranking Republicans—reportedly some had sent word that they could not, in good conscience, attend.

Lyndon praised Dr. Oppenheimer as a leader of learning and a scientist who had set high standards of achievement. Dr. Oppenheimer responded with a reply about Thomas Jefferson and the brotherhood of science, and then, speaking in a low voice, he said: "I think it is just possible, Mr. President, that it has taken some charity and some courage for you to make this award today. That would seem to be a good augury for all our futures."

I wonder if anybody knows how often one has to dare to use that courage and charity and how there are a good many times when you cannot foretell the long-term outcome of your actions and cannot be entirely sure you are doing the right thing. That's the painful thing about this job. In this case, I have the happy feeling that it *was* the right thing and I am glad to see Dr. Oppenheimer come out from under the shadow.

Lyndon got a laugh when he gave the handsome gold medal to Dr. Oppenheimer and then turned to hand the $50,000 check to Mrs. Oppenheimer and said: "The wives usually get hold of the money." In this case, Lyndon was only the agent, because the citation had been signed by President Kennedy a short while before the assassination.

We went on home to dinner at The Elms with Drew and Luvie Pearson, sitting in front of a fire made with Drew's own wood. There were also Justice and Mrs. Arthur Goldberg and Bess Abell, my Social Secretary, with Tyler, her husband. I keep thinking that Justice Goldberg, with his rampant energy and his warm feeling of working for his fellow human beings, his shrewdness and his humor, is oddy removed from the fray of public life in the cool halls of the Supreme Court. I always love to hear Dorothy Goldberg talk about art and we discussed her book. Luvie Pearson talked about her work with a group of women who are teaching the rudiments of reading to underprivileged children here in the District of Columbia. She's the spearhead of the movement. I take off my hat to people who really spend the days of their lives doing something like that.

Saturday, December 7

THE WHITE HOUSE

We are now moved into the White House, at least partially, but we shall be bringing things down for months, as I sort out and store and send to the ranch or storage the accumulation of twenty-six years of living in various houses in Washington.

Mr. West notified us that Mrs. Kennedy had left and this afternoon the house was ready for us to move in. It will be infinitely more convenient for Lyndon and the staff, who have been working in makeshift arrangements, but both of us have loved The Elms and hate to close its door.

The press has been asking, over and over since President Kennedy's funeral, when we were moving in. Several days ago I became rather impatient with that staccato question and simply told Liz Carpenter (now my staff director and Press Secretary), "I would to God I could serve Mrs. Kennedy's comfort; I can at least serve her convenience." Liz told them just what I said and the question seems to have abated for a while. I know it must be difficult for Mrs. Kennedy to gather everything together in the agonizing aftermath of the assassination.

But the call came today to move, and Luci took the two beagles, "Him" and "Her," in her birthday convertible, and I got in another car, taking Liz and Bess with me so we could carry some of the breakable objects. I had our favorite picture of the Speaker, Mr. Sam Rayburn, in my hand. His is the only photograph of a person that we keep in our living room wherever we are, and I wanted it with us at the White House. His face is comforting at this milestone, just as he was at so many happier ones.

When we drove through the gates, several newswomen awaited us. That is a whole new adjustment for me—having every move watched and covered and considered news. I want to be fair, but I am sure that even at this most public address—1600 Pennsylvania Avenue—there are moments which are rightfully private.

Since we stepped off the plane on the night of November 22, there have been relentless demands for interviews—hundreds of them from all parts of the world. We have fended them off and directed them to Pierre Salinger. Now the time has come to lift this burden from his shoulders. Liz has been meeting with various groups of newswomen to seek their advice on the most efficient way to handle their needs. I want a workable formula that will allow us to live happily together—the press and me. I know many of them personally, value their friendship, and I respect their profession. Liz has combined their thoughts into a memo which boils down to two basic requests: "Be Available" and "Never Lie—tell us you can't tell us, but never lie." Well, I see no problems on either score, though I am sure there will be times when I will flinch from so many spectators looking into this glass house. But we can try. We can be cognizant of their needs and considerate of their deadlines.

When we arrived, Mr. West was waiting at the door for us and greeted Luci and me and took us to the second floor. He has worked at the White House for twenty-three years and is now Head Usher—a totally undescriptive title. If he were at court he would be called Head Chamberlain, for his job embraces everything required to make this 132-room house operate smoothly. A few days ago when we visited with Tish Baldridge [Mrs. Kennedy's former Social Secretary], she called him "Mr. Wonderful," and I can already see why. He finds solutions to so many problems with quiet efficiency.

I decided that one of the first things I wanted to do was to meet the people who staff the household. I asked Mr. West to introduce me to all of them, for I want to know personally the people I shall be working with. By now, in fits and starts as they were on duty, I have met and shaken hands with what seemed to me dozens of butlers, maids, cleaning men. Bess Abell, my Social Secretary, went with me, and Liz went off to the East Wing to that ever-ringing telephone from newswomen who wanted to know the details of moving day. I told Liz when the need arises to use the library for briefings and to be sure the fire is lighted, and hot tea ready. During these past few days I have seen Isabelle Shelton, Nan Robertson, Frances Lewine, Helen Thomas, and Nancy Dickerson standing hour after hour at the funeral and then outside The Elms well into the night. They must be exhausted and chilled to the bone.

Late this afternoon Walter Jenkins [Special Assistant to the President] and his wife Marjorie thoughtfully invited us to dinner at their home. There is nothing nicer than being invited out after a busy moving day. So I called Lyndon and we quickly accepted. Perhaps this also gave a breathing spell to the staff here at the White House who must have been carrying on with heavy hearts. We had a nice evening, comfortable with close friends. That is, we were as comfortable as you can be knowing that out in front are dozens of reporters and TV cameras waiting for you to leave. Well, I daresay they are uncomfortable too.

The whole country is still numb from the tragedy and it is hard to sort out the days and encompass all that has happened, but I keep reminding myself of Lyndon, for whom it is hardest of all to carry on. I find myself repeating that "new resolve" which he urged on all of us last week in his speech to Congress. Our challenge, he said, is "not to hesitate, not to pause, not to turn about and linger over this evil moment but to continue on our course so that we may fulfill the destiny that history has set for us."

That, we in this house must do most of all, but as I told Nellie Connally the other day when I talked to her over the phone, I feel like I am suddenly onstage for a part I never rehearsed.

Saturday, December 14

This has been the most restful day since November 22. I slept late and read the papers as much as possible. Then I spent several hours at The Elms. What a job, trying to sell that house I had filled with much love and some taste, I hope, and a great deal of care! It took me three or four months to decorate it and get settled in it. Now I must dismantle it in a couple of weeks, taking into consideration what Lynda and Luci might want when they get married. I must decide what furniture might appreciate in value and what could depreciate, and what I must leave behind in order to effect a good sale for the house.

Today Luci had a handsome young midshipman from the Academy over, LeRoy Bates, and I was so happy to see children and laughter in the White House. There were several young girls here too and just watching them dashing about the halls made me feel good.

Then for dinner, not forgetting the big business of future legislation, we had a representative group and their wives from the Hill: Hale Boggs, Albert Thomas, Wilbur Mills, and Jack Brooks—he's one of the liveliest people I know—Carl Albert alone (Mrs. Albert was ill), the Gerald Fords— he's a Republican leader—and, of course, Homer Thornberry, our own Congressman.

The conversation was about recognizing the Dominican Republic and naming Tom Mann [former Ambassador to Mexico] to—I don't quite know the title—an all-over Latin American Administrator in the State Department. And most of all, the talk among the men was about the Tax Bill, the Tax Bill, the Tax Bill.

In the course of the evening I took the ladies to see our bedrooms and was touched and pleased to see how interested they were. I also discovered some pretty interesting things—for instance, that Carl Albert is quite an authority on the Catlin Indian pictures in the hall. And everyone, of course, loved seeing the Treaty Room with the chandelier which came from Lyndon's old office, P-38, his habitat as Majority Leader and later as Vice President.

So it was a good evening, but what depths of friendship we really have and what feelings of warmth it created remains to be seen. At any rate, the Hill is my Hill, and the people of the House and the Senate who make it up are so many of the people I care a lot about. Besides just plain liking Gerald Ford, it is nice to remember that Betty Ford and I came to the Eighty-first Club together. (That's a club consisting of the wives whose husbands were elected to the Eighty-first Congress in 1948.) I hope there will be a lot more nights like tonight.

Wednesday, December 18

Eva Adams, Director of the Mint, came over this morning with Gilroy Roberts, a sculptor, to show me a head of Lyndon that he is doing. It's a model for the Presidential medal. (Every President must have his likeness struck for the Presidential medal.) They wanted my opinion of it. I think the hardest thing for a sculptor to capture is the eyes, and the eyes were wonderful, and the brow and the shape of the head. (Lyndon, I think, has a rather magnificently shaped head.) The ears were just as big as Lyndon's are and I wouldn't have them the slightest bit smaller. The mouth I didn't really like much. It had an almost too beneficent look, a look I have seen many times and like. But I think for the purposes at hand there is another attribute more true to his life—a certain grimness—or determination. I suggested a slight change in the mouth. Mr. Roberts made the change—and I liked it better.

Next I went up to the third floor to see the school where Caroline's kindergarten and first-grade classes are held. I had been looking forward to this very much. There were between twenty and thirty children in the charming, round room, which looks out onto the Washington Monument. The room is filled with small tables and chairs, its walls gay with the children's crayon pictures. I went around and shook hands with each child and told them my name and they told me theirs. The little girls curtsied and the little boys bowed.

Caroline had on a red Christmasy dress, with Tyrolean green appliquéd designs on it. She stood and looked at me the longest of anybody. That child has the most beautiful eyes. It was almost the last day of school before Christmas, and they'll be picking up school someplace else after the holidays.

Saturday, December 21

I believe I am about to catch my second wind.

At 10 this morning a nice young assistant from Miss Genevieve Hendricks' decorating shop came over with loads of samples of chintz, pretty things, and we explored Lynda's and Luci's bedrooms and the possibility of a little sitting room for Luci and decided what would be pretty with what. We looked into the room here in the White House where they kept the stored furniture and had various pieces moved in, remembering always Lyndon's watchword—"economy, economy"—because I mustn't buy anything if something we already have might do. I think we found some nice things but I have to look at them over and over and then decide.

It was about that time that I got the shattering news. Congress had thrown up a few roadblocks. . . . They were not going to adjourn, so we were not going home Sunday. In other words, things were in just about as bad a state of inactivity with regard to legislative matters as they could be.

I had some feeling of the amount of effort Lyndon must have put into trying to make this a productive day in Congress, his old home. So I went over to his office, knowing full well there wasn't anything I could really do, but just with the same instinct that leads you to call on a sick friend, knowing this was a bad time for Lyndon and wanting to pat him on the back.

Monday, December 23

Gone is the black mourning crepe that swathed the great crystal chandeliers in the State Rooms and draped the high doorways. The flags, at half-mast this long month, now rise—and with them my spirits.

The sense of pall that held the house in hushed quiet has lifted, and we can begin to turn our eyes to Christmas! The mantels are bright with holly and the house smells of evergreen. I have put my small wardrobe of black dresses, worn every day since that day in November, in the back of the closet and put on my Christmas red.

Christmas Eve, Tuesday, December 24

LBJ RANCH

The House of Representatives met very early this morning to pass the Foreign Aid Bill. The bill passed, thanks to a tremendous effort by a lot of people, and this released us from our bondage. So we left Washington about 9:30, choppered to Andrews, flew to Philadelphia for the funeral of Congressman William Green, and from there on to Austin.

The first thing we did in Austin was to go by the Governor's Mansion to see John and Nellie. They were there, lined up on the back porch— John with his arm in a black sling and looking, as cattlemen would call him, "drawn." He appears older and in pain, but he is fine and so handsome. Nellie was smiling again, and there were cute little Sharon and Mark. We had some coffee and a good visit, and continued our journey home.

We decided to visit our neighboring ranchers, the A. W. Moursunds, on the way, and it was just about sunset. Lyndon got in the car with A. W. and there they went, away to get lost over the horizon. How often I have seen that picture; how much I like it; and what a real release. They might do a little deer hunting, but they'll do a lot more talking. I returned immediately to the Ranch to find the house a good deal changed by my friend Nancy Negley, at my request. And most of it I liked very much. The Alexanders (Lyndon's sister and her family)—Lucia, Becky, and Birge—soon came up to join us. And Cousin Oriole, who brought along Aunt Jessie Hatcher, came over from her house. (They are two elderly relatives of Lyndon's.)

There are some changes about the Ranch that I don't like. For instance, there are two enormous silver saucers, pointing to the sky. I suppose they're radar and have something to do with the landing strip. At each entrance gate, there's a little white cubicle of a guard house, with the guardsman in it, who checks everybody who comes and goes. And all around the house, front and back, large searchlights project out into the night, so that we will never be quite settled into the anonymity of darkness. The place is also abristle with Secret Service men aided by Texas Highway Patrolmen. Much is changed. The impact of this, I suppose, will gradually get through to me, and I shall get used to it.

Christmas Day, Wednesday, December 25

Today was a beautiful, clear, bright day. I loaded some poinsettias in the back of the car, got Jerry Kivett, my Secret Service agent, and we went to deliver them to friends. Eventually we joined up with Lyndon, stopped by the Lutheran Church just as the service was over, gave some poinsettias to decorate it, and took one to the Lewis Ranch and one to the Scharnhorst Ranch. Then we just drove around—over the beautiful Hill Country which I love so much.

In fact, we were rather late getting back for the big Christmas dinner, to which we had invited all of Lyndon's kinfolks: Uncle Huffman and Aunt Ovilee; Aunt Josefa, very dressed up and still looking pretty in spite of her many years, and her family, Colonel and Mrs. Paul Kinnison and their three children; Sam Houston, Lyndon's brother, walking very slowly and heavily on his cane; the three Alexanders—and if there is one family member Lyndon needs most and responds to most, it is his sister, Lucia. The Bobbitts—Lyndon's sister Rebekah and her husband—came, and their son Philip has grown about three inches. There was Cousin Oriole, of course, and Aunt Jessie and her family, which consists of her daughter and her husband and two children. Bernie (Bernard Rosenbach, the young Navy ensign to whom Lynda is engaged) was there, looking very handsome and very devoted; and Lynda and Luci.

The usual press contingent was waiting to take a family Christmas picture. One woman reporter asked, "Mr. President, could we go through the house?" I said to Lyndon, "Now, honey, they're coming back again on Friday. Don't you think we'd just better put off the tour of the house, because the gravy is getting colder?" Lyndon said, "No, no, let's go on through the house." So through they went—a swarm, fifty to seventy-five strong, with me trailing along behind them, knowing that dinner was not improving as time went by. Lyndon gave them all ashtrays as Christmas gifts. Finally they departed, and we all sat down to grace and a big family Christmas dinner.

When the family finally dispersed, Lyndon went off to ride around, and I, glad to seek a little of the sunset and quietness, put poinsettias in the car and drove to the Johnson City Hospital and to Cousin Ava Johnson Cox's house.

We came home and opened our Christmas presents quite late. Everybody was there—our household staff, including James and Mary Davis and the secretaries, and there were so many beautiful gifts to exclaim about and enjoy together.

Lyndon invited Uncle Huffman Baines and Aunt Ovilee to go back to Washington with us, and they're looking forward to it very much. And so this is almost the end of the busiest Christmas day that I can remember.

Friday, December 27

Bess Abell, Liz Carpenter, Pierre Salinger, and some Filipino stewards arrived at the Ranch yesterday and got preparations under way for Chancellor Ludwig Erhard's visit—the vast logistics of deciding who was going to stay where, arranging for stewards to manage the Scharnhorst house and the Guest House, and getting ready for the steady flow of people who will be here shortly. Workmen started furbishing the school gym in Stonewall in an attempt to turn that simple village gymnasium into something bright and gay and special for Chancellor Erhard's visit.

Secretary Dean Rusk arrived this morning. Secretary Orville Freeman of the Department of Agriculture and Secretary George Ball of the State Department were already here; George McGhee, our Ambassador to Germany, and McGeorge Bundy came for all the briefings and preliminaries before the German contingent arrived. Two by two and three by three and in groups they huddled with Lyndon and talked, and moved around the

Ranch, while I was busy getting ready for the five busloads of press people, totaling around two hundred, due to descend around 2 o'clock for a press briefing on the meetings.

There were White House press, Texas press, and many members of the German press, and they rolled up in five big Greyhound buses. Pierre acted the top sergeant and piled them all into three school buses which could maneuver ranch roads. Our foreman, Dale Malechek, took the lead-off bus, and I suggested that anyone really wanting to know about the agriculture on the place go with him. I took the second bus and Lynda, that obliging dear girl, took the third.

I picked up the bus microphone and began to tell them about their surroundings—that this was where Lyndon's grandfather settled after the Civil War. He had nine children and he divided his land among them all. I told how we had bought the place in 1951—from one of those children, Aunt Frank Johnson Martin—and what had happened since then, with as many relevant and interesting facts as I could muster. You enjoy talking about what you love, and I love this place.

We saw Lyndon cruising along with the car top down, talking away with Secretaries Rusk and Freeman. Later on he said, "Why didn't you tell me you were going off with the newsmen?" Well, I thought five Greyhound buses loaded with press were fairly easy to spot, so I didn't see why it was necessary to alert him.

Thank heavens it was a glorious sunny day. We entered the barbecue grounds, where Walter Jetton (master barbecue cook and caterer from Ft. Worth) had a bonfire going and big tables full of barbecued ribs with plenty of hot coffee and beer. Everybody helped himself and we settled down on bales of hay or under the trees, eager to pick up any unusual tidbits from the assemblage of distinguished gentlemen who joined us there. Lyndon got up on a bale of hay and talked to the gathering. He introduced Secretary of State Rusk, Secretary of Agriculture Freeman, and also Tom Mann, whose job as Number One coordinator of Latin American affairs had been announced.

The barbecue turned into an all-around press conference, but most casual. After the press and the people from Washington had melted away, we helicoptered over to the Moursunds and I found myself in a car with Lyndon driving, along with Pierre Salinger and two or three other people. We rode around and we saw deer outlined against the sky. We rode and rode and looked at the sky and the deer leaping the fences in the pastures and finally we called in on the car radio to the Governor's Mansion and asked

John and Nellie to come out and join us, which they did. We ended up in A. W.'s "hunting tower," looking into the darkness for the little light eyes of the deer that sometimes appear watching you. I felt as if this was my "time off," as though I were really playing hooky. Then we all went back to the ranch house, had dinner, and sat around the fire, and "told tales" (as my daddy would say), and then we all went to bed fairly early.

Saturday, December 28

We left for Bergstrom Air Force Base in Austin after 9 o'clock to meet the Germans, arriving there on a beautiful blue-and-gold day. There was a crowd of people behind the fence, troops lined up to be reviewed, flags flapping in the breeze, a band, a red carpet, John and Nellie Connally, and then the dignitaries lined up to greet the visitors . . . the Mayor, some of the military, and lots of people from the government.

Pretty soon the German plane rolled in, overshooting the red carpet by a few feet, so there was a slight snafu and they had to hop around to get onto it. John did look white and drained. I keep remembering that he might have to go back for more surgery on his hand. When the cannon roared its customary salute, I thought I saw him flinch involuntarily.

After the review of the troops, both national anthems, a brief speech by Chancellor Erhard and one by Lyndon, it was all over. I began to feel that this was a record I've heard many times, a scene that I had watched all over the world. We got in the helicopter and returned to the Ranch, where there were speeches and a stag luncheon for fourteen of the German visitors, the nucleus of the men who would engage in the hard core of business.

Chancellor Erhard is cherubic of face, very solid, not so formidable as Adenauer, but he looks like a sound man. Gerhard Schroeder, Minister of Foreign Affairs, is a very suave and impressive gentleman. There was Franz Krapf, tall and handsome; we talked about Helga, his wife, who had been my friend in a public speaking class in Washington. He brought me a beautiful German angel, a Christmas present from Helga. And, of course, there was Heinrich Knappstein, West German Ambassador to the United States, and others that I remember—Karl Carstens, and Heinz Weber, who was an interpreter, but a good deal more than an interpreter, I think. And Dr. Ludger Westrick, who occupies a high position in their State Department. This is a solid business trip, so after lunch there were more talks and I stayed out of the way.

This evening Lyndon and the German delegation—about forty—settled in for a beautifully done stag dinner in our dining room, at round tables, with lovely flowers from the White House, and place cards.

Ezra Rachlin, the head of the Austin Symphony Orchestra, brought out Linda Loftis, former Miss Texas and a beautiful girl, naturally, but also a good singer. She sang German lieder to entertain the gentlemen after dinner and Ezra played the piano.

Presently, we exchanged the State gifts. The Chancellor had brought me four beautiful white candlesticks, candelabra really (they hold two candles each), which match the china that Lyndon bought in Berlin. Also, he brought me six lovely china birds, one a magpie. In fact, most of them were birds which I am unfamiliar with. There were two vases for our girls.

We, in turn, gave him the usual sort of things, yet there was one thing which was not at all usual—a little book we had made ourselves, containing some poems by a young German girl, Hulda Saenger Walter, written many, many years ago. She was the daughter of immigrants who came to Texas about 1840 from Germany and settled in Fredericksburg. In her poems she told about how hard her father worked in this new pioneer country. She also expressed homesickness—how much they missed their fatherland. The poems were written in German, in her own handwriting, and we had them translated into English and prettily bound, with a letter, which I tried to make as warm as I could, to Mrs. Erhard to tell her how sorry we were that she wasn't along on the visit.

One more pleasant thing, in the "small world" department, is that when the little German girl who wrote the poems was a grown woman, she came to know Lyndon's mother in Fredericksburg.

Sunday, December 29

The second of the big days dawned beautiful and clear, but so cold that I praised the Lord we were not having the barbecue out under the live oaks. Early this morning Lyndon and I and the nucleus of the German party helicoptered to Fredericksburg and went to the Pioneer Memorial, the octagon house located just off the main street. There we were met by the leading citizens of the community. We passed the statue of Baron von Meusebach, who had brought in 120 German families in covered wagons back in the 1840's to settle this area.

We stood in front of the octagon house and had a little ceremony. Postmaster Bill Petmecky and lawyer Arthur Stehling made welcoming speeches, and the head of the Historical Association of Gillespie County made a short talk and presented a book called *Pioneers in God's Hills* to Chancellor Erhard.

The Chancellor made response and we went on to church services at the Lutheran Church. There was a curious blending of the old and the new in the service. The elderly minister conducted a large part of the service in German, and a handsome, vital, young assistant delivered a brief sermon in English. There was a beautiful choir—all men—who sang "Silent Night" in German. That, I think, was the most tranquil moment of all Christmas.

We returned, to the cauldron of activity that has become our life, to find that the guests were already arriving in the gymnasium. They had been invited for one o'clock, and it was only a little past 11. The German delegation continued their talks and there was no interrupting them—they had come on business. They were in one room, our people in another, and they met jointly in a third room. I dispatched Lynda Bird to the gymnasium to represent the Johnson family and greet anybody who came early.

I took my post at the Guest House to meet and greet a good many guests who had come in by private planes from various parts of the state. There were Mr. and Mrs. Tom Lea (he's a fine southwestern artist and writer from El Paso); John Jones, a Houston publisher; our old friends the Wesley Wests; Wernher Von Braun of NASA and his lovely young wife. There was Bob Kerr, Jr., son of the Senator, and his partner Dean McGee, who flew in from Oklahoma and had a slight accident on the runway. Nobody was hurt but the plane was damaged and it was impossible to fly in or out for several hours because the plane jammed the runway.

And then, very important—I wanted to take care of and make feel very welcome Mr. and Mrs. Harvey Cliburn from Kilgore, Texas, the parents of Van Cliburn who was playing for us. I tried to introduce everybody to everybody else, with the help of Eloise Thornberry.

Throughout the day Ambassador Angier Biddle Duke, Chief of Protocol, was weaving his silken way. He always knows exactly what to do and say and I feel like laying my hand on his shoulder and saying, "O.K., you tell me what next!"

At the appointed hour all of the guests were asked to go to the gymnasium for the barbecue. I stood by the fence waiting for Lyndon and the Chancellor, then jumped in the car in the nick of time, and rode up to the barbecue myself. We found the gym transformed, with red checkered tablecloths and red lanterns on the tables, and bunting everywhere, with the colors of the German flag and the German insignia prominently displayed. As a backdrop for the enormous, handsome piano and Van Cliburn, there were bales of hay, saddles, lariats and a lantern or two—very different things, I'm sure, than he's used to having set off his piano! I steered the Chancellor into the buffet line. We loaded our plates and made our way among the guests to the head table. Twelve or fourteen of the top German dignitaries were there and some of the local people, and thank the Lord, it wasn't my job to seat them!

Lyndon said grace and we began supper. There were beans (pinto beans, always), delicious barbecued spare ribs, cole slaw, followed by fried apricot pies with lots of hot coffee. And plenty of beer. The gym would accommodate only about three hundred people and by the time we seated the German press, the White House press, the local press, the German delegation and our group, it was possible to invite only about seventy-five other people. Among these were Chancellor and Mrs. Harry Ransom and Professor and Mrs. J. Frank Dobie from the University of Texas. From the cattle industry we had asked Bob Kleberg and Jay Taylor.

After the barbecue came the entertainment, and it was a mighty job for Cactus Pryor (our own local emcee from KTBC) to meld together that very diverse entertainment! I think he did a masterful, dignified job. A group of girls from Fredericksburg danced folk dances from the Old Country, including the *Herr Schmidt*. St. Mary's Choir, led by a nun, sang a program of beautiful German songs and then sang "Deep in the Heart of Texas." That caused the Chancellor to smile and lean over to me and say—and he does speak some English—"We know that in Germany, too."

Van Cliburn was of course the star of the show. He was born and raised in deep East Texas, about forty miles from where I was born, and he has become one of the world's greatest pianists. Cactus gave him a splendid introduction, and I was just as proud of Cactus as I was of anybody in the whole show. Van Cliburn played Beethoven's "Appassionata," then a beautiful Schumann love song and some other things that I didn't recognize. Everybody was impressed, especially when Van Cliburn said that he was glad to play for us because he had heard that the Chancellor himself was a pianist as a young man and had expected to become a concert pianist.

Next—and I'd almost swear there was no planned agenda—Lyndon got up and introduced the outstanding German visitors, saying a few words about each one. Then he introduced the outstanding members of our own party and his introduction of Secretary of State Dean Rusk was one of the most eloquent and moving that I've ever heard him make.

Sometime during the evening there were toasts. The Chancellor's remarks—which I didn't understand, of course, until they were translated—were pure poetry. He made a great speech, which made me feel that all the effort had been worthwhile and that maybe we had put a little more cement into the building of good relations. Lyndon's toast was brief but good. I felt our first State meeting had gone well and that we had given the Chancellor and his party a sense of the hospitality of this country in a setting where there were ties of kinship.

Monday, December 30

It seems as if one great crescendo of activity follows another so rapidly that I wonder how Lyndon manages to shift gears in his life from one to another. No sooner had we said good-by to Chancellor Erhard and the German group than the Joint Chiefs of Staff arrived this morning, led by General Maxwell Taylor and including General Curtis LeMay, General David Shoup of the Marines (whose birthday it was and, incidentally, his last day in the service), and several others. They spent the morning talking over very weighty problems and I spent the morning staying out of their way. Dr. Walter Heller, Chairman of the Council of Economic Advisers, and Kermit Gordon, the Director of the Bureau of the Budget, have been in and out of the meetings, putting in their bit during the morning.

Rest at the Ranch is a complete misnomer to me. The airport stays busy, with planes disgorging Cabinet members with important, difficult decisions, budget estimates, crises. This week has been like living in a revolving door. I only know that, somehow, the Ranch manages to be restful to Lyndon. The house has become a joint residence and office. Visitors pour in and news pours out. And these old walls are bursting at the seams!

Lyndon and I went into Austin in the afternoon to attend the funeral of Mrs. Tom Miller. Her death marked something of an ending to certain days in Austin, because if there was ever anybody who loved the town, who claimed the town, and who made the town, it was Mayor Tom Miller, who died a couple of years ago. With the passing of his widow, there was a sense of a final good-by—good-by to those days which had been so much of Lyndon's life as a young Congressman.

Later we went to the dedication of the Congregation Agudas Achim Synagogue in Austin, which is our friend Jim Novy's brainchild. Lyndon had been invited to attend this dedication set for November 24, but it had been postponed, like so many events across the nation. It was a night I'll always remember with great affection. The hall was filled with good Jewish friends whom we have known all our lives in Austin, our constituents for more than twenty-five years.

Jim Novy introduced Lyndon, saying, "I think it was in 1938 that I first met this young Congressman. We can't ever thank him enough for all those Jews he got out of Germany during the days of Hitler." And then he said, "Lyndon, right down there in front of you" (I looked and there were six little boys ranging in age from about four to twelve years) "there's the current generation, and they'll be watching for you and helping you."

Jim went on to describe how a simple man feels about someone who has given his life to government service. I couldn't help remembering that Jim himself came here as a Jewish immigrant at the age of eight and went into the junk business when he was about twelve. He's amassed a good deal of money, and he's putting a lot of it back into the community that helped him and back into causes to help other Jews.

Lyndon was never better than in his response. He began by saying (and I feel just that way, too) that he was glad his first unofficial speech in this office was in a place of worship in his home town. It was a beautiful speech. In spite of my respect for television's power and my recognition that we couldn't have had the livelihood we've had and remained in politics except for the income from my TV business, it's this kind of politics that I really like! Life will be less rich in politics—less rich in other ways—when there are no more meetings on the Court House square and it all takes place before the camera.

Two of the most memorable things about the day were the way, as we started out of the synagogue, person after person plucked at my sleeve and said, "I wouldn't be here today if it weren't for him. He helped me get out." That both frightens you and makes you happy. And second was the nice way, around the fireplace after dinner, that Lynda Bird and Dr. Walter Heller got to talking, and Lynda Bird was deep in conversation with him about economics, the economy of Texas, and the University of

Texas. She upheld her end of the conversation so well, and I could see Dr. Walter Heller responding to her, not only with interest but with respect. It was fun to watch.

The last day of this year began early, about the ridiculous hour of 6:30, with Lyndon getting up to go deer hunting, taking with him our friends Jake Pickle and Don Thomas. I got Lynda Bird off on her trip to Dallas and Luci Baines off to see the football game, and then I luxuriously and self-indulgently went back to sleep. I woke up about 12 o'clock noon—the most wonderful morning I've had in two or three months. After a while the hunters came in and had a big breakfast. The living room was filled with important faces, some of whom had just arrived on the plane from Washington to discuss the endless important agendas.

When they all left, the day was given over to my kinfolks. My cousin Winston Taylor was the first to arrive, then my sister-in-law Sarah Taylor, and my niece Susan with a boy friend. They came about one o'clock and then we waited for Tony and Matiana, my brother and sister-in-law from Santa Fe, who appeared around 2; followed by my nephew, T. J. Taylor III, and his family, Christine and Nancy and Sally. Finally we all sat down to lunch.

Later in the day Lyndon asked me to go to Austin to a couple of parties. But I'd much rather sit around the fire and watch the embers glow and talk to the folks close to me, so I begged off. Pretty soon those going in to Austin said good-by and the family group gathered around the fire, with a glass of wine. We put on another stick of wood and we talked about the Brick House in Karnack (our childhood home) and Daddy's store, and the times we remembered in our young days. Each one of us had a favorite story to tell about Daddy and Mother and Tommy. We relished retelling it all, but mostly we just enjoyed being together.

My last day at the Ranch for who knows how long! We began it by going to St. Barnabas Church in Fredericksburg with Scotty Reston of the

New York Times and Mrs. Reston, Lynda, and Gerri Whittington, Lyndon's attractive young Negro secretary.

The charm of St. Barnabas never fails to please me. The church is a little log cabin, built in the 1850's by one of the earliest German families who came in covered wagons to settle in Fredericksburg. A grapevine in the backyard brought over on a ship from Germany still bears grapes. My introduction to St. Barnabas, eight or ten years ago, came when one of the church ladies gave me a jar of jelly made from these grapes. St. Barnabas retains all of the charm of the old and it is as comfortable as a log cabin can be. I wondered what Scotty Reston thought of it.

Because it's so hard to leave home, we took one last drive around the countryside, going into Johnson City, stopping at the old stone fort and the old stone commissary, where Lyndon's grandfather lived after the Civil War and where they used to gather the cattle herds to start driving them up the Chisholm Trail.

We pointed out to the Restons the portholes in the commissary, through which the settlers stuck their rifles to fire at the Indians, as the local legend goes. And we told the story of Lyndon's grandmother, hiding with her two infant children in the cellar of the log house, while the Indians were stomping around outside, stealing the horses and all of her wedding presents. Then we drove to the little house in Johnson City where Lyndon grew up, which we are having restored as a Community Center, where, hopefully, 4-H youngsters or the PTA, or Kiwanis, or Lions, or ladies' groups, or whatever can hold their meetings. Afterward, we went back to the Ranch and had our last meal at home, our last look out the picture window at the fields stretching away.

We flew in to Austin then, stopped by the Governor's Mansion, and had a cup of coffee with John and Nellie. I know in the ensuing years, there will be many times when John's and Lyndon's paths will have to part, because John is naturally more conservative than Lyndon. But, as far as I'm concerned, their hearts will never part, and I feel that's true for all four of us.

Next, we went out to Senator Yarborough's New Year's reception for the neighbors in his community. I think all the neighbors up and down the street gathered to see us. We're going to need him, we're going to need everybody, we're going to need to make peace all around. If we get any kind of a program across, in this coming legislative year, we cannot spend our energies fighting among ourselves. I hope we don't.

Finally, we wound up out at the airport, where a crowd was gathered waiting for us. Uncle Huffman Baines, Aunt Ovilee, and Aunt Josefa were there, ready for their big trip to the White House. Lyndon gets total credit for the thoughtfulness of doing this for them (and I'll probably get a little bit of the work). But I'm glad he's the sort of a man who does such things, because there may not always be another time to do the good things that you think about.

We got to the White House early and I took Uncle Huffman and Aunt Ovilee up to the charming green and blue room on the third floor. Aunt Josefa was in the small bedroom next door, a room that's completely furnished with antiques—a sleigh bed—just the sort of furniture that delights her. They have a little sitting room between them.

Settling down to slumber, I cast one backward glance to the wide, sweeping hills, the golden sunshine, the gray-green landscape of the Hill Country that I've come to love, and very much of a forward glance to tomorrow, which will begin the working day and the working year.

Monday, January 6

THE WHITE HOUSE

My first big day back on the job! I got Uncle Huffman and Aunt Ovilee and Aunt Josefa off sightseeing in a White House car, with Susan Taylor as their guide. I had introduced them to enough of the staff to make them feel at home, and they are charmed with their rooms.

I settled down from 9:30 to 12:30 to work with Liz, Bess, and my secretary Ashton Gonella. Assignment of duties, settlement of problems, going over things—decisions, decisions.

Then came the big event of the day—the White House staff reception from 6 to 7:30, something I had been looking forward to very much. I had been told we would be meeting everybody—all the cooks, the maids, the laundresses, the gardeners, the waiters, everybody who makes the house tick. True enough, I did meet most of them, but was I disappointed that Zephyr Wright and Helen Williams, our own long-time cook and maid, weren't there.

One of the best things was to meet, before the party started and for just a few minutes' conversation, the people who have been there the longest —Miss Nellie Butler, who had come as a cook during the Coolidge administration, and Miss Edna Rosenburg who had come in 1929; Mr. Isaac

Avery, in the carpenter shop since 1930; and Mr. Edward Morris, who arrived in 1931. There were two from the Roosevelt Administration: Miss Edith Rowley from West Virginia, and Miss Toinette Bachelder, who had met Lyndon when he went to Warm Springs to see President Roosevelt. She was a patient at Warm Springs, and that was how she came to know President Roosevelt and to go to work for him. This is one of the nicest parties I ever expect to have here, because its guests are people I think most deserve to come to a party.

We stood in front of the beautiful Christmas tree, which was decorated with snow crystals, lovely and sparkling in their myriad shapes, and lots of beautiful lights. Because Lyndon was late, Luci stood in line with me and received nearly everybody, and then finally, when her daddy came, she slipped off upstairs to her date.

I believe I can write "well filled" and "well done" after this day.

Tuesday, January 7

At one o'clock occurred one of the most important moments of the day, when I went to the Red Room to stand in line to greet the labor leaders whom Lyndon had invited for a stag luncheon. The "big brass" was on hand to receive them, Dean Rusk of the State Department, Douglas Dillon of the Treasury, Robert McNamara from Defense, Luther Hodges of Commerce, Willard Wirtz of Labor, Director of the Budget Kermit Gordon, Walter Heller from the Council of Economic Advisers, Larry O'Brien, Pierre Salinger, Theodore Sorensen.

I was glad of the opportunity to meet them all and see what they were like. Jim Carey I remembered from a long time back; and David Dubinsky, rather like a pixie; David MacDonald, very big and handsome and masculine; George Meany, walking heavily on his cane; and youthful-looking Walter Reuther.

And then there was Jim Suffridge, whom I remember so fondly. We went around the world together; we had shared a lot of experiences and I like him. And Andy Biemiller, who came here to Congress with us back in 1937.

Over a very proper dinner this evening with Uncle Huffman and Aunt Ovilee and Aunt Josefa, preceded by a blessing, I asked them all about what they'd been doing. Susan Taylor had been taking good care of them, and they had done a lot of sightseeing and visiting with a relative who lives in Alexandria. It's really given me pleasure to know that I have done something for Mrs. Johnson, having her sister and her brother up here to see Lyndon in the White House.

Lyndon, with his indefatigable appetite for work, after having had the labor leaders at noon, was having the Businessmen's Council that evening for a stag dinner. The moment our dinner was over I went to the Oval Room to greet the sixteen guests who had been asked to come upstairs. Alas, the President wasn't there yet, and somebody needed to be.

Roger Blough of U.S. Steel and Frederick R. Kappel, Chairman of American Tel and Tel, had arrived. (I told him we were among his best customers, what with Lynda Bird engaged to a Navy man who was always far, far away, and Lyndon's penchant for the telephone.) As for Mr. W. B. Murphy of Campbell's Soup, I felt like telling him that we had gone around the world living off his soup. I greeted L. F. McCollum of Continental Oil of Houston as homefolks, and handsome, attractive Tom Watson of IBM, who was standing in the corner looking on.

Shortly after Lyndon joined us, we went downstairs to meet all the other guests. The total party was composed of about eighty-nine businessmen and a contingent of government people, including once more (and it looks as if Lyndon is working them almost as hard as he is himself) Dillon, McNamara, Hodges from Commerce, Wirtz from Labor, Kermit Gordon from the Budget, and Heller from the Council of Economic Advisers—enough to provide an exchange of ideas with all these businessmen and to give them an impression of what this Administration plans to do, what its people look like, think like, want—that is, as much of an impression as you can give in a crowd of over one hundred.

Along with Lyndon, I met the rest of the guests: Fred Lazarus, Jr., of the Federated Department Stores, Neil McElroy of Procter and Gamble, whom I remember from another Administration, one-time Texan C. R. Smith of American Airlines, and Dr. Frank Stanton. To Solon Turman of Lykes Brothers Steamship Company, what I really wanted to say and didn't quite know how was: "I just hope you'll save me a trip on that ship I christened!"

After getting them started in to dinner, I happily left them to their business and went upstairs.

At noon today, Wednesday, January 8, Lyndon delivered the State of the Union address. It was one of those days when you have the feeling that everything that has gone before (in the last two weeks at any rate) has been leading up to this pinnacle. So might Sir Edmund Hillary have felt when he at last reached the top of Mount Everest. It seemed to me that we had had long, long ropes stretched up a high mountain and day by day we had been pulling and hauling and this, finally, was the day that we either came to the top and fell on our faces or stood up and planted the flag.

I arrived in the House Chamber a little early and took my seat in the front row, with Luci Baines on my right, and then how glad I was to have Roberta Vinson, widow of our dear friend Chief Justice Fred Vinson, next to her and then Uncle Huffman Baines and Aunt Ovilee and Aunt Josefa. On the other side sat Susan Taylor, and Helen Williams, our long-time maid and friend, and nobody watched it with more interest than Helen. Behind us were the wives of the Cabinet members and the wives of the Supreme Court Justices and also as our guests we had Hobart Taylor and Jay Taylor. I noticed, tucked away on the farthest step in the last little square inch, Wendy Marcus (daughter of Stanley Marcus of Neiman-Marcus), young and eager and ready to "grab life by the forelock."

The familiar Chamber below began to fill up with the pomp and display that always takes place on these occasions. How many times I have seen it! The House members were in their seats. Then with a loud announcement from Fishbait Miller, Doorkeeper in the House of Representatives, in came the Senate. Then came the Diplomatic Corps, getting bigger all the time, and how they finally found room for them all I don't know; followed by the Cabinet and the Court, occupying the front row. In his most pontifical voice Fishbait Miller—and how could there ever be a replacement for Fishbait?—rose and said, "The President of the United States." In walked Lyndon, flanked by old friends of long standing, and went up to the podium in front of Speaker John McCormack and Senator Carl Hayden with the flag behind him. Speaker McCormack, gray and craggy and white-haired, with that wonderful commanding voice, and Senator Hayden—on the Hill ever since Arizona entered the Union, a charming lively face for eighty-five—I wonder how many people in the Chamber were struck with the thought that here stands a President without a Vice President . . .

My favorite line was actually the first one: "I will be brief, for our time is necessarily short and our agenda is already long," but "it [our agenda] can be done by this summer." I want it done so that the House and Senate will look better to the nation as much as I want it to be done for Lyndon's good and the Democratic Party's good. By all odds, the most important thing in the speech to me was this statement: "This Administration, here and now, declares unconditional war on poverty in America. I ask this Congress and all Americans to join me in that effort." There was a heavy accent on education, on retraining, on health. I liked the line about a thousand dollars invested in an unemployable youth today can return forty thousand or more in his lifetime.

I looked around for my weathervane, Dick Russell, and tried to watch his reactions, and in spite of searching for Harry Byrd every time the word "budget" was mentioned, I couldn't find him. I did notice that the Republican applause was pretty sparse, but the applauding in general was awfully good, so good that a very short speech, one of the shortest ever for a State of the Union—I think it was designed to be delivered in something like twenty minutes—stretched out to about thirty minutes.

I watched the press corps, wondering what was going through their minds and what would be coming out soon from their typewriters. Finally the end came—and I let out that long-drawn breath. (Why should it make *me* so tired?) Lyndon turned around to shake hands with Speaker Mc-Cormack and with Senator Hayden and then with Lew Deschler [Parliamentarian in the House of Representatives] and then with all of his old friends as they filed out. Luci and I walked out into the waiting arms of the ladies of the press, and I hope I made sense when I said the speech was a good synthesis of Lyndon's living and working for the last thirty years and then quoted the lines that appealed to me particularly, remembering certainly the one that went: "You must be strong enough to win a war and wise enough to prevent one."

About 5:30 we had a meeting in the family sitting room—Bill Batt of the Area Redevelopment Administration, two of his assistants, and Liz Carpenter along with Mac Kilduff—to talk about my trip to the coal areas of Pennsylvania on Saturday. They spread out the maps and gave me a lot of information about the amount of unemployment, why it had come about, what the Area Redevelopment Administration was doing about it, the chances of success, the things that I might do, what sounded most productive.

The big test of today—actually something that I have been looking forward to—is tea for the ladies of the press, about sixty-five of them, at 4 o'clock. I hope the time never comes when I feel I have to be afraid of them.

As I stood in the Yellow Room, I was surprised to see how many I could call by their first names and how many of them I am genuinely fond of—Bonnie Angelo and Betty Beale and Christine Sadler Coe of *McCall's* magazine, Nancy Dickerson of NBC, Doris Fleeson, the columnist, and Helen Baldwin of the *Waco News*, who had come to Washington because she wanted to write a special article on me and to see me in action. Other familiar press ladies were my gardening friend Isabel Griffin, Gwen Gibson, Frances Lewine and Helen Thomas, whom I feel I know best of all, Florence Lowe and Dorothy McCardle, so sweet in face and manner.

When I saw Sarah McClendon, I thought, "I hope I don't have to start flinching the way so many people do when they see you." And there were Marianne Means; and Speaker Sam Rayburn's old friend Hope Ridings Miller; Ruth Montgomery, who was going over to interview Lyndon on what he thought about me for her book; Josephine Ripley whom I remember happily from my trip to West Virginia, who writes for that rare newspaper that many people look to as one of the best, the *Christian Science Monitor*; Nan Robertson and Isabelle Shelton—I think Isabelle did the first by-lined piece on me that anybody ever wrote—and Marie Smith and Mary Van Rensselaer Thayer.

We made a tour of the second floor, and they all seemed quite interested. But I found out that sixty-five is too many to take on a tour. The next time I am going to limit tours to twenty, preferably, and positively not more than thirty.

Fortunately, I have had time to study about five rooms thoroughly with the Curator, and I could talk about them knowledgeably, I hope, with a few anecdotes. We started off in the Yellow Room, where President John Adams, the first President to live in the White House, used to receive each week in his velvet knee breeches with silver buckles on his shoes and with his wife, Abigail, seated by his side. The usual things—I can't resist being amused as I point out the porthole portrait of George Washington by Rembrandt Peale and comment on the exceeding temerity of a parent in naming an infant "Rembrandt," and then the infant growing up to be a famous painter! It was a particular joy to point out that all of the furniture in the long hall is the work of the greatest American cabinetmakers, circa 1805, in the manner of Hepplewhite and Sheraton, with their own touches added. This hall is part of Mrs. Kennedy's wonderful project.

One purpose of the tea was to set the tenor of press conferences—not as conferences but informal meetings—as an invitation to a relaxed and pleasant atmosphere with an opportunity to meet somebody else who was newsworthy. This time the person was Esther Peterson, whose new job is Assistant to the President on Consumer Problems. The pièce de résistance was to have Esther, whom I introduced, stand in front of the fireplace in the Yellow Room and discuss the mail she has been receiving on consumer problems, along with her plans for her job.

One of the most interesting moments of the afternoon happened in the Treaty Room, where Mrs. Franklin Delano Roosevelt used to hold her press conferences for women only. I asked those who had been present in those days to hold up their hands and there were ten or twelve of the sixty-four who had been there in Mrs. Roosevelt's day. I would much rather have listened to what they had to say than to what I had to say for the rest of the time.

Because I have lived openly and unafraid and quite candidly with people all my life, I think, I found this press party pleasant. I like to show people my way of life.

What the newspaperwomen liked hearing about most were the little personal things, such as the time I walked into the Treaty Room and found Luci's algebra and Latin texts and some frayed notebooks and some chewed pencils lying there on that famous table. Obviously she had been doing her homework in the Treaty Room for several nights. I did think I'd better put a stop to it. It's a little too much of a museum for that.

I wish I had had the nerve to tell them about the first night we moved in. Seeing a beautiful fire laid in the fireplace and remembering how nice it was at my childhood home, the Brick House, to go to sleep by the shadow of the flames dancing upward on the ceiling, Luci and her friend Beth Jenkins decided to light the fire. It was about midnight and something was the matter with the damper. Smoke began to pour through the room and presently out into the hall and you would have thought the British were back again! I just hope Luci is as good a friend of Mr. J. B. West and the rest of the staff around here after that, but I haven't quite cleared that story in my own mind for telling yet.

Saturday, January 11

WILKES-BARRE AND
SCRANTON, PENNSYLVANIA
AND THE WHITE HOUSE

This has been one of the best, or at least one of the two or three best, days I have spent in the White House up to now. Much too early this morning I left on a plane with Liz, Mac Kilduff, Congressman Dan Flood, and Republican Congressman Joe McDade, Bill Batt of ARA, and about forty newswomen—most of the regulars—to see an area in Pennsylvania hard hit by the declining coal industry. I noticed Ingrid Jewell, a Pittsburgh correspondent, who had briefed us in a letter showing that she knows far more about this region than I will ever be able to learn. It was comfortable to look around and see Warren Woodward, formerly of KTBC, now in his new role with American Airlines, but still somebody I can lean on.

We were going to Wilkes-Barre and Scranton, Pennsylvania, the sort of depressed places Lyndon had in mind in his War on Poverty speech. On the way Dan Flood briefed us about how long the anthracite mines had been on the decline, about the mines that were on fire and imperiling homes and businesses, about the unemployment level, which was twice as high as the national average, about 11 percent instead of the 5½ percent that is the national average. More happily, he briefed us on the vigorous work of the ARA in that section, in some cases joined by the Accelerated Works Program and assisted in some ways by the Health, Education and Welfare Committee.

The country was beautiful to look down on, but when you saw the vast scars across the landscape from the mining that is literally a surface mining, you couldn't keep from thinking that God had done his best by this country, but Man had certainly done his worst, and now it is up to Man to repair the damage. At Scranton, we hit the ground running and it was a day of running. The first person I met was Mrs. William Scranton, the wife of the Republican Governor, a charming, able, tactful woman and somebody I would like to know better. She was by my side all day long, helpful, unobtrusive. I'd say her husband has an able assistant in any campaign.

The next six hours were packed with activity. We went to the Courthouse Square at Scranton, crowded with people. There was a presentation of flowers, a welcome by the Mayor, then we pressed on to the public square at Wilkes-Barre. I was presented the key to the city by somebody in place of the Mayor, who was ill. There were more flowers, then on to Goldsmith Mill where a payroll of about a hundred had been saved by the joint work of the community and the ARA. We went to the Wyoming Valley Technical Institute. But it is vignettes and not timetables that you remember.

I asked one man who was learning the trade of painting, what he had done before. He said that three mines had closed up on him and he decided that he had "better get out of that business." He had been out of work for two years and then he heard about the retraining program. Now he was learning painting and he was practically assured of getting a job when he finished. The Institute had a woodworking shop, a machine shop, an auto repair shop, and they were installing a painting and paperhanging shop. They also worked with handicapped people. I saw one man who had one hand and one claw. He had lost his hand in an industrial accident and was learning cabinetmaking. He presented me with a bowl he had made.

One of the things I liked best about the school was that classes went on from 8 o'clock in the morning until 10 o'clock at night. It was a ramshackle old building but they were making a lot of use of what they had. Mr. Ray Taylor, who was running the school, said they had almost complete assurance of jobs for the people when they finished their training. But it was more than the official nature of the visit that I loved. People and people and people stretched out in the cold frosty squares around me. There was a little child with a muffler right up to his nose, and children sitting on top of their fathers' shoulders, and outstretched hands in every direction.

We had lunch at the home of the President of Wilkes College, Dr. and Mrs. Eugene S. Farley, and just as we were about to turn into their drive, I saw a sign that read: "GEORGE CATLIN." I asked if we could stop so I could read it closely. The group of cars ground to a halt, all six of them—six cars in procession almost piled up on each other. You keep forgetting that this is the way it is. It's odd that when you learn about something, you keep on coming across it more and more often. Scranton was the home town of

George Catlin who painted the Sioux, the Dakotas, the Navajos, the Indians of the plain, of Oklahoma and Kansas and the Dakotas. His paintings line the second-floor hall of the White House. He was born a long way from where his talent was to flourish.

We had a short respite for lunch. I have learned that "rest periods" on schedules just disappear. Then we went to Wilkes College, where I was glad that I had a few minutes to meet with some of the students. I found myself in a science room with a group and nobody to introduce me, so I just stood up and introduced myself. I talked for two or three minutes and really felt quite at ease with them. The main feeling was a certain twinge of envy, because they are young and living in a marvelously interesting period of this planet's life.

Then we went to the ceremony dedicating the Science Center at Wilkes College. The main speaker was Dr. Frank Graham, former United States Senator and former President of the University of North Carolina at Chapel Hill and my old friend. You can't beat a Southern gentleman! You could have practically waltzed to his speech (although really it was far too long), and he paid me the usual graceful Southern compliments.

The Science Center is being built with federal funds supplied by the ARA and matched with local money. That is one of the things I liked about the whole feeling of the day, that there were local brains, local initiative, and local money coming in from some of even the poorest of pockets to help meet the serious problem that confronts the region. The aim of the Center is to attract new industries for the depressed areas, and if they produce scientists and technicians from the science and graduate centers, they have an RCA plant and a labor market located here. They can go to work right at home.

One of the saddest aspects of a depressed area these days is that the young people leave their homes in search of better jobs. If a pool of technicians can be produced in the stricken areas, they can provide bait for industries and keep the young folks at home. I think it is heroic that these people are concentrating on electronics, because to step from the coal industry, long a dying one, into the electronics industry, which is geared to tomorrow, is like building their own economic bridges to the future.

One of the interesting but sad aspects was concerned with the fact that local textile mills employed principally women. That meant that in a lot of families it was the woman who was the wage earner and the man who stayed home and cooked the meals and washed the diapers. Just imagine what twenty years of that would do to the sociological aspects of a community.

There was so much to take in, so much flavor, so much history, so much economics! I asked about the strange old houses stretched out along the banks of the Susquehanna River. They looked Victorian—very ornate, very solid, very impressive, maybe a bit Gothic. Somebody said they were the homes of the coal barons of long ago. Mrs. Farley said they called the architecture "Bastard Anthracite."

And so the day wore on, a montage of faces, outstretched hands in the biting cold, children wanting autographs, roses. It was a day I loved living, and finally about 4 o'clock we got back to the Wilkes-Barre–Scranton Airport. I shook a few hundred more hands, said good-by last of all to Mrs. Scranton, climbed on the plane and came home. Was the end of the day reached when we got to Washington? No. I had all of ten minutes to change my clothes and get downstairs for a 6:30 meeting with the Democratic National Committeemen and Democratic women and the State Chairmen and Vice Chairmen, about 150 people. I was glad I could call many by their first names.

After the receiving line we went into the State Dining Room for refreshments. Lyndon actually made me stand up and give them a little greeting and then he found a chair in the middle of the State Dining Room, stood on it, and made a speech about our aims and plans. After that we left the party in the graceful and friendly hands of Margaret Price [Vice Chairman and Director, Women's Activities, Democratic National Committee], said our good-bys to everybody, and got into a helicopter on the South Lawn. In the middle of the receiving line Lyndon had leaned over to me and said, "Would you like to go to Camp David? If you would, get your clothes packed and we will leave in twenty minutes." He had sent somebody else to phone Secretary and Mrs. McNamara who, happily, are used to spur-of-the-moment engagements. They came and brought their son Craig and we flew off into the night, headed for the peace and quiet of Camp David.

Sunday, January 12

CAMP DAVID

We woke up to snow and serenity and fire burning in the fireplace, and the satisfying company of Bob and Margy McNamara. Lyndon went to church—a little Episcopal church down in the village of Thurmont. It was a lot like my own St. Barnabas in Fredericksburg. I am sorry I did not have the get-up-and-get to go with him. Margy and I went for a walk in the 12-degree weather, with every breath blowing out in front of us like a banner. There were frequent calls about Panama from Cyrus Vance and other people on McNamara's staff, but somehow or other at Camp David there is an insulation that keeps you from being terribly worried about what's going on in the outside world.

About 11 o'clock Senator Dick Russell arrived and we sat in the big living room, looking out through the picture window in the valley of Maryland. Senator Russell began to try to get us placed geographically and said, "I think we are close to Antietam here." Then he began to tell the story of a great Civil War battle, where General Robert E. Lee had distributed his orders to his generals but one luckless general had lost his. A Yankee sergeant had found them in the forest, wrapped around a couple of cigars. He took them to General George McClellan. At first McClellan thought they were a hoax, then he acted on them, gathered his troops, and there ensued the bloodiest battle of the Civil War, one of the bloodiest of all times.

Later on as I was telling Lynda Bird on the telephone about how interestingly Dick Russell told it, I said, "Honey, that is one of the reasons I want you up here, because you know so much about history. You like it; you like politics, and I want you to listen to these people I listen to." Lynda said, "Yes, Mama, and if McClellan had rounded up all of his troops and pitched right in aggressively, he could have ended the war two years before he did." I asked Senator Russell about that when I had hung up the phone, and he said, "That's entirely right. He could have."

We had a late lunch, a short nap, a little bowling. We tuned in on my TV appearance in *The Week That Was*, which was a catastrophe. It was filmed last week with Nancy Dickerson when I was tired, and it was about as bad as I had thought it was going to be, although the bits from Pennsylvania were good enough. I liked them. The activities of the week had been good, but in my five minute interview I looked just as old and just as frenetic and just as tired and just as unprepared as I was. If I am not smart enough to get a moral out of this, I am not smart at all. No more unprepared things, no more things when I am not well briefed in what I am going to do!

For once, I read all the articles in the paper about my trip to Pennsylvania, even enough to satisfy Liz. I guess the best thing about today is that I have actually had some time for reflection, time to think about the changes that have come into our life.

One thing—for the first three or four weeks in this job, I was cold all the time. I wanted a sweater when nobody else wanted a sweater. I didn't have any appetite and I lost about five pounds. After I moved into the White House, for a while I found myself walking on tiptoe and talking in whispers. That's about over now. One can't go on doing that. But has there been any sense of elation at any time on reaching the place we now occupy? No. None at all. Just a sense of how hard the road is going to be and the determination to make these twelve months—eleven or whatever they are—as good as I can.

And then there is another thing that's gone unmentioned but not unnoticed by me. It just happens that every night at dinner since November 22, Lyndon has said grace or asked some appropriate member of the group to return thanks. That's a custom I like and have tried to foster for twenty-nine years. Somehow I have never gotten it over, and yet here *he's* the one who does it. Also, he has been to church every Sunday since then and occasionally on days in between—New Year's or Christmas. There have been at least two Sundays when I have missed church but he hasn't missed once. We've been to the Lutheran, the Episcopal, and once we tried to go to the Christian Church but that day there was a gathering of all sorts of denominations. We must go to the Christian Church soon. I am not going to say how glad I am about all this for fear it might somehow evaporate, but I have the feeling that it's not going to.

It would be the understatement of a lifetime to say that a man of good sense doesn't know how much he needs help and solace in this job. Lyndon does know, and I am so glad he's simply and straightforwardly going about seeking it.

Monday, January 13

THE WHITE HOUSE

This morning I woke up to a white world—snow falling outside of our bedroom windows, so thick and white—the biggest storm in six years, the papers said—the magnolia trees heavy with snow, the Washington Monument barely visible. Later in the day the sky cleared and it was the most gorgeous, white, sunny world, but I knew the snow would create lots of headaches. Bess was already wondering and worrying about the guest list for dinner. Who would make it from afar? Liz was wondering if the entertainment would get here from Arizona.

I asked Mary Ellen Monroney and Marny Clifford to come over, and about 2 o'clock we began to lay out the luscious samples of fabrics to finish up Lynda Bird's room and Luci Baines' room. I value their tastes and opinions and love their own homes. I pointed out all of my favorite fabrics to them—for chairs, and stools, and braid on the curtains —and we planned where to hang pictures. We talked the pros and cons of furniture and what we could find in the government warehouse to use. I think these rooms will be charming, especially after they acquire the lived-in look which the children must and will impart.

About 5:15 I had an appointment with Dick Adler to discuss the entertainment for Tuesday night—our first big party in the White House. I'm looking forward so much to having Mr. Robert Merrill sing some arias from Verdi—that, I know, will be wonderful. I confess to a question mark about the Christy Minstrels. I love folk music, but the name "Hootenanny" rather repels me. I guess I'm just too old-fashioned for it, but I can just hear my children, Luci especially, saying, "Moth—er!!"

Then I had to shift the gears of my mind in order to meet Frank Meloy, who came over to brief me on Italy—its recent politics and history, and economics, and on President and Signora Antonio Segni themselves—and to impart all those juicy bits of information he always knows.

After he left I got the word that I could expect Lyndon in about forty minutes. He was going to have a swim first and then would be home for dinner, which sounded too lucky. But anyway, it didn't turn out that way. About 9, I heard that he had returned from the swimming pool to the Cabinet Room, which portended no good; and that he was meeting with Rusk, McNamara, Bundy—about fourteen people—and since I had been watching a program about Panama on TV, that didn't sound very promising.

As the hours went on—9, 10:30, 11—I began to wonder what I could do about it. With fourteen men of such stature involved, I didn't quite dare do anything. I got a bulletin from the office about every thirty minutes advising me that they would let me know when Lyndon started to leave. Pretty soon I asked everyone in the kitchen to go home except two —one to cook and one to serve. That was about 9:30. About 10:30 I ate my own supper, rather forlornly, on a tray and went to bed at 12:30.

This is my problem which I must solve, if I'm to fill a useful role here where I find myself. My personal request to the Lord is that I can somehow be tactful enough, and gay enough, and sometimes even mean enough, to get Lyndon home at a reasonable hour for dinner and bed, or at least to get him to come home, bringing with him the documents of his office, so that he can work here in a more relaxed atmosphere.

It would belabor the obvious to say that on nights like this I think of Lyndon making his State of the Union speech or his first speech to Congress and of the two gentlemen standing behind him on the dais—both gentlemen I love—and I know that he must get through the next twelve months as hale and hearty and strong as possible.

It would belabor the obvious to say that every time I pass that portrait of President Woodrow Wilson—painted when the strains of office lay heavily upon him—it says to me: "Have his portrait painted soon."

Tuesday, January 14

It was not until this morning that I learned the meeting had broken up a little after midnight, and after a little letting down, a talk with his own staff, Lyndon had arrived at 2 A.M. for—shall we call it dinner—too late to talk to me about his day.

Today was the day President and Signora Segni of Italy arrived for their State visit. The day began with the mundane business of getting my white chiffon dress shortened, and then I spent an hour or so reading the background material on Italy, its state of politics and economics, and biographies of the Segnis. I also looked at the pictures of members of the official party so I would recognize them. At noon I drove with Lyndon to the Union Station for the official greeting.

President Segni is rather like an elderly elf, with wispy white hair and a gentle smile, which belies the long years he's spent in the government holding all the top posts there are—Prime Minister, Minister of Agriculture, Minister of Foreign Affairs. Signora Segni is gentle, and easy to be with.

We met them in 18-degree weather, with every breath we blew making a great white cloud of steam. We walked through the lined-up flags of all the fifty states of the Union and onto a little platform where there were the usual greeting ceremonies, slightly snarled up by the cold. A good many musical instruments won't play outdoors in 18-degree weather, and we had to rely too heavily on drums.

We got in the cars for a parade down Pennsylvania Avenue. Though cold, it was a crystal-bright day with gorgeous sunshine and snow everywhere, and the Capitol never looked whiter. The brilliant green, red, and white flags of Italy and our own red, white, and blue flags gave the day a festive air.

When we reached Blair House we said good-by, and I went back to the White House for lunch on a tray and to go over the guest list, and to inspect the State Dining Room laid for dinner. I was very pleased with it. Then I checked out the Yellow Room, fortunately, for even in this house things need dusting every now and then. Finally, feeling dressed up in my white Grecian flowing chiffon dress, I joined Lyndon and we waited for the word to go down to meet the Segnis. When it came we walked down the front steps of the White House, through the glaring lights of the photographers, and into the icy weather, I without a coat, to say hello to two very nice elderly people and the leaders of their government accompanying them.

We took our guests to the Yellow Room. This intimate gathering was always a part of the evening I liked best in the Kennedy days. The Chief Justice and Mrs. Warren were there; Secretary of State and Mrs. Rusk; the Italian Ambassador, Mr. Sergio Fenoaltea; our Ambassador to Italy, Mr. G. Frederick Reinhardt, and his wife; Angie Duke and Robin, without whom such things couldn't go on; and the chief members of the Italian party.

Cocktails were passed and then we exchanged the gifts. We gave them a silver box, engraved with the map of the United States and the map of Italy and a sentence from Henry Wadsworth Longfellow: *"Italy remains to all, the land of dreams and a vision of delight."* (Until about a week ago we'd have called this a cigarette box. Now it is called a "desk box" in deference to the new government reports on tobacco and cancer.) And there was, even more delightfully, a letter written in 1774 by Philip Mazzei, a compatriot of our guest of honor, who was a friend of Thomas Jefferson and Benjamin Franklin, and who had been asked by them to come to this country and look into the possibilities of improving our production of wheat and the introduction of vineyards. The letter was authentic and charming, translated into English along with the Italian and framed in leather.

Next, down that rather terrifying staircase to the tune of "Hail to the Chief," we went to stand in line and greet the guests assembled in the East Room. Besides the Leadership in the government, there were all of the members of Congress of Italian descent—Senator John Pastore, Representatives Pete Rodino, Dante Fascell, Silvio Conte. It was particularly nice to see Victor Anfuso, formerly a Congressman, now a Judge.

The labor leaders were there also—David Dubinsky, George Meany, and Walter Reuther. It gave me a lot of pleasure to see Perle Mesta, looking stunning, coming down the line with my friends Scooter and Dale Miller. And I welcomed Mrs. Charles Marsh, whose husband had played a considerable role in Lyndon's early life. She said something very nice —"Charles is here in spirit, you know."

After having read all about Sardinia being a crossroads of the world, —with the Phoenicians, the Carthaginians, the Spaniards, not to mention the Romans and the Greeks, and Lord knows who all else, having traveled there and left the relics of their lives and civilizations—and after having read about President Segni being a farmer, and of his many careers in government, I found that I need not have worried so much on what to talk to him about because the conversation was pleasant and easy. Mr. Giuseppe Saragat, the Foreign Minister, sat on my left.

The room was lovely! I glowed with pleasure as I looked around. After coffee and liqueurs we went into the East Room for the entertainment. Dick Adler introduced Robert Merrill of the Metropolitan Opera, who sang an aria from *Il Trovatore* and then a selection from Rossini's *Barber of Seville*. I wish I had had time to tell him I was raised on Scotti and Tetrazzini and Galli-Curci, singing all of the Verdi operas, on Red Seal Records.

Then came the Christy Minstrels. Everybody under twenty-five, I'm sure, knows them, but I must say that I hadn't known them before. I just fell in love with them. They're seven young people described as "the face of young America," doing folk music which they sing out with a considerable beat, rhythm, and vigor. I saw President Segni patting his foot and I believe the Christy Minstrels pleased everybody (except, perhaps, the critic Mr. Paul Hume, in the *Washington Post* next day).

We went out on the front porch in the frosty night to say good-by to the Segnis. Then Lyndon said, "I must get back to work." McGeorge Bundy said, "The President just hates to be unemployed."

One little thing that I'm going to have to do for *me* is to have an aide stand beside me in the receiving line. By the time the person's name is filtered to me (I'm the third individual in line), it has become indistinguishable. Either I know the guest already and do not need the name, or I do not get the name. The person goes by and there is not that moment of contact I really want.

This morning began with a session with Mr. West: agenda, how to handle 2 A.M. suppers, because that is the ridiculous hour my husband came home to eat his supper on Monday night. This cannot go on—first because I want him to live; second, because I want him to work well while he's living; and third, because that's no way to run a house.

We decided the one way to tackle the problem was to keep on hand a cooked turkey, ham, and roast beef, things to make into sandwiches, so that whenever we got the word from the office that there were ten or twelve people in the Cabinet Room and serious talks were going on, and the hour reached 9 or 9:30, we could make up a platter of sandwiches and send them over at 10 o'clock, along with big thermoses of coffee, milk, and some candy, because by that time everybody would need to renew energy.

The worst that could happen to me would be for them to break up the meeting just as I walked in the door with the sandwiches and they would be wasted—or else I could eat them for the next ten days for my own lunch! No, that wouldn't be the worst. The worst would be that I'd make them angry. But something has got to be done, because, first of all, I'm thinking of Lyndon. And second, there are some other women's husbands there who might be hungry too.

The second part of the agenda with Mr. West concerned the fact that when the evening waxed along to about 8 or 8:30 and we observed that there was nobody left in the office but Lyndon and one, two, or three staff members, it was obvious that we would not be having real company for dinner. Then we should send home most of the staff, leaving just the cook and one person to serve, which is the way I've run my house all of my life. That way I can gently prod and urge Lyndon as best I can, win or lose, to come home and continue his business talks over dinner.

We also talked about how to clean the beautiful yellow sofas in the Yellow Room, which are really so perishable when heavily used. Next, I tried to call René, the principal chef, and Ferdinand, who made the desserts, because the dinner last night had been so beautiful and I wanted to tell them what a triumph it was. But, alas, both of them were out of the building. I guess they're artists, and artists go about things in their own way. I simply left word that I had called, and I shall try to reach them another time.

We went to the Italian Embassy about 1:30 for the Segnis' lunch in our honor. How I love their gift to us! It is a bust of the Emperor Tiberius dating back to the first century. This will be the most valuable artifact in my small collection—a charming link with history—and how eloquently it speaks of the grandeur of their past.

The guest list was pretty much as it usually is—State Department people, Cabinet people, and the entire Italian delegation. The Italian Embassy reflects the imprint of its own country, which is what an Embassy should do. Dominating the dining room are two enormous chandeliers of Venetian glass—and they are pink and blue, beige, and every pale color in the world, very delicate and terrifically ornate.

I sat between President Segni and the Minister of Foreign Affairs, Mr. Rusk's opposite number, Signor Saragat. The food was so beautiful that I couldn't keep from remarking on it to the Ambassador, who was within ear and eye reach down the table. Each dish that came out was an architectural dream. What a chef they must have! This brought the following comment from the Ambassador, an urbane and charming man: "The most important man in the Embassy is the cook. You can get by with a mediocre Ambassador and a wonderful cook but you cannot run an Embassy with a poor chef."

The Foreign Minister also made an interesting comment in answer to something I said—that it seemed to me, as a pure outsider, that the great monolithic structure, the Roman Catholic hierarchy, was finally beginning to change under the last two Popes. He said yes, that when he went to see the Pope now he wore his business suit, and he did not kneel. His daughter knelt (are women more prone to ritual?), but he did not kneel. It was like going to see anybody else.

I wonder what Lyndon and Mr. Segni talked about in their substantive talks. My feeling is that this visit is a sort of reassurance to us, to the Italians themselves, and to the world that the flurry some months ago about the election and about Italy swerving toward communism isn't serious. The new balance in Italian politics with the Socialists in the government still leaves Italy firmly with the West. At any rate, the toasts couldn't have been more beautiful, or sounded more pro-Western.

We made our good-bys to the Segnis and left. I didn't get to take my head of Tiberius with me, but I'm going to watch to see that it gets delivered to the White House. Later I went downstairs to the Blue Room to greet the Senate and the House members of the Inter-Parliamentary Committee, about forty members from our own Congress and from the Parliament of Canada, at Senator George Aiken's request.

While we were having our sherry in the State Dining Room, Lyndon came in, and with about ten minutes of greetings and conversation I think he got the maximum results. This is what I want him to do—visit for a short time with real warmth, touch as many bases as he can, and save time for the real work.

Next followed a little time to curl up in front of the fire in my bedroom, and talk to Luci. I'm so glad she's going to the Buck Hill meeting on Christianity, because she said: "It's something I've always wanted to do, Mother." She'll be exposed to a lot of young people, both boys and girls, from excellent schools. They will listen to discourses on religion by instructors from major universities. There will be good minds and sharpening of the wits, and there'll be some skiing and some dancing. I think Luci will come back with horizons a bit expanded. Then I had a good talk on the telephone with Lynda Bird about everything from clothes to art.

I finally got a chance to read the wonderful article in *Time* about John Connally—on the cover he looks like everything he is—and what they wrote about Texas is about as close to the truth as one can hope for.

I began to think about how to pry loose my friend from his office and get him home. One of the things that makes me think the Lord has his hand on Lyndon's shoulder is that about one minute after Lyndon's head hits the pillow, I hear his announcement that he is now asleep, with his regular breathing. That happens only with the Lord's blessed lucky ones!

Thursday, January 16

At one o'clock today I had what to me is the most pleasant type of ladies' luncheon—not given for any particular person or reason, but just to enjoy the company and perhaps learn about something of particular interest to women. I asked the Senate wives whom I enjoy, such as Mary Ellen Monroney, Betty Fulbright, Henrietta Anderson, and Abigail McCarthy, and then from a long way off Mrs. Philip Hoff, the wife of the Governor of Vermont, amazingly enough a Democrat. There was also our long-time friend (whose husband Bob is President of NBC) Jean Kintner, and Miss Katherine Quinn, a veteran Democratic worker from Connecticut who I expect knows every precinct vote for the last twenty years. And then, what an utter joy it was for me to meet and have at my own table Helen Hayes, who is in Washington playing in *Miss Dove*.

I have watched her from the other side of the footlights for so many years and just loved her and I found her enchanting in person.

While we were drinking our coffee, Ellen Stoutenberg got up and told us about her life and times with the UN. She had brought down twenty-eight delegates to the Ranch last April. I thought a little information about what some private citizens are doing to show UN delegates, confined to the vast steel and stone canyons of New York, some other part of the United States would be a good idea. I plan to have more of these gatherings of Women Do-ers.

I spent the afternoon waiting for Luci to come in so I could give her the good, good news. I had had a talk with Miss Katharine Lee, of National Cathedral School, who told me that yes, she thought she could re-arrange one of Luci's finals so that she could have it on Tuesday or Wednesday afternoon. That would enable her to get away one day early and have her trip to Wisconsin, a trip that I fear will not meet with the approval of all the members of our family, but which I—maybe I am a softie—very much want her to have.

One of the best pieces of news Miss Lee gave me was that Luci's attitude is getting so much better. She doesn't panic any more on exams. She is organizing her time better. They think that, if the doctor agrees, she might be able to add the course that was dropped when she began to have the eye trouble that has caused a lack of self-confidence, both in her school work and with her family. If she can complete the course before summer, she will be able to go back to Camp Mystic for her seventh summer.

We had an early dinner this evening—7 o'clock, business suit, about sixty-four guests, for the heads of the Senate Commitees and their ranking members and the Leadership on both sides and their wives. The purpose, as it is so often with Lyndon, was really business. He invited John Mc-Cone of the CIA, McNamara, Rusk, and Kermit Gordon of Budget (spelled in capital letters this time of the year!) to brief them. As soon as we had all filed into the Blue Room and shaken hands, Lyndon announced that he would like the gentlemen to accompany him to the little theater where there would be a briefing. I asked the ladies to go upstairs —perhaps some of them might like to see the second floor, the family living quarters. So we all trooped up, except for Senator Margaret Chase Smith, who went with the gentlemen. In the course of the evening Kermit Gordon remarked, "I have seen more of your husband in the last three weeks than you have," and I said that both his wife and I had a complaint to enter, but just so it wound up in saving the country a few million dollars, we wouldn't mind.

Many of the women said they had never been on the second floor before, and they are the wives of the ranking members of the Senate. We saw practically everything, except Luci's room, where she was studying for finals, and Lynda Bird's room. As always, the Lincoln Room attracted the most interest, and I was glad that I had studied the room enough to remember that five pieces of the furniture, including the Victorian settee and two of the little slipper chairs, were original pieces that had been here in the Lincoln Administration. I did point out that this was not the room in which President Lincoln actually slept—that it was my own bedroom where he slept. Later on several women looked at the plaque above the fireplace in my bedroom that designates it as his bedroom, and at the small one below that Mrs. Kennedy added, which reads: "IN THIS ROOM LIVED JOHN FITZGERALD KENNEDY WITH HIS WIFE JACQUELINE DURING THE TWO YEARS, TEN MONTHS AND TWO DAYS HE WAS PRESIDENT OF THE UNITED STATES."

All the time, as much as I enjoyed the ladies, I kept wishing I could eavesdrop on the men, because the evening was designed to acquaint them with what the Administration was trying to do. It was not planned to push or convert or sell, but to lay out the program and indicate what the Administration ought to do, and why, with an invitation for their judgments. Well anyway I hope there will be some residue of good will and a good deal more knowledge of the program.

When we went in to dinner, we were seated at round tables in the State Dining Room and I found myself delightfully enough between Senator Dick Russell, who was on my left, and Senator Carl Hayden, who was on my right. Senator Hayden used a sentence about Horatius at the bridge which I have heard all my life vaguely and never heard accurately. It went something like this: "Lo, I will stand at thy right hand, and keep the bridge with thee." I am glad to have him there.

Most of the guests went home about a quarter to 10. Just a few lingered and went upstairs—the Humphreys, the Fulbrights, the O'Briens, and Lyndon and I. There was nobody upstairs to serve, so I went in the kitchen and took over. Presently they all left and I hoped that would be the end of the evening. It was for me but, unhappily, it wasn't for Lyndon. There was a large stack of papers on Panama for him to read. Dean Rusk had shaken his head and warned me about this as he came in that evening, so it was another 2 o'clock night for Lyndon.

One of my last thoughts of the day was being grateful to Bess for concocting a menu that was about as inexpensive as you could work out for such a large group. There was just one wine and there was chicken. I have a feeling chicken is going to be a frequent feature of our menus at the White House!

At 11 this morning Clark Clifford, our long-time friend and adviser, came in to discuss art with me, in great big red capital letters—to wit, what's going to happen to all of the sprouting varieties of committees which Mrs. Kennedy had established in order to bring the White House to its present state of beauty. There is the Fine Arts Committee, the Committee on Paintings, the Library Committee, and the White House Historical Association, of which only the last is actually an incorporated business entity. The rest of them are rather nebulous, without any precise standing or assurance of continuity.

My desire (and I think Clark knows it and I think that is what he is working toward) is to make sure that there *is* continuity in all of the good things that have been done, preservation of everything that has gone forward. I think the job of Curator of the White House should be an official position, so that the house will not be at the whim of any First Lady.

Clark is going about this in a very orderly fashion, suggesting that an Executive Order be issued by Lyndon establishing the position of Curator of the White House and the Committee on the Preservation of the White House. This new Committee would pick up several of the members of the White House Historical Association. They would be John Walker, Director of the National Gallery of Art; Leonard Carmichael of the Smithsonian Institution or his successor; Clark Clifford himself, I certainly hope; Bill Walton, Chairman of the Commission of Fine Arts; and George Hartzog, Director of the National Park Service. We would have four or possibly more public members, chosen for their taste (and knowledge of furniture and art). Mrs. Kennedy has made a couple of suggestions, which couldn't be more wonderful, and perhaps we might want to increase the number of public members on the Committee from four to six or even more.

I never expect art to be my major concern in the White House, but I expect it to be a growing joy. And the more I learn about the place, the more I love it. Education is a contagious sort of thing. The more you get, the more you like it.

In the afternoon I had tea with an attractive young couple, Governor Edward Breathitt of Kentucky, newly elected, and his young, pretty, and candid wife. It is a joy to see somebody like them starting out in politics. Luci Baines came in from school just as I was about to bid them good-by, her arms full of books, old tennis shoes, and coats, wailing about finals, so I think the Breathitts must have realized we were a fairly normal family.

At 7:30 the Charles Engelhards and the Mike Mansfields came for dinner. Lyndon was late, so I had a good long visit with them before he arrived. Jane Engelhard was as elegant as usual—beautiful and smart—and on top of it, so industrious.

Thank goodness, when reading about White House art I had read that the Engelhards had been the donors of enough furniture to furnish a dining room. The guidebook did not say where it was, but spoke of an oval dining table, a buffet, a large sideboard and a small serving sideboard, made by some of the great cabinetmakers of Baltimore and Annapolis. I asked Mrs. Engelhard where they were and said, "Let's go look at them." It turned out that they were in the downstairs family dining room. She told me all sorts of interesting stories about what the Committee on Fine Arts did, and sometimes didn't do, among them an amusing story about herself and Mr. Henry duPont—who must be all of eighty years old—pushing and shoving the furniture around!

We stopped off in the Queen's Room, which Jane—as I do—thinks is the prettiest of all the rooms, and the Treaty Room, which to me is always a little forbidding and overpowering. I wouldn't be quite at ease in there. Jane said the Treaty Room was one of [Stephane] Boudin's contributions to the restoration and he was a pretty controversial figure around the White House.

A little later Lyndon joined us and we had a pleasant dinner. There were only seven of us, the smallest group we've yet had to dinner in the White House (except at those unreasonable hours of 10 or 11 or 12 P.M. or 2 A.M. or on the kitchen table when I just give Lyndon a sandwich).

This whole day was an adventure of my own—my personal pleasure!

I left early this morning with Wendy Marcus and Bess tourist class on a commercial airline for New York, which seemed to be a fact of considerable interest to the newsmen. We were headed for the Metropolitan Museum of Art, where Mary Lasker met us. She had offered to be my guardian angel through the tour. The Director, Mr. James Rorimer, the Curator, Theodore Rousseau, Mr. James Fosburgh and the President of the Trustees, Mr. Roland Redmond, were on hand too to take us through.

We went to a board room where they had set aside a group of American paintings which they would be willing to lend to the White House for two years. There was a Peter Hurd called "Rancheria," which for simplicity, for the wide stretches of sky, for the look of the country of New Mexico and Texas, was quite appealing to me. (I think I'll ask them if I may borrow it.) One of the dearest pictures was a Mary Cassatt portrait of a mother and child. There was a Childe Hassam called "Golden Afternoon in Oregon" which would bring sunlight to the family living room on a gray winter day.

We spent about an hour walking through the museum. One of the things that appealed to me most was the fact that we came upon group after group of school children—twenty or thirty at a time—with a teacher having them in tow, explaining the pictures to them. I didn't realize that there was so much exposure of school children to art. Is this a new departure? At any rate, it's good for anybody who lives in a town to know the riches of the town—or, I should say, the riches of the world, because they're certainly gathered here.

Trying to see the Metropolitan Museum of Art at one time is like trying to read the *Encyclopaedia Britannica* at one sitting. It can't be done, but it's enormously illuminating to go through with people like Rousseau and Rorimer, who point out not only the significant and wonderful things about all that you're seeing, but also the funny little gossipy things.

From the Metropolitan we went to the Whitney Museum, and there I was met by Mr. John Baur, Assistant Director, and Mr. John Gordon, Curator, who took me on a brief trip through the galleries and then to see pictures they might be able to let us borrow. There were two Grant Woods, in sepia. They were unfinished and depicted the interiors of an

American farmhouse while dinner was being prepared for the threshers. They had a nice, nostalgic quality and I think they would be good for the Fish Room, which is really the President's reception room (so called because a large fish hung on the wall there in FDR's day). There was also a little American Primitive—just made you merry to look at it.

We went on to Mary Lasker's for lunch in her charming house, which is like a setting for jewels—her pictures are the jewels. She had gathered together some interesting guests—Anthony Bliss from the Metropolitan Opera, and our friends who had accompanied us this morning, Ted Rousseau and the Rorimers. Mr. Fosburgh came with Mrs. Fosburgh; Roger Stevens of the Kennedy Cultural Center was there. It was such an interesting assemblage and I felt alien but excited.

Any participation I have in the world of art, in this job that Lyndon and I have, will be because I really enjoy it. But if I can spotlight, serve to bring publicity to—to use a crude word, "advertise" the pleasures of art, whether it be paintings or plays or opera, this will be a service joyfully rendered.

Mary graciously and kindly offered to let me have something from her own house for the White House. I'm just not a natural-born salesman, and I think she'll just have to pick something out and bring it down here and say "This is where it belongs" before I could accept it. Of all the lovely things in her house, to me almost the loveliest is the scene from her living room window, which looks out over the East River with the boats plying their way up and down and the gray stretches of that magic city.

Tonight our friend of many years Abe Fortas, Ambassador Adlai Stevenson, and Mary Lasker joined us—and we set out to see *After the Fall*, the first production of the new repertory theater of Lincoln Center. Because Lincoln Center isn't finished yet the play was performed in the ANTA Washington Square Theater in Greenwich Village.

After the Fall was written by Arthur Miller. I remember seeing *Death of a Salesman*, which I enjoyed tremendously, if you can use the word "enjoy." In this current play—well, he sort of saws off the top of his skull and slits open his heart and lets you look in on the agonies and the awareness of an intelligent and sensitive man during the last three or four decades. He gives his views of the Depression, the Nazis, World War II, the period after—when a lot of people were being called up before Congressional Committees for questioning about being Communists (Miller was one of those called)—and also the two unsuccessful marriages that he lived through, with much pain, and the third that he is just entering on.

The play was highly autobiographical, I think, but if one doesn't write about what one knows about, how one has lived, what else is there? I thought it was *magnificently* written and I want to buy it and read it. There was a line that I loved, about holding the future in your hands like a vase. There were any number of gripping phrases—hammer and rapier use of the English language. It was acted so well by Jason Robards that I wondered why he wasn't a sweating, fainting wreck at the end of it. He carried such a load for about two and a half hours.

Elia Kazan directed the play, whose central character Maggie is patterned after Miller's second wife Marilyn Monroe. The tenderness and agony and torment get to you through the *marvelous* acting. At first I thought I was going to mind it because there were no stage sets, nothing but a big empty stage with some gray cubes here and there where the actors could sit down. But I became so absorbed in the characters that the absence of sets went unnoticed.

I wonder what the critics will have to say about *After the Fall*. I hardly see how they can brand it as anything but superb—and yet, if Marilyn Monroe left a legacy of love, there will be those who will be angry that Miller wrote it, and there will be those who will say it is in bad taste.

After the play we went to the Loeb Student Center at New York University, where there was a champagne supper, and a chance to visit—though only in staccato phrases, with Arthur Miller, Jason Robards, Myrna Loy, and Lauren Bacall. Mayor Robert Wagner came in and sat beside me, and I saw Marietta Tree and Jean Kintner, and Perle Mesta. Perle Mesta is everywhere.

The play and supper were a benefit to help launch the repertory theater and that, I think, will be a good thing. Whatever the critics say, I think *After the Fall* is a magnificent play, although after watching it you're just as tired as if you'd plowed all day—that is, if you've got any feelings at all.

One extra nice thing about the evening—I find it's always pleasant to be around Adlai Stevenson. He escorted me home, probably too late for his hard day's work tomorrow, but not too late for my own enjoyment.

This whole morning was spent in the world of clothes (spelled in capitals). Stanley Marcus and two of his assistants, Kay Kerr and Clara Treyz, had very kindly assembled and brought to the Carlyle Hotel clothes from all over, from every maker, by various designers, with wide variety in prices. I tried on, and tried on, and tried on, and finally bought two outfits. Soon I hope I'll get this wardrobe wrapped up and never have to think about it again until summer.

In the afternoon we returned to Washington, because tonight Prime Minister Lester Pearson of Canada gave a dinner in our honor at the Canadian Embassy. This turned out to be an unusually pleasant official dinner, because it was very informal. There were only about eighteen people there, with men outnumbering women—the Rusks, of course; and the Pearsons; the Charles Ritchies (he is the Canadian Ambassador); the W. Walton Butterworths (he is our Ambassador to Canada); the Dukes; and several Canadian Cabinet members they had brought along.

The Prime Minister's toast was delightful. He told how he barely missed being a United States citizen because, during the war, one of his uncles had come to Chicago, had done well, and he had written to his two nephews who were engaged in the war, and said, "I've got a job for you boys, if you want to come back here and go to work for me." One of them chose to but Pearson did not. He went back to Canada. "Now what if I'd gone on to Chicago," he said. "Who knows, I might have been a Senator from Illinois now!"

He also joked about the fact that there were seven Oxford men and only one Cambridge man at the dinner—the Cambridge man being their Secretary of State. I couldn't help smiling to myself and thinking, "Well, if you can't get to Oxford or Cambridge, it's pretty nice to be able to make it to Southwest Texas State Teachers College!"

After dinner we went in to what Mr. Pearson called the "Santa Claus room." There the Canadian delegation presented me with a green enameled maple leaf pin set with small diamonds—symbolic of Canada—and I love it, because I like things that speak of the country they come from. To Lyndon they gave a saddle, just like the Canadian Royal Mounted Police use—those men who were always the symbol of romance and daring adventure in my childhood.

We found the Pearsons excellent company. They're strong believers in friendship between our countries. Thank God there's one border in the world that, as of now, we don't have to worry about. I gather they too, in Canada, have their difficulties with minority populations, with the French provinces actually talking of seceding from the Dominion. Certainly nothing could conceivably come of this, could it?

Thursday, January 23

Today was one of those days when there was just too much—too many appointments, too much to do, always that sense of running behind. In the morning I tackled the mountain that is my desk, the tyrant that sits there and glowers at me. At 2 o'clock I had a meeting with Cliff Carter [Democratic National Committeeman], Liz, Bess, Mac Kilduff standing in for Salinger, and we tried to make some decisions on my future schedules —what things to accept, what we could do without, what we must refuse. The possibilities varied from a reception for young college editors in the East Room in February and later a big one for the American Society of Newspaper Editors during their annual meeting in April, to how many of the fund-raising dinners Lyndon and I should make it a point to attend. Visits for me to Kentucky, Michigan, and New York were discussed, weighed, most of them decided on. I kept on repeating that I wanted to go somewhere in the South, possibly to Georgia or Alabama for something like the ARA, the HEW, the Accelerated Works Program, or some college event. I have no illusions whatever about how much good I can do, but maybe I can attract some public attention to the accomplishments of those programs, and furthermore, because I am tired of everybody's acting like the South is a stepchild. I belong to the South and it to me, and I intend to say so even if I get a rebuff for it.

We had dinner at round tables in the State Dining Room tonight at the Senate briefing. Senator Tom Dodd was on my right. Gale McGee was on my left and I couldn't have asked for better company. Not surprisingly the menu was once more chicken. There was only one wine, but one wine is enough for anybody.

The intricacies of the Tax Bill today are more than I can keep up with— defeat, victory, defeat, victory—in and out, like cattle in a chute. I really don't know how Lyndon can reach a moment of peace at the end of the day, but you couldn't have told it from his face. He looks relaxed, happy, successful, even after what must have been a rather grueling press conference.

Lyndon sent me one of those messages which I always receive with a slight cringe, asking me to get up and say a few words about Maggie—Senator Warren Magnuson—who came to the Congress when we did in 1937 and is the ranking Democrat here tonight. Lyndon, in turn, planned to say something about Senator Roman L. Hruska. It was easy though to reminisce about our years together—Maggie's and ours—and I was proud of Lyndon's fine and accurate statement about a member of the opposite party.

The surprise of the evening arrived when Lynda Bird got up at her father's prodding and said she had just come from the University of Texas where we had the Number One football team in the nation, to the house where she could listen to the Number One people of the nation, and a few more pleasant little things, just as poised as you please. To my delight she will be living here with us and going to George Washington for this second semester.

About 10:30 folks began to drift away. This is nice until you consider that you arrive back in your bedroom to find the old giant still here—all the mail waiting to be signed! (And then I am keeping up with my promise to myself to take exercises at least three times a week so that, maybe after about six months, I may be a more fit human being.)

Friday, January 24

Today was a day of really leveling on the art project. Clark, Abe, Bill Walton, Pierre Salinger, Liz, and I met in the Queen's Sitting Room to discuss our project. I had decided that was the room where we would be least interrupted. It has become my own little private retreat.

The Executive Order already prepared by Clark, gone over by Abe, considered by Walton, was now presented to Salinger and Liz to evaluate from the news standpoint.

There would be a Curator of the White House as a permanent position. A Committee for the Preservation of the White House was established, consisting of the heads of the National Park Service, National Gallery, Smithsonian Institution, Fine Arts Commission and several public members chosen by the First Lady.

Clark said that Mrs. Kennedy had suggested that two of the public members be Mr. Henry duPont, Chairman of the Fine Arts Committee, and Mr. James Fosburgh, Chairman of the Painting Committee. There couldn't be two with more sterling credentials, and there couldn't be anybody to whose wishes I'd want more to accede, but that left so few members of the public group to enable me to put more of my own personal stamp on the Committee.

And then Clark brought us the news that Mrs. Kennedy had agreed to serve on it herself, which is something that I had asked her the very first day when I went to see her; I think it was the day after the funeral, Tuesday, November 26. She will probably furnish the flame and the fuel for the forward progress of such an organization, so that will be wonderful. Now my job is to look around and find people, hopefully some from the Southwest or the South, with equally outstanding credentials, and I feel some of them must be women. So it gets down to a job of research.

The second part of the agenda was concerned with how to make the other members of the Fine Arts Committee and the Painting Committee feel that they are appreciated; how to retain their talents, their friendship, their future help. The announcement will be made as soon as we can select our public members.

After about three hours of hard work, we said good-by, and I jumped in the pool (which is as hot as a Turkish bath) to try to drain out some of the uncertainties about all that I've been doing, and then I drove to the beauty parlor with Lynda Bird. My moments with her are stolen moments, but they're always good ones.

Monday, January 27

Today was the day we entertained the Queen of Greece. In the morning I did a little work and then started getting dressed. That was when it began to dawn on me that I *really* don't have any new clothes!

A few minutes before one o'clock I was out on the front portico to meet that beautiful woman, that extremely assured career Queen, Frederika of Greece, with her daughter Princess Irene. The handsome Ambassador from their country, Mr. Alexander Matsas, accompanied them. We went upstairs to the Yellow Room, with a small group—Mrs. Carolou, the Grand Mistress of the Court, and two or three more members of the Greek party; Chief Justice and Mrs. Warren, who have traveled to Greece and are always an addition; and the George Balls of the State Department.

The Queen is always one who gets right down to what the State Department calls "substantive conversation," and I could overhear her saying something about Cyprus to Lyndon: "Forty miles straight, between there and Turkey, . . . can get there in a motorboat." Knowing that area is all a sort of a powder keg, and the least match could set off a conflagration, I found myself involuntarily trying to eavesdrop.

The Queen has beauty, brains, and humor but she is also something of a firebrand. She might be difficult for the politicians of her country to deal with, but she is somebody who works at her job and I do admire her.

After cocktails were served (and, incidentally, one never gets time for more than a sip of the drinks one has up there), and the presentation of gifts, we went down the stairs for the luncheon, Lyndon escorting the Queen. I came next with Princess Irene and Lynda Bird. We stood briefly at the bottom of the steps for photographs. I fared pretty well in those, I think. It doesn't always happen!

I may be the only living human being who enjoys a receiving line, but that is the only contact I have with some of the people who are invited to the house, our home for the time being. That is my moment to express a little friendship, a little pleasure, interest, and so I do enjoy it.

From the Senate there were the Fulbrights, the John Sparkmans, the Symingtons, the Harrison Williams, and Maurine Neuberger. Standing in for Secretary Rusk was George Ball. From the House came the Albert Thomases and the Peter Freylinghuysens (looking as if ten generations of aristocrats had produced him)—and thank goodness I had a few minutes to tell Peter how lovely I thought the paneling which he had given to Blair House was—and young Congressman John Brademas, with whom we've spent some pleasant weekends. I was so happy to have Walter Jenkins there from our office, and I hope the party provided an hour's respite from the long hours of work he's struggling with now. And there was sweet little Marie Fehmer, Lyndon's secretary.

And then—oh, interesting sign of the times!—the first guest from my home town of Marshall, Texas, Dr. Thomas W. Cole, President of Wiley College, a Negro. Of course, the guest list included many Greeks who have made a success in this country, who have contributed to the bloodstream of its culture, its business, its achievements.

This was the first time Lynda Bird has been present at a royal occasion—in fact, at any State occasion since we've been here. She was seated next to the Princess. She doesn't say much about enjoying it here but I hope she does. To me it seems such a marvelous opportunity for a young person.

Without a doubt, the most noticed Greek was one of humble origin and of simple achievements, Mr. John Govatos of Corpus Christi, Texas, a friend of Lyndon's since 1931. In the middle of the seated luncheon he got up, walked calmly over, and leaned over the Queen's chair and over Lyndon's chair and chatted with them. He told them how he and his wife were married on the very same day that the Queen and King Paul were married, and how their child was born on the very same day as the Queen's, and how he, when he had known Lyndon thirty-five years ago in Corpus Christi, had predicted that one day Lyndon would be President of the United States!

We made Betty Beale of the *Washington Star* happy, I think, by seating her next to Adlai Stevenson, although she did have some heavy competition from Mrs. Charles Lindbergh, so attractive and quietly magnetic.

Lyndon's toast was charming and true because so much that we are in the Western world goes back to a little Greek town of several thousand years ago. But the Queen stole the show, she was so witty. She said that the Delphic oracle must have left her country and come to ours, since John Govatos was predicting thirty-five years ago that Lyndon would someday be President.

When I bade the last guest good-by, I went upstairs to the Queen's Sitting Room and spent a couple of hours with Mrs. Lindbergh. The interview for the magazine article she was writing had been planned to occupy about one hour, but because I liked listening and talking to her, I myself prolonged it.

I was interested in the diversity between her book *Gift from the Sea*, which was so introspective and delicate, and her later book *Dearly Beloved*, which had humor in it and some bitterness. The characters lived pretty painful lives in *Dearly Beloved*. That they should both come from the same mind intrigued me.

Our conversation was interrupted in order to permit me to run down to the southwest portico and greet Warrie Lynn Smith, throw my arms around her, hug her, and say, "Come in and help us live in this place, dear." Lynda Bird was there and, naturally, Lynda's "unfriends," the photographers.

After Mrs. Lindbergh had gone, I went back to the desk to work. Later Lyndon asked me to join him in the pool. By that time it was 9 o'clock. So I went for a swim with him, for it had been a bad day. Cyprus and Panama, and a few troubles in Texas don't all mix up to make a cream puff of a life.

Sandwiched in the day, and herein lies the crux of my dilemma, because it *has* to be sandwiched in, was a little talk with Luci. She showed me a small snapshot of a sign in Maiden Rock, Wisconsin. Stretched above the street (and probably Maiden Rock is about the size of Johnson City) the sign proclaimed, "WELCOME, LUCI, TO MAIDEN ROCK."

I also had a few words with Lynda, in which she told me more about her walks each night. Last night she walked all the way to the Capitol and back. If I'm going to win the battle to keep us all close together, I'll need to apply equal time to the girls, along with Lyndon's business, and my public duties, and my own pursuits.

Thursday, January 30

One of the highlights of the day was that Mrs. Alice Roosevelt Longworth came to tea, with only Lynda Bird and Warrie Lynn and me. It was one of those afternoons I had promised myself—one of those completely unofficial things, no duty at all, just pleasure. Mrs. Longworth has lived this life I've loved, in this town I've loved, and seen so much of it— has observed it with such a caustic wit and at such close-up range, that I yearned to spend an hour with her. And it was a grand one! I rushed downstairs hoping to meet her at the front entrance to accord her the dignity that is due her age and position—but, alas, I was just a moment late. She had on her stiff, black hat, which is a trademark with her, and a big smile. We came upstairs and sat in the family living room.

It was no trouble to persuade her to reminisce about the days when she was in the house. She told us that it was true that when one of her little brothers had been sick, they had taken his pony up in the elevator to his room because it would surely help make him well! I can understand that so well, because Luci really needed our beagles Him and Her at hand one day not long ago when she was sick.

To show how much this town has changed—that same brother rode his horse, unattended by any Secret Service person, to school a few miles from the White House. She told us about attending a Republican dinner for President Eisenhower—one of the appreciation dinners where several Senators were deploring the sad state of social life, when people jumped in swimming pools with their clothes on and did the "Twist" in the stately halls of the White House. She laughed and she talked about the time her father had an American wrestler and a Japanese practitioner of jujitsu in the East Room, stripped to their waists, engaging in their respective styles of battling, to see which one would come off best. I guess one of the main things I like about Alice Longworth is her spirit and vitality at seventy-nine or thereabouts. She also mentioned a time when she herself jumped into a swimming pool with her clothes on, but it was on board ship and she had on the white, washable summer clothes that were the fashion for strolling the deck in that day.

This was the first time that I realized that her stepmother, not her mother, was the First Lady at that time. President Theodore Roosevelt had been married before, and she was a child of his first marriage. Her mother had died at her birth, or shortly thereafter, and her stepmother was mother of the other five little Roosevelts. She must have been a pretty difficult daughter to raise in the White House, coming in at seventeen. But she has added a lot of zest to Washington and the world. She sounded to me as if she had liked her stepmother and respected her, but that the relationship was not exactly close. Maybe she was just too much of a free spirit. She said that when she was married, the wedding was supposed to take place at 12 noon. At 11 the guests were already streaming into the house and she was still upstairs, not dressed, and her stepmother was about to have a fit because she wasn't prepared to receive the guests. I found myself feeling somewhat sympathetic toward the stepmother.

Mrs. Longworth spoke about how her father hunted peccaries in Texas —I wonder where the peccaries could have been—maybe in the Big Thicket—and how he had roped wolves. She also said that the animal heads that hung in the State Dining Room were not the results of his safaris but were good versions of the heads of American animals he thought ought to be represented in the White House. When an artist wanted to carve a lion on one of the marble mantelpieces in the house, he insisted: "No, indeed, it should be the buffalo, the bison, because that's a native animal."

Lynda and Warrie Lynn sat entranced during the conversation and asked more questions than I did. This is the sort of experience I want Lynda Bird here for, to soak it up. In fact, it was a delicious hour and a half.

I don't know whether I would like to be around when Mrs. Longworth is describing her visit later on to somebody else, because I don't know how we appear in her eyes. She often mentioned her granddaughter, who is off at school, and said that she would like to bring her here to show her the house. That is a request I certainly want to see that we carry out.

The other event that made this an important day was our last dinner and briefing for the Senate. I wonder why I should feel sorry for our hard-working Secretary of State, and for McNamara, and for Kermit Gordon, when, after all, Lyndon is doing all of this, too, and much more besides? Perhaps it's because I'm so used to seeing Lyndon work so hard—also because I think he has a thorough understanding of how necessary it is to work with the Congress. The evening followed the usual pattern—cocktails, briefing, ladies upstairs, to see the family quarters. One of the funny events of the evening was when Mrs. Gaylord Nelson [wife of the Wisconsin Senator] arrived with one heel of her shoe broken half in two, sighing that she was going to have to hobble around over the White House the rest of the evening. I promptly took off my shoe and tried to put it on her to see if we could send upstairs quickly for another pair. Mine didn't fit and then Warrie Lynn, who always comes to the rescue, strolled by and stuck out her shoe. It was the right size, so Cinderella went off to get herself fixed up with another pair of shoes.

Lyndon had Maurine Neuberger on his right and Joan Kennedy, so soft and lovely in a red velvet dress, on his left. He toasted Ken Keating, who was the top Republican present. And it was with a lot of pleasure, if not much advance notice, that I toasted Mike Monroney. There's a lot to toast him about, too. One of the main things was the sheer courage of his voting against raising the price of oil back in the days (was it after or during the war?) when the price lines were being held to prevent inflation. The oil industry, with a good deal on its side, was pushing and shoving for a rise in the price of crude. Lyndon and Mike were the only two Senators from any of the oil-producing states who had the—well, "guts" is the best word —to vote to hold the line.

After dinner we went in to the East Room where there was dancing— and we really had a good time! Senator Strom Thurmond is a delightful dancer, as well as an accomplished passer out of compliments. But it's the most fun of all to dance with George Smathers.

At least we put in a good day and made a good try—and it was fun, too. And, no surprise, we served "Breast of Chicken Washington"!

Today began early. I got up at the dark hour of 6:30 to be able to leave by 7:30 for the Congressional Wives Prayer Breakfast. As I went into the familiar room at the Mayflower Hotel, already full of women, and walked among the tables, I thought of how many times I had done this before. When I got to the head table, I found Mrs. Richard Langford of Maryland presiding, and Mrs. B. Everett Jordan, wife of the Senator from North Carolina, ready to introduce the main speaker, Mrs. Billy Graham, wife of the evangelist. Seated directly in front of us was a table full of Embassy wives. There was Mrs. Chung Yo Kim, wife of the Ambassador of Korea; a lady from one of the African countries, in an exotic native costume; at least one or two from Arab countries who I felt sure must be Moslems. I wondered what all of this must seem like to them?

My greeting was to quote a prayer that I heard on my trip to Greece at the American Farm School, founded by an American missionary near Salonika. This lovely song, sung by the Greek farm boys, had been taught them by the American missionaries.

> *This is my song, Oh God of all the Nations,*
> *A song of peace for lands afar and mine,*
> *This is my home, the country where my heart is,*
> *This is my hope, my dream, my shrine,*
> *But other hearts in other lands are beating*
> *With hopes and dreams the same as mine.*

The song had made a considerable impression on me when I heard it that long-ago day in Greece, and so I brought it out for this occasion. I think it fitted in very well.

Mrs. Luther Hodges, from North Carolina, gave the Old Testament reading, and we sang some old familiar hymns—"What a Friend I Have in Jesus," . . . I have been a member of the Episcopal Church for more than thirty years, yet I still remember and participate far better in those old songs from my Methodist upbringing. I think if I had done a count on those present, I would have found that a sizable proportion of them were Southerners and Westerners. To get up and pray in public and be outspoken about it—well, it comes easier to us, I think. I find myself a little self-conscious about it, but if it is one of the strongest feelings in your makeup, why not say so right out loud?

Mrs. Billy Graham, who is as pretty as her husband is handsome, gave a very down-to-earth talk about religion in the housewife's life, when her days are full of lots of children and shortage of money and plenty of problems. Then the men came in—Lyndon and a few of the leading Senators who had started the Prayer Breakfast, and Billy Graham, who spoke briefly. We made an early departure and back to work. I took Dr. and Mrs. Graham back with me to Lyndon's office. She hadn't seen it and we had a little visit there before I went on to a very important meeting—for me—a meeting with my correspondence staff in the East Wing. There was Bess, and those who work with her; Liz, and those who work with her, especially Wendy, and Ashton.

The whole group numbered about fifteen. I spent about two hours asking questions and talking. I wanted to give them my general philosophy of answering letters and my feeling that a letter to the White House is worthy of a good answer, not just a perfunctory reply. Such a letter is likely to be the only contact that a person will ever have with the President's wife —the one way she will ever know her. I found out a lot about the different categories of letters, and who handles what. I am still disturbed by the fact that I find myself signing a letter that must have been received two weeks or more ago, but I do think this session improved morale, made us understand each other better, and made for a better working relationship.

This long meeting caused me to miss lunch, so I was glad to sit down for a cup of tea with Mrs. Carl Sanders, the wife of the Governor of Georgia, and Mrs. Farris Bryant, the wife of the Governor of Florida. They arrived about 1:30, after a tour of the White House, and we had tea and sandwiches and a visit. Mrs. Sanders gave me a charming little bangle for my bracelet with the map of Georgia and, what's more important, some kind words about Lyndon on it.

Lyndon left in the middle of the afternoon to go to New York for the Joseph P. Kennedy Foundation dinner, but I didn't go with him. I've been away too much from Luci—and it shows. One reward for not going was a talk I had with her. She came in and had dinner with Judge A. W. Moursund and me—just the three of us—and she was all wound up and talked and talked and talked. I learned a lot about my shortcomings and something about my virtues! She's a very interesting, exciting, perceptive, emotional, high-strung little girl, for whom my heart aches. I know she can achieve great things if I can just help her stay healthy enough and level-headed enough, and realize that life is one long series of problems that you handle one day at a time. A. W., the children's trustee, and I had a lot of business to talk about—the house, the ranches—it's a *great* com-

68 / A White House Diary

fort to have him here. I can't say that we settled anything—signed, sealed, and filed away—but at least we put some steam in behind some matters and got them moving.

I said good night to him early and then went in for a very luxurious evening of watching Jason Robards on television in a play called *Abe Lincoln in Illinois*—I can't remember whether it's by Sherwood Anderson or Robert Sherwood! I was very much aware of—and atingle with—the fact that I was watching this excellent play in the room where Lincoln himself had slept. The fire was burning and there were flickering shadows on the ceiling. It was one of those evenings when you feel very much alive and wouldn't want to be doing anything else except *exactly* what you are doing.

Tuesday, February 11

I have been sick the last few days. I hoarded my strength like a miser for the Diplomatic Reception, getting up only to get my hair done, so that I would look as well as possible for the 7 o'clock reception, which was business suit.

About 6:45 the Dean of the Corps, the Ambassador of Nicaragua, came upstairs without Mrs. Guillermo Sevilla-Sacasa, who is still taking care of their very ill little daughter, Julia, just out of the National Institutes of Health. Also, the Ambassador of the Netherlands and Madam Van Roijen came up, because they would be leaving very soon—it was to say good-by . . . and Chief Justice and Mrs. Warren, who are always on hand as helpful standbys and ornaments, and the Secretary of State and Mrs. Rusk. I was delighted that my old friends Senator John Sparkman and Ivo were there. He's close to-the top on the Foreign Affairs Committee.

The Spanish Ambassador, a very handsome man, was in attendance to present a letter to the President, concerned with Spain's recognition of Russia. He and Lyndon disappeared for a while. Then we all came downstairs, preceded by full pomp and panoply of flags. We stopped for photographing at the bottom of the stairs and then walked into the Blue Room to receive, in proper protocol order, the Ambassadors from all the nations, the Chargés d'Affaires, and the four new Ambassadors who were there to present their credentials, the Ambassador of the Dominican Republic and Mrs. José A. Bonilla, the Ambassador from the Kingdom of Libya and Mrs. Fathi Abidia, the Ambassador of Peru and Mrs. Celso Pastor, who replaced the Fernando Berckemeyers who had been here since time began, and the Ambassador from Sweden and Mrs. Hubert de Besche, and then the OAS Ambassadors, who had been held in another room (I hope with ample drinks and plenty of hostessing from wives of Cabinet members), came by to be greeted by us in their turn.

Later on Margy McNamara and I were talking about the reception and she said yes, she thought it had helped to have the Cabinet wives hostessing in various rooms and that she would always be glad to do it. She thought it would be useful for future functions if we could send them in advance a list of guests who had accepted. I suggested that we could get together for a cup of tea and have a briefing, passing out the list of those coming so that each could single out those whom she knew and make them feel at home—or concentrate on those who seem to be left alone and uncomfortable. I think this is a good idea, but one I haven't thoroughly worked out. I did see Jane Freeman busily engaged in talking to several foreign guests and, of course, Mrs. Rusk always does a superb job, along with Phyllis Dillon, who is as kind and socially smooth as anybody could possibly be. If it is "small town" to try to make every guest at a party feel at ease and have a good time, then I'll cheerfully be labeled "small town"! I have been to some elegant, sophisticated parties that were also cold and tiresome. I don't want that sort of entertaining in my time here.

When we finished greeting the last Ambassador, we went into the East Room. The band struck up, and we began a very merry dance. The Dean of the Corps, Sevilla-Sacasa, led off with me, and then I had a whirl with everybody from the French Ambassador to Anatoly Dobrynin of Russia, which I am sure caused all the lady reporters to get out their pads and pencils. (But he was covering the territory, because he got around to Lynda Bird too!) Mr. Dobrynin said that Siberia was a land that I ought to see, that it was endless, and full of vast forests and diamonds. I don't know whether he was using that as a figure of speech or whether he actually meant there was some untold mineral wealth or maybe even diamonds themselves! I was beginning to worry that an Arab wouldn't dance with me, when, delightfully enough, the gentleman from Kuwait, Talat Al-Ghoussein, who has one of the most beautiful wives in the Corps, came up and we executed a waltz around the floor. I suggested to Lyndon, when I had a chance to dance with him again, that he get "geographical"—from continent to continent, so to speak, in his dancing—and I noticed that he did and did it beautifully.

A few, not as many as I would have liked because it's so colorful, came in their native costumes. These were nearly always from the African continent. I remember one gentleman had on a black, beaded hat, and vast robes of red and green and black in a sort of plaid, which he had thrown around his shoulder like a cape or serape, along with a big belt full of ornaments.

There was a good buffet in the dining room—ranging all the way from a steamship round of beef and whole turkeys and hams to our always reliable chili con queso. After dancing with as many as I could, it suddenly dawned on me that I was beginning to get a little weak in the knees from my bout with flu, so I murmured good night. Lyndon stayed and danced until 9:30 and many said that it had been the gayest White House reception for foreign diplomats that they could ever remember.

Wednesday, February 12

The day began with arrival ceremonies for the Alexander Douglas-Homes. Prime Minister Douglas-Home, whose dignity and sense of amusement seem undaunted by the possibility (almost a certainty) that he will be ousted at the next election, which will take place in the next five months, made a pleasant and adequate speech, and so did Lyndon. Then we told them good-by and dispatched them into their limousines and they drove off into the frosty air.

Tonight, the Bill Whites (writer and old friend) came to dinner and we had a good talk about his book and about Lyndon's reasons for going to church. My interpretation was quite simply that Lyndon knew that anybody who lived in the house he lived in, and sat at the desk he sat at, needed help more than man's. And oddly enough, the second reason was that nobody could accuse him any longer of going to church for political reasons, because he was already at the top, so to speak. Bill added, and this was funny coming from him, "I think there's another reason—I think he wants to set a good example." Fine and laudable reason, but hardly what I had expected from Bill.

As always, it was a relaxed and pleasant evening, with just the Whites. It's difficult to find a couple who are equally stimulating, both the man and his wife, and whom you can feel utterly free and easy around, who haven't changed toward us in any way since we got into this job.

This was a morning of meetings and then the Heart Luncheon. In the late afternoon I had two guests, the John Steinbecks, whom I had very much been looking forward to spending an hour with—Mr. Steinbeck, because I'm an old, old fan of his, way back to the days of *Grapes of Wrath* and *Of Mice and Men*, and Mrs. Steinbeck, because when she was Elaine Anderson at the University of Texas, about 1932, I had seen her in Curtain Club plays. Much later she became Mrs. Steinbeck.

It turned out to be an absolutely *delicious* hour. They had spent some six months behind the Iron Curtain, traveling in Poland, Czechoslovakia, and Russia, meeting artists and writers whenever they could in an attempt to explain America to those countries—one of the cultural-exchange ideas. They had many things to say about the Russian people—that they were very hospitable, that they were outgoing, and also that they absolutely, like a stone wall, refused to believe a lot of factual things that you would tell them about our country. For instance, Steinbeck tried to tell a group about the time their leader, Nikita Khrushchev, took off his shoe and angrily pounded home a point on the desk at the United Nations, when he was making a speech. They said, "You lie! Our great leader is a very cultured man; he would never do anything as uncouth as that."

The Steinbecks related one delightful incident about how, when they were returning from some evening engagement, they emerged on the street at 11 o'clock. They could find no taxi and didn't have anybody with them from Intourist. They tried to summon a policeman and get help. They asked for help from first one and then another, as a crowd gathered around them, but were not able to get anyone to find them a taxi anywhere; and *finally*, John Steinbeck sat down in the middle of the street and refused to budge. Then Elaine began to tell the story. She said, "He had on this great big black Russian fur hat and great big overcoat, and he just sat there and said, 'I'm not going to move till you get me a taxi.'" Presently, while everybody stood around, in bewilderment, not knowing what to do, a cultured gentleman walked through the crowd, looked at him, leaned over and asked, "Ernest Hemingway?" Steinbeck said, "No." Shook his head. The man looked at him again and said, "John Steinbeck," and John said, "Yes." The man turned around, gave some swift orders, and in about five minutes up rolled a taxi and they got in, thanked him, and off they went!

Tonight Lyndon is in St. Louis, making a speech celebrating St. Louis'

Bicentennial. It looked like a good night for Mary Lasker and me to sit around and talk about the Arts Committee, the continuation of all the things that need to be done, the places where I may be able to get pictures on loan for Lyndon's office, the Fish Room, and my little study, and perhaps, eventually, for the family room upstairs. So Mary is spending the night.

Tuesday, February 25

Probably the most memorable thing that I did today was to go this morning to call on the volunteers working for Mrs. Kennedy in the Executive Office Building. I was met by Nancy Tuckerman, who took me from room to room—there are about four rooms filled with volunteer workers. There are many Foreign Service workers, and I met at least one Congressional wife, Lucy Moorhead. I was told that there had been a good many more. There were a number of Army wives and there were a lot of just plain housewives, and there were women who speak all sorts of obscure languages. They had been organized and put together sometime during the first week after November 22, when it became apparent that it was going to be impossible for Nancy Tuckerman and a staff of two or three to handle the volume of mail expressing sympathy over President Kennedy's death. One peak day there were 44,000 communications; now the mail has shrunk to about seven or eight hundred letters a day.

Some of the Foreign Service wives with language abilities were translating mail from foreign countries. There were bulging envelopes marked "Yugoslavia," "East Berlin," "Russia" (this last one was not such a bulging one), large envelopes from every country in the world. And then, of course, the most important part of the file was that marked "particularly appealing." Those were the letters that were taken to Mrs. Kennedy to read. They came written in poetry, they came in barely legible pencil on tablet paper, they came in the exquisite language of the cultured and well educated, and they came bearing all sorts of gifts.

I shook hands with everybody in all four rooms and thanked them and told them that I joined with all the people in the country in appreciating the hours and the effort, the heart and the love, they had put into doing this work.

Then I stopped by to see those ladies whom we must have caused so much trouble, the telephone operators. To my surprise there wasn't an enormous roomful of them. There were about eight there—I suppose there are peak hours at which there are more. They were as busy as cats on a hot stove. They hardly had time to look up and say hello, but I did manage to go down the line and thank them all and tell them how much I appreciated their efficiency and their kindness to us in these past months, because we must really have been a chore.

And then I went to the files, located in an enormous room. Our files, at present, take up less than a fifth of the space. The remaining area is still occupied by Kennedy files which will be moved to the Kennedy Library, how soon I do not know. The archivist in charge has been there through many, many Administrations. His work is a science and love with him.

I got back to the White House in time to have a 12 o'clock conference with Walter Jenkins and the indispensable Mr. West in the Queen's Sitting Room to discuss household expenses, my Number Two bête noire. Number One, of course, is keeping up The Elms—still unsold. We went into all the ramifications of what expenses were allotted where, and who paid for what. I came away slightly relieved. We each had some ideas to offer about how to cut down on expenses. We decided to have an additional meeting with Miss Anne Lincoln, the housekeeper, and with our own cook, Zephyr, and we are making a start toward putting this place on a more Johnsonian basis, that is, a somewhat more economical basis.

There was a good picture of Luci in the *Washington Star* today, spelled "Luci." There is quite a flap these days as to which way it's spelled. As for me, why should I object so mightily if my L U C Y chooses to spell it another way? I remember when I was about fourteen, I spelled my middle name Byrd, after I had given up ever managing to be called Claudia!

The photograph shows LUCI standing beside a piano. She's honorary chairman of the National Symphony Orchestra's Music for Young Americans, an annual series of free concerts for high school students visiting Washington each spring. I have the feeling that Luci is getting more and more incorporated into this life and willing to play a part in it, and I look for happier days for us and her.

Wednesday, February 26

I returned from a short trip to New York just in time for big news. The Tax Bill had been passed, completely, irrevocably, finally, *passed—big step—* Victory Number One! The White House was being filled—the East Room

—with all the equipment of TV and they were readying a press conference which was to take place at 6:30. I fixed up a bit and went down with Lynda and sat in the back row and watched the ceremonies. The table and microphone were in front of the great urn of gorgeous flowers that I always think ought to have its portrait painted by some Flemish artist of old.

Lyndon had gathered the people there who had been so instrumental in producing the Tax Bill—Senator Russell Long, who had piloted it on the Floor of the Senate; Senator George Smathers; Representative Wilbur Mills, without whom nothing financial gets done; Representative Carl Albert; Speaker McCormack; the Secretary of the Treasury, Dillon; in fact, leaders of both parties and every committee, and every phase that had anything to do with the Tax Bill. I must say it's pleasant, occasionally, to savor a moment of triumph—and this was one.

Lyndon's speech began: "Today I have signed into law an eleven-and-a-half-billion-dollar reduction in federal income taxes, the largest in the history of the United States. It is the single most important step we have taken to strengthen our economy since World War II."

He went on to say how the legislation was inspired and proposed by President Kennedy. It has been one year, one month, and two days since President Kennedy's first appeal to pass the bill—and I'd hate to count hour to hour all of the calls, the talks, the reading, the work, the effort, the late night hours, that Lyndon has put in during the last three months to get it passed. But it did pass, by the happy majority of 74 to 19 in the Senate, with generous Republican support.

Lyndon's speech tried to explain two things. First, how the new law would mean something to each person, by putting an average of four or five dollars more a week into the pockets of most U.S. wage earners this year, beginning next week. And second, how by releasing millions of dollars into private economy from corporations that would otherwise be saving it to pay their taxes, this would stimulate new expansion and encourage the growth and prosperity of the country. One of Lyndon's highest accolades went to Senator Byrd, who had been staunchly against the bill from beginning to end, but had made it possible for the majority to work its will by letting it out of his committee, where he could have bottled it up, for God knows how long.

The line I liked best in Lyndon's speech was "No one can bury us or bluff us or beat us so long as our economy remains strong." It was a good moment for him, and I loved to see him relish it. I hope he got all the joy out of it that he should have.

Immediately after the signing we were whisked off to Mrs. Kennedy's house, just Lyndon and I, where we met practically all the members of President Kennedy's Cabinet—they had remained on at Lyndon's request—for what was a moving forty-five minutes or so. This was supposed to be a surprise to Mrs. Kennedy. Someone thoughtfully had refreshments on hand.

Lyndon brought to Mrs. Kennedy four of the pens which had been used in signing the Tax Bill: one for her, one for the John F. Kennedy Memorial Library, and one each for Caroline and John-John. And the Cabinet presented her with a gold tray and coffee service. The tray was engraved with the names of the entire Cabinet and also of President Kennedy's closest White House advisers. Dean Rusk made the speech presenting the tray—and a very graceful speech it was. The gift was a sort of housewarming present and it was, of course, given in memory of the President.

Caroline was there, wearing cute new-style stockings, and she had a little friend her own age with her. While they were climbing around over the sofa, I had a nice talk with her. I told her how Lynda and Luci had wanted to come with us, and she said, "Why don't they?" I do think it would be a good idea if they did go sometime. John-John stomped all over the vast amount of tissue paper with which the gifts had been wrapped while Dean Rusk was making his speech. He was also the official opener of the gifts.

As we emerged from the house there were many neighbors on the sidewalk, looking on with great interest, and a lot of flashlight bulbs popping, and of course we were asked lots of questions. I quickly made my way to the car but Lyndon paused long enough to say something graceful to the reporters about President Kennedy having worked so long and so hard on the bill. He said he hoped so much it would bring fiscal integrity, and that we were here to see Mrs. Kennedy and express our happiness at the fact that it was signed. He described the visit as "very moving." I did note that none of the others who came out had much to say. That may have been the way that Mrs. Kennedy would have preferred them to act. But Lyndon was acting the way he is, and the way he would want people to act about him.

As we drove off, he said: "Why don't we run by and see the Valentis?" And so we did. Imagine having the President drop in unexpectedly, when you have a four-months-old baby! Their place in Georgetown is very charming but small. Courtenay was brought down and lay on Lyndon's lap and gurgled for a few minutes, and then went very quietly and pleasantly to bed. What a joy! We had a drink and Lyndon said he just believed he would stay for supper! So Mary Margaret said she could work it out very well indeed, and sure enough, we did stay and had delicious steaks about an hour later.

Summing it up, I think the Tax Bill signing may be the first time that Lyndon has been on television when he felt really good about it. He had a story to tell that reflected achievement—something worth talking about.

The last thought I had before I dropped off to sleep was remembering the inscription on the tray which went something like this: *"In memory of three shining years together."*

Friday, February 28

This day found me returning from Florida, remembering the poignancy of a special hour we spent there. Lyndon and I had gone to Palm Beach to pay a courtesy call on former Ambassador Joe Kennedy and Mrs. Kennedy. I thought of the other times we had been to their house. Once, when Lyndon was a Senator, they had courteously invited us for lunch—Mrs. Kennedy, that is, the Ambassador was not there. And I thought of the time, after the election in the fall of 1960, when Lyndon and I came down so that he could have a conference with President Kennedy, when Jacqueline was just recovering from John-John's birth. Their home is such a beautiful place and now there is so much tragedy there.

I cannot begin to say how impressed I am with Mrs. Rose Kennedy. She must be more than seventy, but she has a beautiful figure. She looks lovely, she dresses superbly, and she kept on talking amiably, just as a good hostess should, welcoming us, talking about the house, the family, people we know, being gracious, and, I think, even grateful for kindnesses that Lyndon has tried to show to all the members of the family since the awful day in November. She skimmed lightly over the fact that her husband has been a complete invalid since his stroke in December 1961. Two of the little Kennedy boys came in. I believe they must have been the children of Ethel and Bobby. I think all eight of the Robert Kennedy children had just been there, staying at Phyllis Dillon's house and recuperating from colds, and these two had remained on longer. We had a glass of orange juice and tried bravely to make interesting conversation with a man who must once have ruled in a sizable province of the world and who now is so removed from the use of power.

Now, red-eyed and weary, about 8:30 A.M. I stumbled into the house and got into bed with the art file piled all around me—this is everything having to do with the Committee for the Preservation of the White House, the Fine Arts Committee, the Painting Committee, Mrs. Kennedy's letter and memo to me, the whole history of the project, which I've been concerned with since the last of November. I wanted to brief myself before I went to see Mrs. Kennedy at 11 o'clock.

Fortified with some—and not enough—knowledge, but a pretty sure intent of what I wanted to say, I set out a few minutes before 11 and arrived at her Georgetown house, which is a mellow, pretty, pink brick, to find outside three or four policemen in uniform and a few interested neighbors congregated on the sidewalk. I guess there will always be people around her house, waiting to see the coming and going.

She greeted me sweetly on the inside. There were no children around. We went into the big drawing room in which there was a small fire—it was really quite cold. The house lacks a good deal being completed. Even Mrs. Kennedy, who knows so much and does so much, can't bring a house to the perfection of warmth and finish in a few weeks' time.

We had a cup of coffee and I told her that I'd had many conferences with Clark Clifford about how best we could preserve and carry on and make permanent the wonderful work that she and her committee had accomplished at the White House. I said that we felt the Committee for the Preservation of the White House should have the following regular members: the head of the Smithsonian, Dillon Ripley; the head of the Park Services, Mr. George Hartzog; the head of the Fine Arts Commission, Bill Walton; the Director of the National Gallery of Art, John Walker; from the White House itself, the Curator Jim Ketchum; and that most important man of all, the Usher, Mr. West. There would also be public members. I told her that Clark had said she had agreed to be one of the public members and that would be the most important thing that could happen to this committee. I said I was so happy that she was willing to serve but I wanted to hear it from her, rather than make the announcement relying on a message through someone else. She said yes, she would accept, and I told her that I intended to follow her suggestion and ask Mr. duPont, the Chairman of her Fine Arts Committee, and Mr. Fosburgh, the Chairman of her Painting Committee, to join the committee, and I did so hope that they would serve.

I said what is very true, that any committee is only as good as the most knowledgeable, determined and vigorous person on it. There must be somebody who provides the flame, who furnishes the inspiration, and I think she is the natural person for this. I want her to do that, and I hope she will. I also told her—remembering what Clark had said to me—that he had had a spirited discussion with her about the dissolution of her own Fine Arts Committee. She has recommended that it be dissolved. I told her that I hoped to continue, in addition, an advisory committee, and to choose for it some of the members of her Fine Arts Committee and Painting Committee. I did not want to lose that reservoir of talent and knowledge and good will and contribution. I didn't want to lose it for the future of the White House, and I didn't want to lose it for my husband's Administration. Even if the restoration could be considered 90 percent finished, history will keep on moving. Other people will come and live in the White House, and if we can do anything to perpetuate what has been done and move forward in acquisitions that is my great ambition.

I thought the meeting was successful enough. Mrs. Kennedy listened quietly and after a couple of cups of coffee and my presenting her with four coins—the first four to be minted in the Philadelphia mint with the head of President Kennedy—one for herself, one for each of the two children, and one which I said she might like to send on to Mrs. Rose Kennedy—I said good-by and came away.

The rest of the day was spent in signing mail, making decisions, handling a lot of tedious things, realizing that the arrival dates on some of the letters were so many days or weeks old that I cringed. To my delight, about 4 o'clock in the afternoon, I got word that John and Nellie Connally were in the outside hall! I wrapped my robe around me and went to sit with them until Lyndon could join us. He'd asked them over for a cup of coffee. It was snowing blindly, and it was beautiful to look at outside the window while we sat and chatted.

John and Nellie said they had to leave in about an hour to catch their plane, and we decided to call and see whether the plane was going to take off in such weather. The plane was canceled, so Lyndon and I insisted they spend the night, saying, "We will put you in the Queen's Room with Bill Stinson upstairs, and we'll ask the Walter Jenkins' to come over and have dinner with us. There will be just us, and it'll be such fun!" Lynda had invited Bernie Rosenbach to spend the weekend with us, so we had young folks as well.

I had that same delightful feeling that you get at the Ranch when the river rises and you cannot get across, and the only thing to do is sit there and relax. And if you're spending the time with people that you care very much about, then what could be better? It's like being lost on a desert island!

Spring 1964

THE
WHITE HOUSE
AND EN ROUTE
TO GREECE

Tuesday,
March 10,
1964 This morning was one of those anticlimactic periods of waiting for the important event of the day—my departure for
Greece for the funeral of King Paul. I picked at my desk
aimlessly, and at one I simply gave up trying to get any work
done and went with Lynda Bird down to the White House
lawn. Spring was coming, the weather was soft and mild,
the sky was blue and full of fluffy white clouds. We explored
the grounds, talked to the gardener, noticed the scilla blooming under the magnolia trees, went past the tennis courts
and found a trampoline, carefully hidden in a surrounding
hedge of holly, where Lynda Bird bounced up and down as
though she were six instead of nineteen. Then we went over
to the Executive Office Building where there is a bowling
alley, and Lynda Bird shot 134, while I, for the first time
that I can remember, broke 100, making a score of 107.

I came back and dressed for the take-off. About 3:45 I went
down to the Diplomatic Reception Room to meet the Greek

delegation. There was my co-chief of the official delegation, President Harry S Truman, with a cane, a homburg hat, and a big smile.

On the lawn I said good-by to Lyndon and we got in the helicopter and flew to Andrews. On *Air Force One* I met the rest of the delegation, and an interesting lot they were: young John Brademas—his father was a Greek immigrant—handsome, successful, one of our brightest young Congressmen, Mike Manatos of the White House staff; John Plumides, also the son of a Greek immigrant, with a South Carolina accent as thick as any Southerner's, a successful lawyer, head of Ahepa, hopeful sometime, I think, of going into politics. There was also Judge John Pappas of Boston, who had, himself, come over as an immigrant at the age of eight.

But aside from President Truman, the most interesting member of the delegation was Archbishop Iakovos, the head of the Greek Orthodox Church for North and South America with about two million members. He was dressed in long, black clerical garb, with a beautiful religious medallion hanging around his neck, and the black pillbox hat from which flowed long black veils. He was heavily bearded, and it took me several hours to discover that behind that beard there was a youngish, handsome man, with a sense of humor and a very interesting mind.

General Harry Vaughan, who came along as aide to President Truman, kept us laughing all the way. Clifton Daniel, the son-in-law of the President, was always gently, capably, and unobtrusively at his elbow to help. Liz and Helen Williams were with me, and Angie and Robin Duke.

After a considerable wait, it was 5 o'clock by the time we were airborne, and I suggested a drink, to which President Truman quickly acquiesced. I began to visit first with Plumides, then Brademas, and then Pappas. The Archbishop awed me a little, so I insisted on giving him sort of a seat of honor opposite President Truman. Presently I moved over alongside President Truman and began to ask him some questions about what it had been like back in 1946 when he instituted the Truman Doctrine in Greece and Turkey.

He said, "It was all the Marshall Plan, an extension of the same plan that we had used in all the countries of Europe to try to help them recover. It's just that the Greeks like the Jews and the Irish can holler louder than anybody else, if you have heard more about the Truman Doctrine than you have the others." About his operation of the Presidency, he said, "Get all the information you can, make up your mind and go ahead—and tell them to go to Hell." By "them," he meant the inevitable armchair critics and the newspapers.

He also said, "There is no gratitude for things past. Gratitude is always for what you're going to do for people in the future." I asked him, "What is the best thing a wife can do for her husband in the White House?"

He said, "Protect him. Don't let people use you. If people bring you some sort of a proposition they want you to talk to the President about, it's all right to tell him, but if you have doubts about them be sure and tell him that." He said that Mrs. Truman always had good judgment and when she had doubts about people, if he didn't follow her feelings he usually turned out to regret it later.

General Vaughan was one of the delightful surprises of the journey. I think his image, as created by the newspapers, has been unfair and incorrect. At one point President Truman looked over at him and said, "See, he kept me laughing. He did more for me than anybody else."

I asked President Truman what he had been doing since he left the Presidency, and he said, "I lecture to young people in high schools and colleges. I've got three lectures, one on the American Presidency, one on the relationship between the Executive and the Legislative bodies, and the third on periods of hysteria in American history."

This last proved a wonderful mine of conversation, which ranged all the way from the witch burnings in Salem to the recent Joe McCarthy days. He told the story of a student in one state, who began his question after the lecture was over with the phrase, "We have a country boob as Governor." Truman interrupted him saying, "The Governor, whoever he is, is the first citizen of the state. If you want to restate your question in a respectful way, do so." He had thirty-two hundred students in the audience that day and he said he believed that he had taught them a little respect for elected officials. And he said that the boy came up to him afterward and told him that he had been wrong.

Then he told about a girl who asked, "President Truman, what do you think the government is going to do about birth control?" He answered, "Ma'am, that is your department."

Immediately afterward, a boy asked, "What if there is an atomic war?" He answered, "I don't know, but one thing is sure. If there is an atomic war, we won't have to worry about the answer to this young lady's question."

He also talked about Presidents in American history who had not "sold for what they're worth"—that is, whose stature in American history is not as great as he thought it ought to be. Among them he mentioned President John Tyler, who succeeded to office after the death of William

Henry Harrison. The formidable Daniel Webster, Secretary of State, came in to Tyler and said, "Now you are the acting President," and Tyler replied, "I am the President. If you do not agree I will find myself another Secretary of State." According to President Truman, that rejoinder did a lot to establish the validity of the succession through the years. I had a marvelous time talking to him.

We had an early dinner and I went straight to bed in the cabin of *Air Force One*, asking Mrs. Matsas, the wife of the Greek Ambassador, to share the other lounge. With the crossing of the time zones, we actually had only four hours to sleep. It was about one o'clock "stomach time," the middle of the night, when we were awakened to get ready to get off the plane for our 8:30 A.M. landing.

Before we went to sleep, some of the reporters came in with the news of the New Hampshire primary, in which both Rockefeller's and Goldwater's chances for the Republican nomination took a pretty bad beating from Henry Cabot Lodge, who was a write-in candidate and away in Vietnam. There was a creditable number of write-in votes for Attorney General Kennedy for Vice President and a higher number of write-in votes for Lyndon.

Wednesday, March 11

GREECE

Arriving at Athens at 8:45 A.M., we were met by Prince Michael, a relative of the royal family, and Madame Carolou, Grand Mistress of the Court. After the playing of national anthems, President Truman and I, in company with Prince Michael, walked down the long line of troops. We then went to our limousines and headed for the Athens-Hilton.

Since it was really about 2 A.M. for me, I had a hard time acting wide awake along the road, but Prince Michael livened things up by searching for a topic of conversation and saying, "President Truman, my grandfather was in your country. He was aide-de-camp to General Grant." President Truman said, "Young man, as far as that little lady over there is concerned, and me too, your grandfather was on the wrong side." Prince Michael was rather abashed, but it gave me a wonderful opportunity to say that although we have had our wounds and suffered deeply, the years have taught us that if we are going to be one nation, we've got to be united, and forget our hostilities. I just hope it meant something to him in terms of Cyprus. *Really*, the more I see of the rest of the world, the *prouder* I am of the United States.

Ambassador and Mrs. Henry Labouisse, our old friends, had also met us at the plane, and presently they joined us at the hotel and escorted us to the Palace to sign the guest book. At noon Mrs. Labouisse had arranged exactly what I liked most, a small luncheon for six—she and I, Liz, Robin, and two very attractive women from the Embassy, Mrs. Herbert Brewster and Mrs. John M. Maury.

We drove out along the shore line of the Aegean to a small restaurant perched high on a cliff. A fire burned merrily in the corner on this crisp, bright day. We began with octopus, which I bypassed, and lobster, which I enjoyed. Next was a delicious fish that only an hour ago had been wriggling in the Aegean, and a good salad of tomatoes, cucumbers, and an excellent Greek cheese. We ended with Greek coffee, which tasted as though it had come from the very bottom of the pot. You practically had to eat it with a spoon rather than drink it and it was very sweet.

Mrs. Labouisse filled me in on much that has happened since I was in Greece in August 1962. Our friend Constantine Karamanlis is, of course, no longer Prime Minister. When the government fell, a caretaker government headed by Karamanlis ruled for a time. And then there was the election. Thinking that because he had given the country a very good administration for eight years, that the people owed him a return to office, he did not pour himself into the campaign with enormous effort, earnestness, and enthusiasm. An old-time politician, Mr. George Papandreou, about seventy-five, who had been Prime Minister briefly long ago, won the Prime Ministership by a sizable majority. Papandreou's son had emigrated to the United States, become a citizen, married an American girl, and was teaching economics at the University of California, in Berkeley. Now his son had given up his American citizenship and returned with his wife to Athens to serve in his father's government.

Since the Prime Minister is a widower, his daughter-in-law Mrs. Papandreou took me around that afternoon, accompanied by Mrs. Stavros Costopoulos, the wife of the Foreign Minister.

They picked me up, along with Mrs. Labouisse, about 4:30 and we drove through the city to a little Byzantine monastery, high in the hills. Although built during the period of the Byzantine Empire, it nevertheless incorporated columns, statues, pieces of marble in the walls, in the garden, as decoration here and there, from pagan days! They had "borrowed" these motifs from some ancient pagan temple, or maybe it's best to say that they've used the temple as a marble quarry for their construction!

Inside the church, which was very small, the walls and domed ceilings were covered with Biblical pictures, still fresh and brightly colored—after how many centuries? There were no pews, only standing positions along the walls for the worshipers, a sort of pen where you would walk in and find a place to lean your elbow. The garden was charming and lovingly tended. You could see the narrow cells where the monks had lived. And there was a big room containing some enormous stones, which had been the olive press. In spite of the cold weather, the almond trees were blooming, very much like peach or pear blossoms at home.

We drove past the Acropolis and arrived on a high hill about sunset with a magnificent view of the Parthenon, and there, against that background, we had our pictures taken—young Mrs. Papandreou, Mrs. Costopoulos, and I. I kept wondering what was going on in the mind of this young American woman—what divided loyalties, what prospects for the future, what hazards she faced. She said something interesting about her husband's economic interest in the future of Greece—how Israel had about the same sort of climate and resources, and had done so much with them. She indicated that they were possibly going to make a study of industrialization along the same lines. One thing is certain, tourism—one chief source of their income now—won't exactly blossom in the climate of mobs throwing stones, along with uncertainty about the threatened invasion of Cyprus.

The Ambassador had told me that it had just been decided that the Queen would receive all the visiting delegations at the Palace tonight at an informal supper reception. I had a difficult time getting dressed. I put on my black evening dress, which is strapless and therefore not appropriate for any occasion connected with a funeral. I draped my black lace mantilla around it, high over my shoulders and throat and coming down low over my arms, and pinned it in the back with a pearl pin—it looked quite "Merry Widow"! Then I took it off and tried on the long-sleeved black jacket I had made for the occasion, which looked rather "Salvation Army," but in a smart way (I hope). Finally I set out with the black lace underneath, and the black jacket thrown over my shoulders, for what was one of the most interesting evenings I have ever spent.

The invitation for 9 o'clock was in French, "Diner Palais Royale Dauphine," and was limited to two members of the delegation, so it devolved on President Truman and me to attend. However, the Ambassador went along with us, as a sort of shepherd, I suppose. Upon entering, Mrs. Caro-lou, Grand Mistress (and oh, what a busy time she must have had!), told me that Queen Frederika wanted to receive me alone. She led me up stairs and down halls, and finally to a very small sitting room, where I found Queen Frederika, dressed most beautifully, in long black velvet, looking so beautiful and yet forlorn; I wished I could have really communicated with her because I admire her and I know what a break in this life the death of her husband must be. But my words came out rather trite. I spoke of her visit to our country, and how sad it was that so immediately upon her return to her own she found herself faced with the desperate illness of her husband.

It was a brief but graceful meeting and then I walked out into the hall. There I encountered one of the most remarkable members of the whole entourage—a very elderly lady, who floated along in a gray habit of some religious order—Princess Alice, the mother of Prince Philip of England.

The guests gradually melted into a vast banquet hall, where there was a long buffet table heavily laden with a great variety of meats, salads, and jellied dishes, with beer and orange juice to drink. There I had the first opportunity of seeing the galaxy of Chiefs of State, and representatives of other Chiefs of State who had come to the funeral, from some thirty or forty countries. Many of the members of the royal contingent I had met on my trip to Scandinavia last October—the King of Denmark and Queen Ingrid, and beautiful Princess Anne Marie, their daughter, who is going to be married to young King Constantine of Greece; spry and elderly King Gustaf VI Adolf of Sweden; King Olav V of Norway; and then from my Benelux trip the very attractive young King of Belgium, Baudouin; and the slight, amiable, mustached Grand-Duke Jean of Luxembourg, and his Grand Duchess, Josephine Charlotte. One of the most solid and impressive members of royalty, Queen Juliana of Holland, was there with her attractive husband, Prince Bernhard.

Among royalty actually on the job, the tallest and handsomest was Prince Philip, the Duke of Edinburgh, husband to Queen Elizabeth and a cousin of King Paul. (I scarcely saw how he had finished handing out the cigars, because it was just this morning he became a father for the fourth time.) Prince Rainier of Monaco was present, looking rather world-weary. Of those close to the throne, there was the brother of the Shah of Iran, taller and handsomer even than the Shah.

A numerous and interesting group were those Kings "out-of-work," or

Pretenders: King Umberto of Italy; the Duke de Braganza, Pretender to the Throne of Portugal; the Comte de Paris à Bourbon, Pretender to the Throne of France; King Michael of Rumania, son of Queen Helen, grandson of Queen Marie, whose handsomeness was blunted by a look of great frustration on his countenance. There was even a Prince Nicholas Romanoff, and I wondered into what segment of the Russian hierarchy he fitted. There was a Pretender to the Throne of Spain, Don Juan, father of Juan Carlos, married to King Paul's oldest daughter, Princess Sophie of Greece.

From a tall, uniformed, heavily bemedaled gentleman behind me—and I think he must have been of one of the royal families no longer in office—I heard a most interesting remark. I wish I could remember it exactly. It went something like this: "There are three sorts of people who speak the same language, who understand each other—wandering gypsies, royal families . . ." (and then I couldn't hear what the third category was, and it intrigues me). Of course, all eyes were on Archbishop Makarios, the representative from Cyprus, and he is not a man to go unnoticed.

Someone kindly escorted me to the only table in the large room. Several chairs were drawn up to it, and I sat there with my plate of food before me, together with Queen Ingrid, President Truman, and several other people whose identity I was not sure of. (One, I think, was the Duchess of Kent.) For the first time I was aware of something diplomats always take notice of in our country, which I always find amusing—that is, they notice how much time a Chief of State spends with particular foreign delegates. Queen Frederika was sitting and chatting with Archbishop Makarios for quite a long time in a corner. And I think everyone was mentally clocking the minutes.

A great clutch of the guests were royalty from small German states, now extinct, but ceremoniously recognized in all royal circles. They were the relatives of Queen Frederika. There was Princess Theodora of Baden; Prince Peter of Schleswig-Holstein; Prince Ludwig of Baden and also Prince Max; Duke Carl of Württemberg; Prince and Princess Welf of Hanover; Princess Marguerite of Hohenlohe; Prince Friedrich Wilhelm von Preussen; Prince Ernst August of Hanover. The list sounded like the map of Germany before it became unified.

President Truman wanted to leave at the earliest possible moment, and Ambassador Labouisse departed to take him home, saying that he would return for me in a few minutes. Eating was unimportant, but looking and listening was very important. I found it fascinating, but I'm afraid I may have seemed gauche to Angie and many sophisticated people, because I walked up to those whom I had met on trips or who had been our visitors in the United States and introduced myself and just chatted with them.

I left early, not unmindful of the fact that it had been about 1:30 when I had arisen that morning, and I gave a thought to Lynda Bird, who, clear across the world, was being hostess tonight to the last of the six groups of members of the House of Representatives and their wives who were coming to the reception for briefing, upstairs tour, and dancing.

Thursday, March 12

I dressed early this morning, in solid black, with my mantilla draped over my maline hat, and set out with President Truman and Ambassador Labouisse for the Cathedral for the Requiem Mass for King Paul.

The entrance was flanked by masses of photographers with flashing bulbs, with a uniformed Palace Aide here and there, heavily laden with medals and ribbons. The dim interior of the Cathedral was rather small, but into it crowded the most brilliant pageantry I have ever witnessed. In the center of the Cathedral, on a raised dais, was the coffin of the King, draped with the royal standard and with the crown and sword on top of it. On the floor, all around the casket, was a raised, velvet-covered platform, on which many lovely elaborate pillows lay, each bearing the coat of arms of a country. Also on the pillows were medals, ribbons, and decorations representing Orders or Honors which had been given to King Paul in his lifetime.

In the front of the church were Archbishop Chrysostomos of Athens, eighty-four, the head of the Greek Orthodox Church, and the most amazing assemblage of high appellates of the church I have ever seen. They were about fifty in number, most of them in long brocaded robes, a different design for each robe, vying with each other for magnificence, bejeweled with medallions and topped with a gold dome of a hat, which, I understand, weighs about seven pounds. A few of the priests wore long black robes and the pillbox hat with flowing veils, and every last one of them had a beard of great proportion.

On the right of the coffin was seated the royal family. Queen Frederika, regal and beautiful, in a long black velvet, flowing coat dress, topped by a heavy veil, was on the arm of the youthful new King Constantine. Beside her sat Princess Sophie and Juan Carlos, on the other side Princess Irene, and behind them all the assembled kin, including lovely young Anne Marie of Denmark, the King's fiancée.

On the left side of the church were lined up visiting Chiefs of State. I never recognized the two gentlemen on my right for sure, but I think one of them was the Prince of Lichtenstein, then myself and President Truman, Queen Juliana of the Netherlands, King Baudouin of Belgium, King Frederick IX of Denmark, King Gustaf VI of Sweden, King Olav V of Norway, and Prince Philip of Britain.

Standing in the rear of the church were all the other delegates from many countries, and how I would have hated to be a Chief of Protocol this day! Not a word of the service did I understand, nor any of the six hymns that were written by John of Damascus twelve centuries ago, except for one line that reads: "There is no difference between King and soldier, rich and poor, just and sinner."

At the end of the service Queen Frederika went to the coffin, knelt, and kissed the cross on top of it. She was followed by King Constantine, who repeated the ritual. And then came the two Princesses. Next the white-skirted, blue-jacketed royal evzone guards (each of whom I think must have been chosen for his good looks) marched in, picked up the pillows bearing the medals, and walked out with them. Then eight more evzones appeared, and how fascinated I was by their costumes. Their legs were covered with long hose or what we might call leotards, and they wore starched, stiff white skirts, blouses with long flowing sleeves, elaborately embroidered blue jackets, little black caps with a great display of tassel, and heavy shoes with huge pompons on the toes.

They lifted the casket and marched out, and my chief feeling was that I wished somewhere in the ceremony someone had said, "Here we are, saying good-by to a human being, a man, King Paul." The casket was loaded onto a gun carriage and pulled through the streets of Athens by one hundred blue-uniformed Navy men. The King had been a great Navy man himself. There was a long, long rope, with a double file of the sailors pulling. This was followed by a riderless horse, a dappled gray, one of the King's favorites, I was told. Then came Queen Frederika, regal throughout, veiled to the waist, walking with her son, dignified, solemn King Constantine, bearing his sword and scepter, and behind him Princess Sophie; then a man who must have been the Queen's brother; and Princess Anne Marie, wearing no veil.

They were followed by a column of royalty, including the King of Sweden, the King of Denmark, and Queen Juliana. And in the next row

I found myself, pleasantly enough, with Prince Rainier of Monaco and Prince Philip of England and just in front of me, Archbishop Makarios.

As we walked the mile and a half from the Cathedral to where the procession ended, at the Athens Hilton, an estimated one million Athenians lined the road. I saw a few women with candles, a few women weeping, but not much evidence of grief. It rather worried me. President Truman rode in a car, I'm glad to say, for it was a long slow walk, requiring about an hour and a half.

Prince Philip said, "We measure our pace to the oldest priest, and he is ninety-two." He proved to be a delightful companion, if one can use such a word in speaking of a funeral procession. I asked him if there was any tradition about the coffin being pulled by men instead of horses, and he said yes. When Queen Victoria died, and the body arrived at the railroad station, they loaded it onto a carriage drawn by horses. The route led up a long hill. The horses began to shy and rear and prance and became uncontrollable, so they unhitched the horses, called in the Navy, applied a long rope, everybody took hold, and away they pulled. And since then, royalty have been carried to their graves by humans.

Once, along the way, Prince Philip asked me if I had ever been to Greece before and I said, "Yes, I had a delightful time on the Island of Corfu with the King and Queen in August or September of 1962." And he said, "Oh, yes! I was born in that house." How involved those royal families are and how difficult it would be to unwind all the strings of relationship—to an outsider, that is!

As we walked along between a sea of faces, whenever there was a cross street I was conscious of a strange noise. The best way I can describe it is as a sort of hiss. Later I heard that the sibilant sound was an effort to hush (sh-sh-sh) people, to make them refrain from chatter, but I rather doubt it. I simply do not know at whom the hissing could have been directed. The royal family and all the principals of State were in a group so very close together.

Just as we arrived in front of the Athens Hilton, an unsettling little incident occurred. The cortege began to break up, and each member of it went to his own car. Archbishop Makarios turned off to the left to get into his limousine. The crowd gathered around him in a great cluster and began to cheer and clap and shout. Mr. Labouisse told me that the Archbishop raised his hands in salute and did nothing whatever to discourage them.

Mr. Labouisse rode with President Truman and me to Taktoy Palace. This beautiful country place, sixteen miles from Athens, is the royal summer home. It is situated in the hills, surrounded by a beautiful wooded, parklike area, in which the family cemetery is located, not unlike the graveyards of many of the old homes in the South. The funeral procession wended its slower way through the little villages, with all the family behind, but the Chiefs of State arrived ahead and walked down the paths to the grove where there was a small chapel and five tombs. We stood around, not knowing exactly what to do.

Queen Juliana, who I think had a very laudable way of helping out and taking charge, came up to us—to President Truman, Ambassador Labouisse, and me—and said, "Somebody ought to be making introductions; somebody ought to be going around seeing that we are presented to each other. We don't know all the people here." She looked around rather nervously and said, "Ambassador Labouisse, why don't you go out and introduce yourself to them and then bring them up and present them to us?" I thought, "What an excellent idea."

So Mr. Labouisse obligingly stepped forward and approached the first couple he saw and brought them up to introduce them. Ironically enough, the gentleman turned out to be Prince Loroton Kantol of Cambodia, whose countrymen just yesterday had been throwing stones at the American Embassy. But not to be daunted by a bad beginning, Mr. Labouisse looked around and brought up the Crown Prince of Ethiopia, whom I had met when Haile Selassie was in Washington. Then he brought Couve de Murville of France, the Foreign Minister Anton Atalla, and the Chief of Protocol Iklil Sati of Jordan, whose King will be coming to Washington soon to visit us.

Queen Juliana's kindly tendency to help out reminded me of how in the Cathedral two or three hours earlier she had looked around and gestured rather urgently at me to take off my right glove, pulling the fingers on her own right hand to show me. I did so and then observed that every woman in the Cathedral within eyesight had a bare right hand but a glove on her left hand. Queen Juliana leaned over and said something like this: "It's just like the man wearing his hat in church." I was grateful, because how else would I ever have known?

Finally someone began to lead the way down the sylvan path, because evidently we were not yet at the selected burial place. Off to the right I could see a cross and a tomb, and another block or two along I could see through the trees to the left another tomb. We passed several others. Apparently each monarch chooses his own burial site during his lifetime. And this line has been going on for a hundred years. The night before at the Palace I had seen a great many women wearing identical gold pins. When I asked what they were, they said they were given for the Centennial Celebration of this ruling house of Greece when they had met the year before for a very happy gathering.

After a walk of about a quarter mile down a graveled path, we arrived at the clearing where there was a newly dug grave, and there we all began another long wait. Fortunately someone presently arrived with two chairs, one for the Princess Alice who—wraithlike in her gray religious habit—was leaning on the arm of Prince Philip. All the kinfolks were gathered on one side of the path, and all the other Chiefs of State on the other. The second chair was given to President Truman, bringing about the most amusing bit of double-talk. To the nice young man who offered him the chair, President Truman said, "You are going to make an old man out of me yet." And the young man, thinking of the fact that it was going to be quite a while before the coffin and Queen Frederika arrived, said, "I'm afraid it's going to be quite a long while." Mr. Truman answered, "I hope so," referring, of course, to his approaching old age.

We waited on that pine-forested hilltop for a full hour. Then down the path came the procession, headed by a Court chaplain, carrying the holy Icon of Tinos, then came King Constantine and Queen Frederika, who had in her hand one small wildflower, a lavender, cuplike flower. Later on I heard someone say, "Oh, yes! Now it's the time for the anemones."

The eight evzones of the Royal Guard who had carried the coffin such a long way through the woods lowered it into the grave, removed the Royal Standard, folded it carefully, and gave it to King Constantine, who kissed it and then handed it to his mother, who also kissed it and held it in her hands. Then the national anthem was played, in mourning time, and a chorus of young boys in long red robes, on the other side of the burial place, sang the anthem. At the end three shots were fired, and Queen Frederika approached the grave, threw in her one wildflower, knelt, crossed herself, and walked out.

The King approached and saluted very gravely, and other members of the family did the same in their turn, followed by the Chiefs of State. When it came our turn, we approached the grave, President Truman and I, and bowed respectfully, and turned and walked back up the path. I thought that this spot which the King himself had selected and on which he had piled sixty-two stones in the course of the years, one for each year of his life, was as beautiful a place as one could find for the last resting, unless it's a certain spot on the Pedernales River.

Then we all turned around and went back to Taktoy Palace; the seven Kings, the former Kings, three Queens, two dozen Princes and Princesses, and all the notables from around the world. Inside, Taktoy looked like a comfortable country home of a well-to-do family, with bright, cheerful chintz, big chairs and sofas, and once more in the long dining room the sort of lunch—by now it was nearly 4 o'clock—spread out on the buffet table that was not unlike what might have been offered at home on such an occasion, when neighbors come in with ham and potato salad, and fried chicken, so that all the visiting relatives will have plenty to eat. But it had been a long day and President Truman was well ready to depart for some rest. I hardly had time for a small plate of food and a few words with some of the passing nobility before Ambassador Labouisse and President Truman scooped me up and out we went, making our last good-bys, uttering our last words of sympathy to the solemn, nice-looking young man who now must assume the burden of being a King, and to Queen Frederika, regal to the last moment.

On the way back President Truman launched into some interesting reminiscences. One of them went something like this. "President Roosevelt was a great President, a fine President, but the reason he selected me for his running mate—the reason he just picked me up out of the Senate and made me run—was because he couldn't stand to see anybody succeed him that he thought could do as well as he had. And he just felt sure I wouldn't."

Throughout all of this talk was the repeated phrase "I want Lyndon Johnson to do well. I know he's going to be a great President. You know, I've been *for* him all these years." Naturally I loved hearing him say that. I think what pleased me most of all about him was his unfailing good humor with everybody, from Kings to elevator boys, and the fact that he has lived through the fire of public disdain to enjoy life with such complete lack of bitterness and such delight in his family and friends. He told me that before he was fourteen years old he had read every book in the library in Independence, and he had read the Bible through three times!

Back in the hotel suite I had time for a bit of rest and a change of clothes, and then went out to what was really an utterly relaxed evening where we could talk it all over. Ambassador and Mrs. Labouisse entertained the delegation, Archbishop Iakovos, Congressman Brademas, Mike Manatos, Judge John Pappas, Mr. Plumides, the Angier Biddle Dukes, Harry Vaughan, Cliff Daniel, Liz, and also Robert Dowling, who was there representing the Mayor of New York, General James Van Fleet, who had played such a great part for President Truman in Korea, retired Ambassador Karl Rankin, and all the Embassy staff, some of whom I had come to know when I was here a year and a half ago.

We loaded our plates abundantly, because a lot of food had been offered but very little eaten until now—by me, at least. We enjoyed a good dinner, and then President Truman played the piano. There were delightful toasts, and at an early hour we all dispersed homeward, and so to bed.

As I record this several days later, I must say that being with President Truman those days has been one of the big pluses of this period of my life. It has been an insight into history for me, a joy to see a man who has lived through so much public rancor and condemnation and has emerged philosophic, salty, completely unembittered, a happy man—and vindicated by history on most of his major decisions.

Thursday, March 19

THE WHITE HOUSE

Whatever happened today, and it's been plenty, the most important thing about it is that it is Lynda's twentieth birthday, which reminds me of a line from Jane Addams. "One generation after another has depended upon its young to equip it with gaiety and enthusiasm, to persuade it that living is a pleasure." And that's one thing that Lynda Bird constantly does for us.

One of the nicest things about the day was a note from Lyndon with some flowers for the mother of the birthday girl. It began, "Dear Fritz" (reminding me of a time very long ago), and ended with a signature that takes me back to the first day we met.

As for that blessed child's birthday, I feel remiss in having given her only that most unimaginative of things—money—and I sat down for a brief visit with her at lunch, where Zephyr did have an angel food cake with pink icing. Today we moved some furniture from the family room at The Elms to the Solarium, in hope of finally getting it fixed up so the girls can enjoy it. And I went out to buy a couple of lamps for Lynda's room. Tonight is the night of the big Democratic dinner at the Armory, to which Luci Baines has agreed to go, planning on wearing her pink crepe dress. For this party I am getting out my beautiful red ball gown.

All of the day was something of a strain, but nothing compared to the bombshell that dropped into our lap late this afternoon. Pierre Salinger walked into Lyndon's office about 3 P.M. and told him that he was going to resign and run for the Senate in California. Lyndon called George Reedy in the hospital, asked him to take the position of Press Secretary, which Pierre was vacating. George accepted and agreed to come over as soon as possible so the announcement could be made. They called a press conference and Salinger told the press of his resignation and his impending departure for California.

Of all the people from the Kennedy Administration, I had felt that Salinger was one of the most professional, most committed to doing a job. Although he is very attached to the Kennedys, I thought we had established a certain simpatico relationship with him. So his sudden departure leaves a big uncertainty in my own thinking.

Ambassador Adlai Stevenson came over and changed clothes in the Lincoln Room to go to the dinner tonight. We all got dressed up in our best and arrived at 8 o'clock in that vast barn, the Armory, now holding fifty-three hundred people. And what a strange dinner it was! I must say that I never saw the Armory looking prettier, but since it was March 19 they had chosen a St. Patrick's Day theme and the place was festive with green-and-white mammoth shamrocks, lyres, top hats, balloons rising from every table, anchored by Irish potatoes, and green-and-white cellophane fringe, and balloons hanging from the ceiling. It all served to remind you of one person, President Kennedy.

Lyndon's speech was quite competent I thought, but not sparkling, and there was intentionally very little humor in it. Many people came up to the table to shake hands with us and obtain autographs, and the nicest moment of the evening came when the waiters brought in a silver donkey with a green top hat and a green bow tie on a float, carrying a huge shamrock which proclaimed: "HAPPY BIRTHDAY, LYNDA." The donkey float also had on it a three-tiered birthday cake with twenty pink candles and sugar roses, the whole thing weighing fifty-five pounds.

Added all together—the financial success of the dinner, the fact that it was for the Congressional Class of 1936, of which Lyndon was a member (although somewhat belatedly, not having arrived until 1937), the presence of so many paid-up ticket buyers from our own state of Texas (I think there were thirty-five from the old Tenth Congressional District), the presence of that towering political figure James Farley as toastmaster, the fact that three good friends, Scooter Miller, Lindy Boggs, and Mrs. Claiborne Pell, were co-chairmen of the dinner—and the charming courtesy to

Lynda—all combined to make it a big evening, a great evening, a tremendous success. But over all there was that peculiar pall—the departure of Salinger, the Irish decorations, the absence of any member of the Kennedy family. All helped to evoke that curious mood.

This morning I had an appointment that I have been looking forward to very much. Mrs. Paul Mellon came at 10:30 to walk around the gardens with me. She is the wife of one of the richest men in the United States, daughter-in-law of the one-time Secretary of the Treasury, Mr. Andrew Mellon, who gave the National Art Gallery and the great bulk of its treasures to the government, owner of a home in Virginia, another in Georgetown, one somewhere in the British West Indies, and wherever else, I don't know. She is one of the great authorities on gardens, on planting in general, and a working-at-it authority, a planning, creative authority. It was she who implemented the things Mrs. Kennedy wanted to get done on the White House grounds, transforming the Rose Garden into a thing of exquisite beauty, changing the flower decorations in the White House into works of art so delicate and distinguished and imaginative, and so charming. I love to walk from room to room and see what the arrangements are each day, particularly those in the Queen's Room.

I was anxious to meet her because I want excellence to be applauded and preserved. We reviewed lovingly every detail of the story of the Rose Garden, walked around most of the grounds, and then we went into the similar garden on the east side. Mrs. Mellon has a plan to transform it into a very dainty, feminine garden and put up a little plaque as a tribute to Jacqueline Kennedy, for all that she did for the White House. I think that no accolade could be enough and I am all for getting it done. I will go ahead with that idea and see what we can bring into being. Mrs. Mellon is an easy, unassuming person; I liked her very much. And although I could by no means match knowledge with knowledge, I can at least match it with understanding and appreciation and let her know how much it means to thousands of people.

Later I asked Lyndon what he thought about the project of naming the East Garden the Jacqueline Kennedy Garden. He thought it was fine. I then tried out the idea on Clark Clifford, legal-adviser-without-portfolio to the White House since Truman days and gratefully continued by us.

He thought it was an excellent idea, but suggested that it might be well to mention it to two other people. I could readily see why.

First was George Hartzog, head of the National Park service, whose job it is to oversee the White House grounds. I tracked him down and he was very much in agreement, although I asked him to make sure there wasn't any fine print lurking in the legislation anywhere that might make it difficult. He called me back and said that there wasn't anything and it would be fine. And then I called Bill Walton of the Fine Arts Commission. (Except for his failure to call on the Fine Arts Commission, Mr. Truman might not have had any trouble with his famous balcony, so I did want to touch that base.) Bill Walton, too, was very much in favor of the idea. It only remained to call Mrs. Kennedy herself. When I did, she said, "No." She said she didn't think First Ladies deserved any recognition, that it was really just her husband and his job that had accomplished anything.

She went on to say the important thing was to have the work continue, to have the garden finished, to have Mrs. Mellon go on, and finally, laughingly, she said, "Well, if she wants to, scratch my initials on a tree, or put a plaque, ever so little, underneath some bench." So now I must get back to Mrs. Mellon with that permission and I think the garden will happen. My main hope is to have the grounds and the flowers in the house continue to profit by the artistry of Mrs. Mellon's hand.

Tuesday, March 24

HUNTSVILLE, ALABAMA

This was a great day! Three or four days' worth all rolled into one, with an exposure to learning, excitement, and the warm and simple pleasures of seeing kinfolks and old friends. I got up at 6 and was airborne at 7, with Liz and about twenty-five or thirty members of the press. We arrived at Marshall Space Flight Center in Huntsville a little past 9 and walked down the ramp of the plane to meet Jim Webb, who had helped plan the visit, and Mrs. Webb. Dr. Wernher Von Braun, Director of the Space Center, was there with his wife; the Mayor of Huntsville; Congressman Bob Jones; and an outstanding employee of the flight center, Mrs. Mary Derryberry, age seventy.

The first, the inevitable event, was the greeting ceremony. There were about three hundred people in front of the platform—VIP's from Huntsville, civic and community leaders, and industrial and business representatives. Jim Webb welcomed me, and then I set the tone of the day, I hope, by giving the reasons I had come. First, because Lyndon authored the Space Act back in 1958, and ever since then it has been his white-hot interest. By osmosis, a lot of his interest has rubbed off on me.

Second, I am proud of the vital role that women are playing in space. About 20 percent of the payroll at Marshall Space Flight Center consists of women, ranging from clerks and typists to aerospace engineers. But the most important reason of all to me is because the space program is one thing that's taking the South into the future. The South, so long mired in its troubles of the past, has taken a long step toward catching up with the rest of the United States in its attachment to the space program. I used the line "The South has hitched its wagon to the stars," and that's one sentence the papers picked up. On all of my trips to the South I want to accent its future and not its past. What better springboard than space?

When the greeting ceremony was over I rode with Jim Webb and Dr. Von Braun to observe the care, feeding, and development of Saturns—rockets that, before this decade is over, will take man to the moon, or so we all fervently hope. We stopped first at the engineering division hangar, where Dr. Von Braun tried to describe to me what I was going to be seeing. At each stop along the way I would meet a new "escort officer," almost always a woman. First there were the wind tunnel models to show what effects wind currents have on rockets, followed by a gyro in a suitcase—that's the machine that keeps the rocket on its proper course—and then we saw a part of the so-called rocket brain. And then a flexible tube, consisting of thousands of pieces of glass with a lens at each end, that takes photographs inside the rocket during flight.

The most interesting thing to me, however, was not the machinery but the people. I kept asking: "Where are you from?" and over and over I would get the names of little towns in Alabama—Vida, Wetumpka, Cullman—or Mississippi, Tennessee, or Georgia. And when I would ask them where they had got their educations—very satisfactorily (to me, that is)—they frequently said Auburn, the University of Alabama, Vanderbilt. Of course there had to be a sprinkling of MIT alumni in there, and always in the background I was conscious—because of their accent and their really quite different look—of the German scientists who had been brought back from the Peenemünde experiments and set down in Alabama at the end of World War II.

We saw a graphic display of the evolution of the Saturn rocket. There were about six Saturns lined up on the base, just like little dominoes beside big dominoes, which demonstrated how much the Saturn has grown in its brief five years of life, though its ancestors go back to Peenemünde.

We saw the mechanism which holds the rocket down until it is ready to lift off its launching pad. This is called, appropriately enough, the umbilical tower. And we saw the astronaut's suit, all shiny silver, and the small craft, rather like a big frog on tall, spindly legs that will some day land the two astronauts on the moon.

Presently we came to what is called the "hard hat" area where Dr. Von Braun, who I suddenly noticed was wearing a Texas Stetson (I think he had had it behind his back most of the morning), presented me with a "hard hat" with the Marshall Space Flight insignia on the front with my name. At the same time he told how he happened to have the Texas Stetson: Lyndon had given it to him when he was at the Ranch for Chancellor Erhard's visit at Christmas!

At noon, gorged with information, or rather with unassimilated exciting facts, and footsore, we arrived at the tenth floor of the center, where I was to have lunch with all my Alabama kinfolks. This was an interlude of real delight. Lunch was a buffet and I wound up by having fifty-eight relatives present, including Cousins Elaine Fischesser, Edwina Mitchell, Guss Hawkins, and Bernice Robinson. The first "kissing kin" I had met when I emerged from the plane was my cousin Lucille Pattillo Thomas and her beautiful daughter, Jean. Lucille had been my special playmate of the years between about six and fourteen, and I was so happy to see her.

Aunt Ellen, a veteran of fifty years of teaching in the public schools, was also there, bless her heart. She is one of those people who keep the family together by writing and telling the rest of us what each one of us is doing. One of the folks I was most glad to see was Uncle John Will Pattillo, eighty-seven, ruddy of cheek if a little slow of walk, who predicted that "Lyndon will beat the other fellow, whoever he is, and make him like it." Elaine and I talked a mile a minute, lickety-split just as we had always done. The years have done little to dull her sprightly spirit.

After lunch Dr. Webb and Dr. Von Braun took me to the static testing center where we entered a bunker and watched the test firing of an eight-engine cluster of Saturn I. Never have I seen such a sight! There were the breathless moments when they counted down to zero, and then a noise that shook the world, the bunker trembled all around me, and flame erupted from the bottom of the rocket in great billowing sheets of red fire. It lasted more than two minutes but it seemed an eternity. Saturn I will be used to send an unmanned Apollo spacecraft into orbit—in fact, one is on the pad at Cape Kennedy now for launching later this spring.

Jim Webb was beside me in the bunker and we looked out together through the narrow slit no wider than a foot. When the firing started and the world shook, he put his arm around me, and the resulting photograph was really amusing. The caption under it read, or so Liz quipped: "Lady Bird, after this is over, let's you and me go out and have a drink."

After a second and somewhat less dramatic firing we returned to the auditorium of the Administration Building for an award ceremony with NASA employees. There were about five hundred workers in the auditorium and it was my privilege to present awards—a thirty-year service award, a twenty-year service award, four invention awards, a group-achievement award, and a sustained superior performance award which I am glad to say was won by a woman in the Purchasing Office. I made a short talk but found it easy because I had been so thrilled by the events of the day and everything that I had seen.

The day was climaxed by a reception, at which Mrs. Webb and Mrs. Von Braun were the hostesses, for Alabama officials and organization leaders. Though it was brief, it couldn't have been warmer or more fun. I walked down the line and shook hands with about two city blocks of folks, not making it to the end of the line, because the Secret Service kept on muttering: "It's time for the plane to leave. It's time for you to leave."

All in all, it was a great day for me, worth several days of a life.

Wednesday, April 8

THE WHITE HOUSE

This should have been a late morning because it was a very late night last night. After the guests from the North Carolina reception had departed and I'd finished about two hours of work, restlessly I went over to Lyndon's office, hoping to jar him loose and bring him home. I found him in the little room with several staff members.

There was an air of excitement and I could tell that something on the Hill was coming to a boil. It was the Farm Bill—a cliff hanger. The Food Stamp plan was tied in with it and the bill had almost been given up as lost by the newspaper people, by Larry O'Brien, by almost everybody. Except Lyndon.

I sat in the office for about an hour and a half while Larry pored over a long list of House members in hand, those committed as being safe for the bill, those irrevocably against it, those who were shaky and could possibly be persuaded, those who were absent and might "pair" if you got to them and could find them an opposite number. Lyndon made call after call after call. It was an interesting performance. Larry kept checking off those on our side or against us, and adding one more on the side for us or who might possibly be for us, until we thought that, by an eyelash, we had it. The bill passed, and finally I succeeding in bringing them all home for dinner.

So today began without enough sleep. At 1:30 came the major event of the day—Washington's good-by and our own good-by to one of America's great heroes, General Douglas MacArthur. Lyndon and I, Lynda Bird and Warrie Lynn, drove to Union Station and there we boarded the train, greeted, and paid our respects to Mrs. MacArthur—a slight woman, gracious, gentle-voiced, and assured—their son, Arthur MacArthur; Mrs. MacArthur's brother-in-law, Colonel Smith, and his wife; Ambassador Douglas MacArthur whom we had recently seen in Belgium; and the General's aide, Major General Courtney Whitney, and Mrs. Whitney. There was also a very solemn-looking Oriental woman, Miss Ah Cheu, who had been young Arthur MacArthur's nurse, and a whole traincar full of relatives and friends, including General Carlos Romulo—what memories of General MacArthur's great days go along with him!

After we emerged from the train we lined up in a solemn single file. Lyndon was on my right, and on my left I found the Attorney General, Bobby Kennedy. He looked tanned, healthier, more relaxed than I had ever seen him. And as we stood there, with the skies weeping outside—it was the third rainy day in a row—a cordon of troops came to attention, flags were at half-mast everywhere, and in the distance sounded the roll of drums. The Attorney General said something that I was certainly thinking, but would have bitten off my tongue before saying. "We seem always to be meeting at funerals," he said. "Yes," I answered. He said, "There've been a lot of them these last four months."

As the casket passed by, flag-draped, carried by eight men from the different services, I felt the next two hours were an echo of the November day of President Kennedy's funeral. At Sixteenth Street and Constitution Avenue the casket was transferred from a hearse to a caisson, drawn by six dappled-gray horses. Immediately following the caisson came a great red flag with five white stars, and as we rode along Constitution Avenue, General Ted Clifton, the Military Aide, told us of how, during the last

World War, five-star Generals came into being. It became necessary to create a rank above four-star General or to institute what in other countries is called a Field Marshal.

And General George Marshall said, "I'll be damned if I will have people calling me 'Marshal Marshall.' Nope, we'll just have five-star Generals, and, no, we won't have any six-star Generals, either." So General Marshall chopped off the rank at five stars.

There was another familiar figure—the beautiful, spirited black horse, riderless, with black boots pointing backward. Once more an echo of a November day. I thought of what Bobby Kennedy had said as I stood next to him. "You're doing a wonderful job. Everybody says so." And then, after a pause, he added, ". . . and so is your husband." I appreciated that very much.

One difference about today was that the crowds that lined Constitution Avenue seemed to be without emotion. No one was crying; after all, General MacArthur was eighty-four. But there they were, under a sea of black umbrellas, silent, to say good-by to one of the most dramatic figures who ever traversed the American stage.

While we were riding together, Lyndon told Lynda about the time General MacArthur awarded him the Silver Star, for action in New Guinea before she was born. And then about a visit he'd had with him only a few months ago, when MacArthur said that if he'd known Lyndon was going to become President he wouldn't have let him go on that New Guinea mission.

The five Joint Chiefs of Staff were supposed to walk from Sixteenth and Constitution up to the Capitol. I kept on hoping they wouldn't, or we might have one or two less, from pneumonia.

At the Capitol steps we got out and stood beside Mrs. MacArthur while the Army band played "Ruffles and Flourishes" followed by a hymn, and then the casket was borne up the long steps by the servicemen into the rotunda of the Capitol, where it was to lie in state. The House and Senate had adjourned and the rotunda was thronged with all the Senators and the Congressmen and many military men. The House chaplain and the Senate chaplain each gave a prayer, and Lyndon placed an enormous red, white, and blue wreath at the foot of the casket.

I had asked Mrs. MacArthur and her son, and the Ambassador and all the kinfolks, to stop by the White House to warm up and have a cup of tea. Mrs. MacArthur accepted, so when the services were ended Lyndon and I departed at once, he to his office and I to the second floor. Presently they arrived, and Mrs. MacArthur, controlled, gracious of manner, reminded me of the General's phrase about her. He had called her his "finest soldier."

We all reminisced about that great day when General MacArthur rose to the rostrum in the House Chamber and made the address to the Joint Session. That was one day I wouldn't have given up my ticket in the gallery to any constituent!

The sun came out and lit up the Yellow Oval Room with full glory. I had the feeling that it was the right thing, the appropriate thing to do, having them there, although I hadn't known them well. But the whole country had really known him well. And this had been a very dignified departure from life, a most respectful good-by.

When they were gone, Hester Provenson came to see me and we put in about two hours of hard work on my speech for the Eleanor Roosevelt Memorial luncheon in New York. Then I curled up in bed and watched Walter Lippmann on television. He was on for an hour, and never a dull moment. What he said about foreign aid certainly isn't going to make it any easier to get a Foreign Aid Bill passed. He really gave ammunition to all those who are against it, for good or bad reasons, or who have come to have their doubts about foreign aid within the last year or two.

What Lippmann said about Lyndon couldn't have been better. He virtually said it didn't make any difference whom Lyndon asked to be his Vice President, because he didn't need the help. When the commentator inquired about the possibility of McNamara and pointed out that he had been a registered Republican at one time, Lippmann rather washed that one out. I think this is the first time I have ever thought of this as an actual possibility.

It had been such an exhausting day, and I was very near the borders of sleep when they came upstairs from the office. Lyndon's endurance is simply fantastic, and mine is not.

Thursday, April 9

NEW YORK AND THE WHITE HOUSE

Today was a truly big day.

I was up early—7 o'clock and had breakfast with Lyndon, who I had hoped would sleep later. My last words to him were: "I could have caught a much later plane if I could only have ridden the shuttle." He said, "Well don't, because we're just about to run into a big strike tonight—a railroad strike."

So, I left at 8:30 on the commercial airline with Liz and Bess for a New York appearance that I had anticipated with both dread and the will to succeed. It was the first anniversary luncheon of the Eleanor Roosevelt Memorial Foundation. I had accepted because I greatly admired Mrs. Roosevelt and because Jean Kintner had asked me. Adlai Stevenson had followed up her invitation with an even more persuasive letter. Jean met me at LaGuardia, took me by the hand, and had me in tow all day.

Headquarters for the Memorial were the New York Hilton, all glass and steel, where the luncheon took place before an audience of twenty-eight hundred, who had paid $12.50 a plate. They expected to raise $100,000 for the Eleanor Roosevelt Foundation. The money will be spent for internships in the human rights field, for cancer research, and for the construction of two memorial wings at the Hyde Park Library.

The first event was a pre-luncheon reception for women who had paid a thousand dollars each to participate. Jean Kintner, Anna Rosenberg Hoffman, and I made up the receiving line, and in walked a guest list that comprised a large part of the power structure of New York—from the financial side, the philanthropic side, those interested in human welfare, and, I imagine, those just interested in society.

Having greeted all the VIP's, we went marching in to the luncheon. Adlai Stevenson arrived from his latest crisis at the UN just in time to go in with us.

The whole luncheon was Jean Kintner's triumph, and very well handled it was. Marian Anderson spoke some words from Mrs. Roosevelt's book *Tomorrow Is Now*, and I found her speaking voice almost as moving as her singing voice. To me the most touching thing of all was Anna Rosenberg Hoffman, handsomely dressed, her fingers as bright with jewels as her mind is bright, reading the last letters that she had received from Mrs. Roosevelt. In these letters Mrs. Roosevelt said that she didn't want her friends to have to provide the money to start her foundation—that she intended to work right on, at least until her eightieth birthday and as long as she could beyond. But if the time came when she could no longer work, she hoped then that perhaps they would . . . Anna's hand and her voice shook.

Not even Adlai Stevenson, with his silver tongue—and what a command of language he has—could quite equal her sincerity. Adlai was introduced as the man with whom every woman in the world would like to have lunch.

Well, actually a great many of them were having lunch with him today. He is one of the most likable human beings I know. He introduced me and had a great many kind things to say about me. And then came the dreaded moment when I had to stand on my feet and say what I had come to say. Having lived those years with the Roosevelt regime, I really felt like talking about them. I recounted a day in 1939 when Mrs. Roosevelt came to a benefit luncheon my Seventy-fifth Congress Club gave to buy a wheel chair for a crippled boy. "Only one person would benefit, but where else do you start except with one person? Mrs. Roosevelt was always ready to *start*. And one person was important to her."

I saluted her belief that sometimes silence is the greatest sin. "All of us are familiar with the people who are the partisans of departed virtue, but are afraid to defend an unpopular truth today. Mrs. Roosevelt never stood with this timid company. She was never afraid to speak up against wrong, no matter how many brickbats it brought down on her head."

Sometimes I think somebody ought to pen an accolade to her generous and understanding husband, who took those brickbats, too, and recognized her for the good she did. My sympathetic feeling for the subject, and the two hours I had spent with Mrs. Provenson learning how to say what I thought, paid off, and when I finished and walked down the star-studded table I felt as if I had acquitted myself well enough—something I seldom feel.

After the heady hours of seeing New York's assembled great, I spent the next hour or so in relatively minor household errands, and caught the 6:30 plane back to Washington. All day there had lain in the back of my mind the dismal gray fog of what Lyndon had said about a national railroad strike. When I reached the White House I found that he was still in his office and that he had made the bold stroke of asking the Railroad Brotherhood and the leaders of the railroads to gather with him and lay plans to mediate their differences, which have been festering for four years. How presumptuous to think he could walk in on an abscess that has been gathering venom for that long and do anything to lance and heal it. But he's not a man to let it burst in front of him without having a try. So he didn't come home. He stayed—until midnight, working with them. That's the late, late stint twice this week. One night the Farm Bill, tonight the railroad strike threat.

The papers can describe it better than I can. The Associated Press said: "It was a fantastic, almost unbelievable day around the White House. . . . President Johnson staged a balcony scene from the Truman Balcony. . . . He and reporters shouted banter and comments back and forth." Doug Kiker of the *Herald Tribune* said: "It was a Spring fever day at the White House yesterday. Consider two press conferences—a chance for poet Carl Sandburg and his brother-in-law, Edward Steichen, to hear and see union and management officials negotiate the railroad dispute. A White House balcony scene."

Actually, the morning began early for me. I took a long, tedious, and "almost last" trip to The Elms, unearthing such things as a picture of me at thirteen, baby pictures of Lynda and Luci, and the key to an apartment we had in 1941! When I was too tired to do any more, I went back to the White House just in time to meet, at 2:30, Carl Sandburg, eighty-five years old, his little wife—with the gentlest, nicest face I nearly ever saw—and Edward Steichen, famous photographer (and patron of our friend Okamoto), and his amazingly young and beautiful wife.

Secretary of Interior Stewart Udall and Lee Udall had been escorting them around Washington and brought them to the White House. Before his arrival I had had brought up from the Library Carl Sandburg's *The War Years* and *The Prairie Years* from his biography of Lincoln, and had read again his poems in Lynda Bird's anthology: "Chicago," "Fog," "The People, Yes." He was shaggy-haired (his hair white, almost in a Dutch bob), rugged, completely untrammeled in his conversation. He had somewhat the same attitude as Lyndon, I thought. He hadn't "heard about the rules." Also, he was a little hard of hearing.

Edward Steichen, with his marvelous beard, was urbane and sophisticated but just as childishly happy to be with his sister and his brother-in-law. He said of Mrs. Sandburg, "That little sister of mine is an angel if anybody ever was." The four of them simply glowed with the pleasure of being alive and together.

We went into the Lincoln Room and I asked Mr. Sandburg to autograph two of the volumes on Lincoln's life, since he is the great master of Lincolniana. I tried to tell him a bit about the furniture and the hand-penned manuscript of the Gettysburg Address, which Lincoln had given to be auctioned off at a charity fair, but you couldn't tell him much, because he did all the talking. When Lyndon came, they had a time dividing it up between them! He looked Lyndon up and down and said solemnly, "You look like you could take care of yourself."

When Mr. Sandburg had smoked a cigar down to the last quarter inch I offered him an ash tray, hoping to save the rug of the Lincoln Room. But he pulled a little metal gadget out of his pocket, clipped it onto the last end of the cigar, and said, "Oh, no, I'm not through yet," and smoked it until there was barely a whiff of smoke left.

Various people came and went and were introduced. Lynda Bird, in from school with Warrie Lynn, arrived and got her book of poems autographed. Luci rushed in, more full of her own plans and dates than interested in Carl Sandburg, and Mr. Ketchum, Curator of the White House, was introduced and then stood in the back of the room to listen. So did Liz Carpenter. You couldn't have separated her from that scene! We went into the Yellow Room and had tea. Then Lyndon took them out on the Truman Balcony. There they looked down and saw a group of reporters standing around the Rose Garden. Lyndon began shouting back and forth to them. The first semi-press conference that ever took place from a balcony, I think!

From there we went down into the garden, because Steichen is a great lover of delphinium. He raises some rare and beautiful strains. He had promised to send me some plants, and I wanted him' to see the garden. Among Sandburg's delightful remarks was: "My brother-in-law wanted to raise a beard and he didn't know what kind of beard he wanted, and so he decided he would copy one after the Prophet Isaiah." Another thing he said affectionately was: "Did you ever hear of a photographer who had a biographer?" (Meaning himself, because he has written a rather extraordinary biography of Edward Steichen.)

From the garden, to my amazement, Lyndon ushered us into the Cabinet Room. Lyndon said he wanted Edward Steichen and Carl Sandburg to see "some tough men operating . . . men who can throw several million people out of work." There were all the leaders of the railroad industry, prepared to spend the next fourteen or fifteen days in negotiations to prevent a strike. It was a unique White House visit!

This evening we dined out, and that's getting to be a rare treat in this house. We went to Phyllis and Doug Dillon's house to a dinner in honor of Undersecretary and Mrs. Henry Fowler. Henry is leaving the government, for the third time. This is his third hitch in three decades, during which he has served in many departments in many capacities. When we got to the Dillons' beautiful home, I felt as if I were entering a door of complete relaxation. Anything that happened was not my responsibility. I was just there to have fun and I did. It was a graceful evening. Phyllis manages to be both efficient and light-hearted and just the sort of woman Lyndon enjoys.

Many toasts were made during the evening in praise of a man who has given a large share of his life to his government, with small remuneration. Henry (everybody calls him "Joe") was sitting on my right and told me the saga. He had first come to Washington in the Roosevelt era for a limited engagement. He must have done a hard job well because he kept on trying to escape from office, and persistently being called back. I loved Lyndon's toast. He said: "Go off and get rich and have a good time—for about ninety days."

Tuesday, April 14

Because King Hussein of Jordan was scheduled to arrive without his wife, I had not expected to participate in the ceremonies at 11:30 this morning. I was busily engaged in desk work when I got word from Lyndon that I had better appear.

The King arrived in a helicopter on the South Lawn—short, handsome, infinitely dignified, with a deep, musical speaking voice. We escorted him and his younger brother, about eighteen, upstairs in the elevator and went out on the North Portico, where an army of reporters awaited us on one side and a similar army of photographers on the other. The long line of flags snapped merrily in the April breeze, the tulips were coming out, and Angie had shepherded the King's party up the stairs so that they were there and lined up ahead of us. Lyndon took the King out, and I took my position slightly to the left of the door.

Lyndon made his welcoming remarks, and the King responded. Then Lyndon, to the surprise of the Secret Service and everybody else, got in the car with King Hussein to drive with him to Blair House. From there Lyndon elected to walk back. He became enveloped in a crowd of passers-by and sightseers, shook hands, and signed autographs, and enjoyed himself.

Meanwhile, I was getting ready to dash over to the Department of Agriculture to open the Food and Home Fair for Consumers. Jane and Orville Freeman were waiting for me, with Esther Peterson and Mrs. John G. Lee, Chairman, Consumer Advisory Council. I said my few words, based on the fact that my life has been largely spent as a purchasing agent for the family. I told them I wanted to get the most and the best for my money, like everybody else.

Immediately afterward, I was on my way with Jane Freeman to the Senate Ladies Red Cross Luncheon in my honor. This was the first time I was to be the guest at this luncheon—after fifteen years of serving as one of the hostesses—twelve times as a Senate wife myself, three times as the wife of the Vice President. Mrs. Peter Dominick of Colorado was the Republican Chairman today, assisted by Betty Talmadge as Co-Chairman.

For lunch we had delicious filets mignons, half of them from Texas, half from Oklahoma, all donated. On behalf of the group, Louella Dirksen presented me with a wonderful charm for my bracelet, with the Senate seal on one side and an inscription from the Senate Ladies and the date on the other. I enjoyed speaking to them, because I knew them all so well. I told them that if I ever wrote a book about my life, the longest chapter would be concerned with our love affair with the Senate!

Among the old-timers present was Mrs. Frances Parkinson Keyes, on two walking sticks. She informed me that she had notified me of her presence in town and had not heard anything from my Social Secretary . . . alas! Mrs. Tobey, our leader year in and year out, has the manner of a duchess with a sense of humor. There was good attendance and a lively spirit, but somehow there was something missing. I don't know exactly what. The *esprit de corps* and sense of drive that prevailed when Lyndon was in the Senate, and which always by osmosis transferred itself to the Senate Ladies and to me, seemed somehow missing.

When the party was over I came back and performed that most signal service of the citizen (second-most really—I suppose voting comes first). I signed my income tax papers. Then I dressed up in my beautiful yellow chiffon evening dress and made ready to receive His Majesty, King Hussein I.

A little before 8, the Warrens, the George Balls, the Dukes, our Ambassador to Jordan and Mrs. Robert Barnes, Ambassador of Jordan Saad Juma and his wife, Jordanian Minister of Foreign Affairs Anton Atalla and Chief of Protocol Iklil Sati (whom I had stood beside at the funeral of King Paul of Greece), and His Majesty King Hussein I and His Royal Highness Prince Hassan came upstairs to the Yellow Oval Room. There was a presentation of gifts. We gave the King a gold clock with the U.S. Seal and engraved inscription, a vermeil pen stand with two gold pens, also with seal and inscription, and a camera and a book of Lyndon's speeches, called *A Time for Action*. Sometimes I am vaguely unhappy that our gifts seem less imaginative and less meaningful than the gifts that foreign monarchs make to us. This was one of those times, for His Majesty gave to me two bracelets from the time of the patriarch Abraham and a little oil-burning lamp that might have been used at any time during a thousand years of Biblical history. To both of us he gave a magnificent Bible, bound in mother-of-pearl and elaborately carved. Following the presentation came the always-thrilling removal of the colors, the forming of the line, and the marching downstairs to the tune of "Hail to the Chief."

We stood in line in the East Room where about one hundred and fifty guests filed by to shake hands. I was honored to have J. Edgar Hoover, who never goes to affairs of this sort but who has always seemed to have a very real respect and personal liking for Lyndon. We had several guests of Jordanian ancestry, including Najeeb Halaby, head of the Federal Aviation Agency. And this was just the right time to have Helen Thomas of UPI.

The King sat on my right and his beautiful English—he was educated at Sandhurst—made conversation easy, although I can't say there was any time that I felt I had made real contact with him. We spoke about his having piloted the plane (a 707) on the way over. I approached gingerly the subject of water, and he said that many of the springs of the Jordan River rose within Israel. For the first time I asked the guest of honor to sign my menu. The autograph was in Arabic; I couldn't read it but the King graciously added "Hussein I."

We went to the East Room after dinner and heard the Dave Brubeck Quartet render four numbers of avant-garde jazz, planned because we had been told that the King was a jazz fan. Afterward we went into the Blue Room for dancing. Since the King had had a long hard trip, he danced only enough to be polite and took his departure. But a lot of people lingered on. One of the bits of conversation I enjoyed was when Jane Freeman said to her husband, "Oh, let's go dance," and the Secretary replied, "All right, you testify for me in front of the Appropriations Committee in the morning at 10 o'clock and I'll go in there and dance with you." An interesting insight came from one of the guests, Dr. Allan McKelvie, who had spent several years in Jordan as a member of a medical team. He said the King had inaugurated a program to have every child in Jordan immunized against polio and that he himself took the first shot. I like all the things I hear about him—his personal bravery and the fact that he gets out among his people.

Altogether, I would say it was a successful, not superb evening, but I wish I could look at it through the eyes of some of the guests and not always through my own.

Next day a society columnist said, "Not one of the 151 guests were seen to yawn once, which may be somewhat historical in review of Presidential entertainment." I am glad that she, and apparently a lot of people, felt that way, but I was not actually in the groove with it myself. I like to hear "St. Louis woman with the diamond ring" sung or played so that I feel like getting into motion—and I could barely recognize "St. Louis Blues." However, I must be improving as an actress because the columnist reported: "but it was Mrs. Johnson who seemed to enjoy the music most. She tapped one gilt-shod foot and kept time with the rhythmic drumming of her fingers on her program . . ." So, good enough!

Thursday, April 16

I got word this afternoon from Lyndon that he was bringing over some of the Texas editors and their wives. At first the forecast was fifteen, then presently it grew to forty, so I sent a quick SOS to the kitchen to get refreshments ready and we'd arrange to serve in the Oval Room.

Most of the Texas editors were old-timers: the Charlie Greens, the Charlie Guys, Bill Hobby alone (his wife, Diana, was at home), Bill Hooten, the Rhea Howards (she is always the ultimate in refinement, and looked very pretty in blue), Walter Humphrey, the Wes Izzards, the Bob Jacksons, the Frank Mayborns, the J. Q. Mahaffeys (he was grinning as usual). I always like to see somebody from close to home. Walter Jenkins, Cliff Carter, and Jack Valenti came over to help out, but Lyndon was completely in charge of everything. He took everybody out on the Truman Balcony to show them the gardens below and the view of the Washington Monument.

After the editors left we had the sort of dinner I had been planning and wanting ever since Lady Jackson arrived (she is Barbara Ward, author of *Rich Nations and Poor Nations*)—just she, Dr. Willis Hurst, and ourselves. She had been staying on the third floor, writing memoranda and speech material.

Lady Jackson talked and Lyndon listened, something he doesn't always do, especially to women. But he is fascinated by her, and so am I. She spoke of the possibility that a lot of the money saved and the people put out of work by the closing of the bases under McNamara's program might be used for some sort of pilot program for urban renewal, to create a model city and surroundings, to experiment with traffic problems. The nice thing about Lady Jackson is that she seems to believe that anything is possible.

She envisions the next few decades as possibly the greatest in the history of mankind. Automation can be turned into a vast blessing instead of a curse, she says. Our natural resources are so great, the inventiveness of man's mind so boundless, that at last we have it in our grasp to build a really new society, offering more for everybody—or at least that's my synthesis, after listening to her.

Friday, April 17

This afternoon was spent in office work and planning for the reception for the American Society of Newspaper Editors—twelve hundred all told, who were converging on us at 5:30 in the Rose Garden.

In my white suit, I joined Lyndon at his office, with Lynda Bird in tow, and an SOS for Luci to come as quickly as possible. It was a beautiful day, thank heavens; the editors filed into the Rose Garden and spread out onto the South Lawn. There was a podium; I said a word of welcome and Lynda Bird did well with her few words. Lyndon launched his speech on a light note with a few jokes, and then he plunged into the story of what faces him: a President's duties, the Civil Rights issue, his war on poverty, amplified by many statistics, and a line I liked very much about "turning tax eaters into tax payers." He quoted that dreadful figure, the fact that about 49 percent of the young men who are called up by the draft are found physically or mentally unfit for the Army! Then he discussed Medicare, the Pay Bill, the railroad talks. (There hasn't been a night when we've come in these last few that my eyes haven't turned to the Executive Office Building, wondering, hoping, praying for the success of what they are doing there—trying to settle the railroad strike equitably.) Lyndon ended with what a good many of those listening probably regarded as an evangelical appeal—for unity, for compassion. "For today . . . under the shadows of atomic power it is not rhetoric but it is truth to say that we must either love each other or we must die." I expect the cynics were smirking, but we may well look back on this decade as a time in which the United States could rise to that kind of leadership—or in failing, fail all.

At the last moment Luci came in and got to say her small word and then we filed into the White House for food and drink in the State Dining Room and dancing in the East Room. Mr. Miles Wolff, the incoming President of the American Society of Newspaper Editors, introduced me to as many people as we could meet, since it's pretty nearly impossible to stand in line and meet eleven or twelve hundred. And Mr. Herbert Brucker, the present President of ASNE, accompanied Lyndon.

There were the Barry Binghams of Kentucky and the young Harry Byrds of Winchester, Virginia. The Hodding Carters, Jr., were taking his father's place—his father is ill. She's Marcia McGhee, George McGhee's daughter, and so attractive. The Otis Chandlers from California were there and the Turner Catledges of New York, Willie Snow, and Mark Ethridge. And *how* delightful to run into David Hall, whom I introduced around as *my* first editor! He was editor of the *Daily Texan* when I got a Bachelor of Journalism degree in 1934. I had a good talk with George Healy of New Orleans about the G. P. A. Healy paintings in the White House, in which I told him I thought there were *six*, and he told me, "No, fifteen!" It was impressive to meet Mr. and Mrs. Joseph Pulitzer, Jr.—and two families of Scripps from the Scripps-Howard chain.

And then we danced, danced, danced! I was cut in on about every third step. I heard later that Lyndon said, between clenched teeth, to Bess over his shoulder: "Get those Aides to dancing!" I doubt if the editors and their wives ever saw so much, or did so much, or danced so much at the White House in two hours' time!

Finally, about 8, they began to melt away. We took the Turner Catledges upstairs for a final bit of conversation, and then had a fairly early but weary dinner; the large envelope of "Night Reading," and eventually good night to the world.

Sunday, April 19

Today was a gloriously beautiful day, with the garden at perfection. We'd asked Secretary and Mrs. Dillon to go to St. Mark's with us, and when Ambassador Stevenson came over about 10:15 in the morning to talk a little business, we abducted him and took him along. Coming in from church Lyndon waved to all the tourists at the gate, even stuck out his hand and shook hands with a few of them.

Adlai had to leave but the Dillons stayed for lunch and the McNamaras joined us. First we had a good walk in the garden, much to the delight of

Him and Her, who romped around us, jumping up and down. This exercise will probably cost me eight dollars in cleaning bills, but it reminded me so much of "Dear Dog" (Beagle himself, who died last fall) that it was worth it.

After our guests left, Lyndon lay down for a nap, and I faced the prospect of telling Bernie Rosenbach good-by. He came in to see me, very tall and slim and sad, and told me that he and Lynda Bird had decided not to see each other any more until Christmas, and then they would decide whether they wanted to get back together again, for dates, if not to be engaged. Bernie said—as I had suspected—the break had been brewing for some time and they only wished they had done it earlier, because they'd gone through a lot of heartache. I know that for me it was painful, because I like him and respect him so much, and because he is going back to that cold, gray ship, all steel and loneliness, and Lynda Bird will stay here surrounded by warmth and family and excitement. My heart aches for him. As he started to step into the elevator, I reached up and kissed him good-by. I'm not at all sure that he's gone out of our lives, but I think that for now this is the best solution.

Earlier I had taken Bernie in to tell Lyndon good-by, but I left before he really did. Afterward, I was pleased to hear Lyndon say how manfully Bernie behaved and to know how much it really mattered to Lyndon. I want him to know and share some of our girls' heartaches, as well as their joys.

Wednesday, April 22

Lyndon whirled off in the helicopter this morning to open the World's Fair in New York. At 4 o'clock I had a reception here for two hundred leaders of the Daughters of the American Revolution, the State Regents and the national officers. This is the first time in eleven years that the First Lady had received the DAR. Mrs. Eisenhower invited them in 1953, and had entertained around four thousand guests, about a four-hour stand. I knew *that* was impossible, but I did want to hold out my hand in some gesture of greeting to them. They have had such bad publicity these last few years and I want to applaud them for their many good programs: the schools they maintain in the Appalachian Mountains and the scholarships they give to youngsters, and their dedication to the preservation of our national monuments. Also, I believe that if you persist in calling the members of any group "bigots" year after year after year, the human reaction would be to begin to defend yourself and harden in attitude.

Mrs. Robert Duncan, the National President, was the first in line, wearing her broad blue ribbon and white orchid and bringing a gift for me. When I opened it, I found it couldn't have been more perfect for my life. Two pairs of white gloves! And then the two hundred ladies filed past, most of them wearing broad blue sashes, many medals, and pretty hats. I do not remember a more friendly group or one more responsive to being in this house.

I chatted with them about Lyndon's mother's great interest in genealogy and how helpful the DAR members had been in rounding up records. Actually one of Lyndon's ancestors was one of the three joint founders of the DAR. She was Mary Desha, a granddaughter of Joseph Desha, brother of Lyndon's great-great-grandmother, Phoebe Ann Desha Bunton. There is a bust of her in the DAR building.

Next was a meeting with Boisfeuilett Jones (our friend and advisor from HEW), Liz, and Wendy, to plan my trip to Atlanta on May 11. While we were talking, Lyndon burst out of the elevator, followed by as many men as the car would hold, headed for the Yellow Room. He called back over his shoulder to send in some coffee while the elevator quickly made additional round trips. About twenty men gathered in the Yellow Room with the doors shut. I thought I had recognized Dr. William J. Taylor, one of the negotiators in the Railroad Brotherhood meeting. I wasn't sure, but I had that sense of excitement that something important was happening!

We continued with our outline of the visit to Atlanta, the groundbreaking for the Communicable Disease Center, the trip to Emory University for the Honors Day convocation, lunch with the President of the college, maybe going to the Capitol to meet the Governor and the members of the House and the Senate, possibly having a reception at the Mansion, hosted by Mrs. Sanders, the Governor's wife, and a trip to the art museum.

Suddenly, like Olympic runners, out hurtled Lyndon and the first spate of men. As he stopped by the elevator, he looked at me and held up his thumb and forefinger in a gesture that I interpreted as meaning success. As the elevator descended, my prayers ascended—"Dear Lord, let this be the end of the strike!"

In a few minutes I got a call from Lyndon's office saying, "Turn on TV and watch the David Brinkley show." I hastened to tune in; in the middle of it Lyndon came on, announced the settlement of the Railwork Rules dispute, with an accolade for the Brotherhood and an accolade for the railroad management—and not forgetting, so like him, a personal word for Dr. Taylor, who had left a sick wife—in surgery the day he was called—to come and help mediate the strike. This will surely go down as one of the good days.

I worked a little longer with Liz, and presently Lyndon came in, exhilarated, on that Olympian peak. I wonder if he was thinking: "Perhaps this is the best it will ever be!"

Friday, April 24

ILLINOIS, INDIANA, OHIO,
PENNSYLVANIA, AND WEST VIRGINIA

This must have been one of the biggest days we'll ever live through in the Presidency. It began at 5:30 A.M. in the Conrad Hilton, with an early breakfast, and then departure for Meigs Field and a chopper to South Bend, Indiana. South Bend was the next stop on the five-state tour that would take us from Illinois to Indiana and Pennsylvania, down into Kentucky and West Virginia, and finally, by late night, back to Washington.

As we rose above that great city on the lake, Chicago, in the freshness of early morning, it was magnificent to see. There were huge ships plying their way across the lake below us, and I was reminded of what Mayor Daley had said—that Chicago is now the largest inland port in the United States. Five years ago it had been no port at all. But vision and daring planning had brought into being this child of the St. Lawrence waterways, and now great ships were carrying out lard and wheat to Europe and all over the world, and other ships were returning with needed imports. What a sizable achievement for the mind of man!

When we arrived at South Bend, about 8:45 A.M., we landed on the playgrounds of Cline School. There we were almost mobbed by a crowd of about fifteen thousand, who gave the police lines a bad time in their enthusiasm to get to Lyndon and shake his hand. South Bend has been hard hit economically since 8700 people were thrown out of work last Christmas Eve when Studebaker ceased production. What we had actually come to see was an example of the way a town can fight back. In Cline School there was a retraining program in operation, fired by local initiative, and aided with federal funds.

We saw three adult literacy classes, and what courage it must take to go back to school when you are thirty or forty years old. But lack of basic education is one of the reasons people who are let out of jobs can't get other jobs. We saw a computer class, full of white-collar workers, taking lessons in how to run office machinery. I asked one young woman why she was studying computer operations, and she said that with typing and shorthand, she knew she could always get a job, but if she learned how to work with these machines she would be capable of getting a better job. To my great delight we also saw a class in practical nursing, and I told them that the world was certainly waiting for their skills. So it is, as anybody who has tried to find a practical nurse for an elderly or ill member of the family can tell you.

We went out the back door into the crowd, and Lyndon climbed up on something and made an impromptu speech. It was really a surging crowd, children climbing up on trees or on the goal posts (it was an athletic field), anywhere they could get a foothold. I saw the police carrying one lady who had fainted out through the crowd. I have found that the best way to behave in such a situation is to be very calm and walk quietly, smiling and shaking as many hands as possible, but moving steadily toward my destination.

Accompanying us on this trip were the Cabinet members who are involved with the war on poverty, Secretary of Labor Willard Wirtz, Secretary of Commerce Luther Hodges, Undersecretary of Commerce Franklin D. Roosevelt, Jr., and Secretary of Health, Education and Welfare Anthony Celebrezze. There were six or more Congressmen along, from the districts that we visited, and in and out during the day, Governors Matt Welsh of Indiana, William Barron of West Virginia, and Edward Breathitt of Kentucky.

From South Bend we flew in the helicopter over the beautiful, rich, black land, with spring blooming—some of the prettiest farm land I have ever seen. I asked Senator Vance Hartke how much that land cost per acre, and his answer was something like this: "It's almost never for sale, but it would be about one thousand dollars per acre if you could buy it."

We landed at a town called Peru, in Indiana, at an Air Force base called Bunker Hill. Here we left the helicopter and got on a fast plane to take us to Pittsburgh. All along the fence there were crowds and crowds of people. Lyndon went in one direction and I in another. We shook a lot of hands, saw a lot of excited youngsters and adult citizens—curious, admiring, hopeful, and some just out for the side show.

And then on to Pittsburgh where, at the airport, Mayor and Mrs. Joseph Barr and that "old Alcalde," Governor David L. Lawrence, met us, and hospitably enough, Senator Hugh Scott, Republican. There were also Senator Joe Clark and David McDonald, the big handsome leader of the United Steelworkers, and six Congressmen or so. Our first stop was to address the National Convention of the League of Women Voters with more than thirteen hundred delegates. I think it came as a last-minute surprise to them, because Willard Wirtz was supposed to be the speaker. He had called up the night before and said, "How about me bringing the President along?"

Lyndon's talk was brief, emphasizing that his program of economic development was aimed at providing work for a half-million young Americans who were now facing a bleak future. He said that he expected the women of America to be the first to enlist in this war against poverty, because it was their children and the children of future generations that were going to live, for better or for worse, with the results of this program.

Following Lyndon's usual prodding, I got up and said a few words—all quite true—that we and the entire country were in the debt of the League of Women Voters for bringing the issues before the people and trying to get everybody to go to the polls to use his right to vote. (It does irritate me very much when I see a state like Texas using only 50 or 60 percent of its voting potential in some elections.) Then we left Willard Wirtz to make the main address.

Now the true phenomenon of the day began for me. We went by motorcade to Pittsburgh's southside section, headed for David McDonald Hall, headquarters of the United Steelworkers' home local, where Lyndon was scheduled to address the union members. Along the way we saw a quarter of a million people, according to the estimate of the Chief of Police, in an eastern industrial town, which I would not have reckoned as Lyndon's stronghold, by reason of our place of origin and his reputation for conservatism.

It began to dawn on me, and perhaps upon the nation as well, that Lyndon was a national drawing card, a national candidate, somebody who captured the imagination of the great masses of eastern industrial cities to a far greater degree than we had realized.

Before we had gone very far Lyndon had transferred to an open convertible. Along the way he made three unscheduled stops, standing on the trunk of his car and, having from somewhere acquired a bull horn, blaring out in a few short sentences his determination to fight the war on poverty—

and unemployment—and to end discrimination. Pretty soon he sent for me and I squirmed my way among the crowd and climbed up on the back seat of the convertible with him, making a mental note that flat-heeled shoes were the best thing for any kind of campaigning!

Inside the union hall another new experience awaited us. David McDonald, in introducing Lyndon, pledged "that the Union shall do all of the down-to-earth work that is possible to elect you this November." This is the first really outspoken assumption that Lyndon is running—and pledge of support—that I can remember.

But looking at the faces of the union members themselves was even more interesting to me. I found myself curiously at home making my little one-minute talk to them, which included that line of Carl Sandburg's —". . . They make their steel with men." It was an exciting atmosphere— the feeling of power this organization wielded in America, industrially and politically, what automation might hold for their future, who would be intelligent enough to turn its threat into the potential good that it does hold—for more leisure, for more material wealth in this country. Most of all I watched the faces for the individual stories they contained.

After the union hall we went back to Allegheny Airport, feeling once more the adrenalin-in-the-blood of the vast crowds along the way, and after more speeches and handshaking at the airport emplaned for Huntington, West Virginia. On the plane at last, about 2:30, we had some sandwiches. I had begun to wonder if the day was going to include any lunch. It had been a long, long time since that 6 A.M. breakfast, and addressing the luncheon of the League of Women Voters hadn't meant a bite for us.

We stopped at Huntington and after the usual airport ceremonies helicoptered into eastern Kentucky to Inez. The landscape changed completely. Could this be the same country as Pittsburgh, Pennsylvania? We flew over beautiful spring-green mountains, dotted with dogwood, the hillside pockmarked here and there by the mouths of small mines. Swift, rocky little streams tumbled in every valley, and rutted dirt roads curled their way along the mountainside.

We landed in a meadow near the community of Inez and drove up the mountainside to the home of Tom Fletcher. Now, all the welcome signs were homemade, crayon on cardboard, a piece of an old grocery box scribbled with something like "Mouth-of-Turkey School Welcomes You, Lyndon," followed by the school band. I wonder if the reporters knew what Mouth-of-Turkey meant? I am sure it was a creek. All those schools had such delicious geographical or folkloric names.

Going up the mountainside the roadway led along winding Rock Castle Creek, crossed here and there by a suspended foot bridge, homemade certainly, and leading to one or two houses nestled against the mountainside on the other side of the creek. In this area mining once was king, but it has petered out and nothing has come along to replace it. Now, two or more generations have lived here, trapped in stalemate and hopelessness.

We arrived at the Tom Fletcher home, chosen to illustrate the human toll the declining mining industry has taken on these Appalachian families. (I always feel that these occasions are too much "on stage," but perhaps it is the only way to help the media tell the story and enable the nation to understand.) The Tom Fletchers, parents and eight children, lined up on the front porch of their three-room tarpaper house—composed, friendly, welcoming, dignified in their own way. Mr. Fletcher had been in mining for many years, had lost his job, had become a sawmill worker, but he often worked as little as three or four days a month. The previous year he had earned a total of four hundred dollars.

Two of the Fletcher children had dropped out of school; that was the worst part. Mrs. Fletcher was a thin, tired-looking woman, with an acceptance that went deep down, not expecting much of life. There was another lady there, who had walked up from a little store in the valley below. She ran the store, she told me, and made a living for her four children. Her husband was ill and hadn't been able to work for years. She had "get-up-and-get" and was articulate. I asked her what that area needed most. She said, and she was quick to say it, "Jobs—we need a business or a factory to come in here." And then she said, "Next, we need a hospital. The closest hospital is over the mountain, in Louisa. If anybody gets sick here they have to go to Louisa and more than likely they don't find hospital beds when they get there."

I remembered that Louisa was the home town of Fred Vinson, who had gone into the great outside world to become almost everything in government and finally the Chief Justice of the United States. So you can't say that this part of the country doesn't raise strong men. The store owner told me that as soon as the children got old enough they left and went to Columbus or Cincinnati, or somewhere else looking for work. She said, "Don't nothing ever happen any more in Martin County." Later someone told me that Martin County had the lowest per capita income in Kentucky and, I believe, in the entire United States.

As the *New York Herald Tribune* reported it: "The President hunkered down on the porch with Mr. Fletcher for a talk." This is exactly what they did. They talked about keeping the children in school, and how the Fletchers managed to live on four hundred dollars a year with eight children. Their living depends largely on "commodities," surplus food, which is passed out on certain days of the month by the federal government in little towns throughout this area. I imagine this accounts for a very limited diet, and enough years of subsisting on it could be the reason Mrs. Fletcher looks so faded and dispirited and why there were no steps up to the front porch of the house. Hoisting myself up onto the front porch, I couldn't keep from wondering why somebody didn't at least go down and saw off a stump and lay it down for a step. And then I realized they must lack the energy. How could I know what it was like to try to raise eight children on four hundred dollars a year?

When we said good-by, the store owner put her arms around me and embraced me and said, "God bless you." Well, that, too, indicates the sort of people they are, and for the children, at least, some way out must be found.

We took a ten-minute helicopter ride to Paintsville and visited the Mayo State Vocational School. I walked into several of the classes. We saw an automobile shop, a lathe shop, a hairdressing class. All the women in our party, Frances Lewine, Helen Thomas, and I, said we wished we could stop there and be customers. How sensible these girls are to be starting on a skill that they can exchange for a paycheck almost anywhere.

We went to the Court House, that traditional place for talking to the folks, and Lyndon made a speech. In the course of it he introduced Secretary Wirtz. Now it happened that poor Mr. Wirtz, not having had any lunch, had gone across the street to snatch a quick ice cream cone with Anthony Celebrezze, so no Willard Wirtz arose to take a bow. Then Lyndon went on to say ". . . And we have with us in the crowd somewhere, Secretary of Health, Education and Welfare, Mr. Anthony Celebrezze. Will he stand up, please?" Both of these gentlemen, at the first call, started sprinting from the ice cream parlor back toward the Court House. Willard Wirtz arrived, dripping ice cream cone in hand, just in time to take his bow as Anthony Celebrezze!

It was after 6 when we left Paintsville for Huntington, flying by helicopter above the green mountains. There the big plane was waiting for us, and Lyndon held a conference with the Governors of the Appalachian states, Matthew Welsh of Indiana, Edward Breathitt of Kentucky, William Barron of West Virginia, and the representative of William Scranton of Pennsylvania, to discuss the proposed Appalachian recovery plan, which would cost the federal government about three billion dollars over a five-year period. This meeting was supposed to last about thirty minutes, but it lasted nearer to two hours.

Then Lyndon made a short, televised speech, and I said a word of farewell. The gist of his speech was what he had hammered away on all day—that poverty and unemployment are unnecessary evils in modern America and that he means to do something about them. The whole purpose of this trip, if I may presume to summarize it, was to draw back the curtain for the American nation on how about 20 percent of its people live; to persuade the public to apply the prod to the Congress, so that the Poverty Bill can pass—so that we can get a foot in the door.

All day long Lyndon had reiterated: "We are going to have a Civil Rights Bill if it takes all summer, and we don't want a Democratic label on it, we want it to be an American bill. And the war on poverty is not a Democratic job or a Republican job—we must do it together."

Saturday, April 25

THE WHITE HOUSE

My interesting news of today is that Mr. and Mrs. J. Frank Dobie [author, folklorist and professor] had arrived from Austin to be our house guests. In my absence Lynda Bird had met them as hostess and taken them in charge. She had put Mr. Dobie in the Lincoln Room and Mrs. Dobie in the Queen's Room, where they were happily settled. I spent a moment or two greeting them early this morning and just before lunch I asked Mrs. Dobie to come in and have a glass of sherry with me. Mr. Dobie had gone over to see Lyndon in his office, where he was going to witness a brief press conference.

I got a call from Lyndon's office saying they would be over in a few minutes and that he was bringing President Truman. I went in the kitchen to consult Zephyr about lunch and discovered that we were having hash! Hash is one of Lyndon's favorite foods, especially with jalapeños, and I knew this would suit Mr. Dobie, but with President Truman on hand I was slightly abashed at the prospect of hash. However, with only ten or fifteen minutes to produce something else, I decided we would proceed unperturbed with hash. Minutes passed and continued to pass. About an hour later, well after 2, Lyndon arrived with Mr. Dobie, two newspaper editors —Walker Stone and Bill Steven—and President Truman. Lynda and

Warrie joined us and we sat down to our inelegant luncheon. And I had the frustrated feeling that if I had taken a sirloin strip out of the deep freeze it could have thawed and been cooked in that hour's time. Oh, well, wrong guess sometimes!

With his ruddy countenance and frosty hair, Mr. Dobie looks a bit like Carl Sandburg or Robert Frost, and talks like a philosophical old Texas cowhand. He was a delightful guest, and ever since my trip to Greece with President Truman I have had an especially warm place in my heart for him.

There was one moment during lunch when someone reminded us of a caustic saying of the Republicans during Truman's Administration—they said that Truman made his foreign policy decisions in the dark. One time he was alleged to have answered that there was one decision he had made in the dark on his knees, and that was the decision on whether or not to drop the bomb. At lunch, he described it this way. He said that when he was informed about the existence of the bomb, its potential, and how it would probably bring Japan to her knees in two or three days, he called in General Marshall and General Omar Bradley and asked: "If we invade the Japanese Islands, how many lives of American boys will it cost?" General Marshall had answered, "Our best estimate is between 200,000 and 250,000." President Truman then said, "There wasn't any decision to make—the decision was made—there was nothing to do but drop it." He went on to say that the hard decisions he had to make while he was President were all made the same way. He'd get the best advice he could, weigh and consider and make up his mind, and then never look back— and that he could go to sleep at night as soon as he put his head on the pillow. Later Mr. Dobie said he had heard President Truman say: "Lyndon Johnson may be the greatest President since Lincoln." This opinion derived from his remarks on the railroad strike achievement. This was similar to so much he had said to me on the trip to Greece.

I looked around, beaming that Lynda and Warrie should be there, soaking up history as it happened. Mr. Dobie described the press conference he had just participated in. (That was the reason they were so late, of course.) It came about suddenly because of the presence of President Truman. Between sixty and seventy reporters gathered in a half-circle in front of the President, with President Truman on Lyndon's right and Mr. Dobie on Lyndon's left. It must have been quite a morning for Mr. Dobie!

Tonight was the night of the Gridiron Dinner, so about 6:30 Mr. Dobie, all trussed up in white tie and tails (which he said he'd had ever since he went to England to teach in the early 1950's and expected to outlast him), was about to set out with Walker Stone for this great stag event of the year. It always amuses me that Lyndon, who makes so many ridiculing remarks about "women wanting to put on a long dress and making us men get into a black tie or a white tie," growlingly puts on the full regalia and goes forth to the slaughter year after year, with not a female present.

I escorted Mrs. Dobie downstairs, with a guidebook in my hand, and did two things at once. I practiced for the arrival of my Art Committee on May 7—that is, while learning more about the first floor room by room, I described the Savonnerie rug, the Waterford chandelier, and the Monet painting given by the Kennedy family—at the same time trying to provide a special guest an intimate tour, complete with anecdotes. Then we went upstairs for an early dinner, just the two of us, to talk of Texas wildflowers, on which Mrs. Dobie is an authority.

Monday, April 27

The day began with breakfast with Lyndon, with Jack Valenti bustling in and out, bringing papers, briefing him on the day's activities. Jack is growing a little wan and drawn himself, I think. He certainly is pouring devotion, good humor, and hard work into his job and my respect and liking for him increase all the time.

At 11 I had an appointment with Madame Indira Gandhi and from the Indian Embassy, Mrs. Avtar Dhar, who happens to be a cousin of Mrs. Gandhi, along with Mrs. Rusk. We had coffee in the Yellow Room, talked about the health of Jawaharlal Nehru—he is steadily improving, Mrs. Gandhi assures me—and about our trip to India a year or so ago. I find it rather difficult to communicate with these intellectual Indian women in spite of their exquisite English. It is possible that, with the departure of Nehru, Madame Gandhi may become the Number One influence in that great sub-continent. Mrs. Rusk, bless her, is never at a loss for conversation to bridge a gap. I lunched with Jane Engelhard and we toured the whole first floor. She chose some vermeil ornaments to go on the mantel in the Red Room, where Mrs. Kennedy had used her own obelisks.

Later in the day I got a plaintive call from Luci: "Mama, you must, absolutely *must* come up to see me in the sewing room, at once!" With minutes to spare, because I was going to Mrs. Kennedy's house (and that was a date I didn't want to be late for), I ran up to the sewing room.

There was Luci, looking adorable in a white dress that she wanted so much to wear to the Shenandoah Apple Blossom Festival. I had told her she couldn't have it, because we had already bought another white dress, and she didn't really need two bouffant white dresses on our realistic budget. But she was so appealing in it and she wanted it so much I couldn't say anything but yes. I hugged her, gathered up the long panel of gold-and-cream fabric that will be the drapery fabric in the East Room, and the drawing of the draperies, and rushed downstairs and into the car to leave for Mrs. Kennedy's.

I approached the stately Georgian house almost with apology, hesitant to trespass on sadness, feeling like an intruder. Jackie met me at the door, in a black skirt, a white blouse, and a big lovely smile. We went into the living room, much prettier now that it had had the touch of her hand the past several months, much more complete—draperies, a rug, a Grecian head here, lovely paintings there.

What I had come to discuss was what I had already told her briefly on the phone. I wanted so much to have her present at the meeting of the Committee for the Preservation of the White House on May 7, and at the tea that afternoon. It would mean so much to everyone.

She said, "Lady Bird, but I cannot return to the White House." I told her then that I hoped that she could write us a little note to guide us and get us started and to continue to contribute to whatever was done by the Committee. She said, "Can't you just tell them for me that I send my best wishes?" Rather hesitantly I agreed.

Then I took from the box the fabric which had come from Boudin a week or so ago. I had never unfolded it myself until this moment. It had been chosen by Mrs. Kennedy sometime last summer and ordered in the fall. The looms in Lyon, France, had started weaving it, and so, by November 22 it was very much on the way. There appears to be no pattern or repetition in the design. It's a long panel of birds, flowers, medallions—motifs that were used in grand houses of the early eighteenth century—the sort of thing, I suppose, that Thomas Jefferson or James Monroe might have chosen for the East Room. The design is exquisite, with a heavy fringe of beads at the top. We both gasped with pleasure as we examined the fabric.

I had a cup of tea. Jackie used the expression that you could easily get "tea poisoning," referring to the number of times one is called on in the White House to meet with a group and have tea. I told her how lovely the garden was. I had brought a picture of it at the height of its perfection. I told her how wonderful Mrs. Mellon was, continuing to keep it up. And then, with that empty feeling that there was nothing that I could really say or do, I said good-by.

In the course of talking about coming to the White House she said, "You know, every place I go reminds me of all the places we lived. We lived all over Georgetown." I wonder if she will go away this summer for a long vacation. That might make it better. I understand they have routed a tourist bus by her house now, and I noticed policemen in front of the house and the Secret Service inside.

I returned to the White House just in time for one of Lyndon's instant receptions. This one was for the labor newspaper editors and was supposedly stag, except that some of the editors are women. So he had asked for my presence.

There was a lovely but painful picture of Lynda and Bernie in the paper today, with a caption under it that read: "The Last Dance." Bernie, reached by telephone, had confirmed that the engagement had been broken. What he said was dignified and correct. I felt sad to look at their young faces. They're dancing together and Lynda is smiling her big (perhaps it's just for the public) smile.

Tuesday, April 28

What a busy month is April! For many years now it has been the crescendo month in my life. Today was the day for one of my Women Do-ers luncheons, and tonight was our black-tie dinner for the leaders of business. The black tie produced a not unexpected growl from Lyndon, but it *should* be black tie, because dressing up makes the evening a lot more special for ladies, and for everybody really.

There were the William Battens of the J. C. Penney Company; Roger Blough, Chairman of U.S. Steel; bluff, hearty Gussie Busch of Anheuser-Busch and his slim, blonde wife Trudy, mother of six children; the Donald Davids—he's Vice Chairman of the Ford Foundation and I would *adore* to get him talking about what the Foundation has done all around the world. Also from Ford there was Henry Ford II. Then the Crawford Greenewalts from the E. I. duPont de Nemours and Company; our friends the Frederick Kappels of American Tel and Tel; the Tom McCabes of Scott Paper Company; David Rockefeller of Chase Manhattan Bank and James S. Rockefeller of the First National Bank of New York City; the

Bob Stevens, formerly in the Eisenhower Administration; and the Walter Touhys of the C & O Railway Company.

I hope Lyndon knows how very proud I am of him, because he can meet the business power structure of the country on equal footing and talk to them in strong, persuasive language. I think they like him. We had dinner at round tables, the Air Force's Strolling Strings arriving with dessert. A note from Lyndon was passed to my outstretched hand under the table by Jack Valenti, suggesting I make a toast. I rose and proposed a toast "on behalf of a grateful nation to the leaders of business in this generous country, who have done so much for so many, and in the doing, have made us great."

We went into the East Room for dancing, with a battalion of handsome White House Aides swarming to the rescue, gracefully taking lady after lady from Lyndon's arm. I hope he got to dance with nearly everybody present. I know he wanted to. How funny that we should do more dancing after fifty than at nearly any time in our lives! And I love it.

The evening was light and gay for the women, and, I hope, explanatory and probing and impressive for the men. At any rate, my husband is making one blockbuster of a try to meld together the various strengths of this country to get done things that he thinks must be done!

Thursday, April 30

Today dawned cold and rainy. Ah, unhappy forecast for Saturday, when the three thousand Democratic ladies will converge upon us on, hopefully, the White House lawn.

The first big event of the day was the Congressional Club annual breakfast honoring the First Lady. How often I have attended this affair, on the other side of the fence! There was a reception beforehand including the wives of the Supreme Court Justices, the Cabinet, and the officers of the Club. This time dear Carrie Davis (long-time worker in the Democratic vineyard) is President. Ruth Burleson of Texas is Chairman of the Breakfast Committee this year, with help from Mrs. George Andrews of Alabama. And Betty Kuchel of California, one of my favorite Republican wives, is Vice President—I imagine that means that she'll probably be President next year.

There were about a thousand women in the familiar ballroom of the Sheraton Park. The red-coated Marine Band played. The tables were decorated with bluebonnets! I wish the light hadn't been so bright in my eyes as I walked down the aisle, because on each side there were so many people I wanted to greet, but I was pinpointed, like an insect in glue, in the brilliant glare of that spotlight as the uniformed Aide escorted me to the head table.

Carrie was her usual easy self, so capable, so much at home, so devoid of any pomposity in presiding. At the end of the breakfast she introduced me for a few words of greeting. I said: "Coming here is familiar territory to me, a little like coming to a family reunion. I remember my first Congressional breakfast, in 1938, when your guest of honor was Eleanor Roosevelt, and since then I've been back every time, with a constituent—the most important word in our vocabulary!" The only thing I missed was some contact, one personal moment, with all of the many women of the House and Senate I knew personally who were out there in front of me. I'd been to First Ladies' breakfasts so many times myself, I knew how carefully the club members used their limited tickets for kinfolks or constituents, and what it meant to them.

When I got back to the White House I heard the happy news that Lyndon had driven to Winchester to the Apple Blossom Festival to be present at the crowning of Luci Baines. Later I saw the picture of him standing on the steps of the high school, while General Curtis LeMay crowned Luci, beaming. Lyndon stood as tall and straight as he always does when listening to the national anthem anywhere, but this time smiling so sweetly. I didn't think it was possible that he could go and I hadn't urged him. In Lyndon's greeting he said, "She's always been a Queen to me."

But when Luci was asked if she'd ever been a Queen before, she said, "No, I've never been *anything* before!"

It rained all day and turned cold, and I wondered if Luci would come back with pneumonia. Imagine walking in an apple orchard at 9 o'clock in the morning, in a sheer organza evening dress, in about 50-degree temperature in a misting rain! I've been delighted to read that she went from event to event, with a sweet word to say: the Women's Horticultural Luncheon; a tea dance at the home of the Richard Byrds; an appearance at a firemen's parade; dinner at the home of the Frank Armstrongs; an appearance at a teen-agers' dance; and *finally* the Queen's Ball at the George Washington Hotel.

Lyndon's wire to the Apple Blossom Festival officials was a classic. It read: "PEOPLE OF VIRGINIA, INTELLIGENCE REPORTS THE CITY OF WIN-

CHESTER IS IN DANGER OF BEING TAKEN OVER BY A NEW MONARCH. I URGE ALL CITIZENS TO BE ON THE ALERT. I HAVE KNOWN THIS NEW RULER ALL HER LIFE. SHE ENTERED THE WORLD WITH A COMMANDING VOICE, AND HAS BEEN TAKING OVER EVER SINCE. BEWARE OF HER BEWITCHING SMILE; UNDERNEATH THAT KID GLOVE IS A STRONG HAND. PAST EXPERIENCE INDICATES THE BEST WAY OF DEALING WITH HER IS WITH TOTAL ATTENTION AND LOVE. [Signed] LYNDON B. JOHNSON."

Well, so much for home-grown royalty.

The next event of the day was a reception in the Blue Room for visiting Japanese Governors and their wives, something the State Department had asked me to do. The eleven Governors with unpronounceable names were accompanied by their wives in exquisite native costumes, with their enormous obi sashes; Angie Duke and Mrs. George Ball represented the State Department. After greeting them we went into the State Dining Room and I passed from group to group, bringing out my small store of identification with the Japanese. Several of the men spoke English, but not a one of the women.

Finally Lyndon and I and Jack Valenti sat down to dinner. Later we returned to the Sheraton Park where Lyndon spoke to the Democratic Women's Conference. There were three thousand women in the hall, and it took us five minutes to walk to the platform. It was almost like a Convention scene with many banners. Margaret Price introduced Lyndon, and he talked to them, at first jokingly and then seriously, about women in government jobs, ending with these words: "I promise this tonight not because you need jobs but because the country needs you."

Among the "old reliables" on the stand were Dorothy Vredenburgh Bush of Alabama, Dr. Mildred Otenasek of Maryland, Doña Felisa de Gautier from Puerto Rico, and Hilda Weinert of Texas.

Thank goodness, all I had to do was take a bow.

Wednesday, May 6

Today was the occasion of the annual luncheon that the First Lady always gives for the Senate Ladies Red Cross unit. And how eagerly we wanted to make it different.

Bess had the grand idea of having the twelve tables, seating 130 guests, set with china representing eighteen different Presidential Administrations, ranging from the George Washington porcelain with the emblem of the

Order of Cincinnati on it to the Eisenhower china, with its elaborate gold medallion. There was a centerpiece on each table from a different Administration. Of course, not every one of the thirty-six Presidents had a special set of china. (When the supply gets so low that you can't seat a State Dinner of one hundred people, then it's time for the current Administration to buy more china.) These were just place settings, the most extraordinary of which, by all odds, was the Rutherford B. Hayes china, with its exotic patterns of wildlife. It is extremely rococo and Victorian, every piece different, decorated with a stag, a wild turkey, buffalos in the snow. There were two tables set with the Lincoln china with its broad purple border. Mrs. Lincoln must have bought a lot of china, or else people into whose hands it has fallen through the years have been excessively kind in returning it to the White House.

The tables were overlaid with pale yellow organdy and had exquisite flower arrangements. I put Mrs. Mansfield, wife of the Majority Leader, on my right and Mrs. Kuchel on my left. Otherwise, people drew numbers to find their places.

At one o'clock I was in the Green Room to receive the Senate ladies, with Cabinet wives on hand to help as hostesses. As usual, there were many old-timers—about seventy-one wives of sitting members and about thirty-one wives of former members. Among them were the wives of the "old greats"—Mrs. Alben Barkley, Mrs. Tom Connally, Mrs. Millard Tydings, and the widow of one whose name only yesterday was on everybody's lips, Mrs. Estes Kefauver . . . Then there were those that are an echo from the past, and you have to think back to remember—Mrs. Charles McNary of Oregon, Mrs. Gerald Nye of North Dakota, Mrs. Kenneth Wherry of Nebraska, and Baroness Silvercruys (the lovely Rosemary with whom I occasionally play a game of bridge). And my Spanish-class friends, Abigail McCarthy, Grace Dodd, and Bethine Church.

There were those without whom the Red Cross unit itself could not get along—Mrs. Charles Tobey [widow of Senator Tobey of New Hampshire], its pillar and citadel; Mrs. Edward Burke, who has been in charge of sewing ever since time began; Mrs. William Bulow . . . And others that mean much to us, personally and sentimentally, like Sarah Clements (Mrs. Earle Clements of Kentucky), whose husband was Lyndon's best captain in his Senate days, and Esther Frear (Mrs. J. Allen Frear of Delaware).

We had a gourmet lunch, beginning with prosciutto and melon, but the conversation piece was the china! I said a few words about the first First

Lady who had inhabited this house and her impressions of it. "On November 21, 1800, Abigail Adams, who had just arrived in Washington to become the first hostess at the White House, wrote her sister, 'My dear sister: I arrived in this city on Sunday the 16th ult. Having lost my way in the woods on Saturday in going from Baltimore, we took the road to Frederick and got nine miles out of our road. You find nothing but a Forest & woods on the way, for 16 and 18 miles not a village . . . As I expected to find it a new country, with Houses scattered over a space of ten miles, and trees & stumps in plenty with, a castle of a House,—so I found it—The Presidents House is in a beautifull situation, in front of which is the Potomac, with a view of Alexandr[i]a. The country around is romantic but a wild, a wilderness at present.' "

After putting them back in time and place to 1800, I asked them to go into the East Room, where we would see Miss·Helen Hayes and her group in a thirty-minute performance from A. E. Hotchner's new play, *The White House*. There was a red-velvet-draped stage with a backdrop of the White House itself, against which George Washington, John Adams, Thomas Jefferson, and James Madison emerged to express their feelings on life in the White House. And Helen Hayes quickly changed from the decorous Martha Washington to the "mind-of-her-own" Abigail Adams, who advised her husband that he should "interest himself in legislation which would abolish slavery, put a high tax on liquor so that there would be an end to drunkenness, and give equal legal rights to women"; and then changed again to the lively, dancing Dolley Madison. The playwright says, "These events are relevant and irrelevant, reverent and irreverent." The dialogue was composed of quotations "from the White House tenants themselves." Truly, it was the best entertainment I've ever had here.

Lyndon came in, spoke briefly, calling the Senate wives "the jewels" of all the Senators, to whom he still feels so close. He said that he never has seen me happier than when I am in their vicinity. And, indeed, this was one of my happiest days.

The last guest had scarcely departed before the next extraordinary event took place. I had heard, but had paid very little attention, that Lyndon was having a press conference that afternoon. It turned out that he was having it on the South grounds at 4:30, with not only all the press invited, but all of their wives and children, diaper stage to college age.

The striped tents were in place ready to dispense refreshments, the service band was playing merrily in front of the bandshell, and the whole

South grounds were teeming when I surveyed the scene from my window and hurriedly went down to join Lyndon. He was already up in the band-shell, answering questions about the gross national product, about the United States in Vietnam, about Republican nominees.

One little boy was crawling between the legs of a man standing in front of him. Another small child had wandered off toward the fountain and was losing his diapers, and hundreds of alert, eager, interested young folks of an age to understand were fixing piercing eyes on the man that their fathers dealt with at news conferences. When the conference was over, Lyndon said he would like to have his photograph taken with all of the youngsters. The Secret Service said they couldn't possibly all get onto the shell at the same time without its collapsing, so he asked half of them to come first. The cameras went clickety-clickety-click; then off marched the first group and then the next battalion walked up the steps.

"Camp meeting" and Ringling Brothers' Barnum and Bailey together couldn't top this afternoon! The letters this affair brought forth from the children and the newspaper stories were hilarious. The best story was by Mary McGrory, writing as though she were a twelve-year-old boy, making more fun of the reporters than of the President. It was all summed up by one little reporter, aged fourteen, who said, "I will always remember this day. Now I feel that I've really known the President of the United States."

My old and dear friend Alice Brown [Mrs. George Brown of Houston] arrived this afternoon and I got her settled in the Queen's Room. We had a quiet, leisurely tour of the first floor and the ground floor. Meanwhile, Alice opened up two pictures that she had brought. One, to my overwhelming amazement, was a Winslow Homer watercolor—"The Surf at Prout's Neck"—and the other a portrait of George Washington by Sully, after the Athenaeum portrait, which was painted by one of the Peales.

I had thought that before the last month of our term here expired I might acquire a Winslow Homer. I never dreamed that one would come this quickly and in this way! It's beautiful and I love it, and I'm sure that it will be the first important acquisition to come to the White House through me.

Finally we had dinner, just Alice and Lyndon and me. I went to bed thinking that this was enough of a day to have lasted a month—I hoped that my guests at noon had noticed the Andrew Jackson urn from the Hermitage, and the James Madison tureen, and the John Adams tureen, and, perhaps, the Franklin Roosevelt china with three feathers and roses that came from the Roosevelt family's coat of arms. And I hope they noticed Thomas Jefferson's Chinese export porcelain tureen with the heart-shaped escutcheon bearing the letter "J." There is such a wealth of history and meaning in this great house.

Thursday, May 7

This is a day that I had regarded as an enormous hurdle—something to tense my mental muscles for, and try to jump over successfully. Lyndon and Lynda Bird had left by helicopter for Andrews for a five-state poverty tour which was to last two days. At 10:30 there was a meeting of the Preservation of the White House Committee in the Yellow Oval Room. I had dreaded, and looked forward to, this meeting very much and had studied hard to try to learn about the subject matter and make it go well.

There were two important highlights of the meeting. One was the showing of the first panel of gold-and-cream damask from which new draperies will be made for the East Room, and the other was the reporting on a new acquisition, a handsome silver coffee urn, which had belonged to the first President to occupy the White House, John Adams.

Then we got onto the important question of having some good copies made of the present rugs in the Green Room, Blue Room, and Red Room, which are exquisite antiques, Savonnerie and Aubusson—very perishable. They are, naturally, rolled back when the tourists come through, but they are on the floor for all parties. It would really make more sense to have some very good copies that would stay down nearly all the time, and bring out of storage the rare antiques for State Dinners and a few very select groups. It was determined by the Committee that Mr. West should get estimates and evaluations of some good copies.

After about an hour and a half of discussion, including a consideration of the financial situation of the White House Historical Association by Clark Clifford, everybody had had his say about the business of the Committee. The meeting came to an end, leaving me with a feeling of relative satisfaction that Mr. duPont and Mr. Fosburgh would feel fairly safe about their achievements of the last three years, and fairly hopeful of what might happen in the immediate future. I showed Mr. Fosburgh the Winslow Homer painting and I think he was as amazed as I am that it should have so precipitously and happily dropped into our laps.

Why, when I'm not the least bit afraid of meeting the tycoons of business, or the titans of labor, or any other sort of people at home or abroad, should I look upon today's meetings with such trepidation? Well, at any rate, at 4 P.M. I fared forth in my simplest and best white dress to the Green Room to receive my guests, the people of the art world. I am pleased that so many of them came—to a tea—about fifty-five, and from as far away as California, Michigan, Chicago, and St. Louis. From Mrs. Kennedy's Fine Arts Committee there were Mr. Charles Francis Adams of *the* Adams family, Roy Davis, lovely Phyllis Dillon, my friend Jane Engelhard, on whom I lean considerably and who flew her plane down from New Jersey, bringing with her Anne Ford, formerly the wife of Henry Ford II. And handsome, urbane Mr. John Loeb, who contributed in toto the furnishings of the lovely Yellow Oval Room.

And there were Mrs. Henry Parrish ("Sister" Parrish), who has done much of the decorating here, and gentle David Finley of the Fine Arts Commission. From the Paintings Committee there was Susan Mary Alsop. I asked her to be sure to slip off upstairs to the third floor to see where we'd put the desk that she and Joe gave. And J. Cheever Cowdin, Mr. Lawrence Fleischman of Detroit, Mrs. Walter Halle, Mrs. William Paley, and Vincent Price.

The Library Committee, headed by Mr. James T. Babb, was well represented. I'm glad, because I wanted both a chance to thank them for what has been done and to recognize the fact that their mission is still in midstream, not yet accomplished.

The Advisory Committee was there in great number also, from Mr. James Biddle, Curator of the American Wing of the Metropolitan, to Mr. Julian Boyd, who is working on the papers of Thomas Jefferson at Princeton, and Lyman Butterfield, who works on the Adams papers in Boston, and to whom I enjoyed talking about our new treasure, the Adams silver urn.

I had invited a number of museum Curators and Directors, ranging from Mr. Gerald Gibson of the Henry Ford Museum in Dearborn, to Mr. John Graham of Colonial Williamsburg, Director of Collections there, and Mrs. John Pearce, who had been Curator at the White House when the project was first established under Mrs. Kennedy.

After I had met everyone in the Green Room they all filed into the Blue Room, where the gilt chairs were placed in a semi-circle and in each seat was a list of the donations to the White House collection since Mrs. Kennedy's last tea with them on December 1, 1962.

I made a brief speech of welcome, because I wanted them to know their continuing efforts are appreciated: "Welcome to this house, to which, under the inspiration of Mrs. Kennedy, you have turned such loving hands. I wish that you could hear the remarks of your most ardent admirers, the myriad of tourists who see your handiwork . . . a number which is expected to top two million this year. One recent Saturday there were 24,400 in this house in one day! You would feel rewarded indeed to hear the oh's and ah's from the girl from Sioux Falls who saved baby-sitting money all year to ride the school bus here. Or the approving remarks of the Curator of the Louvre. Only the other day, museum Directors were here from all around the world, and they were lavish in their praise."

Then I told them the story of the wife of a National Academy of Science member who had gone through and returned to me to say, "Now I feel like a citizen . . ." I continued with something of my own situation, telling them that since January I have been taking my own crash course in the history and furnishings of the White House. I related a number of anecdotes—about how Dolley Madison had ordered a washing machine her first month in the White House, and that in the Van Buren Administration the house was so badly underdrained that during heavy rains the floors of the kitchen and cellars were under water. I told them about President Chester Arthur, who didn't like the furnishings, swept up twenty-four wagon loads, including much of the furniture for the East and Green Rooms, and auctioned it—carpets, curtains, chandeliers, beds, sofas, chairs, pots and pans, all going under the hammer. In fact, the auction was so complete that a newspaper reported "the sale of a rat trap, that caught the rat, that ate the suit, that belonged to Mr. Lincoln!"

I pointed out this could never happen again. Through the years many First Ladies have put their hearts into this house and Mrs. Kennedy's devotion and taste brought the committees together to produce the present and permanent excellence of this house. Now, Lyndon has signed an Executive Order providing for a White House Curator and establishing a Committee for Preservation of the White House. The one thought I wanted to leave with them was that I wanted their continued interest and advice—because this dear house is a living thing and will never really be completed.

I think what interested them most among new acquisitions was the Monet painting, the gift of the Kennedy family, "Morning on the Seine," hanging in the Green Room. And next, perhaps, the marble bust of Joel

Barlow, by Houdon. Several of the members recommended that the sculpture be moved downstairs where more people could see it.

I walked from room to room, and from group to group, with as many words of personal thanks and appreciation as I could manage: to Mr. Shea for the tables; to Mr. Fosburgh for giving us months of his life; to Jane Engelhard, with delight, about how much everybody had enjoyed seeing the china actually on the tables yesterday, and particularly for her gift of Harrison Administration dinner plates with the beautiful wheat design around the edge. And how could I possibly say enough to Mrs. Mellon to express my feeling about the portrait of Thomas Jefferson? Only, I guess, that whenever anybody asks me, I am always quick to say that the two paintings I like best are the portraits of Thomas Jefferson and Benjamin Franklin.

Every foot of the way I felt very much supported by Mary Lasker, by Alice Brown, and by Jane Engelhard. And so a day that I had looked forward to with a certain dread, as a sort of test, passed pleasantly enough— with a certain glow of success . . .

Thursday, May 14

HUNTLAND
MIDDLEBURG, VIRGINIA

There are places the very names of which evoke for me the thought of leaving all cares behind. They are winged names. Huntland is one of them. Huntland is the lovely Virginia home of the George Browns.

I ate lunch with Luci and Beth Jenkins, and discovered that they had stayed up late, talking about whatever it is sixteen-year-olds have on their minds, and playing cards. And then Jerry Kivett (my Secret Service agent) and I went walking. Virginia in mid-May is balm for any trouble! No "Silent Spring" here—the green arch of fresh spring leaves almost met over the rutted country road, a brown thrush flashed through the underbrush; occasionally you would see a bright little chipmunk perched on a rail fence. A flock of crows cawed in the distance across the lush green meadow, over which the dairy cows placidly ambled. And every time you came to a rise, there was the blue outline of the mountains in the distance. The melancholy call of mourning doves announced that it was spring again. There were robins hopping about, and once a cardinal flew across the road.

This was just the sort of aloneness I needed to think clearly—to write out succinctly—my own feelings on what Lyndon should do this August. I called the White House and asked Dr. Hurst if he and Jim Cain would like to drive out and have dinner with me to talk over Lyndon's problems, about which they were going to have a meeting the next morning. They were conferring with Dr. Larry Lamb, who was coming up from San Antonio, and Dr. George Burkley and Dr. Janet Travell from the White House. I wanted to be in on this, because it's important to me too. Maybe I could contribute more understanding if I talked to the two of them quietly, rather than as one in a conference of seven or more.

Dr. Hurst had taken care of Lyndon during his heart attack in 1955 and we have come to feel very close to him. And Jim Cain of Mayo's has been our friend and doctor since the thirties.

While they were on their way, I wrote out for Lyndon a nine-page analysis of what I thought his situation was. First, in case he definitely decided that he wanted to use it, there was a suggested announcement that he wasn't going to run again. This draft would need to be polished up by one of Lyndon's assistants, if used, and any medical items added by the doctors.

"Having, by the end of this present term, finished some thirty years of public service, ranging from my young years with the NYA to the House of Representatives, the Senate, the Vice Presidency, and this latterly ultimate responsibility, I wish now to announce that I will not be a candidate for reelection. I wish to spend the rest of my life in my home state, in peace with my family, for whom the rigors of my duties have left me too little time for companionship. This decision is made easier by the fact that I can feel my conduct of the Presidency, to which I came in such a tragic hour of national rending, has not been without some solid accomplishment, thanks to the grace of God and the sturdy cooperation of the American people. To all those who have helped me throughout these years, my thanks and those of my family can never be fully expressed."

I hope he won't use it—that's that!

Then I put down the alternatives:

If he does run he will probably be elected President. During the campaign and for the ensuing four years he, I, and the children will be criticized and slandered for things we have done, things we may in part have done, and things we never did at all. This will be painful. There will be times when he will be frustrated and torn by the inability of his staff, his family, and ultimately himself to achieve his vaulting ambitions for this nation.

And that, I should think, would be even more painful. There will be times of achievement, such as passing the Tax Bill, and settling the potential railroad strikes, and especially on health and education or conservation matters which could provide satisfaction with no peer I believe. And lastly, he may die earlier if he continues in the role of the Presidency and works as hard as he has been—who can tell? If anything, the last six months have shown us that it is impossible to know what to expect of life.

On the other hand, if he does not run we will probably return to the Ranch and he will enjoy the country he loves, and me, and Lynda and Luci, more than he ever has, and that will be good for all of us.

But there will be a barrage of newspaper stories, of questionings and innuendos as to his motives. People will ask what skeletons hang in the closet, what is he trying to hide, what disclosure will come next? People will believe anything but the truth, and the distortions could go on until we are forgotten.

Next, and much more important, there would be a wave, this time national and not just statewide, of hollow disillusionment, a feeling of "You let us down, Lyndon," among those people who really look to him as the best candidate of the Democratic Party, and perhaps the best candidate in the nation. This would be not unlike the wave that swept Texas after he went on the Democratic ticket with Kennedy, only this time it would be wider and more well founded. And that would be painful.

And then, with the limited amount of time it takes to ride over the Ranch, he could entertain himself with overseeing the cattle, and maybe making a few lectures. But I hardly see how that could contain him and consume his twenty-four hours a day in a constructive way. There might be periods of depression and frustration, as he watched Mr. X running the country, and thought what he would have done instead.

Last, he might live longer if he didn't run for the Presidency. Who can tell? And if he did, would it be worth it?

My final conclusion was that I thought he ought to run, facing clearly all the criticisms and hostilities that would come our way, pacing himself as well as his personality will permit, with Sundays off and occasional vacations, and then three years and nine months from now, February or March 1968, if the Lord lets him live that long, announce that he won't be a candidate for reelection. By that time, I think, the juices of life will be sufficiently stilled in him as he approaches sixty so that he can finish out the term and return to the Ranch, and we can live the rest of our days quietly.

I wrote all this out, put it in an envelope, addressed it to the President, marked it "Personal, please." When Jim and Dr. Hurst arrived, I put it in their hands and asked them to give it to Lyndon when they met the next morning.

We began our talk in the small sitting room, and then went into the lovely dining room, candle-lit, fire blazing (it was chilly for May), with a bowl of lilacs on the table, steaks and wine for dinner! Our girls joined us, and Luci said the blessing. It was wonderful to see how joyously she and Jim greeted each other. She doesn't always like all of our friends, or rather, more exactly, she doesn't "give out" in front of them. But for Tom Corcoran, the Cains, Dr. Hurst, she is the most articulate, out-spoken little girl—a rebel, but delightful. Jim said how much he had loved having her as their houseguest and invited her back at any time.

After dinner Jim and Dr. Hurst and I went into the small sitting room, had our coffee around the fire, and talked about the possibilities for Lyndon. They were planning to give him a thorough medical check-up the next morning, and tonight we discussed only the psychological aspects. Both of them thought that inaction, idleness, lack of command, would be a harder role for him than the long hours and heavy responsibility he now shoulders. They both really thought that he should continue for now.

They promised to call me tomorrow after the conference. I don't know, though, whether either one of them understands the depth of Lyndon's pain when and if he faces up to the possibility of sending many thousands of American boys to Vietnam or some other danger spot.

When I was almost asleep, a little after midnight, Lyndon called me. He had been to a stag party. Lyndon was lonesome; I could tell from his voice. It was a sad-happy talk, balanced between little worries and big ones, and concerned with his restive desire to seek a way out of the burdens he carries.

Thursday, May 21

KENTUCKY

If I had to list the ten best days I've spent in the White House, Thursday, May 21, would certainly be among them. This was the day of my trip to Kentucky. I was up early and out to the airport to catch the chartered Convair at 7 A.M. with Liz and Bess (because we were going to Bess' home territory, Kentucky) and Congressman Carl Perkins, whose district we would be covering; Bill Batt of the ARA; Howard Bertsch with the Farmers Home Administration; and Peter Jones with the Department of Commerce, who had prepared me, by giving me *Night Comes to the Cumberlands*, by Harry Caudill, to read.

We arrived at Blue Grass Field, Lexington, about 8, to be met by Governor and Mrs. Breathitt and their pretty children; Mayor and Mrs. Fred Fugazzi; and Dr. John Oswald, President of the University of Kentucky, and Mrs. Oswald. About one hundred and fifty people were lined up along the fence, and after I said hello to all the dignitaries I went over and began shaking hands with the crowd.

Then began an eight-hour tour by motorcade, on foot, and by helicopter, with my incongruous army of newspaper people and cameramen trailing me, through the beautiful but economically depressed Cumberland Plateau. I love the picturesque names—Troublesome Creek, Lick Branch School, the community of Quicksand, Stray Branch! It was a country of hills and hollows, emerald green with spring, swift rocky streams crossed by foot bridges, and occasionally a hillside blighted by strip mining—the process of simply scraping off the top of the earth with machinery to get to coal and leaving it looking wounded and ugly, with no reforestation.

Governor and Mrs. Breathitt were in the car with me, and as we rode along the highway we passed a school where all the students were lined up by the side of the road. It was the last day of school and many of them were clutching report cards. I couldn't resist—I halted the motorcade, bolted out, shook hands with as many as I could reach—and then on we went to our first planned stop, the home of Mr. and Mrs. Arthur Robertson and their seven children at Warshoal Branch.

Marie Turner, Superintendent of Schools of Breathitt County, was at my side all day, and how lucky that community and area is to have her, because she pours so much into her job. Although she has so little to work with, a lot of the good in this county must be traced to this one woman. When we stopped, she said rather diffidently that it was almost a mile up the creek to the house where the Robertsons lived and she thought we could make it in a school bus, she wasn't sure. I said, "No, I'd much rather walk." So I put on my black boots, which have walked many a mile around the Ranch, and led my small army up the winding path along Warshoal Branch to the three-room house of the Arthur Robertsons.

They were lined up on the front porch—Mr. and Mrs. Robertson, six sons and one little girl, Judy Ann, who—scrubbed and dressed up for the occasion—offered me a bunch of red and yellow wildflowers—"snake tongue" and "rooster comb." I was delighted.

Thin, wiry, gaunt-faced Mr. Robertson was easy to talk to and full of ginger, although he looked as if he hadn't had a square meal most of the days of his thirty-six years. We had come here because he had taken advantage of a seven-hundred-dollar government grant, which paid for materials only, to "winterize" his house, put asbestos siding and insulation in it, dig a well, and build a privy. All of the labor he had accomplished himself. Also because, through help and instruction from the Agriculture Department, he had cleared and put into tobacco about three fifths of an acre of this unbelievably hilly farm. I walked around with him for about thirty minutes and really enjoyed it. He showed me the log cabin they had lived in before he had built the new house. Three of their children were born in the log cabin. He now has a part-time job on the Unemployed Parents Program, setting out pine trees on Stray Branch. Tobacco is his only cash crop, but he has a few chickens and a Poland China hog, and kills about two pigs a year for his family's table; and the most marvelous garden—the potatoes were coming along fine. He said one of his sons had planted the garden and did all the work in it.

The bet we are making—the government, I mean, and it is a large bet, because the federal government has poured about two hundred million dollars a year into Kentucky since 1961 to improve health and housing and for job retraining, school lunches, public works, and similar public service programs—is that you can do this without destroying the character and self-reliance of American citizens.

When you look into the faces of the children, you see good raw material and you know that hope for the future in this area must be found in education, job training, and eventually opportunities for employment from industry, some way of making a living besides clinging to the mortally ill coal industry, in this beautiful part of the world.

Inside the house there was a framed marriage license, a picture of Jesus, some family pictures, a wedding picture. The children were all very clean and polite, but there certainly wasn't a fat one in the lot. One of the little boys, Lonnie, gave me his school picture. I brought it home with me. We trudged out of the hollow, over the log foot bridge, the dusty sweating cameramen carrying packs that must have weighed fifty or more pounds up to the highway and then up to Lick Branch School.

The one-room schoolhouse was very much like Fern School which I attended from the time I was five until I was eleven (near my home in Karnack, Texas). There were twenty-five children here, from the first grade through the eighth. The school is located in a beautiful, leafy, wooded hollow, and once more you reach it by crossing a little bridge. Schoolhouse architecture hasn't changed much. Not only was the schoolhouse the same as the one at Fern, but there was a big pot-bellied stove inside. I told the youngsters that in my childhood the biggest boy always had the job of putting in the kindling, and then the big sticks of wood, and lighting the stove, first thing when we got there on cold winter mornings.

All the children were dressed up, the little girls (and lots of them were so pretty) in stiff, starched pink dresses. Everybody was clean. They were fine-looking young folks, with very Anglo-Saxon names—Bush, Bolling, Watts, Turner. We had a hot lunch, which cost ten cents to all those who could afford to pay for it. If you couldn't pay, you got it free. This is part of the government's lunch program, to help hard-hit regions of Kentucky. Lunch consisted of canned pork, green beans, corn bread, ginger bread, and milk. Before lunch everybody had washed his hands, including me, at a very sensible device, a perforated zinc bucket full of water, hanging from a nail. The water dripped through, into a large garbage can below, and you washed your hands as it came out. We hadn't thought of that at Fern!

The children then put on a puppet show for me, all about "The Little Red Hen." They had a collection of homemade puppets and I thought it delightful that two of them were "Daniel Boone" and "Black Beauty"—so speaks Kentucky! After the puppet show we went out on the front porch and I presented the Lick Branch School with a flag that had flown over the nation's Capitol. They had already provided a flag pole and we ran up the flag while they all gave the Pledge of Allegiance. It was a moment to remember.

I had also brought them a set of encyclopedias, but the biggest event of the day was that electric lights had been installed just prior to my arrival. I was the first person to throw the switch. They said on dark days in that hollow you could scarcely see to read in the school. Sometimes classes had to be dismissed at 2 o'clock on winter afternoons, so this was a big advance.

Finally I said good-by and rode away with Marie Turner, thinking especially about two things she had told me—that when some of the youngsters first came to school in September, they were listless, dull, not very interested, and then after one good meal a day for three or four months, they perked up, showed improvement in their school work, became livelier, even mischievous.

And when I asked her if they had much turnover in schoolteachers, she said yes, a teacher hardly ever stayed longer than one year in these little one-room schoolhouses. It's hard to attract young people to such places—young, vital teachers—who must board with the neighbors, where the facilities are often outdoor toilets, and the roads are so muddy there is not much chance of getting out even on weekends. This made me hark back to the idea of a teachers corps that I'd heard discussed at the White House.

Our next stop was at the Breathitt High School in Jackson, where a new gymnasium was to be dedicated. What interesting rhythm of the bell of history, that this should be on the same site where the old gymnasium was dedicated by Mrs. Roosevelt twenty-six years ago. Three graduates were on hand who had been present then.

The new gym was a clean, bright building with lots of glass, one of a hundred and eighty-eight accelerated public works projects in the Cumberland area, a partnership between local initiative and federal support. I was introduced by an attractive, poised young girl, Trevor Louise Howell, Marie Turner's granddaughter, a senior in Breathitt County's High School, carrying on the tradition for the third generation. I made my first talk of the day to the five thousand guests, including the Lieutenant Governor and Congressman Carl Perkins.

After the speech Mrs. Breathitt presented me with a beautiful hooked rug—an art still practiced by the old people in the area—with a federal eagle in the center. She also gave me a quilt that is an aristocrat among quilts, made with the tiniest little stitches. I wish these crafts could be brought to a wider market, by instituting improved designs in this indigenous art, to help the economy of the depressed region.

At the end of this day, so full of sights and impressions and emotions, one thing Mrs. Robertson had said kept ringing in my mind: "It don't hurt to dream!"

Saturday, May 23

VIRGINIA

This was a significant day to me, because it marked the dedication of the George Marshall Research Library in Lexington, Virginia. Lyndon and I left with Dean Acheson and Mrs. Acheson, Secretary Rusk, Senator

Byrd—in a white suit, as always this time of year—and some staff members. We flew to Roanoke, and from there took helicopters to Lexington.

At the VMI parade ground in Lexington there was a twenty-one-gun salute and "Hail to the Chief." Lyndon inspected the VMI Cadet Honor Guard Company. Poor dear boys, the temperature was in the high 80's, sun bright, and the jackets of their uniforms, their summer uniforms mind you, heavy, thick, long-sleeved wool! I believed it when I heard that discipline is one of the main things they teach them at VMI.

Next we went to a lovely, quiet house, where the Superintendent of VMI, General George Shell, and Mrs. Shell lived. She told us this was the only house left standing when the Yankees burned VMI during the Civil War. At noon we went for a brief visit through the library with President Eisenhower, Mrs. Marshall, Governor Albertis Harrison of Virginia, and a long line of other dignitaries. All of this seemed to be for the benefit of photographers and not for the benefit of those who came to see the library. We posed, first here and then there. What I really wanted to do was to look and plan, thinking that sometime Lyndon might have a library, smaller in scope, but along the same general lines.

And then the ceremony began. I sat next to Mrs. Marshall on the front row in the sun; by now the temperature was about 90 degrees. I was glad I had worn a hat. It was a touching ceremony for many reasons. My particular reason was because I believed implicitly in George Marshall, without reservation. He was a man whose character has seldom been equaled in our government's service. I'm sure that Lyndon agrees.

General Omar Bradley, his old friend, presided. To me one of the most interesting things that General Bradley said was what he told me before the ceremony began: "This is one of the twenty-two things I'm doing because I think they're good to do. Of course, my heart is in this more than any of the others." He went on to say, "Don't misunderstand me; I've got several things that I get paid for doing." He's never one to reach for credit. But that caused me to reflect on the joys of retirement. If General Bradley, retired, has twenty-two things he does as public service, I wonder if we'll ever reach that stage of lying in the hammock at the Ranch, or sitting lazily in a boat with a fishing pole, with nothing more important to do than wait for the fish to bite, or watch the birds fly over?

General Shell welcomed us to the school, and then Governor Harrison spoke. Next came General Bradley, and then General Eisenhower (all day long people referred to him as General Eisenhower, not as President Eisenhower) made the best speech that I ever heard him make. Then came Lyndon's speech, which to me was one of the most touching, beautiful, and impressive tributes I've ever heard him make, or anybody else.

Mrs. Marshall was the center of everybody's attention and although she's getting old and is not very well, you could see that she was savoring this great day to the hilt. And so would I, if I had been she. It was a fitting salute to a towering character; one of the moments in American history I'm glad this job gave me the opportunity to share.

One of the nicest aspects of the day was seeing all those handsome young cadets. Several of them escorted me around at different times and at least three came up and introduced themselves as Texans. They all asked about Lynda and Luci. Looking at the caliber of these young men, I could understand how a great Civil War General said of this institution, just before he went into a battle where they were going to participate: "The men from VMI will be heard from today!"

Monday, May 25

THE WHITE HOUSE AND NEW YORK

I called Mary Lasker this morning and consulted with her on the speech that I was to make in the Museum of Modern Art tonight, on the occasion of the opening of the new wing. She made a couple of suggestions, and very good ones they were. (Mary has that rare quality of making suggestions in a way that, somehow or other, winds up by getting them done.) In the middle of the afternoon I went to New York, going directly to the elegant Carlyle Hotel. The suite I use is yellow and white, all glass with magnificent views of Central Park on one side, and tall buildings on the other side—a fantastic sight! The bedroom is pink and white and blue, exquisitely feminine, and I think of it as the tower of the Fairy Princess.

Tonight is another one of my ventures into the art world, this time occasioned (because I had regretted it in the first place) by a very urgent call from a dear friend, Frank Stanton. It would be hard for me to say no to anything that Frank asked me to do.

Adlai Stevenson picked me up at 7:20 to take me to the Museum, where I was met by the David Rockefellers, the John Rockefellers, René d'Harnoncourt, Director of the Museum, and William Burden, the President. We made a tour of the galleries, passing first through the rooms that house the great artists of the last years of the nineteenth century—

Renoir, whom I like; Toulouse-Lautrec, who amuses me tremendously; and several Degas that weren't dancing. We paused in front of a large mural by Matisse, called "La Danse." The figures, all nudes, seemed to be dancing in mid-air. I saw a painting by Van Gogh of a storm brewing, which must have been painted when he was entering a phase of deep depression.

There were four hundred guests for dinner, seated at round tables, in the most interesting room! It had a red felt carpet and the walls were treated with yellow felt, with facsimile autographs of the artists—enormous Picassos, rather small Lipchitzs, and a Toulouse-Lautrec signature that looked like a Japanese symbol; Dufy, Chagall—all sorts of celebrated names in the handwriting of the artists, and very effective and fascinating it was. That is, if you could take your eyes off the people at the forty-seven tables around us.

I was placed between René d'Harnoncourt, who is six feet eight and a most interesting conversationalist, and Mr. Burden. Mary Lasker was at my table and Jacques Lipchitz, one of the most controversial sculptors (whose work is in the Museum garden) and who had just finished designing the medallion Lyndon will award to Presidential scholars. I wish I had been more knowledgeable about the medallion itself. All I could do was give him a big smile of appreciation.

What impressed me most this evening was David Rockefeller's speech. He's a personable, handsome, youngish man, brother of Nelson, Winthrop, Laurance, and John D. He began to reminisce about how, in his high school days, his mother would invite to tea friends interested in art, and how they planned this Museum of Modern Art, which stands on the very spot of ground where his home stood in those days. The Museum was begun in 1929. What an interesting picture that conjured up! And what an interesting family they are—the Rockefellers—pouring back their vast fortune into art and education and civic life, not only in this country but around the world. I've come upon their tracks everywhere I've been.

After dinner we went to the upper garden for the reception for the artists. But, alas, it was black as pitch, on purpose, because the big moment of the evening would arrive when I pressed the switch and turned on the lights, revealing the new garden and the new wing. In addition to the darkness, the crowd was back to back, so it was impossible to move around gracefully to greet the artists, although one of the lady chairmen took me in tow and attempted to do that.

Presently the ceremony began, with a tribute to the artists by Mr.

Burden, followed by the main address of the evening, written by Dr. Paul Tillich, but delivered by Dr. Wilhelm Pauck in his absence (he was ill). And then it was my turn and I saluted our generation as one engaged not only in a war against the poverty of man's necessities, but in a war against the poverty of man's spirit.

Then I pressed the button. I could practically hear a sigh of relief go up from those in charge, because not everything had gone according to plan. But the moment I pressed the button, lights flooded the lovely garden and lit up the shaft of the building.

I said good-by to the people on the platform and made my way to the car. Adlai Stevenson had invited me to an after-opening party, which turned out to be the best time of all. He lives in an apartment in the Waldorf Towers, most charmingly decorated. And the one hundred or more guests who came in for nightcaps and sandwiches were an interesting cross section of this sophisticated world, including the Richard Rodgers; Marc Connelly of *Green Pastures*; Ken Galbraith, with whom I had an interesting talk about my trip to Kentucky and the idea of a teachers training corps; the Josh Logans; the Fredric Marches; and Roger Stevens. There were also the Ed Weisls and Abe Fortases.

Adlai is certainly a man who wears well, but since he's ten years or more older than I am, I wonder how he can work and think all day in the tense arena he's in, and go to parties at night? But it was the most fun I've had in a long time.

Wednesday, May 27

THE WHITE HOUSE

News of Nehru's death was the word that woke us up about 6 this morning, and great repercussions it will have in the world.

I spent the morning working with Liz, and then went down on the South grounds to greet the President of Ireland, Eamon de Valera. The occasion was bound to be full of sentiment. Who can be more full of it than the Irish? This octogenarian gentleman has had a very full and dramatic life, fighting for Irish independence, and he has much attachment to the United States, where actually he was born.

There was the Diplomatic Corps, the fluttering flags, the national anthems, the review of the troops, Lyndon's speech, and President De Valera's response.

I was charmed by Mr. De Valera who was courtly, happy to be here, sentimental, and he kept on using the phrase "Forty-five years ago . . ." this, and "forty-five years ago . . ." that. He's been to this country six times but the most famous trip was made forty-five years ago when he tried to influence us to arise and help Ireland in its fight for independence from England. His mannerism made me quite conscious of the fact that I frequently say, "Twenty-five years ago . . . ," and I think I'd better stop.

We rode with him to Blair House and on the way there was quite a crowd of people, and frequent shouts of "Hey, Dev! Hi there, Dev! We love you, Dev!" I was not surprised to see Lynda Bird standing among the tourists, unrecognized by anybody, right in front of the White House. She accomplishes what she wants—to walk right out among a thousand tourists and hardly anybody ever stops her.

Tonight we entertained for President De Valera at a State Dinner. He joined us in the Yellow Room with the Ambassador of Ireland and Mrs. William Fay, and his son, a thoughtful, courteous, nice doctor, also named Eamon de Valera; the George Balls; the Angier Biddle Dukes; and the Justice Brennans.

The exchange of gifts included lovely Irish linen handkerchiefs for the children, and for us an Irish linen tablecloth and a beautiful silver coffee pot made in Dublin before our own country won its independence from England. I was particularly pleased with our gifts to President De Valera, because they were as sentimental as the Irish. Besides the vermeil cigar box, inscribed "POETRY, FAITH AND FREEDOM, WE HAVE NAMED THESE AN IRISHMAN'S TRINITY," there was an antique ballot box, an old framed print of New York harbor, the city where Eamon de Valera was born, and a copy of his baptismal certificate with a picture of the church, St. Agnes in New York, where he was baptized.

As a newspaper columnist remarked, "the olde sod" was well represented by Capitol Hill's finest—Congressmen and Senators of Irish descent, as well as the staff we had inherited from the Kennedy Administration. The Irish have certainly put their stamp on our politics.

We had asked the Attorney General and Mrs. Kennedy and Senator Ted Kennedy and his wife, but none of them came—they are off, I think, on money-raising campaigns for the Kennedy Library. However, the Sargent Shrivers were on hand, representing the Kennedy family, and the George Balls took the place of the Rusks, the Secretary having left at dawn that morning for the funeral of Nehru.

I was charmed with Lyndon's toast. He made a graceful reference to

President Kennedy by saying he was one of the many gifts that the Irish had given to America. And then he said, "You and I have a great deal in common, Mr. President, not the least of which is that a lot of Irishmen vote for us—and occasionally vote against us. Furthermore, in our work, we are both surrounded by Irishmen. I have heard it said that there are more Irishmen in the White House than people."

And of De Valera himself, he said, "Few men have had the satisfaction that you have had—not only did you play a leading role in the birth of your nation, you have continued to exert great influence long after Ireland became a significant force in world affairs." And so he has, and he looks like a very happy man now.

De Valera's answer was warm and pleasant, not what we had been led to expect by some newspaperman who wrote that "President De Valera would be marching on Washington, at the head of 20,000 words."

Summer 1964

Today began with working with Eric Goldman on my letter to appear in the new edition of the White House guidebook. At 5 o'clock I went to the East Room for a very special ceremony. It marked the return to the White House of a silver coffee urn, the handsome possession of the first President to live here, John Adams. This is the most historic acquisition since my occupancy. The donor is Mark Bortman of Boston, who came to know Lyndon when he was Vice President. Bashir Ahmad, the Pakistani camel driver, who came to the United States at Lyndon's invitation, was sponsored by the People-to-People program, of which Mr. Bortman was head.

The eighty-odd guests were an interesting assemblage. There were thirteen members of the Adams family present, including Mr. and Mrs. John Quincy Adams and Mr. and Mrs. Thomas Boylston Adams. We'd invited the Massachusetts delegation in Congress and a great many of them came, headed by Senator Leverett Saltonstall. Also present were

Catherine Drinker Bowen, the biographer; the Lyman Butterfields, he is editor of the Adams papers; Clifford Shipton, Director of the American Antiquarian Society; and Miss Alice Winchester, editor of *Antiques Magazine*, a publication Lyndon's mother used to love to read.

The gold chairs were arranged in the familiar semi-circle, with the Adamses on the front row on one side and Mr. and Mrs. Bortman and their daughter and son-in-law on the other. The urn itself, displayed against a background of black velvet, was placed on a stand below the podium for all to admire.

I introduced Mr. Bortman, "whose sense of history and generosity of spirit have prompted this ceremony." His presentation was *dear*. He noted the similarity in the careers of the first occupants of the White House and the present occupants. "John Adams and Lyndon Johnson came from homes that created in them a great strength of character and a strong desire for higher education. Both men had the advantage of genteel but hard economic stringency. Under difficult conditions in acquiring educations, they both had that character which enabled them to become good schoolteachers. John Adams devoted all of his life in the service to his country, as Lyndon Johnson now is doing."

The urn had been purchased by John Adams when he served abroad as our country's envoy and became one of the first important pieces of ceremonial silver used by the second President and his wife in the White House. It bears the initials J. A. A.—for John and Abigail Adams. The urn had been passed down in the Adams family until twenty years ago, when it was purchased by a dealer in New York, who in turn sold it to the Bortmans. They, moved by the significance the White House collections are acquiring, and also, he said, by their liking for Lyndon, had decided to give it to the house where it had been used in 1800.

In accepting the urn I pointed out that not all the gifts that have come to the White House have been as relevant to its history as this one and described the gift from "a far away Sultan 125 years ago, to his Excellency Martin Van Buren, President of the United States of North America, which included two horses with their groom, a bottle of attar of roses, five demijohns of Rose water, one gold-mounted sword, one bottle of diamonds, and one box of mixed pearls and diamonds."

And then, speaking of the woman to whom this coffee urn originally belonged, I quoted a letter that she wrote in November 1800 to her sister when she first moved into the White House. "This House is twice as large as our meeting House. I believe the great Hall is as Bigg. I am sure tis twice as long. Cut your coat according to your Cloth. But this House is built for ages to come. The establishment necessary is a tax which cannot be born by the present sallery: No body can form an Idea of it but those who come into it. . . . Not one room or chamber is finished of the whole. It is habitable by fires in every part, thirteen of which we are obliged to keep daily, or sleep in wet & damp places."

I introduced Mr. Thomas Boylston Adams, the President of the Massachusetts Historical Society, founded in 1791 before this house was built. He is a descendant of both the Adams Presidents—a great-great-grandson of John Adams. He said that he was delighted that the urn had come to the White House where it belonged, but he was "surprised that any of the so-called family loot was on the loose, since the family had relegated the historic possessions to the Quincy house in 1925." (I thought they were all somewhat abashed that some kinsman had had the effrontery to sell it twenty years ago!) Then he regaled us with tales of Abigail and John Adams, from the Adams family correspondence, and presented me with two volumes of these letters for my own personal library.

One of the Mrs. Adamses present wore a quaint hat that tied under the chin. Later on someone told me that she said it was an old one dating several generations back, which she had brought down in a box especially for this occasion. It is delightful to see someone so secure in family prestige that she can actually dress as she pleases—I rather like it. It reminds me of Alice Brown's joke about the lady who asked a typical Boston dowager: "Where do you buy your hats?" The dowager looked at her perplexed and said: "*Buy* our hats? We *have* our hats."

Later Lyndon and I went to the Max Freedmans' house for a birthday party for Bill Moyers who is just turning thirty. Their house is next door to Kay and Phil Graham's, and there is a glorious backyard with a noble tree in it. The tables were spread on the back porch, where we had supper and enjoyed good talk among the small company of about twenty—the sort of richness peculiar to Washington and what I shall miss most when I leave here.

I went to bed thinking how lovely the urn looked on the card table in the Green Room, in front of the picture of old Philadelphia. I wondered what John Adams would have thought of his urn, which is now worth a half-million dollars—or so I read in Betty Beale's column.

Senator Birch Bayh of Indiana and his wife, Marvella, were the spark-plugs of a standing-room rally in the Senate caucus room yesterday for the formation of the Young Citizens for Johnson. "Labor, sports, politics and art were all represented by young people with famous names," said the *New York Times*. Beautiful Charlotte Ford, the daughter of Henry Ford II, sat across the table from John Reuther (nice counterpoint this was), son of labor leader Victor Reuther. Bobby Mitchell of the Redskins football team, pianist Peter Duchin, and Mayor Robert Wagner's son Bob, Jr. were among the group. Luci and Lynda were on hand to show their apprecia-tion for the Young Citizens.

I was pleased with what the *New York Times* said about Luci. " 'This is tremendous,' chortled Luci Baines Johnson. 'School's out, there's so much excitement!' Then she did just what any other teenager would do in a crowd of young celebrities, Senators, Representatives and statesmen—she bounced up and down with a wide grin."

I was impressed that Charlotte Ford said, "I'll do anything you want me to do. Type, pass out cards, anything." Also, she said that she had made up her mind to vote for Lyndon before her father, long-time Republican, announced that he favored him.

This morning we attended a memorial service for Nehru. The setting for the service was fittingly solemn and grand, in the National Cathedral. Lyndon and I went with Dean and Virginia Rusk and Mrs. B. K. Nehru. B. K. Nehru, Ambassador from India and relative of the dead leader, his face a stern mask, followed with Ellsworth Bunker, formerly our Ambassador to India, and Dean Sayre. Assembled were many members of the Diplo-matic Corps, including Lord and Lady Harlech, Soviet Ambassador Dobrynin, and the Dean of the Corps, Sevilla-Sacasa. The Court and the Cabinet were also well represented.

Though I did not feel close to him when I met him in life, I was keenly aware that in death Nehru left a tenser world. He had literally carried India on his shoulders for several decades. Ellsworth Bunker said that Nehru had given the world so much in thought, word, and deed, that we were all much richer for him. He also said that bits of poetry Nehru liked were written down in shorthand on a pad on his desk. Among them were lines from Robert Frost's "Stopping by Woods on a Snowy Evening." "The woods are lovely, dark, and deep, / but I have promises to keep, / and miles to go before I sleep."

The most moving thing to me was the complete sorrow on the face of Mrs. B. K. Nehru, herself not an Indian at all, Hungarian, but a convert to their religion and to their life, and a very close friend of Nehru's.

We returned to the White House for a State luncheon for the Shah of Iran. Handsome, intense, gray-templed, his name appears often on lists of the most attractive men in the world. His beautiful Empress Farah Diba is serene, sloe-eyed, statuesque. I greeted them on the North Portico and we went upstairs, together with the Ambassador of Iran and Mrs. Foroughi, and Mr. Alam, who was Prime Minister when last I saw him, and now is Chancellor of the University. Dean and Virginia Rusk and Angie and Robin Duke were with us. Lyndon was late, but this has been a rough week for him. They had brought us a beautiful Persian rug and we had matching cowboy outfits for their four-year-old son (who was a toddler when I had seen him in Teheran) and for their year-old daughter.

The luncheon had originally been planned as a stag affair, but when the Empress had decided only a few days earlier to come, we simply invited the wives of the men already on the list. I had the Shah on my right and Mr. Alam on my left, and it was a fascinating luncheon from my standpoint. I hoped that Lyndon was enjoying the Empress as much—she's certainly beautiful.

The Shah's eyes light up and he becomes lyrical when he talks about dams and irrigation. I asked him how they were progressing and he said that three dams had been built and a fourth is being built. His aim is one dam per year. I laughed and told him that was exactly the aim my husband had for Texas during his twelve years in the Senate. The rich irrigated land which results from these dams in Iran is used to produce alfalfa and wheat, but they've recently begun an experiment with raising sugar cane, which is proving remarkably successful.

As we sampled the nuts in our nut dish, he asked me if I liked pistachios. I said I adored them, and I had never eaten such good pistachios as in his country. There, they opened easily to the touch; here, I break all my fingernails trying to get into them. He smiled and said: "When they're nearly open like that, we call them 'laughing pistachios.'" I asked the Shah for his signature, on my menu card. He wrote "M. R. Pahlavi." I think I'll ask for signatures at every State Dinner. It will make an interesting collection of autographs if we ever have a library.

John and Elaine Steinbeck came for dinner and how I looked forward to it. I can talk to two people so much better than I can to two hundred and fifty. They arrived before dark and I took them to the Rose Garden for a stroll, and then back upstairs. In an effort to indicate what a psychologically draining job this is for Lyndon, I picked up and read the last letter on my stack. A woman was answering a letter from Lyndon, in which he had expressed sorrow at the death of her son in Vietnam. Her answer was simple, dignified, and acceptant—no bitterness, which made it all the more painful.

When Lyndon came in, I never heard him more articulate or more interesting, though troubles are coming, not in single file, but in battalions. The Turks are on the point of invading Cyprus; the coal industry is angry, wants the government to cease imports of Venezuelan oil.

John Steinbeck talked about his trip to Russia. One telling incident revealed the Russians' antipathy for the Chinese. He said he and Elaine were having dinner with Rada, the daughter of Khrushchev, and her husband in their apartment. They had no servants and when they were removing the dishes afterward, Elaine offered to help take them into the kitchen. She remarked to Rada, "This is the most beautiful china." Rada got very excited and said, "It is not china!" Elaine said, "Of course, I know, I recognize it as Meissen from Germany, but in our country we call all fine dinnerware *china*, it's just an over-all word." Apparently it's a word they don't like to hear.

Steinbeck said he feels that it's blindness that we do not have diplomatic relations with one quarter of the people of the earth, meaning Red China. He made another interesting suggestion. He said it would be a good idea to invite to this country young Russian writers who object to the way their government is being run. Then it would be up to their government to permit them or not permit them to come, and if they did come, he hoped we would give them every opportunity to see us as we are, our best and our worst.

He told a delightful story about his days as a newspaper correspondent in Norway when he became involved with their underground. Danish ships were rescuing captive Norwegians and the Germans were trying to catch them doing it. In the process they used dogs to enter the ships and search out human beings who might be hidden in inaccessible places. Steinbeck suggested sprinkling cocaine powder all along the gangplank. The dogs sniffing cocaine got happy going up, and they couldn't smell a thing from then on!

They brought us a unique gift, one that I shall give up with pain, but I shall give it up, because it is inscribed *Given to the White House Library in the time of Lyndon Johnson, John Steinbeck.* It is a bound copy of *Atlantic Monthly,* dated 1862, which contains the first published version of the "Battle Hymn of the Republic," with those thrilling lines: "Mine eyes have seen the glory of the coming of the Lord, / He is trampling out the vintage where the grapes of wrath are stored." This was significant to him, because from it Steinbeck obtained the title of his most famous book. There is something he didn't know and I didn't tell him, but long, long ago Lyndon—who almost never took time off to see a movie—went with me to see *The Grapes of Wrath* and sat in his seat crying quietly for about two hours at the helpless misery of the Okies. I do not think he has ever forgotten it.

We had a delightful evening and a chance to thank John Steinbeck for probably the best piece of writing that's ever been done about Lyndon, which will probably be incorporated in a brochure by the Democratic Committee for distribution at the Convention. It is true, it is beautiful, and I am very proud of it.

He asked us: "What can we do for you?" And I was quick to say, "You can keep on giving us ideas, clothed in good words . . . help of the same high caliber as that piece of writing."

When they started to leave, Lyndon said, "Where are you staying?" And they said, "Right across the park at the Hay-Adams, so we won't take a taxi, we'll just walk." Lyndon said, "Well, we'll go with you." So out the front door we strolled, and down the walk, along Pennsylvania Avenue to the left, not recognized for quite a little while, and then recognized with astonishment on the part of the few passers-by. We crossed the street with them and said good-by.

Saturday, June 6

The day began on an ominous note. At 4:30 A.M. a telephone call from McGeorge Bundy jarred us awake. No news at 4:30 A.M. is good and this news was that one of our reconnaissance planes had been shot down over Laos. It was a long conversation, and after that a restless rolling sleep for me. I was dimly aware that Lyndon got up and left early. But I, luxuriously, stayed in bed until 10 o'clock. I would have enjoyed it if it hadn't been against the backdrop of that gray-dawn conversation and the mounting anxieties from Southeast Asia.

I went out into the West Hall, where Lyndon, very thoughtfully, was reading the papers all alone so as not to wake me. I had both of our breakfast trays brought there and fetched him some slippers because I had heard him sneezing. Then I got dressed just in time for my 11-o'clock appointment with Mrs. Provenson to work on my Radcliffe speech. We worked in my favorite little room, the blue-and-white Queen's Sitting Room.

It was 1:45 before we ever lifted our eyes from our work. Then I suddenly realized how hungry I was. While I was ordering a couple of sandwiches from the kitchen, Lyndon walked in and handed me something inconsequential. I could tell by the look in his eye that he needed to talk to me, so I followed him out in the hall. He did have something that he wanted me to take to Walter Jenkins right away, but much more important, he leaned over and said: "We've got our planes ready to go in if absolutely necessary. Everybody's in agreement that we can't turn and run."

Poor, lonesome, beleaguered man.

Tuesday, June 9

MASSACHUSETTS AND THE WHITE HOUSE

The dreaded day arrived when I was to deliver the baccalaureate address at Radcliffe. I got in about an hour's work in the morning before leaving for the airport with Liz. On the plane there was Kenneth Galbraith. He came back and jackknifed into a seat beside me, folding up his six feet eight, and we talked about India and what would happen next, and he gave me a copy of his latest book, *The Scotch.*

Once caught up in the stream of a day like this, a day in which there is constant activity and every half-hour you are thrust into confrontation with people who you think are smarter than you are, the dread with which you faced it has to be relegated to the background. You simply put one foot in front of the other and march on through the day.

At the airport, Governor Endicott Peabody and Mrs. Peabody—"Toni," smart, sparkly, capable—met me, along with Mrs. John Collins, the wife of the Mayor of Boston. They had been to Washington for the Irish dinner a little while before. Mrs. Carl Gilbert, Chairman of the Trustees of Radcliffe, was also there. Mrs. Gilbert was in the car with me going in, and she said, "You certainly gave a lovely time to a part of my family, the Adamses, in the White House not long ago." And then added something like: "I suppose the younger lines of the family, such as mine, were not included." I gulped and said, "Mrs. Gilbert, we just did not know how to find all the members of the Adams family, and so we asked the Massachusetts Historical Association for the family list." My dismay was lightened only when I recalled Mrs. Oliver Wendell Holmes' quote in *Yankee from Olympus*—"There'll always be an Adams!" Anyhow, Mrs. Gilbert is Mrs. *Abigail Adams* Gilbert—my "new" Adams will certainly be invited to something else at the White House!

We went to President Mary Bunting's residence, 76 Brattle Street, where a small group of ladies were assembled for a private luncheon. It was a comfortable old house, quiet, genteel, and aglow with books; it almost had that assured look that its occupants have. On walking through the gardens, we had come to a pretty fountain and one of the ladies told me that Radcliffe was where Helen Keller had graduated. This fountain was a memorial to her teacher.

At last came the moment when we drove to the Memorial Church of Harvard University. Along the way I saw the famous Harvard Yard. In the minister's study, I changed to my beautiful black robe with the white velvet bands the University of Texas had given me with my honorary Doctor of Letters degree, on May 30, and joined the processional into the small, quaint, high-ceilinged Memorial Church.

I joined the minister, the Reverend Charles Price, Dr. Bunting, and Mrs. Gilbert on the raised portion of the rostrum below the pulpit, for the brief and simple service—the Lord's Prayer and several hymns sung beautifully by the Radcliffe Choral Society. I spent most of the time eagerly searching the faces of the two hundred and fifty young girls to try to determine what it was that made them different from other girls. Radcliffe is said to be Olympian ground, intellectually speaking, and I was never so awed in my life by both audience and setting.

Presently, with no introduction, I arose, climbed up into the high pulpit, and read the speech that I had worked harder on than any other. One of the lines I liked was "Remember in the most local realistic terms that education is a loan to be repaid by a gift of self." The theme of the speech was that "amid all the worries and uncertainties and the provocative doctrines about the role of the educated woman today, a remarkable young woman has been emerging in the United States. She is your sister, your roommate, and if you look closely enough, probably yourself. She might be called the natural woman, the complete woman. She wants to be, while being equally involved, preeminently a woman, a wife, a mother, a thinking citizen. I urge you to enter outlets, not as the super-woman, but as the total woman, a natural woman, a happy woman. If you achieve the precious balance between woman's domestic and civic life, you can do more for zest and sanity in our society than by any other achievement."

I listed a few specifics. Besides repaying the gift of education by pouring back "your energy and your intellect into your community schools and your children's schools," I called on them to improve the aesthetics of our cities, where 70 percent of the people now live and where a larger percentage are going to live in the next two or three decades. Third, and this I think is very important, I urged them "to make your front line of freedom your front door, that is, to raise happy, well-balanced, level-headed families."

Last, I mentioned the world of politics, where I've spent so much of my life. Although the largest percentage of people eligible to vote are women, the largest percentage of people who actually vote are men, and that's no credit to women. A shining example of a woman who's balanced her life is their own Mary Bunting, mother of four children, President of this celebrated college, who has accepted Lyndon's appointment as a member of the Atomic Energy Commission. She practices what she preaches.

I stopped on the front steps of the church and shook hands with as many of the graduates as came by. One lady said she had attended a graduation at Swarthmore for another child yesterday where Lyndon spoke, and today she was attending the graduation of her daughter where I spoke. I told her she was exposed to double jeopardy from the Johnsons. It was pleasant to see Kitty Galbraith and Mary Bundy, and most of all, to meet the beaming parents and grandparents of the Radcliffe girls. When I actually got down to talking to the people, I thought that the gap between Karnack and Cambridge could be bridged.

We left about 3:30 and just had time to drive by the site along the Charles River that has been dedicated for the Kennedy Library, a gift from Harvard. It is a noble, peaceful setting, in keeping with what will be located there. Mrs. Collins, Mrs. Peabody, and I got out and walked around. They pointed out to me where President Kennedy used to live when he went to school at Harvard, very close by.

And then I hastened back to Washington, for the next event of the day, the State Dinner for the Prime Minister of Denmark, Jens Otto Krag, and his beautiful wife, the Danish movie star Helle Krag.

Back at the White House I made a quick change to what I think is my most impressive dress, a white faille with gold passementerie around the top. A fast comb-out, and then downstairs to the front door, with Lyndon in his white jacket, to meet the Krags at five minutes of 8.

In the exchange of gifts Lynda Bird was so eager to show off the abilities of the talking doll for the Krags' year-and-a-half-old daughter, Astrid Helene, and the hobby horse for their son, that Lyndon and I could hardly get a word in edgeways to present ours, among which was a barbecue set, a wagon with grille. This was intended for their country home, which we hear they love just as much as we love the Ranch. The name of the estate, "Skiveren," was carved on it. Also, we had a turquoise-and-silver necklace, from the Hopi Indians of Arizona, for Mrs. Krag. I think we actually took this necklace off the neck of Lee Udall, because the one we commissioned didn't quite turn out right!

Because the Krags are young and handsome and gay, we had planned this party as a dinner-dance, with Peter Duchin playing the music. For once Lyndon would have to admit that his dinner partner and his dancing partner was really the prettiest woman in the room! But tonight was a night of handsome couples and none more so than the Lloyd Bentsens of Texas—their Scandinavian background making them fit so well with the group.

It was a glamorous group but it would have been hard to find a lovelier girl than Luci Baines Johnson—this was her first State Dinner. Peter Duchin was delightful, but his numbers were a little too long for Lyndon, who likes to change partners about every three minutes.

And then late at night, after everybody was gone, occurred one of my funniest little moments in the White House. In my robe and slippers, ready for bed, I observed that all the lights in the second-floor hall were still on, and I went from one to the other, turning them off. When I got to the staircase that leads down to the State floor, I could hear a few clattering feet below disappearing in the distance, and I could see a great blaze of light going down the steps. If I could step out into the hall only a few feet I could turn off the main lights, but I was afraid the door would lock behind me.

Cautiously I pushed the door open, held it with my foot, reached as far as I could—it was quite obvious I couldn't get to the switch. Some giddy instinct of daring led me to just let the door close gently and to walk over and turn out the lights. Then I went back and turned the knob—sure enough the door was locked tight! I knocked, hoping maybe the guests in the Queen's Room would hear me. I called gently, I called a little louder, *nobody* heard me! There was no sound below now, but there were a few lights still on. I thought about all those funny ads—"I went to the Opera in my Maidenform Bra"—and I thought how awful it would be if I walked through the main entrance hall of the White House at about 1:30, in my dressing gown, and met a dozen or so of the last departing guests. But there was nothing else to do, so with a very assured look (I hope!) I went walking down the stairs, and through the hall where I met only two or three of the departing musicians and staff members. I smiled as if the whole thing were a matter of course, caught the elevator back up to my own floor, and so to bed, thinking this had been a remarkable day in many ways.

Wednesday, June 10

Today we held the ceremony for the Presidential Scholars, one of the projects I've been most interested in since Lyndon has been here. Two high school graduates from each of the fifty states, two each from the District of Columbia and Puerto Rico, and a few at large, totaling 121, have been chosen as Presidential Scholars by a Commission headed by Milton Eisenhower and comprising such people as Senator Fulbright, our own Bill Hagerty, now President of Drexel Institute, Dr. Jeanne Noble, and Mrs. Lawana Trout, the teacher of the year. The students were chosen for intellectual attainment and potential. The idea is to spotlight youthful excellence, to applaud intellectual attainment.

The young people had been given a marvelous day in Washington, beginning with the briefing by Secretary of State Dean Rusk, then a tour of the Capitol building and lunch with their own Senators and Congressmen, followed by a briefing by no less than Astronaut Alan Shepard (I imagine that was what a lot of them liked best) in NASA Auditorium, and then a visit to the Supreme Court where Chief Justice Earl Warren talked to them. At 5:30 they came to the White House for the Presidential reception.

When we entered the East Room, the familiar gold chairs were in a semi-circle. The 121 students and as many of their parents as could come were seated, along with a number of the members of the Commission who chose them, and a glittering galaxy of other guests. I thought Lyndon's speech was one of the best I'd ever read, although, unhappily, his delivery was not up to standard. Later on I found out why. Southeast Asia's problems were nailing him to his desk. He has been in constant meetings with everyone concerned in State and Defense and he could scarcely concentrate on anything else.

He said: "Today—as really never before—we must look to our better minds to show the way toward our society's greatest day. That is your challenge and that is your duty. You are exceptional members of an exceptional generation. You have been born to man's most exceptional opportunity. You are younger than most of the earth's quarrels, and you are older than most of the earth's governments. You are younger than most of man's ignorance, and older than much of his knowledge. Since you were born, man has developed both the capacity to destroy human life, and the capacity to make life worthwhile for all the human race."

And then came the awarding of the medals, the calling of the names and the states of each of the 121 students, a handshake with Lyndon and a big glow from me, particularly as certain of them filed by. I had been reading their biographies. It is expected that an economically comfortable home, with stable and happy parents, is more likely to produce excellence, but there were wonderful instances among them of disadvantaged children who had risen above all obstacles.

There was the Arkansas boy whose father was a machinist and his mother a laundry maid. The school counselor wrote: "He comes from a home so poor, one would hardly believe it. He supports himself by tutoring and he's first in his class of 660, and wants to become an organic chemistry major at the University of Arkansas." There was a girl from Shreveport, whose mother was a clerk-typist and her father "believed dead." She has been shunted between grandparents and aunts, because of a broken home, and when in the sixth grade, had been victim of a serious accident, hospitalized for many months. In spite of that, her grades were excellent and she planned to go to the University of Southwestern Louisiana and become a high school teacher. An Illinois boy, totally deaf, who had won awards in science and in English, and a school letter in wrestling, was scheduled for Oberlin College to become a scientist or engineer.

A girl who was one of the first students to be integrated at Little Rock was praised by her counselor. "She's gained the respect and admiration of her fellow students for the excellence of her work. She plans to attend Radcliffe and be a creative writer." A Negro boy from New Orleans, son of a mail carrier and a teacher, was judged by his school principal to be "the best student we've ever had. He plans to go to California Institute of Technology and become a nuclear engineer."

After you read these biographies you couldn't help thinking: "America, God *has* shed His grace on thee!"

Congratulations over, we went into the State Dining Room for refreshments. And here I think our own planning broke down, because our marvelous galaxy of guests invited to greet the Scholars should have had name tags to identify them. Standing in line to meet them, students and guests, I recognized such people as George Balanchine, Director of the American School of Ballet; Herblock, the cartoonist; Helen Hayes, one of the great actresses of the stage; Willem de Kooning, the painter; Harper Lee, one of my favorite novelists; Walter Lippmann, the columnist; Marya Mannes, the writer and critic; Dr. J. Robert Oppenheimer (how excited all of those young science majors would have been to have talked to him); Dr. Glenn Seaborg and Alan Shepard from the space program; Ben Shahn, the artist; and John Walker, of the National Gallery of Art. I had seen many more acceptances, from celebrated people whom I am not sure I recognized myself—Robert Penn Warren, the poet and novelist; Edward Durrell Stone, the architect. What we should have done was ask them all to wear some identification. Even those distinguished people in art, literature, drama, space, government, and education can get lost in a crowd.

I found this out when I introduced Helen Hayes to one of the young students, and her response was a very sweet, polite, "Oh, I'm so glad to meet you, Miss Hayes. My grandmother is named Hayes." After that I didn't make the same mistake again. I would beam and say, "Oh, I know you'll be so thrilled to meet Miss Helen Hayes, because I'm sure you have seen her on the stage or in the movies many times!" Or, "This is Harper Lee. You have probably read her book *To Kill a Mocking Bird*." At any rate, I cued them in from then on, but I know they missed a lot of the richness of the evening simply from not knowing who was there.

Lynda Bird was hostess for the young people on the lawn, where the red striped tents were set up, and there were hamburgers and soft drinks and entertainment. This was one of the best times for mixing and mingling. I later heard that Leonard Bernstein had a group of twenty or thirty students gathered around him, listening entranced. This was what the occasion was all about as far as I'm concerned. Besides the recognition of excellence we wanted to provide an opportunity for young people of unusual potential to meet with those who have already achieved great things for America . . . something for them to remember always.

Lyndon had been in the West Wing for a briefing session on Southeast Asia with Cabinet members. He had strolled out to mingle with the young people and then turned around and gone back into the West Wing and brought Bobby Kennedy back with him. As the newspapers put it, ". . . then something prompted him to return and bring out Mr. Kennedy." Of course, what prompted him to return was simply that, in many ways, he's a generous and understanding man. He knows Bobby Kennedy has a special rapport with young people and that much of his philosophy has been directed toward young groups. He thought the youngsters would enjoy such a meeting and so would the Attorney General.

My old friend of Karnack days, Dorris Powell, arrived about 8 o'clock. She is a houseguest I have looked forward to so eagerly. I got her settled in the room that the Wests had just vacated and told her to join us on the Truman Balcony off the Yellow Room to watch the entertainment on the lawn below. Mariallen Moursund and her children Will and Mary and I took our seats on the Truman Balcony and watched Sidney Poitier introduce the Gerry Mulligan Quartet, one of the contemporary jazz favorites. Among their numbers was "Blues for Lynda," a composition of their own. José Ferrer gave readings from Shakespeare—not too much Shakespeare, and considerable recollections of José Ferrer. About that time Lyndon arrived, hungry, and we went in for dinner. I excused myself before we got around to dessert, and went back to the porch, too late, alas, to hear Leonard Bernstein, but in time for the Kingston Trio, old favorites of Lynda Bird's, whose music on records I have been hearing since she was thirteen.

I went to bed early, with the self-satisfied feeling that this had been a good day, but there was also an unfulfilled feeling that I, myself, had not added to the young folks' meeting all that I could have. Next time—name tags!

Thursday, June 11

This was a long, full, and interesting day—most of it spent in Philadelphia at the Golden Slipper Dinner. The Golden Slipper is a worthy Masonic organization that devotes its energies to a summer camp for underprivileged youngsters. The return to Washington required a three-hour drive, which I didn't mind at all for it gave me some quiet time to think. My thoughts went steadily back to Lyndon's dilemma; in fact, they seldom leave it. How he could get out, or does he have to go on?

Yesterday the Senate had cleared the way for a vote on the Civil Rights

Bill, by invoking cloture, with about four votes to spare. In ten days maybe the bill will pass the Senate, and then go back to the House. Maybe in two or three weeks Lyndon can sign it into law. That would be a high point on which to make the announcement, but then what? I fear the repercussions so much, not only in Lyndon's personal life, but in the fact that he has become a sort of "father image" in the country, and there's nobody in the Democratic Party quite ready to step into his shoes—not without a few months' build-up. His unwillingness to carry on might bring with it a wave of disillusion, resentment, even bitterness from Democrats and from people everywhere, and that would be too painful to bear. He wants me to help him get out but I think I can only say: "Stay on for now."

Sunday, June 14

We went to National City Christian Church with Secretary of Commerce and Martha Hodges and the Udalls. After the service Martha and I walked around the grounds, leaving the lively Lee Udall in the pool with Stew, Lyndon, and Secretary Hodges. It's a happy thing to me, how much I have come to like President Kennedy's Cabinet. One by one, I have come to feel really close to them and very admiring of them.

At lunch the conversation was about the great cross-country highway system, 90 percent of which is paid for by the federal government, and 10 percent by the state governments. One of the big problems has been that when you draw a straight line across the country—which is the way a cost-conscious engineer would do it—what do you do about a National Park or a Wildlife Preserve, and a historic shrine like the Frank Lloyd Wright house? If you go around them, you may spend millions of dollars. If you go through them, you may grossly sacrifice a national treasure.

Secretary Hodges has ruled that every case has to be decided on its merit, that there can't be an over-all blanket policy that covers all cases. The Department of Interior, with the young and imaginative Stewart Udall at its head, is a loud voice for preserving the wilderness, the National Parks, the shrines, the jewels of America. The Udalls are both Mormons and I couldn't help wondering what it felt like to them to be in the National City Christian Church today.

This afternoon I had another talk with Lyndon, who faces the next five months with the feeling that—well—he wishes there were some honorable way out of it. With Vietnam and Laos and Cyprus—with the summer's turmoil that faces us if Civil Rights passes, including the public accommodations portion, and worse, the boiling over if Civil Rights doesn't pass. Will it be months or years before this change can be absorbed into our society? Whose hand is strong enough and whose head and heart are wise enough to guide us? How can anybody blame Lyndon for wanting to be anonymous, alone, and back at the Ranch? And yet, caught on this pinpoint in history, what exit is there?

About 8:30 in the evening, Lyndon called Secretary Rusk, finding him in his office, and this a Sunday! A few moments later the Secretary came in and handed a wire to Lyndon. Cabot Lodge wanted to submit his resignation as Ambassador to Vietnam and return home.

Lyndon had already been asking the question in case Lodge resigned, "Whom do you recommend?" He had asked advice from McGeorge Bundy, Bob McNamara, and Dean Rusk. Their answers made me think well of this country—the caliber of men suggested, whose willingness to go, in most instances, had been checked out—and also made me know that it would be extremely hard, almost impossible, for Lyndon himself to turn away now and walk out at this stage of the game.

Monday, June 15

This was a day to catch up on work with Bess and Liz, to have about five dresses fitted, and then to go shopping for those little things that you can't do without—purses, gloves, lounging shoes (you can't send your feet out to get fitted for shoes by Helen or some friend, no matter how willing!).

In the afternoon I had an interview with Mr. William Manchester, who has been chosen by Mrs. Kennedy to write a book on the assassination. He's interviewing everybody who was present those five days. I spent two hours with him and it was grueling. It was an exhausting experience to relive those hours, because of the pain involved for everyone and the shame for our country.

We asked the Joe Alsops and the Clark Cliffords to come and have dinner with us. Alas, it's almost a waste to have them the same night, because they're both so amusing and articulate and so much fun. It was a *great* evening for conversation. Among the little gems were the wagers. Joe Alsop bet five to two that Goldwater would get the nomination. Clark

Clifford bet four to one that Goldwater would get the nomination. One of them said that Scranton was not thinking of this election, but of the future. There must be somebody around to pick up the pieces of the Republican Party, somebody who would inherit the leadership, after the ultra-conservatives have had their try and failed.

Joe told us a story that gave me cold chills when I thought that within a week's time Premier Ismet Inonu of Turkey and probably Prime Minister Papandreou of Greece were both coming to lay their troubles at our country's doorstep. He said that he'd been riding along in a jeep, close to the Russian border in Anatolia, with a Turkish sergeant at the wheel. They were on a mountain road. Suddenly the sergeant began to point out a distant pass, raising his hands from the wheel, gibbering and gesticulating in glee. Joe had visions of tumbling down into the chasm, and he said to the interpreter, "What is he talking about?" The interpreter said, "He is pointing at the spot where a battle was fought a thousand years ago that ended the Byzantine Empire. He is saying, 'That is where we killed all the Greeks that are!' "

With a quarrel buried so deep, so ingrained in the bones, how can *we* hope to solve the problems of the Greeks and the Turks living together in Cyprus?

Only the conversation was gourmet, not the dinner. Zephyr was off and dinner was not up to par. Afterward, Lyndon said he needed exercise, and we all went walking with him, on the Southwest grounds, with the beautiful backdrop of the Washington Monument and the Thomas Jefferson Memorial, all the way around the circle, past the fountain, and back up to the Diplomatic entrance.

They all departed at an early 11:30, and after they'd gone, Lyndon said Joe had told him, in effect, if you don't commit troops you're going to preside over the first real defeat of the United States in history. There's no other honorable way out of Southeast Asia, into which we were committed some ten years ago. His elaboration wasn't complete. I suppose he meant if we moved out, the Communists would move in. If we stayed in, it would mean American boys over there . . . it would mean all those letters that tell of the death of an American soldier—each one a wound as you read it—and could it ever possibly end up in a significant victory?

Well, I can't say the evening did anything to solve Lyndon's dilemma— or to smooth his path for the days ahead—although it was a thoroughly delightful social occasion.

I went to bed thinking about the good telephone conversation I had with Lynda Bird and reading how she had enjoyed Hawaii hugely, rubbing noses with Maori children at the Polynesian Culture Center, and then at the Island of Maui where she'd gone skin diving and attended a big luau at the Maui beach home of a sugar plantation owner. She told me they'd had such delicacies as pig's entrails, and lichens or something that grows on rocks! She said she'd had a three-mile boat trip up the Wailua River to a fern grotto, where she planted a five-foot coconut tree in a ceremony at the Coco Palms Hotel, and attended a dinner for young folks. The paper reported that flower leis had to be removed half a dozen times, whenever they got up over her nose! She's taking life at the tide, that little girl, and I'm glad she is.

Tuesday, June 16

Today was the day for another of my Women Do-ers Luncheons. The guest list was long and diverse, including Mrs. Clark Kerr of Berkeley, California, and Marie Turner of Breathitt County, Kentucky.

I had invited an old friend—we'll call her Mrs. John Doe—and hereby hangs one of Washington's funniest tales. This coincidence must have been repeated many times through the years, with many different hostesses. When I emerged to greet the first few arrivals, an elderly, smiling lady put out her hand and said, "I'm Mrs. John Doe." Thank goodness I didn't faint. I hope my face didn't show any flicker of astonishment, but she certainly wasn't *my* Mrs. John Doe. The social office had consulted the Green Book and had copied down exactly the same name but the wrong address. She was a pleasant lady, and an interesting thing about her came to light. She had remarked to one of the other guests that she had been to the White House during every Administration since Taft, except one! It is surprising that such a mistake doesn't happen more often—two people with the same name confused in the social lists.

Our speaker was Mrs. Jane Jacobs, author of *The Death and Life of Great American Cities.* The press was represented by Vera Glaser, of the North American Newspaper Alliance.

This was a successful luncheon, I thought. Although I was a bit thrown by the mix-up over the two Mrs. Does, I felt this was one of those times that shows whether or not you've got poise and inner calm. I introduced Jane Jacobs, saying that the sound of the hammer across Lafayette Park and the usual noonday snarl of traffic, in which they'd probably arrived, were reminders of the growing problem of urbanization that our growing nation faces. I referred to the sentiments of Thomas Jefferson, who warned that if we got piled up in large cities, we would become corrupt. And more hopefully, I cited Carl Sandburg, who spoke of the strength of cities "with their broad shoulders"—and Walt Whitman, who wrote wistfully of the "city invincible, the new city of friends." (I wonder if he really had a city in mind!)

And then, to "get down to brass tacks," as my daddy would often say, I said I felt the questions we all want answered when it comes to urban life are how to keep size from smothering the individual, crowding him into an impersonal and uncomfortable mold, and how to make a city beautiful. These are questions which writer, planner, and citizen must answer, and one of the front runners with the possible answers was Jane Jacobs, who was all three.

Both of us did our talking sitting down. Mrs. Jacobs was a forceful, articulate, salty, occasionally controversial speaker. One of her major objections to the way cities are operated is the fact that you can get practically any size appropriation for a new park, but you can get practically nothing for the upkeep of an existing park. Another is the blight that falls upon cities when a disadvantaged minority group moves into a neighborhood. There's a blackout on mortgages; you can't get houses financed in those areas, presumably because it is expected that they will decline in value. This brought on an interesting but polite exchange with Mrs. Mary Roebling, the banker. From my eternally-hopeful-believer-in-people friend, Tharon Perkins, came the observation (when we were talking about parks and their upkeep) that this problem might be solved by absorbing some of our untrained labor, some of our unskilled out-of-a-job youth. After lunch Lyndon came in to greet us, shaking hands all around—thank goodness I remembered everybody's name!

At 5 o'clock, a ridiculous hour to get dressed in a long formal, I put on my white sheath with the slit up the side, and my new white coat, and left with Lyndon by chopper from the South Lawn, for Andrews Air Force Base. We were bound for New York for the dinner given by the Stephen Smiths, Trustees for the John F. Kennedy Memorial Library, in honor of Mrs. John F. Kennedy. This was Mrs. Kennedy's first appearance at a public social occasion since the President's assassination.

Chief Justice Warren and Arthur Goldberg were on the plane with us; also Jane and Orville Freeman, Bob and Margy McNamara, the Anthony Celebrezzes, and Senator Ted Kennedy, who all the way to New York was wittily and capably espousing the cause of naval bases for Boston. He insisted that more bases had been closed in Massachusetts than had been closed in Texas—but, of course, there *are* a good many more naval bases in Massachusetts.

We went to a reception on the roof of the St. Regis Hotel and stood in line with Mrs. Kennedy to greet about three hundred guests. Jackie looked beautiful in a simple black dress; smiling, composed. She said she was on her way to Cape Cod, where the children would join her for the summer.

The dinner took place in the lovely roof-garden dining room of the St. Regis, all pink and gold, and I was seated between Bobby Kennedy and Stephen Smith. Fredric March and his wife Florence Eldridge were at the table. Charlotte Ford, an exquisite blonde with her hair piled high on her head, was also at our table. So was Mrs. Ernest Hemingway whom I enjoyed talking with about *A Moveable Feast,* which concerns Hemingway's days in Paris in his youth. She said, "If you've spent a part of your youth in Paris, you have it with you always." Lyndon was at a table with Jackie and Jean Smith.

Bobby told me that the guests were all donors of ten thousand dollars or more to the Kennedy Library. He thought that they would have the required ten million dollars for the Library by September. The Library will be built and furnished with funds raised by the Kennedy family and when complete it will be turned over to the federal government. Mrs. Rose Kennedy was there, as slim and pretty as any of her daughters, in a white, sparkling dress.

After dinner there was a program of readings from the favorite poetry of President Kennedy, given by Fredric March. The selections had been made by Jackie, and in the margin she had made notes of why Jack had liked each particular poem. Her charming notes were read by Florence Eldridge and this gave poignancy and counterpoint to Fredric March's reading.

One of the selections began "Now is the winter of our discontent, / Made glorious summer by this sun of York . . ." I want to look it up in my Shakespeare and read the whole scene from *King Richard III.* Perhaps this would help to explain to me the title of John Steinbeck's book, which I like so much.

After dinner we piled into a car, Lyndon and I, with the Chief Justice and Bobby, and one of Bobby's aides. The streets were lined with cheering crowds. We waved and smiled. All the way in from the airport there had been sizable crowds, although our route had not been announced. Announcement of the visit had not been publicly made until about 5 o'clock this afternoon. Helicopters had gone ahead of us all the way, and a good many New York policemen were stationed along the route and at all the overpasses.

Bobby and Lyndon immediately began a very earnest conversation about what the first acts should be, when the Civil Rights Bill was passed. They spoke of the possibility of calling a meeting of Governors from the states affected by the public accommodations measure. There are, apparently, nineteen states, not all Southern states, that do not have a public accommodations law. This would take the onus off the Southern states, if a meeting of Governors from all nineteen states were called to work out measures for a peaceful enforcement and transition. They also discussed appointing a mediator—Lyndon very much wants a Southerner—to handle the complaints when they begin rolling in.

Saturday, June 20

THE WHITE HOUSE

I slept late, self-indulgently, woke to read first the news about the airplane crash—the details are still not clear—in which Ted Kennedy's back was broken. The plane plummeted in an apple orchard, on top of a knoll, just before making the approach to the airport. Miraculously, Senator Birch Bayh and his wife Marvella escaped with minor injuries.

I called Mrs. Rose Kennedy first—maybe that shows the generation I'm in—my mind going back to last Tuesday night, when I had seen her, so slim and elegant and young-looking, in New York. Now she suffers one more blow. Her voice was calm and steady—what a load she has had to carry!

Then I called the Northampton hospital, hoping to reach some member of Senator Bayh's family and wound up with Dr. Thomas Corriden. He reported on Birch and Marvella, but said I couldn't talk to either of them. He asked me if I'd like to speak to Joan Kennedy. She was the first person who used the word "paralysis," dread and frightening word, as something that hung over them but not at all as though it could really happen. Joan was quick to say that Teddy could use both his arms and his legs, but they didn't know yet the condition of the broken bones in his back—and surgery was indefinite. His executive assistant had already died and the pilot had died immediately when the plane crashed.

Later the Boggs came over and I talked with Hale, asking him questions about the progress of Civil Rights in the House. He said they had set July 4 as passage day, and barring unexpected troubles, would achieve it. Now, with victory in sight, everybody's mind turns to the problems that victory will bring in its wake. No solutions yet, not for a decade, or several decades —but tension and trouble, and probably bloodshed lie ahead. But it is a path that has to be taken—a step forward long overdue.

Thursday, July 2

Today is Luci's seventeenth birthday! Seventeen was a very special year for me—the year I began falling in love with somebody new each April! Luci at seventeen is a beauty, much more grown-up and very much more a woman than I was at that age. While Lyndon and I were having breakfast, we asked her to join us. I showed her the nightgowns and robes I had selected—two from which she was to choose one set—and found to my chagrin that the hair piece, which was a very personal and "surprise" gift, had been delivered to her bedroom instead of mine, so she knew all about it. (This latter gift was given partly in self-defense, to keep her from borrowing mine, which she has been doing on special occasions.)

Later in the day Lyndon sent her a sweet note and a yellow rose, and Luci and Lynda and I had lunch together in my bedroom. Zephyr had made a lemon birthday cake with eighteen candles on it, one to grow on, which Luci cut before realizing that she would have to take it down later in the day to show it to the press. Her birthday pictures displayed the cake with a large hunk cut out of it.

The news story I liked best about Luci's birthday reported that she said she was glad to have a day off to sleep late and "wash my hair." But on the other hand she said that her job as optometry assistant to Dr. Robert Kraskin was just "thrilling and I couldn't ask for anything better." She plans to become a medical assistant working in cancer research. That is great. I couldn't ask for anything better!

In the background of today there is always present in my mind, and I am sure in Lyndon's mind, the fact that this is the ninth anniversary of his serious heart attack. For the first few years we passed those milestones stepping softly with great trepidation. Now we act almost as though the heart attack had not been, though Lyndon and I will not forget.

In the middle of the afternoon came the big news of the day—the big news of the last six months and perhaps of the whole year. "Civil Rights Bill Passes House. LBJ's signature makes it a law today. The House voted final Congressional passage of an historic Civil Rights Bill today and President Johnson arranged to sign it into the law of the land within a matter of hours." The vote was 289 to 126.

At 6:30 there was a ceremony in the East Room, the signing of the Civil Rights Bill, complete with TV coverage. All the leaders of Congress were lined up behind Lyndon as he signed the bill with some several scores of pens—each one could hardly have written one single letter. Mike Mansfield, Everett Dirksen, Hale Boggs, Attorney General Kennedy, all the members of the legislative branch or the enforcement branch who were concerned with the bill, were present. It was a dramatic occasion, and there was a really magnificent televised statement by Lyndon.

One odd thing happened. When Lyndon had finished speaking, Hubert Humphrey went up to see whether he could have the copy of the statement that Lyndon had read to preserve for historic purposes, and it had vanished. Some of the newspaperwomen asked me what I thought of the law, and I said my mind went back to the Civil Rights Bill of 1957 and all those many, many nights, some thirty-seven nights, Lyndon had spent working for its passage—at his desk in the Senate Chamber or on a cot in the Capitol and I had taken hot meal after hot meal and change of clothes after change of clothes to him—so this was just another step in a long chain of steps.

As I had slipped quietly into a seat, I noticed Attorney General Kennedy sitting in the front row. This bill that his brother had sponsored so ardently and had pinned so much hope on, that Bobby himself has pushed, has now finally come to passage because, I believe, of the earnest, dogged work and the legislative expertise of Lyndon. I left the East Room feeling that I had seen the beginning of something in this nation's history, fraught with untold good and much pain and trouble.

There were several hours of "wrapping up" business and then a call from Lyndon, making a suggestion as though he had just thought of it: "What do you think? We might just get off to Texas tonight." I was all for it. I was every bit ready. Bags were packed. Willie Day Taylor was standing by to chaperone Luci. We had a bite of dinner. And at 10:30, we got in the chopper on the South Lawn with a high sense of elation, the best feeling of achievement that we have had so far, because the last two weeks have really been productive, with the signing of the Civil

Rights Bill, the Foreign Aid Bill, and a goodly mass of legislation accomplished.

Lyndon and I, Bill Moyers, Vicki, and our Secret Service agents helicoptered to Andrews. We flew to the Ranch in the *Jetstar*, so we didn't have to stop in Austin. Exhilarated with that sense of adventure and youth and release, the perfect beginning for a vacation, we landed at the LBJ Ranch about midnight Texas time. This was one of those rare nights, starry in every way, when one does not think about tomorrow, a wonderful sense of euphoria rarely attained.

Monday, July 6

LBJ RANCH

Today should be full of work and I am in a humor to do it. Three days of play is enough for me. But when Lyndon insisted that I go over to the Scharnhorst Ranch with him, it was one last chance that I couldn't pass up, so I went with him. Jesse Kellam had joined us, his presence always a comfort. He's been by our side since the early thirties as friend and companion, and for nearly twenty years he has managed our family business. We met A. W. there, and then drove around the prettiest ranch of all. I love that new road built precipitously along the edge of the cliff looking down into the valley. The huge boulders that rise on each side almost meet above the road—a perfect place to "hold up a stagecoach"!

There was much talk of the pressing question. Lyndon wants to get out. But there *is* no way out now. As Ed Weisl expressed it, looking at me, shocked, "Bird, I don't know any honorable way for him *not* to run." A. W. was the most subtle of us. He said to Lyndon: "We just want you to do whatever is best for you, and you are the only man that can make up your mind." Jesse was cool and forthright. He said, "Speaking as a selfish citizen, I hope that you will run. And then, when and if you are elected, I hope you will make an announcement right away that you are one President who is going to hold the job down for four years, if you live, and do the best you can for everybody, black and white, Democrat and Republican, and not seek reelection."

These three days at the Ranch have been idyllic. In the long twilight the big clouds come rolling up, first pink and then fading through every shade to silver gray. The katydids make the music of summer and it is the time of fireflies, especially in the grove of trees down by the river. My favorite place to drive is the "top of the Martin" where you can look down on the church spire in the valley below and the fields in between, with Sudan grass waving in the wind, alfalfa just coming up, and, here and there, cows grazing, an occasional live oak tree, and finally to the white nest of houses of the LBJ Ranch.

In the afternoon we got in the helicopter and flew to Austin, having our last view of the Hill Country from the air. Lyndon said good-by rather forlornly into the talking machine to A. W. who was driving along unseen below us on the highway. But A. W.'s voice came back clear and strong, "Good-by, come home soon."

Saturday, July 11

THE WHITE HOUSE

After lunch today I went up on the roof in a bathing suit and lay in a deck chair and read and read—an envelope full of mail that says "Read and File." Then I went down to the pool to swim twenty laps all by myself. Then I walked around the yard with the dogs and tonight I had a rather early dinner with Lyndon, just the two of us.

This weekend he is going through the throes of what may be the last desperate turning away, the desire to escape being the Democratic candidate this fall. But the trouble is he can't find any honorable escape.

The most frightening flags in the wind to me are the occasional letters that come over my desk from parents expressing appreciation to the President for his letter of condolence about their son who has been killed in Vietnam. These are simple letters, quiet, dignified, sad, some even proud that the sacrifice was made for their country, but I know what an unbearable weight a great mass of those letters could be.

Monday, July 13

Now is the time to do something I have long planned—walk around the White House grounds with Mr. Irvin Williams, the gardener, the White House guidebook in my hand, and learn from him and the map in the guidebook the trees that were planted by various Presidents.

Records are a bit dim before 1900, but we do know that Thomas Jefferson had the two large mounds constructed, one on the east side, one on the west side, because he liked to walk in the grounds and wanted the privacy they afforded. And we know that the majestic American elm on top of the east mound was planted by John Quincy Adams in 1826. This is the oldest authenticated tree on the grounds.

Andrew Jackson's magnificent *Magnolia grandiflora* brought from the Hermitage is probably the most famous tree. Grover Cleveland, that enormous man, amazingly enough, had planted two delicate dwarf Japanese maples. Calvin Coolidge, with a great sense of home, had chosen the white birch so familiar to his Vermont. Franklin Roosevelt has two little leaf lindens, still quite small, so short is history. President Eisenhower planted at least five trees that have already been pointed out to me. The gardener said there were several others.

We talked about what tree Lyndon should plant. I want it to be something typical of Texas, but the live oak won't grow in Washington, nor will the Texas pecan. I want a long-lived, disease-resistant, majestic tree-for-the-ages, which is pretty limited when you get to Central Texas. We might plant a willow oak.

Lyndon was very late coming home tonight. I phoned the office and found that he was meeting in his small room with O'Donnell, Valenti, Maguire, Cliff, Walter, at least eight of the chief political cogs in the machine. But that's a good sign, because it means activity and I know that work is better for him than pondering the troubles of the future. It was nearly 11 o'clock when Lyndon arrived with Walter Jenkins and Dick Maguire. We had a quiet dinner, but I gathered there was an air of achievement and "We are on the move."

Then I took my exercises—I, at last, have gotten pretty good about taking them, whereas Lyndon has been *very* good for about three months. Ever since I returned on July 6, Zephyr has been serving his plate in the kitchen, paying strict attention to calories and limiting him to about 1100 a day which, if he doesn't linger by some laden hors d'oeuvre table, is bound to take off some pounds.

Wednesday, July 15

An easy day, with an hour and a half in the sun on the roof outside the Solarium, finishing A *Moveable Feast.*

I walked around the South grounds again today—my most delightful luxury. Tonight Lynda and I went to *West Side Story*, Leonard Bern-

stein's musical. I can't quite get accustomed to being recognized everywhere, although obviously it is my own fault for going in that big black
car and letting it drive up to the front entrance to pick us up at the end
of the play. The simple thing to do would be to go in a small car, park
it as close to the outside gate as we can, and simply walk out like everybody else. I can't live in a cage, and I won't give up doing with Lynda
and Luci and Lyndon a lot of the things I want to do.

We got back to the White House about midnight. Lyndon was looking
at the TV; we've been watching the Republican Convention for the last
three days. It's obvious they are going to nominate Goldwater any
minute. But a little past one my enthusiasm played out and I put my
head in the pillow.

About 3:30 or 4 A.M. Lyndon woke up and I don't think either of us
went back to sleep the rest of the night. He described to me in detail the
problems, the pros and cons, the good points and the bad, of every decision that faces him with regard to this campaign—every sensitive job
to be filled, every spot on the battlefield that needs to be manned. So it
was a wakeful night, with about two hours' sleep.

Thursday, July 16

Today began with hearing Goldwater say on TV, when he was asked
a question about Lyndon, "Yes, I know the fellow." My reaction was
chiefly: "I hope Lyndon doesn't use that tone about *him*," because it
serves principally as a small fire under the supporters of the man slighted.

At 9 A.M. Ken Galbraith came for breakfast, and that's an occasion I
wouldn't miss. We were in the dining room all of two hours, with a rich
fare of conversation. The gist of Ken's conversation was that he considers
himself first a friend of the Kennedy family, but also he is quite understanding of Lyndon. They talked about Hubert, and Ken was friendly
and acceptant toward him. Lyndon urged him to help with any Congressmen that he had influence with to get the Poverty Bill passed. Before he
left, Ken had expressed a willingness, I believe, to write and help out with
campaign material and speeches.

Because I wanted Lyndon to consider two trees, the willow oak and
the Darlington oak, which is the nearest thing to a live oak that will
grow in this section of the country, so that we can choose what he will
plant some day, I walked with him over to the office. In about two

minutes Lyndon had agreed to the willow oak and we had chosen two possible spots, just off the driveway approaching the Southwest Gate, up a little sidewalk toward his office—one on the right-hand side, one on the left—for two possible plantings in September.

In the late afternoon I met James Roosevelt and his daughter Anna in the Yellow Room. Anna is visiting her father from California, and he told me he wanted her to see the White House. I wanted to hear about his memories of the days he lived here. We went out on the Truman Balcony in the gathering twilight. Him and Her and Blanco were racing across the lawn, tourists were gathered at the fence, and the swallows were sweeping across the evening sky.

There is something of her grandmother in Anna—or did I just keep looking for resemblances? She is tall, blonde, sweet-faced, eager. We reminisced about the years from 1933 to 1945. James told me that when his father was first inaugurated, his youngest brother, John, then sixteen and at school, had a ramshackle car of his own. He went out to some gay, late parties after the Inaugural Ceremonies were over. The President had told him he must come in by 12 o'clock, because the gate closed then. He didn't. He got to the gate at 3 A.M., according to James. The guard looked at him with a wry and wary eye when young John Roosevelt introduced himself, and finally said, "Well, no son of a President would ever be riding around in a car like that!" So John had to go to a hotel and spend the night. James says he thinks that's why John is a Republican now.

James also told me that for his father's last Inaugural he did not expect to be present. He was a Marine, stationed somewhere on the other side of the world. His father cabled him he wanted him to come. James answered tersely, "WHEN A MAN IS WHERE I AM AND DOING WHAT I AM DOING, HE DOESN'T STOP TO COME TO AN INAUGURAL." But the next thing he knew, he got orders calling him back to Washington. So he came.

He had not seen his father in more than three months, and said he was astonished at how much he had changed. The President looked old and unutterably tired. Inaugural Day was gray and snowy and bitter cold. After the ceremony his father walked in from the South grounds, chilled, and sat down in a chair. James said, "Father, come on. In just a moment now you've got to go in to the reception, you know. You've got to put in an appearance for a while." President Roosevelt was silent a moment, and then looked up wearily and said, "I think I can make it." He went on to the reception.

Later James questioned McIntyre and all the doctors. They assured him that the tests were fine, that his father was in good health, but James said he did not believe it. He thought they did his father a great disservice, although he said that quickly, almost apologetically, as if he hated to cast any shadow on the doctors.

We talked about the proposed monument for President Roosevelt, which I dislike so very much. It has been labeled "Instant Stonehenge"— a series of pillars starkly stretching to the sky—or perhaps tablet is a better word, with excerpts from Roosevelt's speeches carved on them. The monument speaks nothing of the warmth or character of the man to me. There must be some better way to make his words live. None of the four Roosevelt boys likes the monument, and James said that he was going to go before the Commission and prevent the acceptance of the memorial if he possibly could. I showed Anna all the upstairs rooms, and we had a pleasant time. I was thinking all the while, what a house of passage! But all those who have ever lived here remember.

A little after 8 I went over to Lyndon's office to see if I could spring him loose—but I was not successful.

Friday, July 17

INDEPENDENCE, MISSOURI

A very special day—my day with Lynda. It began with the presentation of the one millionth copy of the White House guidebook to an astonished tourist family—a husband and his wife and two children who were, like several thousand others, making a visit to the White House on a summer day. Suddenly they encountered, as they were purchasing their volume at the entrance desk, a volley of cameras, newspaper reporters, and me. We went out to the Rose Garden and had a picture taken together. How much these million copies are helping in the restoration of the White House, but more important, people in homes across the country are being acquainted with the tradition, the beauty, and the history of this beloved place.

We were all packed, and Lynda, Simone Poulain of the press office, and I left for Friendship Airport for our long-planned trip to President Truman's Library at Independence. Lynda Bird and I had been talking about the trip for two years, and when I was with President Truman on the journey to Greece he promised me a treat. "Come sometime and I'll give you the five-dollar tour myself," he said. So here we were and part of the joy was just being with Lynda.

We arrived in Kansas City humming, "Everything's up to date in Kansas City,/They've gone about as fur as they can go," and feeling gay and silly. There was no crowd at the airport. We felt deliciously alone. We drove to Independence and there, at the entrance to the Library, a simple, brick structure situated on a beautifully landscaped hill, we met President and Mrs. Truman and a large crowd of townspeople and tourists and the press. Here the photographers were in full array, but not the least bit bothersome.

We had the most wonderful trip through the Library anybody could hope to have, with President Truman conducting us. I especially loved the cartoons—those caustic or humorous capsules of history. President Truman told me how many hundred original cartoon drawings he had.

Each one of the Presidents was represented there by a picture and an original document signed by the President. I loved the choice of documents. From Thomas Jefferson was a request to Congress for funds to subsidize the Lewis and Clark Expedition; from Andrew Jackson, a pardon issued to Sam Houston for having assaulted a Congressman, for which offense he was instructed to pay a five-hundred-dollar fine; from Franklin D. Roosevelt was the Pearl Harbor Message, written in his own hand with a good many words scratched out and rewritten; and from President Truman himself was the Victory Day Proclamation.

Something any lover of the White House was certain to notice was the mantel, removed from the State Dining Room in the White House during its renovation—the mantel bearing the inscription of John Adams: "I PRAY HEAVEN TO BESTOW THE BEST OF BLESSINGS ON THIS HOUSE AND ALL THAT SHALL HEREAFTER INHABIT IT. MAY NONE BUT HONEST AND WISE MEN EVER RULE UNDER THIS ROOF."

There was a great mural in the Library by Thomas Hart Benton, called "Independence and the Opening of the West," which I liked very much. But I thought the colors were awfully bright. MY West is muted brown and green and gray, and blue and white. There was also an exact replica of the Office of the President during Truman's term. How many succeeding Presidents may copy this idea?

The most delightful aspect of all, I think, is the fact that in the auditorium President Truman meets and talks to busloads of school children who come all summer long to visit the Library. He says he spends several hours a day, three or four days a week, in the summertime talking to young students about the Office of the Presidency. In a reading room we saw a dozen or so students or scholars using documents from his archives.

One of the most poignant things I saw was a letter from former President Hoover to Truman, thanking him for appointing him to some commission. President Hoover spoke of going back to the work he knew best—public service—after a long interim of not having been called upon in the preceding Administration. Let me remember that lesson.

Finally, we went to a big storeroom, full of the odds and ends that one accumulates in office. I can already visualize how full such a room would be for us. It was a delightful tour, not to be equaled. At its conclusion I gave President Truman a flag that had stood in the study in Blair House during the years he lived there.

Then we went with Mrs. Truman to their old-fashioned white house, freshly painted, comfortably settled among the trees, with a wrought-iron fence around it. How many like it up and down the Main Streets of America! We had a soft drink while we looked at the pictures of Margaret and their three grandchildren, and the Greta Kempton portraits of Mrs. Truman, Margaret, and President Truman. So little does their house seem affected by the years they spent in the White House! Mrs. Truman was serene, happy, assured, rather gingery.

We drove back to the Muehlebach Hotel, where I got the latest news from Lyndon. Before I had left the White House he had been uncertain whether he would go to Texas for the weekend or stay in Washington. The news relayed to me was that he had left the White House in the early afternoon, was already at the Ranch, and wanted me to come on the courier plane.

About 6:30 President and Mrs. Truman arrived at the Presidential Suite and we had a drink—Mrs. Truman, too—and it was a delightful moment when the President put his drink down, went to the piano, and played Chopin for a few moments. He reiterated that he wanted to do whatever he could to help Lyndon. I am so proud that he likes him.

President Truman told us one ridiculous story about a priest who got lost on a walking trip through the Ozark Mountains, stopped at a cabin, and asked the farmer if he could have some supper. The farmer looked at him rather angrily and said, "No. I don't like your religion." The priest explained that he had been walking a long time and was very hungry and he felt sure the farmer would be kind enough to give him something to

1963–1964

*Address to Alliance for
Progress Members in
East Room, November
26, with Mrs. Kennedy
and Mrs. Johnson. LBJ
Library Photo by Cecil
Stoughton, 7A-1-WH63.*

TOP: *Congressman Bob Poage, Mrs. Johnson, Nellie and John Connally at the Governor's Mansion in Austin, December 24. LBJ Library Photo by Yoichi Okamoto, W249-5A.* BOTTOM: *Answering mail at The Elms during the transition, l. to r., Wendy Marcus, Mrs. Oscar Chapman, Mrs. Johnson, Mrs. Eugene McCarthy, Mrs. Everett Hutchinson, Mrs. Hale Boggs, Mrs. Frank Church. LBJ Library Photo by Cecil Stoughton, 16A-2-WH63.*

Family Gallery for Special Joint Session of Congress, November 27.
LBJ Library Photo by Cecil Stoughton, 9A-11-WH63.

LEFT, TOP: *A visit with Edward Steichen and Carl Sandburg in the Lincoln Room. LBJ Library Photo by Cecil Stoughton, 31899-11.* BOTTOM: *Presentation of the John Adams urn in the East Room. LBJ Library Photo by Robert Knudsen, 32634-2.*

RIGHT, TOP: *Warrie Lynn Smith and Lynda on the South Lawn. LBJ Library Photo by Cecil Stoughton, 72-19-WH64.* MIDDLE: *A moment of ease at the Ranch. LBJ Library Photo by Yoichi Okamoto, W262-18A.* BOTTOM: *A Christmas party in the Blue Room for special holiday guests — the city's underprivileged children. LBJ Library Photo by Robert Knudsen, C1061-5.*

FACING PAGE, TOP: *Rafting the Snake River with Grand Tetons in background, with Brent Eastman (l.) and Stewart Udall. LBJ Library Photo, 33026-17.* BOTTOM, *On Pacific seashore with Secret Service agents—l. to r., Woody Taylor, Jerry McKinney, Jerry Kivett. LBJ Library Photo by Robert Knudsen, D2626-30A.*

Procession for funeral of King Paul in Athens, Greece, March 12. Mrs. Johnson with Prince Rainier of Monaco and Prince Philip of Great Britain. LBJ Library Photo, 31691-9.

Lady Bird Johnson met by Lyndon B. Johnson at the conclusion of the Lady Bird Special Whistlestop Campaign, October 12, 1964. LBJ Library Photo by Cecil Stoughton, 412-4-WH64.

eat. The farmer felt a little abashed and said, "All right. Come on in." The priest sat down at the table, ate his supper, and when he looked up at the mantel there was a picture of Pope Pius! So the priest said to the farmer, "Would you please explain to me, sir, why, if you dislike the Catholic Church so much, you've got that picture of Pope Pius up there above the mantel?" The farmer looked at him incredulously and said, "Do you mean that's who that is? Well, I'll be gol-durned—the salesman that sold it to me said it was Harry Truman in his ceremonial Masonic clothes!"

At dinner we talked about the reconstruction of the White House, which took place during his Administration. The Trumans said good-by to us at 9 o'clock. I had enjoyed the visit so much, and the nicest part was having Lynda Bird enter into everything fully. It was time to go to the airport to catch the courier plane en route to the Ranch to join Lyndon. The question arose whether Lynda Bird should fly back on a commercial airline arriving in Washington about 4 o'clock in the morning, or whether she should go with me to the Ranch, always a rather uncertain place to get away from. She decided to fly with me, and we had two swift and pleasant hours—and then down the runway and into the hangar where the white golf cart waited for us.

Friday, July 24

THE WHITE HOUSE

This was a man-killer of a day for Lyndon. At 3:30 I watched one of his confrontations, a televised press conference, the sort of thing you must steel yourself to go through, almost as you would to face a firing squad. I watched it on TV in my bedroom, every nerve aquiver with sympathy. Actually, I thought this press conference was one of the best he has held. Bryson Rash used the expression that Lyndon had "mouse-trapped" Goldwater by leaving him nothing to say about his appointment with Lyndon later in the same day when he said, "Of course we will talk about Civil Rights." They asked Lyndon if he thought this would be a rough campaign and he smiled and said, "All campaigns are rough." I thought he emerged with his scalp and his dignity.

He practically had to leave on roller skates to make it to the Mansion for a reception for labor leaders. Between two hundred and fifty and three hundred of them had been invited for a report on the State of the Nation, comparable to the stag luncheons that Lyndon has held for business leaders. One of the Aides told me he thought they had set a record for shaking hands. Lyndon arrived late because of the press conference, had to leave early because of his 5:30 appointment with Goldwater, and he raced through this reception in a good deal less than an hour.

Yearning for exercise during the evening, I persuaded Lynda Bird to go to the bowling alley in EOB with me, and I did the best I ever have— 117 to Lynda Bird's very good 147 or thereabouts. She doesn't look athletic, but she's competitive and she does well in most everything. I'm improving, I hope.

Later on, we went to Lyndon's office, Lynda and I, and found him in the little room, with some of the staff. Lynda left in a few minutes and I sat down and talked with them. They had been discussing Vice Presidential nominees—Rusk, McNamara, Kennedy, McCarthy, Humphrey, Muskie—the favorite guessing game of the Capitol these days. Finally, I pried Lyndon loose, taking him home for dinner at 10 o'clock.

The nicest thing in this long and eventful day was the news about Luci, beginning with the wire we had sent her: "DEAR LUCI, THREE OF YOUR FANS WILL BE THINKING OF YOU. WE ARE ALL SO PROUD OF YOU." In the paper today was a report of her two performances at Interlochen yesterday—one in the afternoon for all the students of the National Music Camp and their families—about 3600 people—and one at night, an even more successful one, for the public—the proceeds of these concerts go to scholarships for the Interlochen center of music, dance, drama, and art.

The photographs today were delightful . . . Luci and Van Cliburn in camp uniforms—Luci had on navy blue knickers, light blue socks, and light blue shirt—no glasses, thank goodness—and her narration was delivered with pixie gestures of glee, mock fright, or whatever the passage in *Peter and the Wolf* called for.

At the end of the number she decided to give a little impromptu speech. (This is the point at which I would have shivered with apprehension!) I was pleased to find out that it consisted chiefly of telling everybody in the camp how wonderful they were—the orchestra, Van Cliburn, the founder, President Joseph Maddy, everybody. So Luci gets an A for Interlochen!

This morning we went to the National City Christian Church and when we got back we decided to walk around the grounds, with Him and Her on their long leashes racing before us, tugging Lyndon along. At the Southwest Gate about a hundred tourists were gathered and Lyndon said, "Would you all like to come in and walk around the block with us?" while I flinched. I don't know what went on in the minds of the Secret Service agents. But the guards opened the gate, in streamed the people, and down the road past the fountains we trailed, Him and Her utterly delighted until they found a black Scottish terrier in the arms of his owner. Then they set up a yipping and barking—a dog fight on Sunday on the grounds of the White House is not something I particularly want to be remembered for! I tried to hold onto Him's collar, while the Scottie growled ominously, but in a much more dignified fashion than Him. Her, bless her, soon returned to her nice juicy bone and, what with wagging her tail and running around acting friendly with everyone, was the hit of the morning. We strolled across to the Southeast Gate and there was another group of about a hundred. Lyndon asked THEM if they would like to come and walk around with us. I really wish I knew what went on in the minds of those people! All of those who expressed themselves were flabbergasted and utterly delighted.

In the afternoon we looked at Gene McCarthy on television. Handsome, humorous, but a little too verbose. I like a few yes-and-no answers thrown in. In the evening we had a pleasant escape from the White House. We went to dinner at Betty and Bill Fulbright's. The Restons were there; and lovely Phyllis Dillon and the Secretary; and Senator Russell—a rare pleasure to see him twice in the same weekend. Betty has that knack of creating a special aura for a party. Casual atmosphere with interesting people, and her back-porch setting is like being in a summer forest.

The Restons had been at the Republican Convention. I asked him to tell me about it, expecting a large collection of anecdotes and analyses. He said, "Just one thing. Work like Hell." I had nearly finished Bill Fulbright's book *Old Myths and New Realities*, and we discussed his views on De Gaulle and China and the minor accommodations of Consuls and student exchange that we are increasingly making with the Iron Curtain countries.

I never look at Dick Russell without admiration and without thinking of his great talent that I wish were put to more vigorous use. His withdrawal, his aloofness, is his own doing and began sometime after his unsuccessful bid for the Presidency in 1952, which changed him a great deal, or so it seems to me. Nobody can be more charming or express himself more lucidly, and sometimes more humorously.

We returned to the White House in time to meet a radiant Luci, fresh from her triumph at Interlochen and tasting the sweet wine of success. And the nicest thing about it was that she thought all those youngsters were so wonderful.

Saturday, August 1

Mayor Wagner and his two sons, Robert, Jr., and Duncan, arrived about noon today. This is one of the times when it is so marvelous to have Lynda Bird here, because we dispatched her to greet them. They came just as Lyndon and I had to leave for a memorial service for Senator Clair Engle at Fort Myer Chapel.

The Reverend Frederick Brown Harris, Chaplain of the Senate, held this brief, non-denominational service. What a lot of them he has presided over, for the living and the dead! Lyndon and I sat in the front row on one side, and Lou Engle, looking stonily calm, sat with Clair's brother, who is so like Clair. When it was over everybody waited for us to leave, but I asked Dr. Harris if I could step over and say a word to Lou. She has lived through a tortured year. She has been very courageous, and part of the worst of it has been the pressure from California leaders for the Senator to get out of the race.

I had a self-indulgent afternoon. I read a book about Wilson's last days—*When the Cheering Stopped*—not exactly good therapy for anybody who finds himself involved in the Presidency, because it is proof that it is a killing job. Wilson's heartbreak over the failure of the Congress to accept the League of Nations is described. The story is poignantly told, but intrinsic in the failure is his blindness in not working with the Senate long, long before the time for acceptance came. To me, Wilson emerges from the books as a noble and idealistic man, but a man with no concept of the role of the legislative body in the nation's government.

For dinner with Mayor Wagner, we had invited Secretary of Health, Education and Welfare Tony Celebrezze and his wife Anne, so soft-voiced and gentle, and Labor Secretary Willard Wirtz and Jane. (He is fast becoming one of my favorites because he is delightfully witty and incisive.) The two departments of these men are most closely associated with the problems Mayor Wagner faces in New York.

We sat on the Truman Balcony and talked of Mayor Wagner's "three-day vacation." Poor man, he was in Majorca where he had expected a restful two weeks, but he was summoned immediately back into the maelstrom. He believes that the Reverend Martin Luther King is the only leader the Negro people will listen to. According to Mayor Wagner Dr. King has an emotional hold over them that Roy Wilkins and Whitney Young have not achieved.

Mayor Wagner described the heavy unemployment in Harlem. He said the city had promised to give thirteen hundred jobs to youngsters out of school, working in the parks and at various clean-up jobs, but this is just a drop in the bucket. He said the city had allotted a million-dollar budget for a rat eradication program. He spoke, disheartened, of the enormous quantity of public housing in New York City and how the houses deteriorate after the tenants have been in them for a few years. He painted a discouraging picture, but the more he talked the more I felt the city is fighting to solve its problems. As an outsider, I had wondered why New York did not have a people's review board of police brutality. I asked him and he said if such a board were instituted, the morale of his police department would drop to zero overnight.

Tuesday, August 4

Today was a momentous day, and yet so many perfectly ordinary things happened in it. You are aware that great decisions are being shaped, some completely beyond the control of any of us, some that have to be decided by the man closest to me, and yet you go right along doing the trivial things, because you must. First in the morning we said good-by to the Bobby Russell family. We had had a wonderful visit with Senator Russell's nephew and five darling children.

On Tuesday, Lyndon always has lunch with the Secretary of Defense, the Secretary of State, and McGeorge Bundy. (We've come to call them the Tuesday lunches.) Today they stayed a long time. As McGeorge Bundy passed me in the hall afterward, he was looking extraordinarily grave. I remember asking him something which brought forth a portentous answer —one which left me apprehensive, of what, I did not know. But I can't think of anybody I would rather have by our side as we wade into troubles than those three.

In the course of the late evening, cars began to come and go through the Southwest Gate. Lyndon spent an hour and a half in conference with Congressional leaders, with the Cabinet and the Joint Chiefs of Staff. There was discussion about when to issue a statement to television. Lyndon's problem was when to tell the people of the nation what had happened today: Word had come that two United States destroyers had been attacked in the Gulf of Tonkin by North Vietnamese PT boats. One had been attacked on Sunday, and we had not responded. After the second attack, today, we felt we could not ignore it. Lyndon had ordered air action against the gunboats and their bases in North Vietnam.

At first there was talk of making the statement at 7 o'clock in the evening, then at 8 o'clock. Lyndon delayed, wanting to be sure that we had accurate information about where our planes were before word was released to the world. Finally, at 10:40, I brought him, McGeorge Bundy, and Jack Valenti over here to have dinner. I sent trays to the girls in the office. (Bless the staff here for being so cooperative!) George Reedy dropped in for dessert, and finally, after 11 o'clock, Lyndon went on the air to make his statement, following word from the Defense Department that our planes had been launched and Hanoi knew about it.

I thought it was an excellent statement. I liked the lines "Yet our response, for the present, will be limited and fitting. We Americans know, although others appear to forget, the risk of spreading conflict. We still seek no wider war." Lyndon said he had instructed Ambassador Stevenson to raise this matter immediately and urgently before the Security Council of the United Nations. And he said he had met with the leaders of Congress to request them to pass a Resolution making it clear that our government is united in its determination to take all necessary measures in support of freedom and in defense of peace in Southeast Asia.

He ended with, "It is a solemn responsibility to have to order even limited military action by forces whose overall strength is as vast and as awesome as those of the United States of America, but it is my considered conviction, shared throughout your government, that firmness in the right is indispensable today for peace; that firmness will always be measured. Its mission is peace."

When it was over, I had a certain feeling of pride and of release. Perhaps for Truman, Eisenhower, Kennedy, there were long series of such days. Obviously, until now, we have survived them all. But it's a perilous path to tread.

Thursday, August 6

One of the most interesting events this morning consisted of sitting with Lyndon and Mayor Daley—Lyndon propped up in bed, the Mayor in the rocking chair, all of us with coffee—and the Mayor telling us how he hoped to handle the problem of a race riot in Chicago. He said he would not permit his policemen to wear steel helmets. They would simply wear caps—he hoped each one would look like the friend down the block instead of a soldier. He had called in various segments of society—the communications people—newspapers, radio, and TV—Negro leaders, white businessmen, church groups, and talked over problems and possible solutions. He said he did this on a year-round basis, before a crisis became imminent. The crisis is imminent now, because everybody is on edge, waiting to see when race riots will break out in Chicago. All of this was described in a soft, mild, smooth, most determined voice. I would not want to put myself in opposition to that man, and I admire him tremendously.

The television cameras' and newspapers' ability to egg on and stir up dissension and trouble by showing pictures of a helmeted policeman with a big stick in his hand, standing over a fourteen-year-old boy flat on his back on the street, or police dogs jumping on women, has certainly provided some of the yeast in this rising mass of trouble we are having at present. If Mayor Daley can obtain cooperation from the TV networks and the newspapers, then he certainly deserves the Nobel Peace Prize.

At a little past 11 this morning there was a lawn ceremony to greet U Thant. The welcoming ceremony took place, for a change, in the Rose Garden, with the podium on the steps, flag to one side, band under the magnolia tree, guests standing all around. There was no military pomp and display, a very delicate touch, I thought, for a United Nations ceremony.

U Thant spent an hour in conference with Lyndon, and when he emerged I took him on a tour of the flower gardens, followed, to my amazement, by an entourage of ten or twelve people, including Lyndon and Adlai Stevenson. I pointed out President Kennedy's Magnolia soulangianas, the gaillardia or Indian blanket that grows in masses—wild—in

Texas in the spring, the gloriosa daisies which are a fabulous flash of color in all four corners of the garden this summer, the white roses for which the garden is named but which are really very few in number, and the lovely lavender asters which, I understand, grow in U Thant's native Burma.

Her and Him came out and accompanied Lyndon and were more prominently the object of the cameramen's interest, thank Heaven, than U Thant and I. It is rather difficult to carry on a quiet intimate conversation and explain a garden when the tour burgeons into an entourage, so I wouldn't say it was a glowing success. But I showed him some beautiful pictures of the way the garden had looked when Mrs. Kennedy and Mrs. Mellon were first plotting it, and of its spring dress and its fall dress, both of which I think more resplendent than its midsummer dress.

Meanwhile, our gubernatorial houseguests arrived, and I went to meet Bernice and Pat Brown and to take them to their room, and also the John Daltons of Missouri and the Matthew Welshes of Indiana.

In the evening we entertained at a State Dinner for U Thant, probably the last one during our tenure here. We greeted U Thant and the Ambassador from Burma and Madame On Sein on the North Portico a little past 8, took them upstairs to the Yellow Room, along with Adlai Stevenson, Dean and Virginia Rusk, Bob McNamara, the Angier Dukes, the Ralph Bunches, and the Henry Cabot Lodges.

Our gifts to U Thant reflected history current—copies of moon shot photographs taken by Ranger VII just before its strike on the moon on July 31, in a leather case with the Presidential Seal—and history past—a letter written by Andrew Jackson in 1829 to his Postmaster General: "So long as we take the law for our guide and justice the end in view, we will meet with the support of the people."

As for U Thant, he gave us the most magnificent silver tea and coffee service from Burma that I ever expect to see—elaborately ornamented with the animals and flowers of Burma, and with, of course, the elephant in great prominence—rather ironic for a Democratic President, I suppose, but art rises above politics.

This time we all went down the stairs en masse, following Lyndon's instructions, and lined up behind the colors, with Lyndon taking U Thant and I, Adlai Stevenson.

I had U Thant on my right at dinner and the Ambassador of Burma on my left. Betty Fulbright was a great help in keeping the conversation lively. Lyndon had Mrs. Rusk on one side and Mrs. On Sein on the other and, close by, Ambassador Stevenson and the Secretary of State. Sometime before the evening was over I noticed Lyndon leaning over the two ladies, engaging in a long serious conversation with the two men. Oh, the way of husbands the world over! Mrs. On Sein, small and delicate, said not a word and I struggled for some way to communicate with her.

I wore my yellow chiffon gown with the beaded bodice. I thought it would go well with all the white and yellow of the room and the yellow, white, and pink of stock, roses, carnations, daisies, and chrysanthemums in little bamboo vermeil containers on the round tables. Toward the end of the dinner there was that moment of charm and enchantment when the Air Force's Strolling Strings came in. I think that the heart of every guest is always lifted by their music!

Before launching into his toast, Lyndon said he could not introduce all the guests, but that he would like to present two Republicans and two Democrats as being outstanding, each with a few well-chosen words: Senator Fulbright, Chairman of the Foreign Relations Committee, Senator Dirksen, Minority Leader of the Senate, Adlai Stevenson, U.S. Representative to the United Nations, and Henry Cabot Lodge, former Representative to the United Nations.

Later we adjourned for dancing and champagne in the Great Hall and Foyer, and I don't believe anybody had more fun than the Henry Cabot Lodges. She was looking rather thin and worn after her stay in Vietnam, but was gay and gracious.

Lyndon had to leave at the earliest respectable hour after our guest of honor had departed, to talk over the latest developments with Dean Rusk and McGeorge Bundy, but I stayed and danced until about 12:30. And so did Lynda Bird—I think it was the presence of Gregory Peck that lured her in!

Late August

As I record this later, the month of August unrolls in my mind as a crescendo of events: an exhilarating trip to the West—to Idaho, Utah, Wyoming; to New England—Maine and Vermont . . . There were a host of visitors, including John Connally and Billy Graham and the comforting presence of Jim Cain and Willis Hurst . . . I did TV shows with Walter Cronkite and Howard K. Smith. But the end of August approached inexorably and with it the dates of the Democratic Convention. Time ran out to weigh and ponder and consider and there was only time to do.

I spent the morning of August 25 working on mail and some remarks for a Press Brunch scheduled for the Convention, choosing clothes to take with me. Luci had already gone to Atlantic City. Lyndon had lunched with Dean Rusk, Bob McNamara, and McGeorge Bundy about one. Then he spent some time alone in his room with the shades drawn, but he did not sleep. He made many telephone calls. We talked some. It was the same old refrain. He did not believe he should accept the nomination. He did not want to go to Atlantic City. I do not remember hours I ever found harder. . . . At one point during the afternoon I went walking on the South grounds with Lynda. We lay down under one of the big, spreading evergreens and talked and talked. Sometime during the afternoon, I went back inside and wrote Lyndon a letter:

THE WHITE HOUSE
WASHINGTON

The President

Personal

Beloved—
    You are as brave a man as Harry Truman—or FDR—or Lincoln. You can go on to find some peace, some achievement amidst all the pain. You have been strong, patient, determined beyond any words of mine to express.
    I honor you for it. So does most of the country.
    To step out now would be wrong for your country, and I can see nothing but a lonely wasteland for your future. Your friends would be frozen in embarrassed silence and your enemies jeering.
    I am not afraid of *Time* or lies or losing money or defeat.
    In the final analysis I can't carry any of the burdens you talked of—so I know it's only *your* choice. But I know you are as brave as any of the thirty-five.

I love you always
Bird

The answer to my letter came on the night of August 27 when Lyndon stood before the Democratic National Convention and accepted the nomination of his party for President of the United States.

Fall 1964

Abigail McCarthy came over this morning for a cup of coffee.
Among the Senate wives, she is one of my favorites—for character, intelligence, and just plain goodness. She had heard I
was worried about how she might feel about the political
developments and she wanted me to know that Lyndon's
choice of Humphrey for Vice President would make no difference in our friendship. She couldn't have been more clear-
spoken and gracious about it, and she said this would make no
difference in her friendship for the Humphreys either.

But there was that undertone there. For a week or so there
had been a sense of strain among their friends and promoters,
trying to push them on or step up animosity or make them
feel hurt with each other or with us. That's something we've
lived with all our lives—the press and even our friends trying
to pit us against a number of associates with whom we've
worked. Once against Allan Shivers; for many years against
Speaker Rayburn; for years, more or less, against John Con-

193

nally; and later against President Kennedy. One has to learn to ride out such squalls with a smooth sail, and I intend to do all I can to remind both the McCarthys how much we value their friendship.

At 11:30 a group arrived to talk about my proposed Whistlestop tour, which would begin in Washington and continue, as first outlined, forever across the world, or so it seemed to me! The original schedule lasted ten days and covered fourteen states. At the meeting were Liz and Bess; Scooter Miller, who will be a hostess on the train; and Woody Woodward —oh, indignity of all things, this Vice President of an airline has been asked to help manage a Train Trip! Joe Moran, who will be in charge of advance men was there; and the transportation experts from the White House; and two actual train men, one of them a Mr. Dewey Long, who had arranged President Truman's famous Whistlestop tour back in 1948.

We met for three hours. First, by my insistence and after much discussion, we whittled the trip down to four days. Next, we discussed whether the tour should end in Tallahassee, Florida, or go on through Mississippi, Alabama, and into New Orleans. I was anxious to concentrate heavily on North Carolina and give Virginia more stops than we had planned. We all agreed that we should bear down on Georgia. Bill Brawley, who is in charge of the campaign for the Democratic National Committee in the South, was in favor of continuing on, into New Orleans, and that is what we finally agreed on. It was a profitable, long session, and I only found when it was over, how dead tired I was.

In the afternoon I had a long talk with Luci, whom I have been missing. Tomorrow she is leaving for New Orleans to launch a ship. I had so much to catch up on with her and we had a satisfactory hour together. She has grown more this last year than she has in any comparable two or three years before, but I remember age seventeen as being very special.

Finally, just as it was getting dark, I went out to the South grounds for a walk, my favorite thing to do. We had asked Jake Pickle and Sherman Birdwell to have dinner with us. They passed me as I walked around the second lap and got out of their car and walked with me. Lyndon joined us for the third lap and then we went upstairs for a quiet, homefolks dinner, with two who had started out with us in the National Youth Administration days in 1936.

Today I began working on the Whistlestop trip through the South in October. I put in calls to the Governors of the states I would travel through, and to most of the Senators of those states. I thought it was only courteous to let them know I'm coming to their states, and I hope for their cooperation. Governor Albertis Harrison of Virginia said that he and Mrs. Harrison would be glad to ride with me on the train through Virginia and would be co-chairmen for their state.

I put in several calls simultaneously and then I answered them as they came in. Tactically, that wasn't quite the right thing to do. I should have called Senator Byrd before I called anyone else. Dealing with him is a matter of instinct—it's not written in a book anywhere—but I think I have the instinct. This time I didn't heed it. I reached his two daughters-in-law, Helen (Mrs. Richard Byrd) and Gretchen (Mrs. Harry Byrd, Jr.), before I got to him. Helen sounded eager and interested and said she would call me back. Gretchen said she thought she would probably have to accompany her husband to an Associated Press meeting in New York but she would write me. When I found the Senator, he couldn't have been more jovial and courteous and darling, but when I mentioned, in quite a straightforward manner, the purpose of my call, an invisible silken curtain fell across his voice. He said that because of the death of Mrs. Byrd he and his sons had decided not to participate in any public affairs for some time. This is very understandable, and besides, it's not in me to be hurt at Senator Byrd.

Senator Robertson regretted. He was going antelope hunting in Montana—a lovely place, and I'm sure he'll have fun. In North Carolina, Governor and Mrs. Terry Sanford said they would be delighted to be co-chairmen and would ride the train. An immediate call to their successor and somewhat hostile fellow Democrat, Governor-nominee Dan Moore, and Mrs. Moore, failed to find them in. That's one of the many schisms I will encounter, and I shall have to pursue the Moores and invite them to ride the train also. Both Senator Sam Ervin and Senator Everett Jordan and their wives answered right away, "Yes, indeed." They said they would be delighted to ride the train with me through North Carolina, and Senator Jordan had several suggestions about people to call, towns to go to, and things to do.

The most amusing call was the one to Senator Strom Thurmond. Here, too, I quickly gave my reason for the call. I said I recognized fully the many differences that divided him and Lyndon ideologically, but I knew they were both Democrats and I would be proud and happy to have him by my side when I went through the State of South Carolina. Senator Thurmond said he had to make a really basic decision within the next two weeks and, though he thanked me very much, he must regret. That sounds interesting, and we'll see. The decision could be concerned with any one of several things—the old road of Dixiecrat, bolting the party in some fashion, or complete severance with the Democrats and going over to the Republicans.

On the other hand, Senator Olin Johnston said, "Why, yes, indeed, Gladys and I will board the train at the first stop, unless the Senate is in session." Gladys was in the hospital right now, he said, but he felt sure she'd be well enough to get out and go by then. And he certainly wanted to say that he had two daughters who were mighty good hard-working Democrats, and they ought to be in on it. He is a very courageous man and has shown his bravery times without number.

Also, South Carolina Governor and Mrs. Donald Russell accepted as co-chairmen for their state. Mrs. Russell is going to take on the difficult job of being co-chairman for the whole journey, along with Lindy Boggs, lending a lustrous name and, according to all I hear about her, a good organizing ability.

So here we go, marching through Georgia!

Not at all to my surprise, the dearest of them all, Dick Russell, said no, he would very likely be traveling, but that he would be glad to lend us one or two advance men from his staff. He was sure that the State of Georgia would welcome me courteously and happily. He also had advice about where to go. He was interested and I think it very likely that at the last moment he may even ride the train or come out for us. His differences with Lyndon on Civil Rights are those of a man ten years older and deeply imbedded in the mores of his state.

Senator Herman Talmadge accepted if his schedule permits. That is an elastic and dependable phrase, but he said Betty, "for sure," would ride the train all the way with us. I talked to Mrs. Carl Sanders, and she and Governor Sanders are among our strongest friends on the whole route. They will be glad to be co-chairmen for the state, and will ride the train.

And so into Florida. Here I found Senator Spessard Holland deeply engaged in a race of his own, with many dates throughout the month. He thought he could be with us at Tallahassee, but could not be with us the rest of the trip. George and Rosemary Smathers will travel on the train the whole trip. Governor and Mrs. Farris Bryant were among the most available and interested. A call to Governor-nominee and Mrs. Hayden Burns did not find them in at the time.

And now for Alabama, the state most adamantly against us and the state with which I have the most personal bonds. There was no use in calling Governor George Wallace. I doubt it would even be courteous to do so. I called Senator Lister Hill in the hospital, and he and Henrietta said yes, if Lister was well enough they would go with us through the state. Senator John Sparkman said yes, indeed, he would be "mighty glad to"—unless Congress was in session, and, if so, Ivo would go.

And then Mississippi. I was not sure whether I should call Governor Paul Johnson. Senator John Stennis said no, he thought he could do more good in a different way. He is up for reelection, and faces a difficult time, I hear. Senator James Eastland I could not reach. He was in Mississippi.

And then the last state, Louisiana, in which we are to wind up. I reached Governor John McKeithen, father of the attractive Fox Mc-Keithen whom Luci Baines had talked so much about after her ship-christening trip. He too declined. He felt that he had better not be co-chairman for the State of Louisiana or ride on the train. He said that he was "working for the Democrats, you understand," but that he could accomplish more by doing it in another way. I hung up with the feeling that he faced a formidable and angry populace and was not about to take them on in the outspoken bulldog way of an Olin Johnston.

Russell Long was in Tokyo. When I reached Senator Allen Ellender he said yes, indeed, he would be happy to ride with us on the train, getting on in Biloxi, Mississippi, or wherever we decided, and continuing on to New Orleans.

This afternoon the Cabinet wives came in for tea in the Yellow Oval Room. Virginia Rusk, Margy McNamara, Mrs. John Gronouski, whom I had not known well before, Lee Udall, Jane Freeman, Jane Wirtz, Anne Celebrezze, and Mrs. Nicholas Katzenbach. And to represent Muriel Humphrey, her Press Secretary, a young, attractive girl named Pat Griffith. From the Democratic National Committee there were Margaret Price, Carrie Davis of the Women's Speakers' Bureau, and Scooter Miller, volunteer for many endeavors.

The purpose of the meeting was to talk over what we could all do in the campaign for the next seven weeks: to discuss the invitations we were receiving from all over the country, and to decide who could most effectively and happily fill these engagements. Many of them were invitations to me which I must regret, and it would be very nice if we were able to suggest that some Cabinet wife was available. The two most politically active and astute are, in my opinion, Jane Freeman and Anne Celebrezze, both of whom have been making trips to Democratic gatherings for several weeks. Jane Wirtz is very eager and intelligent, but not wanting to make speeches. And Margy McNamara, one of the most valuable of all in certain areas, for instance, Texas and, I would think, parts of Michigan. She is ardently enthusiastic. I do not know to what degree she would be restrained because of her husband's job, but I certainly hope the right kind of appearances will be worked out for her.

AFTER REREADING NOTES AND CLIPPINGS OF 1964

As I read back over my diary and prepare it for publication, I am increasingly dismayed that I missed recording some very important days and nights—including the whole campaign. Alas, there is no help for it. We were living so rapidly that I was simply too busy and too spent to have an hour or a moment with my recorder. The envelopes with the daily calendar, clippings, and mementos are neatly labeled and, alas, untouched.

I remember the nomination, and the election, with no high sense of elation. I felt pride, and great happiness for the thousands of people who had worked so hard, but I think my chief emotions were simply satisfaction in people's faith in Lyndon and a renewed determination to help him use the next four years to the best of his ability and to make some steps forward.

There were moments of high elation during the campaign. I wouldn't take anything for the Whistlestop through the South— forty-seven stops in four days! Scores of times since that October as I have stood in a receiving line someone would come up and say, "I rode with you on the Whistlestop"—and we would clasp hands with a warmth and a rush of memories of that very special time, those four most dramatic days in my political life. And the flying Whistlestops to other points of the country. You see your country at such a time as you can never see it any other way. Thinking back on that montage of depots, faces, signs—such delightful signs—my mind always turns to the little town in North Carolina—was it Ahoskie?—where a woman pushed through the crowd to grab my hand and said, "I got up at 3 o'clock this morning and milked twenty cows so I could get here by train time!"

That may be as close as many of those people ever get to government—to the people connected with government—and I am glad we met and touched.

But for my records, I shall have to be content with the train and plane schedules and the clippings.

Saturday, November 14

Lyndon spent the morning talking with Secretaries Celebrezze and Wirtz. They are the fifth and sixth Cabinet members respectively who have been here to confer with him during eleven days of alleged rest after the campaign. While Lyndon was talking with one, I had a chance to talk with the other, enjoying it tremendously.

Tony Celebrezze has been reading, as we all have, reports in various columns that he is leaving the Cabinet, presumably because he has not been asked to stay on. About the third or fourth time one reads such speculations, one begins to feel a little hurt or frustrated or uncertain, and then, maybe angry. He said he knew I would understand how he felt, because he remembered the sort of stories they were writing about Lyndon in the six months preceding President Kennedy's assassination. I do remember those stories. "What Has Happened to Lyndon Johnson?" and speculations as to whether he would be asked to go on the ticket again with President Kennedy, most of them indicating that very likely he would not. One of the most undignified things that happens to a public official these days is being made a bone of contention by the press.

Lyndon says Celebrezze does his homework, has his heart in the legislative programs of his department, and works with Congress with more diligence and instinctive know-how than almost any department head in the Cabinet. But Celebrezze wants to become a judge when a suitable judgeship opens up. This is a prickly interim, but the facts just have to speak for themselves as they come out.

Tony Celebrezze said that his department was the second largest in the government, both in terms of money handled and personnel. Health,

Education and Welfare is a sort of a Mother Hubbard, covering practically everything. Tony's department is one of the few government agencies whose budget will go up in the next fiscal year, with Lyndon's blessing. Much of the increase is necessitated by new education aid measures pushed through Congress this year, and so earnestly urged by Lyndon. I remember being stopped in the receiving line one evening by an eminent educator, who said to me, "Do you realize that your husband has done more for education than any other President?" Well, that's something I'd like him to be known for.

Bill Wirtz has the ability to clothe his thoughts—and very sharp, clear thoughts they are—in dramatic language that you remember. He outlined his problem this way: Next year three and a half million American boys and girls will become eighteen years old, one million more than this year. Unless we do more about this situation, he said, one out of every seven of those three and a half million will have a door slammed in his face —a job door or a college door. Two hundred thousand of those who will try to get into college won't be able to find a place because of lack of room, and three hundred thousand looking for jobs won't be able to find jobs because of lack of training. He calls his program—that is, what he proposes to do about this situation—Operation Birthright.

Bill has made some of the best speeches during this campaign for the Democratic Party and has made a valuable contribution writing memoranda and material for Lyndon. I have come to feel quite close to him and most admiring.

This is a good lesson in the irreplaceable man. When Arthur Goldberg was Secretary of Labor I thought nobody could ever be as good. I was sorry to see him leave the fray and go to the ivory tower of the Supreme Court. I looked on any successor as bound to be second-rate and not able to measure up. I was wrong. Many different men can fit into the work of this country.

Secretary Celebrezze and Secretary Wirtz left around noon for a press conference in Austin and then were to fly back to Washington. I went down to the little house that was Lyndon's birthplace, to move the furniture around, as Lucia had sent out a truckload of furniture that had belonged to Lyndon's mother. I spent a couple of harried hours with our wonderful maintenance man, Mr. Klein, and James at the house, and then back to the airport to greet our new arrivals from New York—Dr. Stanton, Don Cook, Tom Watson, and our dear friend, Ed Weisl, with Eddie, Jr.

Through the afternoon I worked on plans for landscaping the little house where Lyndon was born. Just as the sun was sinking and the dramatic display I love best of the whole day at the Ranch—sunset— was flaming in the sky, I got in the car by myself—followed, of course, by the Secret Service man. I told "Volunteer" (the code word for the President) that I was driving, and found that Lyndon was at the Lewis place. I drove over there, leisurely. Sometimes it is very comforting to be by oneself. My life does not have enough of that these days.

Sunday, November 15

LBJ RANCH AND THE WHITE HOUSE

Morning dawned gray and wet, with only intermittent sunshine, making it much easier to leave Texas. We slept too late to go to church. About 9 o'clock I joined Ed Weisl, Sr., Frank Stanton, Don Cook, and Tom Watson at the dining room table for breakfast. It would be hard to find a quartet of more interesting men anywhere in America. Ed Weisl is our oldest friend among them—sage, warm, emotional. Ed has a roster of friends in New York in the world of finance, the entertainment milieu, and legal circles that would be hard to equal. He has been our adviser through the years when, as Lyndon says, we needed to do some "heavy lifting."

Dr. Frank Stanton, handsome, blond, always young-looking, is an interesting combination of successful business executive and intellectual— tough-minded enough to bring CBS to the top of the heap, and yet with something of "the artist and the scholar." He is imaginative and a potential pioneer in his own field, somewhat restrained by practical knowledge and appreciation of the balance sheet. Lyndon would love to have Frank serve in his Cabinet. I believe he would be an exemplary public servant, but I do not think he will accept the offer. Too many breaks with his business life would be necessary. And what of his wife? Would she want him to do it?

Don Cook, long-time counsel for Lyndon's Senate committees, off and on for many years, has risen from a modest position in the SEC to become head of one of the largest business corporations in the United States, American Electric Power Service. Now in New York, he is, I believe, leading a rich cultural life, enjoying the concerts, museums, plays and brilliant people that city has to offer—and he must have a sense of having reached the pinnacle of his business career. He is a capable lawyer, a first-class brain, and Lyndon hopes that he will accept a place in the Cabinet. It would give us such a feeling of safety to have a sensitive and important post in the hands of a man of Don's genuine excellence. But here again, to pull a man away from enjoying what he's worked to achieve all his life for a fraction of the salary, not to mention "the slings and arrows of outrageous fortune," is a difficult thing. It takes a willingness to serve that is rare and powerful. I hope very much that Don will accept, but I am not at all sure he will. Again, I wondered about his wife's reaction. Would she be willing for him to make the sacrifice? And then, there is, to us, the newest of this attractive quartet, Tom Watson, head of IBM. Lyndon is asking him to be Secretary of Commerce, replacing our dear friend Luther Hodges. He is tall, slim, handsome, patrician-looking. I admire him and like him and think he would be a substantial, high-caliber, well-received addition to the Cabinet. I believe the first priority in appointments should go to ability and the second to closeness and loyalty. He was a very good listener but had very little to say, albeit always charming throughout his stay.

We had lunch a little after one, and at 2 we accompanied our guests to the airport. I walked with Don and told him how much I hoped he was going to take the job in the Cabinet. He said, "This is the capstone of his career" (meaning Lyndon), and I replied, "But we can't make it good, we can't make the four years really first-class, unless we've got some good troops." Don said, "We'll find them. We'll have to find a way." I'd like to think that meant one of the generals among the troops would be Don. I do not know. Later on Lyndon told me his bet was that none of the three would accept. This is one of the hardest problems a President faces—finding good top executives—and I have sympathy on both sides.

Thinking back on it, I realized I had never spent a weekend hearing more interesting conversation. It had ranged from automation and how to spend leisure time to the theory of the land bridge across the Bering Straits.

We left by helicopter this afternoon for Bergstrom, and then took the plane to Andrews and by chopper to the White House lawn. I changed into my black theater suit en route, and we landed about 6:30 in the early dark on the White House lawn. This was our first return since the overwhelming victory of November 3. We were greeted by phalanxes of cameras and by the Cabinet members and their wives lined up to greet us, with Dean Rusk at the foot of the steps. Behind them were two or three hundred members of the White House staff and their families. To a chorus of "Congratulations! Welcome home! Welcome back, glad you're here!" we walked into the White House. This was very different from the way we entered the White House almost a year ago on December 7, but still for me, personally, there was no moment of high ecstasy.

Lynda, Him and Her and Blanco were close up in the line, but Luci was nowhere to be found. After shaking hands all around, we went to a party for Walter Heller in the State Department, hosted by a number of top officials, including all of the Cabinet. We told Walter how much we hated to say good-by to him and how impossible it was to thank him enough for his years of wonderful work. He's going to be associated with the University of Minnesota, working on a grant from a foundation. I liked what he said: "We have had two perceptive and restless Presidents, who realize the economy's potential." And "I have Potomac Fever," he admitted ruefully. I hope it's true that he will be back, down the road while it's still our road.

Later that evening Lyndon met with some of the staff to talk about a talent search for the best people to help out in these next four years. I left and went to Lynda Bird's room, to find that she'd gone off on a date. So I curled up on Luci's bed—she had just returned from a date—and talked over "the really important affairs of life"—that is, what one's daughters are planning to do.

It appears that Luci is really going to join the Catholic Church. She has been taking instruction and she would like very much for me to meet the priest who has been teaching her. She would like to join the Church as soon as the priest thinks she is ready. I feel a sense of separation, almost as though I were saying good-by to her—as though she were going off to live in "Timbuctoo." And yet I have never seen her happier or more radiant, and I know that for her, religion is a very necessary, deep, and important part of life. This decision has been coming on for about five years—it is no flash in the pan—so I can't say no. How could I make it stick? How would I dare to presume I was right?

Luci herself is so bubbly and enthusiastic, she is a delight. She is a very rich little girl—that is, in the sense of loving life and giving the sense of love to others. Luci describes herself as a "self-starter." And so she has been these last few months. They have been among the happiest of her life, and of our lives together. We have had a sense of sharing, of understanding and enjoyment.

I left a note on Lynda's bed to say I was lonesome—that "there were

BEARS"—an expression we used to use when she was a little girl. Later on she came in and we talked over the difficulties of her possibly returning to the University of Texas where she would occupy a bedroom half the size of her room here, shared with two other girls, where everybody sleeps on the screened porch. No privacy. No place to study. And where would the Secret Service men stay? I am doubtful of the idea of an apartment, unless she knows extremely well the girls with whom she would share it. But I am afraid she is a little too dependent upon us, upon the haven and privacy of home—now this house.

When I look at the newspapers and read, "President Comes Back from Texas," "NATO, Vietnam, Among Problems Crowding Calendar," and I think of all those that I could add to that calendar, I know why there was no sense of elation as we walked in the door, fresh from a victory of over 61 percent, the largest majority since Roosevelt's election of 1936—and even surpassing that in terms of popular vote.

Tuesday, November 17

THE WHITE HOUSE

Today is our thirtieth wedding anniversary. But in spite of that a curious pall of sadness and inertia, a feeling of having come to a standstill and being bound up in gloom, which has enshrouded me for several days, does not abate. This mood is hard to shake, and how hard it is to get to work! For that reason more than any other, I begrudge it. I wore my green alaskine dress and Lyndon and I went downstairs into the Blue Room this morning to have our anniversary pictures taken.

In the afternoon I went out to see Marjorie and Walter Jenkins who are going home to Texas. It was a strange hour—very much the same, and very different. To me, Walter is as much a casualty of the incredible hours and burdens he has carried in government service as a soldier in action. An interesting and heartening note is the barrage of mail he has received in the aftermath, much of it from the general public, which seems so understanding of a man who had, indeed, reached the end point of exhaustion.

Walter has many friends who have called on him through the years, and they have rallied around to offer jobs and help him make a fresh start. It was a sad good-by for all of us. But one good thing, we know we'll always be seeing each other down the road.

Back on the second floor of the White House, I found Mary Lasker waiting to talk about ways in which the Inaugural ceremonies might be given more style and flair and grace, made more memorable—perhaps with a march or a symphony especially written for the occasion. She suggested my asking the members of the Committee for the Kennedy Cultural Center to an entertainment at the White House.

I asked Lynda Bird to join me and her father at the farewell reception at the State Department for Ralph Dungan, who is leaving for Chile to be our Ambassador. We stayed, to my surprise, about thirty minutes. Lyndon seemed in no hurry to leave.

About 9 o'clock we returned from the Dungan reception, and as we got off the elevator on the second floor, violins began to play, the lights were all ablaze, and the hall was full of my favorite friends. I hadn't in my wildest dream expected anything like this—it was a surprise party, a thirtieth-anniversary party, planned and engineered by Lyndon!

The Abe Fortases were there, the Joe Alsops, Liz and Les Carpenter, Dale and Scooter Miller, Justice Tom Clark and Mary, and Tommy Corcoran—it wouldn't have been complete without him—and Kay Graham, making a valiant recovery from her own tragedy, my niece Diana and Donald MacArthur, the Leonard Markses, the Jack Valentis' and the Tyler Abells. And Lynda came with her date, and Luci, dressed up and beautiful, was in and out.

We went into the Yellow Room, where we had cocktails while I opened packages—the most marvelous assortment of presents, including (most important of all) gold-and-diamond earrings—something I have wanted for several Christmases and birthdays and anniversaries—from Lyndon, and an envelope from him covered with travel pictures of faraway places with strange-sounding names and enclosing money with a little note that said: "To go to the place of your choosing to lie under the sky!" There was a framed poem by Luci, beautifully embossed, recalling all sorts of things, from my Daytona suntan to the time Lyndon brought Beagle into our lives, to Christmas Eves at "Maday's" (Lyndon's mother). And a handsomely framed speech that Lyndon had made to the Johnson City High School, which will be just right to hang in the Sam Johnson House in Johnson City. That was Liz's contribution. And from the Fortases, one of those delightful old things—are they called stereopticons? You hold a little boxlike contraption in front of your eyes, and insert a double photograph of Niagara Falls or Mount Everest, which achieves dimension.

In the middle of the table there was a wedding cake, weighing thirty pounds, covered with white icing, wedding rings intertwined, love birds, yellow roses, and about half a dozen pictures from albums, including the awful one of Lyndon and me on our honeymoon, standing on the boat in the Floating Gardens of Xochimilco. There was one after Lyndon's heart attack in 1955, adorable pictures of each daughter, Lyndon and me in front of the Taj Mahal, a montage of memories all done in sugar icing. The party accounted for as wonderful a change of mood as could have been conceived and executed! And it worked, for the evening.

We went to dinner, with me sitting between Lyndon and Tom Clark. After dinner there were toasts all around. I responded, speaking for us— the two Johnsons—and said, "Let's drink to two things: happiness, the sort that's brought to you by the sort of friends who are gathered here tonight (a very special galaxy of friends they were), and courage, just the sort of pedestrian courage that makes you get up in the morning and go on about the day's business, however frustrating and hopeless and endless and imperfect and unsure the course of the day may be."

That seems to be the sort of courage Lyndon has been exhibiting this past year—days of glory, but many more days of just shoving ahead the best he can. And particularly has this shroud of gloom closed around us this last week. Perhaps it's the accumulation of weariness from the campaign. I am sure the departure of able and close friends whom we have come to feel we can work well with has something to do with my melancholy— Luther and Martha Hodges, Walter and Marjorie. . . .

But tonight was a golden night because of Lyndon's thoughtfulness. I hope I have sense enough to cherish the moment.

Saturday, November 21

LBJ RANCH

This was a day you could write a musical comedy about! Lyndon told me when he woke up that he had a man coming from Iowa to present him with a hog—a Yorkshire boar—and what did I think he ought to do in return? Should he give the man a calf—an exchange of gifts—or what gesture could he make? I said, "Well, the least you could do would be to ask him to lunch."

Presently I went out to the airstrip to meet Nancy Negley (my good friend who often helps me with decorating ideas), who was flying in to spend the day with me. We were driving from the main house to the guest house to the birthplace house and the house in Johnson City, and maybe the Lewis Ranch house, trying to fit in many of the things we have acquired on our travels. Most of my marvelous colorful items from Mexico—from the trip of July 1963—are still stored in a closet. I long for a Mexican room at the guest house, as well as a Victorian room, and maybe one we will call the Western room. Anyhow, those places certainly need some personality injected into them and some freshening up. Nancy is just the person to walk around with and conjure up pictures of how those Mexican children painted on tissue paper and matted in orange would look with orange bedspreads and a straw mat on the floor.

Well, we had progressed as far as the house where Lyndon was born and were moving into place a dresser that his mother used during the many years I visited her and were putting on the hand-crocheted bedspread that Lyndon's grandmother had given us as a wedding gift, when we got a call from Lyndon to come on back to the house right away. He said he would like to have lunch as quickly as possible, along with his friends who were delivering the hog.

Back we went, and much time elapsed while we waited. I gathered, through random bits over the intercom, that there were quite a few people at the hog presentation. I told the kitchen that I hoped we were having fried ham (which we were), grits, and homemade peach preserves, and that they'd better set the table for as many as it would hold.

When they drove up, there were three or four carloads of them. Out began to pile a sizable entourage of people. There were Mr. and Mrs. Richard Juhl and another couple of Juhls who had brought the prize Yorkshire boar all the way from Iowa. But it takes more than that to deliver a hog! There was the President of the National Swinegrowers' Association, the President of the Iowa Farm Brokers' Association, two young people who were relatives of the Juhls, another couple whose names I didn't catch, the Farm Editor of the *Des Moines Register*, and a farm editor of another newspaper—eleven in all. They had just finished with ample picture-taking of the delivery of the pig, including in the photographs Secretary of Agriculture Freeman, our houseguest who fitted right into the script.

Lyndon had taken the visitors on a tour of the Ranch, to see the cattle and sheep, the pigpens, the graveyard, his birthplace—all around. Along the way they had been joined by one of Lyndon's cousins, Mrs. Phil Bunton (Hazel Bunton), who had told Lyndon she wanted to come over and see him sometime and had happened to come today. She had brought her husband, her daughter, her son-in-law, her grandchild, and another relative—a group of six, and Lyndon insisted they stay for lunch.

When they started pouring into the living room, my face must have been a sight to see! Luncheon guests turned out to be eighteen in number instead of the two or three that I had expected at the beginning of the morning. But quick word to the office staff, asking them to come to lunch at the second table, left just enough places for the Iowans and the kinfolks. We sat down to a blessing, and an ample farm luncheon, complete with the Secretary of Agriculture.

These people had driven all the way from Iowa in two days—around sixteen hundred miles—when they found that it was possible to make the presentation of the hog to Lyndon today. One couple who had been in Phoenix, Arizona, had interrupted their holiday plans and had quickly driven to the little town of Stonewall. Well, I think everybody had fun and none of them had the feeling that it was an unusual day at the LBJ Ranch. I did notice afterward that the large bowl of White House matches, which I carefully keep filled for visitors to take home if they like, was just about empty.

I had a chance for a bit of a talk with Secretary Freeman. I asked him what must be a very common question for him, why farm population was declining (because now only about 8 percent of the population is actually engaged in agriculture and we feed this country better than any people have ever been fed before with just 8 percent of the folks working at it). I also asked him why the Department of Agriculture keeps on expanding and requiring a bigger budget and employing more people?

I think his explanation deserves to be better known. One reason the department is growing, he said, is the increasing importance of consumer services. For instance, much of the meat bought in an ordinary grocery store or meat market is inspected and graded by the Department of Agriculture. There are many such invaluable consumer services for the protection of health and pocketbooks. Second, the enormous forward thrust of research increases the department's responsibility. For example, orange juice is now frozen and arrives at the table months later, thousands of miles away from Florida or California or Texas, in excellent condition. This is typical of the scientific advancement of food products invented in the research laboratories of the Department of Agriculture. And then there is forestry. I did not realize that the Department of Forestry was under Agriculture, but trees are one of our major crops. Millions of acres of land in the national forests are under the supervision of the Department of Agriculture. There were dozens of other reasons for the burgeoning of the department that I had never thought of.

Of the Bunton kinfolks, I inquired about the possibilities of getting copies of old pictures—of Lyndon's mother and father, his birthplace, the house in Johnson City, of Lyndon as a child—anything that might have human interest or value for the eventual Library, or perhaps just to decorate the walls in the birthplace house.

After they had all departed, Nancy and I continued our decoration, plying between the Johnson City house, the Lewis house, and the guest house, doing small things like hanging my old wooden cookie mold of a hen with ruffled feathers on the wall at the Lewis and placing half a dozen of the ceramic plates from Juan Aldana's factory, Tlaquepaque, with gay little rabbits and owls and deer painted on them. The best moment of all, we hung a handsome picture of Lyndon in the Johnson City house, a photograph which he had given his mother. She had framed it in an antique walnut frame, and it looked fine there. We also went through a collection of things Johnson City people have brought to Jessie Hunter for the Johnson City house, including an invitation to Lyndon's graduation in 1924, a gift from his schoolmate Kitty Clyde Leonard, and a view of a Prohibition parade, circa 1919—banners flying, ladies in long white dresses, on the streets of Johnson City.

It was a delightful day, with just enough accomplishment to lay one's conscience at rest.

BOOK TWO

1965

Winter 1965

New Year's Day began for me with black coffee and orange juice and good resolutions. I'm about five pounds heavier than I'd like to be, and Lyndon is about twenty pounds heavier than I'd like him to be. I hope to cozen, bully, and brag on both of us enough to bring it down in the next two months. I spent the morning in that long-needed, female chore of cleaning closets, finding such things as letters from my father written to me at St. Mary's School in 1929 and brought out in a dusty box from the old brick store in Karnack several years ago. There was also a campaign button for Dick Russell in 1952. The morning's work resulted in one clean closet, many chores laid out to do, and determination to return in the spring without entourage to get this house in order.

213

THE WHITE HOUSE

The State of the Union Message will be delivered at 9 o'clock tonight, the first time it has been given at night since the days of FDR, creating quite a furor with the press corps.

This morning was a morass of desk work—with Bess Abell and Ashton on correspondence and on houseguest arrangements for the Inauguration. There are about twenty to stay now—and what bedlam it will be in Luci's room, with three girls, two in Luci's bed and one on a cot and all of them using the same bathroom, frantically getting dressed for the most important evening in their lives in front of the same mirror!

And then we began juggling tickets for those who would attend the State of the Union. It's a doubtful blessing to be able to dispense favors. I finally wound up with Kermit Gordon on the step seat beside the three of us (Lynda, Luci, and me), and Bill Baxter, our Episcopal minister, on the adjoining one—and at the last minute there was room on step seats for some of the staff wives. I had asked the three top Cabinet wives—Virginia Rusk, Margy McNamara, and Phyllis Dillon to share the front row with me.

Lynda, statuesque and beautiful in her lovely white brocade, Luci in her black velvet suit with a white chiffon blouse, and I in my black brocade cocktail suit went to the Hill together a little ahead of time to take our seats in the front row and greet friends in the adjoining galleries. The State of the Union Message is like an opening night, full of anticipation and excitement.

The Court filed in, the Cabinet, the Diplomatic Corps—this year I didn't see a single one in native costume. I regret the passing of that custom. How can Angie Duke manage them all? There were only about eighty when he came in such a short while ago, and now there are 117 in the Corps. The Diplomatic Gallery is very small. It holds only about thirty-seven people. For the wives of the diplomats it's on a "first-come, first-served" basis.

During the day I had heard that Charlie Halleck had been defeated by Gerald Ford as Minority Leader, Number Two man for the Republicans. No surprise—Gerald Ford is young and vigorous and ambitious—but there's always something a little sad in the passing of one of the wielders of power, though in this case one remembers that it was only six years ago that Charlie Halleck did exactly the same thing to the venerable Joe Martin.

There were dramatic moments as I looked down on the floor—Charlie Halleck sitting alone, and Senator Strom Thurmond striding up to greet him, newly ensconced on the Republican side. John Tower, once more the lone Republican in the Texas delegation, bereft of his colleagues from Dallas and Midland. Somebody said, "Those Louisiana boys are sure taking over," speaking of Hale Boggs and Russell Long, who just won the Number Two place vacated by Humphrey, against the formidable opposition of John Pastore and Mike Monroney. This surprised me in view of Hale's vote on Civil Rights and Medicare and the Democratic Party's losing Louisiana. But everybody knows him as a fighter, and it's so easy to like him.

Fishbait Miller, born for the stage, was already announcing: "The President of the United States!"

And then—how many times have I seen it happen—but in a new role now—Lyndon came in with the leaders of both Parties, everyone rising and applauding—a moment to be savored. The speech he has labored on these last six or seven days lasted about fifty minutes. There were twenty-seven bursts of applause. The Republicans remained quiet, except for lines about national strength and holding down the budget, and there was one moment when Lyndon said that we had cut out waste last year and are going to do better this year, and somebody from their side called out: "Attaboy, Lyndon."

I liked the accent on education, on medical research, and on preserving this nation's beauty—the preservation of the beauty of America along the highways, in the cities, in National Parks—"the green legacy for tomorrow." I hope we can do something about that in our four years here. The end of the speech was sheer poetry, and you could tell when Lyndon got into it that he loved it. It had a lilt and a melody and a cadence—about the rugged, arid land along the Pedernales where he grew up, and how man had made something better out of it. On the way out of the Chamber he looked up and waved to the girls and me. And then we joined him in the Speaker's Room to greet the Leadership.

All in all, I am happy with the speech, though there will be newspapermen who will say it was too "Mother Hubbard," that it promised too much, hoped for too much.

The birthday of Sam Rayburn, still "Mr. Speaker" to me although he died several years ago, was a busy day. At 10 o'clock the dedication of the Sam Rayburn statue in the new Rayburn House Office Building was made. The sculptor was Felix de Weldon and the statue is a gift of the Texas State Society.

The ceremony was held in a small rotunda where the larger-than-life statue stands on a pedestal. Groups of friends and relatives of Mr. Sam's, and many Texans, were gathered, filling the staircase on each side. It was a brief, colorful, nostalgic ceremony, with Wright Patman as Master of Ceremonies, the presentation of colors, the National Anthem, the Chaplain of the House giving the Invocation, remarks by the sculptor. The Speaker's nephew, Bob Bartley, unveiled the statue. And then I gave my short dedication speech. "The first moment Sam Rayburn set eyes on this Hill was a day in March 1913. He arrived from Texas' old Fourth District and stepped out of Union Station to see before him the breathtaking beauty of the glistening white Capitol dome. It was love at first sight," and so on, to the end. "The House of Representatives was his great love. He was at once its master and its servant. There wasn't anyone in the United States who couldn't see the Speaker if they were willing to sit a spell. To the dismay of his staff, he made his own appointments, often on the back of an old envelope in his hip pocket, and he read his own mail.

" 'I'm a Democrat, without suffix, prefix or apology,' Mr. Sam often said." But the ending was what I liked best. " 'All of us are just a little way from Flag Springs,' said Speaker Rayburn. 'You know, I missed being a tenant farmer by a gnat's heel.' " I dedicated the statue to the new members of the Eighty-ninth Congress and to all future Congresses in the hope they would, like Sam Rayburn, serve under the great white dome with the same faith in the people.

Just before it was time for me to speak we had a surprise visitor: Lyndon. Afterward Everett Hutchinson presented the statue—he is President of the Texas State Society—to the government. Speaker John McCormack accepted it in a warm and graceful speech. And then, inevitably, "The Eyes of Texas" and the benediction.

I spent the rest of the day working on the Inauguration, checking my card file of kinfolks, old friends who might otherwise be forgotten, staff, people who have helped us through the years out of friendship or patriotism. It is a tedious task and a thankless one because there are never enough good seats to go around and probably the best thing that could happen to us would be a twenty-inch snow, because everybody would blame the weather then instead of the Johnsons.

Luci blithely informs me that she has worked it out so that Patti McGouirk can come up for Inauguration. That will make four little girls in one room!

This is my first day on black coffee and a hard boiled egg and red meat diet. I have to take off about four pounds before the eighteenth. My total response to it is "ouch"—but it *can* be done.

Tuesday, January 12

The Japanese State Visit took place today. When Prime Minister Eisaku Sato emerged from the limousine, his first words were in English and clearly spoken. He has a quick smile, an easy manner, a stocky build. First the band played the Japanese National Anthem, slow and impressive and rather like a dirge to Western ears, and then ours. I don't think I ever saw Lyndon looking handsomer. Rufe Youngblood and I, both anxious mother hens, had persuaded him to put on his overcoat—a new dark blue, beautifully tailored—and his profile looked stern and strong and solemn. Lyndon welcomed the Prime Minister, who responded in Japanese, which was then translated. We went inside and lined up to receive his party, including our Ambassador Edwin Reischauer and his Japanese wife. Lyndon visited with the Prime Minister and I gather that they hit it off well, for Lyndon had a look of satisfaction.

This evening everything again clicked perfectly and we emerged onto the portico to glaring lights and flashing cameras as the limousine rolled up and the Prime Minister emerged, with Robin and Angie Duke close at hand, and their understudies, Ann and Lloyd Hand, in the background, learning. The Dukes will soon be leaving for his Ambassadorship in Spain.

We took the Prime Minister to the Yellow Room, along with his Foreign Minister, the Rusks, the Humphreys, the Dillons and Udalls, Japan's attractive Ambassador and his wife, the Ryuji Takieuchis, the Edwin Reischauers, and the Dukes. We had found an amusing gift for the Prime Minister—a red, white, and blue mailbox, vintage 1890, from some small town in the United States, chosen because Sato had been Postmaster General of Japan and long in the Postal Service, along with a desk box, pictures, and books. The Prime Minister gave me a beautiful string of Japanese pearls and smaller strings for Lynda and Luci, and to Lyndon a cigarette box fashioned from a piece of Oregon pine Commodore Perry took to Japan when he visited those shores in 1854.

When we filed into the dining room, I took the arm of Prime Minister Sato. The tables were laid with the Roosevelt and Truman china, the vermeil flatware, and there were lovely arrangements of flowers.

Then began the real business of the evening—my efforts to discover whether I could really talk to the Prime Minister! I said that I thought this period we are living in is one of the most exciting in the history of man. "Yes," he said, in English, "I think of today not as the day after yesterday, but as the day before tomorrow." I told him about having seen two young Japanese students in the Lincoln Room a few days before with my daughter, Lynda Bird, who was escorting them through the White House. They had won a trip to this country because they had been selected as the two most physically fit young people in Japan. He said, "Yes, you know this generation is growing taller, a couple of inches more than the past generation." I said, "What do you attribute that to—better nutrition?" He answered: "Yes, in part, but also different housing. They don't sit on the floor so much any more. They frequently sit in chairs. That gives them a chance to stretch their legs." He said, "We noticed when we had the Olympics that our athletes were smaller than athletes from many other countries. I think by the time the Olympics meet again, this coming generation will have just about closed the gap and then down the road the gap *will* be closed."

During dinner there was one bit of byplay that I didn't find so amusing. Lyndon kept looking up and saying something to a butler who would then disappear and presently return with a ten-gallon Texas hat which Lyndon would carefully crimp in the style so important to ranchers of the Central Texas area and present to the Prime Minister. The hat didn't fit, back it went, and out came another hat, which did fit, and then a third hat for the Foreign Minister—all of which elicited peals of laughter. I found it a very odd bit of dinner play and it wasn't until later that I found out what it was all about.

Next we had the toasts. Lyndon spoke of the Japanese and the people of the United States as inventive and creative and he added: "I hope that we may mutually profit from these traits as we work closely together to make the world a better place through technology, a more beautiful place through the arts, and a more rational place through the quest for truth by unfettered minds."

The Prime Minister's toast included a reference to the fact that though there were some frictions which were always more publicized than the areas of agreement, the area in which our interests are not at variance is infinitely greater than the area in which they diverge, and then he got in a bit of adlibbing fun. He said he hoped that some day President Johnson would give him a ten-gallon Texas hat. Evidently Lyndon had had a preview of his toast—so much for the hat incident.

Thursday, January 14

Today was a beginning and an ending. A tentative beginning this morning took place when Sargent Shriver met with Liz and me in the Queen's Room to present a detailed analysis of Operation Head Start. This program will attempt to give one hundred thousand underprivileged children in the five- and six-year-old age bracket a "head start," before they enter the first grade in September. It will include a medical examination, one good free meal a day, and the simplest rudimentary teaching in manners and vocabulary improvement. The course will last eight weeks. Children who enter school from the slums or impoverished homes where neither parent is present most of the time are frequently unable to communicate, because they don't hear and use words at home. And many have never seen a notebook or a pencil. So this is, literally, Operation Head Start and is aimed at the period when psychologists tell us the human being is being molded for his lifetime.

Then we discussed Operation VISTA, which is similar to a domestic Peace Corps. The problem for me is: Which shall I interest myself in and how much? The Head Start idea has such *hope* and challenge. Maybe I could help focus public attention in a favorable way on some aspects of Lyndon's poverty program. Anyway, Sargent Shriver is a superb salesman.

About 7 we had a "farewell" gathering for Martha and Luther Hodges who are returning to North Carolina—the ending I spoke of earlier. It developed into a delightful party about 7:15 upstairs in the Yellow Oval Room—a complete surprise, and the sort of party I like best! Only the Cabinet members and their wives were present, along with about ten of the top staff members and their wives. Drinks and hors d'oeuvres, happy reminiscences and sad good-bys—this was one time I *wanted* to make the speech.

I sincerely hope the country raises up more Luther and Martha Hodgeses and I ended with "rest easy and be happy but don't think you might not be called on again." We gave them a silver tray—all the Cabinet together—and on it were the words "To MARTHA AND LUTHER HODGES, FOR A JOB WELL DONE AND A NATION WELL SERVED, IN ADMIRING RESPECT FROM YOUR COLLEAGUES AND FRIENDS," and the signatures of all the Cabinet members.

About 9 o'clock, still in my brocade theater suit and fur coat, we got in a helicopter, grabbing Him in passing, and left for Texas.

Tomorrow we will have a visit from the Lester Pearsons of Canada at the Ranch, with just the honor guests and the Secretary of State of each of our countries. Then there will be three days to hammer out the Inaugural speech and take all of those phone calls about who *hasn't* got what tickets.

We have asked the Medal of Freedom winners to the Inauguration, and a group of Arts and Letters people—architects, singers, writers, painters, dramatists, actors, dancers, poets, conductors, composers—have been invited as "guests of President Johnson," ranging from Edward Steichen to Paul Dudley White, Van Cliburn, Todd Duncan, Isaac Stern, and Herman Wouk.

Friday, January 15

LBJ RANCH

I rushed out to the airstrip just in time to meet Secretary Rusk's plane this afternoon. He was bringing with him McGeorge Bundy and Mary, always favorite houseguests, and Mr. Paul Martin, Rusk's opposite number, the Secretary of State for Canada. A few minutes behind them arrived beaming Prime Minister and Mrs. Pearson. There were informal remarks of greeting out by our airplane hangar in front of the gathered newspapermen, and then we got in the helicopter and flew to the West Ranch. I took Mrs. Pearson and her secretary and Mary Bundy with me and the four of us drove around until twilight, seeing at close hand three armadillos, herds of deer grazing in the valley, a ballet of deer jumping the stone fences, and the beautiful outline of the hills against the sunset.

In the car I heard Lyndon ask John and Nellie to come to dinner over the Ranch intercom. We drove home in time to change, and all gathered in the living room. The talk centered on Churchill who has lapsed into a coma and there is said to be no hope for him. Everybody reminisced about how the great man's life had touched theirs. We wondered how anyone could use words eloquent enough to express what Churchill meant to the twentieth century when it becomes necessary to make such a statement. Mr. Pearson summed it up when he said, "Only Churchill himself would be equal to the occasion!"

Mr. Pearson is a raconteur also. He told about a gathering in Canada with a Russian delegation, among them Gromyko, during a particularly tense time following a spy episode that had caused strained feelings. Gromyko wanting to stay on a bland and safe subject inquired, "Do you raise apples in Canada?" "Yes," said General Andrew McNaughton, the Canadian opposite number. "What are your best brands?" asked Gromyko. Without hesitation and with honesty General McNaughton replied, "Our best brands are Northern *Spies* and McIntosh *Reds*."

Then he told a story about how Leland Stanford, the famous philanthropist, was visiting President Charles Eliot of Harvard University and he said, "How much would it cost today to build Harvard?" President Eliot said, "It would take a hundred million today!" Mr. Leland Stanford turned to his wife and said, "Mama, we can do it."

John Connally told the story about himself and Lyndon, as young naval officers in San Francisco, about to set out to some unknown destination in the South Pacific, going into a little shop owned by a Japanese who was selling out his business before going into a detention camp. They bought some lovely things for Nellie and me. (I still have and cherish my pearls.) John went on to say that he and Nellie were out there just before last Christmas and went into the same shop, found exactly the same proprietor. He remembered John's face. He was delighted to see him, told him that he knew the other man had become President of the United States. About that time the shopkeeper's wife pinched him and said, "But you don't know who this young officer is now?" The man did not and was delighted to discover that the other young man of twenty-three years ago was now the Governor of Texas.

But Pearson topped it when he told of a London tailor that he had visited only twice in his life. The first time was in 1917 when as a young lieutenant he bought a suit—a military uniform from this London shop —and then he went back to the same shop in 1964. The man who made it was still there! What's more, he opened his books, turned back his records to the very day in 1917, told him his measurements and how much he had paid for his uniform. Both proprietor and tailor were still on the job! That speaks something of England, something that the world has come to expect of it, rather.

THE WHITE HOUSE

Today is the first of the big days! I began it by going upstairs to have my second cup of coffee (after breakfast with Lyndon), with Aunt Jessie and Ava Cox, to see if I couldn't lend them a stole or evening purse or some gloves. These stolen nuggets of time with kinfolks are nice moments in the three-day Inaugural marathon. The plane ride up was treat enough to make Aunt Jessie say, "I tell you, I may not ever get to Glory Land, but I feel like I have seen part of it!"

Just before 3, into my red silk alaskine dress and putting on my fur hat, I left for the National Gallery of Art with Liz for the Distinguished Ladies' Reception. As we rolled into the driveway, I saw Ida May Cain from Rochester and her daughter, Stephanie Cain Van D'Elden from California, and that's the way it was all afternoon. In the crowd of five thousand ladies, I kept seeing dear old friends from the far corners of this country. There were four short receiving lines and nobody knew who was going to be in which one, but in the marble elegance of the National Art Gallery, banked with azaleas and fountains, who would mind waiting?

Wives of diplomats had been asked to come in their native dress. A troupe of them came down my receiving line, each with a personal hostess. There were graceful saris from Nepal, a flowing blue and silver *boubou* [a native shift] from Niger, one from Senegal that reminded me of the enormous poufs of nylon (imported from Paris) that I saw in Senegal when I was there for their Independence celebration. Judge Sarah Hughes came down the line, and Mrs. Donald Russell of South Carolina. She and I had a big kiss for each other. In fact, by the time the evening was over I looked as if I had the measles—there were so many pink lipstick spots all over me.

I later found that there wasn't anything to eat at this reception, but one guest commented to a newswoman, "You can get hors d'oeuvres and a cocktail anywhere, but when do you have a chance to see Rembrandt, Picasso, and Lady Bird all at one time?" Having the reception in the Art Gallery was an inspiration. *Half* of the five thousand ladies, it seemed, wore mink turbans, as did I. I don't know whether I am setting the trend or following it.

Back at the White House I visited with my crew of girls in Luci's room and curled up on the sofa for a few minutes with Warrie Lynn, who talked about Luci and her plans. Luci wants Warrie Lynn to be one of her sponsors when she is baptized into the Catholic Church. Warrie Lynn, no proselytizer, is urging Luci to wait and wait and to be very sure.

I set out with Lyndon for the pre-gala dinners at the Shoreham and the Sheraton Park, renamed for the occasion the "Sheraton Texas" because it was headquarters for all of the Texans. There were about three thousand guests at the "Sheraton Texas" where John Connally introduced us. Another eighteen hundred at the Shoreham, all members of the President's Club. We made brief stops, quickly wended our way through the tables smiling and waving on all sides. Lyndon made brief humorous remarks, ending up on a serious note, "Now is the time for hope and rededication." Hubert had gone to the two other pre-Inaugural dinners. Leonard Marks, who has handled our appearances so competently, drove with us.

Lyndon and I arrived at the Inaugural gala on time, which is more than about half of the audience managed to do. They convoyed us into a waiting room where the walls were hung with pictures of our predecessors —Kennedys, Eisenhowers, Trumans—in galas of other days, and then when the crowd was at hand we went in to the tune of "Hail to the Chief" and an impressive welcome into an Armory made gay with thousands of bright blue streamers from the ceiling, enormous bouquets of red, white, and blue balloons, bold gilded eagles, and American flags rippling in a manmade breeze.

Richard Adler, director of the show, had accumulated such a galaxy of stars that it forced two Broadway shows to close down for the night. Carol Channing came down from *Hello Dolly!* to be one of the emcees, and Barbra Streisand from *Funny Girl* to sing. Dame Margot Fonteyn from England's Royal Ballet flew in from London with Rudolf Nureyev, who now looks like one of the Beatles. Alfred Hitchcock turned out to be the lion of the evening. And Woody Allen, that forlorn, undernourished little comedian, stopped shooting a movie in Paris and flew across the Atlantic for about five minutes of jokes. I found him hilarious, and I am no lover of comedy on the stage. The way he looks—you want to give him a blood transfusion. I was in gales of laughter at his monologue about the man who shot the moose, strapped him to his car, and the moose awoke in the Holland Tunnel, so the man decided to take him to where he knew there was a costume ball going on and introduced the moose with that muttered gesture I have used so often—"know the bla-bla's, don't you?" because he didn't want to say, "This is a moose!"

Julie Andrews and Carol Burnett sang a wonderful medley of musical comedy songs ranging from *Naughty Marietta* to *My Fair Lady*, and Harry

Belafonte won everybody with "Michael, Row the Boat Ashore," and that sad nostalgic song about September. As exquisite and perfect as Margot Fonteyn was, there was a foil at the opposite end of the dancing spectrum that was just as good as she was—a member of the Mexican Folklorico, a dancer with a deer head, complete with antlers, strapped to his own head portrayed a wounded deer and his dying struggle—to me the most startling performance of the evening. Bobby Darin sang a song which, he said, the Army Reserve dedicated to the Secretary of Defense, "Mack the Knife," one of the few allusions to the contemporary political scene. Another was Hitchcock's message ostensibly addressed to the GOP on last November 4. "Good evening friends, do you have that 'morning after' feeling? Did you feel your group had all the cavities?"

Wednesday, January 20

Inauguration Day dawned beautiful and bright. The great day had come. I began dressing and at a quarter of 9 was ready to leave with Lyndon and Luci for the Interfaith Prayer Service at the National City Christian Church. An invited group were bidden to listen to brief prayers for the day, the man, and the country by ministers of many faiths: Dr. George Davis, the host minister in Lyndon's own church; Bill Baxter, my Episcopal minister; Dr. John Barclay from Austin; Rabbi Norman Gerstenfeld; and a Roman Catholic Monsignor, The Right Reverend Monsignor Joseph L. Manning, who had accompanied our own Archbishop Robert Lucey from San Antonio.

We had also invited the Court and the Cabinet and the principal figures of government along with the principal figures of Johnson City—the Winters and Stubbs, Mabel Stribling, Minnie Cox, and the Jimmy Leonards—and our long-time friends Earl and Weeze Death from KTBC, and many to whom it would really mean something. In fact, I had spent hours trying to think to whom, sentimentally, this *would* mean something. There was not an empty seat at the Prayer Service.

After the service I asked to see the seating chart of the platform for the Capitol ceremony and Leonard Marks showed it to me—and here occurred one of the most hilarious moments of the day. Bess and I had spent hours putting our portion of it together and I was satisfied that everything was in good order, until I looked at Row B and saw the name "Mrs. Fern Baines." I got a slight case of the shakes. I told Leonard, "Now, I've got Aunt

Ovilee Baines and Aunt Josefa Baines Saunders but we just don't *have* a Mrs. Fern Baines." I had visions of an empty seat on the second row. How would I account for it? Leonard said he had insisted on getting the list typewritten and not in anybody's handwriting. He had it proofread by Bess and by himself and he just *knew* it was correct. I said, "Well, we'll just say, 'Poor Cousin Fern, she came down with pneumonia and she couldn't make it.'" Only later did I discover the answer to this mystery.

Wonder of wonders, Luci appeared on time, looking lovely in her navy blue and white outfit with the perky white hat and Lynda was regal in her light blue suit and Robin Duke's fur hat. I was satisfied with my own American beauty ensemble, with a bit of sealskin that tied under the chin and the off-the-face hat. I appreciated the luxury of the silk-lined black gloves and a small and elegant alligator bag which Mariallen had given me. We rode down Pennsylvania Avenue, Lyndon and I in one car—the one with the bulletproof glass top and sides—crowds were already thick along the avenue—the children rode in a car rather close behind. I had reminded them to use every moment to look at the people on both sides —to wave at them—to recognize anybody they knew with a special look that would let them know they were recognized, because this would be our only moment of contact with many of them who had come from all fifty states.

Soon we were on the Inaugural stand. Muriel next to me and then Lynda and Luci and Lucia and Birge and Becky, and Tony and Matiana. On the front row on the other side, Senator Everett Jordan, Speaker and Mrs. McCormack, the four Humphrey children, and Aunt Jessie and Aunt Josefa. The rest of the kinfolks and officials made up the group on the Inaugural stands.

There they stretched in front of us, the people we were working for. Thousands and thousands of them, so many of whom we had met face to face in their home towns—Rising Star, Texas, or Doland, South Dakota. I looked for familiar faces. And it was a long way back before I began to find them—A. W. with earmuffs on, Wesley West, Melvin Winters from our Hill Country.

The Invocation was given by Archbishop Lucey, long-time crusading liberal of the vintage of Maury Maverick. He and Lyndon had known each other longer than Lyndon and I had known each other. The Archbishop has always worked with zeal among the Latin Americans of San Antonio. Leontyne Price sang "America the Beautiful." It was a rich voice and a rich song—one of the high moments. Rabbi Hyman Judah Schachtel gave a prayer. Next Hubert stepped forward—for once his exuberance was under wraps. He looked positively stern. I thought there was almost a tremor in his raised hand. Speaker McCormack administered the oath and then Muriel kissed him. Reverend Davis delivered a prayer.

Then came the moment toward which all the days for the last year had been heading—will it or no—the moment when Lyndon would take the oath of office as the thirty-sixth President of the United States. This time the Chief Justice administered the oath. I was touched that Lyndon wanted me to hold the Bible for his swearing-in. We used the Bible Lyndon's mother had given us for Christmas in 1952, just after we moved to the Ranch, and I stood facing the throng between the Chief Justice and Lyndon while he took the oath.

Lyndon's Inaugural Address of eleven hundred words required, so the newspapers said, twenty-two minutes to deliver. And how many hours it had taken to write! Even while we were getting dressed to come to the ceremony itself, he had been rearranging the part about liberty, justice, and union—Jack Valenti bounding in and out of the room like a rubber ball—taping over certain phrases on the teleprompter. I wouldn't have interrupted them if the building had been on fire.

The line I liked best in the speech was the one about always trying. "It is the excitement of becoming—always becoming, trying, probing, falling, resting, and trying again—but always trying and always gaining." And I liked the symbolism of "Even now, a rocket moves toward Mars. It reminds us that the world will not be the same for our children, or even for ourselves in a short span of years." Also, I liked the beginning where he put emphasis on responsibility lying just exactly where it does—on each of us.

The Mormon Tabernacle Choir sang. Lyndon himself had invited them, to the dismay of the Inaugural officials, I think, because they represented 375 bodies and there is hardly room for an extra flea in the Plaza where the Inauguration takes place. My traveling friend from the Greek trip, His bearded Eminence Archbishop Iakovos, rose to give the Benediction. And then there was the "Star-Spangled Banner" by the U.S. Marine Band, and it was all over.

Lyndon and Hubert were escorted up the steps between the assembled House and Senate, people they had worked with so much of their lives. Muriel and I and all the others in the stand went inside to the Inauguration luncheon, at which Senator Jordan presided. It was held in the old

Supreme Court Chamber and I was so glad that the order not to have any more luncheons in this historic old chamber had been overridden by Senator Jordan, in his capacity as head of the Rules Committee. It was there that I found out about Cousin Fern Baines! Leonard came up to me and said, "What do you know, she turns out to be Hubert Humphrey's married sister! How is that for a political mutation?" He also said that the crowd was the largest in the history of the Capitol. According to the Chief of Police, one million, two hundred thousand, were in the square and lining the parade route.

After lunch we got back in the bulletproof limousine, like a bubble of glass, and rode down Pennsylvania Avenue, waving at the filled bleachers, the lined sidewalks, and the jammed office windows. How amazing that I should come almost face to face with Maurine Kranson Feiger, a friend of Marshall High School days, for the third time during these three days! I'd been glad to get a moment with Leontyne Price in Everett Dirksen's office between the ceremony and the luncheon. I introduced her to as many of the relatives and Senate wives as were within reach. I heard that the lone spectator watching the parade from a balcony on an upper floor of the Justice Department turned out to be J. Edgar Hoover. He has seen a lot of us come and go.

We arrived at the White House reviewing stand about 2:30 and found —what an innovation!—a clear, thick glass barrier in front of us and small stoves by our feet. Instead of the Spartan two and a half hours in the piercing cold we had expected, it was going to be quite cozy.

Coming down the avenue, Lyndon had seen the Southwest Texas Strutters who accompany the band from his own alma mater. He nad stopped the procession, got out of the car, and crossed the street to shake hands with three or four of them. When we first walked into the stands we encountered Him and Blanco on leashes, waiting expectantly at the foot of the steps. Lyndon took Him's leash and escorted Him into the reviewing stand, where that happy dog took up his place in Lyndon's big leather-upholstered viewing chair. (He was soon returned to his keeper, but the crowd liked it.)

There had been quite a discussion as to which band would lead the parade—little San Marcos Southwest State College Band, from Lyndon's alma mater, or the proud orange and white Longhorn Band of the University of Texas, and I, even though an ardent University alumna, was belligerently in favor of San Marcos leading. As it turned out, San Marcos was the first of the state or school bands to pass by the President. And then there were two and a half hours of fifty-two bands and fifteen thousand marchers! The parade was shorter, however, than any Inaugural parade in memory, which makes Howard Burris, the Parade Committee Chairman, a diplomat as well as an executive.

Texas had a float that was a replica of the LBJ ranchhouse, with a plastic Pedernales River, and a toy dog that waved his tail, representing Him. The float I liked the best was Georgia's, which was a miniature "Lady Bird Special," painted red, white, blue, green, a sort of vintage "Toonerville Trolley," and out of its windows waved attractive young girls in LBJ campaign uniforms. Many of them were the daughters of the real hostesses on the Lady Bird Special, including Christy Carpenter playing Luci, and Patsy Derby, my young Alabama cousin, playing me!

There was more "jumping up and down" at the parade than at any Episcopal church service, to paraphrase Lyndon—because the flag went by every few moments. Sometimes I nudged Lyndon and the girls to let them know that it was coming, and to retrieve their attention if a Governor approached in his open convertible, because we wanted to accord them the dignity and welcome they were according us by their presence.

Some of the far western states had marching units or floats of bearded buckskin-clad men with boots and big hats and long rifles—frontiersmen, trappers, hunters—one of the funniest was a man being dragged on a frontier-type stretcher, behind a horse, with a quivering arrow protruding from his chest, laid out cold. As he passed the reviewing stand, he sat up straight and saluted! The audience howled. There was a brandy-keg-toting St. Bernard mascot of the Chicago Fire Department, marching along in a Texas hat. I heard later that Him set up quite a yapping when he saw him, but to no avail.

During the parade various people joined us briefly. The McNamaras came while the military units were going by and also General Earle Wheeler. Lyndon signaled Sargent Shriver and his three children who were watching it from the other side, one of the children perched on top of his daddy's shoulders. They came over and sat with us a little. Margaret Truman and Clifton Daniel came down when the Missouri float went by. Miss Kate Loney, Lyndon's first teacher, who now lives at Rough and Ready, California, was brought in for a few moments. In fact, there was quite a parade of Governors, labor leaders, VIP's, little and big—nationally known variety and Johnson City variety.

Dale and Scooter Miller were in the front row and as the parade drew to an end they must have been about ready to breathe a vast sigh of relief, since they were in charge of the Inaugural proceedings. White House waiters filtered through the stand, passing snacks and hot bouillon and coffee. Lyndon kept jumping up to greet friends back in the stands, former Postmaster General James Farley and evangelist Billy Graham. Between Lyndon's departures and returns and the Governors going by in their convertibles, saluting us and we them, and the passing of the flags, it was an active two and a half hours. The most remarkable thing of all about the parade was that it was over on time, at 5 o'clock. Cheers to Howard Burris! Everybody began filing out of the stands to get ready for the numerous parties.

At 9:15 we left to go to all the Inaugural balls, with Lynda and Luci and their dates following us. We went first to the Mayflower, the most civilized ball, because it was the smallest. We greeted those in the President's box and then went out into an area roped off with velvet ropes and danced, changing partners every few seconds. At one point Lyndon surprised Margaret Truman Daniel by lifting her bodily out of her box to the dance floor and twirling her around the room. We stayed only about forty minutes—the first of five stops—a regular marathon. Next, to the Statler-Hilton and then the Armory, where there were thirteen thousand people. Tonight the decorations had all been changed, instead of blue streamers there were enormous bouquets of bright flowers hanging from the ceiling. When we left the box and started down to the dance floor, it was like plunging into a University of Texas-Oklahoma football crowd. I felt dreadful to see how the Secret Service had to push against the crowd to make the few feet in which we danced possible. After a few changes of partners we went back up to the box. Lyndon tried to use the microphone to thank everyone and it didn't work. (The first goof for three days that I am aware of.) He talked without it and then presently it came on with a blare!

Next we visited the Shoreham, which was full of Minnesotans. At each place we stayed about thirty minutes, and then at last came the Sheraton Park, where all the Texans were congregated. Lyndon made a delightful little speech. "Never have so many paid so much to dance so little! . . . One thing I can say about the Great Society—it sure is crowded." He had been in fine spirits all evening and changed partners as rapidly as possible, dancing with Muriel, Lynda, any Cabinet wives who were handy, and the wives of those who had particularly helped with the Inaugural. I glanced over my shoulder, hoping that he would find Scooter and Dorothy Marks.

I was really quite pleased with my upswept hairdo, which I hadn't worn in twenty or more years, and the yellow satin ensemble with only one drawback—it is much handsomer with the coat on, more regal. But add about thirteen thousand human bodies and you have a Turkish bath!

The Presidential Box was filled with notables—to give everybody something to look at and talk about when they got home, in case they couldn't find room to dance. Like Cinderella we tried to make it home by midnight.

Thursday, January 21

Today was by all rights a day that both Lyndon and I deserved to stay in bed all day, but perhaps you don't come down off the mountain of excitement so quickly. Lyndon had a meeting of the Leadership at 10 and I got up at 9 to meet Margaret Truman Daniel and her two little boys. Homer Gruenther was showing them the White House, including the beagle—Him—the swimming pool, everything on the first floor, their grandfather's balcony that I love so much, and their mother's bedroom and sitting room, which are now our kitchen and family dining room. I had a nice visit with them over a cup of coffee, always trying to accumulate tales of what it was like when another family lived here. I asked Margaret. She told me, instead, one of her father's favorite tales about Calvin Coolidge. Senate Majority Leader Joe Robinson of Arkansas was having breakfast with President Coolidge. Mrs. Coolidge's aristocratic white collie sat down beside him and looked up at him with mournful, solicitous eyes and President Coolidge said, "He wants your bacon." Senator Joe Robinson picked up his one slice of bacon and offered it to the collie, who ate it appreciatively. Senator Robinson kept looking over his shoulder for the butler to come from the kitchen and offer him another piece, but he never came.

Lyndon's meeting with the House Leadership in the Yellow Room included Speaker McCormack, Carl Albert, Hale Boggs, Hubert Humphrey, as well as Lyndon's staff members, Horace Busby, Valenti, Moyers, Doug Cater, and all the Committee Chairmen. Just before they were ready to leave he asked me to come in and greet them. Others were powerful though aging Judge Howard Smith of Virginia, my friend Mendel Rivers of Charleston, Mills of Arkansas, as well as three Texans—Wright Patman,

Tiger Teague, and George Mahon. They had a lengthy session on how to start the legislative program. Humphrey and some of the staff lingered after the Congressmen left and there was an absolutely marvelous conversation. I remember, at one point, Lyndon leaning over to Larry O'Brien and saying, "John Kennedy is watching us up in heaven and we are going to wrap up all of his legislation and put it in a package and tie it up and label it JFK." Whatever it is labeled, if this impetus keeps rolling, there are going to be some laws passed.

Lyndon asked Hubert to call Muriel to join us for dinner. I called the Thornberrys and the six of us had a delightful time. I have no illusions that a President and his Vice President can maintain unbroken, day after day, a completely simpatico relationship. But it is pleasant that we have it now.

Sunday, January 24

BETHESDA NAVAL HOSPITAL

Winston Churchill died about 3 o'clock this morning. And so the old warrior is gone. Lyndon had entered Bethesda in the early hours of Saturday morning. I learned that the staff had awakened Lyndon to tell him. Dr. Wilbur Gould told me later that his temperature rose immediately and that he thought it was directly attributable to the word of Churchill's death. But all this I learned later in the day because I slept like a log until 10 o'clock. I had taken a room above him, and I went downstairs in my robe to have my breakfast in Lyndon's room. He was very quiet and he let the doctors work on him instead of telling them what to do. In fact, he was so orderly a patient that I knew he must be feeling bad.

The doctors called me aside and very firmly told me that they were strongly opposed to Lyndon's going to Churchill's funeral next Saturday. They said that he would probably feel well enough to go, but he would still be weak and would be a prey to any germs that came along, and that if he contracted any other infection it would be harder to deal with. They skimmed around the word "pneumonia." A very real objection to his going to Churchill's funeral would be the sheer emotional impact. I believe it would be wise not to go.

Jack Valenti was in and out all day. Lyndon signed some letters—he signed the Budget Message. He teased Jack about being out of town when he needed him. Jack had gone to New York for just one night—on the one night Lyndon needed him.

Tomorrow I shall have to start returning calls and thanking those who sent flowers. Tomorrow I shall go back to work. I am comforting myself that this enforced rest could be a boon to Lyndon. That he could even lose a few pounds. If only he doesn't let the speculation of the columnists and his own sense of rising to duty cause him to go to Churchill's funeral.

Wednesday, January 27

THE WHITE HOUSE

We came home Tuesday morning, and last night was not a good night. An old enemy returned. Lyndon sweated down two or three pair of pajamas. This has been a symptom of his illnesses for all the years I have known him, so I should have expected it.

Today was a day of office work for me, interlaced with working on my income tax. I'll always wish that somewhere in my life I'd taken that course in accounting as planned! With Ashton sick, my bookkeeping is a shambles.

For Lyndon it was a day for two major decisions. One, not to go to London, which he announced at a 5:30 press conference in his bedroom to a small group of newspapermen, saying that the doctors had warned him against going on the theory that he was susceptible to reinfection. So he was naming Dean Rusk, the Chief Justice, and Ambassador Bruce to represent him. The other decision was to name the Acting Attorney General, Nick Katzenbach, as his Attorney General. At the same time, he named Ramsey Clark as Deputy Attorney General, which to me is the next best thing to the Number One spot. There is no doubt that Katzenbach is able, for he has handled Civil Rights well. He will ride out the storms now brewing, drawing less lightning than any of the other people under consideration. Lyndon called him and asked him to bring his wife and come over for a talk, and they arrived a little past 7. Lyndon is working while he recuperates.

Today was full of family news, too. It appears that Luci, on her own, had given an interview to a Chilean newspaper woman who sold it to *Ebony*, which printed a long article, complete with many pictures. A summary of it appeared on the wire services in the Washington papers. In the interview Luci included such juicy bits as explaining that her father has become quite economical since he became the President and that he is terrible about waste. If a member of the family really needs eight hundred light bulbs burning in a room in order to study better or to read or do something useful, he doesn't care, she said, but needless expense annoys him. She gave her own ideas about youth, race, her family, love, and politics. About race—"the problem will be solved only when Negroes are neither loved, hated nor accepted, but rather by a natural living together without any intellectual or emotional effort made to forget color." She added that she did not want to sound like a well-fed preacher sitting in the White House! She told about how she wanted to become a nurse, that she almost burned down the White House the first night she slept here by lighting a fire in the fireplace when she really didn't know how, and then she gave a too intimate but accurate analysis of her relationship to politics. She said she formerly thought of politics as the most despicable, lowest, and most compromising activity in the world but the assassination of President Kennedy had changed her feelings. Politics had once isolated her from her family. Her father didn't come for suppers at 6 o'clock like most fathers; her mother didn't have enough time to spend with her— but after the assassination she had come to understand her father better— his commitment, his giving for the life of public service, and she decided she wanted to join in the commitment too. So that was when her political life of campaigning trips and speeches began. As she expressed it, she became "integrated into the life of this reunited community in the White House."

Sometimes Luci reminds me of Christopher Robin—"And the look in his eye seemed to say to the sky, 'Now, how to amuse them today?'" Every day, something new with Luci! She is a lark, a sprite, an imp. And you might as well try to bottle sunshine as to suppress her. Tonight she baked a cake for a friend's birthday—about eight inches high, four layers with lemon filling in between, and soft, fluffy seven-minute icing. She came out proudly displaying it to the Katzenbachs and to her father, who had come out to sit with us in the West Hall while he talked to Nick about the decision to ask him to become Attorney General.

We had a long and interesting evening with the Katzenbachs. He and Lyndon discussed the imperative need to make Washington a law-abiding city and how to go about it.

I felt at the end of today like a jug into which rich wine was being poured until it was full to the top and overflowing and simply couldn't take any more.

The day began with Mr. and Mrs. Laurance Rockefeller coming for coffee. I had wanted to talk with him in an informal way—exploring why he had put so much of his life and intelligence and money into beautification and recreation. Getting on the subject of beautification is like picking up a tangled skein of wool—all the threads are interwoven—recreation and pollution and mental health, and the crime rate, and rapid transit, and highway beautification, and the war on poverty, and parks—national, state, and local. It is hard to hitch the conversation into one straight line, because everything leads to something else.

Laurance Rockefeller is going to be the Chairman of a National Conference on Beauty which Lyndon is calling for mid-May. There are many of us desperately interested in something positive coming out of this program, something besides a lot of words and proliferation of committees. I do think now is the time—what is the line about "nothing is so strong as an idea whose time has come"?

About 4 o'clock I shifted gears to the war on poverty. Sargent Shriver had asked me if I would invite to tea the Advisory Council of the War on Poverty. We met, about thirty of us, with tea and cocktails in the Blue Room—the members of the Advisory Council from all over the country, plus the five Cabinet members whose work is particularly related to the war on poverty—Tony Celebrezze of HEW; Orville Freeman of Agriculture; Nick Katzenbach, the Attorney General; Stew Udall of Interior; Bill Wirtz of Labor; and Margy McNamara, whose husband is deeply concerned, and who is, herself, a member of the Advisory Council—and some agency heads who are involved, such as General Lewis Hershey of Selective Service (who has been around here about as long as I have) and Robert Weaver of the Housing Department.

We wound up in the Red Room, many of us sitting on the floor, everyone talking. One of the best spokesmen was Dr. Otis Singletary, whom I had met on the Whistlestop in North Carolina. He's director of the Job Corps and says that applications to join are coming in about six thousand a day. Describing the young men who apply, he cited one who, when he got off the bus at the Catoctin, Maryland, Job Corps Center, asked suspiciously, "Where are the fences?" He had thought it must be some kind of corrective institution. The official replied, "There are no fences. If you thought there were fences, why did you come?" "Because," the boy replied, "I just figured this is my last chance." Dr. Singletary said, "So many of these kids have a sense of overwhelming defeat—of having their last chance."

On the Advisory Council were men of such stature as Ken Galbraith— he said he was there to listen to Sarge Shriver and me conduct the Seminar. An interesting observation from Galbraith during the course of the discussion was, "What we are trying to do is to take human material that is potential waste and transform it into usefulness." There was also A. Philip Randolph from Labor, and Archbishop Lucey, long experienced in dealing with the poor of this world.

I asked the group, "Do you think we can make it work?" It was Tony Celebrezze who gave the dramatic answer. He said that years ago in a slum area of Cleveland, Ohio, a schoolteacher gathered up from the streets boys from poverty-stricken homes who were wandering loose, "just waiting to get in trouble." She said, "Let's have a club." They played basketball, discussed civic issues, and held debates. Since the teacher was a Republican, it was named the Theodore Roosevelt Club. "In the years since then, one of the men has become a Judge, three are lawyers, one is an architect, one a doctor, one a dentist, two are CPA's, and one was the Mayor of Cleveland and now sits in the President's Cabinet!" You had only to look at Mr. Celebrezze to know he had lived this story.

As they filed out, Sarge asked me if I would consider and sponsor the program Head Start, an honorary Chairmanship, not supposed to lead to any work. After this heady meeting I am more inclined to say "Yes," although I don't like being just "honorary" anything. If I take it on, I want to work at it.

Later upstairs I found Mary Lasker who talked with me about the beautification program and my Women Do-er's Luncheons. She was full of excitement. She says that President Johnson's State of the Union message marked the first time any leader of a nation has used the word "beauty" in a national address, the first time one has called for the beautification of the whole country as a part of his program.

Lyndon and I left for the Shoreham Hotel where he was to receive the Democratic Legacy Award from the Anti-Defamation League of B'nai B'rith. We arrived about 10 P.M., Lyndon still in a business suit, and without dinner. We were met by Dore Schary and Abe Feinberg, and moved in hurriedly, greeting Cabinet members and waving at a few Congressional people at their banquet tables, and then Lyndon delivered his speech.

Thursday, February 4

Today began at gray dawn, about 6:30, with coffee in bed before we dressed to go to the Congressional Prayer Breakfast. One of the things I remember out of the day were the brief encounters with very special people—Adlai Stevenson, Barbara Ward. I got a call from the office that Ambassador Stevenson was waiting to see Lyndon, but Lyndon was delayed, and perhaps it would be a good idea if I would come over and talk with Adlai, "and bring a birthday cake." It was his birthday. That wasn't too easy to do in five minutes, but someone in the kitchen produced one with a candle on it in jig time, and I went over to Lyndon's office. I was delighted that Lyndon was held up on the telephone for several minutes, so I had a chance to talk with—or rather listen to—Adlai. He talked about the failure of Russia and several other countries to pay a portion of their dues to the United Nations. And he made the complex situation understandable. Apparently these countries do pay all of their regular dues, but they don't pay "peace-keeping dues," or their proportionate cost for armies to the Congo and some place else, perhaps it's the Gaza Strip. You'd think from the papers that they never paid anything, but they announced originally that they were against sending the army to the Congo, would not be held responsible for paying any portion of it, and they have stuck to that, placing a burden on the rest of the countries that is hard to work out. Then we talked about China and I was rather flattered that he talked seriously to me.

I went back to the second floor and Barbara Ward and I had lunch. We talked about urban renewal and she discussed the concept of the garden city, the work of Edmund Bacon, city planner in Philadelphia, and the renovation that has taken place there. She told me the romantic story of a Greek named Doxiadis, a master city planner, and of his proposed development in Louisville of a marina and a medical center right on the river. I asked her in what countries in the world she found the most hope. Much to my pleasure, some of the hopeful countries of the world, according to Barbara, were in Latin America. "Venezuela," she said, "and

Chile, and perhaps with luck, Brazil." And then she said: "Outstandingly, Pakistan! Your old friend, Ayub Khan, and the vigorous nature of the Pakistanis themselves, are really building that country. You can notice the difference in the three years we've been going there."

In the late afternoon Lyndon had a guest—Senator Dirksen. I left them in earnest conversation in the West Hall, two brother artisans in government, heads close together, and went downstairs to intercept some guests I'd asked for a swim and drinks.

Nearly two hours later when I returned alone to the second floor, to my surprise, I found Lyndon and Senator Dirksen in practically the same postures. They asked me to join them and I was struck, sadly, by how thin and ill Senator Dirksen looks. But the minute he gets to talking, I forget all about it, because I am mesmerized as that great organ voice rolls along. He said, "You don't mind if we denounce you once in a while, do you, Lyndon? You can explain that better than when someone on your side of the aisle denounces you. . . ." Lyndon went on to give him his advice about how he, Lyndon, had operated as Minority Leader under Eisenhower: "I announced in the beginning that I did not believe in the past policies, that the business of the opposition was to oppose, that I was going to be with the President every time I could, when I thought what he was doing was for the best interest of the country. And I was going to oppose him, with dignity, when I felt his policies were not going to produce the best for the country. But I wasn't going to say ugly things about him, nor about his wife, nor about his dog, nor his grandchildren."

There is something terrifically right about watching them talk to each other. Both of them have spent their lives in the Congress, they understand it, though they may necessarily be disappointed in each other, from time to time.

Friday, February 5

Today wound up a busy week. It was my day for the Women Do-er's Luncheon, the one that is the kick-off of the beautification program, with Mary Lasker as the speaker. A little before Mary came I got word that Lyndon was in the Diplomatic Reception Room with the young people of the Senate Youth Program, sponsored by the William Randolph Hearst Foundation, and consisting of students from every state in the Union. Two or three from each state are brought to Washington each year, and given a thorough review of their government at work because of the leadership qualities they've shown and their interest in government work.

There Lyndon was in the middle of the circle of more than one hundred young people, eyes fixed on him, delivering a lengthy speech on why he wanted all of them to get into government. He added that when he got out of government, he was going to spend his retirement promoting in young people an interest in government service. I'm glad to hear it and I applaud.

Then back upstairs to the luncheon. Among the guests were Senator Maureen Neuberger, long an advocate of beautification, with special emphasis on controlling billboards; Mrs. Newbold Noyes of the *Washington Star*; Lee Udall, whose husband is spearhead of the beautification program; Mrs. Erastus Corning, President of the Garden Clubs of America; and the Dean of a Minnesota college, a friend of Hubert. The guests for the Women Do-ers Luncheons come from among my own friends and include women known for their interests and achievements in whatever we are going to discuss. Suggestions are occasionally made by a Congressman or a staff member.

Conversation was lively at luncheon. Mary Lasker—vivacious, competent, attractive—gave a speech and showed her splendid pictures. In a nutshell, her program is, "masses of flowers where the masses pass." Water, lights, and color—masses of flowers—those things spell beautification to her. I was surprised to see, when it was over, that Mary, that most sophisticated, most intelligent of women, was a little nervous and unsure when it came to speaking, so I don't mind so much it happening to me.

Tonight was another late night, 10:20 when Lyndon came home for dinner. I'll have to do something about Zephyr—her days are too long. But how can I speak of that when what I really ought to do is something about Lyndon? Only it's so much harder to do anything about him.

Monday, February 8

It's odd that you can get so anesthetized by your own pain or your own problem that you don't quite fully share the hell of someone close to you. Dear Lyndon has been facing the agony of hour-to-hour decisions, in a situation deadly close to a spreading war, and I have just been worrying about getting through an interview with *U.S. News and World Report* this morning so that even though I knew about his problems I couldn't help share his predicament.

Well, everything comes and goes, and so did this interview. When it began at 11 o'clock, I was curiously calm and fatalistic. We sat around President Grant's Cabinet table in the Treaty Room and six reporters asked me questions. There was a tape recorder and a stenographer. The session lasted for about two hours, and there were times when I had the feeling that I'd pulled out a true thought, dressed in rather fresh and interesting language; other times I was quite sure I was rambling, disjointed, and dull.

When it was over, Bess and I had lunch and talked about the mail, which is voluminous. There were more than thirty-five hundred letters the last week in January about Lyndon's hospitalization. The moral is "Don't get sick." And, of course, Luci's mail is running about five to one above Lynda's, much of it based on the rumors of Catholic instruction, and many of the letters hostile.

Tuesday, February 9

The scowling clouds are darker, if anything, for Lyndon. In Moscow there was an attack on the U.S. Embassy—rocks, ink bottles, and broken windows—and the police standing by.

But on the second floor, routine went on. Luci's history class, along with her teacher, Mrs. David Acheson (Dean Acheson's daughter-in-law), came to tour the White House, and Luci took over on the second floor and did her own conducting, including her bedroom and the kitchen. (It makes her so angry when *I* let anybody even peep in her bedroom.) I met all sixty-two members of the class and said a few words of welcome. It always startles me when I realize how much such things mean to Luci. Later she told me that Mrs. Acheson had been a friend of Margaret Truman. She seemed to feel that Margaret Truman had just counted those seven years of her father's Presidency out of her personal life. She just waited through them, doing whatever she could to assist her mother and father, but sort of putting her own life in cold storage.

John Walker of the National Gallery came to see me, excitedly confirming that the transparency I have from Mr. Dietrich shows a real John Singleton Copley, of the best early American period, done before he went to live in Rome. It's of a little boy with a squirrel. So I'll write immediately and say we would love to borrow it for the White House. I hope there's no slip-up on it. And he was equally enthusiastic, as Mr. Fosburgh and I are, about buying the beautiful Thomas Sully portrait of Fanny Kemble. He wasn't even startled by the twenty-five-thousand-dollar price.

Tonight is the first of ten Congressional receptions we have planned—eight for the House, with about fifty Congressmen and their wives at each, and some of our staff and two for the Senate. And it is my desire—as an alumna of Congress—that the parties be warmly hospitable for the wives and meaningful for the husbands, theirs and mine.

We met our guests in the Red Room. My light blue dress seemed just right for photographs, and each and every one of them paused for a picture with us—some to be treasured, I'm sure, some to be laughed at by a few sophisticated people, who consider this a "country" thing to do. As soon as we'd had a quick drink, Lyndon took the men off to the East Room to be briefed by McNamara, still much too wan, and Ball, standing in for Rusk, who's getting some sunshine in Florida, thank Heavens. I took the ladies down to the movie theater, to see *The White House Story,* a film about the thirty-two families who have lived in this house, the thread of history liberally sprinkled with anecdotes. When the men finished their briefing, we joined them in the State Dining Room for a light buffet.

I followed Lyndon to the second floor a little past 9. He had asked the Humphreys and the Larry O'Briens to join us for dinner. Hubert was his usual exuberant self. He had a new reason why he wasn't sent to the Churchill funeral. He said it's because (so they're saying) "Hubert just can't look sad." They are good foils for each other, Hubert and Lyndon, and Lyndon was never more amusing, reducing the day's problems to salty, picturesque summaries—but the problems are mounting.

Thursday, February 11

How many things are launched under the name of a tea! I met the Committee on Beautification in the Blue Room. Mary Lasker and Libby Rowe, Chairman of the National Capital Planning Commission; and Tharon Parkins; Stewart Udall, the real captain of the project; city planner Victor Gruen; master architect Nathaniel Owings, father of the Pennsylvania Avenue Plan; Walter Washington, head of Public Housing here; Mr. Commissioner Walter Tobriner; Charles Horsky, the White House adviser for National Capital Affairs; and Bernie Boutin, who used to be head of GSA and has now gone on to be head of the National Organization of Home Builders. A man who must have been a surprise to some of those sitting there was Adam Rumoshosky, Director of Marketing for the American Petroleum Institute. What are there more of than filling stations? And if each of them, or many of them, should adopt even the idea of neatness, what a boon it would be, and it would be even greater if they had a minimum of landscaping and some excellence in design! Also present were Bill Rogers, President of the Federal City Council (he used to be President Eisenhower's Attorney General); Katie Louchheim (no meeting would be complete without her); Admiral Neill Phillips, President of the Committee of 100 for the Federal City; Mrs. Kit Haynes, President of the National Capital Garden Club League; Bill Walton, Chairman of the Fine Arts Commission, so amusing and likeable; and that Number One conservationist, Laurance Rockefeller.

Fortified with tea, we went into the Red Room, and Stew and I sat on the couch, with everybody else in a circle around us. I began, alas, by reading (and herein lies one of my great dissatisfactions with myself) the statement that I had in my hand. Fortunately, the first part consisted of quoting a British diplomat's account, written in 1913, of what Washington looked like to him. This account had been published in the paper recently; so, hopefully, it didn't seem too awkward to be reading.

". . . your admirable river [the Potomac] is quite as beautiful," said Lord Bryce, "as that which adjoins any of the capital cities of Europe, except, of course, Constantinople, with its Bosphorus. No European city has so noble a cataract in its vicinity as the Great Falls . . . You have such a chance offered to you here for building up a superb capital, that it would be almost an act of ingratitude to Providence and to history and to the men who planted the city, if you did not use the advantages that you here enjoy." He ended with the prediction, "So someday the people are going to set the true value upon all these things . . ."

I added, "I think I have here in front of me today, you who set the true value on these things." And we went on to talk about what we might do to implement, to supplement, and to be a catalyst for action. I told them about the wire from the Vice Mayor of Norfolk. Norfolk is going to send us five hundred azalea bushes to plant in Washington, because Luci is their azalea queen this year.

And there was a letter from Secretary Freeman advising me that, out of the Department of Agriculture's inventory of shrubs, a few hundred azaleas, magnolias, and rhododendron were available. I talked about some specific things, big and little, that we could do—make a showcase of beauty on the Mall, which would be *used* by the American people, instead of just looked at. Take the small triangles and squares with which Washington abounds, now quite barren except for a dispirited sprig of grass, and maybe a tottering bench, and put shrubs and flowers in them, through the volunteer help of neighborhood associations or business firms (it would take some cutting of red tape to do that); perhaps have a volunteer committee of landscape architects to draw up plans, so that we can have continuity and good taste and a wise choice of plants. I then turned the meeting over to Stewart Udall, who began to elicit suggestions from all the members. Bill Walton recommended that we adopt New York Avenue as well as the Mall. The meeting ended with Stew's appointment of small committees to come back with suggestions, in their separate fields, as to how to proceed.

I rushed upstairs, about 6:20—the butlers and I were going to be equally busy getting ready for the second Congressional reception at 6:30. This time, we met them in the East Room, and then went into the Green Room. They were still tidying up in the Red Room from the committee meeting thirty minutes before!

Friday, February 12

Lincoln's Birthday marked a first in the White House, a celebration of the anniversary by inviting Lincoln scholars, Lincoln historians, actors who had played the role of Lincoln on stage or in movies, Civil War buffs—especially heads of the Civil War Centennial Commissions in many states—to the White House for luncheon. It was Dr. Eric Goldman's idea, and a very imaginative one, I thought.

The occasion began with Lyndon receiving the Gold Medal of the U.S. Civil War Centennial Commission in the East Room, and then we met the guests in the Blue Room. Among those present were Major General U. S. Grant III, whose sister had been born in the White House and whose father had been assigned to serve with General Custer; historian Bruce Catton; authors Paul Horgan, Oliver Jensen, Mark Van Doren; many university professors whose specialty is Lincoln—among them Frank Vandiver of Rice University in Houston—actors Gregory Peck and Raymond Massey, who had played the granite-faced Lincoln on stage and in films.

At the luncheon we had used the Roosevelt, Wilson, and Truman china for the table settings, and each round table had a piece of the Lincoln china in the center—its deep purple decoration, reflected in flower arrangements of heather, iris, freesia, and chrysanthemums. Lyndon's luncheon speech was measured, calm, and strong. "The man Abraham Lincoln . . . is forever shrouded in legend and hope," he said. "But his challenge to us sounds clearly across the years: love justice, extend liberty, remember you may be wrong, but act when you believe you're right."

In the middle of lunch I thought, "What an audience to take up to the Lincoln Room!" and sent Lyndon a note suggesting it. When we finished lunch I went up to the Lincoln Room, and as people drifted in and out, Mr. Ketchum and I gave a little word picture of the history and uses of the room then and now. One of the historians had offered to send me a letter written by Mary Todd Lincoln to place in the room! Afterward everybody departed to get in buses bound for the Lincoln Memorial, where Lyndon was to place a wreath.

I was proud of the whole day, and I think even columnist Mary McGrory was impressed. Later she wrote that Johnson had kidnapped Lincoln, taken him away from the Republican Party, stealing their last ornament of glory, as if it weren't enough to defeat them so soundly last November.

At 5 o'clock I had a meeting with Clark Clifford and Bill Heath on that phantom that I want to clothe with flesh—the Lyndon Baines Johnson Library. Bill presented us with a proposal that is almost too great to comprehend! The University of Texas wants Lyndon to deposit his papers there, and they propose land, a building, and a School of Political Science, or Public Affairs, to be named after him. It will cost several million dollars and will involve setting aside additional money to maintain the school. The plan must be explored from many angles, but it is a solution I know now I want to reach. Busby sat with us and was full of good ideas and good judgment.

Lyndon came home for dinner about 9, and I told him what we'd done. He suggested, "Why don't you get Bill Heath for dinner?" I observed that lots of people had eaten by 9; and sure enough, when I called Bill at his hotel, I think he had gone to bed. Nevertheless, he came quickly and we sat down to dinner at 11—Bill, Lyndon, and Lynda Bird. We talked until 12:30, Bill outlining his plans to Lyndon, and Lyndon showing as much interest in the establishment of the school as the library. We talked about the difficulty of getting competent men to serve in the government. Lyndon thought it would be wonderful if he could call upon well-trained men for the Cabinet or for Agency jobs—from Texas, from the Southwest, from the South, as well as from the little strip of the eastern seaboard, California, and the very few schools spotted in between. Of California, he said, "The whole airplane industry went to California because one professor went there, an eminent authority in that field, and the industry followed him." We really got caught up in his enthusiasm for this Texas training ground, for bringing others to it from all over the world. He talked of the people he would like to get to come down to lecture if such a school ever became a reality in his lifetime. It was a glowing, wonderful evening. If only something real could come about from it!

Valentine's Day, Sunday, February 14

Luci came bounding in this morning, to give her daddy a box of peanut brittle for his Valentine—no thanks from me. It's fattening! She and Lynda Bird had given me sweet Valentines. And I'm delighted that I got a card from the Secret Service—who knows you better?

We went to the National City Christian Church, and when we returned home, Lyndon went to bed. I was restless and had no wish to sleep. About 2:30, Lynda and I went to the National Gallery and spent more than an hour looking at the drawings of John White, who accompanied the expedition to Roanoke Island and painted all the flora and fauna, and inhabitants, from sand crabs and pineapple (he must have encountered those on some West Indies stopover) to Indians in war paint.

We looked in on the Flemish artists, Rembrandt and Frans Hals, and Van Eyck and Rubens. Lynda gave me the benefit of all her art courses, a thumbnail sketch on each. Sources of joy that are free, and imperishable—music and art . . . I want her to own all such riches. Every now and then a little flurry of whispers followed us, and glances were exchanged between the other tourists, but mostly, I think, we were quite incognito.

We had asked the Bob McNamaras, and the Bill Fulbrights, and Tom and Nancy Mann, to come for dinner. A success story is hard to come by in the foreign field these days, but it looks as if Latin America—and I speak perilously and timorously—would qualify as a success story, and the chief architect is Tom Mann. Lean, ascetic, with a sort of Lincolnesque face, and a bit hard-boiled, I believe he has added some tough realism to the idealism of the Good Neighbor principles, and the ability to say no. During the course of the evening he used the statement, "The policies of

Cordell Hull were necessary in the thirties, all right in the forties, they were tolerable in the fifties, and they are impossible in the sixties."

Ah, how comfortable the job of Senator looks from this vantage point! Bill Fulbright can disagree with everything that happens, and he doesn't have to come up with the answers of what to do.

Thursday, February 18

This morning I went to the warehouse with Mr. West to see the collection of White House furniture not actually in use. In one area were those things accepted by Mrs. Kennedy and her committees for the White House during the renovation of 1961 and not incorporated into the house before her departure. Then a larger collection of things that had been brought in by Theodore Roosevelt in 1902, and put away during the Truman renovation, about 1950. The biggest group of all was the furniture used briefly by the Trumans and then by the Eisenhowers during the eight years of their Administration. These pieces had been sent to storage by Mrs. Kennedy.

There were some strange oddments—a trunk that must have dated from around 1817, with "JAMES MONROE" on the front; and, when you opened it, you saw that it was very carefully built to pack and carry the famous vermeil that Monroe had purchased in Paris and that still adorns the table when we have State Dinners. And a wheel chair, perhaps the one that President Wilson had used during his long, last weary months in the White House. What a lot of ghosts this old warehouse holds!

Spring 1965

Life is lived these days against the backdrop of air strikes by
our planes in Vietnam, attacks on our Embassies—this week
it's another in Moscow involving stones and ink bottles hurled
by mobs of students and other dissidents—and a rising murmur of the press here in Washington about secretiveness or
not enough press conferences. But we still read that more
than 80 percent of the people approve of the record Lyndon
is making. It's like shooting the rapids, every moment a new
struggle, every moment a new direction—trying to keep the
craft level and away from the rocks, and no still water in sight.

I worked at my desk and was in small meetings until about
3:30 and then took a break to go to the circus. Ringling
Brothers had invited six thousand underprivileged children
who have rarely if ever had a chance to see a circus before,
and they had invited me. I was delighted to go because I
wanted to say "thank you" to them for their generosity to all
these youngsters. The children had come in buses, station

wagons, and on foot from settlement homes, nurseries, churches, and elementary schools to attend the show, all of them selected by the United Givers Fund.

Two clowns led me to my seat, and I found myself between Joyce Waffen, a bubbly little blonde, and Towana Johnson, a quiet, decorous Negro child. And in a sea of children. Jerry Kivett was practically invisible somewhere behind me, and Liz nowhere to be seen, but the press and TV, with a forest of cameras, were right in front of me. When I saw how pleased Joyce was at having her picture made, I thought even that was a good idea. Presently the press disappeared, and I enjoyed "the greatest show on earth," with a very appreciative audience, for two hours. The children enjoyed the cotton candy—everyone got a cone—almost as much as they enjoyed what they were viewing.

Sunday, March 7

We went to the Christian Church—Lyndon and I and Lynda and Paul Dresser. The coffee hour afterward always turns into a receiving line, and in no time at all half the states of the Union had been represented by the churchgoers who filed past. Lyndon has an absolute talent for finding the most lovable little girls or boys and striking up a conversation with them. This time was no exception. There was a little girl in a red velvet dress—I later found her name was Kimberley Fry—completely uninhibited, who liked nothing better than to be picked up by Lyndon and bounced and kissed, all to the delight of the photographers. They were also delighted as we filed out of the church to see Lynda Bird with a date and soon were telephoning Liz as to his identity.

Tonight the Bill Whites came to dinner, and the Jack Brooks and Congressman Pickle, and Clark Clifford (Marny's cruising the Caribbean with old friends from St. Louis days) and the Jack Valentis. In talking about a certain Congressman, someone remarked, "He couldn't pass The Lord's Prayer in the House," and Jack Brooks said, "Not even if the Lord returned and spoke in favor of it." It was one of those easy evenings when you feel you can talk about anything and not be afraid it will wind up on the front page.

For some time I have been swimming upstream against a feeling of depression and relative inertia. I flinch from activity and involvement, and yet I rust without them. Lyndon lives in a cloud of troubles, with few rays of light. Now it is the Selma situation. Negroes are demonstrating for the right to vote, and the cauldron is boiling. In front of the White House pickets are marching—a not-unusual sight, but in this context there is more poignancy than before, I think, because Lyndon is a Southern President, because he received such a great vote from the Negroes last fall, because the right to vote has been the key to the whole Civil Rights issue that he has hammered and hammered on since 1957. But this was only one of the intractable problems. I am counting the months until March 1968 when, like Truman, it will be possible to say, "I don't want this office, this responsibility, any longer, even if you want me. Find the strongest and most able man and God bless you. Good-by."

In talking about the Vietnam situation, Lyndon summed it up quite simply, "I can't get out. I can't finish it with what I have got. So what the Hell can I do?"

Tuesday, March 9

The second meeting of my Beautification Committee was held today in the Yellow Room, where Nathaniel Owings showed slides of the history of the Mall, beginning with the original grand design of Pierre Charles l'Enfant. (L'Enfant sent Congress a bill for ninety thousand dollars for his year-long work on the City of Washington, and finally collected, I believe, three thousand dollars.) And then we progressed to the changes during the nineteenth century. Quite recently, there was a steam plant right in the middle of the Mall! Van Buren had been one of those Presidents with extensive plans for the Mall, but he got no place. The McMillan Commission in the early 1900's helped bring l'Enfant's vision closer to fruition.

Mr. Owings' plan includes a Sculpture Garden and outdoor restaurant in the large empty square between the Museum of Natural History and the National Gallery of Art. He wants to banish automobiles from the Mall area, divert traffic through tunnels underneath, build underground parking, use minibuses and your own feet for transportation up and down the Mall, have a reflecting pool at the Capitol-end of the Mall similar to the one in front of the Lincoln Memorial, and preserve the tapis vert, the long green ribbon that stretches majestically from the Capitol to the Lincoln Memorial. All of that is fine, but I hope very much to add some masses of color in the meantime, because the great plan as proposed will take a decade to finish.

About 11:30 we started out in gay, striped minibuses for our first planting—all thirty of us, Mary Lasker and Libby Rowe close at hand with me. We made our first stop at the Smithsonian Museum of History and Technology, where Dillon Ripley showed us his charming plan for awnings and tables and chairs on the terrace. Beginning in June the Museum will serve light refreshments and have music for visitors.

And then we stopped at the Mall where, bordering a heavy traffic area that crosses the Mall, there is a new bed of pansies, a long carpet of purple and gold. I planted a symbolic few to finish it.

The next stop was at one of the park triangles close to the Capitol, right in front of the HEW building, where Maryland and Virginia Avenues and Second Street converge. It is one of the 761 little parks—triangles or squares or circles—formed by the way l'Enfant first drew up the city. It was quite gray and dismal, with a little scabrous grass and a couple of leaning benches, but one or two nice trees. Nash Castro of the National Park Service had planted some very respectable-sized dogwood trees. (I was delighted that my report after my first trip down there—that they were just "little switches"—had caused him to plant some larger ones.)

Next our entourage of committee and press bounced along to Greenleaf Gardens, a housing area of modest brick row houses, where a small crowd of the neighborhood folks were gathered to greet us, including two school bands, which performed loudly and enthusiastically, if not perfectly. This is Walter Washington's bailiwick and his great enthusiasm. In fact, it was he who had talked me into saying a few words here. He introduced me and I made a short speech, with little children wandering around, the band at attention. The gist of the whole stop was what I told Stew Udall: that all of our efforts will fail unless people in these neighborhoods can see the challenge and do the work on their own front yards.

It was a good start, a good morning.

But not for Lyndon. It was a day of tension and strain, with once-quiet little Selma dominating the news. To some extent the tension has eased. The marchers, led by the Reverend King, walked the prescribed distance—I believe it was across the bridge I have driven over so many times—and then turned around at a specified point and followed the Reverend King back, in accord with the court order. (I heard later that he did not know when he turned whether anyone would be following him.) Restraint of these forces was a victory for him and for the nation; this was sanity, a temporary lid on the volcano to grant time for the good sense of the nation to take hold, and we have a strong Voting Rights Bill in Congress to save us from catastrophe.

Despite all the troubles, Lyndon was feeling good when we met for the Congressional reception at 6:30. This was the ninth of the lot. It was the usual working session, a long briefing that ended after 9, with the ladies starving for refreshments. John Connally was in town and later joined us and stayed after the Congressional guests departed, talking long in the bedroom with Lyndon. It was not until later that I learned about the ugly aftermath in Selma—the beating of the Reverend James Reeb that sent him to the hospital, making infinitely more dangerous the forces of tension and destruction in Selma and across the country. So it was one step forward and two steps backward.

Thursday, March 11

My day was divided among work on the Presidential Library, the Diplomatic Corps, and the tenth and last Congressional reception. It was played against the background of loud, incessant chanting from the Civil Rights marchers, parading with banners in front of the White House.

During our morning meeting Buzz answered the phone—to hear the startling news that some of the Civil Rights marchers had walked into the White House with the tourists, taken seats on the ground floor, and refused to budge. A sit-in in the White House! There were twelve of them, mostly young people. There was a brief hurried discussion about how to proceed with the tourists. It was Lyndon who decided to let them keep coming in and not close the White House, but to route them in such a way that they would not encounter the demonstrators. This left the protesters in quiet seclusion, alone on the ground floor, with a minimum number of White House guards. I would have loved to have had a peek, but that would have destroyed the whole solution.

For me, the second event of the day was to go to lunch at the Venezuelan Embassy, where Mrs. Enrique Tejera Paris, one of the loveliest young wives of the Diplomatic Corps, had invited the wives of all the Latin American Ambassadors to be with me. I had accepted several weeks ago, first, because I want to get to know the wives of the Diplomatic Corps better, and second, because Mrs. Tejera Paris is a member of my old International Group and I know and like her.

The luncheon sounded innocent enough, to meet all the wives together, and it was only later that I discovered, through the State Department, the hurdles along the way. One was that Mrs. Sevilla-Sacasa of Nicaragua, who is the wife of the Dean of the Corps, would probably feel she should have been the first to extend such a courtesy. This I solved (I hope), and once more it was Liz who thought of how to do it, by asking Mrs. Sevilla-Sacasa to accompany me in my car to the luncheon. I enjoyed the ride very much. Mrs. Sevilla-Sacasa is quite a woman—the mother of nine, refreshingly outspoken and really quite funny, a change in diplomatic circles. Another difficulty, I discovered, was that Venezuela, alas, does not have relations with some of its Latin American neighbors and, therefore, how could it invite the wives of all the Ambassadors? Solution: those wives just happened to be out of town at the time, thank Heavens. And most of the OAS Ambassadors' wives did come.

At 6:30 was the Congressional reception. One of the problems this time was how to get the guests past the twelve demonstrators, but they had departed, after some urging—very civilly done, I am told, by the police—around 6 o'clock.

We followed the pattern set by earlier receptions—briefings for the men, theater for the ladies, with a movie on White House art. Then upstairs for all the ladies who wished to go to the second floor, and into the State Dining Room for refreshments. We were very late in being joined by Lyndon and the Congressmen tonight. It was 9:30 when they emerged. These briefings have gotten longer and longer.

When the news came that the Reverend Reeb had died, Lyndon and I excused ourselves for a helpless, painful talk with Mrs. Reeb. But what is there to say? When we went upstairs we could hear the Congressional guests and the music still playing below; and out in front the chanting of the Civil Rights marchers. What a house. What a life.

The Ides of March, Monday, March 15

Today I am dieting. Endless cups of black coffee, one egg for lunch; I did sit down with Lyndon and Walter Lippmann, but for the conversation, not the food. I had a moment with Mr. West and Mr. Ketchum to discuss a letter from Mr. duPont about a possible offer of a lovely Aubusson rug from Mrs. Edward Hutton. We decided to accept it. We have had to get alternates for the Red Room and the Green Room. This will make an alternate for Mary Lasker's rug in the Blue Room.

As the afternoon wore on, the tension began to mount for everybody in Lyndon's office and especially for those concerned with the speech he was to make to the nation this night on the growing turmoil in our land. I called Mary V. Busby to ask if she would like one of the step seats I use in the Gallery, and she said yes indeed, she would. The four ministers with whom Lyndon had conferred—Monsignor George Higgins, Rabbi Uri Miller, the Reverend Eugene Carson Blake, and the Reverend Robert Spike—were guests in my Gallery, and I am very proud that J. Edgar Hoover accepted an invitation to sit in the front row with me. I asked Ramsey Clark and Diana MacArthur—Civil Rights is one of her big interests—and Governor Buford Ellington of Tennessee, and the Burke Marshalls—he, so recently retired, pitched right back in to work when the crisis began to mount.

At 6 o'clock the speech was being brought over to Lyndon a page at a time. He was going over it, scratching out lines, giving directions to Jack, who looked pale, harassed, his wonderful good humor almost at the breaking point. I could very nearly hear him groan whenever Lyndon marked out a line and wrote in something else. This was still going on at 7 o'clock, and he had to be on the stand delivering it at 9. It was about then that he said, "Let's close it up the way we closed the one [the State of the Union] where I talked about growing up in the Hill Country. Let's talk about teaching the Mexicans in Cotulla, the first job I had after I left college." That job had taught him what poverty and prejudice mean to a young person.

Thanks to Marvin and Jack, I can now divorce myself far more from these tensions than I could a few years ago. Paul Glynn handles Lyndon's clothes, which I always used to take care of, and the operator gets people on the telephone.

It was 8:45 when I left with Lynda and Governor and Mrs. LeRoy Collins. Governor Collins has worked so hard as mediator all through the South. We went ahead of Lyndon to the Capitol and hurried to our Gallery, too late to see the pageantry of the entrance of the Diplomatic Corps, the Supreme Court, the Cabinet, the Senate. As I entered, the Chamber rose to applaud and I was as pleased as a sixteen-year-old. Back home to the Hill, and the Chamber rising for *me!*

And then Fishbait Miller's stentorian voice announcing, "The President of the United States." And in came Lyndon, marching down that familiar aisle, accompanied by long-time comrades-in-arms. I thought I could sense in the beginning he did not have the teleprompter. They hadn't finished in those last few harried minutes, and the speech I held in my hand—the copy of it—came to an abrupt end two thirds of the way through. I looked at the Press Gallery, and I did not see copies in their hands. I suppose it simply did not reach them.

But the speech was good, and the delivery was great! I doubt that he had time to read it over even once in the finished version. The best part of it was toward the end when he talked about his first teaching job in a small Mexican-American school in Cotulla, Texas. "My students were poor and they often came to class without breakfast, hungry. They knew even in their youth the pain of prejudice. . . . Somehow you never forget what poverty and hatred can do when you see its scars on the hopeful face of a young child. I never thought then, in 1928, that I would be standing here in 1965. It never even occurred to me in my fondest dreams that I might have the chance to help the sons and daughters of those students and to help people like them all over this country. But now I do have that chance— and I'll let you in on a secret—I mean to use it." I don't believe there was anyone in the Chamber who doubted him. Through the years I've always insisted he's his own best speechwriter.

They gave him a rising ovation at this point. In fact, there were two rising ovations in the course of the speech. I don't believe I ever saw that before. There was, of course, also one at the beginning and one at the end. My eyes skimmed across the Chamber. The Democratic side was most generous in applause; the Republican somewhat slow, the hands of some rather like the flippers of a seal. The bellwether of the Southerners, Senator Russell, was not there. He's in Puerto Rico recuperating from an illness. And I did not see Senator Harry Byrd. But in one row were Smathers, McClellan, and Ellender; and I saw practically no response from them.

The speech was too long. It ran forty-two minutes and would have been better at twenty-five. But all in all it was a magnificent speech, and the next day I was not surprised to see several newspapers and commentators call it "his finest hour," "his best performance," and such. The gist of the speech to me was concentrated in one sentence, calling on those communities who wished to avoid action by their national government, to "open your polling places to all your people." The solution for them would lie therein.

I said a respectful good-by to J. Edgar Hoover, good-by to the ministers, and walked out waving to the Cabinet wives. We went to the Speaker's office for awhile with the Leadership, and then home. Back on the second floor, Governor and Mrs. Collins, Jack Valenti, Larry O'Brien, the Busbys, and some other staff and I sat and talked about the whole performance and the whole course of affairs. It's like coming down off the mountain— intense strain and effort, putting everything into the performance, and then unwinding.

Governor Collins left a seventy-five-thousand-dollar-a-year job to take a twenty-five-thousand-dollar one that alienated all of his old friends and would give anybody ulcers. But somebody's got to do it and thank goodness there are people in this Republic who will. He told us of how a man who had been his barber for thirty years had refused to cut his hair the last time he was in Tallahassee. His pretty little wife, so typically Southern, said, "Well, you'd better be glad he didn't get that razor in his hand, with you sitting in that barber chair."

Larry O'Brien talked about Mayor Curley of Boston, in whose campaigns he had worked as a young man. All of them thought it was a wonderful speech and wonderful delivery. One or two were concerned about the length, as I was.

I have the feeling that tonight marks the end of a three-day comet, a rising spiral of activity on Saturday morning, sparked by what, I do not really know, perhaps will power. Saturday, Sunday, Monday, a crescendo of activity and effort, culminating in tonight. And now what can be done has been done, and we shall see.

Sunday, March 28

CAMP DAVID

What a glorious night of sleep! I treasure it for Lyndon as I would a four-carat diamond on my finger. We all gathered around the breakfast table about 10, having disposed of the idea of going to church. I, a great advocate of going to church, was delighted to omit it for once. We ate as if we were never going to have another meal. First came scrambled eggs and fried eggs, with home-cured bacon, thick and luscious. I had had my mind set on grits, and sure enough in came a big dish of them, followed by a dish of hot pancakes and more bacon, and syrup and melted butter. We threw discretion to the winds and had a banquet.

The day has seen another shot in the arm for the beauty program. We gave out the story of Mary Lasker's gift—9300 azalea bushes, flowering dogwood, and other plants to put along Pennsylvania Avenue.

Later Lyndon talked about the circumstances under which he started to college. He made one abortive attempt in which he went for a few weeks, made bad grades, and quit, with his father scornful and his mother weeping. Then followed several years of adventures—to California, running an elevator, working in a café, in a law office, and then, finally, back to Johnson City working on the highway driving a truck.

One Sunday morning his mother came into his bedroom to find him sprawled out on the bed with a broken nose, which was spread all over his face. To hear Lyndon tell it, he had been to a country dance the night before, "had gotten into a fight with a Dutch boy," as he expressed it, "over a girl." The boy had broken his nose—at least he and a group of companions had pitched in together and had given him a considerable beating. And there lay Lyndon—a pretty sight. His mother must have thought, "a truck driver by day—a brawler by night!" She began to cry. She said, "My son, my first-born," and then she began to talk to him about working with his mind and going to college. She must have gotten under his skin because he said, "All right, Mother, you write a letter for me to help me get a job, and I will go to college." On the other hand, his father administered a completely different sort of medicine. He said, "No need of your going. You can't make it. You haven't got what it takes to get a college education. Just keep on, and you might be a pretty good truck driver." I expect that was calculated. At any rate, it did the job.

Lyndon left for San Marcos with twenty-five dollars borrowed from A. W. Moursund's father, who had the Johnson City Bank. Later he borrowed fifty dollars from the Blanco Bank from Mr. Percy Brigham. So he was off to college—San Marcos State Teachers College. (Dr. C. E. Evans was the President.) Lyndon's father dictated a letter which Mrs. Johnson sent to Dr. Evans, asking him to give Lyndon a job. He got the job—working on the campus, cleaning it up. It is the rockiest, hilliest campus I have ever seen.

Lyndon soon discovered the paths by which Dr. Evans went to and from his duties, and Lyndon always managed to be along those paths working with extra vigor at exactly the time Dr. Evans came by. Dr. Evans noticed him and within six weeks he was working in Dr. Evans' office. His meals at Mrs. Gates' boarding house cost sixteen dollars a month for two meals a day, lunch and supper, or ten dollars for one meal.

The day was full of such delicious reminiscences.

NEW YORK AND BALTIMORE

Today began at the Carlyle in New York. Bess and I went with Mr. Fosburgh to the Frick Museum, where the lighting system makes dark pictures come alive, to see if such a system could improve the paintings at the White House. I decided it would and we made arrangements to get plans and estimates from the best lighting people. I went to the airport and was headed back for Washington on the 5:30 plane. But we had some trouble. It took us forever to get in. We flew in pea soup and uncertainty. Finally, we landed at National Airport and were at the White House just moments before I had to join Hubert and Muriel to drive forty-five miles to Baltimore for the big event of the day—Lyndon's speech in Baltimore at Johns Hopkins University, one of his major efforts to explain Vietnam to the United States, to the people he works for, and hopefully to more of the world. Lyndon wanted the girls there and they went, carrying schoolbooks along in the car and studying en route.

The speech was at 9 and we filed into the auditorium just in time. It was an impressive speech. There was a simple statement: "We will not be defeated. We will not grow tired. We will not withdraw, either openly or under the cloak of a meaningless agreement." After a thorough exposition of our strength and determination, there was the other side of the coin—what peace could mean. As a cynic might say, the carrot held out with the stick. Lyndon talked about the vast Mekong River project which can provide food and water and power on a scale to dwarf even our own TVA. He said, "For our own part, I will ask the Congress to join in a billion dollar American investment in this effort as soon as it is underway." He called on the UN to help and for all industrialized countries, including the Soviet Union, "to join in this effort to replace despair with hope, and terror with progress." And toward the end there came something which is almost a signature to his speeches lately—a reference to his own life, and how rural electrification changed his part of the country.

I had the high, thrilling feeling that we have taken the initiative. We are beginning to really explain to the world about Vietnam, about what we can do, about the promise of this epoch in history—that we are on the move against the negation of war and communism. It was exciting. I felt as if the stalemate had had a firecracker put under it.

LBJ RANCH AND SAN MARCOS

We arrived at the Ranch last night about 10:45 on the *Jetstar*. On the way down Lyndon talked of the harvest of legislation. He said that never has there been such a hundred days. And what a week this has been! Thursday, the House passed Medicare, 313 to 115; the Committee reported out the Civil Rights Bill, quicker and stronger than ever expected; and then the success of the Education Bill. This was a week to put a golden circle around, so let us remember it, because there will be many ringed in black; but this week we tasted the heady wine of success.

Today is the twenty-eighth anniversary of Lyndon's election to Congress. Sarge and Eunice Shriver, Ann Brinkley, Lyndon, and I helicoptered over to San Marcos to Camp Gary, a ghost of World War II, to the dedication of the Job Corps Camp in the old auditorium. This was why the Shrivers flew down. The nearly one hundred boys in residence are taking courses in automobile mechanics, shop work, landscape gardening, cooking, and baking. There were prayers and speeches but, for once, not too many. Dr. Singletary, who heads the over-all program, introduced Sarge Shriver; Congressman Jake Pickle introduced Governor Connally, who introduced the President.

Strangely, a speaker's platform sometimes offers time for reflection, if you are there as a spectator. I couldn't escape the drama there on the stage before me! Back in the middle of the thirties there had been just such a Job Corps as we were here dedicating, but it was called the National Youth Administration in those days. Congressman Jake Pickle had worked for it, Governor John Connally had helped pay his way through college making seventeen cents an hour with the NYA, and President Lyndon Johnson had been the Texas Director of it (not to mention Mayor Ellis Serur, who had welcomed us, and Federal Judge Homer Thornberry, both alumni). The old NYA helped lift a generation of boys out of the Depression and here they were thirty years later—these products of the NYA—putting all their energies into a Job Corps for another generation of boys who were in danger of being dropouts from life. It was the sort of day that makes you glad you are in the government, in the place you are, and have this chance.

As for the speeches, the Congressman, the Governor, and the President had hot competition from the three young men of the Job Corps who spoke—one from Georgia, one from Louisiana, one from Oklahoma. One of them, a young Negro, spoke without notes in a very straightforward and persuasive manner. Lyndon ended his own speech with a dramatic reference to the two Presidents who were looking down on us now and smiling at the day's achievements—President Lincoln and President Kennedy. It was well done, though melodramatic, and I had to blink hard to keep from crying. Leaving, we glimpsed familiar faces in the crowd—Mrs. Ed Cape and Jesse Kellam, again so much a part of our lives in early NYA days. It was a good feeling—that this was a going concern, that the boys, scrubbed and in their white shirts, were there to learn and would come out better able to face the world, and that there was a good staff capable of teaching them.

Sunday, April 11

LBJ RANCH

Today was a gold-star day in our lives—the signing of the Education Bill at the little one-room schoolhouse down the road. About 2:30 several school buses and two large chartered Greyhound buses rolled up, debarking Lyndon's former students from Cotulla, and from Houston, and his former classmates came in cars from all around this locality. It was delightful to greet Gene Latimer, who had studied under Lyndon when he taught public speaking in Houston, and have him sit by me at lunch, still boyish after thirty years, and to see tall, still slim L. E. Jones, graying, looking quite distinguished and confident, successful—not the awkward, brash, out-at-the-elbows young man I had known. One former student even called in and said he wanted to fly his Piper Cub in from Yazoo, Mississippi. We gave him permission to land, but, alas, I never ran into him.

Senator Gene McCarthy has been in Austin making a speech at the University of Texas, "An Intellectual's Place in American Government." We had asked him out, and Congressman Albert had come down—both of them to watch the signing of the bill this afternoon and then to fly back with Lyndon.

Bess and Lyndon and I had gone up earlier and surveyed the grounds of the little one-room schoolhouse, called the "Junction Schoolhouse." Mr. and Mrs. Bert Alford of Oklahoma now own it and live in it through the summer months, but it was vacant this weekend. They had given us permission to use the premises for the bill-signing and we had mowed the grass. Fortunately there was a lovely display of yellow and purple flowers around the stone steps that led up to the entrance. Bess had found some of the old double desks that were used in the school and had put one or two out front. It was an accurate, corny, warm setting for the signing of a great education bill, one of the landmarks, one of the victories, one of the real triumphs to be cherished by the Johnson Administration.

We converged on the place about 4 o'clock—around three hundred people—students, classmates, a few passing tourists, a sizable press, Lyndon, Lynda Bird, Miss Kate Deadrich Loney, Lyndon's teacher in the "primer" more than fifty years ago, and I. Among us was a Strawberry Princess from Poteet, who had arrived laden with baskets of gorgeous strawberries as a gift and who had had her picture taken with Lyndon. She was an emissary from Mr. Sam Fore, again a "landmark" in Lyndon's early years when Lyndon had asked advice from this sage South Texas editor. With his dying breath, Mr. Fore will be promoting some local product or person, making his contribution to his community and his state—and it has been sizable, what with a President and a Governor and a Federal Judge among "his boys."

We had brought up a picnic table and benches from the Ranch. Lyndon sat down at the table facing the TV cameras. Miss Kate, dignified and very sweet, sat down beside Lyndon. He made a short speech about what education had meant to him, about the bill, giving much credit to the Congress, about how much he wanted to further education through the entire warp and woof of our nation. Then he signed the bill and gave the pen, the only one, to Miss Kate. A brief ceremony, but a moment to remember.

Lyndon announced to the group of newspapermen that he had just made Admiral Raborn head of CIA and Dick Helms his Deputy. That announcement was the second big news of the day. Miss Kate lingered, but the rest of us set off to the lake in the helicopter to catch every minute of the sun.

Lynda said, as I have often said wryly, that we rush madly to rest, that we are always in a moving vehicle, and so we are. But what nicer moving vehicle than the boat going slowly, the Llano River turning scarlet with sunset and Pack Saddle Mountain silhouetted sharply against the sky, and a luminous three-quarter moon when we looked down toward the Colorado! As we lay on the deck of the boat, the sweet fragrance of the bluebonnets—buffalo clover is what they really are—was heavy in the air. Lyndon said, as he had yesterday, "This is what I call Heaven." He told

Carl and Senator McCarthy that he was going to be a teacher, come back here and live. He is getting more and more enthusiastic about it.

Later Lynda Bird and I found willing bridge partners—Carl, Senator McCarthy, Mariallen Moursund, five of us cut in and out. Playing bridge is my favorite way to end a day.

Good Friday, April 16

Lyndon and the McNamaras were up early. Bob McNamara is always a 6 A.M. man when here. They were out riding over the Ranch before I was awake, inspecting the coastal Bermuda, the tanks, the graveyard, the schoolhouse. A little past 8, I pulled myself out of the bed and joined them; we drove to the Scharnhorst. Dale Malechek was putting a large bunch of sheep in the pen for shearing, with several cowboys to help him. One of them was Ernest Stubbs, with his fine-looking young son, Clay, who was home from A & M for the weekend. In Levi's and boots, he could have walked into a Western movie without a bit of make-up. The whole scene was like a stage setting. Dale's two little boys were solemnly helping, and even Clary came bouncing up on her Shetland pony.

Lyndon keeps talking more and more about retiring. That has been a symptom this past week, and he talks joyously about it. For the first time, I am about convinced that he could. I have always believed that he had to stay lashed to the mast until the last gasp of breath, but I think that he is changing.

Saturday, April 17

At noon, Lyndon met with about forty reporters. I had ordered cookies and coffee put out on the front porch, but here I got a D minus as a hostess, because telephone calls from Lynda and Luci kept me inside; and there sat the cookies and coffee. Out in the yard was the press with no one to welcome them, and then right on time, Lyndon emerged and made his statement. They dived for their cars and we have cookies to last a week!

I gather Lyndon's statement was planned as a countermove, a chess play, to Senator Fulbright's speech about Vietnam—which was approximately this—that we ought to cease bombing for a few days to give a chance for negotiations to start. By seniority he has the position of being our party's leader in the Senate on Foreign Affairs and he is diametrically opposed to Lyndon's policy in Vietnam—a ham-stringing situation for a President. Lyndon's statement repeated that we have asked for talks on peace. There is no answer—no answer from Hanoi, no answer from Peking. You cannot talk to people who do not want to talk. We will not get out; we will not stop bombing unless there is an indication that they are willing to talk. He reiterated our readiness for negotiation but emphasized that it takes two to negotiate and both must be willing; then he said that due to the pressure of Congressional business, he would postpone impending visits from President Ayub Khan of Pakistan and from Prime Minister Lal Bahadur Shastri of India and any other until the early fall. Foreign Aid is up before the Congress. It is going to be hard enough to pass it anyway. It may be impossible, and the repeated presence of foreign Chiefs of State and their possible public expressions here might not be helpful to the sensitive business of guiding the bill through the Congress.

We had an evening of boating, and looking, and talking banking and politics and ranching, and laughing at old-time stories. On these evenings Lyndon is a raconteur par excellence. Many of his phrases make me wish I had a tape recorder handy. They are so earthy and colorful and true and fresh, though often rough. I am grateful for these times of relaxation. I want to prolong them. I look at him in profile. He is much too heavy. I do not know whether to lash out in anger or sarcasm, or just remind him for the nine hundred and ninety-ninth time. But now I see him yearning toward the days of peace and retirement, toward a life much along the pattern of these last three days.

Monday, April 19

LBJ RANCH AND COLUMBIA,
SOUTH CAROLINA

The mood is broken; the vacation ended. Lyndon awoke early to begin working hard. He must have spent three hours on the telephone talking foreign problems with McGeorge Bundy and then a long session with Dale telling him everything that the Ranch needed, all the things that ought to be done, fences, grass, water—being an executive. Dale must have been weary before he ever got started with the day's work.

We had a quick lunch with the staff, then choppered to Bergstrom.

I had asked Will Edward and Elizabeth and Nancy and Alfred Negley to ride up with us on *Air Force One*. They were thrilled. On the way up, Lyndon continued his marathon of work with staff and with the four newspapermen who were aboard—the pool. He talked about Vietnam. "If they bomb our barracks or the Saigon Embassy, we never hear anything about it; but if we bomb a radar installation or munitions depot or a bridge, the papers give us hell for it. We bomb a bridge and ammunition dump, they are steel and concrete and have no blood. China says stop bombing Vietnam, so does Russia. Of course, they would! It is not all right to bomb people in the North, but it is O.K. to invade the South . . . How can an American Senator or an American newspaperman or an American student tie the hands of our fellow American military men? Are they duped; are they sucked in?"

We had made the decision before we left Texas to stop in Columbia, South Carolina, for a memorial service for Senator Olin Johnston, who died yesterday. We arrived at the airport a little before 5, a very different arrival from the last time I was here on the Whistlestop train—October 7, 1964—the first place I had encountered real cold hostility and continuous heckling because of recent Civil Rights Bills. I recalled it had been difficult to handle. I had been mad, and yet determined, somehow, to remain cool. I said, "This is a free country. You have a right to express your opinions, and now I have a right to express mine. Will you listen?" Fortunately, it worked at that time. Senator and Mrs. Olin Johnston had been with us. The Senator met us at the first stop in South Carolina and had ridden all the way, looking wan and ill, but a fighter to the core, with courage and dedication to the Democratic Party in the face of his own people who were angry and vocal against him. I will never forget how he strode across that stage in Charleston, South Carolina, and roared at them, like an irate father, defiant, commanding—a wonderful stage appearance—and Gladys Johnston was no less courageous.

This time two of the same people were with us—Governor and Mrs. Russell met us at the airport. They went with us to the State Capitol where Senator Johnston's body lay in state in the rotunda. We met Gladys and her daughters, Sally and Elizabeth, and their husbands and her son. Gladys felt as thin and frail as a bird when I put my arms around her. She, too, has been very ill, but she was steeled and brave. It was a simple service. Their long-time minister and the Governor spoke. I am very glad that we could be there to pay homage to a great Senator and, yes, also to the State of South Carolina. For this son of a tenant farmer, this one-time mill hand—no riderless black horse, no roll of drums, but a suitable farewell in the Capitol, where he had been Governor longer than any other Governor and then had gone to the Senate for twenty-one years.

San Jacinto Day, Wednesday, April 21

THE WHITE HOUSE

This was a memorable day, primarily because Alice Roosevelt Longworth came to tea and brought her grandchild, Joanna Sturm. She is fiercely undaunted by old age, bristling with the quality of aliveness. It's said of her that she has an acid tongue, but I like her. We reminisced over tea, and she obviously enjoyed herself, recalling the days that she spent in this house. She related that once her little half-brothers and their friends were playing hide-and-seek in the attic (what is now the third floor) and that President Roosevelt, hearing the noise, went upstairs to investigate. It was nighttime, and he was in his pink pajamas, rotund and blustering. One of the youngsters looked up and said, "Here comes Cupid!"

She told us she had had her appendix out in the Queen's Room, lying there on the bed the doctor brought from Baltimore. Then she was moved into what is now the Lincoln Room to recuperate. She said her step-mother had three good party dresses; and, since the press was not present at their receptions and entertainments, the White House gave out descriptions of them. They would describe a dress for one reception as "blue-gray silk" and for the next as "light blue moiré silk with a lace portrait collar," and so on and so on. The same dress was described a dozen different ways!

Mrs. Longworth had not, however, enjoyed having dates in the White House. She had always gone out to the home of a dear aunt who lived here in town, where she felt freer. Lynda was with us and enjoyed talking to her and eliciting stories of the past. She knew so much of the history of that day. This visit had been planned especially for Mrs. Longworth's grandchild, but I think that both Lynda and I enjoyed it more.

This afternoon we went to the Italian Embassy for the return engagement of Prime Minister Aldo Moro. Alas, the very graciousness of the hosts in asking so many guests resulted in a crowd that was overwhelming. The painted eighteenth-century doors of the Italian Embassy, with its rainbow-hued Venetian glass chandeliers, were completely obscured in the welter of humanity through whom we pressed—Ambassador Sergio Fenoaltea, Lyndon, Prime Minister Moro, Mrs. Fenoaltea, and me—with the photographers in stumbling retreat in front of us and friends on each side getting a hurried greeting or, in the case of Virginia Rusk, backed to the wall by the crowd, a kiss from Lyndon. The whole affair took little more than thirty minutes. Prime Minister Moro is an amiable, earnest man. One likes him. But a reception is no occasion to learn anything about him or his country.

Lyndon had invited the Max Freedmans (he is the correspondent for the *Manchester Guardian*) to join us for dinner. I had the luxury of a quiet visit with Max before Lyndon arrived, and then the conversation revolved around him. Lyndon brought with him George McGhee, just over from Germany for a few days, and the conversation was good. I asked George about the possibility of a united Europe—a feeling that I had sensed was in the air when I had been to the Scandinavian countries and the Benelux countries in the fall of 1963. The apogee of that time is past, George thinks, De Gaulle having effectively prevented it. Germany is a crucial country, and Germany is still willing but no longer anxious, and the time for union to happen is diminishing day by day.

Lyndon took his text on Vietnam and in vivid, down-to-earth language, very clear and impressive, summarized our position vis-à-vis Vietnam and the ten-year course of the struggle. I knew he was working. I knew he wanted to explain it from his viewpoint to Max, and maybe Max in turn, by osmosis, could explain it to his readership. Lyndon has been hammering away this month on TV, in press conferences, with individual columnists, to groups of Congressmen, to every forum he meets, trying to put Vietnam in true perspective, to win the war of words in which we have faltered even more than on the battlefield itself.

When you are so close to the scene, it is hard to tell when something starts, but I believe I have seen it start these last few weeks—a seizing of the offensive, not only of planes and gunfire in Vietnam, but here at home in telling about it, in convincing people.

Tuesday, April 27

Lyndon had asked Governor and Mrs. Allan Shivers to have dinner with us; and, for once, we had a reasonably early dinner followed by the briefest appearance—only forty-five minutes portal to portal—at the annual dinner of the U.S. Chamber of Commerce, honoring Bob McNamara. With the Shivers, we drove out, walked in just in time to listen to the honor bestowed on Bob, to hear his brief rejoinder and for Lyndon to say his few words—how he does admire and depend on Bob.

The evening had that peculiar quality for me, and I believe for the other three, of pleasure, release, gratification, that two who have been torn asunder by politics are once again friends. Lyndon and Allan Shivers had begun as friends, had gone through a knockdown, drag-out fight in 1956, in which fire-eaters on both sides of our divided Democratic Party in Texas had rejoiced and tried to bloody up the schism—but here they were, talking in a relaxed and comfortable manner.

Looking back on it, Lyndon's life has been extraordinarily free of losing friends in the thirty or more years that he has been in politics, having to hold the reins firmly and having to make choices. He has managed to keep or return to most of our friends. . . . If we lose friends in our present job, I hope we can return to them someday.

Tuesday, May 4

THE WHITE HOUSE

Back from my three days in Texas, my desk was in a hopeless state. Lyndon looks tired and worn. The Dominican troubles have taken their toll. At the Ranch I had watched his TV report to the nation on the Dominican Republic on the reason for the American presence there. I saw a twenty-minute news clip of it. He had a cold; he was obviously very tired; the teleprompter didn't work, I soon became aware; but with great earnestness, clearly and solemnly, he explained why we were there—to save lives, to prevent a takeover by a Communist regime that did not represent the country but was dominated by outside forces. I felt a wave of sympathy —what the last two or three days must have cost him in terms of sheer physical endurance. But I remembered gratefully the way Dorris had expressed it. She said, "I'm so glad he talks to us, he tells us what's going on." For over a month, he's really been talking to the whole 190 million the best he knows how. If *not* talking has been a failure of the Administration in the last year, two years, or whatever, it has ceased to be a failure now.

Also, he has gained three of the twelve pounds he had so proudly lost. When his weight reached 226, it really struck home to him, because that was more than he weighed ten years ago when he had the heart attack. In a little over a week's time, he had brought it down twelve pounds.

Once in gear, his will power carries him along like a tank. His undoing is those 10 and 11 o'clock dinners, before which he has had little lunch or no lunch, and tea and melon for breakfast. And so he's ravenous and eats hugely, especially desserts.

Because of being out of town for several days, and because it's the merry month of May, I had a horrendous schedule today. First I went down to the State Dining Room to meet a group of Metropolitan Opera singers, headed by Risë Stevens, who were touring the White House. Next I went to the Red Room to greet two workers for Project HOPE and accept tickets to the HOPE Ball. Then I went to the Blue Room to hear Mrs. Luther Terry and John Walker of the National Gallery explain about Pictures for Patients—reproductions of great paintings to be made available for hospital patients to hang on the walls of their rooms. Then I went to the Green Room to meet the Multiple Sclerosis Mother of the Year, Mrs. Allen Somm, and her husband and child. And then downstairs to the library to say hello to two happy, elderly people, a lady and a gentleman, who were delighted to tell me all about the Episcopal Home for the Aged. They wanted me to come to the fashion show which raises funds for the Home. Then out to the Jacqueline Kennedy Garden, where representatives of the Bethesda Chamber of Commerce showed me a big colorful photograph of their sixty-six-thousand-dollar beautification project. A cross section of citizens—architects, businessmen, Chamber of Commerce boosters—have been working on it for several years.

I'm sure when the history of this period is written, the volunteer spirit, particularly in this country, will stand out as a phenomenon. Volunteers, foundations, automation, space, and the war on poverty—what a decade, what a remarkable generation I live in!

I was so glad to do all of this—the projects were all so worthy—but it *was* an assembly line and my haste may have seemed ungracious to my guests. I told Liz not to permit such a pile-up to happen again—five or six in a row! Then I was off to a big event of each spring for me since 1949 —the Senate Ladies Luncheon.

Back at the White House, I met with Mr. James Babb, who has carried the load for the White House library, and with the other committee members, friends, and donors of the library, to thank them for bringing it to its present state of completion, except that it isn't *really* complete. Because as long as life goes on and people write, there will be books to choose from and add to the shelves.

We were joined by a cross section of celebrities from the world of books—authors, publishers, and critics—for the ceremony to award the first National Medal for Literature, which went to Thornton Wilder for the whole body of his works. It turned out to be, for me, one of the most congenial and, in a way, lustrous gatherings that I have ever had in the White House. I was delighted to be with Thornton Wilder, and I thought he was a happy choice. He left me aglow with his remarks, and I felt at home with these people.

This was one of the cultural events, of which Eric Goldman and Roger Stevens are the midwives, that I go along with happily. Of all the talents I wish I possessed, the one I most envy is the ability to make words march and sing and cannonade and speak with the cool voice of reason.

It was after 11 when Lyndon came home and, weary and haggard, he had dinner. He talked about the Dominican Republic affair, and finally got to bed, but not to sleep, well after midnight.

Wednesday, May 5

This morning I greeted the Junior League Garden Club in the Rose Garden and thanked them for all they are doing. And then I went to the Trinity AME Zion Church, in the very poor Cardoza area, to see a pilot project for Operation Head Start. Here three-, four-, and five-year-olds are given a medical examination and one hot meal a day and busied with such things as painting, dancing to the guitar music of returned Peace Corps volunteers, and going on field trips to such places as the museum and the zoo, the post office and the supermarket, to learn something about the world around them.

The children, most of them Negroes, one Chinese, a scattering of whites, were all scrubbed and clean and dressed in their best. Nearly all of them seemed to have the capacity to grow. The main thing they try to teach in Head Start is how to communicate. When the children first arrive, there is little response to the instructors or to each other. They come from an area where juvenile delinquency is about twice as high as that throughout the rest of the city, and the dropout rate at the high school in Cardozo is between 50 and 60 percent.

The primary reason for my going is that next Sunday, Mother's Day, Operation Head Start is going to announce that it hopes to reach six hundred thousand children in about two thousand communities throughout the country. By attracting even a little more attention to the program, perhaps we can get more volunteers. The more you see of these young ones and what happens to the likes of them as they grow up and reach teen-age and maturity, the more you believe that the fruitful, hopeful time to start work is in Operation Head Start.

In the middle of the afternoon there was a long work session with ABC. Make-up, cameras, reading of script, an attempt to break me in, I suppose, to the formidable business of doing the beautification show. My part in it is vaguely dissatisfying—because I really want to lift and soar with poetic words of my own—and, alas, they don't flow out on cue.

Another important event of the day was the Diplomatic Reception—black tie—for the entire Corps, 114 countries, a battalion from the State Department, the press, and the White House itself.

This party was being given against the backdrop of tenseness and at least two trouble spots, Vietnam and the Dominican Republic. At 9 o'clock the OAS was to meet to decide whether or not they would join the U.S. in sending troops into the Dominican Republic. Gallant Sevilla-Sacasa, Dean of the Corps, bending low over my hand, was, of course, the first in line. The representatives from Great Britain, Ambassador and Lady Patrick Dean—because they have only recently come to this country—were near the end.

At the last moment Bess had informed us that photographs had to be made of each diplomatic couple coming down the line. That was one complete, unalloyed mistake. Nobody understood, and it caused a horrendous traffic jam. Finally Lyndon and I gave up. He engineered all those he could reach into standing quietly while a picture was made, but most of them wandered off.

Nine o'clock brought the departure of all the members of the OAS, and shortly thereafter, Lyndon's. I decided to pour all the gaiety and energy I could into seeing that the rest of the Ambassadors and their wives felt as much at home, had as good a time as I could provide. From the State Dining Room, where the buffet was laid out, to the East Room, where the dancing was taking place, I walked purposely, looking for those I knew, or didn't know, who seemed lonesome.

Meanwhile, Dobrynin of Russia and Dean Rusk sat on the sofa in the Red Room for over an hour talking quietly, while people passed, casting glances over their shoulders, wishing, I suppose, that they could eavesdrop.

Walking through the East Room, I saw that the Ambassador from India, Mr. Nehru, was alone. He is one of the most distinguished-looking men in any room. I quickly went over, took his arm, and asked him if he didn't want to see the really lovely view from the south portico. So we went out to survey the Washington Monument and the Thomas Jefferson Memorial—I had asked that the doors be opened from the Green Room, the Blue Room, and the Red Room, and alerted lots of my friends to suggest that people stroll out and see the lighted fountain, surrounded by tulips, and smell the wisteria. The Ambassador and I talked of his wife's speeches and the way they have put so much of India into their Embassy, its furnishings, its art work. But we didn't have a word to say about Kashmir.

I decided that next time I would ask a corps of special friends—people who speak French and Spanish—who would single out their quarry and make them feel "at home" and special, I want the Diplomatic Corps to feel that their one reception a year in the White House is personal, something to remember, not just a formal exchange of courtesies.

Thursday, May 6

I dashed into Garfinckel's with exactly five minutes to buy a black patent purse, and made it to the Shoreham for the Congressional Club brunch, another high point of the year, the annual party of the Congressional Club, which I have been going to since 1938. As I pulled up to the entrance, Mrs. Alvin O'Konski, the Republican Chairman and Mrs. Chet Holifield, her Democratic co-Chairman, met me at the doorway with conductor's caps on and big grins! That set the tone of the day. They had used the Lady Bird Whistlestop as the theme of the brunch. Each table was centered with a toy train engine, with a little red and white canopy and a bird perched on top of it.

For this theme to have been chosen by a Republican Chairman and okayed by all the Republicans on the Board is, somehow, especially pleasant, for the Whistlestop was hardly bipartisan.

The Marine Band was playing "Chattanooga Choo-Choo" and later "The Yellow Rose of Texas" and "Hello Dolly!" And all of the audience —this time there were a thousand, more than I ever remember—were in a party mood!

With the two tickets I had received for the girls, I had invited Mrs. Emmet Redford and Mrs. Barefoot Sanders. I remember all those years in the House and Senate when I used to hoard my tickets and parcel them out to my very favorite constituents. I remember so well standing in the hall, hoping that I would at least be able to get close enough to a Cabinet or Supreme Court wife to introduce my constituents. When I went in, in the Club's well-staged manner, last of the guests of honor, to the blare of music and on the arm of a very erect red-coated Marine, I tried to look from right to left at all the Congressional Club members with their very special guests to make it as personal as possible. But the spotlight was so blinding I couldn't see anybody. Their traditional gift to me was truly special. It was the original of the cartoon of the Lady Bird Special train. And if I looked as if I were having a good time, it is because I was!

Tuesday, May 11

VIRGINIA

Today I made my long-awaited "Landscape-Landmark Tour" into Virginia in the big Greyhound bus with all the Cabinet wives (except Mrs. Rusk—who had other duties). What fun it is to be off with them on a trip that promises a good time and real talking, as well as work. The Laurance Rockefellers were with us, and the Roger Stevenses, and the Rex Whittens of the Bureau of Public Roads, and Nash Castro from the Park Service. There was also a State Senator from California, Fred Farr, who was particularly knowledgeable and interested in the aesthetics of highways. And a pool of reporters—just behind us was a press bus with some forty or so reporters from all the media, including ABC, NBC, and CBS. Nan Robertson of the *New York Times* said it was "as relaxed as a family outing in the country," and so it was. We had come without our hats, soon slipped out of high-heeled shoes, moved around the bus from person to person, while we drank coffee and munched homemade cookies that Mrs. Rex Whitten had brought along.

Margy had her camera and I had mine. The first stop was for the dedication of the Dumfries Wayside Shelter. Silver-haired Governor Albertis Harrison, Jr., the very prototype of a Governor, and Mrs. Harrison met us there for a ceremony dedicating this complete facility for the tourist —picnic tables under an attractive little roof, a barbecue pit, water fountain, and rest room—against the backdrop of native trees—many dogwood, with a few azaleas planted, as Mary Lasker would say, "like lipstick on a woman."

There was a small crowd, a few speeches, the unveiling of the stone which attested my dedication of the shelter. They hope to have a tourist facility like this on all the major Virginia highways, located every twenty or forty miles. The shelter had a verse I like on it—"THE ONES WHO TRAVEL FAR ARE DOUBLY BLEST/ FIRST, WITH A CHANCE TO ROAM AND THEN TO REST."

Next down the road we saw a blazing exhibit of azaleas, dogwood, pansies, marigolds, planted by the Associated Clubs of Virginia for Roadside Development. I spaded up the dirt to plant a dogwood. This is the Year of the Shovel for me! The woods were laced with dogwood, white and fairylike in the brilliant morning.

The chief lesson of this morning is the opportunity of seeing what has been done with Interstate 95, which has a broad right-of-way and complete control of access, by selective cutting, by skillfully maintaining the best native trees and shrubbery, by planting the banks for erosion control, by preserving the vistas. This highway is a beautiful drive, even if it frequently comprises six, or even eight, lanes. It is a model of what can be done, and the median strip is a great plus.

Briefly we got off of Interstate 95 to go down to Highway One, to compare the two roads, one a narrow right-of-way with uncontrolled access. What we saw was a tunnel of filling stations, billboards, neon signs, and dilapidated little buildings. And yet these enterprises are conveniences for people, and this is private enterprise. What is the answer? Some control by government and some raising of taste levels? But the contrast of frenetic billboards on one road and only nature on the other was a significant lesson.

At noon we arrived at Charlottesville, our luck still holding with the lovely weather, and climbed Jefferson's mountain to Monticello. Many times I've been here, but never in this fashion, trailing forty newspaper people with heavy camera equipment, and met by the Trustees of Monticello.

No house speaks so much of the man who built it and loved it. Like everybody else who has been here, I particularly love seeing Jefferson's inventions—the revolving chair, the chaise longue, the duplicating machine —great-great-grandfather of Xerox. His "solitary" I had never seen before; nor had I been up to the topmost floor underneath the dome, with its beautiful views in every direction. You wonder if he had in mind being an artist, the room looked so much like a studio.

I did find myself looking at the house with new eyes, the eyes of someone who someday might leave a simple house—not anything so great in our history as Monticello, but one to which other generations of American tourists might come—so I gave a thought to the future as I drank up the past.

We had sherry under the great tulip trees, and I took movies and wandered around the grounds and talked with Mr. Henry Taylor, the columnist, whom I found delightful, although he may no doubt have cut us to pieces many times in the past. I remember him as an acerbic critic of FDR and of all his followers. We had lunch on the terrace overlooking the University of Virginia. The menu was superb: Virginia ham, Sally Lunn bread, an oyster recipe that was supposedly Jefferson's own and delicious, and Crème Brûlée. I threw discretion to the winds and ate everything.

There were some speeches. In mine I spoke of my great liking for Jefferson's having put the phrase "pursuit of happiness" in the Declaration of Independence, and of the four Thomas Jeffersons in my own family. I gave a seedling of a flowering horse chestnut tree—a white one—that grows on one of the mounds on the South Lawn—a mound which Thomas Jefferson had designed for what he called "The President's Park."

We got on Laurance Rockefeller's plane and flew to the Bristol Tri-Cities Airport, and went from there by car to Abingdon, riding with Congressman Pat Jennings and Bob Porterfield, manager of the Barter Theatre, whom I found charming and full of good stories.

As usual on such trips, the three hours' allotted rest time collapsed into one hour. Rain was falling as we drove up the streets of Abingdon but we were preceded by two high school bands, and there was a sizable crowd of local people along the sidewalks. As we approached the old Martha Washington Inn, we saw the yard was full. We went up on the porch for a welcoming ceremony—roses for Muriel, yellow roses for me, greetings from the acting Mayor, a talk by Bob Porterfield. I just took a bow and introduced the Cabinet ladies and the Roger Stevenses and the Rockefellers.

Upstairs I found my room, furnished with antiques. This old and charming building was once a school, attended by Edith Galt Wilson, and Eleanor Roosevelt's father once lived in Abingdon. I had a canopied bed and someone had placed a funny little picture of Lyndon and Lady Bird Johnson, circa 1937, on my bedside table, with an exquisite bouquet from the local garden club.

I did snatch about an hour's rest, and then a nice young girl performed a miracle on my hair. I dressed in my peach theater suit, clutching my magnolia seedling from the Andrew Jackson magnolia, and led the nine Cabinet ladies across the street to the Barter Theatre, each carrying whatever her "barter for admission" was—her jug of sorghum or a bucket of tomatoes and squash—to go into soup, not to be thrown at the performers! One chief purpose of this trip was to give an award to Roger Stevens for his contribution to today's drama.

Roger Stevens, Bob Porterfield, and I went backstage and when the curtain rose, there we were, lined up in front of Caesar, Cassius, Brutus, Calpurnia, from the cast of the current offering, *Julius Caesar*, to present this award which has gone to a star-studded group since 1939, beginning with Laurette Taylor and including Ethel Barrymore, Helen Hayes, Tallulah Bankhead, Fredric March, Cornelia Otis Skinner, and Mary Martin. This is the first time it has been awarded in the Barter Theatre, although not the first time, I believe, by a First Lady. Bob Porterfield was a friend of Mrs. Roosevelt's and she'd been to the Barter. I believe she had presented the award once.

I borrowed a line from the play and said, "Friends, Romans, countrymen, lend me your ears. We have come to praise Roger Stevens." For once I got a laugh! The small, quaint theater was full; the award itself included a Virginia ham, with a platter from which to eat it, a scholarship for two young actors, to be chosen by the man receiving the award, and an acre of land on the mountain close by.

When *Julius Caesar* was over, we went across the street to the Ballroom of the Martha Washington Inn, candle-lit, flower-bedecked, festive, and had an after-theater supper party. By this time I was starving. If they hadn't brought on Virginia ham, I would have gone out to the kitchen to hunt for some. And fried chicken and spoon bread! What can there be about such a day to make one so hungry? Maybe trying to learn about everything that is put before you and projecting your appreciation of it and your interest in it does take muscle and effort, although it doesn't always look as if it does.

Tuesday, May 18

THE WHITE HOUSE

Today began with coffee with the Peter Hurds on the Truman Balcony, discussing Lyndon's portrait. My goal this year is to achieve some of the physical things that will relate to history. Lyndon will make his own record, good or bad, but to preserve it some things must be done. One thing I want is a good portrait of him. Most of all, I want the establishment of a library, and that is up to the University of Texas at present.

Third, and this is a small item, I want the little house that was his boyhood home in Johnson City to be restored and opened to the public.

Mr. Hurd and his charming wife, Henriette, sister of Andrew Wyeth, and I talked about the difficulties—especially of finding time for sittings. We all decided it would be ideal if the work could be done at the Ranch. The dining room, with its huge picture window and the north light, would be the best place for sittings, maybe two hours a day, preferably in the morning. I emphasized the difficulties there would be with our "sitter"—many arising from his own personality, more from the nature of the job he holds.

But the most important thing in my day was the beginning of the ABC-TV project, which I hope will speak to the whole country and sow some seeds of interest in nationwide beautification. I have never been more scared of anything or felt less confident or competent to undertake it.

I rushed to the Rose Garden, late, for an announcement that Lyndon was making to an assembled group of newspaper reporters and poverty program people about grants to Project Head Start. Over sixteen hundred grants will be made to form about 9500 pre-school centers that will serve 375,000 children this summer for eight weeks.

On the steps leading down to the Rose Garden, behind Lyndon, were four of the children who are going to be enrolled in the Head Start program—youngsters with their mothers. One came from Gum Spring, Virginia, and I am glad we haven't forgotten the rural areas. Sargent Shriver was there to explain Head Start, when Lyndon had finished his own speech.

One thing they expect to discover among these 375,000 children is one hundred thousand eye difficulties, and this is what Luci is interested in. I hope her work equals her interest, and I think it will. Lyndon was entitled to be out of sorts with me for holding him up a good five minutes while I was walking around the grounds. He just said, "Next time be on time when we are holding a meeting which you are going to be in on." A measured admonishment, dear man, from somebody who had been up until 5 o'clock wrestling with problems of the magnitude he has.

Then to get dressed for the return reception of President and Mrs. Chung Hee Park of Korea at the Mayflower. The table was magnificent, and Mrs. Park looked like a flower in her brilliant red Korean dress with white "birds of good omen" embroidered around the hem. I was told that the birds symbolized Mrs. Park's good wishes for the happiness of the President and the First Lady of the United States. The only trouble was that there were thousands of people in a room meant for mere hundreds. The population explosion is certainly getting to politics. Lyndon towered over most of them and made his way purposefully enough, while Mrs. Park and I did our best to follow, speaking to the right and left, smiling and shaking hands, totally ceremonial, with hardly a chance for a personal encounter.

Friday, May 21

Something happened today that may be of utmost importance in the art future of the nation's capital. I had asked Mr. and Mrs. Joseph Hirshhorn to come down from New York for lunch with me, inviting them intentionally for thirty minutes before the other guests came so that we could have a quiet, personal tour of the State floor and the second floor.

Mr. Hirshhorn has the greatest collection of modern sculpture in existence, according to Dillon Ripley and Roger Stevens, as well as an outstanding collection of paintings, including thirty-two Eakins. For some time the Smithsonian has been talking to him as, I understand, have many other museums, including the Tate in London, in the effort to persuade him to will or give his collection to them. He has agreed in a letter to give it to the Smithsonian if they meet certain requirements—a separate and suitable building bearing his name, assurance of good care, and other requirements.

I had asked the Roger Stevenses, the Dillon Ripleys, the Sam Harrises, and the Abe Fortases to join us for lunch. (Fortunately the Fortases turned out to be old acquaintances of Mr. Hirshhorn.)

I had met Mr. Hirshhorn briefly before and gathered that his is one of those great American success stories, an immigrant from humble beginnings, with intelligence and drive, who seized an opportunity offered in this marvelous land and acquired great wealth, all in his lifetime. He has been collecting art for forty years. When he began, he didn't have much money. But he bought vast quantities with instinct and taste, and picked out many things that were going to last and appreciate—that's Roger Stevens' estimate.

At any rate the Hirshhorns came, and we had a delightful time. He enjoyed seeing the White House collection, and I love showing it to people who enjoy it. I hope, of course, that one of the thirty-two Eakins Mr. Hirshhorn owns will come to rest in the White House, and have charged Roger Stevens, Dillon Ripley, and Abe Fortas with that hope, because

I am the world's poorest salesman. What a situation I find myself in! A First Lady should be a showman and a salesman, a clothes horse and a publicity sounding board, with a good heart and a real interest in the folks in "Rising Star" and "Rosebud," as well as Newport and whatever the other fancy places are. Well, the last—real interest—I do have.

Lunch was pleasant—with some discussion of the proposed building. Mr. Hirshhorn will contribute a million dollars toward the housing of his collection. Roger Stevens estimates the building will cost ten million. A design has already been drawn by Nat Owings. Much of the Hirshhorn collection is sculpture and will fill and adorn the Sculpture Garden. The building will house the paintings and other objects.

In the middle of lunch Lyndon came in, met everybody, thanked Mr. Hirshhorn, and boldly said what I had been wanting to say and couldn't —that it was wonderful that the people of the United States were going to be able to enjoy his art works, but that it would be downright selfish if the White House itself didn't get an example. Mr. Hirshhorn could appreciate him, I think. They are both aggressive and strong.

Mr. Hirshhorn loves his art—he calls the sculptures his "children."

This Hirshhorn gift may open a great chapter. We will see. Dillon Ripley used the expression that it was the greatest art gift that has been made —that is, if it *is* made—to the United States since Andrew Mellon gave what formed the nucleus of the National Gallery in the thirties.

I sandwiched in a little talk with Luci about her invitations for graduation. It turns out she is determined not to send any. She said: "Mother, it's just a request for a present. It's phony, hypocrisy—I'm *not* going to do it. Oh, yes, I'm going to see that certain people get there, like my friends here in town, but I'm not going to send out invitations." Well, I lost that battle.

Toward evening the helicopter was on the ground; the holiday spirit was in the air; we were headed with a group of friends for Camp David. In a few minutes, Lyndon joined us and off we went in a very relaxed mood. I think the Dominican situation must be easing up. I do not know how much to believe in the newspapers, but Lyndon's spirit is lighter and his face less weary, less lined with trouble.

Summer 1965

Luci's graduation day—red-letter, great day in our lives!
The ceremony was all pomp and pageantry. What a beautiful instrument is the voice of Dean Sayre. Frail, scholarly-
looking Bishop Creighton was there, and also Bishop Hines,
solid and masculine, from Texas.

The class filed in, Luci looked lovely in a long-sleeved
white lace dress that she had designed and Lucinda, the able
White House seamstress, had made. Her hair was black and
glossy, her face angelic, uplifted. When they called out the
cum laudes, she was not among them, but to her credit, her
grades have been better and better each semester for the last
year and a half—and that under the shock of the change in
our lives.

I was proud of Lyndon's speech. He warmed up to it by
saying that he would miss the small consolation of knowing
that no matter how much homework the night held for him,
Luci had brought home more from National Cathedral. And

then, asking the pardon of young and lovely girls for the solemn talk of an old man, he launched into a foreign policy speech. One of the lines I liked best—and he interpolated it—was when he said very emotionally how happy it had made him that Luci had decided to learn nursing and spend her life helping people.

It was a strange speech, delivered on the floor of the Cathedral, not in the pulpit. There was no introduction at all, and at the end, no applause, of course. A robed official—a sort of an acolyte—with a big mace (I know so little of church hierarchy and vestments) started to lead him back to join us. Lyndon walked away from him. I had a dreadful moment when I thought he was probably going over to shake hands with all the assembled sixty girls, but what he did was go over and kiss Luci and she looked as if all the angels had descended from Heaven and formed a ring around her.

Then he sat with us for the rest of the ceremony, which was impressive, thrilling, patriotic, and so very personal for all the parents, including us. So bound up was I in the pomp and circumstance, it was hard to realize that this was the end of five years of National Cathedral School for Luci —the end—and the best.

Outside, Lyndon talked to some of the clergy, extolling the virtues, most sincerely believed, of the faculty of NCS—Miss Katharine Lee, Mrs. Geraldine Wharry, Miss Elizabeth Fry, all of them—what they have done for the girls, what they have meant in their lives. Then we went to the lawn and congratulated the graduates, standing in line a while with Miss Lee. We hugged and kissed Helene Lindow. Her lovely mother and father were beaming too. Walter and Bennetta Washington were there —their daughter had been one of the cum laudes, and so had Marlene Johnson, the only two Negroes in the class.

Today was Luci's day! Her hair was like a raven's wing, and her face was radiant. She had sat up until 4 o'clock the night before autographing *Miters*, the school yearbook, and a little steel engraving of the White House as a gift for each of her classmates.

Youngsters had swarmed over me for autographs—I didn't mind a bit. The air was full of confusion and emotion, tears and laughter, and beaming parents.

The rest of the day deteriorated into hurry and confusion and overtaxing of my strength. For the first time I realized that I was very, very tired and cross with too many people. Mrs. Ethel Smith and Mrs. Archibald

1965

President Lyndon B. Johnson, Lady Bird Johnson, Vice President Hubert Humphrey, and Muriel Humphrey greet crowd while walking away from the podium after the Inaugural Address. LBJ Library Photo by Cecil Stoughton, C25-61-WH65.

LEFT: *Preparing to leave for Inaugural ceremonies at the Capitol. LBJ Library Photo by Yoichi Okamoto, A25-2A.* BELOW: *Arrival ceremonies for Italian Prime Minister Aldo Moro on the South Grounds, April 20. LBJ Library Photo by Cecil Stoughton, 34277-13A.*

LEFT, TOP: *Senate Ladies Luncheon held annually at White House — here with special guest, Mrs. Dwight D. Eisenhower. LBJ Library Photo by Robert Knudsen, C1972-2.*
BELOW: *With Liz Carpenter, Bess Abell, and Ashton Gonella. LBJ Library Photo by Yoichi Okamoto, D3094-4.*

RIGHT: *Planting a Japanese cherry tree on the banks of the Potomac. LBJ Library Photo, 34199-11.*
FACING PAGE: *Tackling a deskful of correspondence in the First Lady's bedroom. LBJ Library Photo, 32686-19.*

Brown of McMillen, the decorators, had come from New York to spend the afternoon or whatever it took to work on the big things in the Reception Room (once the Fish Room), Lyndon's office, and the Cabinet Room. This whole project should be given weeks and not harried minutes. I'm fighting for time, maybe a losing battle. In the afternoon a staccato of interruptions—Bess about the Arts Festival coming up June 14, which I look forward to with so much apprehension and uncertainty; Liz about the Virgin Islands trip; Ashton with mail to sign.

Meanwhile Luci's friends, Stevie Steinert and Bill Hitchcock, had been excitedly chattering to me about a surprise party for Luci in the Solarium, beginning at 9 o'clock. They had collected a list of her friends—somewhere between thirty and forty-five of them—they had some rather clumsy decorations done by themselves—cabaret tables, chairs, and candlelight out under the stars off the Solarium.

But how to get Luci up there? Luci had decided that she was going to Camp David, taking some friends, and Ashton to chaperone. In typical Luci fashion, she was being very late getting ready to go. Very much at home with them, she had decided to go with her hair rolled up in curlers, simply because it "just wouldn't dry in time." She had on shorts and a sloppy shirt. It was 9 o'clock, the guests were coming in. Stevie was on pins and needles, everybody was tiptoeing into the Solarium, and Luci was under the dryer in her room!

Lyndon was downstairs having a stag party for General Eisenhower. They astonished us by opening the door, putting their heads in the Reception Room. I introduced Mrs. Smith and Mrs. Brown to General Eisenhower. He looked wonderful—hale and hearty and happy—and it makes me look forward to retirement. I am so glad that he and Lyndon can be friends. Lyndon looked as weary as I felt—I with no reason, he with every reason—so many sleepless nights.

So Lyndon and about fifty men were having a stag party downstairs, and Luci was coaxed upstairs on some pretext to the Solarium, where all of her friends jumped up shrieking their congratulations!

Stevie got up and delivered a small speech. "Because of our great love for you and our interest in your future career, we have decided to buy you equipment to follow your profession." He produced a large and very complete Nurse's Kit. And then he said, "Georgetown, in view of its appreciation that you are coming over there to learn nursing in the fall, has sent you over a body to work on!" In came a stretcher, carried by several of Luci's huskier friends—a white sheet, covering a body—the sheet was lifted back—there was Beth Jenkins home from Marquette! Stevie raised her up, Luci shrieked, they hugged and kissed, the whole room exploded! It will be one of the unforgettable moments.

Thursday, June 3

ST. JOHN, THE VIRGIN ISLANDS

I woke at the reasonable but not self-indulgent hour of 8:30, had breakfast, and looked forward to five free hours before time for the harness of hairdo and gloves and off for the commencement address at the College of the Virgin Islands.

There is a long slope down to a perfect little horseshoe of white sandy beach, lava rock to the left, and straight in front the blue and green Caribbean, changing color with the depth, brilliant in the sunshine, mountains on the other side. I went to the beach and lay on the sand, swam far enough out to get good and tired, swam back and tried snorkeling. Getting in and out, one had to watch for the sea urchins, myriads of them, black balls varying from the size of a lemon to a cantaloupe, long black spines sticking upward in all directions.

Bess, Tony, and I got our snorkeling masks on and into a motorboat with a lifeguard named Randolph. The coastline is dotted with these lovely little horseshoes of white sand. At the second one was a promontory of craggy rock, and off it Randolph said there was good snorkeling. First I tried the all-over mask and the fins. It was one of life's marvelous experiences—a new world! Sea fans, fragile as lace, gray and purple and green, waving gently in the current. Coral, some formations as big as an elephant's side and perfectly round, exactly like the convolutions of the human brain—thousands of years in the making, they tell me. Tall plants called gorgonian stretched upward some eight or ten feet, as well as I could judge, beneath the water—and it is probably deceptive—long finger-like tubes, twenty or more of them, swaying in the current, for all the world like those plants you see in horror movies at a cannibalistic feast, wrapping themselves around the victim if he comes too close and devouring him. I swam through millions of tiny silver fish—I don't know what happened to them because I didn't feel them, but they were there.

Tube sponge, like hollow purple fingers sticking upward, and some coral that was orange in color and much that was yellow, and every now and then a bit of red.

I thought the fish were the most wonderful things! There were lots of little bright yellow fish, young blue tang, they called them—as they grow up they change color. Rock beauties, yellow about half-way back and yellow tails, and the rest of them brown. "Four-eyed" butterfly fish—oval, almost round, a bright black spot surrounded with a white ring close to its tail, one on each side, for all the world like an extra pair of eyes.

But the most beautiful were the queen angelfish—yellow and blue-green, variegated, so bright you could almost hang one up and use it for an electric light; and the banded butterfly fish—gray-white with precise bands. Each time I saw a new one, I wished I could tell somebody about it, it was so exciting. Most of them are quite thin, although some seemed as long as two feet. Perhaps most startling of all was a fish whose every scale stood out—you could almost count them—shades of yellow, orange, amber, brown, some black, and underneath, pinky red, the red-bellied angelfish.

But duty waited for me. I put on my prettiest new dress, white and cool-looking, with blue-green beads at the sleeves, and we took the boat for St. Thomas. Governor and Mrs. Ralph Paiewonsky escorted us up the hill to the College of the Virgin Islands, and if you ask five people how many there are in the student body, you will get five different answers. I finally decided there were about 275 full-time students, eleven graduates, and a number of night students and part-time students. They very sensibly teach them the occupations they can make a living out of on the Islands: hotel administration, construction, business administration, engineering.

First I met and congratulated the eleven graduates. To the tune of "Pomp and Circumstance," played by the Christiansted Honor Band of St. Croix, slow as a funeral dirge, we marched up the high hill—the faculty, the graduates, the Trustees, and I, by this time in my long black gown with the white velvet band of my degree from the University of Texas.

From the hilltop was the most glorious view for the commencement ceremony. The blue Caribbean stretched before us, mountains rimming the bay. There was an excitement in being present at the first commencement of a new institution.

There were several short speeches and Governor Paiewonsky introduced me. My brief message was that I was glad that they were preparing to keep their brains and talent at home by training them at home, so that they will be able to give the Islands the leadership needed in the expanding decades ahead.

I stood in line with the Governor and Mrs. Paiewonsky at the reception and various University officials took turns introducing me. Here I got the surprise of my life, because I would have sworn the crowd before us did not number more than two or three hundred. I stood in line for an hour and a half, and I believe at least two thousand people filed past.

The interesting, the thoroughly delightful thing to me about the reception was the variety of the people—some well-dressed, sophisticated, elegant; some modestly dressed, poorly in fact, but equally dignified, equally at home, poised and sure of themselves. There were a good many Danish names left over from the days of Danish dominion, but most of the population, it seemed to me more than four fifths, were Negroes.

When the last guest filed past there were hasty good-bys all around, and I went back to the boat and three days' freedom. My thoughts went to Luci. As I was getting my hair done I had a breathless call from her. "Oh, Mother, the most wonderful thing in my life has happened. Daddy wants me to go to Chicago with him and play First Lady." I said, "That's just wonderful," but I was a little surprised that she was delighted to play First Lady. And then she went on to say, "Oh, no, that's not it at all, Mother. Beth is here, and she is going back to Marquette and they're having a big college weekend—they're having dances and all sorts of parties, and she brought down a boy with her—someone named Pat Nugent— and he's just tons, Mother—he's a tough guy!" ("Tough" means great, wonderful, nice, attractive, it seems.)

She wanted to spend the night in Chicago after her daddy's speech was over with friends of Beth's and then go on to Milwaukee and spend the weekend with the William Feldsteins, who had had one of the barbecues for Young Democrats during the campaign. She had stayed with them then; she had traveled with them, she said. They had been very fond of her. "They are very nice, Mother, very reliable." Actually I remembered they had been to the White House and I had had several nice letters from them, so I didn't feel too averse to calling them and asking them if it would be convenient to have a little girl spend the weekend with them. The problem was, Daddy was leaving in an hour, would I do it right now? That is the way Luci's life goes!

I called the Feldsteins, nobody answered. Then Luci called back frantically and said that one of her agents, Jim Goodenough, who had left her detail, had gone to settle in Milwaukee. She'd *adore* to stay with him and his wife, and she *knew* it wouldn't trouble them in the least. So I tried to reach him, or rather his wife, to no avail. The number didn't answer.

I was getting frantic, too. Then I asked Jerry to help me. He found Agent Goodenough, the agent said yes, indeed, Luci could stay with them, but he thought that he could locate the Feldsteins—perhaps she'd enjoy it more with them, they'd have more room. Sure enough he did, talked to Mr. and Mrs. Feldstein, they did sound delighted. I called Luci back and she got off in the nick of time—the greatest weekend of her life.

Thursday, June 10

THE WHITE HOUSE

Today varied between being hilarious and serious.

At 10:30 I was to leave with the ABC crew to shoot film on the Potomac River, which meant Jean Louis for hair at 9:30 and make-up with Lillian Brown and getting geared up with my little microphone in pocket, and then to the river.

For the occasion John Secondari had engaged a boat—a quite elderly boat—that must have spent some part of its time hauling fish or even garbage. From the first moment of the day we were "snake-bit"—everything went wrong.

Always I am accompanied by my straw bag—necessary, ubiquitous container which carries sun oil, scarf, my own camera, maybe a big hat. Today we forgot it. The top deck of the boat was broiling hot.

It was hard to maneuver the boat to the locations where we had either the good view we wanted or the bad view we wanted of the banks. Everywhere we went we were directly under the air flight pattern from National Airport. Since this is the busiest airport in the United States, every one of us was ready to swear. Just as I got to the most earnest or poetic part of the script, "roar . . . rrr" would go a jet overhead.

They had brought along a lunch, and we all sat below deck and ate while John Secondari, an accomplished raconteur, told us tales about filming near the Dead Sea in a daytime temperature of about 125 degrees. He also described a film he hopes to do of Cortez. (I wish he would bring the whole company by the Ranch if he does it! I've grown very fond of them all.) I was their guest at lunch and they had a "director's chair" for me, with "THE FIRST LADY" inscribed on its back. This will be one of my prize possessions in my own little archives.

After lunch we went back to work, and pretty soon I began to have the feeling that something was going wrong and that nobody was anxious to tell me what it was. Finally it was inescapable. They had to tell me. We had been having engine trouble for some time. The boat had stopped dead now. We could not proceed. We could stay where we were and shoot the rest of the film, with the boat drifting, in spite of the anchor, steadily toward the shore. We kept on doing takes—Simone dashing around like a kitten on a hot stove, the Secret Service talking on their little machines and conferring with each other and Simone and shaking their heads, as the boat drifted and drifted toward the shallow shoreline.

I noticed the police boat, which had been accompanying us at a distance, drawing nearer and hovering quite close. Finally, my Secret Service agent said, "We are just going to have to take you off. This thing is going to be grounded any minute. No, no, it's not dangerous." But it appeared this would result in a call for help to some kind of patrol, a lot of attention from the shore, and probably a ridiculous newspaper story if I were on board. But we didn't have much left to do of the script. John Secondari and Mr. Harry Rasky and my friend "Indian Joe"—all of them were so eager to do one more take—one more take. Over and over we were doing small bits. Mr. Secondari was probably cursing under his breath, and I trying my best to keep a straight face while I said, over and over from the script: "Who knows, someday John Smith's sturgeons may return to their native home!"

A few minutes passed after the time that the Secret Service had wanted me to get on the other boat before the cameras stopped grinding, and I said farewell to my marooned friends, stepped into the police boat— it would hold only my Secret Service detail and Simone and me—and waved them good-by from our glorious day on the river. We were soon back at the White House.

Rebekah Harkness, who is making a gift to the White House of a portable stage for the East Room, came for cocktails at 6, bringing a couple of executives from her Foundation—Aaron Frosch from New York and Gerald Wagner of Washington. The idea of the portable stage was born when Mrs. Harkness came to a White House dinner and watched the entertainment in the East Room afterward on a thoroughly makeshift, heavy, unprofessional stage.

Mrs. Harkness was quite beautiful—slim and sleek and elegant—an inhabitant of that glittering world where one moves from a home in Antigua to an apartment in New York to a cool country home in Connecticut or a ranch in Wyoming—and where one knows many people in the arts and literary circles along with the financial world. If I sound like a child with my nose pressed against the glass of the candy counter, I am rather. I think it's a fascinating world. The beautiful pin like a pixie angel which Mrs. Harkness wore had been designed by Salvador Dali! It was crude of me to have admired it, quite probably, but I was interested to find out that Salvador Dali designed jewelry.

While we had cocktails in the Yellow Room, they admired the Cézannes. Mr. Jo Mielziner came. He had designed the stage himself, and a model was brought in by Bess and set up for us to look at. The new stage will blend so well with the beauty of the East Room. It is all aluminum for light weight but the off-white color, the fluted Corinthian-column effects, and the curtain which will be the color of the new East Room draperies will be heavenly for the White House shows. It weighs just one third of what the present stage does. When we are shifting from a 3 o'clock tea for 600 4-H children to a State Dinner with the stage all up just a few hours later, I am sure everybody in the White House will rise up and call Rebekah Harkness blessed!

The next hour represented a great change of pace. Father Montgomery came to talk to me about Luci. Luci joined us. I asked him the steps—one, two, three—of how one entered the Catholic Church. I had already told him before, and I made it plain once more, that this was not my wish but that we had waited nine months—almost a year—and all I had asked Luci for was time to consider—to make sure it was what she wanted. He told me that the first step was Baptism and that Luci wanted to be baptized on her birthday—July 2. After that would come her First Communion, which could be the next day and quite private indeed. Sometime later, whenever they decided she was ready, her Confirmation—possibly a month or so later. There would be two sponsors. Luci wants Warrie Lynn for sure. She hasn't made up her mind about a man sponsor. Later on, when she is actually confirmed, there is another sponsor who stands up and speaks for her. For this she has chosen Beth.

We agreed that, because we didn't want a religious matter to turn into a sideshow with the press, the ceremonies should be as quiet, as simple, as dignified as possible. Normally these would be held in St. Matthews. I preferred and suggested any other church, because I cannot escape the memory of President Kennedy's funeral there. But it seems St. Matthews is the parish to which Luci will belong.

We decided that we would not tell anybody else except Lyndon, the sponsors, and three or four friends Luci wants to invite. And, of course, Lynda Bird. None of my staff would be advised but I would hand out a two-sentence factual statement about it a few minutes before Luci and her father and I got in the car to go to the Cathedral.

I cannot be happy about it, but it is true that Luci herself has been happier this last year—a more cooperative, understanding, and working daughter, student, and citizen—than she has been in her whole dear little life. Maybe her earnest search is at an end, because it always has been a search, from the time she used to walk across the street in Austin on a Sunday morning as a very little girl, dress not quite buttoned up in the back and hair ribbon in her hand, to ask Mrs. Coleman if she could go to Sunday school with Evelyn at the Good Shepherd.

Always she wanted to go to Sunday school and there were times then when I wasn't feeling very well, but Luci managed to go by herself. There has been a thread of that through the years, chosen the Chaplain at Camp Mystic for three years—and so utterly ecstatic about it and so serious. And joining the club on religious study when the time came at National Cathedral School to join a club . . . Being chosen to go to Buck Hill Falls, Pennsylvania, for a religious seminar—one of the few juniors at NCS who had shown the interest which results in their selection.

It was a late night for Lyndon, 11 when he came home to dinner. Such a capacity for concentration and for continuing work! Sometimes it makes me almost angry because he's spending himself so, but then, I don't know a better thing in the world to spend yourself for. Today had been one of those days, made up of long sessions with Maxwell Taylor, Rusk, McNamara, William Raborn, Ball, and McGeorge Bundy and General Wheeler. It's really strange—the idea the press has of Lyndon's lack of interest in or lack of grasp of foreign affairs. He spends so many more hours of his day working on foreign affairs than on anything else. From my own small viewpoint, it looks as if the problems internationally—the problems of the world—are so much more insoluble than those of these United States. We can work on domestic problems and make a dent—a rather wonderful dent—but the great world is more complex.

Tuesday, June 15

I will have to remember today as Black Tuesday. I would have preferred the complete oblivion of sleep until noon, but I awoke fairly early. Lyndon's dark countenance was dour and grim. I tried to comfort him without too much effect. His feelings were made up of many things; disasters of the Arts Festival were a "pebble in the shoe," but the real rocks are the constant black background of Vietnam and Santo Domingo. And today, the death of young Bobby Russell, forty, handsome, father of five beautiful youngsters, and the beloved nephew of Dick Russell. When Lyndon is wracked by grief, he shows it—in his face, in his voice, or, even more likely, in his silence. It was a bad day.

I called in Liz and Bess to have a post-mortem on the Festival of the Arts, and we discussed the one-by-one hammer blows of the front-page stories—*New York Times, New York Herald Tribune,* even the *Washington Post.* All of them seemed to delight in faulting their country and their President. They accented only Robert Lowell's not coming, John Hersey's coming and lecturing, Dwight Macdonald's passing around a petition for his fellow guests to sign, disapproving of the President's foreign policy. There is some uncertainty as to whether he got four or seven signatures out of three hundred guests. I'll take a 293 to 7 majority any time!

But do you think that was the news? No, it was the fly on top of the feast, and indeed, feast it had been. We had thrilled to Helen Hayes, Marian Anderson, Roberta Peters, the whole cast of the *Glass Menagerie,* Catherine Drinker Bowen, and poet Phyllis McGinley—all "playing" on the White House stage on one day.

It seemed to me only the women reporters saw the event in perspective —Isabelle Shelton, Marie Smith, Gerry Van der Heuvel. For once I read all the stories, the second time in my life I remember doing it. (The other time was when Lyndon's boyhood home was dedicated.) Much to Liz's grief, I seldom read them. Today I couldn't wait for the issue of the *Evening Star* to come out.

All the women saw it in perspective, gave the good things their due and the small dissensions their due. All save one—Mary McGrory, an excellent writer. Hers was as cruel and cutting a story as ever I remember.

I think Phyllis McGinley's line about "those who wear tolerance as a label, and find some other views intolerable" fitted the whole occasion.

Poor Dr. Goldman. He has worked so hard. And yet the total result must have been a towering headache, if not heartbreak.

Lyndon had asked me to substitute for him in receiving the Inaugural Committee workers this afternoon. They were going to present me a gold medallion for him, a silver one for the Vice President, and the first copy of a book that will go on sale for ten dollars to help pay the expenses of the past Inauguration and build up a nest egg for future ones. This provided a chance for us to say a last thank you—sort of a reunion—and that was something I was glad to do.

I went down to the East Room at 5:30 to see many familiar faces, and I stood in line with Dale Miller to greet the guests as they drifted in. Lindy Boggs, the Oscar Chapmans, advance men from the Lady Bird Special, the Howard Burrises, the Warren Woodwards, the Jack Hights, all the Committee chairmen and many of the hard workers.

Lyndon suddenly strode in and said, "I think you've already had all the speeches, but I just want to tell you, Dale, it was the best Inauguration any President ever had." He shook half a dozen hands and went back to his office in less than five minutes. Not so Hubert Humphrey! He was with us the whole time, got up and made a speech in which he said, "I enjoyed every living minute—and, lest I be misunderstood, I wouldn't mind doing it all over again!" to the amusement of everybody.

Thursday, June 17

This was one of those incredible days that would make a book. Lyndon had agreed that we should invite all the astronauts' families, wives and children, to spend the night at the White House.

We met them at the helicopter, and who should emerge first but four-year-old Pat McDivitt, followed by Mike and Ann McDivitt, and then Colonel and Mrs. James McDivitt. Mrs. McDivitt, also named Pat, peppery, gay; Colonel McDivitt scrubbed, crewcut with a nice smile. And then the Ed Whites: Bonnie Lynn, in a pink dress that looked as if it had been made for Easter, and Edward III, and handsome, manly, and taller, slim with not an extra pound, Colonel White and pretty, blonde Mrs. White, another Pat.

We went into the Rose Garden and Lyndon pinned a NASA Exceptional Service Medal on the astronauts and Charles W. Mathews. McDivitt's parents, White's parents (he's a General), a coterie of kinfolks, and a whole Rose Garden full of press looked happily on, all keenly aware that this was a moment to remember.

Lyndon used the occasion to speak once more of peace. Every day he is trying to take the peace offensive in any way he can. He termed the three astronauts "the Christopher Columbuses of the twentieth century" and said their work had nudged the world toward greater international cooperation, because "men who have worked together to reach the stars are not likely to descend together into the depths of war and desolation." He talked about how much we would all prefer to see men riding together in a spaceship to new adventure, to discover a new world, than to shoot down each other's planes as we had had to last night. This time he referred to activity over Vietnam. He also said that we have now pulled even with the Russians, closed the gap in manned space flight.

After he had awarded the medals, the astronauts gave him something that will be a prime exhibit in the Johnson Library if ever there is one: a small framed American flag that they had carried on their four-day, sixty-two-orbit flight. They had been permitted only sixty ounces of luggage and this was part of it. The flag represented a step toward Lyndon's space dream of the late 1950's which he has fought for for eight long years.

The most charming part of the ceremony came when Lyndon leaned over to give a little medallion to the smallest of the McDivitt children, Pat, and said, "We want you to eat supper with us and spend the night—you and all your families—because down home that's the way we show affection." I think everybody there liked that as much as I did.

I looked out in the crowd, and who should I see but Jacqueline Cochran! Nobody who flies has played a greater role in our lives than Jackie Cochran. Once she flew Lyndon to the Mayo Clinic when he had a kidney stone and our fate hung on a thread at a crucial point in his 1948 campaign for the Senate. Would he go to the hospital for a six- or eight-week operation—no campaign, no Senate—or, as it turned out, have the good fortune to have the stone removed by the rarest kind of expert at Mayo's and be on his feet in three days? I know I gripped Jackie Cochran's hand with special warmth. She is an ardent Republican now, but I hope and believe she still likes us.

And after promising to return with all their families for a quiet, personal showing of the White House and to be our overnight houseguests the celebrities left to participate in the parade and to receive greetings at the House and Senate.

I went upstairs to untangle what had become a very tangled skein indeed. I called Bess and Patsy and Ashton, and we planned the rest of our day, because we had three groups of visitors—the astronauts, our former Ranch foreman and cousin, Corky Cox, and his family, and Art Vickland from my business firm in Austin and his family. Bedding down thirteen guests of different sexes and ages can be quite a problem, not to mention the sudden realization that we had to pick up Dr. Jim Cain and put him somewhere—where? Lynda's room, which is vacant. Perfect! He's a member of the family.

I dressed to greet the astronauts, all beaming, buoyed up by excitement, and showed them to their rooms and took them on a tour of the White House. By 6 P.M. seven little astronaut children were splashing in the pool, the meals were ordered for the Solarium, and a Walt Disney movie laid on while the grown-ups prepared for the evening.

A little before 8 I got ready to go to the State Department auditorium. Chiefs of Missions and their families, along with many heads of the State Department, had been invited to view the movie of the astronauts' trip in space, described by the astronauts themselves. Lyndon had told me that he wanted to accompany me, and he came striding into my room like a whirlwind with a beagle and, of all people, Governor Tom Dewey of New York! This was the first time I remember meeting Governor Dewey, but he looked not a day older than my memory of him in 1948. They had been talking about crime. Governor Dewey had given hours of his time—and it's not the first time—to make plans to attack and eradicate crime in the District of Columbia, as sort of a model for the nation. It had been a two-fisted tornado sort of a day for Lyndon, one hand in a fist lashing out against crime, the other hand extended toward peace, offering the exploration of space through joint sharing of knowledge, the benefits of the rich technology of our country to other countries, asking others to share the adventure with us.

We all went to the State Department auditorium for what must have been a most singular event. The astronauts narrated the film in soft, gentle, matter-of-fact voices. Colonel White, bulky in his space suit, stepped out into a bright blue void. Below him you saw a great spherical mass. You could see the umbilical cord which connected him. He described his feelings: "I wanted to be darned sure I didn't lose the lens cap on the camera. I knew I might as well not come back if I did that!" McDivitt in the craft was an excellent cameraman, too. White said, "I took some big steps. I stepped out on Hawaii and onto California and then I stepped right on Texas, Mr. President." It was a thrilling, incredible, heart-in-throat moment, our astronauts miles above the earth, one floating around in space! And it had been only eight years ago, not even that, one October night in Texas, when Lyndon and I had heard of the Russians' first shattering trip in space.

Once more, Lyndon used this opportunity for a peace plea. Rusk thanked all the Ambassadors present for the contributions of many of them to the space flight. Their ground stations had helped service and guide the flight. Some of them had vacated radio frequencies to help clear transmission for the astronauts' broadcasts.

And then Lyndon delivered the shocker of the evening. He said, "This may not make me too popular with your families. But I am going to ask you tonight—in the very next few hours—to take the Presidential plane and travel outside this country again." While Pat McDivitt and Pat White and the two Colonels sat open-mouthed, he asked them to go along with the Mathews and Hubert Humphrey to Paris to the American Air Show, leaving at 4 A.M. Pandemonium broke loose! Staff members crowded around Webb and then around Lyndon, making plans for the flight, for getting Muriel Humphrey—who was in Minnesota—to fly back to join them in time.

In moments we were upstairs on the top floor of the State Department for the reception, shaking hands with diplomatic members of at least sixty foreign nations. After about a half an hour we gathered up Governor Dewey and went back to the White House, still without dinner, and here began the funniest part of this crescendo of a day. When the astronauts' wives came in, I took them back to my office-dressing room and opened up the closet where my evening dresses hang, because what does any woman think about when she hears she's going to Paris—clothes! The purpose of the visit was to show the French and the world the achievements of the United States in outer space, but nevertheless clothes must be thought of, too.

Mrs. McDivitt and Mrs. White were both size ten. That's great—so am I. We called Helen and suggested that we have a fashion show and see what they could wear. They would need one evening dress apiece, surely, just for insurance. Maybe "Le Grand Charles" might invite them to a reception. Then there was the coat problem. Mrs. Mathews was a size fourteen. Lynda's closet yielded a fourteen. I asked Helen to get the washing machine ready—they'd been traveling for several days and were bound to need to launder things. And then I told the people in the kitchen to get some dinner on the table as quickly as they could for a starving, bewildered Governor Dewey. What a household he must think he'd descended into!

Leaving the fashion show, I went to the dinner table at a little past 11. Lyndon, Governor Dewey, Hubert, and I had dinner, with Colonel White and Colonel McDivitt and Mr. Mathews. And Dr. Jim Cain sitting by—he had been roped into going to Paris as the doctor. And Lloyd Hand was moving quietly in and out making plans.

Lyndon told Governor Dewey he must spend the night and they would finish their conversation in the morning. Hastily I re-counted guests and rooms in my mind and said, "The Lincoln Room, of course," and I would bring him pajamas and a toothbrush. Alas, Lyndon's oversized pajamas would just have to do!

It was during dinner that I realized the full impact of their discussion. We had merely touched on it—the discussion that Lyndon and Tom Dewey had had during the day about crime. How determined Lyndon is to combat crime—how generous Tom Dewey has been in trying to help.

It was during dinner that the final act of the whirring circus took place. Lyndon called Mrs. Arthur Krim, asked her if she could fly to Paris in about four or five hours to act as interpreter for the astronauts. (She speaks seven languages.) Just jump on a plane and come down and spend —we couldn't say spend the night—rather, take a nap, in the Queen's Room, and then depart with the Vice President, the astronauts, and Jim Cain before gray dawn! She could. She did.

I took Tom Dewey up to the Lincoln Room, and I think he thought the day had been just as hilarious as it had been to me. But I know when I've had enough, so I crawled into bed, leaving Luci to cope with the cock-crowing hour.

Friday, July 2

THE WHITE HOUSE AND NEW YORK

Today is Luci's eighteenth birthday, and the tenth anniversary of the severest trial that we ever knew—Lyndon and I—for it was ten years ago today that he had a heart attack.

I suddenly discovered I couldn't, after all, go around slouchy and sloppy and happy in my self-appointed vacation. So harnessed and enslaved can one become, trying to look one's best! So I got a rush appointment with Mr. Per and went over for a permanent—a sort of psychological surrender.

I got home just in time to have lunch with Lynda in my bedroom—a meal we gulped down off trays while I handed papers back and forth to a secretary, saying, "Tell them this," "Tell them that," and in between writing out my statement for the press—the simplest and shortest possible

—to announce what was happening today—that "Luci Baines Johnson is being baptized into the Catholic Church at 2 P.M. at St. Matthews Cathedral. . . . She has been taking instructions from Father James Montgomery since last September. . . . The President and Mrs. Johnson and her sister Lynda were present at the service, together with a few friends."

Dear Lynda—her mind was on many things. I was conscious I wasn't quite reaching her. It was a fragmented hour. She feels depressed, I think, more than I do, about Luci's becoming a Catholic.

Lyndon and I had tried to do this with dignity and in a very personal manner, discussing it only with Luci and Father Montgomery and Lynda Bird and the young people whom Luci had asked to be her sponsors. I never thought we would succeed. But as 2 approached, it looked as though we were the only ones who knew it.

Lyndon was standing by—Lynda Bird and I were dressed. We were waiting for Luci. If only we could get through the next hour in a dignified, inconspicuous manner. Just as I was handing Liz the envelope with the short, simple statement about Luci's Baptism, in walked Luci, about as inconspicuous as Brigitte Bardot. She had on a lovely white lace dress— it would have made a fine wedding dress—her black hair shining, her eyes full of stars, a rosary and a prayer book clasped in her hand. Liz took one look at her and said, "My God, I've been with you through pierced ears, a Sting Ray car, that party where you had beer, and now what is this?" We all melted into laughter. Liz looked at the announcement. I said, "Tell all your press folks in another fifteen minutes or so."

Father Montgomery was standing at the street door of St. Matthews waiting for us. We walked in quickly, but not hurriedly, and went to the front of the church. With James Montelaro and Warrie Lynn in a beige dress and a beige mantilla standing by, and Father Montgomery officiating, we went through the ceremony of Luci's step into Roman Catholicism.

There were a few elderly ladies in black dresses, very much absorbed in their own prayers. There were a few nuns here and there, a dozen or so worshipers who paid us little attention. And then we rose and went back to the baptismal font. The priest tipped Luci's head backward and baptized her, speaking only a few words, and then he smiled and said: "Congratulations." We all kissed her. Lyndon shook hands with Father Montgomery. I noticed that Lynda Bird left swiftly with tears in her eyes and was down the steps and into the car before the rest of us emerged.

All the Betz family were there, including a relative who is a nun. And of course, Beth Jenkins, besides Pat Nugent and two or three more friends from Marquette. I walked out the door deliberately, not swiftly and not slowly, because I didn't want there to be anything furtive about this, and yet I did not want attention called to it. I did not see a camera in sight. The whole thing had required less than fifteen minutes.

Luci remained for her confession. Lyndon and I and Lynda Bird drove home . . . I could not help but think we went in four and came out three.

All plans had been made for Luci's birthday party in the Solarium upstairs with about thirty of her best friends. Lots of them were house-guests. Beth and her boyfriend, Lynda Bird and Dave, Warrie Lynn, Pat Nugent, one or two others from Marquette. I had called Willie Day Taylor, who is so close to our girls, to come over and be "Mama."

Casting a slightly forlorn look over my shoulder in this fragmented life of mine, I boarded the helicopter at 3:20 for New York with Lyndon. He was going to address the National Education Association—thousands of teachers gathered from all over the land—to propose the Teachers' Corps for areas in the United States that are economically or culturally deprived.

On board *Air Force One* was Senator Wayne Morse. Lyndon spoke to him easily, jocularly. I spoke. And Carl Albert—dear smiling Carl—the "Little Giant" they call him. And handsome, urbane, Ambassador Lodge.

We motorcaded into Madison Square Garden—the streets lined with cheering people, the bridges overhead as we passed the World's Fair crowded with people looking down and waving. It was a clockwork-timed, in-and-out trip, and soon we were back on the plane headed for Texas.

Senator Morse had gone his own way, and Ambassador Lodge had departed for Boston, but Carl Albert and the Homer Thornberrys were in the main cabin with us.

There is always plenty of "shop talk" when Carl and Lyndon are together. Speaking of his ambitions to help Negroes during his tenure as President—whatever his tenure may be—Lyndon said, "If Martin Luther King wants to catch up with me, he has got to get up early and march fast."

Lyndon admires Judge Thurgood Marshall and spoke of the possibility of asking him to be Solicitor General, and then if he proved himself outstanding perhaps when a vacancy on the Supreme Court opened up, he might nominate him as a Justice—the first of his race. In talking about the Congress, of course, we soon got around to Judge Howard Smith of Virginia and the difficulties he was placing in the path of passing the Area

Redevelopment Administration Bill. Carl said, "I want to wait a few more Thursdays." (I don't know what Thursdays mean—I guess it's just when the Committee meets and reports.) Lyndon said, "We can't beat the Russians with Judge Smith in charge," continuing, "we have got to get our program between now and October 3. And then next year we'll tackle transportation and a few more things and wrap them up and get out of here before Easter."

I looked out the window and there was a new moon—the last moon cycle I had spent partly in the Virgin Islands, with complete surcease and delight. Now we flew toward Austin. Politics, the legislative procedure, the grist of this familiar mill, filled these three hours.

Lyndon said, "I have been in public life thirty-four years. But of all the things I am glad to be the architect of, it is putting the Catholics and the Protestants and the Jews together in the Education Bill."

When we landed at Bergstrom we were met by Colonel and Mrs. Frank Bender. The moon was up and the last rays of sunset streaked the sky. Lyndon was yearning for the lake—for the boat. And so he said, "Let's go to Haywood." It aroused no enthusiasm in me. The nights have been sleepless lately. Lyndon, the Thornberrys, the Benders, and the Moursunds went for a boat ride—and I went happily and sleepily home to the Ranch.

Tuesday, July 13

LBJ RANCH

Nancy Negley arrived at 9:30 to help me with a full day of decorating— one of the main things I came to the Ranch for. I had the walls of the dining room lined with paintings that had never found a home, and there were lamps, decorative objects, the sort of things that one accumulates from a political trip to Brownwood or a State visit to Thailand, a wide range that might add color or interest to this house or to our family quarters in the White House. We roamed from room to room, beginning upstairs and moving, placing, deciding, having the sort of good time that only a born housewife can understand.

The most significant part of the day, of course, had been an interruption which Liz in a most motherly fashion had herded us into—not that I was going to forget it, but Liz reminded us at least three times to convene around a TV set and watch Lyndon on his news conference.

There were three main pieces of news. First, the appointment of a new

U.S. Solicitor General—that's the third-ranking post in the Justice Department and it's Thurgood Marshall, the first Negro to hold such a post —the grandson of a slave—a man with a wonderful record that Lyndon feels he can surely be proud of. And second—and this gives me particular pleasure—Leonard Marks is to be the new head of the USIA, replacing Carl Rowan. His work on educational television in Pakistan and Pango Pango, on the founding board of the Communications Satellite Corporation, and his brains and energy all make him a good choice. The *New York Times* described him as "bouncy and brilliant." We need that sort in this Administration—or in any Administration. And then third, a very attractive woman, Penelope Harland Thunberg—Ph.D., Phi Beta Kappa— has been appointed a U.S. Tariff Commissioner.

The most dramatic part of the conference was the reference to Dean Rusk. The press has kept needling him these last two weeks—almost trying to undermine him or to seek his resignation. They asked Lyndon if he foresaw the possibility of any such resignation in the months to come. The President replied, "None whatever. I think you do a great damage and a great disservice to one of the most able and competent and most dedicated men I have ever known—Secretary Rusk. He sits to my right in the Cabinet Room, he ranks first in the Cabinet, and he ranks first with me."

I felt like rising from my chair and applauding.

Later, when Lyndon called, I could tell him I had liked it and all the parts I liked particularly—maybe a little slow, maybe not enough spice or laughter—but solid good. I would depend upon that man if I were John Citizen looking on from my living room.

The press has been boiling these last few days with Schlesinger's account in his book of how Lyndon became Vice President. Everybody's got to have his say about that . . . Everybody but us.

Wednesday, July 14

Sometime in the early afternoon a tolling bell was heard—a sound that arrests first your heart and then your thinking—a flash came over the radio that Adlai Stevenson had collapsed walking in a park in London— in Grosvenor Square—and had died almost immediately. After that the day went on just as we had planned, but my mind was absent. I kept thinking about the mortality of man—of even the most important men—

and about the times I had spent with this man. How very much I liked him! How would the UN get along without him?

I know how heavily this blow must fall upon Lyndon—the death of someone who, in spite of how very different they were, he liked and respected—coupled with Lyndon's own heart attack and the rushing imperative to appoint someone to fill Adlai's post.

The skies were cloudy and we could hope for rain. We needed it very much. But personally, I hoped it would hold off until 10, because we had invited all the professors from the University of Texas who had worked together on the small book called *A President's Country* for a barbecue. This is a wonderful word picture of our native land, its flora and fauna, its geology, the story of man's time here. I'm proud of it.

We had cocktails and spareribs around the pool and "noches specials." And a rediscovery of Texas—some of the best conversation I've had in weeks. No protocol was possible. So we filled our plates with barbecue and just sat down at tables of six or four. It was a good evening.

I received calls from both Lynda and Luci this afternoon—Luci, saying she was going straight home from work to comfort her daddy, to be on hand for anything she could do for him; Lynda, in tears, talking about Adlai and how much she had liked him, and the last time they had been together. And then a long talk about her stay in the Grand Tetons, which has lengthened from three or four days to a week. Brent Eastman, the young man whom I had found so attractive this summer, has made it an interesting time for Lynda Bird—on the raft ride down the Snake River, at a square dance, at a campfire picnic. Her conversation was full of him.

So I went to bed feeling older and tireder and my thoughts swinging toward Lyndon for whom today's burden had so many implications. I called him, but it wasn't a very satisfactory call. I cannot comfort people over the telephone. I told him I wanted to cut short my trip and come back for the services for Adlai.

Friday, July 16

The day began early and without any night before it. The plane was late leaving Dallas, and I was sleepless. We reached National Airport a little before 7 A.M.

As I walked into the second floor of the White House, I paused a moment outside Lyndon's door, wanting to go in and yet the unkindest thing I could do would be to deprive him of any sleep he could get. I tumbled into my own bed and gratefully slept like a stone until almost 10. Then I got up to put on the black silk dress I bought last February and had never yet worn, having in the back of my mind when I bought it the grim, unacknowledged thought that as time passes, more and more, I need a black dress for funerals.

I found Lyndon in the hall deep in conversation with Bill Fulbright. Already the next step weighs on him—to find Adlai's successor. I helped Luci find suitable clothes and then we were off—Lyndon and Luci and I and Senator Fulbright—to the National Cathedral.

Bishop Creighton and Bishop Moore met us at the door. About two thousand mourners—and I mean the word "mourners" literally—were there. There was a lovely sentence—a cheering sentence—used by one of those who spoke. "We are a vast company, we friends of Adlai Stevenson." Although it appears over and over in the stories about him that his life was full of disappointments, I can never really accept that. He enjoyed life too much. He contributed too much for me to think of his as a life of disappointments.

In the vast vaulted Cathedral, a casket draped with a flag—no flowers close by—looked very small and lonely. To me the Cathedral is inescapably cold, and yet there was much that was beautifully fitting—the anthem, "Let Us Now Praise Famous Men," and most of all, "The Battle Hymn of the Republic"—"Mine eyes have seen the glory of the coming of the Lord." And that line, "As He died to make men holy let us die to make men free," no doubt falling into each one's heart with its various shades of meaning.

The eulogy was delivered by Judge Carl McGowan—one of Adlai's close friends—I think at one time his law partner. Though it lacked the eloquence that Adlai himself imparted to all his speeches, there was one line I particularly loved, "For our biggest stakes we put forward our best."

I know many minds were going back to Adlai standing in the pulpit of that Cathedral, such a few months past, delivering his eulogy on Winston Churchill. Watching Lyndon next to me—his face weary, grave, knowing how he had lived with this since the news came on Wednesday and how much funerals drain him—I could only reach out my hand to touch him.

The service closed appropriately with the national anthem, and we were walking down the aisle behind the family, seeing fleetingly the desolate face of Marietta Tree and the frankly weeping face of our good friend Anna Hoffman, and Bill Benton, Bill Blair, and the whole assemblage of diplomats. Down in front we spoke to the family. Mrs. Ives was so very sweet, saying that Lyndon had done everything from the beginning. I murmured a few words to the three sons—Adlai III, John Fell, and their attractive wives, and Borden. And then we stood aside to let the family go by and returned to the White House.

I had a good long-distance talk with Lynda. Her code name with the Secret Service is "Gypsy" on this trip. Ordinarily her name is "Velvet"; Luci's, "Venus"; mine, "Victoria." I like all of them but mine. And the center of operations at the Ranch is called "Volcano." I contend that the Secret Service doesn't lack poetry or imagination, although I am disappointed about their verdict on me!

I hunted up Luci who was in the Solarium with Pat Nugent. He's found a job in Washington and is spending the summer here, and he and Luci are together constantly. But in a happy fashion—quite different from her earlier stormy romances. She is now on top of the world, a lark, a sprite—sometimes very intuitive, deeply feminine and quite mature. Before dusk I walked around in the back yard—the South grounds I should say—and stopped by Lyndon's office to urge him to come home.

On a summer evening the most attractive place in the White House to me is the Truman Balcony. I settled down there as the light faded and phoned Abe Fortas. While I was talking to him, Lyndon came in, picked up the phone, and asked him if he and Carol wouldn't come down and have dinner with us. Since it was after 9 it was no wonder they had already had dinner, but they said they would come for coffee. The four of us sat out on the Balcony for dinner and talk of serious import. Lyndon went over possible people for Ambassador to the United Nations. He spoke of Clark Clifford—wonderful negotiator. And surprisingly, to me, of Arthur Goldberg, also a wonderful negotiator. But does anyone ever leave the Supreme Court? Lyndon said of Goldberg that he's the sort of man who would cry if he saw an old widow woman and some hungry children. He feels that quality would be useful in dealing with underdeveloped countries and poorer nations. We said in unison, "But what of the Arabs?" Lyndon thought we couldn't let anyone dictate to us—whether a Jew or a Catholic or a Negro or a person of whatever ethnic background—who sat on the Supreme Court or held any other government job.

And then he talked to Abe about a place on the Supreme Court when and if there was a vacancy. It must be Olympus to any lawyer. Abe was moved, quiet, grateful. Carol, a lawyer herself, believes in her husband like an ordinary housewife, and she felt that he would make a good Justice. Before Lyndon leaves this office I would like so much to see that happen. I think he would be a credit to the Court—and yet we would be the loneliest people left in time of trouble.

Late at night I thought of some of the things that had been said in the headlines about Stevenson—"The gentle wit in the political rough house" . . . "The greatest, the best-loved loser in the whole history of American politics" . . . "Adlai—the magnificent failure." I see no sense of failure whatever. And there was that word so important these days in politics—"style." One Harvard professor mourner had said Adlai had style, that he had prepared the way for Kennedy.

Saturday, July 17

THE WHITE HOUSE AND CAMP DAVID

Today began with an attack on the Augean stable—my desk. No wood was visible on my desk top, which was completely covered with papers. I spent all morning working on mail, except for two excursions to the ground floor to greet our weekend guests, the John Steinbecks and the Billy Grahams—both of whom I enjoy and like—but they are dissimilar, to say the least.

Lyndon had asked them. We are going to Camp David. Sometimes I don't know whether his choosing of people to bring together is by innocence or by design. They are both great workers in today's vineyards, to their rather different audiences, it seems to me.

I convoyed each couple to the third floor suites they were to occupy, excused myself and got back to the desk, with an interlude for a talk on finances with Luci. How different those children are about money—Lynda handles hers so carefully, so well aware of what everything costs, and can look very nice in a dress three years old. Luci *adores* clothes, buys so many of them, her money vanishes like snow under the Texas sun. And yet . . . "I just don't have a *thing* to wear, Mother," she says, and it's always true. Last year's clothes are never quite right for that butterfly.

It was 3:30 before we sat down to lunch, the Steinbecks, the Grahams, and Lyndon and I. I still try to give Lyndon a cup of hot bouillon ahead of time, when lunch is so late, and I've gotten past worrying what the guests think, because the tyrant that rules his life is not social correctness but work.

I was dying to find out what had happened to Billy Graham's proposed trip to Alabama. I hadn't read a word about it in the papers, and I knew it was a bold, actually a courageous, thing to do, because his meetings are always completely integrated. The temper and climate in Alabama, since he first talked in April about his trip, have been hot. I just asked him a tentative question—"What have you been doing since I saw you in April?"

"Well, I went to Alabama," he said, "where I held meetings in Dothan and Montgomery and Birmingham." And on and on he went. The smallest meeting was in Dothan, five thousand people—it doesn't seem to me that Dothan has any more people than that! All the meetings were fully integrated, all very peaceful—the largest had eighteen thousand people with not an incident, not a ripple. Sometimes, he said, "there was even a feeling among the highly organized people who run the crusades that the white people made a conscious attempt to sit beside Negroes." He said the local papers carried the story, with full play, all except the Dothan paper, which is very hostile. There television helped him—with wide coverage—"But here comes the question mark," he said. "There was practically nothing reported on the national wire about it." I knew I had not seen one word about it here in Washington. Lyndon accuses me of never reading the papers. It's true, I don't scour them as he does, but I had not read even one little notice. What strange commentary on the taste of this decade, that a success story is not news. If it had been a march or a riot, or a minor incident, there would have been a big headline. If we want to cure ourselves of some of the strange sicknesses that beset us in this age, one good medicine would be to make a success story, an achievement, real news on radio and television and in the papers.

A little after 4, we all left for Camp David, with Governor and Mrs. Ellington, the Watsons, and several staff members complete with families, including one little boy aged five weeks. What an entourage the Johnsons are!

As soon as everybody was assigned a cabin, and how smooth and helpful Commander Howell is about arranging us, I got into slacks and beat a beeline to the bowling alley. Lyndon played a marvelous game, and won. I was dogged and pedestrian—a disappointing score but a determined player. Marvin and Marion are so nice to have along for any kind of work or play. Capable, handsome, fun, both of them.

Elaine Steinbeck and I talked about Austin and the University. It's because of her that the University has acquired many of the first editions, the very special works of the playwrights. The University is a place you can quickly love and she has turned her love into building for it, by adding such literary treasures. John Steinbeck, with his cane and beard, and bright colored shirt that reminded me of the Virgin Islands (I found they were devotees of the place, as I am), was an exotic note among us plainer citizens. Elaine is a thoroughly attentive, bolstering, charming wife. She's the sort of woman who makes things go socially. For instance, she had expressed immediate pleasure when I told her that the Grahams would be their neighbors across the hall in the White House—"I've always wanted to meet them," she said. Billy Graham does, in fact, look almost too good to be true—so tall and handsome, athletic and intelligent, natural, persuasive, terrifically organized and businesslike—to my thinking, a force for good in this country, and someone I enjoy being around.

Billy Graham himself used an enlightening and amusing expression when he spoke of Harry Luce coming down to see him once. "He spent three hours with me," he said; "he wanted to see if I was real." No laughter, just straightforward.

Some of the guests walked, some of us bowled, and Nick and Lydia Katzenbach joined us for dinner, immediately establishing an affinity with the Steinbecks. When it comes time to arrange seating, I always think how comfortable it is to have Bess. But I seated the Ellingtons and the Katzenbachs in the appointed spots and from there on everything was very informal.

After dinner we watched the NBC movie *The President's Country*, only this time without sound. I think the finished product, the script, music, can be a good backup, a good complement, for my beautification program. And then I went back to watch *Gunsmoke* and the younger folks stayed up to see a movie called *How to Murder Your Wife*.

Sunday, July 18

Today began with a religious service in Hickory—all the buildings at Camp David are named after trees—conducted by Billy Graham. All the guests were there (except Luci and Pat Nugent who had gone to Mass), as well as the servicemen and their families attached to Camp David. Billy Graham is certainly an interesting phenomenon. He would have been a success in any field, I believe, but I'm glad he's chosen preaching because he can reach out and touch such a wide audience.

Lying on the grass around the pool were the Nick Katzenbachs and the Steinbecks, talking books and Russia, and what I used to call, in my university days, "Life with a capital L." I asked Nick about some of the techniques, some of the things we could do to combat crime in the District of Columbia. He's full of ideas—like a hundred-thousand-dollar insurance policy on each policeman, which would mean that a young policeman with a family would have some sense of assurance that if he were killed in the line of duty his family could go on living, would be protected. Another is to get college education for policemen, try to recruit college-educated men into the force, or offer night courses to policemen.

Another category is wide use of electronic devices, such as two-way radios which criminals themselves now employ. I asked Nick about repeaters among young criminals. He used some horrifying figure—I believe it was 70 percent. However, he said, there was now a greater effort to send young first offenders into some kind of a home condition, where they would have some training, some corrective supervision. And when they were let out of there, Nick said, the repeaters dropped to 40 percent or 30 percent. This is a war—the war on crime—that Lyndon wants "won yesterday." Nick thinks that maybe we can make a dent in it in two or three years in the District of Columbia.

I went bowling with Lyndon and the Grahams (Billy was an excellent bowler), the Watsons (Marvin rolled a good, straight ball and a reliably high score, just like the man himself), and John Chancellor (who is practically the champion in this group, except for Lyndon).

Lyndon wants John Chancellor to take the job at Voice of America. He believes we're not telling our country's story to the world well. John is, I think, walking a tightrope between what attracts him and what pays more money. I told him I hoped he would earnestly consider the USIA post. He looked quite solemn and said he would.

Lyndon and I watched Secretary John Connor on *Meet the Press*. He was assured, had done his homework, had just a little nuance of humor. I thought he was great. Lyndon picked up the phone and told him so, as soon as he finished. But I liked it even better when Lyndon called the telephone operator and told her how much she added to the smoothness and efficiency and good functioning of his life, and would she please thank all the operators. That's when I beam.

The Alabama story and my talks with Billy Graham have been one of the most interesting things of the weekend to me. He says Dr. Frank Rose of the University of Alabama is a great friend of his, a builder of that institution—and several times I've heard that now. There are, I believe he said, twelve or fifteen Negro members on the faculty and about one hundred twenty-five Negro students now (you never hear about *that*).

Wednesday, July 21

THE WHITE HOUSE

I had a session with Abe Fortas. He read the proposal of the University of Texas about the Library. I discussed with him his own decision of last Friday night not to accept a Supreme Court post and asked if it were irrevocable, because Lyndon would have to make the appointment soon. With a wry smile—a sort of sad look—he said it had been a bad day. His decision was based on the fact that he had about forty-two lawyers in the firm and more coming on and lots of other employees and their families —about one hundred sixty-eight people—for whom he was responsible, in a way. His greatest hope was to stabilize the law firm, to get plans settled for the lawyers in about two years. And then—just maybe—there might be another such chance as this one, he said. To desert them now was a hard decision. And second, he said, "If the President was faced with any real troubles, I would want to be around to help him. And if I were on the Court, I could not. That was the difference between the possibility of a Court job and the Attorney General job." I told him if he had any doubt at all he had better let Lyndon know right away—if his letter was not irrevocable.

I dashed off, late and harassed, to the beauty parlor, using my time under the dryer to read the guest list for the reception for the White House Conference on Education scheduled for 5:30. I went over the topics of discussion, the VIP's, and tried to get in the mood to meet them.

I had known Lyndon had had a meeting at 11 with McNamara, just back from Vietnam, and Dean Rusk and McGeorge Bundy. And their cars were still there when I got back at 5. So it had been a hectic day for him—no time to concentrate on education—not even for a galaxy of visiting Governors and university professors.

He was to meet the fourteen Chairmen and the Vice Chairmen in his office at 5 for their report on the achievement of the Conference; thirty minutes later we would all move out to the stage for his speech to hundreds of guests—Cabinet members, Ambassadors, Governors, educators

—ranging from James Conant of Harvard to Nick Garza, the Principal of Brackenridge High School in San Antonio.

To apply oneself with complete concentration to the problem of Vietnam and then shift the gears of one's mind to the major workers in the Conference on Education while they discussed the results of the panels on jobs, dropouts, automation, skill obsolescence, reeducation, teacher education, the role of the states to the university and higher education, overseas programs, foreign students, educating the handicapped, pre-school education, school desegregation, innovations in higher education—while knowing that eight hundred people are waiting for you on the lawn— would make me throw up my hands and leap out the window. So I felt like cheering Lyndon for getting there at all, apparently calm and only about fifteen minutes late.

We walked up the platform to "Hail to the Chief." I recognized California Governor Pat Brown, Tony Celebrezze, Terry Sanford—the former Governor of North Carolina—and Whitney Young of the Urban League. Lyndon made a good short speech with an opening line welcoming them to "the first White House teach-in" which drew a roar of laughter. He said the results of all their deliberations would be distributed to government agencies and to Congress and will hopefully produce action. Arthur Goldberg was on the platform with us. Lyndon introduced him and asked him to stand, and acknowledged his great sacrifice in taking this new UN job.

Perhaps the highlight of the evening was a proposal to establish a series of Adlai Stevenson scholarships to study international relationships. Lyndon shook hands around the group for about fifteen minutes, and I stayed for another hour and a half greeting Dr. Frank Rose of the University of Alabama, amazing Sister Jacqueline, whose personality fairly shoots sparks, Barnaby Keeney, President of Brown University, and John Gardner, Chairman of the whole Conference.

I directed everybody to the Jacqueline Kennedy Garden or the Rose Garden and I tried to make them all feel at home. After seeing Luci strolling around with Pat Nugent meeting people, I slipped upstairs about 7:30 and waited for Lyndon to come for dinner. When he came, he brought Jim Hagerty of ABC, and Bill Moyers and the Jack Valentis. The six of us sat on the Truman Balcony and discussed the profession of being Press Secretary to a President—a job not unlike a bullfighter's, it seems to me.

I like Hagerty—crisp, positive, professional. Lyndon has always liked him. He told us we would do well to get someone who understood television to help us, someone who could give the kind of assistance Robert Montgomery gave to President Eisenhower. He also gave Bill advice about timing of releases, the number of releases. They had a lot of laughs. Jim and I talked about my ABC show with John Secondari on beautification. (How I do like Secondari and all his crew! But I wonder if we have gotten the message across to the women on the other end of the set in Gadsden, Alabama, or Portland, Maine.) We talked about upping the release from Thanksgiving afternoon to an earlier time to take advantage of the possibilities of fall planting.

It was a working dinner full of laughter and good suggestions and reminiscences. I remember Jim saying that he never entered the gate of the White House without having a special feeling. I do; I always shall.

Bill Moyers—slim, quick, so very intelligent—is riding a wave of euphoria of compliments from all sides. And they came from Hagerty as well about his handling of the news office. There was talk of President Eisenhower and his way of conducting business. There is nothing like getting in the job yourself to become more understanding of the men who had it before you! President Eisenhower has been very helpful, and I know Lyndon has lived to bless the days in the Senate when he cooperated with him with courtesy and respect.

Friday, August 6

NEW YORK AND
GREENWICH, CONNECTICUT

Today I spent hours trying on, fitting, trying on, modeling, trying on, filling in the holes in the wardrobe I had last year, deciding what would take the place of last year's most useful this or that.

I talked to Lyndon, telling him I'd be back by dark, ready to do anything he planned. He reminded me of the signing of the Voting Rights Bill. This ceremony was to be in the Capitol, where in 1957 he had made his first sizable stride pushing the Civil Rights movement. It would be a dramatic moment. Alas, I completely forgot to watch it on television but later I was proud to know that Luci had not forgotten. She was right there, by her daddy's side, walking in with her hand in his.

I was satisfied and glowing, but at the same time confused and uncertain, with that feeling a woman has who has shopped a lot, when we walked out of the Carlyle, headed for Greenwich, Connecticut, to see the Joseph Hirshhorn sculpture collection. Mrs. Hirshhorn had called me the day before and invited us. I was torn between wanting to go and realizing we'd only have about an hour there, if I were to get home in time to spring Lyndon loose from his desk for a two-day weekend; that is, to leave for Camp David by 8 o'clock. My presence can sometimes make the difference in getting him off.

Seeing the Hirshhorn collection in an hour is something of an insult —it should be savored slowly, luxuriously, like a candle-lit banquet, instead of gulped like a hamburger. But my philosophy is that there is only today, and what I don't do now, I may never do. So we went.

The countryside was beautiful, in spite of a drought in New York, green and lush, and rolling. Lynda was with me and I was a little concerned that my twenty-one-year-old was going to bid me good-by at the airport and go back into New York and spend the weekend having dates. She had been to Arthur discotheque the night before and came home with stories of the people she had seen, such as Carol Channing in her white velvet bell-bottom trousers trimmed in red and a middy blouse top, with a huge alarm clock hanging around her neck, and two-inch artificial eyelashes.

About 3, we reached the Joseph Hirshhorn residence where the winding driveway led through clumps of rhododendron and tall elms up a gentle hill, topped by a dignified residence, rather English in style. There, all similarity to anything I have ever seen before ended! Right in the middle of the circular driveway, in a plot of green, stood five or six huge figures in chains, Rodin's "Burghers of Calais," with expressions of agony, dignity, endurance, self-sacrifice.

Our host, all of five feet two and bouncy, was at the driveway to meet us, with his attractive, young wife, the Curator and his wife, and his lawyer, Sam Harris, and his wife. For the next hour we had an exciting experience, pelted by impression after impression—a classic, timeless piece of Greek sculpture, and then a modern piece—some waving wands of aluminum that were bolted together for balance but swaying in the wind. There were many, many Henry Moores. Mr. Hirshhorn says that he has more of them than any collector in this country. His favorite is "The King and Queen," seated on a bench in the center of his rose garden, not at all clearly defined figures of a man and a woman, but with the series of lines and molding that express, nevertheless, a certain dignity and quiet and importance. I found fascinating one I called "the hungry dog" by Giacometti—a lean, emaciated dog that looked as if it were made of some igneous rock, fried and bubbled and pitted, material that was left in the bottom of the pot when the burning was over. There were Alexander Calders—a huge stabile and many smaller pieces—sculpture by Rickey, Lachaise, Maillol, Brancusi, many more Rodins—many I never heard of. I was delighted to encounter the French Impressionists' works in sculpture (I'd only known their paintings)—Matisse, Degas, many Daumiers.

But nothing that I saw was more interesting than our host himself. Mr. Hirshhorn told me he had been collecting for forty years and delighted in finding art which had not struck the eye of the world, acquiring it at a moderate price, watching it appreciate in value and bear out his judgment.

About every fifteen minutes Bess would murmur: "If we are going to catch that plane, we have to leave . . ." Our hostess offered us a drink and we snatched it up and kept on walking, none of us willing, least of all me, to stop and think about planes or drinks. The setting, too, was exquisite—the beautifully kept lawns, sloping off into misty vistas, visible between tall trees, a rose garden, boxwoods.

There is talk that the Tate Gallery in London is wooing Mr. Hirshhorn with promises to build practically a second Taj Mahal, and that several New York museums are seeking the collection. It is said to be the most outstanding one of modern sculpture in private hands.

We went inside and I saw a couple of his Eakins paintings. He has more than thirty—the largest collection of them in private hands—very commanding character portraits, with something of the quality of the Flemish masters. There were Robert Henris and a fine Childe Hassam, all misty and delicate.

Finally, we were off in a whirl of good-bys, heading for the White House and then Camp David.

Thursday, August 12

NEW JERSEY

Today was like a campaign day. I had wanted to see Project Head Start in operation. We chose New Jersey because I could see two contrasting projects, and because New Jersey had been the first state to enlist in the war on poverty. Helen brought me coffee a little before 7, and that was the last easy moment of the day. The plane was full of newspaper people. There were the regulars, and unexpectedly, Eugenia Sheppard, who writes about fashions. I looked self-consciously at my coffee-colored linen trimmed in white.

Soon we were in Newark, with Mayor Addonizio and Governor and Mrs. Hughes at the foot of the ramp. Mrs. Hughes proved a most outstanding person in that crowded day, combining good common sense, infectious humor, and industry. We got in the motorcade, and Dr. Charles Kelley, who is the New Jersey coordinator for Head Start projects, took us to the Cleveland Elementary School in the heart of a congested Newark slum—concrete, screeching trucks, and heavy black population, with signs on the stores reading: "BEDBUG SPRAY SOLD HERE." Head Start has one hundred and fifty children enrolled in this area. Mr. Maurice Feld, the teacher in charge, took me through, and Mrs. Mildred Groder, white-haired, commanding, very dignified (Liz called her "the grandmother of all Head Start programs"), went with us. She is head of Head Start for the whole Newark area.

Two small starched and scrubbed Head Start children, Dawn Rudd and William Purdie, both Negroes, met me and escorted me to their homes across the street. They lived in an old tenement, with faces now projecting from every window; the stoop was newly painted with bright green paint—some of it rubbed off on Liz's shoes. It was like company coming to anybody's house—you get ready, you spruce up! I met Dawn's mother and William's mother, who told me how much better he got along with other children at home since he had started school, and that he had learned to dress himself.

Back at the school, we visited two classrooms of five-year-olds and watched one group sitting around wide-eyed on the floor while a teacher's aide read to them. In one corner was a make-believe kitchen, with pans of flour, salt, meal, milk, and oatmeal. The youngsters are learning the words for ordinary things common to a kitchen. They are fed one balanced meal a day, receive medical and dental care, inoculations, and are given hearing and speech tests. They are learning how to pay attention, how to get along with others, learning new words, and going on field trips to such ordinary places as the grocery store, the post office, the police station, and the zoo—places many have never been. Their world is so narrow, and in their homes—frequently broken homes with one parent or an aged grandparent on relief—the vocabulary is often limited to grunts or profanity.

We held a makeshift press conference in the classroom, with Sarge

Shriver, the Governor, and the Mayor doing most of the talking. I answered such questions as what we hoped to get out of this—we, the government, we, the people. We hope for fewer dropouts thirteen years from now, for children able to grow up with a prospect of being responsible citizens, taxpayers, not tax-eaters. Some of these are third-generation welfare folks. You have to start somewhere to break the cycle, and this is the time, the malleable age. Many of them are bright-looking youngsters whose lives can be changed, but I emphasized over and over that eight weeks is a drop in the bucket, a flash in a lifetime.

Our next destination was Lambertville, the second of the Head Start projects. There we went to a hilltop called, for no reason I can understand, "The Commons." It was a place of tarpaper shacks, dirt roads, outdoor toilets, and a general appearance of shiftlessness.

We stopped at a little Mennonite church. Reverend Warren Wenger, the pastor, is one of the few who have a rapport with the parents of the children who are in this Head Start project, and Dr. Kelley and Sarge especially wanted the parents to participate, to meet them, to have me meet them. The little church was as bleak and poverty-stricken as any I have ever seen in the backwoods of East Texas or Alabama, but it opened its arms to people in need. I was impressed by the teacher in charge of the Lambertville project, Mr. Angelo Pittore. He was so earnest, devoted, full of life, excited by the improvement in the children in the course of eight weeks. I met them and their parents, and it was then that the real impact of Head Start reached me. Some were factory workers, some migrant farm laborers who work in the truck gardens and corn fields along the Delaware River and who live in the shanties and trailers on The Commons. I do not want to turn America over to another generation as listless and dull as many of these parents looked. I yearn for better from their children.

We then had a half-hour of movies made by Mr. Pittore, just as unprofessional as my own home movies, but an ingratiating record of the field trips the children had made. They were shown visiting a farm, having a picnic by the banks of a pond (one little boy fell in), filing into the grocery store and accorded the treat of a candy bar, taking a sightseeing trip on the river. The children were animated. They kept giggling and whispering and pointing: "There's Susie, there's Jim." But best of all was the interest of the teachers, the aides, and Mr. Pittore himself. Lambertville has a population of forty-five hundred in contrast to the urban project I had seen in Newark.

We headed back to Morven, the New Jersey Governor's Mansion, already seventy-five years old at the time of the Declaration of Independence. Mrs. Hughes led me into her own room where I got the not-so-restful news that we were leaving for Texas when I got back from New Jersey. I changed into my blue linen (a good idea, with Eugenia Sheppard along, that I'd brought a fresh dress for tea!).

A tent had been set up on the lawn and several hundred New Jersey educators, clergymen, and Head Start officials had already held a seminar on their problems, their achievements, and how they could carry the work of Head Start into the school year. Governor Hughes spoke, also Dr. Kelley, and a mother who was a volunteer in the program. The last line of her speech was the most moving. One of her charges, who had come in silent and listless and had blossomed during the five or six weeks, reached up his hand to take hers as she was leaving and said, "I love you." Dr. James Murphy of Princeton University's Institute for Teachers of the Disadvantaged discussed higher education's responsibility for training teachers for this sort of program. My speech was a montage of the letters I had received from Head Start workers all over the country.

One of the happiest moments of the day had been my arrival at Morven. At least eight of the ten Hughes children were waiting for me—some his, some hers, some theirs! They are a remarkable family and my admiration for Mrs. Hughes grew minute by minute. We talked in the car about the need for raising the level of the dignity and prestige of service jobs—maids, gardeners, housekeepers and the like. The unrealistic emphasis placed on the desirability of white-collar work or professional work and the stigma attached to homemaking jobs is wrong. All of us who run households don't feel less dignified for the cooking and cleaning we have done.

Back in Washington Lyndon's day had included everything—a ceremony attended by all of the Hoover family making Herbert Hoover's birthplace a historical site; the swearing in of Cabot Lodge; a fiscal talk with Henry Fowler; interviews with Ed Morgan and old friend Sam Gilstrap back from Malawi, where he served as Ambassador. Then he had dinner on the *Sequoia* with thirty-five Ambassadors from countries scattered around the world—a three-and-a-half-hour session in which he moved from one part of the boat to another, covering the crowd in as personal a way as possible. I felt worn out just to hear it recounted, but he arrived at Andrews jubilant, almost refreshed by activity.

We were home at the Ranch by 2 o'clock our time.

Fall 1965

*Thursday,
September 2,
1965*

Today began another phase in the building of the Lyndon Baines Johnson Library. Bill Heath, Max Brooks, Roy White, and I flew to Independence, Missouri, to see President Truman's Library.

When we landed in Independence, I thought our pilot must have made a mistake. It was a dirt runway as rural as the Winters' strip at Johnson City. But there was one happy result—no press awaited us. Feeling like conspirators on a real adventure, we piled into the car and drove to the Truman Library. President Truman awaited us on the steps, standing quite straight, cane in hand, with a big smile. Mrs. Truman was beside him. (I always feel her first interest is rightly to take care of *him*, and second, whatever guests they are meeting.) I was so happy to see them, and introduced my fellow travelers. This time there were a few cameras and one or two people I thought I could identify as press. Dr. Philip Brooks, Director of the Truman Library,

312

so knowledgeable and so devoted to his job, was with us the whole way.

Then President Truman gave us the tour, with Max asking all sorts of architectural questions—storage, humidity, traffic routing, vaults for documents that were still restricted. Bill Heath looked at it all with the eye of a plain tourist and of a regent who is about to spend several millions of the University's money in erecting a building to house a similar project. And I going along with a curious mixture of thought divided between two currents: The first, seeing President Truman, now really growing old, and Mrs. Truman, who is quite hale and hearty and so sensibly solicitous of him, listening to the drama of President Truman explaining the Library, the story of his life, and observing his pride and pleasure in it, and wondering to myself whether someday Lyndon and I would be able to present such a picture . . . And the other current of thought—Max's, Bill's, and Roy's, who had never before seen a Presidential library—which was, "So this is what a Presidential library is like. Can we do it better? Is it worth the sizable commitment we have made to it?" And, looking at it through their eyes, I wondered how it could be a better reflection of the man, the period, and his influence on the period.

Some things I began to see with new eyes—the Presidential papers themselves, gray, anonymous, box after box, identically bound, hidden from the world on shelves behind locked doors, awaiting the very few scholars who come—the public comes in thousands and the scholars in trickles. Some more dramatic use ought to be made of those papers, I thought. They could be secure behind glass but some use could be made of color. There could be some displays highlighting the outstanding achievements of a President's years. Putting it in terms of Lyndon, there might be a display on the Education Bill—what led up to it, what it would mean to John and Mary Citizen of 1975.

Mrs. Truman asked us if she could take us to lunch, and of course we were delighted. We went to a place called The Old Apple Farm, set in an orchard of crooked apple trees, a rambling farmhouse with many small rooms, with candles and low ceilings and Early American antiques. I wondered if the food was going to measure up—it did! We had apple fritters, roast chicken, an enormous lunch, with Mrs. Truman talkative, easy, and the President reminiscing and telling jokes. He's really very fond of Lyndon. Mrs. Truman asked me if I ever saw Roberta Vinson and how Wilma, one of the maids at the White House, was doing. We talked about the grandchildren and of Clark and Marny Clifford.

When lunch was over, Mrs. Truman announced quite firmly (and I would have been shocked if he had countermanded her order) that she was going to take President Truman home now, his legs were wearing out a bit. We all said good-by, with many thanks, and I, especially, thinking how glad I would be someday to be in their shoes, to look so calm and content and happy as old age approached.

We returned to the Library for another hour's session with Dr. Brooks, mostly on storage facilities, and to see how the building itself is set on the fourteen acres of land (very gracefully, in my opinion) with the Seal of the United States to the left of the columns in the front, the Seal of the Masonic Order to the right. (Looking at it from a distance, I had decided it must be the Seal of the State of Missouri.)

Next we flew to Abilene, Kansas, and once more landed on a quiet and rural airstrip. This time word of our coming had preceded us and there were many cameras and microphones as our car pulled up in front of the Library a few minutes before the closing time of 4:30. I said a few words of explanation and interest and pleasure in seeing the libraries, identified my companions, and moved inside as quickly as I graciously could where Dr. William Aeschbacher, Director of the Library, met us. This was my first trip to the Eisenhower Library, and indeed, I found it was a complex, composed of three parts: the Library itself, which houses the papers, a vast, handsome building of marble that surrounds a small courtyard. More than a block away, across the Mall, is the Museum, a much less expensive-looking structure. Then, finally, the old Eisenhower home, with the most atmosphere of the three—authentic Americana of the first quarter of the century—warm, middle class, nostalgic, speaking to many of us of our yesterdays.

The Eisenhower Library was dedicated two years ago but it is not yet open to scholars. It apparently takes years for archivists to declassify and open the papers in a Presidential library. The Library was, at this point, magnificent but empty of people. I could see Bill Heath falling back and saying to himself, "Is this what a Presidential library can be like?" And my own feelings were reinforced that the legislation, the bills, the actions, the decisions of a President, his effect upon his times, must be displayed more dramatically, whether in a showcase relating events that led up to the passing of certain legislation or certain decisions, or by some audio-visual method, maybe a film of the times, such as they have at Williamsburg, Virginia.

We visited the Museum, which has heavy accent on gifts from Chiefs of State, and rich and wonderful they are—swords with thousands of diamonds and rubies in them were the special choice of many monarchs, notably the Moslems. Most charming to me was a display entitled "The Girl That He Married"—pictures of Mrs. Eisenhower from debutante age on through their White House days—a truly delightful grouping. A display with a lot of potential, which I would like to follow with some variation, was a panorama of the homes that President Eisenhower had lived in, beginning with the little one where he was born in Denison, Texas. The Curator told us that the Museum had around 125,000 visitors a year.

In my opinion there should be a melding of both library and museum, a melding from which they would both profit and both become more alive, more vividly used as an instrument to record and remember history. I think it would be useful to have the library where the traffic is, where the scholars are, where students come on a university campus, and not so far off the beaten track, even though there were sentimental reasons for placement of these Presidential libraries.

It was a pleasant journey back to the Ranch, flying over the flat, rich lands of Kansas as sunset came—such marvelous fields of grain—sunflowers everywhere, as big as salad plates. You can see why it's called the Sunflower State.

In summing up our impressions of the two libraries, Max said: "It's a challenge—more than I had thought—to see what we can make of it." And that's what it is to me. I want to use every artistry of architects and archivists and staff and family who have loved and saved things through the years, to make ours tell the story of our period of time.

Friday, September 3

This was a day of waiting and uncertainty. This will be the last long weekend of the summer but how could Lyndon come to the Ranch with the steel strike hanging like a sword over his head? About 4 I got word from him to turn on my TV. I switched it on with mounting excitement, and there he was—jubilant, calm, never looking stronger. He announced the settlement of the steel strike. He introduced Mr. I. W. Abel and Mr. Richard C. Cooper, representing respectively the steelworkers and the steel companies. Weighing the cost to the nation in the weeks to come if the strike had continued, this moment could be considered a high point in the craft of his Presidency, beginning that November day.

I put in a call to Lyndon, loved the racing excitement in his voice when he came on. He said he would leave by 7 o'clock for Texas. And then he put Mr. Cooper on and Mr. Abel, and I had a chance to say thank you for their long hours of hard work and patriotism.

Too excited to get down to work, I drove in the sunset to the Lewis Ranch and wandered into the back yard, where the enormous fig tree has practically enveloped it. The figs are getting ripe, sweet, and delicious. Later I drove past the boyhood home and picked up Jessie Hunter, and we went on to Haywood.

How I have relished the hours of being alone here! Quite still, no calls, no necessity of responding to anybody's needs or moods. A little aloneness is necessary in my life, an ingredient that's been very much missing for nearly two years. Aloneness and housekeeping have marked these last two weeks. Strange ingredients for happiness, but necessary sometimes for my own personal self.

When the helicopter set down, Lyndon was still riding a high wave of success. We had dinner, fried fish, right away—a sort of a victory offering to the Conquering Chief. It was only later that I found out he had worked until after 2 A.M. and then read until nearly 3 this morning.

This week has been such a week that it almost frightens me to think of the time when there are no more rabbits coming out of the hat, no more victories wrought by any magician out of a set of facts that seem to promise only grim failures. This week has seen not only the victory in the steel strike, but also a near victory for Home Rule in the District of Columbia. A vote in the House is assured. What's held it up all these years has been inability to get the Home Rule Bill out of the House District Committee. Now there will be a vote on September 27.

But failure is for the future, and tonight is for success.

Tuesday, September 7

LBJ RANCH AND JY RANCH, WYOMING

Today was a day I will long remember. It began about 4 A.M. at the LBJ Ranch and ended almost twenty-four hours later at the JY Ranch in Jackson Hole, Wyoming. Lyndon woke me about 4 o'clock saying he was having awful pains in his stomach. Coming quickly out of the fog of sleep, I was so frightened I said I was going to call Dr. Burkley. He vetoed that so firmly that I did not dare override it. "Let's wait a while . . . no . . . not this time of night."

The next three hours were a montage of thoughts and emotions. The pain subsided and returned, and he turned and tossed miserably. Dawn finally began to seep into the windows, but the only joy it brought me was that soon I could call Dr. Burkley. We didn't actually talk about what was most on my mind, and I assume on his—could this be the beginning of another heart attack? Although his illness behaved like a stomach ache or kidney stones, with nausea and misery, so had the heart attack. For a long time—months, years—I have been keenly aware how lucky we have been. There was a necessity to be calm while frightened, to bridle anxiety whenever you opened your mouth—a familiar feeling.

Finally I did call Dr. Burkley. He was there in a few minutes. As far as I could tell, he too thought it was kidney stones. I can only say that it developed rather than was discussed that I should go on to the Garden Club meeting scheduled in Jackson Hole very quietly and that Lyndon should rest as much as possible and return to Washington in the afternoon. By sheer chance, Dr. Willis Hurst was going to be there. I had known he was coming and had felt deprived, because for the second time he had come when I had to be out of town. They would get Jim Cain. They would make all the tests and investigation they could at the Ranch beforehand.

Meanwhile, what would we say to the press? What would we say to our houseguests? It was Lyndon's feeling that as long as we really knew nothing, we should say nothing. I began to get ready, moving automatically, uncertain, worried. But not to go now would be a statement that something was the matter. When I was getting ready to leave, I leaned over and said to Lyndon, "You know this has been an especially wonderful weekend for me, don't you?" He answered, "Only we didn't have enough time." I thought of that moment during the weekend when we had started to go off by ourselves, for a ride, and somebody had come up, somebody he needed to see, wanted to see, had to see, and presently there were five or six of us in the car.

It was decided that Arthur Krim would ride with me, and that most perfect of houseguests gave no indication this was a change in plans. My last glimpse of Lyndon was of him stretched out on the bed with the wires of an electrocardiogram machine attached to his body. I am glad I am a controlled person, and I do not believe there was a flicker on my face of what was going on in my mind, as I talked with Frances and Helen about the trip. We flew to Kansas City to join the big plane, leased by the press. There I found Nancy Dickerson, Doris Fleeson, Dan Kimball, Betty Beale, Karen Klinefelter, Wauhillau LaHay, Maxine Cheshire, and of all people, Art Buchwald! Josephine Ripley of the *Christian Science Monitor*, Norma Milligan, and a few more I didn't know, along with cameramen, and our indispensable Nash Castro. And, best of all, my Lynda Bird, who was sound asleep.

I had looked forward to her coming. I wanted us to have a few days together before school started and I thought it would be very pleasant for her to meet some of the young Rockefellers. Laurance had told me he planned to have a group of them at the house while we were guests.

Lynda Bird suggested a bridge game, and Betty Beale, Wauhillau LaHay, Lynda, and I had an hour of one of my favorite self-indulgences, which naturally I enjoyed since I made a little slam. The time may come when I am totally self-conscious around newspaperwomen and consider them my natural enemies, around whom I must be on guard and silent. Mostly, up to now, I have had an easy camaraderie with them. They have done little to me personally that I could call unfair or untrue—often they're nicer to me than I deserve—and I am always aware, when I see one of them with a typewriter balanced on her knee in an airplane in turbulent weather, knocking out a story—the facts of which were gotten on the run or in a crowded caravan, perhaps—that it's a hard job.

We were late, first twenty, then forty minutes late, and then I stopped asking when we would get in. The fog grew denser and Liz's knuckles grew whiter, gripping the chair. But about 2:30 we came in for a beautiful landing at Jackson Airport against a background of great black clouds and soaring mountains capped with white.

The welcoming party had been waiting for us for more than an hour. Governor Clifford P. Hansen and his pretty wife in a pink suit, Congressman Teno Roncalio, Mrs. Fred Mauntel of the Garden Club, and Mary and Laurance Rockefeller with their son Larry and a friend of his, Jerry Reese.

It was a forty-five-minute ride from the airport up the valley to the JY Ranch, and all the way I was thinking, as I talked with Mary and Laurance Rockefeller, how soon could I call Washington?

Divided between my silent worry over Lyndon and my elation at the beauty of this place, I arrived at Honeymoon Cabin, a real log house whose picture window framed Elk's Lake and two towering peaks of the

Tetons. There was a roaring fire, and the most inviting-looking chaise longue in front of the window that seemed to say: "Come, spend your three days here!" Brent Eastman had called. Lynda had asked him to go to the dinner with us.

At the Lodge I met all the head-table guests. Senator Clinton Anderson and Henrietta were there. I was so pleased to see their familiar faces. There were a number of American Forestry Association people, several officers of the American Conservation Association, Mrs. Mauntel of the National Council of State Garden Clubs, and Governor and Mrs. Hansen. Senator Anderson was presented with the American Forestry Association's Distinguished Service Award at the dinner and the President, Mr. Peter Watzek, said of him: "His service to forestry is unexcelled by any living man." I was so glad that honors were being paid to him now.

In the middle of the dinner Jerry Kivett leaned over to me and said, "The President would like to speak to you immediately." My heart thudded, but my voice said casually and politely (I hope) to Mr. Rockefeller on my left: "Would you excuse me, please, a minute?" I went into a private room where there was a phone and heard Lyndon's voice, natural and hearty enough to be reassuring. I hadn't been able to reach him in the three hours that I had been at Honeymoon Cabin. Dr. Hurst was with him; they had made X rays; they thought it sounded like gallstones, he had had some bad times, but he felt better. He was going on with the appointments he had but he was not going to make any more. He would not make any statement yet. Jim Cain would arrive at the White House and they would have further tests the next day.

He told me to make a good speech and to give all the Garden Club ladies and the conservationists his thanks and greetings. I was relieved to hear him sounding so much like himself, relieved that we had had Jim Cain and Willis Hurst at the White House so often that their presence would cause no flurry, relieved that he gave me the nugget of truth upon which to hang an excuse for my disappearance—that he'd sent them greeting and instructed me to "make a good speech."

I walked back in to the table, pounds lighter and years younger, and soon after followed a very kind introduction by Laurance Rockefeller: "The Constitution of the United States does not mention the First Lady of our Land. Our statute books give the position no specific power or authority. Yet it can be a position of tremendous influence." He went on to add some nice words about me. Then it was my turn. I did my best to an audience in tune with the subject matter and quiet enough to hear a pin drop. I felt satisfied and glad of every hour I had spent on the speech, particularly the personal portions. And then I went with Mrs. Mauntel to the front door and shook hands with all of the five hundred guests as they emerged, finding many old friends from some campaign trail or trip across the United States.

Work over, and feeling at least a remission of anxiety about Lyndon, I left with the Rockefellers for the ride to the JY Ranch. A moonlight night in the Grand Tetons, and two free days ahead of me! I am looking forward to visiting with them, as well as the trails of the mountainsides. Also the young people, Larry and his friend Jerry Reese, and their nephew John D. Rockefeller IV, called Jay, who is about six feet five inches, and beautiful, blonde little Sharon Percy, whose father had run for Governor of Illinois, and Stephen Rockefeller, who is Nelson's son.

Back at Honeymoon Cabin I lit the fire in my bedroom and drifted off to sleep with that most luxurious of accompaniments—dancing firelight on the ceiling and the crackling of the wood.

Saturday, September 11

THE WHITE HOUSE

Today actually began about one A.M. I had arrived at the White House from the Grand Tetons a little before midnight to find my husband, my supposedly sick husband, to whom I was returning with concern and compassion, gone—gone to New Orleans to survey the damage wreaked by Hurricane Betsy.

He had left about 5 and was due back after midnight. There was nobody at all—nobody whom I could ask how he felt. So I sat down with the accumulated mail to wait for his return. He came along about one A.M., looking exhausted but talking of nothing but the hurricane damage. He began checking the Departments (even at that hour of the night) about whether food was being flown in and if enough medicine and cots were available. He told me of the man who rushed up to him and cried, "I've lost my baby!" Lyndon's face contorted just as the man's had, as though he were about to cry. He said it was horrible.

Day by day the press stories from the Grand Tetons had become less and less beautification and more and more Lynda and Brent Eastman. I almost wished I had climbed a Grand Teton myself in order to top the Brent story. I wonder if the newswomen realize how embarrassing this sort of thing can be for a young man who has three dates and shows a girl the country he loves, and for a young girl who is essentially a sensitive and private person.

Luci and Helene Lindow are going to New York with Lynda, with Ann Hand to chaperone, and select clothes. Luci came in to say that this was the first Saturday night since she was eleven that she hadn't had a date. What a lot of satisfaction that girl gets from being a girl!

Sunday, October 3

THE WHITE HOUSE AND NEW YORK

Lyndon and I had a late breakfast and then got ready to go to the National City Christian Church.

When we walked in I came face to face with Judge and Mrs. Tom Ferguson from Johnson City. With sheer good luck I recognized them in this faraway, unexpected place, greeted them warmly, and we sat together. Afterward in the coffee hour as we stood in line and shook hands with the huge congregation—and even long after Labor Day there are many tourists from all over the United States, mostly the South it seems—Lyndon leaned over and whispered to me, "Why don't we ask Dr. and Mrs. Davis and the Fergusons to have lunch with us?" In his impulsive way, he gathered them up and the six of us returned to the White House. Lyndon insisted that they get their suitcases—in fact he sent for them—and move into one of the guest rooms, although he explained we would not be there. Then he said, struck by inspiration, "Why don't you all come up to New York with us?"

It would be chilly before nightfall—Mrs. Davis didn't have a coat. I lent her one. And so, thrilled and elated, the six of us set out by helicopter —another exciting experience for our four guests—and then *Air Force One* for New York. Luci and Pat were along because tomorrow is the day the Pope spends in our country. The plane was loaded with government officials, including the Mike Mansfields, going up for one of the most dramatic hours of this year's Congressional session—the signing of the Immigration Bill—that long-fought-for measure ending the national origins quota system governing immigration. It took place—where else? —in the shadow of the Statue of Liberty. And if anybody shouts it's corny, well, make the most of it! (I learned later that some Congressman in a long list of what he hoped were humorous suggestions of where to sign bills had listed the Statue of Liberty for this very bill.) The ceremony was a jewel of an hour that I won't forget.

Our chopper landed on the little island where a crowd of Cabinet officers, Senators, Governor Rockefeller, both Representative John Lindsay and City Controller Abraham Beame, each in the race for the Mayorship, and Mayor Wagner met us. There was a coterie of outstanding citizens whose fathers or grandfathers had come to these shores as a part of the "huddled masses yearning to breathe free" and who themselves had added muscle and brains to America's greatness. And some tourists had just caught the ferry and come over.

Lyndon spoke against a backdrop of the New York skyline as he faced the Statue of Liberty. It was a windy day, and the flags were snapping in the breeze. Anna Moffo sang "America" and as her great voice rang out "thy purple mountain majesty, above the fruited plains" and as my eyes turned from Lyndon's face to the flag, to the great old statue, I was caught up in the magnificent drama of the moment. It was good history and good theater and there was many a wet cheek in that crowd.

The participating Congressmen filed by to receive the pens Lyndon had used in the signing. And then came others with a very real reason for being there: Arthur Goldberg, whose father was a Jewish peddler from Russia; General David Sarnoff of RCA, who had poured much creativity into the stream of America; and picturesque Jacob Potofsky of the Garment Workers Union. I remembered when I had asked him how old he was when he came to this country, and he replied: "It all depends. I was eleven, sixteen, and thirteen." He had given his age in three different ways to suit the necessities of the occasion—once when he had signed up as an apprentice to learn a trade and had to be a certain age to be eligible, once when he filed his immigration papers, and once for a religious ceremony—and I think this must have been the correct age, thirteen—a Bar Mitzvah.

As we turned to walk out of the crowd, Lyndon shaking hands to right and left, I found myself face to face with Erich Leinsdorf, our own small part of that great American story. About 1938 Lyndon had helped rescue Leinsdorf, a young Jewish conductor, from the maw of Hitler's Germany and brought him out to the then peaceful island of Cuba and eventually to "the golden shore" that the lady with the torch symbolizes. (And now he has gone as high in his profession as a musician can.) We stopped, embraced, gathered him up, and we all got in the car, bound for the Waldorf

Towers in a long motorcade through thousands and thousands of New Yorkers who thronged the street.

What a complicated weekend for New York! I think the happiest man on Tuesday morning is going to be the Chief of Police, unless it's the Mayor. I remember what Mayor Wagner said about Khrushchev's visit having cost—I'm afraid to mention the sum, but it was in the neighborhood of a million dollars for the extra police hired to protect him. Here they were again—hundreds of policemen on the streets today to protect the President, and tomorrow there would be a legion to protect the Pope.

Finally we emerged into the quiet of the Waldorf Astoria Towers suite with Erich still in tow. The Goldbergs were having a dinner party in their suite for us. It was a day of being awash with emotions. And if there hadn't already been enough, I could hear the chant of demonstrators below us. We looked down to see a small crowd marching back and forth across from the hotel. I felt sure they were protesting the United States' policy in Vietnam and the Dominican Republic. I thought I could see people coming up to argue with them. I was ready for the sort of civilized evening of good conversation, good food, and good friends that I could anticipate with the Goldbergs. But I could not enter that hotel suite without remembering Adlai Stevenson, so recently the light of any gathering. And somehow I was sad and a little lonely.

It was a blue ribbon gathering—the Nelson Rockefellers, Speaker and Mrs. McCormack, Dean and Virginia Rusk, Cardinal Spellman—rotund and affable but growing uncertain on his legs—the apostolic delegate with whom Jack Valenti is quite friendly. Fanfani who is now President of the UN General Assembly. And U Thant, the Secretary General. The Mansfields, the Javitses, and the Bobby Kennedys. The John Rooneys. Mayor Wagner and his new wife—how good it is to see him happy again! Anna and Paul Hoffman. Jimmy Roosevelt. And beautiful Anna Moffo with her husband Mario Lanfranthi. And our good friends the Ed Weisls and the Arthur Krims.

On my right was Cardinal Spellman, who doesn't hear very well. He said he knew about the Lyndon Baines Johnson Library and that he had contributed to many Presidential libraries in his day and he would be glad to make a small donation to this one.

Lyndon had suggested to Arthur Goldberg ahead of time that he hoped it would be a quiet, informal evening—no toasts. And Arthur, who is never at a loss for words, was not quite sure that he meant what he said.

He turned to me for advice, and then he quickly followed it by saying, "I thought I might just repeat the words of an old Hebrew prayer." I jumped at that excellent solution. No response is needed to a prayer, surely. (At least no earthly response!) So at the end of the dinner, very eloquently he recited a Hebrew prayer for peace, asking for wisdom for the leaders of the nation—not unlike some of the passages of the Episcopal prayer book.

After dinner we went into another room and Anna Moffo entertained us with several of my favorite songs—"Greensleeves," "Summertime," and one from *Madame Butterfly*, the most plaintive one of all.

Dorothy Goldberg is putting her own stamp on the Embassy. One room contains several of her paintings. Once long ago she had promised Lyndon a painting and he never lets her forget it. He renewed his request.

There was a sense of excitement in the air, even for the most Protestant of us, because tomorrow is the day the Pope is coming.

Tuesday, October 5

THE WHITE HOUSE

All day long—through work on my ABC film, appointments, a beautification ceremony—I went with the sense that I am moving automatically through the prologue toward the real beginning.

At 5:30 I met with Liz and Bess. They had no idea what I was going to tell them. I said that at 6 Bill Moyers would announce briefly that Lyndon had had a gall bladder attack the night of Labor Day. Repeated tests and X rays had indicated the wisdom of removing the gall bladder and he would go into Bethesda for surgery Thursday night to be operated on Friday morning.

When I finished I felt as if I had just delivered a time bomb that I had been carrying. We began to plan how to handle the barrage of mail and the flowers—using cards to be printed or engraved with the Seal, settling the fact that I intended to go to the hospital and stay there the whole two weeks of Lyndon's stay, canceling my few engagements after Thursday night and letting them know why I was not going to accept any more engagements for an indefinite number of weeks. The mounting stacks of invitations have been getting unexplained "No's" from me for days, with Bess and Liz increasingly restive and puzzled.

I went hurriedly with Marvin, Jack, and Dr. Burkley to Bethesda to look at the suite—the first time I had seen it—raced through with Dr. Davis, asked that a reclining chair be brought up from Camp David, plenty of hard pillows, the TV set to be installed. I would bring family pictures and a favorite painting from Lyndon's office to make it more homelike.

We hurried back to the White House so that Marvin and Jack could attend the stag dinner—another of the series involving Cabinet members, businessmen, leaders in the fields of education, the ministry, and the arts —all gathered for briefings, dinner, and then the talk-and-write routine at the table. I wonder if in any other Administration there has been such a constant mixing of the diverse brains of the country as at these stag dinners—with explanations of why we are doing what we are doing, and what it will mean to *you*, John Citizen—to *you* in labor and business? Lately, new facets have been added with guests as varied as David Susskind and Dr. Wayne Dehoney, the President of the Southern Baptist Convention, and Dr. Barnaby Keeney, the President of Brown University. I think it is one of the most exciting things that Lyndon has done.

With the stag dinner going on downstairs, I settled down comfortably on the sofa with my own two guests, the doctors Jim Cain and Willis Hurst, for a quiet talk of evaluating the operation; but I lost them to a higher priority, for Lyndon sent word asking them to join him.

I received word that Stew Udall and Bill Mauldin, attending the dinner, would like to come upstairs to present a cartoon to me. Bill had tucked under his arm the original of the cartoon of a highway winding its way through a thicket of billboards, one of which said, "Impeach Lady Bird"! (Imagine me keeping company with Chief Justice Warren!) They both autographed the cartoon and rejoined a much more compelling company downstairs.

I left a note for Jim and Willis to come swim with me. I had forty laps—enough to wear off some of the emotional fatigue—and then I came back upstairs feeling sure that Lyndon must have come up (it was nearly one). I opened the door and started into his bedroom. Aghast, I found it full of men—Gregory Peck, Hugh O'Brian—ten or twelve more —with Lyndon on the table getting a rubdown and holding them in conversation at the same time. I shrieked and backed out. What a household! And what a moral to always have your hair combed and give that comfortable old bathrobe to the Goodwill charity organization.

There was a signing in the East Room at 10 A.M. of the $340 million bill providing grants to regional medical centers fighting heart disease, cancer, and stroke. Lyndon had referred to it as setting up "a bunch of little Mayos" around the country ". . . so Dale Malechek and Alvin Sultemeier can get to them." This was a bill-signing I wanted to see—one of those I am proudest of. Lyndon and I walked in with everybody seated, and I took my seat in the front row, along with John Gardner of HEW and Lister Hill, the father of all the medical legislation in the Senate, and the Surgeon General. And behind us were Mary Lasker and Florence Mahoney.

Lyndon's speech was a beautiful tribute to the men who worked in the restoration of health to other men. He never once mentioned his own problems, making it all the more dramatic. But he threw in an impromptu accolade to Lister and to Mary Lasker. Mary has for years conducted a one-woman crusade to enlist the federal government in health research and in shortening the distance between the fruits of research and the patient.

Lyndon was having a whirlwind of a day. After the signing, he had had a walk around the White House grounds with the dogs, shaking hands with tourists, followed by taping a speech, seeing a delegation from Appalachia, popping in at the National Press Club luncheon for cartoonists, consultations with his economic advisers—as though to show the world how tough, how indestructible he was on the eve of going to the hospital.

At 5 o'clock there was a reception for the new members of Congress —that is, the Democratic freshmen, who have done so much to assure the success of Lyndon's programs in this Congress. Once more we were seated in the East Room—it takes on more and more the aspect of a seminar room in an unusual university . . .

Lyndon welcomed, praised, and thanked. And then Larry O'Brien took over with charts that showed the seventy bills that went into the hopper at the beginning of the session, their progress in June, the status now, how many had passed or were awaiting Committee action, and how many were yet to come up on the floor—only four I believe!

We went into the State Dining Room for cocktails and a buffet, and for one of the few times in my White House tenure I did not linger at a party. I had a quick drink and at ten minutes past 6, saying good-by to nobody, I went upstairs, asking Lyndon to follow me later.

Upstairs was quite a different party—one I had looked forward to for oddly sentimental reasons. It was the acceptance of the Jacob Epstein bust of Winston Churchill which is being presented to the White House by his wartime friends. Actually, it was Averell Harriman's idea. I have become very fond of him, partly because he seems so indestructible (handsome at seventy), works hard in his country's service, and remembers his old friends—witness the monument to FDR and now this bust of Churchill. Among the other donors were David Bruce, Ambassador to Great Britain, and wartime comrades-at-arms, Generals Carl Spaatz and Frederick Anderson—the latter had flown all the way from Europe just for this hour—and General Ira Eaker. General Eisenhower couldn't be present but had sent a sweet note. A special guest was youthful, pink-cheeked Winston Churchill, the grandson of Sir Winston, who is touring the United States.

It was an evening of nostalgia. Anna Roosevelt and her husband, Dr. James Halsted, were there. And also the Franklin D. Roosevelt, Jr.'s. And Bill White and Eddie Folliard. There's no greater admirer of Winston Churchill than Bill White, who had been in England as a war correspondent before and after D-day. There was the widow of Edward R. Murrow, and the British Ambassador and Lady Dean, and Kay Halle who had been instrumental in getting legislation introduced to make Sir Winston an honorary citizen of the United States.

We had a short ceremony with a graceful tribute by Averell Harriman. Then Lyndon joined us and spoke briefly. Sir Patrick Dean made a response. Then I felt moved to express myself. Usually I am dragged by duty or shoved by Liz, but this time I *wanted* to talk.

I told Anna Hopkins Baxter—the daughter of Harry Hopkins—about a picture of her, age seven, with her father and President FDR that had hung on Lyndon's walls all the years that he was in the House of Representatives. I told David Bruce—our Ambassador to Great Britain—how enchanted Lynda Bird was with his wife, Evangeline, when she had called on us.

Everyone left early, and Lyndon vanished back into his office. I had a few moments with Luci who sometimes behaves like a free psychiatrist. Tonight she delivered me a lecture on our reactions—Lyndon's and mine

—to the approaching operation. She feels we are unduly controlled and unemotional. One thing about Luci, she is very sure of her verdicts. She is opinionated, uncomfortably intuitive, and a joy to have for a daughter.

Monday, October 11

BETHESDA NAVAL HOSPITAL

This was a busy day at the hospital. In the morning Hubert visited Lyndon and I went to the dentist's office for the first of a series of protracted sessions. If some future civilization three thousand years from now digs me up as a mummy, they will certainly find a record of the latest in dentistry circa 1965!

By every barometer Lyndon seems to be progressing well. My chief fear is that he will return too soon to too much work. There are no rabbits in the hat; he is no superman. I know how much of his success is made up of 2 o'clock nights, of dogged determination, and of calling forth from himself and from everyone around him the last ounce of strength. I don't want him to begin that again on sheer nerve. In six weeks he can build up a backlog of strength. But everything was going so smoothly, I thought I could take off for two important destinations—the beauty parlor and the foot doctor. The first stop—the White House swimming pool for thirty quick laps, with Bess and Ashton walking up and down beside the pool, asking for decisions on engagements—all regretted—and on special correspondence and office problems.

I returned to find Clark Clifford in the room with Lyndon. They were discussing United States aid to foreign countries and the United Nations. Lyndon said, "I would like to tell Goldberg 'we have got a billion dollars in chips in your pile and don't you put them in until you can win the hand.' "

His heart makes him want to use the affluence of this country to feed the hungry and cure the diseased, but he is getting increasingly concerned that what we send away may be wasted or misused and that other nations take our help for granted. He believes that Goldberg is a combination of warm humanitarian and shrewd trader who can make aid more effective as a tool.

Of his own feelings he said, "I am just like a dog on a point." He has not slept enough. With an hour-long visit with Dean Rusk, who brought good wishes from the leaders of the Soviet Union, together with bringing him up to date on a number of matters, it had been a long day for Lyndon.

The day we were to leave the hospital began with bad news. The Rent Subsidy Bill had been scuttled without opportunity to work on it—some sort of blunder, some legislative maneuver that I did not understand, but Lyndon's face darkened. He had been convinced the bill had every chance to pass. At least he wanted to fight for it.

On the way out we stopped in a ward full of Marines wounded in the fighting in Vietnam. Those who could stand and one in a wheelchair gathered around Lyndon, and most of those in bed propped themselves up on elbows. What followed was touching. Lyndon told them simply and movingly how proud he was of them all. "And when I feel pretty blue at night, and I issue the orders that you carry out, I do it with a heavy heart." And then, "Whenever we cease to love it [our country] and whenever we cease to be willing to die for it, and whenever we are willing to throw in the towel, why then some other society will come along and take us over." I could not read the expression in the eyes of all of them. There was tense interest everywhere and in many, I believe, strong emotions. I could not hold back my tears.

Then we wheeled and started down the corridor fast and out the door, saying good-by to all the hospital heads on the steps. Up on the left we heard voices, and there were streamers hanging out the windows, and heads stuck out and hands: "Good luck, Mr. President—from the boys in 4-C." "Vietnam, O.K." "Good luck from Ward 4-D, LBJ." They were waving and shouting, "We're with you." "The military is behind you." Lyndon called back, "They fixed me up. I'm in good shape. Now *you* get well."

Thursday, October 28

LBJ RANCH

This morning we had breakfast together and went for a walk—just the two of us—past the dam and on to the birthplace and the cemetery and the school. We crossed to the spot where Lynda and Luci were always picked up by the school bus going into Johnson City during our first years out here. And then we walked back past the church almost to the entrance—nearly three miles—talking all the way about things we wanted to plant or repair or change around the Ranch. Never will a home be finished! In the late evening we drove to "3 Springs" over a road—or rather a non-road that it was unbelievable a Continental could navigate—and finally arrived at the brink of a great bluff. Below us, the Pedernales wound across a wide bed striped with sandbars.

A. W. and Lyndon and I got out and sat out on the rocks. Up the river on our right the sunset slowly faded through all the shades of red. It shows that winter is coming on. It's not the great splashy palette of a summer sunset.

Far below us to the left the river on the rapids made a steady, rhythmic noise. And Lyndon talked about how when he was a little boy he used to come on picnics to the swimming hole right under the bluff below us. I wish I could set out with an adventurous friend and walk the whole course of the Pedernales until it enters the Colorado! I'll never be satisfied after having been down the Snake River until I've become a river runner.

Back at the Ranch Marie called me in and I found to my dismay that the Peter Hurd portrait had been unpacked and set up for all to see. I had intended to leave it packed until Peter arrived. I hoped that the three of us—Lyndon and Peter and I—could look at it together in the best light at the best time. This was an unplanned, inauspicious beginning; from face to face around the circle of family and staff I read the message of disappointment. I must confess I did not like the background, too violet. Nor the figure. And the hands were not Lyndon's gnarled, hardworking hands which have so much strength and so much fight in them. But I did like the head. The expression was searching, hopeful—there was nobility in it. But Lyndon could find nothing good about the portrait at all.

I looked at the large size of the figure and remembered with puzzlement how I had taken Peter Hurd on a tour of the White House last July when we first started these plans to look at all the Presidential portraits. We had especially looked at the backgrounds and sizes used, and I pointed out the Thomas Jefferson portrait by Rembrandt Peale as the same scale I would like for Lyndon's portrait. Peter's portrait was disappointingly large.

Saturday, October 30

It was one of those awful days that make you cling to the words of an old Greek philosopher: "Have confidence. There is nothing terrible that lasts forever, or even for long." Or to remember Euripides' lines: "The end men looked for cometh not. And a path there is, where no man sought."

The day began with an absolute barrage of news stories on the radio, on the television, and in all the papers, about Luci and Pat coming to the Ranch to seek the permission of the President to marry. I wonder, if the government of Soviet Russia had fallen, would the news have received such concentrated attention? Such a spate of words and speculation about one girl and her personal life! A "friend" in Austin was quoted. Pat's father was interviewed (he handled it very well). Pat's friends were interviewed. Poor Jim Moyers, here in his debut as Press Secretary (understudying Bill who had to be away), was badgered and besieged with questions until 2 A.M. and then waked up again before daylight.

Helen Thomas was the most determined of all. Lyndon said, "I am just going to wait until this dies down and at a quiet and appropriate time I'll talk with Pat and Luci." I could tell—though he had been out of the hospital a little over a week—he didn't yet feel really fit.

Then I began the second hard round of the day—getting Peter and Henriette Hurd into the convertible with Lyndon—top down—to ride around the Ranch. I like them both so much—picturesque, sophisticated, but simple. They love so many of the things I do, including the land. And we had to tell them that the President did not like—indeed, hardly anyone liked—the portrait that Peter had worked so hard on. There it lay in the office, while everyone walked on tiptoe around it. So it wasn't exactly a relaxing ride.

After lunch—unable to postpone it any longer because the Hurds had to catch a plane to Albuquerque—the four of us went into the office and unveiled the portrait. My sympathy was mostly for Peter. But next for Lyndon, because I understood how he hates to hurt anybody, and also how the last two days have eaten into him about Luci. But he had to tell them the truth, and there was no comfortable way to tell it.

He told it without embellishment. Peter said he could not improve on the head. He thought the head was as good as he could do. When Lyndon said he did not like the eyes, Peter made a good case for the dreamy expression in them. "This man was looking off into the future— this man had vision." I did not like the background and this he said he could change, and would. He was the first to admit that the body, and especially the hands, were not good, because he had not had enough sittings. And that is quite true. To paint hands—and Lyndon's hands are a very important part of him—Peter said it would take several sittings of an hour each. But there was no need to do this if the painting were to be made smaller; one of the chief problems is that it's much too big.

Then there was the Capitol in the background—my idea—an allegory. "I am a creature of the Congress," Lyndon has often said. That is where he came from. And I still think it is a good idea, though I had in mind a sort of misty hint of a Capitol dome. This, Peter is simply not the artist for, he explained. Some could, but he couldn't. He is a realist in painting. And the parapet that Lyndon was standing against has no meaning to me.

It was a gruesomely uncomfortable half-hour. But there is one thing one has a right to express oneself on—and that is one's own portrait. Henriette, in the manner of any woman who feels her husband is attacked or his ability questioned, could hardly keep from showing that she was incensed. Peter was so nice, and my heart went out to him. The final conclusion was that Peter would work on the background, reduce the painting in size so as to omit the hands, and perhaps leave just the Capitol dome lighted. And we would look at it again.

I went out to the car with them and said good-by—hurt, sorry, and incapable of handling the situation with the grace, yet honesty, that would give an air of ease for all my guests in our tangled skein of troubles.

And then I fled, gathering up Lynda who is often my recourse in time of trouble, and Ashton and Dr. Young. We went down to the guest house, sat under the live oak tree in the bright autumn sun, and played bridge for an hour and a half. About 5 I got an imperative message—the President was going to the Nicholson place—would I please join him? I would. We helicoptered over and drove around over roads that were never meant to be traversed by anything except a jeep. We talked ranches and fence crews and upkeep on the houses of the Nicholson, and cattle and grass. It was Lyndon's recourse, just as bridge had been mine.

After dinner I leaned over to those at my end of the table, knowing that I was going in to watch my Saturday night indulgence, *Gunsmoke*, and said, "I hope you will excuse me in a minute. I have an engagement." Luci gave me a wry smile and said, "Couldn't you use another word?"

Tuesday, November 2

Dawn—gray and dreary—and early. We had planned to be the first in Johnson City to vote, so we were up at 6:30. My weight was so encouraging—115¼—that I felt very brave and had just black coffee.

Lyndon and I drove in, arriving at Johnson City at 8 at Pedernales Electric Co-op Building where the polls were. The sidewalks were lined with press and cameras. We walked rapidly in, got our ballots from Judge McNatt, and to the flashing of camera bulbs, we marked and deposited them—the first and second votes of the day. Though the skies were dreary, Lyndon's spirits were expansive.

As we left, the press fell in behind us—an entourage of about twenty cars—and like the Pied Piper we led them out the highway going to the Lewis place. Lyndon called back to Bill Moyers that if he wanted to bring them with him he was welcome to do so and to tell them all we were going home by a country road, riding by the Lewis place and maybe the Hartman Ranch. Bill brought Jack Horner, Frank Cormier, Merriman Smith, and Forrest Boyd. The hills were brightening with sumac, but our golden Indian summer was gone.

I often wonder what these Eastern reporters, these city boys, will remember about their Johnson City interlude—winding over the caliche hills behind the President who stops to telephone instructions to a foreman about a sick cow or a cattle guard or a fence crew or seeding a pasture. It must be as unintelligible as Urdu to them.

At lunch I put Merriman on my right and enjoyed talking to him about his twenty-four years covering the White House. He told a story about a bill that got lost in Truman's years. Apparently it fell off of Clark Clifford's desk and into the trash basket and got burned. It was a big appropriation bill and Speaker Sam Rayburn had to push it through the House again.

Everybody was in a gay, expansive mood—and nobody mentioned Luci.

After lunch I did something I had been wanting to do these past two years. I asked the telephone operators—just as their shift changed—to come in and have tea with me and tour the house. Beverly Cole, Mary Crowe, Mary Hoffer, and Ruth Krell. Beverly Cole has been with the White House since the days of Roosevelt. Martin Anderson had sent us a big box of orchids from Orlando, Florida, and I gave them each one and we all laughed because the height of their social life here in Johnson City is to go to Charles' Restaurant.

We gathered around the dinner table at 8:30—Birge and Lucia and Cousin Oriole, the staff and Lyndon and I. Everybody was happy and relaxed. I look back on these last few days at the Ranch and think of the moments I have savored—yellow roses in a copper basket that came from the flea market in Paris posing for a still life on our coffee table which was once an oak tree in Sherwood Forest—the gleam of firelight reflected in the glass doors of the old pine corner cabinet that President Kekkonen of Finland gave us—seeing a roadrunner—paisano—not more than ten feet away yesterday at the Martin place, long, awkward, humorous (I never knew they were black-and-white-speckled before)—and the mist rising on the river when I wake up before the sun is up. The tempo of life must be slow sometime for you to really savor its moments.

Wednesday, November 3

Today was a complete departure from our days of quiet. John Gronouski and his family were coming down for him to be sworn in as Ambassador to Poland. And Larry O'Brien was to be sworn in as Postmaster General in front of the Hye Post Office.

The morning again dawned gray and misty, and it was obvious the plane could not land at the Ranch. Our guests would have to land at Bergstrom and drive here. That would entail more than an hour's delay. There would be at least fifty newspaper people arriving at our door in a few minutes. What would we do with them? Let them wait in the cars? Offer coffee in the hangar? We finally decided that we would open the doors and ask them in out of the rain—what else? So we reduced the size of the dining room table to the smallest dimension, shoved it against the window, pushed the chairs against the wall, put out two enormous urns of coffee, and kept a steady stream of cookies traveling from oven to platter to table. Lyndon conducted a tour of the rooms. Eloise, Homer, and I moved from group to group chatting. And finally the Washington visitors arrived.

First, John Gronouski was sworn in, standing in front of the fireplace, with his wife beside him. Homer, in his capacity as Federal Judge, very dignified, with sonorous voice, administered the oath. Lyndon rearranged the two Gronouski children—Julie and Stacey—"Now wait a minute. Let's get these children in here. Get under that Bible so you will be in the picture." He praised John Gronouski for taking on this new assignment and said his mission is to build new bridges, not just to Poland, but to the people of Eastern Europe. "He carries with him not only the official papers of an Ambassador . . . but my great personal confidence . . ."

Then we all piled into cars and drove to Hye, where the Post Office is located in a store with red, white, and green gingerbread trim that a newspaperman described as "so authentically a general store that it could serve as a movie setting." The next hour was deliciously funny—filled with nostalgia with a capital N. As one newspaperman wrote: "President Johnson spun crackerbarrel stories while cows bellowed beside the highway and city boy Lawrence O'Brien joined the Cabinet as Postmaster General in a homespun, front-porch ceremony at a country store and Post Office."

Across the street is the old cotton gin where Lyndon had jumped into the loaded cotton wagons, and in an adjoining field he had played baseball with the nine Deike brothers. One of the brothers, Levi, is the current Postmaster of Hye. As many of us as could gathered on the porch for the swearing in, which included the line in which the Postmaster General promises to handle all money faithfully and properly!

Lyndon began his speech by saying that this was where he had mailed his first letter fifty-four years ago—to his grandmother. And that Larry O'Brien was going out to try to find that letter and deliver it! "This little community," he said, "represents to me the earliest recollections of the America that I knew when I was a little boy. It was a land of farms and ranches and people who depended on those farms and ranches for a living. . . . Since then, I am fearful that this way of life has slowly passed. . . . But the price of progress must not be two Americas—one rural and one urban, or one northern and one southern, or one Protestant and one Catholic."

In the little crowd that had gathered in front of us, a baby babbled every few moments; a huge cattle truck roared by; and one or two carloads of surprised passers-by pulled over to the side of the road and got out to see what was going on.

I made sure that the Postmaster's wife, Mrs. Deike, and Mrs. Glidden, covering the event for the Johnson City *Record Courier*, met the stars of the day. When everybody had shaken hands all around, I took Elva O'Brien and Mary Gronouski and their families and we drove back by the house where Lyndon was born, and then to the Ranch for lunch. I was proud of the dinner tables set with our Mexican dishes and amber glasses. We had the enchiladas I've been dreaming of since I started to reduce and chili and pinto beans and tamales.

John Gronouski was seated on my left and I enjoyed hearing him talk about Poland and how it serves as a sort of listening post for what is going on in Red China. Poland recognizes Red China and Poland recognizes the United States. Every few months there is a meeting between the

Red Chinese Ambassador and the American Ambassador, which provides a unique opportunity to try to pierce the wall of silence between us. John is studying Polish. His background as an economist heightens his excitement at this job. As soon as lunch was over, our guests had to leave, and we went to the airstrip to bid them good-by.

This afternoon Lyndon had had a long drive with Bill Moyers and the newspaper people. He brought them home for dinner. In discussing foreign affairs, Lyndon said to one of them, "The truth of the business is that this country is in trouble because we cannot any longer make things bigger and better than other countries. We have put Germany and Japan back in business and they are selling their heads off."

At dinner when Lyndon saw the spinach come in, brought by the Filipino waiter, he gave a grimace and said, "Do I have to eat that stuff again?" By his own orders he has been having it two meals every day. The little Filipino waiter, affable and anxious to please, but not understanding much English, hastily grabbed it up and said, "Tapioca?" We all roared with laughter. One word I am sure they are learning from their sojourn with Lyndon is "tapioca."

Tuesday, December 14

THE WHITE HOUSE

I worked at my desk this morning, and, looking out the window, saw the assembled troops waiting for the "pomp and circumstances" ceremony for the arrival of a Chief of State. A little before 11 o'clock I rushed over to Lyndon's office to accompany him to the ceremony, and Colonel Cross escorted us out on the lawn. With clockwork precision, up rolled the big black limousine with Pakistan's green-and-white flag flapping from one front fender and the Stars and Stripes from the other. Out stepped Chief of Protocol Lloyd Hand with handsome, smiling Ayub Khan, one of my favorite Chiefs of State. He is very much a man, with the presence, dignity, the look of strength, that fit him for the role of leader. He and Lyndon have a natural affinity for each other in spite of international troubles. I turned around to greet Minister Zulfikar Bhutto, who has had some rather acid things to say about the United States. Bhutto is quite young—educated in California, interesting looking—but seemed to have a "chip-on-shoulder" manner, or was I being influenced by what I read about him? I was surprised to find former Ambassador Aziz Ahmed, the

Number Two man under Bhutto—himself very able and a good deal older than Bhutto.

Later, I worked an hour on the Christmas album which I am giving Lyndon for his present this year—pictures going back to 1936. How endearing the old ones have become in one's fifty-year-old eyes! Lyndon came home and asked Luci and me to have lunch with him. Though we had already eaten, we pretended and had clear soup. He launched into a long conversation with Luci. He's going to send the child and "Paddy" Nugent up to spend a part of Christmas with Paddy's family. Luci could not have been more thrilled with a star in her hand.

Lyndon returned to reading reports and talking to staff, and I worked again on the Christmas album. Some of the titles just rolled out. The picture of Lynda and Luci asleep on Christmas Eve, 1948—Luci with thumb in mouth and Lynda with a big smile—was a natural for the caption: "While visions of sugar plums danced in their heads."

With a pang, I saw the picture made in Mrs. Johnson's house on Christmas Eve, 1957. It marked the end of a tradition, though none of us knew it then, for she died the following September.

Tonight for dinner I wore my gala dress—white satin and sparkles. The house was beautifully decorated for Christmas! In a lightly falling mist we went onto the North Portico to greet Ayub—cameras flashing to right and left. Lyndon is always very considerate in the crush and the confusion of those moments. He gathered Bhutto and Ambassador Ahmed and Begum Ahmed into the picture. Then we went up to the Oval Room.

This is always one of the most pleasant parts of a State Dinner. Tonight there were fifteen of us—Ayub's party; Hubert and Muriel; the Balls substituting for the Rusks; the ebullient Goldbergs; slight, Alabama-born Walter McConaughy, our Ambassador to Pakistan; and the Lloyd Hands—Ann looking like a girl out of a Botticelli painting, in a pale pink chiffon with sparkles and a high-piled hairdo.

It soon became apparent that the mood of the evening was business. The men gathered in clusters and talked. I dislodged President Ayub for a moment to present our gifts with a little explanation. One was a picture taken in space from a satellite as it flew above Pakistan. There were books for Ayub Khan's wife, who had remained at home, and a tiny television set. And then they were back talking again. This kept on and on, with Bess looking in hopefully and Lloyd trying without success to get us moving. At last President Ayub Khan turned to me and said he had brought "some small gifts." Actually this was the formal presentation, for two very elegant Oriental rugs had already been spread out on the floor and we had been walking on them all evening. In addition to his gift of the beautiful rugs, we also received a length of lovely brocade. Luci bounced in, wearing a very short skirt and flats, just in time to receive two boxes—one for her and one for her sister. Then Lloyd ushered us out the door.

We went downstairs to "Hail to the Chief." And then—I shall always be impressed by it—the entrance to the great East Room, the moment of expectation as the President, the First Lady, and the visiting Chief of State arrive to greet the guests. I always feel a little detached, like a spectator, surprised that I am there.

I did my best to make the receiving line personal and chatty, but I was conscious that we were running about thirty minutes late and that restrained me. There was one long table set for twenty and the rest of the 137 guests were seated in the happy arrangement of round tables of eight.

President Ayub was on my right, Bhutto on my left. Dorothy Goldberg and Jane Freeman were seated next to the two honor guests, so I never had to worry about the flow of conversation. Ayub and I talked about their new capital, Islamabad, which Doxiadis is laying out, and about China. He said, "I think the great tragedy of today is that there is no dialogue between your country and China." He beamed when I told him what Barbara Ward had said about Pakistan being a shining example of an underdeveloped country which is making great strides forward. We talked about birth control. He said their program is really getting under way this year with acceptance by the people. It's in no way at odds with their religious scruples, and its progress is hindered only by the people's lack of information. They are working to keep population growth within bounds the country can handle, and it has complete government backing and sponsorship.

And then I talked with Bhutto. It turns out that the housing development of Korangi, which we saw when we were there, is his brainchild. It was one of the most interesting things we saw on our trip—ambitious in size, so well planned to suit the terrain, low in unit cost. Lyndon wanted to adopt it and bring it back to use in poverty areas in parts of our own Southwest. I remembered I had learned a new word there—ekistics—the science of city planning. One thing Bhutto said I thought was revealing. He mentioned that on some visit he had made to the United States—I judge it was when he represented his nation at the funeral of President

Kennedy—he had said something that he understood "made the President perfectly furious." I looked at him blankly, for I had never heard anything about it. I doubt that Lyndon had ever heard of it either. Actually I thought he looked quite intelligent and likable but acted almost as though he were determined not to be liked. Quite different was Ayub—so calm and reasonable and strong looking. And yet some of the fire, perhaps, was gone.

When Ayub rose to make his toast, it was, as Isabelle Shelton said, as though he were speaking directly to the President, as if there were no one else in the room: "I am only talking to a friend now. May I have the liberty of doing so with a great heart?" It was a very simple, candid, touching expression of the way things are between us now. He spoke of our warm and friendly relations in the past, and then said: "It hurts me to say that our relations have, to a certain extent, been soiled, and I think that has happened because of a lack of understanding of each other's difficulties and problems." He thanked us for our help, and said that he is the first to admit it, "not only in my heart, but in front of my people." And then, "In a period when the world has shrunk, peoples' expectations have risen. They want the good things of life quickly. The people are not prepared to wait. They are impatient. Therefore, there is great pressure . . ."

I could look at the face of Bhutto, multiply him by ninety million—but Ayub says there are one hundred million now—and feel something of this pressure. Ayub was continuing, "Lately, unfortunately, we have been bedeviled with a major conflict. My endeavor has been to live in peace with our neighbors—especially with our big neighbor, India. We need peace not only for the sake of peace, but also for the sake of doing a very noble task of improving the lot of our people." It was a touching, stirring speech. He makes you want to be his advocate.

Lyndon took him straight upstairs with a few of his Ministers for further talks while I led the guests into the Red Room and Green Room for coffee and liqueurs.

Lyndon and Ayub talked about thirty minutes upstairs, and when they returned we went in for the entertainment, which was called "Music for the White House." Gregory Peck was the narrator and the Westminster Choir, assisted by the Marine Band using a number of old instruments that had been under lock and key at the Smithsonian for the last one hundred years, sang a medley of tunes that were popular in the eighteenth and nineteenth centuries: "George Washington's March," "Sea Engagement,"

"These Things Shall Be," ending with John Adams' "Prayer for the White House." The young people of the Choir had ridden in a bus all night from New York, had been housed in Army barracks, and had spent the day in practice for the evening's entertainment.

The concert was a fine idea, but somehow, it seemed to me, the whole evening lacked sparkle. I felt the lag although I have never been more anxious for a Chief of State to feel graciously welcomed and for the hours of talk to be productive. President Ayub left immediately after the entertainment was over.

I went upstairs to find that however the party had seemed to me, it had seemed a brilliant success to our houseguests. Oveta Hobby, the Tom Miller, Jr.'s, Ed Hartes, and Jess McNeels were all gathered around Lyndon rehashing the events of the evening. This is the best time of any party, and I am glad we have begun inviting special friends to spend the night at the White House.

Monday, December 20

This was one of those near-perfect days when I would rather be right where I was, doing what I did, than anywhere else imaginable, even Caneel Bay or the Grecian Isles. The White House was beautiful with evergreens and the great Christmas tree in the Blue Room. It was decorated with gingerbread men and drums and toy soldiers. The gingerbread was real as high as anyone could reach, and farther up it was ceramic. There were garlands of popcorn and miracles of lights. It was a beautiful work of art. We had invited the children of all our friends, the staff, of course, my dentist's and doctor's families, all of the Clark Clifford grandchildren, some twelve or so, to see it. In the East Room there was the crèche. Mrs. Howell Howard has spent several nights putting it together—a marvelous collection of eighteenth-century Neapolitan figures, some earlier, that she has spent her lifetime collecting. She has given her other collection of figures to the Metropolitan Museum of Art in New York, but each year she displays a crèche in the White House, a practice begun for Mrs. Kennedy in 1961. I had sprigs of mistletoe from Texas hanging over the doorways, from the Diplomatic entrance with its lighted trees flanking the door to the Great Hall with its tall evergreens. The whole house bespoke Christmas at every step and I felt like skipping and humming "Deck the halls with boughs of holly . . ." as I walked through it.

No matter how much planning ahead we do, about five or six days before Christmas Lyndon gets frantic, thinking about all the things he wants to do for all the people he loves, and heaping work on all those around him, and issuing orders, "Recheck the names! Plan gifts! Get it done!" I know this results in many midnight hours for secretaries, merchants, picture framers, parcel post deliverers—and me. But after more than thirty years I, at least, should know what to expect.

This evening we gave a State Dinner in honor of Chancellor Ludwig Erhard of Germany. We opened up all the stops and the Christmas carols rang forth. We met the Chancellor at the door of the Diplomatic entrance, with a sixty-member chorus from the American Light Opera Company lining the steps to the balcony above. These graceful mansion stairs have seldom been used for their full drama. The lighted trees down front and the carolers giving forth with infectious joy got the evening off to the gayest of starts. I tried my best to look into the eyes of each singer, up and down the stairs, to telegraph the message "thank you."

We went upstairs to the Yellow Room for the exchange of gifts. Chancellor Erhard had brought a hunting rifle for Lyndon, an engraving of George Washington, and clocks for the girls. Then we went back downstairs to the East Room for the receiving line.

Chancellor Erhard's wife was not with him and when we went in to dinner he was on my right, with Gerhard Schroeder, the Minister of Foreign Affairs, on my left. Lyndon's dinner partners were Mrs. Heinrich Knappstein, the Ambassador's wife, and Mrs. Humphrey. The dinner was in the grand tradition—lobster and roast duckling and, at the end, a beautifully decorated chocolate yule log.

I found the Chancellor good company, with better English than I had expected. I remarked that I had read that 20 to 25 percent of the population of West Germany were people who had come from the other side of the Iron Curtain. He said, yes, that they had come at a time when there were hardly enough jobs, enough houses, enough to eat, for those who normally live there. Absorbing the émigrés into the social and economic life had been quite a job. He is in good part the architect of West Germany's post-war reconstruction, and I was so interested in hearing him discuss it. Always a reliable subject with every Chief of State is: "How I would like to visit your country!"

During dessert the University of Maryland Madrigal Singers, dressed in colorful Renaissance costumes of ruby-red velvet, moss-green silk, and dull gold satin, strolled among the tables singing sixteenth- and seventeenth-century Christmas carols. We were all caught up in the enchanting story-book atmosphere.

In his toast Lyndon told Chancellor Erhard that he would shortly send to Europe a Commission to discuss joint explorations in space, leading to probes of the sun and Jupiter. In a much lighter vein he said, "There is no truth to the rumor that your reputation as an economist prompted us to invite you to visit us at Budget time."

Erhard delivered his toast in German, which was then translated. He gave the United States credit for having extended the hand of friendship which enabled Germany to get back on its feet after World War II. He then said, with unusual candor, that the United States is making great sacrifices to defend the security of the people in Vietnam. "But that is also our security. . . . I feel ashamed, because what we can contribute is very modest compared with what you do." I am sure before he gets out of town Lyndon will ask him in as forceful a manner as possible how much more they can contribute.

Lyndon used his toast, as he does everything these days, to talk about peace. "There will be peace in Vietnam the very moment that others are ready to stop their attacks." He reaffirmed that we are going to keep this country moving forward with The Great Society.

For the entertainment of the evening we moved into the East Room where I introduced Robert Merrill. Bless him, he was performing for us for the third time. Tonight with the Madrigal Singers he sang "Silent Night" in German and English, asking all of us to join in. I was so happy and so relaxed that when I finished my introduction I dared to wish our guests a "Sehr Fröhliche Weihnachten"—a most Merry Christmas.

Almost on the stroke of midnight the Chancellor left. We accompanied him out to the front door, where a light fall of snow was drifting—the last perfect touch. It was really Christmas!

BOOK THREE

1966

Winter 1966

I woke with that inescapable feeling of drama: What will
Saturday, this New Year hold for us all? Tom Mann flew in about
January 1, 11:30. He had been to Mexico as a part of the Herculean
1966 appeal for peace that has been mounted since the Christmas
ceasefire. Five roving emissaries have gone to some forty
countries, urging them to apply pressure on Hanoi to come
to the peace table.

Lyndon and I with Tom Mann, Jesse, Tony, and Matiana
started driving to Enchanted Rock. We have lived in Stonewall thirteen years, and I have heard about it all this time
but never been there.

Tom said that in all the years he had known Mexico
and its politicians, he had never found them so friendly
to the United States. Our conversation was constantly interrupted by the talking machine in the car with long
calls from Bill Moyers and Joe Califano about reports
from all the peace seekers and about price increases in

345

steel. The other five of us were immobilized while Lyndon was talking.

It was a misty day—not one for exploring and mountain climbing, but as we climbed the hills the country rolled away from us on all sides and we could see the tree-dotted hills and ravines and granite rocks and little running streams. In an hour we reached Enchanted Rock, the largest granite outcropping in the United States except for Stone Mountain, Georgia. As we walked up the great dome we crossed innumerable faults, clearly defined, and tiny little fissures, in which life—never-to-be-defeated life—kept on growing: diminutive yellow flowers the size of a match head or a wee cactus. Occasionally we would see a small group of dwarf live oaks that had somehow found a pocket of soil.

After awhile I began wishing Lyndon would stop climbing, and Tony, too—both of them had once had heart attacks—but there was no heading them off. We climbed on and on, because the top kept receding. Finally, at the very top of this world, we saw the small round bronze piece put there by the National Geodetics Survey, and from there we looked off to all the horizons. One felt one owned the world in every direction!

We went home by a back road, off the pavement and sometimes even off the gravel, and arrived hungry as bears at about 3:15. Appetite is the best sauce. We had ham and black-eyed peas for good luck at New Year's, and corn bread and buttermilk. I realized the pleasure that comes all too seldom in our civilized, affluent life of being really hungry and then getting satisfied.

At Lyndon's insistence, we all trooped to St. Francis Xavier Catholic Church for Mass about sundown. The church was an experience. All the families had brought their babies and there were plenty of them, several crying. Father Schneider's accent was heavy German, but we could understand the warmth of his welcome. He expressed his pleasure that the President and the First Lady were there and blessed all of our party, and all our work, with such genuine pleasure that I felt good we had come, even if my knees were paralyzed from the wooden kneelers.

And then back to the Ranch. We found Lynda and Warrie Lynn weary, full of excitement, both chattering at once. George Hamilton had flown in from London at 8 o'clock New Year's Eve, and had left at 12 New Year's Day. Excitement is a new mood for Lynda, and it becomes her. She looks radiant, happy, in the swift current of her life.

Today was just what New Year's should be, family, kinfolks, dear friends. Besides Tony and Matiana, Winston Taylor had come down and dear

Mildred Stegall. I had never thought I would eat again, but Gene brought in the big turkey, handsomely decorated, for us to admire, and about 9 o'clock we had the traditional dinner. Nobody in the world makes better dressing than Zephyr, and sweet potatoes with marshmallows, and cranberry sauce. Afterward we had a session at the "Johnson Bijou"—*Ship of Fools*, which turned out to be a wonderful movie, but the audience gradually drifted away—Lyndon to sleep, Winston and Tony to do the same. Lynda Bird had already seen the movie, and Luci took Pat back to San Antonio. But Matiana and Mildred and the staff and I enjoyed it.

Monday, January 3

THE WHITE HOUSE

Lyndon slept little. In the morning he said he had thought just as long as he could about Vietnam, and then he thought about the Budget for awhile. Sometimes I think the greatest bravery of all is simply to get up in the morning and go about your business.

The Paul Reveres are riding all over the world. Hubert has just returned from a five-day trip to four countries; Goldberg has been to see the Pope, De Gaulle, and Wilson; Harriman is traveling on and on, country after country. There are no real flashes of hope. But there is, I believe, a feeling in the country that we are doing all we can, sort of a tour-de-force peace offensive that leaves no door unknocked.

I asked Lyndon if he would go swimming with me. While we swam he told me all the things that faced him in this week—Budget decisions, the State of the Union Message, and the dreadful decision that if nothing, nothing, nothing comes of the peace offensive—when to resume the bombing.

Wednesday, January 5

I wish we could do something about these sleepless nights. Lyndon said he slept from 12:30 to 2:30 and then turned and tossed the rest of the night. And yet he gets up and puts in a full day's work. As Lyndon left this morning he turned to me and said: "We've lost the steel fight; we may lose the war." There comes a time when there is nothing to do but go ahead grimly, and that's how today felt.

When I came upstairs I heard a scream in the hall on the second floor and saw Gloria, the maid, running full steam out of Luci's room, followed by Luci who had a large yellow-looking rat in her hand. I jumped straight up in the air and dashed into another room. By that time Luci was overcome by giggles and I saw that the rat was quite dead. She said that he was preserved in Formalin. He had a sort of zipper arrangement on his stomach whereby you could open him up and fit in all of his insides, and he was part of her zoology course in school. The things Luci has added to this old house would make a book!

At noon the papers reported that the steel companies had settled for $2.75 instead of the $5.00 they had demanded. So my spirits lifted. If not total victory, it was at least a measure of success.

But the brickbats were not over. A story in the newspaper reported: "Airman Nugent gets transferred to Washington . . . will not be separated from his fiancée Luci Johnson by military service for the next six months after all." It was a routine, run-of-the-mill transfer, of course. But there was one delightful thing in the paper—a picture of the five puppies clambering out of a huge basket, with Him standing sullenly beside them wondering, I expect, how anybody found them so attractive when he was around.

At 5 o'clock I had a nice interlude. Howard Taubman of the *New York Times* interviewed me about how I felt about art in general—painting, drama, books—and about how my feelings and the President's feelings were reflected in this Administration and in the legislation it had helped to pass. I talked about my desires for this house to acquire representative great American paintings—a Copley, a Benjamin West, a George Caleb Bingham, an Eakins, an Innes perhaps. I showed him the paintings we had acquired: the Winslow Homer, the Sully, and the Mary Cassatt. We talked of the contemporary paintings that have been hung in the West Wing where the dictum about hanging only artists who have been dead twenty-five years or more doesn't apply. I have no idea how I sounded to Mr. Taubman, but it is a subject I enjoy and love to hear about and to talk about.

I tried to explain that I go to a Van Gogh opening and to the Barter Theatre in Abingdon, and to dedicate the new wing of the Modern Museum of Art, and to hear *La Traviata* at the Met, and have a reception for Thornton Wilder to receive the award here at the White House— because I *like* to. I enjoy it. It comes naturally and yet if my doing it —and this does sound presumptuous—helps to make it fashionable, makes other people want to do it, helps others to have the opportunity of being exposed to new joys, new experiences, then I am glad. I kept on thinking afterward of all the things I should have said.

With my hair dripping wet on the way to Jean Louis I encountered Lyndon, Jim Cain, and Ambassador Ken Galbraith getting out of the elevator. Lyndon had asked Ken to head the Peace Corps about a week ago. He had sounded as if he really might do it, but then said, "I have to talk to my wife," and that's when a man wants to put on the brakes. The answer on the Peace Corps was "No" because he is about six months short of finishing a book in which he has his whole heart and mind invested. Galbraith went on to say that if Lyndon ever had a job that absolutely had to be done by "a sort of a fringe liberal considered dangerous by some," he wanted to do it. I asked for an hour of his time in the future to talk about the School of Public Service at the University of Texas, and then I fled to Jean Louis, wishing I were invisible en route.

Tuesday, January 11

This day began in the early hours of the morning with a long talk. Lyndon woke up, as he often does these nights, and we talked about the prospects for the years ahead. They are so fraught with danger and with decisions whose outcome we cannot see. I am torn between two feelings. One, the healthy one, that I should enjoy each day in this job and live it to the fullest. The other, that the end of the term is like a light at the end of a tunnel. And my advice to Lyndon is so mundane and uninspiring: stay healthy, laugh a little, remember you are as tough as other Presidents who have lived through the same or worse.

The important event of the day for me was the reception and dinner of the National Wildlife Federation sponsored jointly with the Sears Roebuck Foundation. I was to deliver four of their awards—little statuettes of a whooping crane—and to receive one myself for my interest in conserving wildlife and beauty.

At the dinner in the Statler Ballroom, Judge Louis McGregor, President of the National Wildlife Federation, was on my right, and on my left was James Griffin, President of the Sears Roebuck Foundation. Stewart

349 / BOOK THREE: 1966

Udall was the Master of Ceremonies and Secretary Freeman the main speaker. I think of them as the Beautification Twins. General Electric won an award for imaginative engineering, unusual research, and successful development of equipment and techniques to preserve America's natural beauty. I asked the award winner just how much was being done to bury power transmission lines in new housing developments, and he said it had increased 400 percent in this last year—a glowing statistic. But I just wished I knew how to turn it into a future picture in Austin, Texas, for instance.

There were awards in various fields of conservation: water resources, soil, wildlife, air, forests, and one as conservationist educator of the year. This went to a young man named Johnny MacJohnson of Union Springs, Alabama, most of whose work had been done in 4-H and Future Farmers, with high-school-age youth. Nelson Rockefeller won the award for "dynamic leadership in developing and promoting an approach to water pollution abatement, which has set an example throughout the nation."

I passed out the whooping cranes and checks to the winners. When I received mine, I announced that the check would be given to landscape the new automobile entrance of the National Zoo. There was an excitement about being with a crowd of people with a sense of comradeship and mutual purpose and congeniality in this gathering.

The day had had its quota of annoyances—three or four stories about "gumshoe practice in the White House." Our effort to reduce the number of chauffeurs from one hundred to sixty had succeeded, but at the price of logging every trip made by anybody who rode in a White House car —who and where to—in order to eliminate social and personal chauffeuring. This requirement is abrasive to everybody who has grown accustomed to the happy ease of stepping into a chauffeur-driven car. The number of telephones has also proliferated far beyond needs. They too must be cut back, to the number of lines actually required by need and not by status. Nobody likes economizing and the tough guy who gets it done gets cut up on all sides.

Wednesday, January 12

Today was the day of the State of the Union Message. It is always as full of tension as an opening night, as fraught with unpredictability as a birth. In 1964 we lived through it on the tidal wave of emotion produced by the death of President Kennedy, supported by that adrenalin of determination that such catastrophe pours into your blood.

In 1965 we were on the crest of the great victory of the November election, bolstered, assured, the people behind us, a sort of peak in our lives perhaps, and here in 1966 maybe we are in the trough of a wave; erosion and frustrations have set in and now is the time for just dogged toughness.

I kissed Lyndon good-by and Godspeed, and the staff began to come into the room—Jack Valenti, Jake Jacobsen, Marvin Watson. Last night, I had read the final draft of the domestic part of the speech, had suggested a little sentence about thrift and common sense in the conduct of the war on poverty, with due respect for spending the taxpayer's dollar. So, I deliberately wanted to remove myself from the boiling center of things today.

I spent the day with Brooke Astor, Mary Lasker, Walter Washington, and Nash Castro on beautification—looking at Washington's schools (repeatedly Buchanan) and talking about playgrounds and community parks— driving around Hains Point and dreaming of a future full of alleys of cherry trees beside the water. It was nearly 6:30 when Lyndon came in for "lunch," bringing some staff with him. What a day it must have been. We were to go to the Capitol separately—I went ahead with Luci and Pat, and the staff wives I had asked to sit in the Gallery with me.

There is no doubt about it, the State of the Union Message, for better or for worse, is always one of the great shows of the year. We all rose as Lyndon came down the aisle, walking briskly, smiling to right and left. It is always an endurance contest for me. I wonder what it is like for him?

There were strong reassurances in the speech—we would go on with the Great Society to carry forward with full vigor the great health and education programs enacted last year . . . we would make a strenuous effort to meet the growing menace of crime in the streets. There were some surprises—a proposal for a four-year term for the House of Representatives. It must have been something of a bombshell when Lyndon said that we should help nations trying to control population growth by increasing our research and by earmarking funds to help their efforts. This is the first time a President has declared himself on the birth control issue. One of the best lines was: "We must change to master change."

There was a clear recital of the enormous effort we have made in the last weeks of 1965 for peace: "In 1965 alone we had three hundred private talks for peace in Vietnam, with friends and adversaries throughout the world. Since Christmas your government has labored again, with imagination and endurance, to remove any barrier to peaceful settlement. For twenty days now we and our Vietnamese allies have dropped no bombs in North Vietnam. Able and experienced spokesmen have visited, on behalf of America, more than forty countries. We have talked to more than a hundred governments, all 113 that we have relations with, and some that we don't. We have talked to the United Nations and we have called upon all of its members to make any contribution that they can toward helping obtain peace."

The audience was cold and lethargic. It is true there were about fifty-seven applauses, but they were not roars of enthusiasm by any means. There was almost no participation by the Republicans. After all, this is 1966 and an election year. I watched in vain for approval from old friends —Dick Russell, Senator John McClellan—scant occasional expression from Senator Mike Mansfield.

When it was over I breathed a sigh of relief, although there was nothing that reassured me it would be an easy year or a good year from listening to the State of the Union Message or from looking at the Congress in front of me. We went down to the Speaker's office, where I met Lyndon and kissed him, wishing I could convey solace and reassurance. We shook hands all around—the usual first-of-the-year greetings. The pervasively friendly atmosphere seemed missing from that normal social interchange. Or am I imagining?

I went to bed feeling it was not a triumph, not one of the greatest ones, but I was proud of it. And a last thought before I drifted off to sleep was a funny one. We had had an enthusiastic discussion in the Red Room, Mary, Brooke, Walter, Nash, and I. We had gotten to talking about the shortages of labor for park maintenance and highway beautification and nurserymen and about the shortages of plant material itself. And Mary said with an absolutely straight face, "How are we going to get the nurserymen to have enough stock to plant the whole United States?" That's the way it is. Controversy and frustration one day and enthusiasm like a sailboat racing before the wind the next!

Tuesday, January 18

This day was a crescendo of activity. Lyndon and I went down to the East Room at 10 o'clock for the swearing in of the first Negro member of a President's Cabinet, Robert Weaver, Secretary of Housing and Urban Development, and his Undersecretary, Robert C. Wood, who comes from

MIT. It must have been an emotional moment for many of the people in the room and the Negro leadership was well represented—Roy Wilkins, Dr. James Nabrit, Whitney Young, Walter Washington, Louie Martin. It was one of those moments when a sense of history hung in the air. The acceptance by the Congress and the country has been good; our hopes are high.

After the swearing in, Lyndon brought the Weavers and the Woods and their three children and Whitney Young and Louie Martin upstairs. We had coffee in the West Hall and talked. Then I went downstairs to the State Dining Room to meet two hundred members of United Jewish Women from Pittsburgh, whom Lucy Moorhead had asked me to receive. I welcomed them, received a plaque, and then stood in line to meet every single one, to a chorus from them of "You look so much better than your pictures!" Later I went down to the Diplomatic Reception Room to meet Dr. Elisabeth Schwarzhaupp, the Minister of Health for the Federal Republic of Germany, the only woman in the German Cabinet, accompanied by Katie Louchheim and the capable Mrs. Hanna Kiep from the German Embassy, who goes on and on, no matter how the Ambassadors come and go.

No sooner had they left than Mrs. Rusk and Ann Hand arrived with six Ambassadors' wives, most of whom were entitled to sue the State Department for the pictures of them that were sent to me in their advance information. They were Madame Charles Lucet of France, whom I already knew from our days in the International Club; Madame Vu Van Thai of Vietnam, who arrived at Christmas and is suffering housewifely troubles of getting children settled in schools and her household arranged; a lively lady from the Dominican Republic, Mrs. Milton Messina; Mrs. Michael Lukumbuzya from Tanzania, who has nine children, the eldest of whom is ten, in a native dress of a long gingham swathe vaguely resembling a sari. Her English was perfect—she spoke Swahili also—her manner calm and dignified. And there was Mrs. Farhan Shubeilat, wife of the Ambassador of the Hashemite Kingdom of Jordan. Mrs. Shubeilat is handsome, feminine, charming.

And then attractive Mrs. Ernst Lemberger, wife of the Ambassador of Austria—it is a hard act to follow her predecessor, gay Mrs. Wilfried Platzer. After tea I showed them the Yellow Room and the Lincoln Room and the Queen's Room. But somehow the tour wasn't as good as it should have been.

And the day was not yet over. As soon as they left, Clark Clifford and Bill Heath arrived. Bill announced the action of the University of Texas in naming a committee of four—himself, Dr. Norman Hackerman, Dr. Harry Ransom, and Frank Erwin—to make recommendations on getting the School of Public Service under way. They were going to form an advisory committee from the faculty.

A little before 8 everybody had gone. Lyndon was back in his office at work. Luci wafted in on a breeze, happy as a lark, saying, "Mama, I probably aced it!" (her zoology final), and with "Mr. Nugent" in tow she went happily out to dinner. When people ask me if I am glad about my little girl's getting married, if I think she is old enough, what can I possibly answer? How could I know the answer now, or five years from now or ten years from now? And how could I presume that it is not good when she has been so happy for many months?

Sunday, January 23

I suggested we go to Lyndon's church today. Dr. Davis is a comfort to him, and I seek out comforts for him like a mother seeking medicines for a sick child. I get angry at him when he reacts to the poison in the newspapers, but I find *myself* reacting at barbed words toward anybody I love, such as Luci and Pat. Lyndon laughed at me and said, "You are just like George Smathers' brother"—that's a family joke. Nobody else would know what he meant. I did exactly. For years Senator George Smathers had been railing whenever any columnist—it was quite frequently Drew Pearson —took out after him. His banker brother would say, "Now George, you just ought not to pay that any mind, nobody reads it much, it doesn't matter." And then suddenly, inexplicably, one day Mr. Pearson took out after George's banker brother for some action on the part of his bank. Brother was immediately furious, distraught. Lyndon said, "You can tell me how to handle it, but then when they take out after Luci it's a different matter." I laughed too—the week's stories shrank down to their proper size and I am once more convinced we shall go on living.

On Sunday I always try to read the interminable papers on my desk. Today I found results of the much discussed security check on telephones. As a result of our study of all the contacts in the White House, one unexpected thing (at least to me) came out—the amazing total of more than fifty-one thousand "unfriendly contacts" during the year of 1965 was revealed, ranging all the way from abusive telephone calls and threatening letters to 166 picketings—over three hundred "unwelcome visitors" at the

Main Gate—112 of whom were actually arrested or committed for mental observation. Last and most extraordinary—seven persons were apprehended climbing the fence! Of all the things that beset us, physical danger is the last I would worry about.

I had given Lyndon a list of people, any of whom I would like to see for dinner, and quickly put in calls, and we wound up with a delightful group coming at 7 o'clock: the Tom Manns, the Kermit Gordons, the John Macys, Tyler and Bess. Then when I awoke about 6 I found that Lyndon had added the Vice President. I am always glad—I remember how it felt when Lyndon was Vice President. I like for Hubert to be continually reassured of our fondness for him and our belief in him. Although I remember the hilarious remark that Lyndon made about him once—"If I could just breed him to Calvin Coolidge". . . no explanation necessary.

As the guests began to arrive, we were glued to the TV in the little West Hall watching that miracle of Telstar showing Dean Rusk being interviewed by newspapermen in Rome, Paris, Bonn, London—a commentary on humankind that none of us gave any real thought to the miracle of Telstar itself and yet what hope that must hold! If man can do this, can he possibly turn his talents to solving disputes short of destruction? Rusk was magnificent. I would like to give him an A plus and my undying gratitude as a citizen and as the wife of the President in whose Cabinet he plays such a part. He even managed to get in one little note of mild humor when some correspondent handed him a double-barreled question about Rhodesia and South Africa and he said, "If you don't mind, I'd like to take my crises one at a time."

These evenings are serving the purpose I wanted—to make our Administration feel more closely knit—more a part of each other. Of course Hubert livens up any evening. Just as everyone was about to leave, there was talk of sending a medical team and an agricultural know-how team, headed by Freeman himself, to Vietnam. Another and different phase of this mighty search for peace. The question is, "Are we getting it across to the world?"

A little vignette of the evening's conversation was Lyndon saying to the men, "The thing I want most is a Tax Bill by April 15." Then he kept on predicting the dire prospects, legislative-wise, for 1966—measure after measure would fail. "We will not pass much this year." Kermit Gordon said mildly, "It seems to me, Mr. President, this was the way you were talking in January 1965."

From the children there is good news. Lynda Bird thinks she is doing pretty well in her finals. She interrupted a telephone call from me to say, "Mama, you'll just have to wait, George is calling." He is part of the wine of life, exciting and heady. Two bits in the paper today: One was that the First Lady never would compete with the best dressed! Another was that "the Beautiful People" are all heading for Acapulco and in the list of the beautiful people was Lynda Bird's name.

Luci is happy too—in spite of the press stories. (Incidentally, she is praying for them—the press people, I mean!) She came down off Cloud 9 last night long enough to bring in a large box to open up in front of the McNamaras and the Krims and show us the result of her day of shopping. She and Pat had been looking for their silver and china and crystal. Her taste was beautiful. Exquisite Limoges—white with a chaste gold border— for her formal china. And Old Maryland for her silver. Everything except the Limoges, she assures me, will be an American product. But she has her heart set on the Limoges.

Thursday, January 27

NEW YORK

I spent the day in New York in the world of fashion. I hope I'll get enough clothes not to have to go back again soon. But while I am in the White House, I want to look as well as I can, for Lyndon and for this role.

Brooke Astor (Mrs. Vincent Astor) and Jane and Charles Engelhard gave a dinner party for me, in Brooke's exquisite apartment which is filled with paintings. I think I recognized a Matisse and a Fragonard. The flowers were pale apricot tulips and pear and cherry blossoms that belied the snow outside. I wore my favorite green evening dress. As I stepped off the elevator there was Jane Engelhard, always magnificently dressed, and this time wearing a dress in black, exactly like mine! She had on magnificent diamond earrings and necklace to match, which she casually described with the phrase, "a piece of the chandelier fell off." Brooke Astor wore a white lace dress, at once the essence of innocence and also provocative. She is a gay, vital person who embraces life and works with and enjoys those things her Foundation helps. For me she is one of the happy additions to those I came to know in 1965.

There were enough old friends there to make me feel at home: the Laurance Rockefellers; Phyllis Dillon; and people I had met, but wanted to know better—the John Loebs who gave the Yellow Room at the White

House; and the Henry Parrishes, she's "Sister" Parrish who decorated for Mrs. Kennedy; the Arthur Houghtons, he is the President of the Metropolitan Museum of Art; the James Hesters who had been at the White House the night before; the Edward Warburgs, he is one of the founders of the Museum of Modern Art; Ogden White, a member of the Board of the American Museum of Natural History; Ted Rousseau of the Metropolitan; Osborn Elliott, of *Newsweek*; Diana Vreeland, Editor of *Vogue*; and Clayton Fritchey, the perennial bachelor. It was Charles Engelhard who told me the most delicious story of the evening. He was describing the courtship of his stepdaughter, a beautiful girl, Jane's child by a former marriage, by a young Mr. Reed. Time came for the two families to meet, in the polite exploration of each other's background. Charles decided to say to Mrs. Reed, "You know, I think I should tell you that Jane and I are Democrats. Ardent Democrats." Mrs. Reed replied, "How interesting. We know another one, Averell Harriman."

There were toasts, charming and witty and sweet, by Brooke, Charles and Jane, and a reply that I wanted very much to be adequate; if I had been a bit more daring I would have raised my glass in a toast to "a woman whose taste in clothes I have always admired!"

Saturday, January 29

The names of the people I have been seeing on this trip to New York are rather like those on the doors outside the boxes of the Golden Horseshoe in the old Metropolitan Opera House. Today we went to lunch with Jeanne Vanderbilt in her jewel of an apartment exquisitely done with chintz and books and flowers and a fireplace, with a terrace that overlooks New York.

I sat between Truman Capote and Alan Jay Lerner. The alchemy of image has turned Mr. Capote into a legend and I was interested to meet him. He was small, slight, with a speech impediment that surprised me at first, and then I completely forgot it because he was so interesting. We talked about his book *Other Voices, Other Rooms*—he had written it at nineteen. He described his style as the sort of thing that happens to rocks when water flows over them for years and years and they get smoother and smoother. We spoke of Harper Lee and he told me he was the little boy who came to visit in the summers in *To Kill a Mockingbird*. Alan Jay Lerner, who wrote *My Fair Lady*, said that it is likely to run for sixteen years in London, so used are the British to seeing plays over and over that they like. Later Mr. Lerner took us to a matinée of *On a Clear Day You Can See Forever,* and for me this was an enchanted two and a half hours.

A number of people asked for autographs and there was clapping and standing up when I came in and out, so that I felt rather on stage myself. Afterward we went backstage to meet all the actors. There was so much I wanted to say to them. The main actress had the most mobile face I have ever seen. It was a triumph—her change from the elegant lady of 1794 to the rather plaintive little soul of 1966. I was unhappily tongue-tied and couldn't really tell them how much I had enjoyed it. There were lots of pictures all around, and then Alan Lerner took us out to the car and we were off to the railroad station, dropping the Vanderbilts at their apartment.

A blizzard had set in during the day and it was impossible to fly. We took the 6 o'clock train. With a snow plow in front of us from Baltimore on, and three changes of engines, we were to be the last train in during the night. Finally in the unreal world of a heavy storm we were in Union Station about midnight. We had to walk past the eleven cars. There was a freight car on another track with a door open and lights on inside. I could see three oblong boxes, seven or eight feet long. On top of one there were sprays of flowers—rather wilted gladiola. I suppose their destination was Arlington. It was hard to think then of anything else.

Saturday, February 5

THE WHITE HOUSE

Lyndon left today for Hawaii to meet with Thieu and Ky and other high officials of the Vietnamese government plus our Ambassador and General Westmoreland to discuss the situation in Vietnam, especially the non-military side of pacification and economic development. Will I always be sorry that I didn't go? It was a man's trip, or so I told myself, and Lynda was coming in tonight, with George Hamilton. It would mean a lot to her to have me here.

At noon I went down to the Diplomatic Reception Room with Lyndon, to say good-by. A long-haired, bright-eyed little girl of about sixteen, Katherine Westmoreland, the daughter of the General, came running up, an algebra book and a muumuu in her arms. She was going to fly to

Hawaii with Lyndon. Mrs. Westmoreland was celebrating her birthday with her husband in Hawaii, and wouldn't it be wonderful if her daughter could fly out to join them? Katherine's idea of the trip was expressed when she flung her arms around Lyndon and kissed him and said, "Now we can be a family again!"

Because we've turned the second floor into a shambles with electricians and carpenters, and had rugs and furniture slipcovers removed to be cleaned (this always happens somewhere in the house when the President is away), I decided that I would take my dinner guests to the family dining room on the State floor, and we would have cocktails in the Red Room, with the fire—the first time we have ever done this, and a delightful "first" it was.

I had invited Leonard Marks and Diana and Donald MacArthur. Leonard was ebullient about his trip tomorrow to Hawaii and then Saigon. We talked about the audio-visual requirements for the Lyndon Baines Johnson Library.

Lynda and George arrived a little before 9 for dinner with us. George, looking handsome and tired, was just off the plane from Europe. Luci, meanwhile, was cooking chicken in the family kitchen for her own dinner party of six, to be served in the Solarium. As I passed through the second floor, she implored me to taste the gravy.

Zephyr had delicious steaks for us, which were served on the Grant china—we've never used it before. The fire was a perfect foil to the snow outside. Immediately after dinner Lynda and George went off to go dancing.

Sunday, February 13

Tonight Lyndon talked about his trip to Hawaii. He'd been greatly impressed with Westmoreland, actually rather impressed with Ky. He talked about some of "our side" of the story of what happens in Vietnam which, for some reason, never seems to get in print. For instance, how our expert medical service, plus the boon of helicopters, makes it possible to get to a wounded man within an hour, and get him into a hospital in not longer than three hours, which so greatly reduces fatalities among the wounded.

He talked about the SEATO Treaty, which had been passed by the Senate in February 1955, 82 to 1; Langer was the one against it. Incidentally, Johnson and Kennedy did not vote. Lyndon was in Mayo Clinic having a kidney stone operation and Senator Kennedy was absent with his serious back trouble. "Now," Lyndon said, "we are trying to carry out the contracts they made." We were discussing the debate in the country, on the Vietnam policy, as opened up by the debate in the Senate. At lunch, Lafayette Park had been full of picketers. The White House was picketed 166 times last year. Lyndon said, "This thing is assuming dangerous proportions, dividing the country and giving our enemies the wrong idea of the will of this country to fight."

General Maxwell Taylor had been tremendous on TV. We called him to tell him so. He said, "I was just warming up for the Senate Committee."

One looks at the bombing pause in retrospect—those thirty-seven days when we were hopefully setting the stage for peace or for getting together at the conference table—running all over the world, asking everybody to join in peace efforts. Was it a good idea or not? As of today, one doubts it, but I still believe that it's a national proof of going the last mile, being willing to make every effort. The effort had the support of Fulbright and Morse, though little credit we had from them for pursuing it.

Sunday, February 20

Weekends are a sort of safety valve in our lives, a time to rest and recoup and have fun.

The week had been a terrific strain, trying to assess the effect across the nation of the Vietnam debate. There had been increasing hostility in the newspaper columns, for days and weeks it seemed, and then, on Thursday and Friday, I had the feeling that it was our inning—that we won with General Maxwell Taylor and Secretary Rusk.

Nevertheless, I did not go to sleep Saturday night until 2:30. I finally went to my room and read, and read, and read, and turned out the light at 2:30.

We went to St. Marks. It is still a "church in the round," but there were no surprises as there so often are at St. Marks until perhaps, one might say, we started out and little Coco McPherson came up and took Lyndon's hand, bringing along her friend, Janice, a ten-year-old Negro member of the choir.

We emerged from the church, four of us, hand in hand. And as we went down the sidewalk, we saw Helen Thomas. Lyndon said, "Helen, you know Coco McPherson. Coco, if you don't watch out, she'll be announcing your wedding." And at the car, he said, "How would you all like to ride over to the White House with us and see the dogs?" They said they would, and the four of us piled in. We had just asked Bill Baxter and his wife, and Harry and Clay McPherson, if they would like to come for lunch, and they were going to follow us.

But the four of us rode off with all the cameras clicking. At the White House we took the two little girls over to Lyndon's office, and he gave them pencils and keepsakes. And then we found the dogs and went upstairs, and the dogs tumbled all over them. The children had a hilariously good time. Coco said, "This is the best time I've ever had in my life."

We watched McGeorge Bundy on television. He was precise, razor sharp. In the light of Senator Kennedy's espousal of the Viet Cong being included in a coalition government, before and not as the result of an election, McGeorge Bundy's quotes from President Kennedy about similar situations in Communist-infiltrated countries were particularly acute and incisive.

We'd called up on the way to church to ask if McGeorge and Mary, and Clark and Marny, and Mary Margaret would have dinner with us. And so with that pleasant prospect to look forward to, I lay down for a luxurious nap.

Purposely, I refrained from calling Lynda. She'd arrived in New Orleans Friday night to meet George, and was being chaperoned by Lindy Boggs, who is certainly a family friend to my children. Lynda had outlined to me the parades, the balls, dinner in the old French Quarter, the plantation of friends in Slidell, so many fascinating things, that in a way I didn't want to interrupt Lynda's independence or her time, or seem like a hovering and concerned mother. I balance between trying to remember that next month she will be twenty-two, with the right to independence, and that her father is President of the United States, and that anything she does may reflect on him.

We'd asked everybody to come early, deliberately aiming at an early bedtime. McGeorge and Mary came at 6, and the Clark Cliffords soon after; Mary Margaret was already there with her adorable child, who affords Lyndon much pleasure now by being totally unrelated to any of the troubles of his life, totally happy, and totally concentrated on him. She and the beagle puppies are two pleasant safety valves for him.

We called Trudye and Joe Fowler. Joe had been to the Carol Channing party and there was a hilarious picture of him doing a dance called "The Monkey," I believe, with Carol, who wore white ski pants. He had cast a look at the people at his table as he arose to dance and said, "Do you think this will shake the dollar?" Having been off for one night of gaiety, Joe was deep at work in a pile of papers, but he agreed to quit and come over and have dinner with us.

So it was a pleasant party of nine. I moved from Clark, talking about the Library, to Mac Bundy, talking about how sad I was that he was leaving and how grateful I am for what he's done.

Lyndon talked about Vietnam—in fact, that is about two thirds of what we talk about these days. He talked about the individual feelings of every mother who has a son in Vietnam, and in comparison, about his feelings. He said, "There's not a mother in the world who cares more about it than I do, because I have two hundred thousand of them over there—and they think I am in charge, and if I am not, God help them—who the Hell is!"

Tuesday, February 22

It was a short night for those around the White House. Lyndon got in from his office about 3:30 A.M. and was up at 7.

Unable to control the large events of the day, I applied myself to the small—worked at my desk and on my Alabama speech, and succumbed to a shot of B-12 long recommended by Liz.

There was one leavening moment, however. Luci came in, mad as a hornet, discussing an article in something called *Women's Wear Daily*, which had given the three Johnson ladies pretty poor marks as dressers. Luci was inclined to blame it on Lynda Bird's bobby socks and loafers and was quite heatedly annoyed.

At 11 o'clock I went to bed, but I asked Dr. Hurst to stay up and talk with Lyndon. Lyndon did come home a little past 11:30 and had dinner.

It is an endurance contest, this job. I count the months and the weeks until the time I have set, but I have not the force of character, and not really even the desire, to try to make Lyndon work less hard. It is worth every last atom of whatever he has to give it.

TUSCALOOSA, ALABAMA

Today was a good day from beginning to end. Up at 7 o'clock and then off at 8 with Liz and my Mexican straw bag (one always accompanies me), on one of the many trips that have been such vivid highlights of my time in the White House.

Our trip was to Tuscaloosa, Alabama, to address a Leadership Conference of Women, sponsored by the American Association of University Women, the Alabama Federation of Business and Professional Women's Clubs, the Alabama Federation of Women's Clubs, and the League of Women Voters, taking place at the University—and to a considerable degree, I expect, aided and abetted by Dr. Frank Rose.

The setting was not without its drama. Tuscaloosa is the home town of the imperial wizard of the Ku Klux Klan, Mr. Robert Shelton, and he had issued some sort of statement complaining about the University of Alabama allowing such "Pinko tripe" as my speech on the campus. I was also arriving a day after the announcement that Mrs. George Wallace was going to run for Governor to succeed her husband.

So, if the stage was set for drama for the newspaper people, merely because it was a visit into the South by the wife of a liberal President, who herself has ties there, the day was only set with prospects of delight for me. And I was right. We had a chartered plane full of newspaperwomen —Frances Lewine and Helen Thomas, the regulars; Winzola McLendon; Jim Free of the *Birmingham News*, our only man, except for some cameramen; another Southerner, Margaret Shannon, of the *Atlanta Constitution*; three members of the radio-TV media, Fay Wells, and Barbara Coleman, and Betty Lee Hanson; Norma Milligan of *Newsweek*; two from USIA; Josephine Ripley of the *Christian Science Monitor*; Isabelle Shelton; and Nan Robertson. Sometimes I think I spend more time with and know better the newspaperwomen than anybody else in town—and mostly I like them.

At 11 o'clock we arrived at the Tuscaloosa Airport where we were met by tall, impressive Dr. Frank Rose and his wife; the Mayor of Tuscaloosa, Mr. Van Tassel, and his wife, with a lovely bouquet of charmingly arranged spring flowers; and Mayor Quarles of Northport. The fence was lined with several hundred people, including lots and lots of Girl Scouts and Brownies (later I learned why such an unusual number)—a few Negro women, waving United States flags, faces of all ages and types, all smiling. I shook hands with a fenceful, and then we drove to the campus, where a white-pillared mansion serves as a residence for the President of the University.

The welcoming ceremony took place on the balcony—a superb setting! The house overlooks the spacious quadrangle and there are enormous trees, going back to the College's founding days of 1830. Surrounding the dignified, red brick, Georgian-type residence stand the older buildings, the very heart of the University. There were a band and a few hundred students. The only sign I saw was a double one which proclaimed on one end, "WE SUPPORT LBJ ON VIETNAM," and on the other, "DRAFT LADY BIRD FOR GOVERNOR OF ALABAMA."

Dr. Rose introduced me as the "University's most famous ex-student," in no wise deserved (though I did attend for one summer), but it was a mighty pleasant beginning. Then he introduced two fine-looking young people, a young man who is the President of the men in the student body, and an attractive young woman who is President of the women students. (Segregation still exists in that field, evidently!)

We went inside to the high-ceilinged elegance of the old house. It was built in the 1840's, when there were only a few dozen students at the University. They planned ahead, those early Alabamians. I was reminded of what Thomas Jefferson said about the White House, something like "Big enough for two Popes and one Emperor, planned for the ages." The mansion was one of two buildings on the campus to survive the Civil War, when everything else was burned.

We walked over to the Child Development Center, where Head Start teachers are getting on-the-job training, and regular students are preparing to become teachers. There was a room full of five-year-olds seated at low tables, in tiny chairs, having their lunch or listening to stories. They and I were equally shy with each other. The young teachers were an attractive group of young women and so were most of the young people I met on the campus. Dr. Rose has a contract to train Head Start teachers, not only for Alabama, but for several adjoining states which have not been so quick to seize federal opportunities in this line.

Back at the mansion, we had a glass of sherry and talked about the University. "Are you having any problems like those they have in California—wild, way-out, trouble-making students?" I asked. Yes, he said, some, but very few really. One thing they've done is to supply more blood per capita for the Armed Forces Blood Bank than any other university. The student body numbers about twelve thousand; the tuition is marvelously low, and there is a President's Fund, which has enabled Dr. Rose to help poor but promising students through school.

I was enormously impressed with him—a soft-spoken, able, assured, tough man, who has kept up the closest kind of liaison with the federal government in order to obtain immediately for his university any programs, grants, or other help being offered. Also he makes about two trips a month to Washington, he says, on Civil Rights business.

There was a floral arrangement of the most beautiful camellias I've ever seen, in every shade of pink, white, rose, red—some as large as salad plates. Spring had not quite come to Alabama—there had been snow just a few days ago. But the camellias in the back yards were coming out, and I'd seen a few vagrant jonquils.

After our meeting I changed into my green silk dress, mentally counting the dozens of times these same newspaperwomen had seen me wear it, and went forth to make my speech, feeling somewhat braver than usual because of the hours I have put in on it. Dr. Rose escorted me up to the platform of the large gym. It was rather overwhelmingly full: Alabama women leaders on the main floor, and the women students who had been invited in the balcony. There was only a sprinkling of Negro faces. I looked around for cousins, but, alas, I saw only one—Patsy Derby's mother, very pretty and dignified in a flowered hat.

This auditorium was the one where the famous confrontation had taken place between Governor Wallace and Nicholas Katzenbach. They had stared across a chalk line at each other, after Wallace's statement that he would stand in the door and block any Negro student. Now there are between fifty and two hundred Negro students enrolled. The authorities are not quite sure of the number, since there is no question about race to be filled in on entrance papers.

I got through the speech, fighting the "battle of glasses" all the way (I succeeded in doing without them), finding myself actually shaking at some points, because I was intense about what I was saying, believed it, and wanted them to like it, wanted my voice to carry enough of a selling message to get them to like it. I was quite pleased when they began to applaud when I mentioned Senator Lister Hill and Senator John Sparkman. It is always a moment of enormous relief to me when a speech is over.

Later, at the mansion I stood in line for hours—there's nothing like a Southern receiving line! We visited; I liked it; and there were some delightful little vignettes. One woman confided that her name was just as difficult as mine—"Sunset." I thought that was a bit Freudian of her parents.

The League of Women Voters told me that they had set up poll tax booths in supermarkets and in the lobbies of schools where PTA meetings were being held. "We have to go where the people are." What a good idea. Over and over, the most constant, repeated rhythm was "We like your beautification program . . . We're doing this . . . We're planning that project in our community."

I found out why there had been so many Girl Scouts and Brownies at the airport. One of the ladies told me that they had just staged a "clean-up campaign" on the route that we would travel from the airport to the university. When I got back to the airport, I said "Thank you, thank you, thank you!" to dozens and dozens of Brownies and Girl Scouts. An adorable little girl made me a charming good-by speech and presented me with flowers and a kiss.

By 5:30 we were airborne. The newspaperwomen crowded around; they had acted as though we had been going into some alien land in Alabama, where they had expected all sorts of dramatic turmoil. As far as I was concerned, it had turned out just as I expected, and I was expansive and jubilant, even euphoric, as we flew home.

We arrived at the White House a little past 9:30, and I went immediately to find Lyndon. He was in his office, the little one, with Dick Russell. I'm always glad to find Dick Russell with Lyndon. Whatever lack of red-hot enthusiasm he may have for the Great Society, when the going is rough and Lyndon needs the advice of an old hand, a wise old hand, Dick Russell will usually be there.

Spring 1966

Texas Exes were celebrating Texas Independence Day a day late and their honored guests were the Board of Regents. We had invited them to come for tea at 3:30, so the Chairman, Bill Heath, accompanied me into the Yellow Room and stood by me to introduce his fellow members of the Board: the Walter Brenans, Dr. and Mrs. Frank Connally, and the Jack Joseys of Houston—none of whom I knew well. Frank Ikard, the fifth regent, was there and, of course, Chancellor Harry Ransom and Hazel. Alas, Bill Moyers, who is President of the Texas Exes this year, couldn't come, but pretty Judith Moyers did, and the Secretary Treasurer of the organization, the Harold Kennedys. Several other Texas Exes were there: the Jake Pickles; the Horace Busbys (I hadn't seen them in a long time and was anxious to get caught up on news of their country house); Liz and Les Carpenter; Jake Jacobsen; and Christine Stugard (very much a Texas Ex).

Tonight we gave the Congressional Reception for about a thousand people, as important as all ten of the receptions last year rolled into one. We'd done everything we could to make it special. It had been Lyndon's suggestion to have the Leadership and the Committee Chairmen, the Cabinet, and some of his staff upstairs thirty minutes early, for a greeting on the family floor. A battery of photographers was grouped in the hall, and they were frenetic with activity as Bill and Betty Fulbright came down the line. Amusingly, theirs wasn't the picture used in the paper the next day—it was one of Majority Leader Mike Mansfield and his wife Maureen, mistakenly identified as Mrs. Wilbur Mills.

We had decided to make a different, offbeat picture in the Lincoln Room. So the Leadership filed in there, with Lyndon and me and the Hubert Humphreys, in front of the bird's-nest table. Grouped behind us were Senator Carl Hayden, President Pro Tem; Tom and Betty Kuchel; the Senate Minority Whip, Senator Everett Dirksen, with Louella; Mike and Maureen Mansfield; Hale and Lindy Boggs; Speaker McCormack with Miss Harriet; Carl Albert; and the Les Arends, he the House Minority Whip. It was a memorable picture, the only time I remember such a one in the White House.

The upstairs gathering had three ingredients for a convivial party— guests who have something in common, music, and cocktails. When Lyndon and I came down to the Blue Room just a little past 7 to greet the other eight hundred guests, I felt as gay as my red dress looked; and by evening's end so did everybody else. Dorothy McCardle's headline next day ran: "HAWKS AND DOVES COME BACK TO ROOST . . . The doves and the hawks were billing and cooing at each other last night at the White House reception." Betty Beale reported, "Senate Leader of opposition, Everett Dirksen, led the Marine Band in 'Danny Boy,' while singing it at the same time." "Vice President Humphrey, just back from Vietnam, danced gaily with Mrs. J. William Fulbright, while Senator Fulbright whirled Mrs. Humphrey about. And Senator Strom Thurmond showed up with the Peach Queen of Georgia." The best line was "and all the Senators and Representatives acted completely at home."

The buffet table was laden with a steamship-round roast of beef, fresh shrimp, Fritos with chili con queso dip, ham in hot biscuits, and brownies and éclairs. I had elected to have a receiving line. Perhaps it is more chic to move around among the guests, but I would be one of those shy guests who wouldn't go up to the First Family and say hello. The line lasted an hour, with time for a hug for a lot of old friends. And, of course, the guests who were not there also made news: Senators Wayne Morse and Bobby and Teddy Kennedy.

It was 10:30 before all our guests departed, and that in itself is a badge of success for a 6:30–8:30 party.

Betty Beale summarized Lyndon's conversation with the newswomen. "This has been a rather unbelievable ten days in the records of the Congress. We passed our Economic Aid Bill with less than forty votes against it. I just suggested the Asian Bank last April, and a billion dollars for Asia was passed yesterday. We had a vote on Military Aid in the House, and lost only four votes, and in the Senate we lost only two votes. We had a vote on rescinding the President's power, and lost only five. Then we had the Tax Bill and it was 130 to nothing." Dorothy McCardle quoted him as saying, "Among some 2,000 votes cast in the past 10 days, there have not been more than 200 votes against any of my bills." And he ended up by saying, "It's been a good, productive period."

Thursday, March 10

I had coffee with Lyndon about 8:30 this morning, but these days I feel as if I'm part of a staff meeting. Jake Jacobsen, Jack Valenti, Marvin Watson, Bob Fleming, and, swiftly in and out, Bill Moyers come to his room when he first wakes up; and, while he drinks cup after cup of tea, give him reports, ask decisions, analyze the business of his day, discuss yesterday's triumphs and troubles, and go over the appointments. It is a pattern of intense mental strain, totally unrelated to the luxurious idea of breakfast in bed. And I wait my turn to get a word in edgeways.

My day included a Spanish class, briefings on the projected April trip to the Big Bend Country, and more desk work.

About 10 o'clock this evening I began phoning Lyndon's office, hoping to get him over to join us for dinner. (He had had a murderous day, which included a meeting with the Leadership in the Yellow Oval Room that lasted for several hours. I had encountered him after 8 o'clock, going back to his office.) It was ten minutes of 11 when he arrived, and we sat down for a family fare of stuffed peppers and cornbread. Oveta Hobby and Jim and Ida May Cain were with us.

It was a pleasant evening, what was left of it, though how Lyndon could have opened his mouth after the day he's lived through, I don't know. But he gave us a thumbnail sketch: problems of the Guatemala election; the turmoil in the Dominican Republic; De Gaulle's ultimatums; and the tightrope Harold Wilson walks. It's like a string of firecrackers, always another one going off.

I decided to treat myself to a visit to the National Art Gallery with Ida May today. Feeling delightfully truant, we drove to the National, where John Walker and Carter Brown were waiting for us at the entrance. The collection Paul Mellon and Mrs. Mellon Bruce have loaned for the twenty-fifth anniversary of the National Gallery is a retrospective of more than two hundred French Impressionists. They range from Corot to Picasso—Monet, Manet, Cézanne, Degas, Boudin. The exhibition is not open to the public yet, so the paintings weren't labeled. I had a good time seeing whether or not I could identify them. I would guess at the artist and then walk up close and look at the signature to see if I'd been correct. (Secretly I hoped that Johnny Walker and Carter Brown were as impressed as I was when I was right!)

Paintings *do* begin to speak to you after a good many years of exposure. I could tell when Van Gogh was getting into his last period, when he was going mad. I found many Monets that weren't misty at all. In fact, one of my favorites was of a very clear, bright garden, with huge golden sunflowers and two little children going down a path. And another Monet, showing a girl on a hilltop, and you can almost feel the wind in her hair. One of the dearest of all was a little Mary Cassatt girl, plumped on a couch, looking at her little dog, both of them planning some devilment.

We spent a pleasant hour and as I walked out, I saw groups of school children, people smiling and waving at me. I smiled and waved back but for the most part I was inconspicuous.

I asked the houseguests to meet me about 9, for a drink. (How late our hours must seem to other people!) Lyndon came about 9:15, but in no hurry to go in to dinner. He enjoys Oveta Hobby very much, as well as Ida May and Jim. Oveta and Jim are leaving tomorrow morning for Vietnam; they had been briefed all day and they were full of questions.

Lyndon told them what he hoped they'd do in Vietnam; what he hoped this government could do, the imprint we could leave. "I would have a fast inoculation program." (He keeps on talking about the life expectancy of thirty-five in Vietnam and how sores caused by lack of cleanliness and skin diseases are a major scourge of the country.) "I would find out what the simple three R's are out there, and I would get them started in school. I want to do something about the conditions that have caused this war." He spoke of what our agricultural know-how, our technology, could do for Vietnam and of Orville Freeman's mission over there. "We are going to help them raise two-hundred-pound hogs in place of their one-hundred-pound hogs. Our sweet potato vines produce twice as many pounds of sweet potatoes as their vines do. Our only purpose there is to keep those people from being eaten up. I want to get *out* of there more than anybody, including the Marines."

And then he spoke of President Eisenhower. "Since I have been President, the man who has helped me most, and asked the least, is President Eisenhower."

At one time Lyndon described himself: "I'm like a prize fighter in the ring. The right fist is the military, the left fist is aid—medical, agricultural, educational."

He's put in a towering week of work on it. Tomorrow will be more, with about forty-six or forty-seven of the Governors coming for all-day briefings.

Sunday, March 13

One thing about our life, you never can tell who you'll find in Lyndon's bedroom. I walked in this morning for coffee—Lyndon had made a surprise visit the night before to the Gridiron Dinner—and who should be sitting there but Richard Nixon! He had come down for the dinner. He was looking relaxed and affable and well-tailored. Lyndon was stretched out in his pajamas, drinking tea, and they were apparently enjoying their visit.

Lyndon mentioned three names that some of his best people thought were the three outstanding military men in the country, capable of leading our forces anywhere—Westmoreland, Goodpaster, and Abrams. Everything he has to say of Westmoreland is filled with respect and pride.

Mostly they talked about the international situation, especially Vietnam, where Mr. Nixon is, generally, in strong support of Lyndon. He said that opponents say we are risking World War III in Vietnam, that we are risking war with China in Vietnam, but that is not so, we are avoiding a big war. He said that the Chinese are cautious, and the Communists are cautious. If we are going to have any discussion with China, it should come now, rather than later, three or four years from now.

Mr. Nixon looked prosperous, vital, at home in the world, and it sounded as if Pat were enjoying life too. I told him I hoped she would come to the Senate Ladies Luncheon some time. On leaving, he said, "Mr. President, you know this is campaign year and I'll be getting out, speaking up for the Republicans. They'll need all the voices they can get. But there won't be anything personal about you in what I say about the Democratic Administration."

Thursday, March 17

Today in the White House we had the type of program I love. It was the presentation ceremony of the National Gallery of Arts awards to twenty-five teachers. John Walker described the award winners—they came from various levels of education, kindergarten to college—as exceptionally successful in enriching the lives of young people through an understanding of the visual arts.

The winners were in the front row, and I joined them. John Walker made some very graceful remarks, including a kind word about Lyndon's interest in the arts: "At no time in our history have a President and a Congress done so much to create an America in which the arts have their proper place." When he finished, he called off the names of the award winners, and I rose to congratulate each of them and hand them the handsome gold medal—the five-hundred-dollar-prize money would come later.

He read the citations for each of them; they were a thrilling, varied group, including the very elderly and erudite Dr. Erwin Panofsky, one of the greatest living art historians, whose roster of achievements, awards, textbooks, and memberships in such bodies as the British Academy would cover a page. And Dr. Howard Conant, who also occupies an important place in the art world.

From quite another side of America was Mr. Wilbur Stilwell of Vermillion, South Dakota. The very name of his home town thrilled me because I like to think that there are people all over this country who make it interesting and exciting for young people to get acquainted with art, and I like to recognize and applaud them all—whether from Vermillion, South Dakota, or Rosebud, Texas, or Verbena, Alabama.

And there was a couple, the John Sochas of Minneapolis, who received the award jointly. Both were teachers, and between them had a total of sixty years teaching art.

One of the most exciting accounts was about Mrs. Alvin Bippus, of Toledo, Ohio, who has made museums so interesting for children from kindergarten through the eighth grade that the average Toledo child now makes *six* visits a year to the museum. Art cannot exist in a vacuum; it's people liking it that makes it important. My hat was off to Mrs. Bippus.

And then there was Miss Marie Larkin, whose award honored her original thinking in the field of art education for children. "One of the greatest needs of our society," she said, "is to teach people to be intelligently alone with themselves, and the art museum provides a source for all in that respect." That struck a very responsive chord in me.

All in all, it was a thrilling series of citations for various works in the world of art, and I was most proud to participate.

After the last award was made I received everyone in the Blue Room and then we went into the State Dining Room for refreshments. Irish whiskey for St. Patrick's Day, the first time it's been served in the White House, I'll bet, and not a soul wanted tea!

A few minutes after the guests left, Charles and Jane Engelhard and Senator Mansfield and Maureen came up with Lyndon for a short celebration of the Senator's birthday, and after an all-too-brief half-hour with them, I had just enough time to put on my new gold brocade dress from Pakistan, for the Mellon dinner at the Sulgrave Club.

Pictures were taken as I entered but no news coverage is allowed inside, a rigid rule of the Club since time began, which makes for a genuinely relaxed evening. The invitation had said a small dinner party; there were about a hundred—Cabinet members, patrons of the National Gallery, society figures.

At dinner I enjoyed sitting next to Paul Mellon, who talked about the genesis of the National Gallery in 1937, his father's collection, his decision to turn it over to the country. The most amusing of the toasts, which followed a delicious, beautifully done dinner, was made by Mr. Mellon himself. He finished with a limerick, which he authored and which I liked because it covers my predicament:

"I never with confidence know,
If Van Gogh is Van Gock or Van Gogh.
I admit to my shame,
This chameleon name,

Makes my hi-brows feel terribly low.
But a friend of mine said, off the cuff,
You might say that his name was Van Guff,
But regardless, I fear,
What he did to his ear
Was playing a little too rough!"

The opening was scheduled for about 9:30. We were late getting there —in fact, it was close to 10:20 when we arrived, Mr. and Mrs. Paul Mellon and John Walker driving with me. We went up in the elevator, the same one which wouldn't run the night of the Mona Lisa opening. John Walker says he still has a Mona Lisa ulcer!

When we arrived at the exhibition in the magnificent Gallery, there were about nine thousand people filling the halls, and rooms, and court-yards, listening to the music of three orchestras. To rise to the occasion of this great spectacle, I had worn my Inaugural coat over my Ayub Khan gown, but it was a "Cinderella" affair—I had promised to send the coat on the earliest morning plane to Lynda Bird so she could wear it that very night to a cocktail party in Hollywood.

It was a purely public show. About forty-five minutes of flashing bulbs, smiling and greeting, walking and making, I hope, appropriate remarks, saying good-by to John Walker with "I can congratulate you on a marvelous quarter of a century of beauty and service for the Gallery." And one of the nicest things I remember was a toast to Andrew Mellon, who made it all possible.

All in all, it was a day precious to me, afforded entirely by my role here in the White House, and not earned by my knowledge or myself.

Monday, March 28

The visit of Prime Minister Indira Gandhi from India took place today —a day that was bright and clear and cold. My voice had sounded like a frog last night. This morning it still did. So I asked Dr. Young to give me some pills. A little before 11 o'clock, dressed warmly in my off-white coat, and last year's roller-brim straw hat, I joined Lyndon in his office. If one did it well, one could make a career of dressing for this job! And at the appointed moment we went out on the South Lawn for the arrival ceremonies—always a breath-taking experience. The wind was snapping the flags, the troops were at attention, tourists lined the ropes. And up on the balconies above us trumpets blew and drums rolled as the long black limousines pulled up to the entrance. Out stepped Prime Minister Indira Gandhi in an orange sari with a black Western coat on over it and a scarf protecting her head from the biting wind. There was the inevitable picture, me presenting her with roses, and then we walked up on the red-carpeted platform. How orderly to have names taped on the floor (that is, if you can read English).

This is the first time since I've been in the White House that we have received a woman Chief of State. Add to this the particular alchemy of the Nehru name and the size of the Indian country as an Asian democracy and you have a day alive with drama.

Thank goodness we won the battle with Lyndon as to whether or not he would wear an overcoat. He did. Lyndon greeted Indira Gandhi as the leader of our sister democracy. And she recalled warmly his visit to her country but warned that our two nations could not take each other for granted or allow our relations to drift.

For the State Dinner the Humphreys and Rusks arrived a little before 8; I left them in the Yellow Room to stand nervously by the telephone waiting for the signal from Blair House as I tried to synchronize time with Lyndon. We met the Prime Minister at exactly the right moment as the limousine rolled up under the Portico. She was dressed in a dark purple sari, very elegant, with a big gold-leaf design. If I had only two words to describe her, I think I would use "composure" and "assurance."

Upstairs in the Yellow Room we exchanged gifts. She had brought two fine rugs, a sari and purse for Luci (they go with her eyes), and a handsome red sari for me, as well as books on the art and history of India. She also gave us a saddle. I could find no stirrups and wondered how the rider managed. It is red and yellow and embroidered and decorated. All of the gifts had the stamp of Indian artistry and handicraft.

With the receiving line over, we went in to dinner. We had worried about the menu and were relieved when we found it didn't have to be vegetarian. The first course of seafood was delicious, the breast of pheasant only fair.

Lyndon was courtly with Mrs. Gandhi, and in his toast he quoted her father. In her reply Mrs. Gandhi said: "I should like to quote something which you yourself have said . . . 'Reality rarely matches dreams, but only dreams give nobility to purpose.' . . . [Poverty], Mr. President, is really our major problem. Years ago when we visited the villages to persuade people to try for a better life, they turned to us and said, "There can be no better life; God wills it this way. This is our lot and we have to suffer it.' Today not a single voice will be heard like this. There is only one demand, that we do want a better life."

Sometime in the course of the evening, Nehru leaned over to me and said, "Your husband is a passionate man." He was referring to Lyndon's pursuit of his beliefs, his ideas in working out a program. What a good word to choose; particularly astute on such a brief acquaintance. Passion has propelled Lyndon all his life.

Saturday, April 2

THE BIG BEND PARK, TEXAS

Presidio, Texas, had been known to me only as a place on the map that the weatherman usually reported as the hottest place in the United States —often around 103. Its airport had been billed by Liz as one where you had to buzz the runway to get the antelope off before you landed. The runway is an abandoned World War II Army installation, now used infrequently by the scattered inhabitants of this arid land. The truth of Liz's story was proved when a departing private airplane later collided with an antelope, doing considerable damage.

We did see a herd grazing peacefully within yards of the runway. A crowd had assembled around the little speaking stand—some thirty-five hundred—more than half the population of all the towns and ranches for miles around. All the Mayors were lined up in a long receiving line as we got off the plane. The wind was blowing and the Sul Ross College Band was playing "The Yellow Rose of Texas"; all the little children were grinning and waving homemade signs, "WELCOME LADY BIRD, UDALL, AND YOU ALL."

John Ben Shepperd, who has played many roles in restoration and tourism in Texas, was at my elbow escorting me everywhere. The keynote of the day—the keynote of the country—was set for me when the presiding Mayor made his brief speech and said: "Ordinarily on an occasion like this, the Mayor presents the guest with a key to the city. But we don't have any key because we don't have any locks on our doors. You're mighty welcome." They gave us sombreros—the whole party, including the seventy-odd newspaper entourage!

I shook hands with just as many as I could get to, because one lady from Marfa, Texas, had said, "Nobody ever stops here. All they do is fly over us."

There was a Sheriff's posse in quite authentic cowboy clothes, mounted, ringed around the airport, with the backdrop of mountains behind them.

Soon we were off, headed toward "Pancho Villa Country"—the two-hour drive to the Big Bend—crossing the famous old Comanche Indian Trail. The scenery was an ever-changing panorama of mountains and what looked like volcanic flows, swirls of tumbleweed, a few struggling bluebonnets, cactus and yucca, and finally great expanses of nothing at all except creosote bushes with little tiny yellow blossoms on them. It was a harsh, forbidding land, hostile to man, a land of arroyos and mountains, barricaded by boulders and armored with plants that "either stick or sting or stink," as somebody has written. A few public-spirited citizens—among them Amon Carter—gave, begged, and badgered money and finally turned over to the federal government this wild stretch of wilderness to be preserved as a National Park.

Occasionally on the lonely landscape we could see a few cottonwood trees and a windmill that spelled mankind—life. Somebody had had nerve enough to dig a well and to build a house and try to eke out a living. The cottonwood tree is a true symbol out here to me. It says, "Here man is."

Very rarely on this two-hour trip along a really great highway did we come to a settlement. Once a filling station. Once a little community. In each case I am sure every living human being was out by the side of the road waving, grinning, carrying a sign. One sign was so funny I had to stop to shout "Thank you!" Six young girls, all Latinos, had encased themselves in cardboard boxes, a hole at the top out of which their heads appeared, a hole at the bottom for their feet, and on each box a big letter, so that when lined up they read, "MRS. LBJ." They were all jumping up and down yelling, "Welcome, welcome."

A little after noon the terrain began to rise, and just as the mountains were beginning, we stopped at Panther Junction at the headquarters of the Big Bend National Park. They have an Indoctrination Center and in it exhibits that tell the story of the land's geology, history, plant and animal life.

Lunch was served by the Odessa Chuck Wagon gang—barbecue, frijoles and slaw and iced tea. And I was never hungrier! I have a fault to find with so-called banquets where one is the honored guest—you don't get to eat. Just as I started to take a bite George Hartzog motioned to me to "stand up, please." There was a little ceremony. I handed him a check for a Golden Eagle Park Pass. Back to the table and one good bite—and then it was up again for the presentation of a landscape of the Big Bend Country, done by a local artist. I was delighted to have it, but still hungry.

I got back to the table and other guests kept coming up to be introduced. There was mariachi music; a tall Mexican in an embroidered hat with a serape over his shoulder sang the plaintive songs of Mexico. The time came for me to stand up and have my picture taken with him, wearing his hat with his serape draped over my shoulder. Every time I arose for a ceremony the unceasing West Texas wind would blow away my napkin or deposit a little more sand in my plate.

Back at the table I wolfed large mouthfuls of the beans, barbecue, drafts of the iced tea. And then it was time to have my picture taken with Stew Udall and the Odessa Chuck Wagon gang and tell them how wonderful the barbecue had been!

We were soon back in the cars and off up into the Chisos Mountains to the Park basin, which was our destination. Here the land began to rise more sharply. We were leaving the endless, hostile desert country and going up into the Chisos Mountains—*chisos* is the Spanish word for ghosts— why they are so named, I do not know. Could it be because they are so lonely? And to the vegetation was added the juniper tree—so well known to me as the bane of the rancher's life. And two other kinds of junipers I have never seen before: the weeping juniper, whose branches droop as though they are about to draw their last breath of life; and the alligator juniper, with a very rough, scaly bark. And an occasional madrona tree.

A little after 2:30 we arrived at the Park basin headquarters, with rustic facilities suited to the terrain. I had a small but pleasant cabin and thought what a nice place this would be with two or three other people that you loved dearly—to walk and walk, and ride and ride.

I changed into blue jeans, red-checkered shirt, and sombrero. And then all of us—the Udalls, Park naturalists, Secret Service men, and seventy newspaper reporters—gathered at the beginning of "Lost Mine" Trail for a two-hour hike. Here it became evident that we were the victims of our own success. We had two diametrically opposed, incompatible elements. Into the wilderness of these majestic towering crags—this eons-old graphic story of the geological history of the earth, this solitude—thundered the motley crew of one hundred. (As Isabelle Shelton later put it, "At Big Bend you couldn't see the wilderness for the people.")

There soon stood out one character—a newspaperwoman in bright red britches carrying a bright red umbrella as she climbed the mountain. We all remember her as the "girl with the red umbrella."

Stew and I set the pace and a naturalist came along beside us to tell us about the wildlife. The bird life was enormously abundant. One, the Colima warbler, is found only in this area. And most interesting to me, he described the "relic forest" of maple, quaking aspen, Douglas fir, and ponderosa pine with huge trunks. By some strange mystery of nature, they have survived from a much earlier time, when the climate was different here. On the other side of the mountain they are reachable by horseback. They are simply a freak of nature, hundreds of miles from any others of their species.

On the way up, surrounded by the marvelous vistas, Stew and I both said at once, "On a clear day you can see forever!" And you can. In one direction you see into Mexico. It's a wild, free land and it does something to you. To the west was a spectacular view—"the window"—a cleft between two mountains. Through it you could *really* see forever. There was another mountain range far in the distance. And to the east, behind us, rose a gigantic mountain called the "Castle."

As for "Lost Mine" itself, it was a quicksilver mine, if it ever existed. Perhaps it is a legend, though there is quicksilver in the country nearby.

At the top of the trail we all stopped—the newspaper folks got out their microphones or tapes or tablets and I gave a brief word-picture of the way I felt about the day.

At the end of the day we gathered on a mesa top, gay with red-checkered tablecloths and a campfire glowing. Everybody was in a merry mood. High spirits were contagious. We all swapped tales about our experiences of the day, while a magnificent drama was proceeding in the sky around us. Sundown and twilight—the unceasing play of lights and shadows and the nuances of colors in the sky and on the sides of the mountains. Sometimes I think the Lord made up in this Western country for what he didn't give us in rainfall and in verdant vegetation with the glory of the sky. It was the most superb theater, fit subject for a symphony or a poem —but for me just an hour of delight that was almost tangible—of the heightened feeling of being alive.

And then the final, magnificent touch! Above the "Castle" rose a full moon. It hadn't been on the agenda. Not even Liz' agenda. As it rose, the campfire grew brighter—Navaho rugs were scattered on the ground around the campfire. A group of boys from Sul Ross College called "The Believers" began to sing folk songs. Joe Frantz, former Chairman of the Department of History at the University, began to weave together the story of the place—why the West, this part of the West, is what it is . . . . its history . . . the tribal Plains Indians . . . the Spanish conquistadores, the westward thrust of the Anglos, wild tales of Pancho Villa. He told of the region's economy, the determined homesteader, the cattleman, the Mexicans making candelaria wax, the whole philosophy and feel of the West.

Cactus Pryor was the emcee of the evening and he hobbled out of the dark in a long beard and ancient cowpuncher clothes and introduced Brownie McNeil, President of Sul Ross College, with the observation: "You see, nearly all our entertainers tonight are Ph.D.'s." Brownie plucked a guitar and sang frontier songs that ranged from old English ballads originating in the Appalachians to right-off-the-range ones like "Little Joe the Wrangler."

Meanwhile, the full moon rose higher and higher above the "Castle" —the campfire died softly—everybody settled comfortably in his Navaho blanket and succumbed to the spell.

What a night to remember!—sheer magic, and a day worth five ordinary days of living.

Sunday, April 3

Palm Sunday began early. I was up before 7, dressed in blue jeans, checkered shirt, heavy sweater, and tennis shoes, and down to the basin. The Odessa Chuck Wagon gang were already pouring scalding "six-shooter" coffee from big black pots and loading plates with hot flapjacks and home-cured ham and thick bacon. They had sour-dough biscuits too —although they had trouble making them rise in this high altitude.

Reverend Robert Davis, chaplain of the Park, stood at a rude pulpit and conducted a simple, brief Palm Sunday service. Behind him loomed a great, rugged upthrust of rock, rising to the sky—and all bathed in the incredibly clear, fresh light of morning. Next I planted a piñon tree, perfect shape, a wonderful little specimen about seven feet high. A new Park concessions building is going up which will have a picture window with a view toward a divide in the mountains. This piñon will frame one side of the picture.

Then we were in our cars headed for the place where we were to board the rafts for the trip down the Rio Grande. It was a long ride—everything here is long. This is a wild, forbidding, hostile-to-man kind of country, and magnificent. You feel you want to match it. I do not think that I will forget it soon. We were descending constantly from an altitude of six thousand feet in the Chisos Mountains and from the country of piñon pines, oaks, and juniper to the lowlands, which are principally of mesquite and cottonwood. There is nothing so green as a cottonwood in the early spring! And the wind sings in its little rustling leaves. The desert was full of all kinds of cactus, Spanish dagger, agave, lechuguilla, so tall. And most exotic, the ocotillo, which looks like about a dozen long coach whips stuck into the ground, spraying out in a weeping fashion. After it rains in the spring, small bright-red blossoms appear down their spiny stalks with the tiniest little green leaves. Here and there were the luxuriant bell-like blossoms of the big yuccas.

Mostly, though, it was the wildest country I ever saw. There were acres —miles of terrain called "desert pavement." The earth looked like broken-up cement, stacked in slabs, pinkish brown, arid beyond belief, as far as you could see. *No wonder* they send astronauts out here to train for a possible landing on the moon.

A delightful sight I saw was a road runner up in an ocotillo—all of six feet off the ground. Those weird, awkward birds can hardly fly. I yearned for a camera. This area is a geologist's show case, twice covered by an inland sea. Some of the fossil remains of sea life are visible—dinosaurs, and even a giant crocodile—a head of one has been uncovered recently. He must have been fifty feet long. There's evidence of mountain-building by volcanic activity through the untold centuries. If you just knew what you were looking at, it would be infinitely more fascinating than it was.

Finally we reached the spot on the Rio Grande River where our rafts were staked out. There were twenty-four rafts—five or six persons aboard each—on a trip that took us over five hours down eleven miles of the Rio Grande, though it seemed at least *fifty*. Isabelle Shelton reported: "There probably hasn't been such a motley flotilla since the British marshaled every available craft for the evacuation of Dunkirk."

In all of last year less than five hundred people had made the raft trip down all of the three canyons—Boquillas, Santa Elena, Mariscal—Mariscal was ours. And here we were—one hundred thirty-nine tenderfeet in one trip. The Big Bend never saw anything like it.

Later, Stew said: "You have had a wilderness experience. I think you will look back five, ten, or twenty years from now and remember this as spectacular." Isabelle Shelton answered, "It may take the Big Bend area longer than that to recover from the invading mortals."

I went in a yellow raft, with Stew and Lee, Jerry Kivett, and two Rangers—which gave us four fine paddlers. Stew is a natural outdoorsman.

They had put an inflated rubber seat for me in front, the most comfortable spot on the boat. But that set me aside as having special treatment. Something that I haven't learned to master is avoiding the VIP treatment, frequently more trouble than it's worth.

The country was marked with great soaring cliffs that rose up on each side like giant pipe organs or cathedral spires, battlements of some long-ago civilization, or the vast escarpments of another world in which the dinosaurs might still be living. Sometimes you would even see a cave. Occasionally in just a cupful of soil on the cliffside a cactus would be growing. Sometimes even a blooming strawberry cactus or yucca, or ocotillo, or even a stunted piñon. And along the banks, there was river cane, which the Mexicans use to thatch their huts. But mostly there were just the awesome spires of the canyon walls pierced by centuries of wind, eroded by centuries of water, with all sorts of tales to tell to a geologist. And above the canyon walls the bluest sky.

Sometimes in the heavy shadows of the canyon walls the sky was almost purple and it would be quite chilly. And then in the sun it was broiling hot. In a moment of silence we would hear the sweet call of the canyon wren. Once we saw a peregrine falcon, and many times the "high-rise apartments" of cliff swallows. And always we were conscious that right on the other side, often within spitting distance, was the boundary of Mexico . . . Once we came to a spot where the Comanche Trail used to cross the river, where the Indians used to come down from the North, to steal all the cattle and horses they could get before crossing into Mexico.

The river is shallow nearly everywhere in this area. Sometimes there were rapids. They were the delight of the photographers! The rafts rolled and twisted, and the oarsmen fought to guide them. Some of them overturned. Ours, with our expert paddlers, never did. Sometimes the river deepened to twenty feet, in calm pools shaded by the canyon walls. And I remember the homesteaders' stories of the thirty- and forty-pound catfish they used to catch in these pools.

Always there was the component—those one hundred thirty-nine people —laughing and shouting and falling out of the rafts by accident in the rapids and on purpose in the good swimming holes. The star of the show was the press lady with the red pants and the red parasol. She gripped the parasol the entire five hours of the trip down the canyon and was the second most photographed person along. But she had a runner-up, a young newspaperwoman in a black-and-white polka-dot bikini, with a figure to suit it.

There were always cries of "Man overboard!" And I remember while shooting down the rapids I saw one man clinging to a rock and fighting a losing battle to maintain his grip against the swift rush of the water. I never knew what happened, but apparently he got safely to calm water. (The only casualty of the trip was a man who slipped in his bedroom in the hotel on the first night, getting up to answer the telephone in a hurry. He sustained a broken ankle!)

We stopped at Rattlesnake Bar, so christened by Liz, where we had a box lunch. What a many-faceted job is "advancing"! Somebody had to think about getting those portable johnnies down the Rio Grande ahead of us and set up in discreet spots. Everybody was happy and full of laughter, and even Betty Beale, the most unlikely candidate for such a tour, loved it. But Liz Carpenter was heard to remark at the end of the day that from now on she only wanted to go to places where the Rocke-fellers had the concessions.

By mid-afternoon we had emerged from the canyons into a flatter country. Buses were waiting for us, and after another hour's drive, with everybody quite weary, we reached the Rio Grande Village Camp Ground. Then we went out into a big grove of cottonwoods that surrounds a little lake with a fine view of the Sierra Del Carmen Mountains in Mexico—every shade of lavender and blue and misty white and mauve. Here we had sizzling steaks, preceded by Marguerita cocktails, and a good reclining spot on the grass. Nash Castro joined us and Dick White, the Congressman from this district. I met several of the local ladies (and "local" covers a pretty wide area in this country!) who had made the flower centerpieces for our tables, which were once more bedecked with red-checkered tablecloths.

There was guitar music—songs of the country. Udall handed out to the reporters and photographers a certificate announcing them to be members of the "Original American Wet-bottoms."

Isabelle Shelton's last word was: "Only the fit survive."

Tuesday, April 19

Today was one of those overwhelming but rewarding days when waves of people swept over the White House and over us and that is why I call April "the month of people." There was an afternoon tea for thirty-six hundred Democratic women, in Washington for a three-day conference and workshop.

The first wave—approximately twelve hundred ladies—came in at 2 P.M. All the guests were dressed in white gloves and their Sunday best and overflowing with Democratic goodwill. I moved among the crowd in the State Dining Room—shaking hands on my right and left and in front of me and behind me, saying to those that I couldn't reach, "Welcome, I am so glad you're here."

There were the usual responses of "Hello—You look so much prettier than your pictures"; "I'm your neighbor from Lampasas"; "I'm from Alabama"; "We love your husband"; "God bless you." That last one is repeated over and over—it never ceases to be fresh to me. Pandemonium broke loose when Lyndon came in.

Dorothy McCardle wrote: "Rancher Lyndon B. Johnson got corralled at his Pennsylvania Avenue dig yesterday afternoon. Everyone whooped it up with the excitement of a group of teenagers hailing a Hollywood crooner." And the United Press reported: "Giggling like teenagers, the women rushed up to Mr. Johnson, kissing his face, shaking or kissing his hand and trying to tell him where they were from."

How the staff and the Cabinet wives and all of the hostesses moved that many people in and out is a triumph of logistics! I only hope it was done as gracefully and hospitably as possible. But everybody I could see had a big smile, no matter how squashed he or she was. And I tried to have the biggest one of all and to thank everybody for coming and hoped the workshops had been useful.

Images melt into a sort of a montage. I remember seeing a woman with a small baby, three or four months old. She deposited the baby on the dining room buffet table while she helped herself to a glass of punch and cookies. During one interlude Bess had said to me in her calm voice that she thought it would be better if I didn't go into the Red Room and the Green Room, but concentrated on the East Room and the Hall and the Dining Room. Later I heard that as Lyndon and I were converging on the Red Room, the crowd surged forward, ash trays were swept to the floor in splinters, the Presidential Standard staggered outside the Blue Room, an antique lamp toppled in the Red Room. Someone bravely rescued the musical score of "Lafayette's March" as it slipped from a nineteenth-century music stand. A bust of Henry Clay toppled over but fortunately was not damaged.

When the second group had visited, Lyndon deftly led the ladies through the Blue Room onto the great porch and down the steps toward the buses to have a photograph taken. That was an effective good-by to this group, but within minutes I was back downstairs for the third wave. This time I concentrated on the Dining Room, the Hall, and the East Room. In a crowd like this I find that it is wise to move as calmly and leisurely as I can, with an intimate smile and a direct look into as many eyes as possible.

Isabelle Shelton reported: "The energetic President and the indefatigable First Lady exhibited some of the finest broken field running off the professional football field as they skillfully maneuvered through the jammed, packed Red, Green, and Blue Rooms, shaking hands fore, aft and in between." She had a hilarious exchange between hats. (Often hats and heads are all you can see in this crowd. You can't tell what hands belong to what heads.) " 'I caught him, I kissed him,' an orange-hatted woman shouted triumphantly. 'I'm losing my hand!' squealed a green hat, as the crowd veered. 'Watch out for that Mack truck,' a blue turban warned a yellow cloche. 'Poor little thing, she's almost smothered,' a pink straw bowler said compassionately of the First Lady. 'Why doesn't she get out of here—they'll kill her,' said a halo of white flowers." One of the funniest stories was about the lady who hadn't been close enough to the President to kiss him, so she settled for kissing the Presidential beagles on her way out!

I loved it! I'd like to see them all. I'd fly back from anywhere to get here for it.

Summer 1966

LBJ RANCH Today is the Democratic primary runoff and we had come
Saturday, home to vote and for Lynda Bird's graduation. Yesterday,
June 4, flying home on *Air Force One,* Lyndon had said, "It's been
1966 the best week we've had in a long time. . . ." Three things
have happened: One, a peaceful election in the Dominican
Republic. We could unleash our hope a little further. Two,
the soft landing of Surveyor on the moon. That was an almost
unhoped-for victory that put us ahead. And three, the turn of
events in Vietnam, with the government asking for UN
supervision of elections.

Together Lyndon and I went to the polls in the Courthouse a little before 4 this afternoon. In my mind I will
always have a picture of us walking into that Courthouse in
the summer of 1941. Whatever has happened to me in the
interim, nothing has ever been more dramatic than Lyndon's
race for the Senate in 1941.

George Hamilton is here, and Lynda and he left early. I

386

told Lynda I would be in the crowd, beaming, for the graduation ceremony tonight. She laughed and said, "Mother, I'll be the one in the black gown and black shoes." (There will be twenty-four hundred of them.) She's made light of it the whole time—at first, didn't want to go herself—although I believe deep down in her heart maybe she *did* want to go, but it is such a mass production affair—"Mickey Mouse," as she calls it—not quite the sophisticated thing to do anymore.

Lyndon and I went in by helicopter and arrived at the University one minute before the faculty started the procession. It was a beautiful summer night with clear skies and cool breezes; about ten thousand parents and friends of graduates were seated on the mall in front of the great Main Building. Lyndon and I slipped in quietly and took a seat next to Warrie Lynn Smith's parents. Lynda Bird had been adamant: "Either come just as parents or don't come!" I looked at my program and there was Lynda under the cum laude group in the College of Arts and Sciences. It had been thirty-three years since I had graduated and the campus was full of ghosts. The solemn processional entered, and all the parents craned their necks to look eagerly as the graduates walked down the aisle toward Dr. Harry Ransom at the speaker's podium and then filed left into their seats. In a minute I saw Warrie Lynn with the little blue tassel that indicates she's an education major.

Signs of the times—first, babies crying during the ceremony. Young marrieds on the campus—a third or more of those in graduate school, Lynda tells me. This would have been as rare as an elephant when I was on the campus. Another sign, degrees in "Aerospace Engineering"—B.A., M.A., Ph.D.—I wonder how long they have been going on? My heart rose in salute that my University was so quick to meet the times. I, who am a little over fifty and was born and raised in "deep East Texas," have seen the most miraculous change in the life of our country. Another interesting sign of the times was the heavy percentage of Ph.D.'s from the Middle East and the Far East, most of all from India. Pakistan was represented; Japan and China were represented heavily.

The Commencement speaker was Francis Keppel, former Assistant Secretary for Education in the Department of Health, Education, and Welfare. He was witty, left a few deep thoughts with us, and was brief—all virtues. He urged the graduates to serve some branch of government at some time in their lives, to have the rewarding experience of helping with the unfinished business of society.

And then it was over and the lights of the tower turned orange. My heart was in my throat and I knew Lynda's was as the University band struck up "The Eyes of Texas," with most of us singing, old ones and new ones, all across those well-loved acres.

Lyndon and I hurried out so as not to be caught in the crowd. Lynda Bird joined us at the car.

We dropped by at the party that Jesse and Carolyn and Tom Curtis were giving for Lynda. I thought it was a great tribute to Lynda that Chancellor Ransom and his wife came to the party. Anne Clark and the Ambassador were there . . . A sprinkling of Lynda's Zeta sorority sisters . . . Mrs. Frances Hudspeth, who has been irreplaceable in Lynda's life in the University . . . Bill Hitchcock and Joe Batson, the sort of good friends you would tell your troubles to . . . The Deathes and Erwins, and the wives of her Secret Service men. A cozy little group of about fifty-five or so from the many sides of her life. We left Lynda and George at the party and later heard they'd had a silly, gay time riding around town in Warrie Lynn's date's car, a red ambulance—1946 vintage!

One of the sweetest things of all was a card from Mrs. Nolen, Lynda's teacher from early days of high school. Lynda Bird translated the legend in Latin, "Someone has remembered you across the years and believes in you."

Monday, June 13

THE WHITE HOUSE

Today was the day of Tom and Mary Clark's party for Luci, the first "wedding party" ever held in the U.S. Supreme Court. Mr. and Mrs. Nugent had come in Sunday and were staying in the Queen's Room.

For a week we have had "Operation Children," with the house overflowing with seventeen houseguests: Betty Ann and Dick Stedman and their three; Mary Rather and her two nieces, Nancy and Betsy; my nephew, Thomas Jefferson Taylor III, and Chris, and their Sally and Nancy. And then, a last-minute addition by Lyndon, the James Davis family from the Ranch, taking over Helen's rooms. Patsy Derby had been the tour director, each day dispatching them for sightseeing, or arranging hot dogs and watermelon on the South Lawn, and movies in the theater. It has been as much fun for me as anyone, for these are special people, and we love sharing this house.

Even the new Gallup Poll has not marred the week: "PRESIDENT'S STANDING LOWEST IN THIRTY MONTHS. Fewer Americans today express confidence in the way President Johnson is handling his job than at any previous time during the 2½ years that he has been in office." In May it had been 54 percent. Now it is 46 percent who approve. Not that the disapprovals have grown—only one percent. But those that have no opinion have grown from 13 percent in May to 20 percent in June. It was interesting to note that the happy Eisenhower in his eight years only fell to 49 percent at the lowest. Whereas Truman, beset with Korea and hitting it head on, had fallen to a low of 23 percent at one point.

The frosting on the cake was the party at the Supreme Court. The Davises were now departed but Tom and Mary invited the rest. The party began at 7 P.M.—a reception buffet—with the receiving line standing in the great stilled dignity of the Supreme Court hall and the party in two conference rooms, with the guests spilling out into the courtyard around the splashing fountain.

Luci and Pat went on ahead of me. With all of the family joking about Luci never being anywhere on time, she arrived five minutes early, looking lovely in her new white dress of embroidered lace encrusted with brilliants. I arrived on the stroke of 7, bringing Mr. and Mrs. Nugent and Father John Kuzinskas. Lynda came at a time of her own choosing. Her growing independence is a marked thing. Her hair was in a chignon and she wore a black cocktail dress, and looked distinguished, and a little Spanish.

We have no older and dearer friends than Tom and Mary Clark. Our ties are built of times we've shared and admiration for their real goodness. All the Supreme Court members came, with the exception of Bill Douglas who was off making a speech. Several of the bridesmaids were there: Sharon Chapman with her mother and father; Helene Lindow with her parents; Charlotte Sizoo and hers. I was delighted to see Perle Mesta. Someone remarked it was "old home week." There were so many people in fact who, as Luci says, "had a part in making Luci!" And she's right. At the head of the list I would put Miss Katharine Lee and Miss Elizabeth Fry of National Cathedral School, who spent the whole evening and seemed to enjoy it so much, and Mrs. David Acheson. And very flattered I was that the Speaker and Mrs. McCormack should come to Luci's party.

At the last minute Mary, in her generous way, had included all my Alabama kinfolks, the Hill Corys and Patsy's mother, Minnie Wade Derby. And of course, those that are closest of all to Luci—Willie Day and Ashton. A good deal of the White House staff, all of whom had loved her and had been sweet to her, were there too.

Ambassador and Anne Clark were there, and the young Ed Weisls. And quite a number of the Texas Congressmen. About twenty-six of her friends from Georgetown School of Nursing hovered together in a crowd, like pretty little quails—I tried to meet every one of them. When Lyndon came in they crowded around him wanting autographs. I hadn't known for sure whether Lyndon would come or when, but he arrived a little past 8, and he was the one I was happiest of all to see.

Tom Clark gave the sweetest toast about having known Luci and Lynda all their lives, and their parents for ten years longer than that. And then he gave Luci a charm of the Supreme Court and Pat a pair of cuff links.

My first memory of the Court is coming here with Cecille Harrison in the summer of 1934. The building was snowy white, glittering in the sun—just finished. There were still a few carpenters and workmen in the hall. But we could go through—at least there were no guards to stop us. And Cecille and I explored the entire place—even sitting in some of the Justices' *chairs*. Furthest from my dreams was that I should ever return there for a party given by one of the Justices in honor of my daughter and the young man she was going to marry!

Thursday, June 28

Today began with a sense of elation and ended on a solemn note, followed with fear and prayer. I had an early appointment with Charles Palmer of Warm Springs, Georgia, and Madame Shoumatoff to view her sketch of the portrait of Franklin Roosevelt. We went into the Lincoln Room to set it up on an easel and Madame Shoumatoff lifted off the covering. There he was—a young, strong, magnetic leader—many years and millions of worries away from the dying President she had painted at Warm Springs. For once I looked at a portrait and loved it at first sight. Madame Shoumatoff will complete her work in a few months.

My day was filled with a Beautification Committee meeting to view Nat Owings' model of the Mall and an awards ceremony giving plaques to winners in three categories—commercial, public, and neighborhood. Using the White House as a podium—hopefully—to thank, to applaud, to advertise, to rally citizens to action in improving our environment, gives me joy.

This evening Marvin Watson brought Senator Dick Russell to the house. We had a quiet dinner, just Lyndon and Dick and I. There were two hours of discussion of the military future of the country—the Senate and its problems and personalities and new faces. The air was alive with a sense of change, of a big decision having been reached. It had been gestating for days, weeks, espoused, attacked, examined, explored from every angle in the long meetings with Rusk, Ball, Rostow, and the military men. I asked no questions but I felt the decision had been reached —to bomb the enemy's fuel depots.

When Senator Russell left, Lyndon called Luci and said, "I want to go to church. Are any of your Catholic churches open?" Luci said: "The monks live in their church." She called one of them. We could go there. In a few minutes we were on our way—Lyndon and Luci and I—to a dark, silent church in the southwest part of town deserted except for us. We were let in by a monk in a long belted robe. (Luci told me he was a Brother, not a Father.) We went quietly to a pew and knelt. And each with his own thoughts took his troubles to the Lord. I was sitting back in my seat a long time before Lyndon got up. Then we filed out. The Brother acted as though this happened every day of the week—courteously showing us to the door. Nobody at all knew.

Wednesday, July 13

Luci and Pat got their license today. A White House photographer went along. They stood in line just like everybody else and were not recognized at first. It turned out that the photographer was not permitted to take pictures, but his presence caused them to be recognized. Somewhere down the line the anesthesia is going to wear off and I am going to realize that this is for real.

I went with Lyndon to the Navy Yard this afternoon for the commissioning ceremonies of the *Oceanographer*—the floating laboratory which will make a six-month, round-the-world tour in search of the secrets of the sea. In his speech Lyndon invited eleven nations—including the Soviet Union—to have their scientists join in this round-the-world expedition. One of its main purposes is to search for marine food, because of rising world population and mounting protein deficiency in many countries. The Secretary of Commerce and Mary Connor were there.

We were piped aboard—the first time that's ever happened to me.

Dr. Donald Hornig, Lyndon's Science Adviser, told me one example of what the ship would do to produce useful results. He said great schools of sardines for years had run off a certain coast, and then one season they ceased to be there. It was a great loss to the fishing industry. No one knew where the sardines had gone, or why. Then scientists discovered that the currents of the ocean and temperature of the water had changed. The sardines had found themselves another home in the deep a few hundred miles away.

I never cease to feel that I am part of a new frontier here. There is so much happening, so much important work of infinite promise whose results I hope to see someday.

I spent the rest of the afternoon working with Ashton and Bess. At 6:30 I had a meeting with Bruce Thomas and Nash Castro, Joe Bruno, Liz and Mr. West, on the Truman Balcony to discuss how to keep the White House available to tourists and still functioning for the growing number of Presidential activities here. The White House is many things: museum for the public, home for a family, site for official entertainment. Sometimes these activities conflict. There is a steady influx of State visitors —arrival ceremonies and luncheons. There are award ceremonies to Medal of Honor winners, students, scientists. There are innumerable bill signings.

In 1964 a million eight hundred thousand people visited the White House. In 1965, because it was closed more often, there were only a million seven hundred thousand. In the first half of 1966 the White House has already been closed eight times and the hours shortened ten times. Each time it is closed in vacation months, six to ten thousand people go away disappointed. This wrenches me and I am trying to get the cooperation of the appointments office—of everybody—to alleviate the situation.

Marvin Watson, that most beleaguered man, joined us and was very helpful and understanding.

Nash Castro suggested that on days when the house was closed for a State luncheon, tourists might at least walk in the driveway or the Pennsylvania Avenue entrance and guides could produce a narration about the house, and this is an excellent vantage point for taking pictures. And I (who am a chief culprit in having the house closed all day the Friday and Saturday of Luci's wedding) had the idea that we would open it on Monday from 8 until 4. It is never opened on Mondays. This is what Luci would want.

Very pertinently, sales of guidebooks are also falling. Twenty percent of those who passed through in 1964 bought a guidebook; only 16 percent in 1965; and in the first six months of 1966 sales have dropped to 11 percent.

That hits Mr. West and me because the proceeds from book sales pay for the reproductions of rugs, re-coverings of furnishings, and the eventual great necessity for drapes in the State Dining Room. For the new book coming out in the fall, *The Living White House*, Liz suggests a fanfare of publicity to help increase the sales.

It's always a good feeling to lay your hand to the problems of the day, to think you've accomplished something, or at least tried. To me there is nothing more physically or mentally tiring than ignoring my work and letting it pile up.

Lyndon had taken a group of Ambassadors and Prime Minister Harold Holt of Australia out for a stag dinner on the yacht *Sequoia*.

About 10 Lyndon and the Prime Minister, who is one of the most peppery characters I have met in my experiences with Chiefs of State, came in. The Prime Minister told delightful stories about his travels. Once when his plane landed, a harried-looking official had come on, staring at the passengers in the plane, and leaned over to him and said: "Can you help me? I am supposed to meet the Prime Minister from Australia and I don't know his name." Upon which Holt stuck out his hand and said, "Holt's the name." Such light, deflating jokes on one-self always take the pompousness out of a situation and blunt the arrows of possible enemies in the audience, I think.

Sunday, July 17

This was a mild, soft, early evening, the sort that is an antidote for the struggles of the week for Lyndon. And for me it was especially precious because we were all four together. And those days are numbered. Today's paper had a story of Luci's bridesmaids in pink, including a sketch, and a negative story about Lynda Bird's return: "ELUDES PRESS AT AIRPORT."

It's an old story by now and I should know it well. There's a sort of conspiracy by the press, by one's friends, by the public, I'm sure. For years they pitted Lyndon against Speaker Rayburn but that never worked. Now increasingly, as John Connally is reaching a summit of prominence, they are trying to stir up a fight between him and Lyndon. Sometimes it's abrasive, but I believe it will never produce anything between those two. And now in a way, it's daughter against daughter. Luci has certain qualifications that make her wonderful with the press and Lynda has characteristics that give her a bad time with them. The moral is, we must be careful—no rifts within our inner forces. I believe we are too strong and too close for that.

The Cabinet ladies joined to give a party for Luci at Margy McNamara's home. We lunched at round tables on the patio, close to a tinkling fountain underneath some dogwood trees. It was a good, happy, easy time. I feel close to and shall want to keep these women in my circle of friends when we depart from this town.

After lunch, Margy gave Luci a small silver serving tray with the signatures in script of all of the Cabinet wives, just the right size for the household of a young bride and just the sort of thing she loves most.

I had invited Alice Roosevelt Longworth to come to tea with Luci and me this afternoon at 4. I had planned it as a meeting of the bride of half a century ago with the bride of 1966. I hurried to the Diplomatic Reception Room about five minutes of 4 to meet her. She was wearing the big brimmed hat that is her signature—this one in brown. I wonder where she gets them. All the same, decade after decade, and just right for her. She wore a brown print dress—and she was an explosion of vitality and interest for more than an hour and a half. We had tea in the West Hall. While I sat in silent admiration of the gallant way she has battled the years, she talked of home life in the White House. She said her stepmother had permitted her father to bring a limited number of guests to dinner unexpectedly— up to eight at the table—and they ranged from big game hunters to Catholic cardinals.

She spoke of how she and her husband had driven out to Friendship for their honeymoon. It was in the country then, and as they left the White House grounds headed for their honeymoon destination they saw one of the White House aides—Douglas MacArthur. Mrs. Longworth said she wore an absolutely awful going-away dress, and she said also that nobody bothered them on their honeymoon. They were not followed by a tumultuous press. She said that in those days the details of a wedding were not given out to the press. They had to make up things, and this accounted for ridiculous stories about her wedding.

Lyndon came in and kissed her and had a word or two. He likes her and she him, I believe. I expect because they both recognize in each other a strong untamed spirit. As I watched Lynda on the sofa, listening to Mrs. Longworth, I thought—she is the sort of person who would like to do some of the things Mrs. Longworth has done so freely.

Wednesday, July 20

Lyndon woke about 5. Neither of us could go back to sleep so we talked—about each of the children and their various problems, about all the troubles that beset Lyndon and about his future, about me and the things I want to do, both between now and the time we leave this house and then for the years afterward. Home and husband, grandchildren, wildflowers, travel, running rivers, hunting for pictographs, and covered bridges and outdoor summer pageants. There is so much I want to do.

Later after a morning of clearing my desk I met with some advisers and staff, including Inspector Glenard Lanier, Agent Bill Duncan, Mr. Milton Semer from Lyndon's legal department, and Bess. The problem is where to park seven hundred wedding guests on Saturday, August 6. Bess had hoped we could close off Pennsylvania Avenue between Fifteenth and Seventeenth Streets and use the space for parking. A peace organization has already requested from the National Park Service a permit to picket in Lafayette Park that afternoon. The Park Service has suggested two other locations, but if they are insistent they will give them the permit to picket beginning at 6 P.M. Another group started marching, as of yesterday, up and down the sidewalk with banners along the White House fence. The area is under the jurisdiction of the District of Columbia—not the Park Service. The Student Nonviolent Coordinating Committee, I think it is—led by Stokely Carmichael—has expressed its intention of picketing as close as possible to the Shrine of the Immaculate Conception. I have nightmares of our East Texas friend Hugh Powell (product of another day, a different milieu) as he walks across Lafayette Park planting his fist on some wild-eyed protester's jaw! But we have lived in this house with picketing nearly every day for months and months beginning last year. Only when it becomes extremely raucous do we notice it.

My advisers finally decided we should request reserved parking space around the Ellipse and direct guests the two or three blocks that it would take them to come in by the Treasury entrance. About 95 percent of the guests would come in that way. Only the Cabinet and Supreme Court members and those few with limousines will come in through the front entrance. They, poor public servants, are inured to picket lines. The funny things (and the sad things) that have happened in putting this wedding together would make a long story!

This has been as grueling a day for Lyndon as I can remember—meetings with sub-Cabinet-level officers from AEC and AID, and Export-Import, and NASA and USIA and the Arms Control and Disarmament Agency. Then a meeting with members of the Midwest Governors Conference—Roger Branigin of Indiana, Otto Kerner of Illinois, Warren Knowles of Wisconsin, James A. Rhodes of Ohio. Next a luncheon, stag, for President René Barrientos of Bolivia, and now the press conference, full dress with television. I've begun to think of these press conferences as a sort of trial by combat and I approach them as though I were riding in a tumbrel to my execution, although of course it isn't really me—it's Lyndon.

I sat in the front row. It was a hit-and-miss affair on Vietnam and inflation, spiced with one funny moment when the irate male reporter from *Women's Wear Daily* asked if the President didn't think it was unfair that his paper was barred from the wedding. Lyndon's expression would have done credit to any actor on Broadway. With an apologetic smile he said he would prefer to just "step aside" from discussing arrangements for his daughter Luci's wedding. Later he said what he really wanted to say was that except for wearing a pair of striped trousers and that hot swallow-tail coat and picking up the bills, he didn't have anything to do with it. I think every father in the country would have had a fellow feeling!

Saturday, July 23

INDIANA, KENTUCKY, AND ILLINOIS

Today was a great, roaring day, covering three states. It is hard to describe it because it was a montage of faces, a changing kaleidoscope of activities. And by 1 A.M. Sunday when it was all over, we were so weary that everything had somehow melted together.

In the morning I went with Lyndon to dedicate the AMVETS Building. Speaker McCormack and I unveiled a bronze bust of Lyndon. Lyndon then gathered up Senator Yarborough and off he went with us on *Air Force*

One, with a delegation that included—or during the day picked up— Governors Branigin of Indiana, Kerner of Illinois, Edward Breathitt of Kentucky, Senators Birch Bayh and Vance Hartke of Indiana, John Sherman Cooper and Thruston Morton of Kentucky, and Paul Douglas of Illinois, and a great array of Congressmen.

We landed at Indianapolis, where, because the airport was under construction, there was not supposed to be any crowd. But thousands had gathered. Then we drove to downtown Indianapolis, where some forty-two thousand people filled a huge circle and poured out into the streets which radiated into it. In the middle stood a great dominating monument, at the base of which Lyndon spoke. A sea of faces, signs saying "WE LOVE LUCI," "WE ARE BACKING YOU ON VIETNAM," "WE HAVE A DATE IN '68," a wedding bell with "LUCI AND PAT" on it, and in the distance a sign, "VANCE SPEAKS FOR US." We went to the Indianapolis Athletic Club where Lyndon attended a stag luncheon for some four hundred and seventy-five men, hosted by the newspaper magnate Mr. Eugene Pulliam. I went to another room to a luncheon for ladies given by Mrs. Branigin, after which she presented Luci with a Paul Revere bowl from the people of the State of Indiana.

Then we were off for Fort Campbell, Kentucky, for the most memorable scene of the day. There Lyndon awarded medals to twenty-two veterans of the 101st Division returned from Vietnam, saw weapons captured in Vietnam, and spoke as Commander in Chief. What I remember most was a simulated attack—helicopters coming in at treetop height in lines as precise as ballet dancers, the swiftness with which men debarked, picked up soldiers where the big pink flares had been left burning, and were off in seconds. It was breathtaking and frightening. I remember the huge parachute, mottled green and brown for camouflage in the jungle, used to drop such matériel as a truck. And I remember the sense of awed silence I felt when I tried to speak to the wounded men in wheelchairs.

Soon it was time to fly on. (This is what I would call "a four-shirt day." After every speech Lyndon is wringing wet, and at least four times today he changed shirts.)

We went by Convair to Lawrenceville, Illinois, for an airport rally. Once more, thousands of people, in this heartland of America that's not supposed to be our territory. Only once did I think I saw an unfriendly sign. I believe it had the words "PRESIDENT GOLDWATER."

We drove across ten miles of lovely open country. They say they've had a drought, but the corn was beautiful. The wheat had just been harvested and the fields were a crewcut gold. At Vincennes we went to the George Rogers Clark National Historical Park on the banks of the Wabash River, where Lyndon spoke to a crowd of forty thousand about Vietnam, urging Americans to "Stop, look, and listen as you hear the voices talking about what's wrong with your country." He said he had not heard many commentators lecture the enemy about bombings by the North Vietnamese of hospitals for American servicemen in South Vietnam.

Once more we were on the plane, to Louisville for an airport rally. And then to Jeffersonville, Indiana, by motorcade, to present a beautification award to the local Post Office. By this time we were an hour late, and it was past 9. And here, on his ninth speech of the day, Lyndon threw the text aside and launched into his best campaigning style. I felt the bond build up between him and his audience, although they had been waiting for him two hours and it was close to 10 P.M. They cheered most when Lyndon said, "It may be old-fashioned, but I still believe that my country does most things right." A mournful foghorn sounded from the Ohio River as Lyndon "shouted out his gospel" and over and over they applauded and urged him on.

For the first time in a long time, I wrote out one of my little notes: "Great speech—but time to stop." We motorcaded back to Louisville and the plane. This time I did not stop to shake hands anymore, as I had done all day, Luci in one direction and I in another—"Thank you for coming out to meet us." "You sure have beautiful farmland here." "Somebody as little as you had better be careful in this crowd." To a lady on crutches: "You are brave to try this." To one of the thousands taking pictures: "I do that myself. It's hard to get them when your target keeps on moving."

And what do they say? "We are praying for you." This over and over— "Tell your husband we believe in him."

Some might say it's a shallow, meaningless experience. To me it is curiously elating, and I guess it is as simple as this: If they like us, I like them and want to show it.

Then we were back in the plane, for the last time today, and very weary. But we felt excited, and I was satisfied and proud of Lyndon. Then I heard about what I believe was the most important speech of the day. The one at the stag luncheon, where Lyndon had said that riots must stop. That our country cannot abide civil violence. For such riots start a chain re-

1966

*State of the Union
Address, January 12.
LBJ Library Photo by
Frank Wolfe, C1160-4.*

FACING PAGE, TOP: *Tree planting at Hains Point with Mary Lasker and Mr. and Mrs. Laurance Rockefeller, April 13. LBJ Library Photo by Robert Knudsen, C1656-31.* BOTTOM: *Members of the Committee for a More Beautiful Capital tour Washington. LBJ Library Photo by Robert Knudsen, C1654-15.*

ABOVE: *After-hours in the Oval Office with the President and Secretary Rusk. LBJ Library Photo by Yoichi Okamoto, A2124-9a.*
LEFT, TOP: *Exchange of gifts in the Yellow Oval Room during the visit of India's Prime Minister Indira Gandhi, March 28. LBJ Library Photo by Yoichi Okamoto, A2188-23a.*
LEFT, BOTTOM: *With Alice Roosevelt Longworth and Russell Train. LBJ Library Photo by Robert Knudsen, C1500-5.*

OVERLEAF, LEFT: *Mr. and Mrs. Patrick Nugent departing for their honeymoon, August 6. LBJ Library Photo by Robert Knudsen, C2716-14a.*
RIGHT: *The President and First Lady arrive in New Zealand for first leg of Far East trip, October 17–November 2. LBJ Library Photo by Frank Wolfe, 3530-28.*

LEFT: *Transferring from the helicopter to Air Force One. LBJ Library Photo by Yoichi Okamoto, A3056-9.* BELOW, TOP: *Toasting with a native chief in Pago Pago, October 18. LBJ Library Photo by Yoichi Okamoto, C3479-27.* BOTTOM: *Korea turns out to greet the President and First Lady, October 31. LBJ Library Photo by Frank Wolfe, 3750-37.*

OVERLEAF: *Lady Bird in a yellow formal gown posing in the White House. LBJ Library Photo by Robert Knudsen, C9959-23a.*

action, the consequences of which fall most heavily on those who begin them. The riots in the streets do not bring about lasting reforms. They tear down the very fabric of the community. They set neighbor against neighbor and create walls of mistrust and fear between them. They make reform more difficult by turning away the very people who can and must support reform.

Back at the White House we were all on that sort of peak of excitement which makes sleep hard to achieve. So it was 2 A.M. when I fell asleep, feeling infinitely proud of Lyndon—of his spirit and his strength and his determination against the odds that face him.

Wednesday, July 27

THE WHITE HOUSE

Only ten days now until Luci's wedding! No matter if he goes to sleep at 2 A.M., Lyndon wakes up every morning a little past 7.

I called Warren Woodward and he joined me in the Queen's Sitting Room, with Bob Kollar, Luci's Secret Service agent. We talked an hour about the plans for the honeymoon and decided Woody should make four reservations—Luci, Pat, two Secret Service men—from New York, Sunday morning, August 7, on Pan-American for Nassau. Woody will pay cash and reserve them in the name of a fictitious person.

When Woody left, Bob Kollar and I talked a little longer, about the actual departure. He favors the tunnel that leads into the Treasury and asks us to avoid using suitcases that have her initials on them. We ended by deciding to borrow Bob Kollar's wife's suitcases. What a joint honeymoon this is going to be!

And then I had a multitude of phone calls to make: to Rusty Young about the flowers for the Shrine and for the White House; to Mary Kaltman about meals for all the houseguests, beginning this weekend and extending to the weekend of the wedding, with something cold in a buffet for the night of August 6 because not all the guests will simply melt away to a honeymoon.

There are funny things, too, which have happened in putting this wedding together. The other day Bess and Simone gathered twenty-five startled tourists from the sightseers' line to stand them as props in a little roped-off enclosure in the East Room to enable them to measure the size of the area for the number of reporters who would cover the cake-cutting ceremony at the wedding. They were very obliging although they had no idea why they were stand-ins.

It's an unpredictable obstacle course. Anybody planning a wedding in the future in the White House had best read up on the problems faced by his predecessors.

Lyndon was taking Ambassadors to dinner on the *Sequoia*. So I had dinner with Luci and Betty on the Truman Balcony. I talked with Luci until quite late. She described the strings that bind her in her life as the President's daughter. "I'd adore to go to Europe, but I would not love the criticism it would cause. I love to go paddle-boating on the Tidal Basin. Nobody minds if I go paddle-boating, so I go paddle-boating."

Her thesis is that she gets joy from simple things that nobody can take away from her—playing with the puppies, making fried chicken-potato salad picnics for her friends, baby-sitting with Madeline Montelaro's two-year-old while Madeline has the new baby. The essence of it is that Luci loves life. She does not feel frustrated because of the things she can't do as the President's daughter.

Monday, August 1

The settlement of the airline strike—which we had celebrated on Friday—came unglued Sunday. I stayed close by to try to comfort Lyndon.

There was magnificent confusion in the Lincoln Room; Priscilla, Miss Treyz, a covey of bridesmaids trying on the pink dresses, being fitted, posing. Jean Louis had been down early, doing Luci's hair for her pictures in her wedding dress. We had decided to "secure" the first floor so that not even the butlers or maids or passing workmen or signal corpsmen could see that great treasure—the wedding dress—as she came into the East Room for the pictures.

Then Luci came into the Lincoln Room—her black hair piled high. In front of Alice Roosevelt Longworth's mirror, Priscilla hooked on the train that gave the final perfect touch. Helen said, in a soft breath, "It is the most beautiful dress I have ever seen, and it is you, Luci."

Even the closet looked like a wedding. There, side by side, were twelve beige-and-white striped kits, with pink tissue paper foaming from them, containing the wedding shoes and gloves—final touches for the bridesmaids. The kits were Stanley Marcus' gift.

At noon I found to my chagrin that so secure was the securing, there was not a soul in the kitchen to cook me a scrambled egg!

I went downstairs to see Luci. In the gold and white East Room, where she was posing for her formal bridal pictures, I met a blaze of light.

The Nugents had arrived at 2. I welcomed them over the phone and told them I would leave my car for them to go to the Harriman party, accompanied by Bess. I would catch a ride with Luci and Pat because we had been asked to be there by 5. I delegated the job of getting the President to the party on time to Marvin, and Luci and Pat and I left for the Harrimans'. We arrived thirty minutes ahead of the invited guests so that we could have the presentation of the Diplomatic Corps' gift to Luci and Pat by Ambassador Sevilla-Sacasa, the Dean of the Corps. The great package was elegantly wrapped, and as Luci brought out piece after piece of the silver tea service in Old Maryland engraved, she and Sevilla-Sacasa beamed in delight. The exquisite joint gift had enabled every country—all one hundred fourteen members of the Corps—to feel that they were participating. It had almost worked. Luci has received only a sprinkling of gifts from Chiefs of State. As we have tried so often to express through the Chief of Protocol, this is a personal family event, *not* a State occasion.

The Harriman house rambled on and on, rather like a country house. There were French doors that opened onto a terrace which was covered with a flowered tent in case of rain. And then the garden went down and down to other terraces, resplendent with glossy-leaved giant magnolia trees, and pink and white crepe myrtle bushes. Round tables covered with pink cloths and pink-flower centerpieces were scattered among them. On the very lowest level I glimpsed the blue coolness of the pool, with a dance floor and a small orchestra on the other side. A beautiful setting!

The Ambassador and Marie Harriman and Luci and Pat and I stood in the receiving line for about ten minutes and then I left it to the central figures for the rest of the evening. Luci looked lovely, I thought, in her brilliant pink chiffon with the jeweled neck which flowed like a cage, although I can't get used to that two-inches-above-the-knee hem level!

Nearly every one of the one hundred fourteen countries was represented —Chargés d'Affaires if the Ambassadors were out of town. Averell told me that all of the Soviet bloc countries had representatives there.

A little before 7 Lyndon came. I found out what it is like when the President is expected. Someone comes in, in great excitement, "The President is due in ten minutes." Another rushes in, "The President is due in four minutes." Another, "Time to come to the front door, the President is driving up." He was smiling and affable, whatever it cost him, because I know it must have been a hellish day.

We were back at Lyndon's office by 8:15, and I left him with Joe Califano, knowing it would be a late evening. Legislation on the Hill had gone very badly. Congress, so determined to do something about the strike, was going to follow the brave course of directing the President to "use his discretion" to end it. Then Lyndon will be faced with the necessity of signing or vetoing the bill. This seems like a sharp and skillful knife to insert between the President and Labor to excise their support from him. But I personally have one armor—there is nothing I want . . . Even that is not quite true, because I do want to retain the place in history that I think Lyndon has merited in his more than thirty years of public service.

I went back to the White House and joined the Nugents and the young people in the Solarium—Patti, Betty Beal, Hitch, Sharon, the Rays. We've set up a permanent dining room table for the week there. The table will be loaded at night with chafing dishes of food that will stay hot for people as they come and go, and with cold things for lunch. Tonight's beef stroganoff and rice was welcomed by 9:20.

Tuesday, August 2

This was a day that caused Bess and me to flinch—a State Dinner right in the middle of the wedding preparations, with the house already bursting with pink tulle and confections for the reception. It was enough to give apoplexy to the staff.

President Zalman Shazar of Israel and Mrs. Shazar arrived in one door as the last of the bridesmaids came in the other.

Down in the kitchen Ferdinand and two assistants were making the sugar concoction that will turn into the roses to decorate Luci's seven-layer wedding cake.

Meanwhile, a delivery truck rolled up bearing a huge piano for Rudolf Serkin to play tonight at the State Dinner. He brings his own piano to concerts! He had a quiet practice period on the stage. Maybe he was the only quiet person in the house.

Sometime in the morning I went down to the basement where the wedding gifts are on display. A silver bun warmer had come from President and

Mrs. Truman, and my brother Tony Taylor had sent a set of sherbet cups that had belonged to my mother at the Brick House. Luci was delighted that Willie Day had parted with her heavy iron skillet already seasoned with long use.

I was touched to see the many crocheted pot holders, handkerchiefs edged with tatting from the "general public"—sometimes from little girls of seven or older ladies in nursing homes who know Luci through the newspapers or television.

I stopped by the first-floor corridor to see the display of White House brides that Jim Ketchum has arranged—from Maria Monroe in 1820 through the niece of President Woodrow Wilson who had married Isaac Stuart McElroy and who had sent us the cake box and the brooch that she wore at the wedding. It was a charming display, but it kept on saying to me, "Save, save—remember to leave to the White House, to the Johnson Library, and very especially to Luci and to us, interesting things from this wedding." There was so little, really, in the display—pictures of eight brides, one invitation, an autographed place card of Woodrow Wilson's, signed in pencil.

I stopped by the kitchen to see what I could find for lunch. Zephyr said she had already fed nineteen—there wasn't a bit of cold beef left. So I settled for bacon and eggs again.

Lyndon called then and said: "Could you find Luci and Pat and bring them over to the office or find me wherever I am? I need cheering up. And I want to give them their wedding present."

I rounded them up, and we went. He was in his office. He had bought a generous-size Government Savings Bond which would mature in seven years, and on the envelope he had written: "To our children who bring us so much joy and strength." If one can be sure of anything in this world, it is that those two will have need of something special seven years from now—the "just-perfect desk" to put in the bay window of a house they may be building, or an antique chest to lend character to their living room, or maybe a vacation. I was gratified that Luci had requested a Government Bond for her wedding gift. She remembered that we'd told them when we first married we had started buying a bond every month and had kept it up for years and years. You never know whether seeds fall on fertile ground and will bear fruit. It's always a pleasant surprise when they do.

I wore my most elegant dress—the printed chiffon—for the State Dinner. And at twenty minutes of 8 I was madly phoning Lyndon's office to get him over to get dressed so we could meet the President of Israel on the front Portico in ten minutes. He is the swiftest dresser in the world! We could have done it if he hadn't gotten hung up on the telephone but we were down a few minutes late—exactly at the moment the big black limousine, fluttering the flags of the United States and the Star of David, drove up and out stepped the elderly, affable President Shazar and his soft-spoken wife, Rachael Shazar.

There was the traditional gathering upstairs for meeting and gift exchanges and we altered the routine of the stairway entrance to the one hundred ninety guests below, because of the ages of the guests. Sensibly, we took them by elevator.

How I have loved the entertainment at the White House! Drama is my first love and musicals with fine choreography, and always ballet—and tonight I felt proud of Mr. Serkin's wonderful program.

My main feeling at the end of the day was satisfaction that the staff had overcome all the obstacles of giving an elegant State Dinner in the middle of a wedding. Henry Haller, our new Chef, is all that we had hoped —and believe me, this week is a test!

Wednesday, August 3

The house was humming today. As I went up and down in the elevator, a painter, oblivious to the comings and goings of all of us, was touching up the gold leaf—it had just been painted the week before and a huge piece of plumbing material carried upstairs had damaged it. Washable curtains all over the house had been down for laundering and were going back up.

The Lincoln Room is the habitat of Priscilla and her two fitters, and foams with vast clouds of pink tulle that the bridesmaids will wear and a rack full of long pink dresses. Under the hem the name of each bridesmaid is embroidered with the occasion and the date. A sewing machine whirs in the corner opposite the desk that Lincoln used at his summer home in the outskirts of Washington.

The first big event of the day was Luci's party for the staff. It was an unqualified success. The guests included the one hundred or more cooks, butlers, people from the dispensary, laundresses, and the crippled pantry boy who is one of Luci's favorites—she helped comfort him through the accident when he lost both his legs; the doormen, of whom Preston Bruce is the dean; the girls from Lyndon's office—Yolanda, Marie, Vicki; Juanita

Roberts, Lyndon's top secretary for many years; Mildred Stegall, who has been with Lyndon since he was in the House of Representatives; all of the doctors—Dr. Burkley, Dr. Fox, and Luci's beloved Dr. Young—and Miss Chapowicki from their office; and two of Luci's special favorites—Bob Knudsen, who has photographed her around the clock and around the continent, and Jim Ketchum, the Curator, with whom she has a particular rapport, who helped her research her paper on the furniture and art of the White House. And of course it would not have been a party without Zephyr. And Mr. Traphes Bryant—it is hard to say who tried the most to console whom after Him was killed—Luci or Mr. Bryant. And Luci's very special friends—all of the telephone operators. They took turns, four or five or six coming, staying twenty minutes, and then others taking their places. Miss Beverly Cole and Miss Mary Crowe are two of the real old-timers. And Margaret Deeb, who, though Luci doesn't know it, has lived with the black book for the last three months. It is the "Bible"—it contains all the information about the wedding. And Kristin Anderson who is in charge of answering Luci's mail and looks scarcely older than Luci herself.

I've seldom enjoyed a White House party more and Lyndon had come in to enjoy it too.

Luci's party for her bridesmaids was at 6:30 in the Solarium. The Solarium has made history in a small domestic way during the time Luci has used it. I've especially cherished the time she's enjoyed here visiting with the children of our friends, like Kathleen Carter and Beth Jenkins. Tonight, it was full of pretty girls dressed in slacks and shifts and ready to relax. The buffet table with a yellow-flower centerpiece was amply spread with crabmeat crepes—my favorite—and tomato baskets filled with chicken salad and fresh fruit garnished with sugared grapes and mint leaves. Luci's "signature picture" on the windows with the impish, grinning face that Helene had drawn more than a year ago for Luci's eighteenth birthday party still looked down on us.

Mrs. Nugent, who is at home with these young people, and I sat on the sofa and watched the opening of the gifts. Luci had stacked them in a basket and went from bridesmaid to bridesmaid—to Lynda Bird first—and gave them gold charms and bracelets with a little floral bouquet centered with deep pink rubies—tiny ones—on each charm the name of the bridesmaid and the words "A *bouquet of friendship and love—Luci— 8/6/66.*" There were squeals and hugs and tears.

By 9 the party was over and everybody could have gone to bed. But nobody seemed in the mood. We went downstairs to the theater and watched an old movie, *Home from the Hill*, because I had told Lynda Bird I would like to see George Hamilton who appeared in it. In the middle of the movie Lyndon walked in with Mr. Nugent. They had been to the ball game to see the Washington Redskins and the Baltimore Colts. Pat and his father, for Pat's bachelor party, had taken all the young men who will be in the wedding to a private room at the stadium—"The Dugout"—where they had had a spread of hamburgers, hot dogs, and soft drinks and watched the ball game—a unique and certainly a harmless bachelor party.

Saturday, August 6

Luci's wedding day dawned clear and bright and beautiful—all we could wish. What I remember of the morning was a montage. I put on my white hostess robe that Lyndon had bought me in Paris ten years ago and went in to see Luci. She was eating breakfast while Jean Louis combed her hair.

A vintage screen rescued from the musty storehouse had been stretched across the East Hall, concealing what had become a beauty parlor for the day. There were tables, mirrors, chairs, hair dryers, and chattering bridesmaids in robes with their hair being teased into high hairdos, and Jean Louis running in and out.

I had asked Helen to be the guardian of the fifty-eight-year-old rosepoint lace handkerchief made by Luci's great-grandmother Ruth Ament Huffman Baines, for the wedding of her own daughter, Josepha Baines Saunders. This was Luci's treasured "something old," a link with her grandmother's family. "Something new" was her wedding dress. (Will it be the "something old" for a bride in the future? I hope so.) The rosary, given by Pope John to Lynda Bird, was her "something borrowed." Her "something blue" was a gold locket tied with a blue satin ribbon that had belonged to Mrs. Nugent and contained baby pictures of Pat and Jerry, Jr. And she actually wore a sixpence in her shoe—the first of many she received—a gift from the general public. Lynda Bird was running around the East Hall singing, "Get Me to the Church on Time."

I dressed early and went upstairs to see Mrs. Nugent. She looked lovely in a blue-lace dress.

Downstairs in the State Dining Room I saw the exquisite chandelier intertwined with clumps of delicate white flowers—freesia and a trace of greenery. It was dreamlike.

Lynda and the bridesmaids left on time, followed by Lyndon and Luci. He looked so handsome. A cutaway was meant for a tall man—a commanding man. Mrs. Nugent and I were in the car following them. At the bottom of the long steps, Mrs. Nugent disappeared on the arm of an aide to go to the elevator. Then I was climbing the stairs with an aide in the hot noon sun on this most sweltering day of the summer.

Inside the church we went to the bridesmaids' rooms to wait. I was already wilting. There was Corky Hand, starched and solemn in a white suit. Some adult was holding the white satin pillow, lace edged, on which the rings reposed—Luci's twin small bands, and Pat's big band—securely tied with ribbons until the fateful moment. Bader Howar was there in a long white dress, clutching her flowers in a straw basket. Mrs. Nugent and I were the first down the aisle—she, at her request, between two Marines—a salute to her other son, Jerry, who is in Vietnam. A message came from him: "Mr. and Mrs. Pat Nugent: Congratulations Paddy and Luci. Sorry I cannot be there but you know how it is. See you in September. Best wishes. Jerry." And he had toasted them in C rations!

I walked down the aisle as though in a play, thinking not such deep thoughts as "This is the last moment she belongs to us alone," but looking at the pageantry of the altar and the mosaic of Christ above it, swept along on the tide of music from the organ, caressing with my eyes the white bouquets of flowers that marked the ends of pews and the topiary trees with white roses and white carnations. (One of the minor crises was to discover that Luci was allergic to carnations, so we had to switch to roses near the altar.)

I felt a warm tide of love as I walked down the aisle. So many were there who had meant so much in Luci's life from the moment she entered the world! Our missal had been marked "stand," "sit," "kneel"—one of the thousand and one logistic triumphs for Bess, who knew that we, sitting in the front row, would have difficulty following the ritual.

Down the aisle they came! Phyllis Nugent first and then all the bridesmaids—each one lovely. At last came the moment for Luci and her father. When she reached the foot of the steps leading to the altar, Luci turned to her father and patted him on the shoulder. He gave her to Pat, and took his seat beside me. Bess said, "I do not remember him looking at his watch one single time during the service, which lasted longer than an hour." (To his eternal credit!)

The missal was worth all the artistic effort that had gone into it—the elegant binding, the gold drawing of the Shrine on the outside, the words on the first page, *"Bound by the strength of their love, their hope, their joy, in their life together, marriage becomes a golden chalice, capable of containing all their trials and happiness when taken as one in the name of Jesus Christ."* Never once as far as I could see did Pat and Luci fail in the complete dignity and grace of their deportment in the interminable ceremony. At one point I saw Helene Lindow rise from her kneeler and disappear into the wings. I knew she must be faint.

Hale Boggs read the epistle in a clear, commanding voice. I was glad that so good a friend, so strong a Catholic, had been chosen by Luci to do it. I strained—we all strained—to hear the answers to the questions put to the bride and the groom, but we could not.

And then there came the fateful moment when I saw Lynda at her kneeler put her head down completely. From then on I watched only Lynda. I turned the pages of the missal to see how much longer the ceremony lasted. We were on page 19—the Lord's Prayer. I prayed for it to be over soon. A priest went across and spoke to Lynda. She shook her head. I was tensely hoping for Dr. Young and smelling salts. I knew there were smelling salts close by for such emergencies. Any movement on my part would be too conspicuous. And then suddenly, she slumped to an almost sitting position at her kneeler. Another priest approached—she shook her head. He brought a chair. She did sit in it, and gradually her head came up. I could see her father straining, wanting to go to her, knowing that he couldn't. And then the priests were offering Holy Communion, using the Texas chalice.

Very soon it was over. At the last moment Archbishop Patrick O'Boyle read a telegram of congratulations to the young couple from Pope Paul, sent, I believe, in the name of the Secretary of State at the Vatican.

Luci and Pat—arm in arm—her face with a look of transport and Pat dignified and steady—walked toward us. Lynda rose with her head high, in command of the situation, and joined the best man. When Luci reached me, she stopped and kissed me and gave me a rose from her bouquet and kissed her father, crossed to the other side of the aisle and kissed Mrs. Nugent and gave her a rose. And then she and Pat were walking joyously up the aisle.

The bridesmaids and the groomsmen came down, two by two. As Susan Ray passed I thought she looked as though she would faint any moment. She almost reached the door and then was propelled to one side for smelling salts. Lyndon and I paused on the way out, so that when we emerged we were part of the crowd, making our way down the steps. Luci, in a billow of white in the bubble-top with Pat by her side, was waving to the people who had gathered to see her. I myself did not see the pickets. I understand they were there somewhere.

Back at the White House we had a few minutes on the second floor to recoup before we all grouped in the Green Room—Luci and Pat, the two sets of parents, all the bridesmaids and groomsmen. And then out onto the Portico for the wedding pictures. Pat and Luci, the Nugents, Lyndon and I, stood at the railing facing the battery of all the nation's press and TV, thoughtfully concealed behind a band of blooming trees and flowers (which they will contribute to the city's parks tomorrow). Then all the bridesmaids and groomsmen descended the winding stairs (their names had been pasted on the steps in the "dry run" the day before) for the group picture.

Upstairs I took my little rose Luci had brought me from her bouquet and went into the Yellow Room with the family Bible. I sat down at the desk and wrote in the Bible, given to us by Lyndon's mother the first Christmas we spent in our forever home, the Ranch. Carefully I wrote the names and place and date of Luci's wedding. I pressed the rose on that page.

It was a little after 2:30 when we gathered in the Blue Room to form the receiving line. Lyndon, with Luci and Pat next to him, and then Mrs. Nugent and me and Mr. Nugent at the end of the line. This was so I could explain to both the Nugents and they to me that "This is Ann Pittman, one of Luci's fifth-grade friends," and "This is Ag Neff who owned beloved Camp Mystic," and "This is Dr. John Washington who has taken care of Luci from the day she was born." And they could tell me who all the Waukegan cousins and aunts were and the great flock of clergy. Never has there been such a hugging-and-kissing receiving line! And I would have had it no other way. Long and tiring, true. But dear and forever-to-be-remembered by me—and I think by many. As one reporter aptly put it, "It was shoulder-to-shoulder with the notables, with lesser known figures, neighbors of the Nugents, former neighbors of the Johnsons, doctors, dentists, lawyers, preachers, camp counselors, ranch workers, college classmates, relatives." And that is what I loved about it! . . . And each with a bond to Luci.

In the East Room the cake rose like a great glistening Taj Mahal—seven tiers decorated with swans, white roses, and lacy arches like cathedral windows between the tiers, the whole edifice topped with a bouquet of lilies of the valley.

Luci picked up the cake knife and began to cut a slice from Ferdinand's work of art. She gave me the first piece after a bite for Pat, and they went on the dance floor. From this point it was all medley and confusion to me.

At a little past 5 I went upstairs to check on "Operation Departure." For the first time in this day of wonderful precision I came face to face with a crisis of planning. Luci's going-away costume had gone away! We had planned for most of the suitcases to go with the first Secret Service man to their honeymoon destination; those that would be needed for the night were taken to the getaway car. Luci's going-away costume—a beautiful deep pink with a pink floral turban—was to have remained behind in the closet. But it had been taken away accidentally.

Luci was adamant. She would *not* throw her bouquet in her bridal dress and then slip quietly away in an inconspicuous old school outfit still in the closet. After a great struggle we frantically sent for the dress and hat. Fully an hour passed, while guests milled around downstairs, dancing, eating, drinking champagne, waiting impatiently on the lawn. Liz came in with a harried look, wanting to know what she could tell the press. She needed to "put the lid on" if Luci had departed.

It was after 6 when Luci, glowing in her recovered going-away costume, and Pat and Lyndon and I went to the first-floor balcony. Below on the lawn were ranged all the bridesmaids and remaining guests—each with a bag of rice tied in pink net. Luci carefully threw her bouquet. It fell closest to Lynda and she retrieved it. Rice filled the air. With a wave and a hug and "Mother, you've given us the most beautiful wedding" breathed in my ear, and reaching up once more like a little girl instead of a bride to kiss her father—Luci and Pat were gone.

But not quite gone. "Operation Departure" was from then on nobody's business but the Secret Service's and Luci's and Pat's and mine—or so I believed. A few minutes later I went to Luci's room to find her gone. That child who takes forever to dress had, in five minutes' time, put on an inconspicuous dark dress and Jean Louis' wedding gift to her, a half-hairpiece that looks like casual shoulder-length curls. She hadn't left the house. She was somewhere waiting for word that all was in readiness.

I went upstairs where Mrs. Nugent had gone to take a rest. She was curled up on the sofa, and there was Luci beside her, looking like the Luci who ought to pick up an algebra book and a Latin book and get off to school. We waited tensely for the phone to ring. In a minute the call came. Luci kissed us both and dashed off down the hall. I followed her to the elevator and watched it go down. I knew that she was supposed to go to "B"—or so I thought—and that they would go out through the tunnel into the Treasury and into the basement garage. There would be the inconspicuous black sedan and, crouched on the floor of the car, they would begin the drive to New York to spend the night at Mary Lasker's town house.

Down went the elevator—from 3 to 2 to 1 then back from 1 to mezzanine. My heart almost stopped. I do not know what happened. I shall have to wait till she returns, if ever, to find out.

I had gathered kinfolks and some of our oldest friends in the Yellow Oval Room. We had three television sets and we all grouped around them, resting our feet, having a drink, and watching the day we had lived through.

We heaped our plates from the Daniel Webster buffet in the family dining room—the very first buffet of that sort I remember having here in this house. Then back we went to the Truman Balcony to exchange our special remembrances of the day. The Truman Balcony was flooded with memories and love as we said good-by at an early hour. I had one ear cocked for news over the TV or radio about the children's whereabouts and I was relieved that no word had come.

By 11 the great, great day was over—happily, beautifully, to our hearts' delight—a part of the memories of this great White House.

Saturday, August 20

NEW YORK, RHODE ISLAND,
NEW HAMPSHIRE, VERMONT,
AND MAINE

It was a day filled to the last quivering minute with scenery, signs, sensations, and crowds of people—at airports and in parks—on our five-state tour of New England. It began early at the Nevele Hotel in Ellenville, nestled in a valley of the Catskill Mountains. At every airport the fences were lined with thousands of people. Many of them were children, and nearly everybody was smiling. There were lots of signs—many homemade —nearly all friendly. School bands led by pretty girls with batons briskly played their welcome. When Lyndon approaches such a crowd, he is likely to turn in one direction, quickly shaking hands as he strides along, smiling a quick greeting, a long handshake, a stop at a pretty child. And I usually go in the other direction, because if he doesn't get to see them all, seeing me is at least something of a substitute.

Some people don't shake hands—they cling. There is always the little boy sitting on his daddy's shoulders, another little boy shinnying up a tree or a flag pole, and there are always the solemn-faced youngsters too small to reach above the fence and I try to lean down and talk to them. I never have the feeling that crowds can be dangerous, except in stepping on each other's feet and perhaps in pushing against a small child as Lyndon and I try to move through.

There is, on the other hand, a current of feeling that you can almost touch between the President and the crowd—of interest, of excitement, of almost a sustaining strength. But knowing its power I can understand something of the danger if that feeling changed to hostility.

There is always the patient-faced old lady, the rough-handed factory worker, the farmer whose face is browned by many summers. Do I imagine that he looks more philosophical than the rest? The little girl who simply couldn't get on another freckle, the sobering young men in uniform—these crowds are wonderful montages of America. I have so many vignettes in my mind—two in particular. One, a group of nuns, standing at a corner jumping up and down in giddy excitement, their black habits bobbing, shrieking like teen-agers. And another, a group of little girls in leotards or fluffy ballet skirts waiting for the President's car. Apparently a dancing class in a nearby building had turned out to await his arrival.

The first real speech of the day was at Rhode Island University in Kingston. There was a platform in the quadrangle surrounded by the old buildings. I have a memory of red brick and ivy and a sea of faces. And in the right-hand rear of the quadrangle a slowly moving line of demonstrators against Vietnam. One huge sign, "STOP ESCALATION." Others I could barely see except for the words "BOMB," "VIETNAM," "PEACE." It was a good speech on restraint in Civil Rights demonstrations. The Molotov cocktail, Lyndon said, destroys far more than the police car or pawn shop. It destroys the basis for civil peace and social progress. And also, speaking of Civil Rights demonstrators themselves, no one needs the law more than they. Further on, he emphasized that breaking the chain of poverty will require time. "We deceive ourselves and we deceive the poor as well, if we imagine there is some magic sword, some system of federal funds, that can cut this chain and cut it with just one stroke."

My only objection to campaigning in New England is that it is so heavily populated that there is never time to catch your breath between stops. There were only thirty minutes before he spoke at a luncheon of the Navy League at Manchester, New Hampshire. It was a good speech on Vietnam. I remember particularly the lines, "Perhaps it reflects poorly on our world that men must fight limited wars in order to keep from fighting larger wars; but that may be the condition that exists today." There was a young soldier in the crowd and when I saw Lyndon introduce him and ask him to stand up, I knew from the boy's face that it was a complete surprise. He was just back, wounded, from a tour in Vietnam. He became a part of the speech.

Our next stop was Burlington, Vermont, where we were met by Governor Philip Hoff, his wife, and their three children. We boarded helicopters and went to inspect a tri-town water system—the first of its kind in the United States, financed jointly by the State of Vermont and the United States Department of Agriculture. This was Senator Aiken's special project, and he had asked Lyndon to come and dedicate it. Senator Aiken feels that such systems will soon be as much a matter of course as are REA projects.

It was beautiful country! Lake Champlain below us, sparkling clean—beautiful. What a contrast to Lake Erie and its pollution. The Green Mountains on one side and in the distance the Adirondacks in New York. And below us farms so lush and green and manicured that they looked like country clubs.

Vermont is a land you fall in love with. Someday I am going back and hunt for covered bridges and visit their museums and follow autumn from Maine through Vermont all the way down to Virginia.

We arrived at Battery Park—an absolute picture of a place—elm-shaded, peaceful, bordering on Lake Champlain with a view behind us that made me want to sit backward on the platform. There were militiamen, I suppose in the Revolutionary-day costume of Green Mountain Boys, standing at attention at each side of the platform.

Somewhere during the day, Lyndon had begun asking me to stand up and say a few words. I cannot even remember whether I did here, but I know that I was most moved to do so here because I simply loved it. There were lots of signs—some thanking me for my part in the beautification program. Lyndon's speech here was on beautification and conservation. "We are a people whose national character was forged in the out of doors among just this kind of God-given splendor," he said. "I want to pledge to you this afternoon . . . that we are going to retain that splendor in America."

Our next hop was to Brunswick Naval Air Station in Maine. There we embarked on a twenty-four-mile motorcade to Lewiston. I sat next to Senator Margaret Chase Smith. She had been with Lyndon on the Naval Affairs Committee for many years, and later on the Armed Services Committee, and there is a bond between them, a great respect and liking untrammeled by the difference in parties. Senator Edmund Muskie and Lyndon rode together as we approached Lewiston City Park. Lewiston is a small town. There was a gingerbread bandstand decorated with red, white, and blue bunting, bearing the date 1861, and a statue of the Union soldier. There were flags and balloons everywhere, and someone had put a flag in the crook of the soldier's arm. On the left there was a water fountain, vintage 1890, and it all looked like a page out of history.

Lyndon's speech here concerned inflation. He said that what America needs now is a strong dose of self-discipline.

I am continually surprised these last six years at how at home, at how in tune, I feel with New England. Growing up in Texas, it was a legendary land on the other side of the moon to me, and I thought I would feel an utter stranger. But I am charmed with it.

We motorcaded to Portland and often there were crowds along the way on the main turnpike and jammed along the overpasses. Somewhere Lyndon stopped the motorcade at a Dairy Queen. (He's been doing this all his life!) There was a sign, "DAIRY QUEEN WELCOMES LBJ!" but this welcome was no more eager than his own for two heavily piled cones of ice cream.

When we reached the State Pier at 8—an hour and a half past schedule —there was a large crowd. With a final burst of energy I shook hands with a long line and then staggered gratefully up the gangplank of the USS Northampton, to the shrill tune of the pipes. But this was not the end. Lyndon suggested we invite all the Senators and Governors aboard to have dinner in our dining room! I summoned James Symington. We checked the list, dispatched messengers to deliver invitations, set up two long tables in the main salon, and arranged the seating. Everybody had a drink and we all sat down to a good lobster dinner, what else?

A day like this is an exhausting seminar on the geography, economy— the look of the land and people who make up our country.

THE WHITE HOUSE

I spent today shopping in New York but I caught the air shuttle and was back at the White House by 5. I was at loose ends and bored with my own lack of achievement today for I couldn't seem to settle anything.

About 9:30 P.M. I walked into the West Hall to find Lyndon immersed in a stack of papers. There was a pretty little package on the table in front of him—a small valuable-looking package. He said very casually: "There is something you will want to open." I assumed it was a birthday present to him from somebody, since the day after tomorrow is his birthday. I opened the box and there was a diamond ring—beautiful, round—a dream of a diamond—the very one I had picked out as the one I would like to have if I could ever have one. I dissolved in laughter and tears. I didn't think—with the wedding and all the expense—I would have it before I got out of the White House, if ever . . . A "nothing" of a day, except one wonderful event.

All these years I've taken a rather condescending view of women who wanted or needed diamonds, saying something like this: "A diamond is just a shiny rock that advertises that a successful man cherishes you. And I already know that, so I don't need it." Now I find myself, at fifty-three, proud to have that "shiny rock," delighted to be told that I am cherished.

LBJ RANCH

This is Lyndon's fifty-eighth birthday. I woke to the drumming sound of rain on the roof. It rained all morning and by mid-morning we had had an inch, and that was the first of Lyndon's birthday presents. The second was that he told me that he had had the best night's sleep in a long time.

We sent platters of cookies and gallons of coffee to the hangar, where the press—arriving in buses from San Antonio—were marooned by the rain. They came inside, finally, to sit on every possible chair, on the cushions on the hearth, on the piano stool, or to stand in the corners, around the bridge table, while Lyndon sat in his big reclining chair and I beside him. He talked for nearly an hour. "A purely Johnsonian performance," one newsman recounted. He was counting his blessings and finding them plentiful. The blessing that he considers the best is "the opportunity (he) never had before of waging war on the enemies of mankind—poverty, ignorance, disease, ugliness—and waging it with some success."

Off and on during the morning I had been on the phone with Jesse, checking on other guests that I had asked him to call—among them the Frank Erwins, the Don Thomases, the Tom Millers from Austin, and our Blanco County neighbors the Bill Heaths. The Moursunds and the Winters from Johnson City, of course. And Lynda Bird had invited Joe Batson.

About 4 they began to arrive, and about three carloads of us started out in tandem, or as Lyndon would describe it "Round Mountain fashion," men in one, women in one, followed by Secret Service. I've never seen the Ranch so green in August. The rain is a benevolence from Heaven. There are not many flowers—just the goldenrod along the river and the sunflowers in the fence rows. And there is snow-on-the-mountains—everywhere —especially in the meadows.

We had the birthday dinner at the Ranch in the evening, with thirty-two of us. I seated John on my right and Nellie on Lyndon's right, and everybody else just found a place and we concentrated on barbecued beef and ribs, brown beans and slaw, hot homemade bread—followed by angel food cake and homemade peach ice cream, with a wonderful chocolate cake that Mariallen had brought Lyndon with his brand on it. Without thought of discipline or diet, we ate, with fine Roman abandon.

It was late when we went into Lyndon's office to open his presents. The office staff had commissioned paintings by G. Harvey of the Ranch house and of the house where he was born. I gave him a seaman's chest—a crude wooden chest in which a German immigrant family had brought its worldly goods to this country in the 1840's. My present was no great hit. He said, "If I live long enough I guess Lady Bird will get enough of these chests!" I am chagrined with myself. There must be something I could give him that would surprise, excite, elate him. The only thing I can think of is to learn how to do my hair, keep my lipstick perfect, and be devoid of problems.

Neva and Wesley West called from Houston. Altogether it was as happy a birthday as one could want. And I offered up my own thoughts of gratitude to fate, to the Lord, that we had lived to have such a birthday.

Fall 1966

This was one of those days when the greatest courage is to get out of bed and start tackling the day's work.

We woke up to an assortment of headlines: "DEMOCRATIC POLICY COMMITTEE RECOMMENDS MOVING TROOPS OUT OF EUROPE." Apparently the decision was unanimous—with such names as Dick Russell and Russell Long and Mike Mansfield on it. With no evidence that the Russians plan to pull back their forces, this seems like playing poker with a serious adversary and showing him your hand before you begin betting. Then there was also a story in the *New York Times* with details about a proposed tax measure, including removal of the 7 percent tax credit for plant expansion. All these details were known to only two or three people. How did they get in the paper?

I talked about our California trip with Liz over a hamburger in my bedroom. And then I had a long session with Lonnelle Aikman of the *National Geographic*, who is doing

417

the script for the new book, *The Living White House*, giving her some anecdotes about our life here, particularly Lynda's and Luci's part. There was one amusing thing in the paper today and that was a delightful picture of Luci, carrying an enormous grocery basket which they say totaled $30.13, causing Pat to wince. Luci's whole behavior reminds me of Clark Clifford's estimate of the wedding. "The only thing we could have done to make it better," he said, "was to plan it for the summer of 1968."

This afternoon we went to the wedding and reception of Bob and Margy McNamara's daughter, Margy. It was nearly 6 o'clock when we left. Lyndon returned to his office and I went to sign mail. I worked and worked and time passed and Lyndon did not come home to dinner. Finally near 11 I had a little piece of steak, and then, at last, I got a call: "Won't you come over to Lyndon's office?"

I went over and there he was with about a half-dozen men—among them Congressman Carl Albert, looking very weary, and Joe Califano, still looking bouncy. Carl told me he "didn't see how Lyndon could do it." Nevertheless Lyndon was in excellent form. I thought of how the day had begun—the morass of problems as we read the morning paper. And I thought, this man deserves what he gets in terms of achievement. There is certainly no royal road to success. It is work, work, work. I implored the men to come and eat stuffed peppers and black-eyed peas and corn-bread and buttermilk. And just before 12 I got the three of them to sit down—Carl, Joe Califano, and Lyndon. The rest of the staff melted away. It was a very country dinner. And then for Lyndon, night reading, and for me, sleep.

Labor Day USA Style, Monday, September 5

MICHIGAN, OHIO,
AND PENNSYLVANIA

Labor Day was aptly named—a crescendo of work from morning till past midnight. We helicoptered to the National Airport this morning and flew to Detroit with a contingent of Michigan and Ohio Congressmen. When we arrived at Wayne County Airport, we were met at the foot of the steps by Governor George Romney. He was very courteous and I consider his being there to meet the President a mark of good manners.

My impression of Detroit has been one of a city satiated with political figures, too sophisticated to care whether a President visits. Speaking in Detroit on Labor Day is a long tradition. The Labor Party in its heyday could turn out a crowd of one hundred thousand in Cadillac Square. That heyday is long past, I think. There was no parade today. There was a scattering of people along the street but no great turnout. Cobo Hall was respectably full, some five thousand people.

A newspaperman told me later that the proverbial crowd for the Labor Day speech in years past had been brawny men in blue shirts and women in ginghams. Now there were almost no blue shirts. Nearly everyone had on a coat and tie and looked prosperous. Labor has moved into the middle class, and that's good.

There was a heckler who interrupted Lyndon's talk with shouts of "Let's settle the war in Vietnam!" His neighbors began to shush him. Suddenly, in the middle of his speech, Lyndon departed from his text—"Those troops will come home, their bases will be turned over for constructive peacetime purposes, as soon as that vicious aggression stops. And I may add to all whom it may concern. If anyone will show me the time schedule when aggression and infiltration and 'might makes right' will be halted, then I, as President of this country, will lay on the table the schedule for the withdrawal of all of our forces from Vietnam." The great hall responded as one man. They rose to their feet in a prolonged cheer that laid to rest the heckler for the rest of Lyndon's speech.

We had a hurried bite aloft on the thirty-minute flight to Battle Creek. There were an estimated sixty-five thousand people along the way to the Battle Creek Sanitarium, and none of them more thrilled than I! I had been here forty-two years ago with Aunt Effie for a long stay at the Battle Creek Sanitarium where she was a patient.

Lyndon's speech was part of the celebration of the one hundredth anniversary of this health center—famous in its day and still functioning. Memories rushed through my mind of the great white building with its parklike surroundings, and of Dr. John Harvey Kellogg, quick of step in his eighties and always dressed in a white suit, conducting calisthenics for everybody gathered out in front of the building before breakfast. I remember sitting in the dining room and hearing a ripple of excitement run through the crowd—"There goes Senator La Follette." A lot of famous people came here in that day. Not surprisingly, it was smaller than I remembered, things usually are forty years later, but otherwise very much the same. Lyndon spoke in front of the Main Building on a platform. After saluting Battle Creek Sanitarium and its one hundred years, Lyndon spoke of the health achievements of this Administration and of his aspirations to give to the world the medical knowledge we have accumulated.

The freshman Congressman he hoped to help, Paul Todd, was at our side every moment. There was no direct plea to elect him—just praise for his good work, as Lyndon had been doing all along with the members.

We hurried back to the airport for the short ride to Dayton, Ohio, which last week had been boiling with enough racial unrest to call out the National Guard. There was no sign of it, however, when we arrived at Cox Airport where thousands of people were lined up along the fence. Some of them, I heard, had waited as long as eight hours. A school band had been playing briskly for an hour before we arrived. Lyndon and I were first off the plane, with Governor James A. Rhodes close behind us. Always at hand was the Congressman he hoped to help there—Rodney Love. Lyndon walked, we shook hands. Senator Frank Lausche, that authentic maverick of the Democratic Party, met us and went with us the rest of the day—a real barometer that Lyndon stands well in Ohio.

We drove to the Montgomery County Fair Grounds where there was a huge, good-natured crowd. The holiday atmosphere prevailed everywhere. And the day was a case of "it gets better as it goes along"—with Lyndon's enthusiasm rising in direct ratio to the crowd's enthusiasm and size.

Some prize steers were lined up for us to see—polled Hereford and Black Angus. Then we were on the stage facing a grandstand jammed with people, and between us and the grandstand a solid mass of humanity that flowed on out toward the left.

Lyndon spoke on youth and the need for all young people to enter public service for some period in their lives. Suddenly in front of us, out of the sea of humanity, a banner went up: "Thou Shalt Not Kill." We could see scuffling around a small group, with the police moving in and linking their arms around them. Later I heard that there were about thirty-five in the group.

From Dayton we flew to Columbus, Ohio. We were already an hour late when we started driving to the Fairfield County Fair Grounds in Lancaster. Dark was falling, and it had been a long time since our light lunch. The airport was crowded and a solid bank of people was lined up all along the streets. Lyndon stopped again and again, even in the dark, getting out of the car and using the bull horn to say a few words. At a halt, people began to run pell-mell toward his car. I would put the window down in my car and smile and shake hands with those who stopped and stuck their heads in and asked, "Is that Lady Bird?"

The night was deepening and the stops mounted—eight, nine, ten. I asked Jerry to go up and tell Lyndon that we were two hours late and I didn't want him to be exhausted. No sale! We stopped for the eleventh and twelfth times. I heard a message over the intercom from the advance man at the Lancaster Fair Grounds: "Sir, the crowds have been waiting for three hours and it is beginning to rain," in the most plaintive voice. Still we stopped, for the thirteenth time, and for the fourteenth time.

Once I heard over the intercom, "Is there a Dairy Queen place anywhere around?" "No." And then an urgent plea to have something waiting when we reached the grandstand at Lancaster. I could have eaten *anything*. I could imagine how Lyndon, who had poured energy, words, smiles, and handshakes, out into this unending crowd for some solid ten hours or more, needed the lift of some quick energy.

At last we reached the fair grounds. We must have been two hours late. As we rode around the race track to the speaker's stand, I was moving like an automaton but Lyndon was still exhilarated. One newsman said, "If crossroads Ohio were his meat, Lancaster was the President's triumph. He was their kind of President, and they were his kind of people, in Central Ohio." And indeed it was true. The applause was wild, the people were all smiling. It was a magnificent climax to the day. The rain, miraculously, had stopped just before we reached the fair grounds. As far as we could see there were people in all directions. There were twenty-six school bands, the Congressman's wife, Mrs. Walter Moeller, leaned over to tell me.

Finally, weary, elated, we were on the plane. I felt like a vessel into which more scenes, people, emotions, had been poured than it could hold. But it had been a triumphant Labor Day. And instead of depleting him, I had the earnest feeling that it was actually an injection of confidence and strength for Lyndon.

Wednesday, September 7

THE WHITE HOUSE

Tonight we had a reception in honor of the winners of the Tschaikovsky Competition. While I was putting on my red lace dress, Lyndon called and said, "What's this about my having to introduce them? Nobody told me. I am so tired I don't think I can do it. Won't you do it?" My heart sank. I urged him to go on and do it, feeling cruel with every word I said.

The guests were all seated in the East Room by 7:10, and I was waiting anxiously for Lyndon, who came swinging along, his fatigue hidden. I went straight to a seat in the front row, and he to the podium. And here occurred the only flaw of the evening—the spotlight failed to come on. In complete darkness he spoke in his warmest vein, welcoming the young winners of the Tschaikovsky Competition. (I relaxed when he pronounced "Tschaikovsky" correctly. I always *stumble* over it.) He told them that they were a "national treasure," that they wore the brightest badge of all —the pride and admiration of their countrymen.

Then came the performance. Van Cliburn was the Master of Ceremonies. Erich Leinsdorf was invaluable as a sort of a shepherd in charge of all the young winners. I had called on him when we first began to plan the evening.

The first winner was a bass baritone, Simon Estes, a tall, handsome Negro who sang an aria from *Eugen Onegin* in Russian followed by a spiritual, "Sometimes I Feel Like a Motherless Child." Next came a cellist, Stephen Kates. His second selection, "Capriccio," was a brilliant piece of showmanship. And then Veronica Tyler, elegantly gowned and beautiful, who sang an aria from a Puccini opera and a spiritual, "He's Got the Whole World in His Hands." The fourth winner was Misha Dichter, a pianist, whose "Danse Russe," by Stravinsky, made the walls rock. I was delighted to see that Lyndon was enjoying the music. He was applauding heartily for every performer.

Then it was time for the last, Jane Marsh, the first-prize winner, a soprano and the second American to take the highest laurels in the Tschaikovsky Competition. (Van Cliburn had been the first.) She sang three numbers, none of which was familiar to me. "Ain't It a Pretty Night" was an excellent vehicle for her voice. She then sang a Tschaikovsky lullaby, followed by an absolutely wild song from Puccini.

The parents of the thirteen winners had been invited to the reception. Alexander Zinchuk, the Minister Counselor from the Embassy of the USSR, sat in the front row in the absence of the Dobrynins who are in Moscow. The guest list, star studded, included composers, performers, conductors, producers, critics, writers, and represented all segments of the music world. From the world of entertainment came Elia Kazan and the David Susskinds, and Peter Duchin, who had played for us at the wedding, and his wife, Cheray.

When the receiving line was over I told Lyndon, who seemed to have gotten over being tired and had hugged John Steinbeck as he came down the line, that I was going in to visit with our guests but he could go back to work. However, he went in to the buffet and joined the most chattering throng I've practically ever heard there. It was a happy party!

Wednesday, September 21

CALIFORNIA

Yesterday I dedicated Point Reyes as a National Seashore and this morning I breakfasted in bed, with the incredibly beautiful view of San Francisco harbor spread out below me, and the ships coming and going. It spells romance. Nothing gives me the wanderlust more.

I was dressed and ready to go a good hour before time to depart for the airport and there was San Francisco with all its wonders untapped. I called Liz and said, "Let's see what we can crowd into this hour." So we set out to visit Lombard Street, with its terraced gardens and hydrangea hedges, some of its houses old and quaint, some modern with a glass wall or balcony that sought the view, and the hibiscus espaliered on the wall —bougainvillea in a riot of color—a brilliant fuchsia with a lovely weeping habit of falling over the garden walls. I am sure that anybody who lives on Lombard Street reads good books and drinks good wine.

Next we went to Ghiradelli Square. It was an abandoned chocolate factory until some imaginative businessman hired the architect Lawrence Halprin who brought it to life. It centers around a vest-pocket park with a winding stair and eucalyptus trees. Antique shops, book shops, craft shops, restaurants, and a theater lined the sides of the square, so you could shop by day and dine by night. There were a few tourists about, and one who was taking pictures said to me, "Lady, I need somebody in my picture, would you move to the other side of the fountain so I can get you in it?" I did so. I am quite sure she didn't recognize me then— and perhaps never.

We boarded the cable car—that old-fashioned trolley that valiantly works its way up the steep hills of San Francisco, and rode to the Fairmont Hotel. The newspaperwomen were milling around in the lobby asking, "Where have you been?" I was delighted to tell them and for once felt fairly articulate. On the way to the airport with Bernice Brown, the Governor's wife, I was impressed by the splendid tree-planting program in downtown San Francisco. They look like topiary trees. Mrs. Brown described to me how their committee—the Governor's Committee on Beautification—had spent four days touring California by bus, stopping at many cities to see their success stories, their good entrance plantings or river fronts, or vest-pocket parks. What a *good* way to spread ideas—to spark one city's thinking about another's.

We left on a chartered plane with the Udalls and the press and arrived at Monterey a little after noon, where Governor Brown and Senator Fred Farr were waiting at the foot of the ramp. We motorcaded to Colton Hall —a mellow old adobe house, pinkish-beige, Spanish-Colonial architecture, with columns and a gallery, and winding stairs on each side, on which ladies in costumes of the 1840's were gracefully posed and waving. It was here in 1849 that California's first Constitution was signed. The Mayor of Monterey, Mrs. Minnie Coyle, joined me on the speaker's stand. There were Mayors from all the surrounding towns and in front of us as far as we could see a happy holiday crowd.

There were balloons rising in the air, bands playing, and gloriously abundant California flowers in every direction. The sponsors and volunteers of a Head Start group had lined up the little five- and six-year-olds by the fence with outstretched hands, and Boy Scouts and Girl Scouts with flags galore formed an honor guard through which I walked to the speaker's platform.

My speech was recognition and applause for them all. "I wanted not only to see the natural beauty of your country but also to salute the citizens and leaders in government who have taken action to preserve this natural heritage. Your coastline, which is your immediate pride and pleasure, is also the nation's coastline, our common western edge. What you have done with it makes all your countrymen applaud. We have misused our resources, but we haven't destroyed them. It is late. It is fortunately not too late, and I know that the people of Monterey Peninsula know that conservation, beautification, call it what you will, is more than just one tree, or one historic building, or one scenic highway. It is a frame of reference, a way of life." It was a short, simple speech with a salute to Governor Brown and Senator Farr, and then, at last, I planted my chestnut tree seedling which had traveled all the way across the continent.

We were late and Liz was prodding us but we made one more short stop—it was Carmel Mission. This mission was built in 1770—one of a string built by Father Junipero Serra, and his bones remain here. It has been restored much as it was then. The old bell in the tower is the one that called the Indians to prayer before our Revolutionary War. All around the quadrangle stood a great crowd of squealing, chattering school children, bright faced and merry, in striped uniforms, and every few feet a smiling sister in her habit, shepherding them.

Everywhere were the lush and brilliant California flowers—bougainvillea, hibiscus, fuchsia, eucalyptus trees. The Governor and Bernice and I waved to the children, and we paused briefly to see the tomb of Father Serra and then hurriedly the motorcade pressed on to the Big Sur Scenic Highway, seventy-two miles of fine, shining thread, a road leaping, bridging, and weaving between a mountain range and the Pacific Ocean. As we rounded every hairpin curve, another view of towering cliffs and rolling surf below came into view.

We stopped at Hurricane Point, close to Bixby Bridge, and there was a huge boulder poised above the Pacific. It bore a plaque with the words of Robinson Jeffers from his poem "Continent's End," "I, GAZING AT THE BOUNDARIES OF GRANITE AND SPRAY, THE ESTABLISHED SEA MARKS, FELT BEHIND ME MOUNTAIN AND PLAIN, THE IMMENSE BREADTH OF THE CONTINENT, BEFORE ME THE MASS AND DOUBLED STRETCH OF WATER." . . . And then a few words saying I had dedicated the highway.

Governor Brown, Senator Farr, Nat Owings, and I each made our brief remarks, and then the four of us stood at the edge of the cliff with the Pacific below us. Ranks of cameramen charged toward us, each jockeying for a better position, inching forward, moving each other aside, and suddenly there was Liz standing in front of us, saying, "No! no! gentlemen; you will not take a picture; I will stand right here until you move ten feet back!" She stood like Horatius at the Bridge, and they, incredulous at first, finally edged back, and back, and back, while I breathed a sigh of relief. We had, unconsciously as they advanced, backed closer and closer to the sheer brink.

This coast is a country of artists and poets and writers: the Robinson Jeffers of yesterday, and the John Steinbecks of today. Someone told me only rich people live here—or people with no money. They come on motorcycles and live under the bridges or in tents or in parks, and we did see a few of them along the way, looking very much at home, and I don't blame them—it is a land you can love—it beckons.

It was a long day and I was getting tired, and the whole thing becomes a blur. I remember the Big Sur State Park and redwoods—the only ones I had ever seen—great giants to me, reaching to the sky. The Governor said they were only about one hundred years old and not like the real patriarchs to the north.

Late in the afternoon we could see high up on the mountain to our left San Simeon, the home of the late William Randolph Hearst, now a California State Park. We approached it over dry-looking ranch country. I saw some of the zebras that Lynda had told me about—ten of them grazing placidly to our right. We kept winding up the mountain to the white, turreted castle with its sentinel cypresses framing the entrance.

We drew up at "Cottage A"—the biggest misnomer I can think of— in itself it was a castle to me—and there was Bess, calm and busy, with word that we had about thirty minutes to get ready for the evening. I raced to the bed, which had come out of some medieval castle. The ceiling above me was an expanse of ornament—carved, painted, gilded, extracted from a medieval palace.

The evening that followed was straight out of the Arabian Nights. A little after 7, dressed in my white satin ensemble, I strolled out in front of the castle. The Governor and Bernice joined me and we started down the steps toward the Neptune Pool. Facing us at the end was a Greco-Roman temple with majestic pillars and a carved façade; behind it the mountains and a sunset sky. The pool was lined with white marble, studded with antique green-marble mosaics in a pattern, and all around it there were life-size marble statues that represented Venus rising from the sea, and a colonnade where we took our stand. Three or four hundred guests filed by—leading Californians, including conservationists, museum directors, college presidents, Pulitzer Prize winners, movie stars, entertainers, socialites, big businessmen, and members of the Hearst family.

While we were greeting the guests, there was a water ballet behind us, and the whole thing was like one giant movie set. When receiving was over we walked to the terrace before the façade of the castle and there, under the stars, were tables covered with yellow linen and centered with hurricane lamps surrounded by flowers. It was a "barbacoa," as they say in California, and I soon realized my white satin was too dressy.

Danny Kaye as Master of Ceremonies for the entertainment began with some gentle jibes at his good friend Stew Udall, and then launched into a take-off on the disjointed phrases of a political speech. (I flinched for many of mine!) A boys' choir sang; there was a Latin guitarist. The whole evening was a fantastic dream, and I had the feeling that I was living in a world that was gone and would return no more, in the castle of the last American Baron. I went to sleep and good dreams, and no movie stars or tycoons or political figures of bygone days came to haunt my slumber.

Friday, September 23

Today began a little after 6 A.M. in Tony's house in Santa Fé. Carried away with the feeling of how bright and beautiful the garden was and how much we would love to share it, late the night before Tony had asked all the newspaperwomen to come out and have coffee and rolls at 7 the next morning. It was 10 o'clock then, but Tony said, "Never fear, Palo here is a 'can-do man' as the President would say." Palo grinned and somehow the delicious rolls and hot coffee were waiting for us in the garden at 7 o'clock as my weary fellow travelers straggled in.

We were in the cars before 8, headed for San Ildefonso Indian Pueblo, Stew briefing me along the way. San Ildefonso dates from the fourteenth century—a cluster of adobe houses around a dusty plaza with a huge cottonwood tree. There are three hundred Indians living in the Pueblo. In one home, Head Start children were being fed, bright-eyed, solemn, silent. In another home we met a family and saw how they lived.

The most interesting experience of all was a visit to the home, studio, and workshop of Maria and her son, Popovi Da. Many of the residents of San Ildefonso are pottery makers but Maria is an artist of renown and her talent was inherited by her son. They told me the meanings of the designs on their pottery—the eagle feather, the clouds, the mountains. She has revived an ancient process of her people in making black-on-black pottery, and has won numerous international ceramic prizes.

When we were back in the cars we headed into the Sangre de Cristo Mountains to see the golden aspens. I had yearned to come to Santa Fé for this sight and it had been a struggle to keep it in the schedule. As we wound up into the mountains, we could see great slopes of gold, in contrast to the dark green of the ponderosa pines and the Douglas fir. When we got into a great grove of aspens, it was magic to look among their white trunks and up through the gold leaves to the blue sky, shivering in the tiniest breeze like fairy castanets.

The only trouble with this trip was that there was not enough participation. I like to row and swim and walk, and wonderful as this was, it was all riding and looking and learning.

Back at the Ranch by mid-afternoon I caught up on the news of Lyndon. It had been a busy four days for him, too. He had appointed Nick Katzenbach to the Number Two spot in the State Department, vacated by George Ball, and Eugene Rostow to the Number Three spot and Foy Kohler to the Number Four. He had gone out to dinner each night, once to Mary Ellen and Mike Monroney's, with Florence Mahoney and George Wood. How I would have *loved* that evening. He had rounded out 1037 days as President—the length of time that President Kennedy served. They have put furrows in Lyndon's brow and weariness in his heart, but all in all it has been a great thousand days.

Thursday, October 6

At 3 o'clock I went down with Lyndon to the East Room for his press conference. My role was to sit in the front row and look pleasant, and yet these conferences always affect me as though I were going into battle. Lyndon looked calm and assured. He announced the appointments of Sol Linowitz as Ambassador to the Organization of American States, Llewellyn Thompson as Ambassador to the Soviet Union, and Ellsworth Bunker as Ambassador to the government of Vietnam. He outlined our coming trip to six countries. We will leave on October 17. The journey will take seventeen days and cover twenty-five thousand miles and will include New Zealand, Australia, the Philippines, Thailand, Malaysia, South Korea, and a refueling stop in Alaska. The important business is the Manila Conference of all nations involved militarily in Vietnam. The agenda will be military and non-military aspects of the war and the search for peace. It will be the longest trip made by any President since Eisenhower's trip to India, Pakistan, and Afghanistan in 1959. Lyndon announced that I would go along, mostly to be with him, and in my spare time to look at historic spots and inspect conservation and beautification projects.

The questions, when they came, were not primarily concerned with the trip. They were inquiries about the conservative candidates in the South, particularly gubernatorial candidates, the stock market, the Cities Bill, rioting in the streets. I was glad to hear the one about the Great Society from Ray Shearer of NBC because it gave Lyndon the opportunity to say:

"We have recommended approximately ninety bills to this session of Congress, after having the most productive session, the last session, in our history. We have passed through both Houses about seventy-five of those ninety bills. I would suspect in the next ten days we can pass another ten. When you pass eighty-five bills out of ninety recommended, I think that is a pretty good box score."

His command of facts, his orderliness of presentation, the strength of what he said, made me very proud. I wish there could have been a little more change of pace or humor.

As I left, one of the newsmen said to me: "Mrs. Johnson, because you were sitting in the front row in that chair, we thought maybe he was going to nominate you to be Attorney General."

Thursday, October 20

NEW ZEALAND AND AUSTRALIA

I awoke early today in the Governor-General's house, Wellington, New Zealand. I was filled with a sense of anticipation and excitement—didn't want to miss a moment—so I walked downstairs. On the stair landing there was a stained-glass window with the Windsor Crest: *"Dieu et Mon Droit"*; and in the great hall downstairs crests of the families of the former Governors-General. Our host, Governor-General Sir Bernard Fergusson, could have walked right out of the pages of a book—tall, erect, with a rubicund face, a monocle, and a bristly white mustache. He is too perfect to believe. His father had been Governor-General, and both of his grandfathers. Lady Fergusson, his wife, was very slim and tall and elegant.

The side halls were lined with pictures of the former Governors-General, and the dining room chairs were done in needlepoint—as part of the preparation, Lady Fergusson told me, for the long-ago planned visit of King George, which never came to pass; Queen Elizabeth saw the chairs when she visited very much later. I had just started outdoors when Sir Bernard and Lady Fergusson joined me. They showed me the tennis courts. My old friends the Japanese cherry trees were beautifully in bloom. There were lilacs and calendulas and calcilarias—it was spring in October here!

We drove down the winding road from Government House, which was lined with school children, scrubbed and wholesome-looking in their uniforms, and out the gate with its imposing arch to the road by the harbor. Impressions I will always remember about Wellington: the beautiful harbor, the steep hills covered with white daisies and yellow broom, purple flowers, masses of wild nasturtiums and calla lilies. The streets were lined with Victorian houses in pastel colors that looked as if they had been the same for the last six decades. A pleasant country and content, or so it seems from a few hours' view.

Our morning was planned around parks and flowers. We went to the Lady Norwood Rose Garden and Begonia House. Then to the top of the hill where we boarded a cable car—a venerable sightseeing vehicle of wood and shiny brass with open windows—and we went down a breathtakingly steep track with a gorgeous view of the Wellington harbor below, with the Secret Service men hanging on to the outside of the car. Back at the Embassy residence, I joined Lyndon for the downtown motorcade to Civic Square.

Describing our arrival the newspapers said: "The staid city of Wellington gave him the warmest, most boisterous welcome in memory that a foreign head of state has received in New Zealand. Sixty thousand people lined the streets to see President Johnson drive from Government House to Parliament in his open-top limousine this morning. Authorities said the crowd was bigger than that which turned out for Queen Elizabeth when she visited Wellington three years ago."

Lyndon stood up in the car and waved and smiled and shouted and shook the hands within reach and did nothing to speed up the journey, so that it took us nearly an hour to drive to Parliament House. For me, it meant being divided between enjoying what was obviously a wonderful welcome from these people we had been warned were staid and cold, and being uncomfortable about Mrs. Keith Holyoake and her guests who were waiting for me at Wareham for our luncheon.

Our reception was overwhelming, but that is not to say that there were no objectors. Outside Parliament House was a group with signs—the now-familiar "Hey, hey, LBJ, how many kids have you killed today?" And of course, "Withdraw from Vietnam." But they were few in number.

After lunch we drove to the airport where we said good-by to the dignitaries. Almost everybody here is Lady this or that, and once more, as in Jamaica, I had that feeling of being an impostor when I signed my name in the guest books that were everywhere: *"Lady Bird Johnson."*

We departed in a New Zealand airplane with the Prime Minister and Mrs. Holyoake to the tune of a thousand New Zealanders singing a beautiful Maori farewell song, with Lyndon having one last foray into the crowd to the delight of the people. On this flight to Ohakea Airbase, we had one of the most pleasant interludes of our visit. I found that Prime Minister Holyoake is not only a botanist but a man of humor. As we passed over the green, verdant country he said, "Look your last. When you get to Australia, it will be all dry."

From Ohakea we went by car across rolling, lush farm country, to a sheep farm. The farms were divided into small fields or "paddocks" filled with the fattest sheep I have ever seen, and marked off with fences or thick impenetrable hedges of furze. We saw the sheep sheds and the precision operation of shearing—a farm worker gripping a sheep magically with his knees and one hand, while with the other he operated electric shears that in less than two minutes cut the fleece off in one whole perfect blanket, leaving the sheep as naked as a newborn babe. The sheep seemed as docile as a rag doll, but the minute he was turned loose, he pitched and reared and ran out of the chute, and I realized what skill was required to hold him while he was being sheared.

We then returned to the airport and took flight for Canberra, Australia. On this trip the difference in time is incomprehensible to me, but the clock said it was 6:15 when we arrived in Canberra. It was sunset and chilly. I gratefully wore my gray coat, stepping out of the plane with a great sense of excitement and expectation to see this country Lyndon had talked about for twenty-four years.

At the bottom of the steps we were met by the Prime Minister and Mrs. Harold Holt, both of whom had visited Washington, and the Governor-General and his wife, Lord and Lady Casey, a remarkable couple— the sort of people who have made England great—and bustling, ebullient Ed Clark and Anne. As we stood ramrod straight for the national anthems, I looked at the bleachers in front of me, filled with people, and behind them, suddenly in the fading light, there appeared a perfect rainbow, happy augury. I had a swift little thrill when I first saw troops wearing that tilted Aussie hat.

There was a twenty-one-gun salute. Lyndon reviewed the Honor Guard and then he spoke: "When I first came here a quarter of a century ago, I thought that I had not left home at all so much did your plains, your hills, and your bush country, your cattlemen, your cattle and your sheep remind me of my native land of Texas." This set the tone for the next three days. Lyndon spoke of the business at hand: "I cannot say that miracles will occur at Manila. I carry no magic wand." Then on to the long hard business of the war against hunger and disease and ignorance. The papers said the airport welcome was "a near-riot. . . . Throughout, the President gave an impression of controlled power. Though conducting himself with poised dignity, protocol apparently means nothing to the tall Texan."

I got in the car with Mrs. Holt; Lyndon and the Prime Minister made their way into the motorcade. Then began the hour-and-a-half-long ride to Government House for the official call on Lord and Lady Casey. On the way Lyndon stopped nine times to speak to the crowd, and I became familiar with Australian responses, "Good on you, mate," a salutation that would translate "Good for you, pardner," and then the crowd cheering, "Hip Hip Hooray," and singing, "For he's a jolly good fellow."

Lady Casey invited me into a private room and we had a few minutes' conversation alone, a gracious gesture. Mrs. Holt told me how the Queen handled the crowds. She said she waved with her left hand for a while and then with the right. She was interested in Lyndon's response to the crowds. She said, "Your husband is a romantic man." He *is*. Mrs. Holt is a jolly, brisk, natural person, very refreshing. A businesswoman, she owned her own dress shops until Mr. Holt became Prime Minister.

The Holts had invited us on an impromptu basis to come to the Lodge, their residence. I was dead-tired, Lyndon was exuberant, and when Mrs. Holt suggested that she give me a plate of supper (fresh garden asparagus) and send me straight home to the hotel, I kissed Lyndon good night and slipped out, but not before I had met a young, soft, well-mannered member of their household—a baby kangaroo, right in the middle of the living room.

Tuesday, October 25

THE PHILIPPINES

Manila was a feast of the picturesque and colorful, of ancient history and vivid contemporary emotions, of scenes that I wanted to remember so much that I felt as overstuffed as a Strasbourg goose.

I joined Mrs. Ferdinand Marcos and the other First Ladies at the conference for coffee. Mrs. Marcos presented each of us a mahogany chest filled with handicrafts of her country. Then we stepped into a small air-conditioned bus and began a tour of the city. First to Luneta Park—an impressive center-of-the-city open space on which Mrs. Marcos has concentrated her beautification efforts. It is a fecund country—everything grows. There had been much recent planting—blossoming shrubs and ornamental trees. It was beautiful, and I was full of praise for Mrs. Marcos.

It was fun to notice what all the other ladies were wearing. Madame

Cao Ky was in an all-white silk suit with a matching turban, very elegant. She was the only one of us who was a match in youth and beauty for Mrs. Marcos, who wore an exquisite embroidered terno of piña cloth. So many of these Oriental ladies are like butterflies. Mrs. Holt in her green-and-white shift and I in my pink linen were quite simple in comparison.

We went to the Intramuros Restoration Project, where great walls built by the Spaniards in the sixteenth century—now crumbled from war damage and decay in places, covered with moss—are being restored. We visited St. Augustine Church built in 1599. One of the things that impressed me most was that during the Japanese occupation in the 1940's hundreds of Filipinos survived internment for four years within these cramped walls, carrying on all the business of life inside the church—cooking, eating, sleeping, making do with whatever sanitary provisions there were. It seems only yesterday . . . Lyndon was in Congress and Lynda Bird was a year old.

Then on to another church—Santa Ana—where archaeological diggings were being conducted by Dr. Robert Fox. A sizable crowd had gathered around the entrance to the church, and we were almost mobbed by young children and shouting, cheering teen-agers as we inched our way to the inner patio. The Filipino people are volatile and expressive and their press the freest and the most aggressive I've ever seen. So many papers, so many columnists!

The Restoration is being sponsored by Mrs. Marcos herself. She had arranged for us to watch the progress of a new dig—once an ancient burial site. The area was roped off inside the patio of the old church. There were partially exposed skeletons—some in a curled-up position—some earthenware vessels that indicated the Philippines had had trade relations with China as much as five hundred years before the arrival of the Conquistadores—about the twelfth century. One of the exposed skeletons in the dig was curled around a small household stove. I noted one of the skeletons appeared to have filed teeth. And when I pointed it out to Dr. Fox, he was pleased and said, "Yes, you're right. That was a very ancient Philippine custom." Then very close to the top of the dig there were Spanish tiles which dated around 1700. It was a most awesome cross section of the life of man, spanning nearly a thousand years.

Several times along the streets I noticed bamboo screening—barricades like fences of palm leaves. I do not know whether these screened off construction or a row of shanties or what. These screens were part of the city's cosmetics for the Summit Conference, I suppose. There were signs on some of the stone walls that had a foreboding look. One of them said, "FIERCE VULTURES." And another said, "WOLVES." I was told that they were put there by gangs of young hoodlums.

We spent a marvelous afternoon visiting an estate owned by the Zobel family in Calatagan—a countryside of verdant rice fields, coconut and banana plantations, pastures of Charolais and Santa Gertrudis cattle—romantically beautiful country ringed by mountains and, every now and then, a glimpse of the sea. The family's elegant country house was full of ancient porcelain and earthenware—Chinese, Thai, early Philippine—which had been dug up from the site when the house was built.

While we were touring the six Chiefs of State—Prime Minister Holt of Australia, Prime Minister Holyoake of New Zealand, Prime Minister Thanom Kittikachorn of Thailand, President Chung Hee Park of Korea, Lyndon, and their host President Marcos—were closeted in Malacañang Palace discussing all the military, civil, and diplomatic dimensions of Vietnam and hammering out a statement that would present their common aspirations for the future of Asia: to resist aggression and improve the economic life of the people. Once more that unfair division of labor between a Chief of State and his First Lady!

The Barrio Fiesta, which made a festive ending to the Summit Conference, took place this evening. I have rarely seen a night to equal it. Mrs. Marcos had had made to my measurements a native dress called the "mestiza terno"—champagne-colored with big puffed sleeves and low neck, and an apron or overskirt, elaborately embroidered, which was traditional for the Barrio Fiesta. Lyndon was presented with a barong tagalog—the thin embroidered shirt with open collar worn outside the trousers.

We rolled up to Malacañang Palace, once the residence of the Spanish Governors, later occupied by American Governors General. The great banyan trees were hung with paper lanterns and the building itself, with its multitude of arches, was outlined in light. When we alighted from the car we were escorted to a light buggy called a "tilbury" drawn by a white horse whose harness was garlanded with flowers. Lyndon was asked if he preferred a driver or would he drive? He drove. I sat beside him, not without a qualm or two, because the grounds were swarming with merrymakers. Off to the right a cockfight was going on, watched by some of the guests, and beyond a parade was forming and there were six tilburies with their prancing horses—one for each Chief of State.

We drove up to the great formal entrance of Malacañang. There were more "Blue Ladies"—Mrs. Marcos' hostess committee—with fragrant leis of sampaguita for each of the First Ladies. We took our places in a box to watch the "santacruzan"—a religious procession and one of the most colorful pageants I have ever seen. Intermingled in the procession were men carrying long bamboo poles on the ends of which huge paper lanterns swayed and bobbed. It was a wild, colorful, wonderful mixture of the strains that make up the Philippines, the Pacific Island background, the Spanish, and the modern West, with a blending of a gay fiesta and the emblems of religion.

We walked through the grounds, moving among rows of booths which displayed a variety of Filipino foods. Fish, pork, and chicken had been cooked in many fashions—some wrapped in banana leaves—as many as fifty different dishes, including one called "balut," an unhatched duckling parboiled in its shell.

We took our seats at a long table in the Hall of Heroes with our backs to the Pasig River. Then came dish after dish, bizarre, hot, and spicy. Sometime during the dinner a bevy of beautiful young girls came in with trays loaded with tiaras made of tiny white flowers. They placed a tiara on the head of each First Lady. But that was not all. There was also a crown of flowers for each of the Chiefs of State. Lyndon accepted his graciously, thanked them very much, and acknowledged it with a smile for Mrs. Marcos. In a few moments it was lying by his plate.

Soon there was general dancing among the three thousand guests. One of the Bayanihan Dance Troop members asked me to dance. I managed to survive—not very gracefully. But the delight of the evening was to watch Mr. Holyoake, still wearing his flowered tiara, dancing gaily, like a jovial Roman Emperor! The orchestra had been playing best-known tunes of all of our countries—"Waltzing Matilda" for Holt of Australia; "Arilang" for President Park of Korea; "Deep in the Heart of Texas" for us; the Maori Farewell Song of New Zealand for Mr. Holyoake.

Sometime during the evening I obtained the autographs of most of the Chiefs of State and their wives. Mrs. Marcos' was dearly put, "To Mrs. Johnson—Love—Imelda Marcos." And I hope someday I will look at it and think that this was a night not only of pageantry, color, and vivid entertainment, but also the night when something important began. The Summit Conference Pact had been completed late this afternoon. The Barrio Fiesta was late getting under way, because the men finished their communiqué so late. Here, at the banquet table, signatures to the final document were added by several of the Chiefs of State.

THAILAND

We were supposed to leave Manila this morning but we were delayed longer and longer by the difficulty of setting up the telephone call between Dr. Burkley and Jim Cain. Finally we got through. Jim had been talking with the throat specialists and Willis Hurst, and any others concerned, and the general feeling was that Lyndon should go ahead with the operation to remove the growth in his throat and to repair the incisional hernia resulting from the gall bladder operation. Jim and probably the other doctors would come to Washington when we got back and set the exact time—it would probably be after Lyndon had had a week or so of rest.

We arrived at the airport about noon, where our hosts—alas—had awaited us in the sweltering heat, and it was wheels up for Thailand, a three-hour flight to U Ta Pao, and we were escorted by sharp-nosed F-105's—three on each wing. The Prime Minister and Ambassador and Mrs. Graham Martin were there to meet us. In a helicopter we flew low over the country-side for the forty miles to Bang Saen. We saw orange-roofed Buddhist temples and monasteries, coconut palms and an oil refinery. There was a field of something I couldn't identify—white, flat areas, like a tennis court, where farmers were spreading out something to dry or mounding it in white piles. I asked, "What is that?" The Prime Minister said, "That's tapioca." I burst out laughing and said, pointing to Lyndon, "Here's your best customer!" The Prime Minister told me that tapioca, indigenous to Thailand, grows as a root and is a staple of their diet. The Thais make a stew out of it with pork and vegetables. It's the main dish in the homes of most peasants.

Our helicopter landed on the beach close to the Lam Tam guest house, the Prime Minister's summer residence. Bang Saen is a seaside resort which nestles between the wooded hills and the picturesque curving bay. There are resort cottages overlooking the gulf—many of them used by Thai officials and wealthy people looking for escape from the heat of Bangkok.

Mrs. Kittikachorn welcomed us, and I was presented with a garland of fragrant jasmine—white and rose and wine and apricot and yellow, in a precise formal pattern made from a million tiny petals. The residence could have been in Florida or California. It was low and rambling and white and very open. There were many verandas and terraces. The grounds were beautiful, with palms and bougainvillea and tropical flowers and a lovely assortment of orchids. The waters of the Gulf of Siam lapped at the edge of the lawn. All the time that we were there we could see a ship plying off shore. Up it would go, and then back. It was some time before it dawned on me that it was a United States naval vessel—a sort of an honor guard because of our presence there.

Mrs. Martin asked what I would really like to do, and I told her I would like to drive around, perhaps with somebody who could speak Thai so we could talk to the people. The wife of one of our officials there who speaks the language came with us. We set out for a ride around an old village with houses made of teak, standing on stilts on the edge of the water. There were "spirit houses" everywhere—brightly decorated little houses—pink and blue, elaborately ornamented—about the size of a bird house, standing on stilts—one beside almost every residence. These houses are to entice the spirits so they will leave *your* house to you.

I asked the driver to stop so I could get out and use my movie camera. I stepped to the side of the road and was just putting my foot into some bushes when Mrs. Martin shrieked, "Snakes! Don't! Come back!" I could see that she was really upset. Feeling rather casual about it, I explained that we had plenty of rattlesnakes in Texas, and there was hardly one under every leaf out there. She answered, very likely not, but these snakes were kraits and cobras. I was duly respectful immediately. I have heard that if a krait strikes, it is instant death and nothing can save you. I stood in the road and got pretty good pictures.

We stopped at one of the Buddhist temples which appeared to be made of an infinite number of tiny pieces of tile—orange ones on top, green shiny ones and blue ones in a design along the walls. It was open, like a pavilion or summer house. At the corners of the roof were the little points going skyward like the tails of snakes. I saw a monk in his bright-orange robe but he paid me absolutely no attention. There was a big plaster Buddha, grinning amiably under a little pagoda roof, with incense burning in front of him.

On the way back I cried, "Stop. There's a monkey on the little wall!" Sure enough it was—a gray monkey with a long tail. I got out and took his picture, and several of his friends joined him. They are wild monkeys, Mrs. Martin told me. They don't bother the people, and the people don't bother them.

Later Mrs. Martin told me that Air Marshal Dawee Chullasapya and his wife, Khunying Aree, had invited us to visit their island a few minutes away by helicopter. They had a glass-bottom boat and a good sandy beach.

I found this irresistible. As we landed on a hilltop on Crystal Island, they were there to meet us, Khunying Aree in a bathing suit. They looked like any American family having an afternoon at the beach. We got in the glass-bottom boat and looked down into a forest of coral—an underwater jungle of cathedrals and spirals, but there were no bright-colored fish doing a ballet among the coral. My hostess proposed that I try one of her bathing suits and have a swim in the Gulf of Siam. I swam far out toward a shrimp boat that had a face with eyes painted on the prow. Marshal Dawee followed me, pushing a rubber float. How unbelievable, to be swimming in the Gulf of Siam with a companion named Dawee.

Too soon it was time to go. I said good-by and climbed the hill and flew home over the sunset sea, looking down at the fish traps, like long arrows, and boats with painted faces, and the billows of pink clouds that gradually faded into gray and then into night and stars.

Saturday, October 29

BOROMABIMAN PALACE,
BANGKOK, THAILAND

Today we made a tour of the Klong. Mrs. Martin, our Ambassador's wife, accompanied us. We went to the Royal Landing, boarded the Queen's own launch—forty feet of gleaming mahogany, shining brass, and white scalloped canopy. Khunying Molee Khoman, the wife of the Foreign Minister, was along, and a lovely young woman whom I had met previously, Wiwan, the daughter of Prince Wan. She is in the Foreign Service and is an excellent interpreter. The wife of one of the Embassy staff was fluent in Thai. Two Ladies in Waiting represented Queen Sirikit, who couldn't be with us because she had a bad cold.

The Klong is a slow, narrow, winding stream, the heart's artery of this exotic capital. People live beside it, trade on it, bathe in it. It is lined with houses—two-storied, made of teak with banisters and rails, orchids in pots on the porches, roofs of tin or tile; with schools that are bursting with children; ancient moss-covered temples whose ornate domes reach toward the sky; little shops that sell hats or coffee or meat and fish. Today it was teeming with life, with hundreds of Thais lining the bank, smiling, waving.

The Klong itself was full of traffic. (What Liz called the "Thai Navy" followed us, and behind them a huge lumbering boat full of the press, with their cameras frantically trying to record these wonderful pictures.) But the real traffic was the people trading. Small wooden boats with a square lip at the front and back, into which the people stepped as easily as I would step into my living room or kitchen, so much at home on the Klong are they. In the boats were their wares: bananas, coconuts, oranges, papayas, crab apples, a stack of roast duck, orchids . . . orchids . . . orchids, vegetables I couldn't identify—some of them looked like squash—shallots, greens, and whole boats loaded with hats for sale. Soon boats began to come alongside us and a woman would offer me a gift of orchids or a basket of oranges or a cluster of bananas. Within an hour we could have gone into business *ourselves!*

Wee Won told me that most of the houses had their own orchards and garden patches behind them where people raised the things they sold. Sights I will remember: a glimpse into a house where I saw a picture of the King and Queen on the wall; in another a small hammock swaying gently, suspended from a beam—a baby's cradle; a sign saying "Cock Fights" and another "Fish Fights"; a white cockatoo swaying on his perch in a love apple tree; a cage of rabbits, but I was told they were not being sold for meat but for pets; a woman cooking her family's meal over a little charcoal stove. Some of the boats were large, obviously lived in by families who probably live and die in their boats on the Klong.

We passed two sawmills with stacks of lumber—teak, I was told, and a coffee shop—a sort of social center, but to me the whole Klong is a social center. Once we saw a man who was up to his chest in the Klong calmly lathering himself with soap—the only one, I think, who did not notice us. There was an old woman who came up to the boat with her gift, and her smile revealed teeth that were quite brown from chewing betel nut.

Many of the groups of boys and girls that we passed had on uniforms of Girl Guides or Boy Scouts or Brownies or Cub Scouts. They were all singing and smiling, and two of them fell in the water, in their excitement. Several times there were tourists, and once, inevitably, someone called, "Welcome to Thailand, Mrs. Johnson. We're from Texas!"

Often along the way there were golden altars decorated with flowers. At the edge of the Klong I noticed a cluster of people sitting cross-legged on the ground. This, I was told, meant they had great respect for me: one keeps one's head below that of a revered person. The real experience for me was the varied tapestry of life, the crowded, teeming life of the Klong itself.

Later at a colorful ceremony, Lyndon received an honorary degree from Chulalongkorn University, witnessed by the Thai Cabinet, including Prime Minister Kittikachorn and as many of the eight thousand students and professors of the University as could crowd in. Beginning in 1938 at Southwestern University in Georgetown and in the twenty-eight years since, I have participated in a lot of ceremonies for honorary degrees. But the Thais take the prize for having the most suitable kind of academic robes. The top professors filed in and then His Majesty, King Bhumibol Adulyadej, escorting Lyndon; everybody had on a robe made of net—sheer, cool, just right for the climate. Lyndon's and the King's robes were banded in gold and red braid, others in pink and silver. They made a beautiful sight. I wish Lyndon could wear this robe at any June academic ceremony from now on where there is no air-conditioning.

The King is a slight, dark, intense young man who seldom smiles. He wears dark glasses because of an eye injury and you feel that he is very earnest about his country and works hard at his job. There is an air of constraint wherever he is present, or so it seemed to me, with everybody being very deferential and dignified.

The King himself gave Lyndon the citation and in Lyndon's speech he made an appeal to the leaders of Hanoi to lay aside their arms and sit down together at the table of reason. He spoke of all the things we could do—constructive things for health and education if we could lay aside our arms. Then he signed the International Education Act, which will bolster international training and research at both graduate and undergraduate levels in American colleges. I was told it was the first time any American legislation has ever been signed on foreign soil. There was one line in his speech that rang in my mind all day: "The central tragedy of our times is the human and material waste that goes into war."

Then Lyndon stepped out into the flag-waving crowd of smiling students (not a protest banner in sight). He was swamped by their reaching hands and engulfed by their cheers. I thought of the warnings we had had all along that the Thais were "a very retiring people who would not express themselves." Lyndon was enjoying it but he was mindful of the King's presence, which always imposes the necessity of being restrained, so he made as little of it as possible, reaching for a few hands, and smiling into all the eyes his eyes met.

I drove with Mrs. Martin across the campus to the Red Cross Building. There Queen Sirikit met us. She is one of the most beautiful women I have ever seen—a sweet face, gentle, composed—every time I see her I remember that I have read she is one of the world's best-dressed women.

I was presented with a Medal of Merit from the golden bowl in which all things are given to one. On my first trip here I thought you were supposed to *take the bowl!* This time I knew better. The Queen talked with me about her work with the Red Cross, the need for more hospitals, and I told her of the Senate Ladies Red Cross Unit, and asked about her cold. It was better.

About 5 o'clock I put on my yellow lace dress—my "Luci's wedding dress"—and Lyndon and I went to Government House for Prime Minister and Mrs. Kittikachorn's reception. With three days in Manila and two days here, I am beginning to feel very much at home with the couple. He is always smiling and she is comfortable and very pleasant. It was a beautiful party, in a large spacious hall. They led us around the room, introducing us to various groups. There was the "American community"—businessmen representing Singer Sewing Machine and the petroleum companies—and government officials, and many Thais.

After champagne and toasts we returned to the Palace about 6. I made a hurried trip to Sala Sahathai where we are giving a banquet tonight in honor of the King and Queen. I talked with Barbara Keehn who has been working on it for several days. She looked harassed. It isn't easy to run a party thirteen thousand miles from your base. She has decorated the hall with swags of yellow bunting and is using round tables and menus and place cards engraved and written at the White House, transferring as much of the East Room and the State Dining Room as possible to this exotic city.

Then I hurried back to the Palace to see the nice hairdresser. After having known me this long she and her assistant have finally stopped approaching me on their knees—a custom which made me extremely uncomfortable.

Just before 8, we greeted Their Majesties at the front steps. The Queen was in ruby red, high neck, long sleeves, girdled with gold with an enormous gold ornament in the front and lovely chandelierlike Thai earrings.

The high point of the evening, I thought, were the toasts, both of them. Lyndon borrowed from Lincoln: ". . . the first offer of assistance between our countries was made in 1861 . . . by your great King Mongkut." (That was the King's great-grandfather—the one in whose household Anna served as tutor; the offer was made to President Abraham Lincoln.) Lyndon explained that King Mongkut knew we were in a Civil War. He wrote to President Lincoln offering to send him some elephants. Mr. Lincoln thought seriously about the proposal, and then he wrote a letter to King Mongkut. He thanked the King and said he would happily accept the offer, save for the fact that the climate in our country was too cold for elephants to prosper. The whole point of the story was that the disposition of our two countries to help each other goes back well into the past. Lyndon said, "Your Majesty, President Lincoln closed his letter to your great-grandfather more than one hundred years ago with these words: . . . 'wishing for Your Majesty a long and happy life, and for the generous people of Siam the highest possible prosperity . . . , I commend both to the blessing of Almighty God . . .' I find myself tonight unable to improve upon those words."

After the toasts, jazz artist Stan Getz and his troupe, who had come over from the United States especially for this occasion, played a medley of jazz for us. It is well known that the King is a jazz buff and has, upon occasion, gotten up and played an instrument right along with the band.

We bade the King and Queen good night about 11:30, urging them not to get up to say good-by to us, as we would leave the country tomorrow morning at a very early hour.

Sunday, October 30

MALAYSIA

At 9:45 A.M. local time we arrived at Kuala Lumpur, called familiarly "KL" by world travelers. I thought by this time I had seen everything in arrivals, but I hadn't. Stepping off the plane onto the usual red carpet, we were met by the King, His Majesty the Yang di-Pertuan Agong, and his Queen and by Prime Minister Tunku Abdul Rahman, our old friend from Washington visits, a very worldly, poised, charming man, himself the son of a Sultan. What made this arrival ceremony so different was the glaring contrast of the old and the new. In front of us was a handsome new airport building of glass and steel. In delicious contrast we were escorted down the red carpet under gold silk umbrellas elaborately tasseled, the symbol of royalty, and seated on a raised dais under an elegant canopy, the Queen and I. I had been given a basket full of orchids by a little girl. There was a twenty-one-gun salute, the two national anthems, and flags everywhere.

Next came the meeting with Diplomatic Corps and government officials, and the speeches. Lyndon congratulated Malaysia for building a free and prospering countryside that can relieve the poverty and apathy on which communism thrives. He spoke of Malaysia's own struggle against the Communist guerrillas which, he said, shows that military action can stop Communist aggression and also that peace as well as the war can be won.

The fourteen-mile drive into the city with Mrs. Stephanie Bell, our Ambassador's wife, was intensely interesting. She gave me a capsule account of the history, economy, and customs of Malaysia. On my left there was a forest of rubber trees, so different from what I had imagined—tall, slim, white trunks mottled with gray, their foliage very high; a few feet up on the trunk there was a chevronlike mark from which the rubber dripped into a cup at the bottom. The work of collecting from this cup was done mostly by Indians, Mrs. Bell told me. The ground was a carpet of ferns.

We traveled on the best roads in Southeast Asia, she told me, and they would compare favorably with any in this country. There was a wide, high median strip, and evidence of landscape planting along the road. We saw signs that said, "SELAMIT DATANG, PRESIDENT AND LADY JOHNSON," and alas, the largest billboards I have ever seen.

I asked about the people who made up Malaysia. Mrs. Bell's answer, and later the Tunku's, was rather unsettling. Not a majority of Malaysians —between 45 and 50 percent—and about 35 percent Chinese, 10 percent or more Indians, the rest a mixture.

The country is trying to ease its expanding population problem by hacking new land out of the jungle. Lyndon was taken to see a village of two hundred families where six years ago there was nothing but jungle and a few Communist guerrilla fighters. I heard the strange story of their form of government. Under the British Rule there were nine Sultans of nine major states, and five smaller states. The British left the Sultans intact, with all the trappings of grandeur and considerable power, but they had a Governor-General in each Sultanate, who lived in a Government House. When independence came fourteen years ago, a system was set up whereby the nine Sultans chose from among themselves a King who would rule for five years, and then be succeeded by whomever the Sultans chose, a revolving kingship. The Tunku is a strong figure, and apparently a well-loved man. He is called simply "Tunku," which means Prince, by everybody.

Kuala Lumpur is a beautiful city surrounded by heavily forested mountains. Its public buildings are a remarkable contrast of the comfortable dignity of a British past and the startlingly modern new Parliament Building, the national Mosque, and the Museum. The Palace is a big, comfortable white house, reminiscent of the Victorian era of British Rule, with many porches, high on a hill. The King escorted me upstairs where there was a large reception room in which chairs were precisely arranged along two sides and at both ends. The King took Lyndon to one end and seated him on his right with a couple of dignitaries flanking them. I sat close by, next to the Queen, who is a beautiful, poised woman. Members of their government and the American party filled the other chairs.

And then an official, their Chief of Protocol, I suppose, advanced in a very ceremonial way, extending to the King his gift to Lyndon—a very elaborate dagger. I felt a slight chill. Lyndon quickly reached in his pocket and gave him a coin, telling him about the old story in our country that when friends make a gift of a knife the giver must accept a coin in return, so the friendship won't be cut. To me the Queen presented lengths of beautiful brocade. Jimmy Symington approached the King decorously, presenting our gift, and then backed away in a sort of shuffle in order not to turn his back on him, causing me to have to suppress a giggle.

Luncheon began with a clear soup, at the bottom of which lay two round white eggs which glared up at me like baleful eyes. The Tunku explained they were quails' eggs. I daintily avoided them. And from then on it was an "ours" and "theirs" affair. Very considerately they proffered us luscious-looking small steaks, green peas, cauliflower, and also a complete meal of their own exotic dishes. The main course was curried rice, yellow with saffron with little raisins in it, accompanied by a large platter of nine delicacies—chutney, little chips of salted fish, shredded carrots, and other things I couldn't name—and to cover the rice, a hot, spicy meat dish that you might have found in Mexico. The Tunku kept warning me that it was hot, and I kept on insisting I was raised in a country where one ate hot things. Up to now my digestion had held out wonderfully, and I had sampled in each country with eager curiosity the dishes of the land. Dessert finally came and I flashed a look Lyndon's way. It was tapioca!—but not as we know it. It was quite firm, in a gray-white mound, served with two sauces, a white one that was milk of coconut, and a black one that resembled chocolate and tasted sweet, but the flavor was unrecognizable. And then there were fruits. The Tunku took pleasure in peeling them for me and explaining what they were. One looked like a large brown nut and when he removed the thick husks there were little orangelike segments, bland and sweet. Another looked for all the world like a large strawberry with thick hairs. And then my old friend around the world—bananas—very small, the size of a man's finger.

Lyndon had been enjoying his conversation with the Queen. He boldly asked her how she had met and married the King. She told him that she had been married when she was sixteen without ever having met him, a match arranged by her parents and his. The King had been married before and had children her age; one of his daughters was her special companion.

I envy Lyndon the ability to get into such conversations but I can think of no way to ask them such interesting questions as "Can a man have several wives?" "Does the husband still obtain a divorce by just saying three times 'You are divorced'?" "What are the rights and economic situation of the women who get divorced in such a manner?" Later I did ask Mrs. Bell, who told me the old Moslem order still persisted, that there were some changes in the wind, an organization to demand more rights and status for women.

In the afternoon Stephanie Bell and the wife of the Minister of Home Affairs came to pick me up, and we went on a tour of Kuala Lumpur. The Mosque was a beautiful building, a marriage of the past and the present—blue tiles, lacy fretwork, and a slim minaret.

On our drive something unnerving happened. I was so caught up in looking at the buildings and scenery that I forgot the crowds looking at me. I asked the car to stop a moment so I could get a picture of the Parliament Building. Suddenly out of nowhere the car was surrounded by a throng, mostly youngsters. I had rolled down the window to take a picture. The people surged forward, and we were enclosed, and Jerry reached back and rolled up the window, for one fluttering second almost catching a thin, brown, clawlike hand that was reaching in. Jerry said, in that voice that he used the night of the bomb incident at the San Francisco Opera, "I think we'd better stay on schedule, if you don't mind, Mrs. Johnson. You are due back at the residence at about this time." I simply murmured, "All right." I was not proud of my own performance. That hand had reached in only in welcome, and I was annoyed at myself that I hadn't calmly and quietly looked from face to face, smiling into their eyes, instead of hurrying away. Later I found there had been a small demonstration; a group of young Chinese had raced up and down the streets, tearing down American flags before we came by. It involved only a handful of people, but one had been shot by the police and killed.

The Tunku gave a sumptuous dinner for us in the beautiful Parliament Building. Midway during the meal the entertainment began, with classical Malaysian dancers. I highly recommend this timing as a civilized custom for eighteen-hour days. It shortens the evening and spices it too. It was a sort of montage of the history of Malaysia. One dance was definitely Indian, another reminiscent of Thailand, and another purely Chinese with figures inside a dragon, then another Malaysian.

It was an interesting evening with a highly articulate host. Theirs seems a hazardous sort of government and yet what it has to show for itself, after only fourteen years of existence, is substantial indeed. A very interesting volatile country, altogether fascinating. I hope I shall come back someday.

Monday, October 31

KOREA

At 7:40 A.M. we departed for Korea, facing a six-hour flight.

Somewhere between Kuala Lumpur and Korea, we flew above Vietnam, right over Saigon. There were U.S. fighter planes accompanying us then. As we approached the "Special City of Seoul," I saw alongside one wing three fighter planes flying in perfect formation, and alongside the other wing three more—a thrilling entry.

Nothing was ever like Korea in all the visits in all of my life! We arrived about 3 o'clock local time. Ambassador and Mrs. Winthrop Brown came aboard the plane, and for the second time on this trip I felt that I was in the hands of very special friends—first the Clarks in Australia and now Mrs. Brown, who had been Peggy Bell of Austin in whose home I had visited when I was in the University back in the 1930's. The Browns are among the most able Ambassadorial couples I have met, and I don't know a job where a man needs a working wife more.

They escorted us down the steps of the plane, between railings festooned with flowers—a mass of flowers from top to bottom—and we were facing a sea of men and women and children, the first emplacement of the two million Koreans who welcomed us. President and Mrs. Chung Hee Park were at the foot of the steps. A squad of ROK Air Force jet fighters zoomed out of nowhere and flew low overhead, leaving streamers of red, green, blue, yellow, and pink smoke, and the bands played our two national anthems. We stood very erect, and the cannon boomed out the twenty-one-gun salute. Anybody whose pulse didn't race was a child of dullness indeed. Standing in a jeep, Lyndon and President Park reviewed the troops. It was thoroughly done, quickly over.

President Park is a slight, dark, strong-looking man. I believe him to be a good friend and a formidable enemy. He looks as if smiling doesn't come easily to him, but he was smiling most of the time this afternoon. He lacks the hero image and glamor, yet there is something commanding about him, something very firm, and I would lay my bet on him. Mrs. Park is smiling all the time, a womanly, gracious, gentle person. She is among my favorite First Ladies who have ever come to visit us in Washington.

During the speeches I raised my eyes to see what the terrain looked like. There in front of us were the austere, forbidding mountains rising dark against the sky; the years 1950–1953, when Korea was a painful word to Americans, loomed darkly in my mind. That was a time of stress and uncertainty, and wrenching national decisions, when about thirty-four thousand Americans died in those same mountains. And now this country, Korea, is one of the success stories of Asia. I hope I shall live to see the same thing happen with the beast that we wrestle with today. Perhaps it was this bond of association that made Korea the most dramatic stop of all for me, although from the very beginning the country seemed stark, almost drab, with little grass and few trees to relieve the grim mountains and the great city.

It was past 3:30 when we got in the limousine and led by our escort of thirty-one motorcycles began the ten-mile drive to the heart of the city. It was a tremendous, emotion-packed two hours. Sights I will never forget: A sea of faces on all sides, and whenever we came to an open square the tributary streets were full of people as far as my eyes could see, and in all the windows above me. The amazing variety of signs, homemade, many of them with pictures of Lyndon: "WELCOME KING OF KINGS," "THE GREATEST LEADER OF THE WORLD," "THE FRIENDLY HANDCLASP WE WELCOME YOU," "WE LIKE LBJ WITH ALL OUR HEARTS." Many seemed to be right out of a Western movie, picturing Lyndon in cowboy boots and a big hat with two guns, saying, "WELCOME, TEXAS GIANT," "GALLOP, COWBOY," "THANKS, TEXAS BOY, WE LOVE YOU," and one hilarious one, "TEXAS BULL WE LIKE," and even one that said, "WELCOME BLUE BIRD." There were big posters of Lyndon and President Park everywhere. It was a man's country.

Once on the edge of town Lyndon made his way through the crowd to a rice paddy, and I saw him balancing atop a narrow dike while he reached over to greet workers in the field. Eight times he stopped to shake hands, standing in the door of the car waving and talking. Once he sat on the roof waving Korean and American flags while the crowd around him went wild. I soon saw that I was no match for this crowd. To get into it was to be swallowed up and devoured, so I stayed inside the bubble-top car with

Mrs. Park and the interpreter, venturing out only to receive flowers and bend over and greet children and wave and smile and nearly get run over as they made a dash for Lyndon, and then back into the car where the stack of flowers grew higher and higher on the shelf behind Mrs. Park and me. We passed a huge monumental arch which Mrs. Park called the South Gate, and on every inch of it on what appeared to be steps were standing girls in colorful native costumes.

Emotions grew higher, the roar of the crowd louder; there was no end to the signs! Lyndon in a mandarin hat, "LEADER OF THE WORLD," "ARCH-ENEMY OF COMMUNISM," "OUR BOSOM FRIEND," "LADY BIRD FLY HIGH," "YOU OUTPOLLED ALL YOUR OPPONENTS IN OUR GALLUP POLL," "PLEASE COME PRESIDENT JOHNSON, APOSTLE OF PEACE," and one whose philosophy was a bit mixed up, "WELCOME TO THE KING OF DEMOCRACY!" Another delicious one, "WE LOVE BRAVE JOHNNY." There was not one single hostile demonstrator or hostile sign.

Between the South Gate and the City Hall Plaza we were showered with confetti and flowers. The air above was thick with fluttering confetti and our windshield covered. At the Plaza when we thought emotions had reached their peak, and there could be no more, we heard the roar of the massed crowd, estimated at 350,000, and a chorus of two thousand girls in bright traditional dress sang the "Arilang" song. High in the air above us floated two giant flags, the Korean and the American, which were anchored by balloons.

Here the Mayor was to receive us and give us the Golden Key to the city. We climbed the steps to the reception platform between two columns of girls in pink satin scattering rose petals, and at the top I turned to face the mass of people. It was an awe-inspiring sight. They swayed like wheat. Some were pushing to get closer, and those in front couldn't move. I could see that some—the girls in the singing chorus—were being trampled. The crowd was on a razor edge between ecstasy and frenzy. It was frightening. Here and there I saw police moving in, making people sit down, carrying out fainting girls on their shoulders.

President Park was speaking impassively. He said the Korean people were welcoming the American President as their closest friend, their most honored guest, the foremost political leader of the free world in this century. "We have been much indebted to you as comrades in arms," and looking at him and at these people I believed him when he said, "Please be assured that ours is not a nation which will indefinitely continue to be indebted to others, but rather is a nation which knows how to requite its obligations, which has a keen sense of responsibility, and which abides by good faith."

Mayor Kim presented the real Golden Key to the city of Seoul to Lyndon. (The Mayor's nickname is "Bulldozer" because he gets things done.) While we were seated waiting Lyndon's turn to speak, he leaned over to me and said, "You've got confetti in your hair. Take your comb and get it out." I shook my head, not wanting to comb my hair in front of thousands of people, and to my embarrassment he took out his comb, leaned over, and flicked it out piece by piece. I was annoyed—so much for my sense of good public relations! It was the thing that caught the eye of the Korean press, all the women, especially, and was repeated to us approvingly over and over in papers and on the radio. Apparently to them this gesture meant that he was solicitous of me, careful with me, and they liked it.

In his speech Lyndon said, "To an American, the free soil of Korea is hallowed ground." He spoke of the Americans who had died in the bitter battles of 1950 to 1953, of our two partnerships against Communist aggression, then and now, of the South Korean soldiers beside ours now in Vietnam, and of Korea's remarkable economic progress through it all. When it was over we made our way from the crowded square, and left by helicopter for our residence at Walker Hill, exhausted by the emotional pitch of the last two hours.

By now we had made a complete circle of the seasons, leaving Washington in the fall, going to the spring of forsythia and tulips in Australia, and here in Korea back to the golden gingko trees and bright red maples— the last of them we had left in October Washington.

This evening I wore my green "Princess Margaret" evening dress and a long cloak made of Korean fabric that Mrs. Kim had given me to the State Dinner given for us by President and Mrs. Park. We left in a helicopter with the Browns for the Blue House, the Korean White House or Presidential residence, and were greeted by President and Mrs. Park at the front steps. I would swear the band was playing "Dixie"! In fact, in all of this roaring, tumultuous day we were curiously accompanied by well-known, old-time American songs. It was just as though somebody had gone through Seoul with sheet music—"Fifty Favorite Songs of America." I had heard "Oh, Susanna," "Way Down upon the Swanee River," "My Old Kentucky Home," and over and over and over "The Yellow Rose of Texas" and "The Eyes of Texas." This was one example of the infinitely industrious way they had gone about making us feel at home.

Later I was told that Blue House had been painted just three days before our arrival and also the Capitol, as well as the Korea House and the Art Gallery. The Blue House was spacious and handsome, but there was something austere and spare about it, a characteristic I sensed in everything about Korea—its buildings, as well as its people.

There was a receiving line in the Grand Reception Room, where we met the two hundred guests, and then we went into a private room for the exchange of gifts. Somewhere, I don't quite remember, except that it was at a quiet moment, we met one of the Parks' daughters, a shy, sweet girl, and this lent the visit another touch of the sincerity that so marked it—the sharing of their home life with us. Mrs. Park gave me two lovely brocades, one yellow (and she explained she had selected it because she knew it was my favorite color) and one embroidered with lilies of the valley, the flower of happiness.

From Blue House we went to the Capitol Building where we were greeted by Prime Minister and Mrs. Chung and then up the curving red-carpeted staircase—I held on to President Park's arm, for a staircase in long dress and high-heeled shoes is always a mental hazard to me—into the Main Hall for the State Dinner. The four of us were seated side by side at the head of a long horseshoe table. The walls were festooned with flowers. There was a lovely miniature screen at each place—it was the menu card —folding panels of wood and silk with a peacock crest embroidered at the top, and the menu in Korean characters and in English.

Everything was served in bowls—delicate blue-and-white bowls or small dishes. Nothing that I would call a plate. The glassware all bore the peacock crest. And silver chopsticks! I understand that everything was bought new and especially for our visit. We had abalone soup and ambrosia casserole and mustard-spiced vegetables with such strange unknowns as fried seagreens and toasted sealaber. As always, throughout this part of the world, there was rice. Honeyed pine nut nuogat and that simple, old, familiar fruit, apple, were served for dessert. The rice wine, about a thimbleful, was strong and stinging, but glasses were not refilled. In fact, I had the feeling that Koreans do not eat heavily or drink heavily.

Dinner ended with ginseng nectar, and toasts with champagne. But the evening was not yet over. We drove next to Citizens Hall, where we were escorted to a box, to watch a program of Korean folk dancing, which began sedately enough with typical court dancing, beautiful girls dancing gracefully with flower crowns on their heads, a dance dating from about A.D. 600.

The tempo changed. The "Miller's Song," and then the "Twelve Drum Dance," which is a form of Buddhist monk dance, where the dancer races around the stage to beat on twelve separate drums, hurrying madly from drum to drum, striking each with all his might. I leaned over to the President and said, "That reminds me of Lyndon trying to get all of his work done."

It was a veritable crescendo of activity, but we hadn't seen anything *yet*. The evening closed with the "Farmer's Dance," the traditional festival music of the Korean farmers celebrating a rich harvest. Dressed in bright costumes, the farmers whirled onto the stage, each with long streamers of ribbon attached to his hat, which, as he danced, floated, looped, circled around him in a madly increasing tempo. The dancer would use his neck with all the ability one would use his arms—to the left, to the right, whirling the ribbons like a wheel with a tour de force of skill and sheer physical strength. The dignified audience loved it. As our star took the center of the stage, bounding, somersaulting, twirling ever faster and faster, his neck miraculously keeping the ribbons spinning around him, they began to clap, they cheered, it was like watching a football game. Finally, the dancer dropped from exhaustion, and the next one took over. The Farmer's Dance was a wonderful finale for the evening.

Miraculously, it ended on time. We gratefully said good-by and helicoptered to Walker Hill to spend our first night in this "Special City of Seoul" which had greeted us with the biggest crowd ever to turn out in Korean history. This was no personal tribute but a tribute to what Korea itself in association with the United States has achieved in the last fifteen dynamic years.

Wednesday, November 2

SEOUL, KOREA, AND WASHINGTON, D.C.

I woke early in Emerald Villa at Walker Hill. Time has ceased to have relevance, and I am a machine. The end of the journey is in sight. I am glad and I lean toward it. And yet I want to drain, absorb, live, every moment, every emotion, because nothing like this journey will ever happen to me again.

I went with Lyndon early in the morning—the Deputy Prime Minister accompanying us by helicopter—to the National Cemetery. It was a chill, autumn day. The sky was gray, the mountains forbidding. The aides advanced in front of Lyndon with a huge wreath of gold and white chrysanthemums and he stood with bowed head for a long moment. I do not envy the thoughts of a President at a time like this. The smell of incense burning in front of the flag marked it as a foreign field. I raised my eyes to the solemn martial music, looking out on the acres and acres of somber gray tombstones with the forbidding mountains in the background.

And then we were in the helicopter headed for the National Assembly. Lyndon spoke to a stern-faced, intent, very masculine audience. Lyndon said he had seen millions of faces during his tour, "And I have been deeply encouraged [by the trip]. So I leave today with a deep sense of confidence in the future of Asia and the Pacific." He stressed his belief that "a new Asia" is evolving, and how he hoped that a great historian would tell the story of Korea and its emergence in the last fifteen years. He called it a "modern miracle." His main theme was that the Communist strategists of the 1950's were encouraged by the indifference, the fear, and the weakness that had permitted the aggression of the 1930's to move so far so fast. But in Korea in the 1950's they were stopped, just as they are being stopped in Vietnam today. He spoke movingly of the Korean soldiers fighting side by side with our men now in Vietnam.

And then we were off to go to Blue House for coffee and good-bys to President and Mrs. Park. The grounds of the Blue House were in their brilliant autumn dress—the maples scarlet and gold—and Mrs. Park was out front in a beautiful golden dress, all smiles. A most womanly woman. It was a brief, official visit. But Lyndon somehow manages to conquer language barriers and to talk directly—particularly if he likes the Chief of State, as he very certainly likes President Park.

We left with President and Mrs. Park in the helicopter for Kimpo Airport in the middle of the morning and flew low over the city that had been almost leveled by warfare in 1950 to 1953, and now was surging with vitality—block after block of new buildings . . . Then over a countryside that was pale gold with the ripe harvest of rice. Straw was in stacks. Sometimes there would be people carrying it. President Park told us that the average farm was three acres!

Then we were at Kimpo Airport for the last great surge of emotion—the farewell—full honors with a twenty-one-gun salute, our two anthems, and hundreds of children in bright Korean dress waving flags and singing first the "Arilang" song—a haunting melody that's sad and sweet with a note of pathos. It will always remind me of Korea.

And then a girls' chorus singing "The Yellow Rose of Texas." Adorable little girls in red satin kimonos with brilliant striped sleeves, and elaborate coiffeurs, came up to give us flowers. Lyndon leaned over to kiss them; they were irresistible. Lyndon got into an open jeep with President Park and reviewed the troops. He told the crowd that we had fallen in love—he and I—with their country. And that we would stand side by side in Asia. It was one of the most moving ceremonies.

Then we were off into the gray autumn sky.

We flew over Japan—an expanse of mountains. I saw one of the great sights of my whole life—Mount Fuji—rising like a dream from a soft ocean of white clouds. It was a perfect cone rising into a blue sky—its top capped with the most sparkling white snow. There was an utter silence of perfection about it that was somehow unreal—dreamlike—a sight I shall never forget.

We spent a brief night in Alaska and the next morning flew on homeward. Amazingly (to me) it was another November 2 because sometime in the dark hours over the Pacific we had crossed the International Dateline.

As we approached Washington the weather began to get very bad. Never in all my life and travel have I been on a big plane that tossed and twisted and plunged like *Air Force One* did then. Thirty-one thousand miles of good flying, and within an hour of home I was scared white. I looked at Ashton and she looked ready to faint. Liz, who hates to fly, was sending inquiries to the pilot. I was holding on to the arm of the State Department man next to me. I am sure he had blue bruises the next morning.

The flight seemed endless, but at 8 we finally set down at Dulles, on a windy, wet evening. There was the familiar red carpet and the familiar red bouquet of roses—the last for a long time. The members of the Cabinet were lining our way and the Diplomatic Corps and other high officials had come to greet us. I looked up and saw a big banner across the terminal saying, "WELL DONE, MR. PRESIDENT." There was a twenty-one-gun salute. The "Star-Spangled Banner" rang out. And if anybody in our party didn't get goosebumps, they must have been unconscious. Home!

Thursday, November 17

BETHESDA NAVAL HOSPITAL

Today, our thirty-second wedding anniversary, we awoke in Bethesda Naval Hospital. Lyndon had come in late Tuesday and had been operated on early yesterday to repair the scar resulting from his gall bladder operation and to remove the polyp in his throat. Thank the Lord, the growth was benign. I felt as if I'd been holding my breath and could suddenly release it.

This is the fourth stay I can remember here, beginning in 1955 with the long stay of six weeks.

Ashton came over in the morning and I dictated and signed mail—my room a bedlam—going out to visit Lyndon several times in the morning. The paper said he "maintained a brisk pace." It seemed intense to me for the first day after the operation.

President Eisenhower came to see Lyndon and stayed forty-five minutes. Lyndon enjoys President Eisenhower, and I think it is mutual. There is nothing that would generate sympathy and understanding for a President like holding the job yourself. Lyndon's office—the role of the Presidency—has grown for all who have held it.

Later Carl Albert came to visit, still recuperating from his heart attack in September. Lyndon, in bed, had a meeting with the "big four" of fiscal and budgetary matters: Secretary Fowler, Budget Director Charlie Schultze, Arthur Okun, Chairman of the Council of Economic Advisers, and Bill Martin (William McChesney Martin), head of the Federal Reserve Board.

Sometime during the day the pad and pencil disappeared, and he was talking once more as much as he liked—a little hoarse and quiet, but in great spirits and good humor, joking with the doctors until Jim Cain's and Dr. Hurst's laughter rang down the halls; the others are getting to know him, too, well enough to laugh with him, and he is keeping Mary and Marie giggling.

I went out to do some chores and when I got back to the hospital I found that Lyndon was sleeping and that Hubert and Muriel were waiting to see him. I brought them into the living room to chat with me.

While we were talking, a message came that Lyndon wanted me to come into his room. We were quite alone, just the two of us. There were six boxes spread out on a table by his hospital bed. He said, "I want you to look at those, and pick whichever ones you like best." I opened box after box—my eyes wide with amazement. They were diamond earrings! I only half-protested that they cost too much, and that we really shouldn't, and then I selected the pair with pear-shaped drops. I put them on, and out we went into the big conference room where on the table was a beautiful cake made by Ferdinand at the White House that said "32 *happy years*," and gathered around it was a cluster of the newspaperwomen who most regularly accompany me: Helen Thomas and Frances Lewine, Isabelle Shelton, Wauhilla LaHay, Marie Smith, and Nancy Dickerson—some eight or ten—and a dozen photographers; Marie Fehmer, Marvin Watson,

Bill Moyers, Dr. Hurst and Jim Cain, Lynda and Luci and Pat, and the Humphreys.

It exploded into a real happy time. Lyndon cut the cake and I told everybody how happy I was, and Lyndon answered with some lovely compliments. There I was in my earrings and nobody said a word—not even Helen Thomas! I don't know whether it was from politeness or whether because in all those years they hadn't seen me wear fine jewelry and they just thought they were paste!

Everybody had coffee and cake, and Hubert proposed a toast to us with coffee, and Nancy Dickerson answered with compliments from the press. Marie Smith gave us a book, *White House Brides,* one for us and one for Luci and Pat; those two young folks gave me a darling card that said I would receive fifty pounds of bluebonnet seeds, which I immediately translated into one hundred dollars, beaming at their generosity and worrying at their improvidence at the same time. Lyndon refused his slice of cake, saying, "Make mine tapioca," to the hilarity of everyone.

And then the press was gone, but it was only the beginning of the evening. Planning and executing it all, in about two hours' time, to my complete surprise Lyndon had invited a dozen good friends. We settled down to a good visit with our guests and our children. What a day for a man who was just one day away from surgery, and what a day for any wife to remember as her thirty-second wedding anniversary.

Monday, November 28

THE WHITE HOUSE

Today is the first day of my Washington interlude without Lyndon. During the morning Liz came in and we went downstairs to see the blown-up pictures of some of the scenes in *The Living White House,* which—well-recorded by press and television—we hope will help sell the book. Bess came, bringing the guest list for the launching party. My first thought on waking and seeing the gray and dripping sky was that I might lose some guests because of plane trouble and I did, but there was a marvelous list of acceptances and a party spirit in the house. And besides that, I spent a good morning working. Sometimes I think I function better in a fairly regimented life.

Bess and I went over the scenario for the afternoon. Much time has been spent on this party. It has been carefully planned, to give some intimate moments to me and those who have lived in this house, or have ties with it, and to give those special guests, the descendants of White House families, a chance to stroll through the family quarters, or the third floor, and reminisce and recall.

I practiced the few words that I would say, put on my new mint-green alaskine dress and went down for the party to launch our addition to the White House books, *The Living White House*.

The guests were all seated in the East Room—the descendants of Presidents, the *National Geographic* people who had produced the book, the old-time newspaper reporters who had covered the White House for many administrations. I had also invited a good many staff people—my own folks who really make it "The Living White House" for us. Dr. Melville Bell Grosvenor talked about how the book came into being, and David Finley of the White House Historical Association, which is actually producing the book, spoke, and then it was my turn. I expressed my gratitude to Dr. Grosvenor and all the *National Geographic* staff and most especially to Bruce Catton who wrote the foreword. I had especially asked him to, and I was so grateful that he did. I told the little story about President Coolidge walking one day with a Senator friend from Missouri. In a joking mood the Senator said, as they approached the White House, "I wonder who lives there?" "Nobody," said the President. "They just come and go." I was thrilled that many who have "come and gone" had returned for this occasion.

Then I asked Mrs. Eisenhower to accompany me and we went into the Green Room for the receiving line of the descendants. Mrs. Eisenhower was just as gay and informal as ever, looking not a day older. And she was the biggest attraction of the afternoon. She stood with me and greeted them as they filed by. First, the Princess Cantacuzene, who was Julia Grant, the granddaughter of President Grant, age ninety. (The guests ranged from ten to ninety.) And Marthena Harrison Williams, Benjamin Harrison's granddaughter; and Mrs. Van Seagraves who is Sistie Dahl, Anna Roosevelt's daughter, one of the grandchildren who lived in the house during FDR's time; and a gentleman named Laurence Gouverneur Hoes, who was a descendant of both Madison and Monroe.

Mrs. Eisenhower had brought with her her daughter-in-law, Mrs. John Eisenhower, and three of her charming grandchildren, Mary, Barbara Ann, and Susan. There were two Roosevelt sons, Elliott and John with his wife; Mrs. Mary Virginia Devine, a Harrison great-granddaughter; Mrs. Frederick Manning, President Taft's daughter, who was wearing a silver, pearl, and diamond pendant brooch that President Taft had given his wife on their Silver Anniversary.

From the Green Room the White House families and I went into the Blue Room for a group picture. Then they all dispersed. Mrs. Eisenhower went into the pantry to see the butlers and emerged later saying, "I just wanted to see all the boys." That further endeared her to me. She looked fondly around the place and said, "You know, I lived here longer than anywhere else." Her warmest memories were, she said, of the christening of their youngest grandchild, Mary Jean, in the Blue Room and of the family celebration at Christmas after the General's heart attack. How well I understand that last, the feeling of well-being and renewal.

I stood in line in the Blue Room to receive all the rest of the guests. I met two other descendants, Mrs. John Harlan Amen, who had been Marion Cleveland, the daughter of Grover Cleveland. She was born in the White House during their second Administration and had lived here for a year and a half; and Mrs. Richard Folsom Cleveland, the daughter-in-law of President Cleveland. There was Diana Hopkins, now Mrs. Allin Baxter, who had lived here with her widowed father, Harry Hopkins, in the hectic days of FDR's time. Among the veterans of the press were Bob Allen, and Gould Lincoln, and Bill White.

The receiving line over, I went to the State Dining Room where it was very evident it was a good party! Nearly everybody had a story to tell and everybody wanted to listen. Each of the honor guests had a little circle around him. I moved from group to group, gathering amusing vignettes. Princess Cantacuzene said, "I received here in the Blue Room"—and while my mind raced to subtract the years, back to President Grant, she added, "at the age of two months in my nurse's arms beside my mother! . . . And then I returned to be the houseguest of the Coolidges." Sistie Dahl Seagraves said that she remembered "putting Post Toasties in the beds of some of the guests and being roundly scolded by Grandmother"—Mrs. Roosevelt.

Mrs. Manning, President Taft's daughter, said something that I appreciated very much—speaking of the late Senator Robert Taft, her brother, "My happiest memory is to think of Robert and Lyndon running the Senate. They did it very well."

Mrs. Marthena Harrison Williams, the granddaughter of Benjamin Harrison, nearly topped them all with a memory from yet another Administration, that of Lincoln. "We have the last signature of Lincoln. Our grandfather was appointed Territorial Governor of the Northwest Territory by Lincoln. He was in town to see the President but had to return to Nebraska," she said. "His reappointment was found signed on the top of Lincoln's desk, the morning after his assassination, the last document signed." Benjamin Harrison heard about it on the train going west.

I had a very interesting moment with Mr. Hoes, the descendant of the Madisons and the Monroes, who spoke of a splendid Madison portrait which he had. I had known of its existence through Jim Ketchum. I took his arm and walked him over to look at the present one, painted forty years after President Madison's death, a poor excuse of a portrait. I think he knows how enthusiastic I am about the possibility of getting a good one.

Thursday, December 1

NEW YORK

I left for New York on the shuttle at 11 with my ubiquitous Mexican straw bag, signed a large stack of pictures for Christmas to the staff during the forty-minute flight, and read my little speech over a couple of times.

I spent a couple of hours on beautification planning with Laurance Rockefeller, Mary Lasker, and other fellow workers. In the afternoon I had a visit with McGeorge and Mary Bundy and told them of our visit to Los Baños, the Rice Institute in the Philippines. In his good-by to Dr. Robert F. Chandler, the head scientist there, Lyndon had summed up the hope for Asia with a delicious line. He said quite cheerfully, "Well, Dr. Chandler, if you just keep on producing better strains of rice and Margaret Sanger's folks keep on doing what they are doing, this old world might be saved yet."

A little after 6:30 Liz and I fared forth to the Plaza for the Awards Dinner for the National Institute of Social Science. This organization of leading industrialists has for fifty years been giving an award for distinguished service to humanity to a rather varied group of winners—four or five or six each year—lustrous names in diverse fields. Tonight I was one of those privileged to be so honored.

Frank Pace met me, with a warm and cordial greeting. We met rather casually a group of the members of the National Institute of Social Sciences. I gathered they were the old-timers or Board of Directors. I was impressed and grateful at how many of them spoke to me quite earnestly of my small work in conservation-beautification. I knew I was meeting a great tapestry of New York. Unfortunately I couldn't identify all the strands of threads, although I recognized many of the names in the program list of members. They ranged from Charles Lindbergh and Dr. Harry Emerson Fosdick to Eva Le Gallienne, Mrs. August Belmont, and Arthur Hays Sulzberger.

We had a delicious dinner of too much, beginning with lobster bisque, very rare prime ribs, and ending with cherries jubilee—vast change from the Ranch and Mary's simple good cooking.

Then it was time for the citations. Frank had put me first. I think very likely it was Liz's suggestion. How glad I was, because that meant I could enjoy the *rest* of the evening. And from a theater standpoint it was the best thing to do, because mine was the least impressive speech. I regretted it because I *had* worked on it, taking the first draft—it was a beautiful bunch of words—and turning it into something personal, painting two pictures of what I had personally experienced . . . The mood of that night in October 1957, when we heard that the Russians had put Sputnik I into orbit—the mood of colossal, impossible obstacles facing us—stunned silence. And then only nine years later in my own front yard, the ceremony of giving awards to the astronauts and scientists and industrialists who had brought the Gemini program to successful conclusion. Now we had 430 satellites in orbit. So, man *can!* And that was the spirit that I wanted everybody to have as we faced the seemingly insurmountable obstacles of our crowded, ugly, traffic-ridden cities and what to do about them.

They gave me a nice moment of applause. I sat down vastly relieved and listened to some good speeches by the four other award winners. Keith Funston was handsome, suave, competent, and intentionally humorous in his talk about the handling of money—a skillfully read speech.

General David Sarnoff read his also. He talked about the vast technological achievements of this century and the perilous gap that lies between them and our ability to get along with each other and to spread the fruits of those advances to all the earth's people. There was a marvelous line: "In most of the world life is still an earth-packed floor, an empty bowl, and a premature death." What a bare-bones sentence, and how strong! When he sat down I congratulated him on it most earnestly, and he gave me the copy of his speech.

Next there was Danny Kaye. And he didn't read a word! He simply talked from the heart, impassioned, humorous, charming, about the world's children, about UNICEF. It was a *dear* speech. He is a giving man. But I was feeling a little apprehensive—they weren't closing the evening with Danny Kaye; Cardinal Spellman was still to come. I need not have been.

He topped us all! Like Danny Kaye, he read not a line. And with the assurance of his years, in great humor, he told us about his attempts to be a chaplain. And then about his visits to troops wherever they were, across the seas at Christmastime for the last many, many years. I think it is about thirteen years. And he said that he would be going to Vietnam in two weeks for still another Christmas. It was a warm, touching, delightful close to a sharp, interesting evening.

Tuesday, December 13

THE WHITE HOUSE

Today was a full, vivid, exciting day at the White House. We were up early and I held myself resolutely to my desk, signing Christmas pictures. Downstairs the Christmas decorations are up. That is when my heart begins to sing . . . They are so beautiful. I hope I have the grace to know that every day I spend here is a privilege. And never more so than at Christmas.

Sometime during the morning I became aware snow was falling. It is the most magical experience. I love it. I shall know I am really getting old when my heart doesn't beat a little faster and a smile naturally break out when it starts snowing. Soon the magnolia trees outside my window were heavy with the white burden, and the whole South Lawn was blanketed. The sky was gray—it looked as though it would never stop. And I wondered what this would do to our party for the Arts Council tonight . . . Well, it did it. I had hoped that the party would be one of the most glamorous we had ever had—and we had a blizzard on our hands!

A little before 6 Bess and I went over the list. There were a good many cancellations. We invited some last-minute staff people. Then I began to get dressed. An elaborate up hairdo by Jean Louis. He is so amusing and takes such pride in turning me out looking as well as I can. I decided to wear the elegant Philippine dress, beaded from top to bottom, with teardrop beads—an iridescent green—very lovely and very heavy. Lynda was getting an up hairdo, too, to go with her long apricot brocade with sable around the hem.

A little before 8 we went into the Yellow Oval Room and met the Roger Stevenses, Hubert and Muriel, and Lyndon's very special favorite—Gregory Peck and his lovely wife. And towering, humorous René d'Harnoncourt and his wife, the William Pereiras, and Leonard Bernstein.

The setting was Christmas and the theme was the arts. But very much of the talk was about "How did you get here?" Actually the snowstorm had cost us many guests that I missed: Van Cliburn, Marian Anderson, Edward Albee. The guests of honor were the members of the Arts Council —twenty-six of them, including the outgoing and the incoming members. And others in the world of drama and literature and music and architecture and the dance. The adventurous guests who managed to get there at all had many stories to tell. Duke Ellington canceled when he lost his luggage coming down from New York, but Bess told him to come on, in whatever he had on. He got a tux from somewhere, but arrived in a pink shirt—the like of which has not been seen before, but was just right for the mood. The Howard Taubmans, when they got to the airport and found that no more planes were flying, decided to take a taxi, and they came all the way from New York in a taxi, with the Harold Princes. Eleanor Lambert changed into her evening clothes on the train and came direct from Union Station. Mike Nichols had left Los Angeles at dawn, the storm detoured him to Pittsburgh, and he phoned us that he couldn't come. But then he hopped a train and got to the Mayflower at 9:30 and into a tux and arrived at the White House about 10 P.M., still wearing loafers.

I was so happy to see Agnes De Mille, Jean Dalrymple, and Rebekah Harkness. Actor Sidney Poitier and author Harper Lee added to the galaxy of stars. Isaac Stern had regretted, he had a concert in Philadelphia. However, his wife came. And before the evening was over, here came Isaac, having rushed straight from the concert to the station, caught a train, and arrived about 11.

It was a party to remember! Lyndon made a splendid toast. He said he wanted American art to be enjoyed at the grass-roots level, just as it is by the top-hat crowd. After dinner, which ended with a baked Alaska entitled "Flaming Muses," we adjourned to the Green Room and the Red Room and the Hall for coffee and liqueurs. Then I introduced Gregory Peck and gave a few words of thanks to the Arts Council—a thumbnail summary of their achievements. Their trips have sparked new life into community theaters and brought sixteen professional theaters into being. As a result of their activities, touring groups of dance, opera, and ballet have been initiated. Gregory Peck introduced the entertainment, an act from *The School for Scandal* by Sheridan, by the APA Repertory Company, delightfully costumed, with the theme: "The more things change the more they are the same."

Alexander Schneider and his chamber music group entertained us with a serenade by Dvořák. I was proud of our printed program with a quotation from John Adams in 1780 which said in substance that he must study politics and war, so that his sons can study mathematics and commerce and agriculture, so that their sons can study painting and poetry and music.

After the program the music in the rotunda swung into dance tempos and I found myself trying to grow a foot taller in order to dance with René d'Harnoncourt, chatting a moment with lovely Maria Tallchief, and following Lynda proudly with my eyes as she moved with so much gaiety yet dignity among all these people who are really very much "her people."

Lyndon went upstairs a little before one, and I stayed a good while longer. There were sounds of merriment from below until well after 2. It had been a glowing evening—from the beginning, when the American Light Opera Company had serenaded us all once more from the stairs with their Christmas carols, on through the last hilarious story of "How I got here through the snowstorm!"

Friday, December 16

The merry mood of Christmas which began Monday with the newspaperwomen's party and continued through the Arts Council dinner and the party for the staff and the lighting of the Christmas tree Thursday is dissipating under the onslaught of hostile press articles.

Yesterday came the announcement of Bill Moyers' departure. The Manchester book and ugly stories about it are dominating the newspapers. Mrs. Kennedy is filing suit to block publication of the book. The "credibility gap" (that coined phrase) is rapidly gaining acceptance through repetition, and the critical Democratic Governors' opinions are filling the papers. Nevertheless, life goes on and so does Christmas.

The Annual Children's Party was held this afternoon. The children began arriving about 4—one hundred fifty of them, from Friendship House and the Boys' Club of Columbia Heights, St. Vincent's Home and School, St. Ann's Infant Home, the Washington Hearing Society, the YWCA, the Boys Club of Alexandria, and Barney Neighborhood House. They were all dressed up, quiet and solemn, many of the little girls wearing white gloves and hair ribbons, and very prim and well-mannered. I looked in on them from a distance before I came down to the East Room where they were finally all assembled stiffly in chairs, ready to watch the puppet show. I came in and sat in the front row with a floor full of children cross-legged in front of me. One of them soon got up and sat on my lap. Lynda, down the row from me, was being very helpful and was being clambered over by several children. The puppet show was given by the Chandler brothers—Marc and Chris—who held us enthralled for about thirty minutes with their magic little figures—a Spanish dancer, a very sad little boy, and many others.

When the show ended, I invited the children to come into the State Dining Room for cookies and ice cream. The tables were children-size. I sat at one with a little girl named Linda. We ate ice cream shaped like Christmas trees and munched decorated cookies and drank punch, and there were plenty of second helpings without asking.

Lynda was at another table, and there were lots of teen-age hostesses, daughters of government officials and members of the Cabinet—Lisa Connor and Christy Carpenter and little Lisa MacArthur who was very capably busy answering questions, many about where was the bathroom. The most important question at my table was "When is Santa Claus coming?"—at least after the second go-around of the cookies.

Santa Claus was Sandy Fox, disguised with pillows and a white, silky beard. After about the sixteenth question at my table, he finally appeared and the stampede began. Santa asked us to follow him into the Blue Room where the Christmas tree was. But it was more of a race than a following. Safely ensconced on one side of the room, Santa dispensed trains and trucks and dolls with wardrobes, and a joyous pandemonium ensued. Lynda Bird settled quarrels, and got toys for the quiet ones who didn't get any, and at last the floor was a wasteland of paper, and every child had one or more toys.

Dorothy McCardle wrote, "Thomas Jefferson and James Madison rocked in their frames, the Christmas tree in the Blue Room teetered, Santa Claus wiped his brow and staggered back. The Children's invasion of the White House was over for another year."

After the children had gone I went back upstairs to wait for the departure for Texas. It was one of those times when you feel suspended in space. The things that you work with have been packed and departed or put away. You need to do needlepoint or read a book.

Lyndon was in serious talk with Ambassador Lodge, McNamara, Ambassador Goldberg, Governor Harriman, and the Vice President. He brought them over from the office. McNamara soon left—"Margy is waiting for me," he said. The rest of us sat down for dinner.

Lyndon had not come to the Children's Party this year—the first time he's ever missed it—a barometer of how serious is the mood. It was a little after 9 when Lyndon and Lynda and I left in the helicopter for Andrews and departed Washington in *Air Force One*. It was a swift and pleasant and fairly light-hearted journey, in spite of the rising tide of ugly stories, which you can feel in your bones. Before midnight we were at the Ranch, and I could feel that Christmas had begun.

Saturday, December 24

LBJ RANCH

After lunch Lyndon and I left in the *Jetstar* with Jake Jacobsen, Dr. Burkley and the Secret Service to go to Kelly Air Force Base on a poignant visit for Christmas Eve, to greet wounded GI's who were returning to Texas.

We landed and met Congressman Henry Gonzalez, and spoke quietly to a small group who were lined up behind the ropes waiting at the base. The plane came in—an ambulance plane. Lyndon went aboard and met the men and then came down looking solemn. We stood at the foot of the steps—he and Lynda and I. She had joined us, after spending the night with Warrie Lynn Smith.

And then they began to file down the steps—twenty evacuees, including two children of servicemen stationed in the Far East—with bandaged arms or legs and silent, stunned faces. There was utter stillness—never had the war felt so close—a strange war. Suddenly, as the first man approached the bottom of the steps, the small crowd burst into spontaneous applause. And then behind me there was a happy sound, "There he is, there's my boy!" and a pretty lady brushed past us with: "Please excuse me, Mr. President." A litter case came down the steps and a young man raised his head and grinned. His mother kissed him and then she turned to us and said, "I am sorry, Mr. President, but this is my boy. We just heard last night that he had been hit." How incredible! All those thousands of miles away and then suddenly this afternoon he was home. He was Private First Class Alex Hudson III. His father seemed stunned, but his mother was happy just to have him home. They loaded him into a big ambulance in a sort of a hammock, and his mother sat holding his hand.

The last of the twenty came down, and silently they went their ways and the clapping died. Then the three of us boarded the *Jetstar*. I felt buffeted by emotions, deep respect for those young men and for an organization that could get them all the way from Vietnam to San Antonio within hours of being wounded, and sympathy for their families and a shattering sympathy for anybody who has yes's and no's to say about this war—McNamara, Westmoreland, Lyndon.

Back at the Ranch a fire was blazing on the hearth and it was dark. The house was beautifully decorated—it was Helen's doing—with balsam rope along the mantelpieces in the big living room and the den and wound around the stair rail, mistletoe hanging from the light fixtures, and holly from the White House in a big brass bowl on the dining room table. There was a great bowl of eggnog and lots of cookies on the sideboard in the dining room. Christmas carols were playing. Lyndon invited in the Secret Service and the military personnel.

We all filled our cups with eggnog. And I showed them the red-velvet nose on the deer head, which had been put there each year since 1952, and the red-satin Christmas stockings with our names on them, which Neva had given us, hanging from the mantel.

Tony and Matiana were helpful, visiting with real interest with all the people who work around us. Sometime or other Lynda had disappeared and had flown to Dallas to meet George. We had a late dinner when they returned, and we sat down at the table—Lyndon and I, the Taylors, the Nugents, Lynda and George, and Jake and Marie.

After dinner we went into the office and the onslaught on the Christmas tree took place. Mary and James and their three children and Gertrude and Lee of our household staff joined us and it was an hour of pandemonium. I had an album of wedding pictures from Luci with an incomparable inscription. She has a gift of expression that will serve her well in life. And a folder of Daumier lithographs from Lynda with a hilarious one about the budget—a fat woman being wrestled into a corset (this represents a French budget in 1769). A watch from Lyndon and something I particularly enjoyed, a jug of wine from our neighbors the Burgs, and a copy of Dickens' *Christmas Carol* from someone on the staff.

As midnight approached, the floor was a shambles and everybody had his presents, though not all of mine were opened till two days later. We realized that if we were going to make Midnight Mass we had to hurry. So I changed quickly from a hostess gown into a dress, and into the station wagon with Lyndon driving, Luci and Pat, Lynda and George, Marie and Jake, and Matiana and I set out for St. Francis Xavier at Stonewall.

BOOK FOUR

1967

Winter 1967

THE Now is indeed "the Valley of the Black Pig." A miasma of
WHITE HOUSE trouble hangs over everything. If I had to draw a graph of
Thursday, when it began, or when it at least seeped through to me, I
January 5, would say about December 10. All during December there
1967 was the constant grind with the budget. Once Charlie
Schultze of the Bureau of the Budget, looking very intently
at Lyndon, said, "You will go down in history as the man
who kept this nation together fighting a limited war." He and
Lyndon were talking about the difficulty of doing that. The
temperament of our people seems to be, "You must get
excited, get passionate, fight it, get it over with, or we must
pull out." It is unbearably hard to fight a limited war.

There are the big troubles of Vietnam, and the growing
threat of inflation, and a whole flock of little troubles like
gnats. Today Peter Hurd is breaking into print once more
about the portrait. My sympathy and disappointment and
regret are rapidly dissipating as he launches into more and

469

more interviews. And Bill Moyers' departure is giving the press a picnic.

There are stories indicating that Bill has really brought in all the fine, fresh, bright, liberal ideas—an attitude hardly calculated to endear him to the rest of the staff, many of whom are also liberal and bright—and that his departure will be a loss from which it will be impossible to recover. Bill's departure will, indeed, be a sore loss. I remember with affection those long hours of work, years of friendship, Bill's keen, fast mind, laced with wit. We are going to miss him so much, and I hope that we and he and all the staff will weigh this wave of publicity judiciously and philosophically.

I spent the morning working on a possible answer, brief, to Peter Hurd. The picture was too large. Last summer I had taken Peter to stand in front of the portrait of Thomas Jefferson here in the White House and told him I hoped it would be that size. The Capitol is too brilliantly, unrealistically lighted. Actually, the dome floats in the night like a great pearl. I thought we should have ready a brief statement and then no more.

And then I worked on the list for the Vice President's dinner. About 2 I simply went to sleep for nearly two hours. A funny reaction to trouble.

Later I recorded in my little sitting-room office. In came Lynda, fresh from Acapulco—the very spirit of 1967—wearing mesh hose and little-girl flat shoes, and a very short, very bright coat and dress, looking so chic and gay. She told me about being the houseguest of Merle Oberon and her husband, Bruno Pagliai. John Wayne had been there too—Lynda liked him so much. She says he is very conservative, but that he had spoken kindly of her father—and Dolores Del Rio who, she says, is beautiful and such a lady. Lynda does as she wishes, within the limits of decorum and good judgment, and is becoming much more mature. How I do love her!

Muriel came over about 7. She had asked me earlier if she could cook a steak for just the four of us. I suggested we bowl and then just drop by the office and see. We went to the bowling alley, and she beat me roundly two and a half games, shooting 137 one time to my 105 or so.

Lyndon called and he said yes he could go to the Humphreys for a steak. We picked up the Vice President and the four of us arrived at their apartment a little before 10. We all felt that things couldn't get much worse, so we might as well take off a couple of hours and enjoy each other. We analyzed the Senate and its leadership, past and present, the coming session of Congress, the things we needed to do. It was a spirit of drawing together in time of trouble. We moved in a simple, un-Presidential sort of way— no motorcycles, no doormen. I don't think anybody even knew we went. It was kind of a night out!

At 12 o'clock we were back in the White House, and tonight Lyndon did not do his night reading. Tomorrow will be time enough to take up the problems.

Today is the day of the State of the Union Message. Not until it is over do you really feel the New Year has begun.

Sometime this year I must decide on a china pattern for the Johnson Administration. I went into the China Room to make note of the dinner services I particularly like. I like the symbolism of the Benjamin Harrison china with corn and wheat around the border, spelling the land of plenty. The Woodrow Wilson set, the first American china, has a simple elegance in the service plate that will be good for all time, I think, as does Franklin Roosevelt's, with the restrained symbolism of his own coat of arms in its border of plumes and roses. The Thomas Jefferson set I like best of all, but it is Chinese export. And the James Monroe with its medallions, so rich in allegory, so imaginative. Done in the spirit of the sixties, something like the Monroe china would be wonderful—or else it would fall flat on its face! It would take a daring First Lady to choose it. I like the seal in the Lincoln china.

Lyndon went over his State of the Union speech in the theater nearly all morning and then had lunch about 1:30 P.M. I worked on the mail with that sense of hanging in time, of waiting, for everything leads up to the State of the Union. Lyndon continued to work on the speech until almost 8:30 P.M. and then had a bowl of vegetable soup.

It was a drama-charged atmosphere we walked into on the Hill a little past 9. Along the drive to the Capitol I saw flag after flag at half-mast. An old and respected member of the House had died today, Congressman John E. Fogarty of Rhode Island, head of the subcommittee through which most of the legislation on education and health passes. His death will be a severe loss for the Administration. He had died right in his office. On the Hill today there had been a death and an expulsion. Adam Clayton Powell had been expelled from the House in an atmosphere tense with violence and hatred. I do not remember another Congressional expulsion in the history of the Republic. Actually there is a committee which is supposed to spend four or five weeks judging his case before it is decided, but it was weighed as an expulsion today in the newspapers, and Adam Clayton

Powell stormed out onto the steps, surrounded by his supporters, some of whom wore black masks, and called the legislators inside the biggest bunch of hypocrites ever elected.

The Capitol was more brilliantly illuminated with floodlights than I ever remember, and it seemed to me there were more policemen. The air was charged with excitement composed of many things, including the much blown-up Republican victory in November. Another element in this many-faceted picture was the seating of the first Negro Senator since Reconstruction days—Senator Edward W. Brooke of Massachusetts, whose coming in was attended with as much adulation and excitement as Adam Clayton Powell's going out was with anger. Among all the feelings in the air, somehow the jovial camaraderie of most years was missing.

Lynda and I slipped into our seats early, and in fact before the House knew we were there. Some of them turned just as we were about to sit down and saw us, and a ripple of clapping broke out, and all the men on the floor stood. I smiled and surveyed the room, picking out friend and foe and question mark, and so many I didn't know.

What a rainbow my guests were in the front row—Mrs. Charlie Schultze wearing willow green, Mrs. Gardner Ackley in a sort of canary yellow, Jean Kintner in a brilliant red-velvet coat, Judith Moyers in pale gold and Elspeth Rostow the most stunning of all, I thought, in a pink coat over a white dress.

And now it was time to begin, the moment of truth toward which so many hours of work and decision had been beamed this last month, and on which so much hinged. It was a quiet, measured speech, delivered in a time and in a chamber of passion. Lyndon told of his conviction that this nation could stand firm in Vietnam and pay for it and could move ahead with the war on poverty. "Let us be remembered," he said, "as a President and a Congress who tried to improve the quality of life for every American." He asked for a 6 percent surtax on most incomes. There was tough emphasis in the paragraph beginning "Let us fight crime," and that got the most applause of anything. My eyes roved the Chamber. There was loyal and frequent, but I cannot say wildly enthusiastic, applause on the Democratic side, and almost none on the Republican side, except for the Vietnam reference, where the clapping was strong. Senator Fulbright sat silent, above it all, the whole evening. Bobby Kennedy was stony-faced. He applauded once, two or three light claps. It was a cold audience.

When Lyndon reached the line about conservation and beautification, he raised his eyes to the Gallery, hunting me, and I smiled back. As the hour approached 10:30, my eyes went from the clock to the number of pages left in the script. No, he was not going to finish in an hour. The message lasted an hour and nine minutes by my watch.

Then it was over and we rose and streamed out. There they were in the hall, the Ladies of the Press. "What did I think of it?" I thought it was a strong speech. It embodied the hopes and the dreams and the determination of a lot of the American people. To me, the line stating that this was "a time of testing" summed it up.

Then the elevator door closed and I was safe and silent. We went to the Speaker's Rooms where it is customary for the Leadership to gather. Lyndon was already there. There was a quick round of greetings with the Cabinet, Hale Boggs, Mrs. McCormack, and then I was out the door with Lynda, following Lyndon. We headed back to the White House and went swiftly up to the second floor. The television sets were on and the tables were spread with an inviting buffet. All of my guests in the Gallery joined me with their husbands, and some other staff. Everybody gathered around a television set to hear the commentators and the reviews. There were some plaudits within the House Chamber, here at home, and on the telephone, but there was no chorus of praise and support. It was, indeed, a "time of testing."

Everybody was hungry and we filled our plates with ham and turkey, macaroni and cheese, and salad, and a Christmas confection that had been a gift sent to us at the Ranch, which I had thriftily incorporated into the menu. So had the smoked turkey been a Christmas gift, which I had brought to the White House from home. The training of a lifetime is not easy to toss aside.

And then a little before one, everybody drifted off. We felt as though we had climbed one more mountain with great exertion, but the view from the top was foggy. The year had, indeed, begun.

Tuesday, January 17

Tonight was the annual dinner for the Vice President, the Speaker, and the Chief Justice. Our honor guests came a little before 8 and I met them in the Yellow Room—the Chief Justice and Mrs. Earl Warren and their family and the John Dalys and Mrs. Carmine Clemente were first to arrive, then the Speaker and Mrs. McCormack and his handsome nephew, Eddie McCormack, with his pretty wife. "Miss Harriet" used a cane, walking with great difficulty, with unfailing devoted assistance from her husband, the Speaker. It was only later that I found that today a campaign had been launched to unseat him from his position as Speaker, a challenge on the Hill, a column by Drew Pearson. Last to come were Hubert and Muriel, she looking very sharp in a white dress, and a group of his family.

Then Lyndon came in, bringing Mike Mansfield and Senator Dirksen with whom he had been conferring. Among the wives at least, the fresh spirit of reunion, of getting back together in January, is still abroad, and there was talk of the first meeting of the Senate Ladies Red Cross, with about sixty in attendance and for the first time a Senate wife, Louella Dirksen, introducing her daughter who had joined the group—her husband is Senator Howard Baker from Tennessee. I miss the meetings of the Senate Ladies. Some Tuesday I will drop in.

This is always one of the happiest parties of the year. Everybody knows everybody. All the Cabinet, including the newly sworn-in Secretary of Transportation, Alan Boyd, and Flavil, and all the Supreme Court, the John McClellans and Russell Longs, and Everett and Louella Dirksen, affable Tom Kuchel with pretty Betty, Mike and Maureen Mansfield, and the young and attractive Walter Mondales, Hubert's former colleague. There were two Governors, Nelson Rockefeller and Happy, very soon to have their second child, it seems, and young and attractive Governor and Mrs. William L. Guy of North Dakota.

It was a slow line, what with eight of us in it and half the people pausing to hug and kiss each other. There were lots of special friends of the Humphreys and the McCormacks and the Chief Justice, invited for the occasion because it was their party. Minnesota, California, and Massachusetts were well represented. I delighted particularly for them to share it with those they love.

The entertainment world was especially well represented. Tonight offered the most star-studded entertainment the White House had seen in a long time—Carol Channing doing thirty minutes from *Hello Dolly!*, and with her were the composer Jerry Herman and producer David Merrick, whom she calls "the money man" of the show. From my earliest memories of the great of the stage, there were Alfred Lunt and Lynn Fontanne, aging but elegant, and Joan Crawford—there was a marvelous transformation from this afternoon, when she had come to discuss the beautification program with me. Her simple, black daytime dress could have been anybody's. Tonight her shocking pink dress and coat announced her presence from one end of the East Room to the other. There were the Douglas Fairbanks, Jr.'s (he a legendary figure to me), and Al Hirt—a big Falstaffian character with a beard—the great jazz man from New Orleans. From the education world there was Dr. Victor L. Butterfield of Wesleyan University in Middletown, Connecticut; George Meany of labor came, and C. R. Smith of American Airlines—he leaned over a minute and I thanked him again for his generosity to the White House. (He gave the Thomas Moran painting.) The press was there in full force—the Dan Rathers and Victor Riesel and Ray Shearer—he covers us so constantly in Texas I feel especially easy around him, and the same for the Jack Horners and the Bob Youngs.

When the lengthy line was at last over, Lyndon took Muriel and Mrs. Warren to the State Dining Room. I went into the Blue Room with Hubert on my right and the Speaker on my left. Next to him sat Mrs. McCormack. They are never separated at dinner parties. In fact, in all the long decades of their marriage, he has had dinner with her every night! David Merrick and Lynn Fontanne spent most of the evening talking to each other. I caught one phrase, "When have you seen Noel?"

I was fascinated by Lynn Fontanne, her hair piled on top of her head, wearing a regal, flowing gray chiffon as queenly as her own manner, and a handsome jeweled pin—it looked as if the Czar of all the Russians might have given it to her. Even in her late seventies, she creates the illusion of beauty. I had looked up some of the things she had played in and found that they took me all the way back to my old favorites: *Design for Living, Idiot's Delight,* and *There Shall Be No Night,* the most stirring war play I remember. I spoke about them briefly. She told me she was doing *Anastasia* for TV in March.

The conversation naturally gravitated to the theater, and Hubert—no surprise—came up with the liveliest stories of all, stories of a traveling company coming to the Opera House in South Dakota. (It *would* be named the Opera House. What dream of glory caused them all to be named that—in Marshall or Johnson City or that little town in South Dakota?) They borrowed his mother's davenport and rug every year, and the family got free tickets to the play in return. Hubert was in great form and carried the table with him.

We had Sole Nina, and Pheasant Muriel. (Hubert said the wild rice should be named after him.) And then a Chocolate Soufflé Harriet . . . My heart always lifts with the U.S. Army Strings! I feel their music is a special gift to the guests. But next came a problem we haven't solved when we have a dinner in two rooms. Those of us in the Blue Room cannot see the President when he rises for his toast. So the murmur of voices continues and we always lose his first phrase or two. Lyndon's toast was splendid tonight! I liked especially the lines, "It was the richness of this American earth that made us powerful and affluent in this land. It was the fidelity of men like these that made us free." "These" were the honorees —the Vice President, the Speaker, and the Chief Justice. In his reply Hubert left off being funny and was serious in recalling FDR's last written but unspoken words, the gist of which I recall, "The only limit to our realization of tomorrow will be our doubts of today."

The Speaker, when his turn came, was a tall and commanding figure. He called the White House "this Mansion of destiny to which few are called," and said, "our leader today is a man bigger than life, a man close to the soil and to the Bible, a man fitted to the largest scales of human progress." Chief Justice Warren's reply I can characterize mainly, just as I can him, as one of good will.

Lyndon and I and the six honor guests took our seats in the front row in the East Room. In every chair there was a program with a green-gold seal on the front and a delightful picture of Dolly and the synopsis of what we would see—thirty minutes from Act II of *Hello Dolly!* It was enchantment! The waiters did their gallop, the costumes were hilarious. The audience kept time with their feet or leaned forward and then the awaited moment when Dolly swept in, in pink and crimson and cherry red satin and beads and a bushel of feathers for a hat. It was one of the gayest times I remember in the White House—and over all too soon.

Then the band struck up "Happy Birthday" and a huge cake was wheeled in, as pink and cherry and crimson as Dolly's own dress. This was the fourth anniversary of the opening of the show and Carol herself has performed in it over a thousand times.

She introduced the heads of the cast, each one with a quip, and then turned to the audience: "I am deeply grateful for the Great Society because apparently you know how to spread it around." This was an obvious reference to the lines in the play, "Money is like manure. It doesn't do any good unless it is spread around." That brought down the house, but before they could recover, Lyndon said, "We've got to close down this show before Senator Dirksen takes it over," and then he reached out and took the Senator by the arm. Senator Dirksen ambled up to meet Miss Channing and she quickly said, "Many people say we sound alike," and the audience roared again.

The guests filtered out into the Great Hall and the Marine Band struck up dance music; Lyndon led Carol out on the floor. Her feathered hat covered his face as they danced. Rather than join in, nearly everybody made a circle and watched. The night really had been a night of politicians rubbernecking at theater celebrities and show people rubbernecking at politicians. Well, this was a combination not to be missed! Then Hubert took over with Carol. Doug Fairbanks asked me to dance. He talks as charmingly as he looks. He spoke of his visits to the White House beginning with the early days of FDR, how he used to make a few trips for FDR—information gathering. He smiled conspiratorially and said, "I was not Number 007, maybe Number 003½."

Before 12:30 Lyndon left and I soon followed. He said, "If you would like to get the houseguests up, I will slip on a robe and we will have a nightcap." Those who were spending the night in the White House met in the Yellow Room and Ed Clark and his daughter, Leila, joined us and for an hour we reviewed the party. No two couples enjoyed it more than the Roy Whites, to whom it is the greatest pleasure to offer hospitality, and the Jack Joseys, he a member of the Board of Regents of the University of Texas, an attractive couple, not too blasé to be really thrilled at being in the White House. This is the cozy, intimate part of a White House visit, so I tried to make it for each of the couples a personal moment of talking and listening.

Lyndon was in great form, telling the Menzies' stories for Ed's benefit, recounting our stay in Australia for them all, and it was 1:30 before we went to bed—he to his night reading and I to sleep. The year 1967 had begun auspiciously on the social front, at least, albeit surrounded by a swarm of troubles on every other side.

Monday, January 23

Tonight we had invited the second half of the Senatorial hundred for the briefing, as is Lyndon's custom. We divided them pretty much on seniority. The new ones were with us tonight: handsome Mark Hatfield, young and attractive Ernest Hollings of South Carolina, stern-faced, Lincolnesque Senator Clifford Hansen, and youthful, good-looking Charles Percy. Percy's wife looks like a girl herself. Senator William Spong of Virginia is new to me and so is Senator Robert Griffin of Michigan, an interim appointment after Pat McNamara's death.

The first-line team was there to greet them—Bob McNamara, Dean Rusk, Charlie Schultze, Gardner Ackley. The line moved quickly and then Lyndon asked the men to join him in the East Room for a briefing and I took the ladies upstairs to the Queen's Room. Tonight's program was to be about youth: the quality of today's generation, a controversial subject, with entirely too many columns in the newspapers devoted to beards, pot, LSD, and draft-card burners. This was to be the other side of it, the opportunities, the achievements, the activities of another kind of youth.

There was Jay Rockefeller, leaning over slightly from his six feet six, and beaming. He's recently moved to West Virginia. He asked me at once, with a true politician's instinct, if either Mrs. Bob Byrd or Mrs. Jennings Randolph were in the group. I pointed out Mrs. Bob Byrd to him and steered him in her direction for an introduction. This was my first time to meet Bob Taft III. He looked short and stocky compared to Jay's beanpole height. He was smiling but he looked nervous. Nobody was more so than I.

Lynda was the moderator. She introduced Bob Taft, pointing out that he would be speaking in the shadow of the beautiful portrait of his great-grandmother, Mrs. William Howard Taft. He talked about his three years in the Peace Corps in Tanzania and in a few moments it was apparent that he was good. He was that sort of speaker that old Governor Jim Ferguson described as "get full of your subject and let 'er fly." He was enthusiastic. He had loved his years with the Peace Corps. He made the experience come across as exciting, full of pitfalls and frustrations, and certainly no cure-all for the world, but when he finished I felt proud of him and of America and at ease about our evening.

I had taken out insurance ahead of time by calling on some special friends—Vide Bartlett, Gretchen Byrd, Mary Ellen Monroney, and Margy McNamara—to ask questions when the speakers finished. Tonight I needn't have. The questions erupted, and after a moment or two we had to suggest that we wait until the second speaker had finished and then ask all the questions at once.

Jay Rockefeller unfolded to his full height, smiling over at his fiancée, Sharon Percy, and his mother-in-law-to-be, who were on the sofa, and beginning with a humorous reference to Bob's great-grandmother up there on the wall, he said, "I had a relative who was interested in coming here to live once, too." Everybody in the room loved it! From then on they were in his hands. He described the life at Emmons, West Virginia, so graphically you could feel the coal dust under your fingernails and see the rickety front porch where the perennially unemployed father of nine sat and whittled. He told the story of two boys—one who had made it after about three years. Jay had been his friend and tried to help him. He was now on his way to college. He told of another who had not made it, who never would make it, and would be on public welfare for the rest of his life. When Jay finished, Mary Ellen leaned over to me and said, "That young man is going to be in the White House himself one day." The questions flew. It was just that atmosphere of spark, of excitement of give-and-take, that I wanted to create.

About 8 I received word that the gentlemen were ready to eat so we drifted downstairs to join them in the State Dining Room. I spent most of my time walking around to visit with guests with just a bit of hors d'oeuvre instead of a plate. Some of the Senators were most complimentary. One said it was the best briefing he had ever participated in—had more meat to it, very candid, he said, with time to ask questions. There was that beaming atmosphere of a good party and I felt happy.

I went upstairs a little past 9 and the guests did not linger. They are busy people. It is well for us all that these parties end early.

Thursday, January 26

Forty-six Mayors, the Executive Committee of the U.S. Conference of Mayors, were meeting in Washington and I had asked them to come for tea at 4:30 today to tell me what was going on back home in the field of beautification and conservation. I was at the door of the Diplomatic Reception Room to meet them at 4:30 and here they came, marching up the driveway, shoulder to shoulder, John Collins, the Mayor of Boston, in his wheelchair, in the vanguard. I hurried out to greet him.

There were many I had met in their home towns—Mayors Ivan Allen of Atlanta, Thomas Currigan of Denver, where we had had such a delightful visit last fall, bouncy Herman Goldner of St. Petersburg, Richard Lee of New Haven, who had given me an in-depth tour of his city, Roy Martin of Norfolk, Virginia, who spoke glowingly of the two Azalea Queens in our family, and James Tate of Philadelphia, often my host there. Surprisingly, there were three Mayors from Alabama—from Tuscaloosa, Gadsden, and Mobile. We reminisced about the fire station in Mobile that I dedicated during the Whistlestop. But most of the Mayors were from large towns.

The meeting was informal, held in the Red Room—crowded, but it is a good room for getting talk going. I said a word of welcome and then Jerry Cavanagh of Detroit took over as a moderator in a most informal manner and called on about five of the Mayors to speak of what was happening in their home towns.

First there was John Lindsay of New York. His is the stormiest problem city in the United States, I am sure, and he gave a graphic presentation. Fountains are one of his objectives now that the water crisis is over. Mayor Alfonso Cervantes of St. Louis told us about the great arch—a monument to the city's century and a half of life—and I believe it was he who said that St. Louis had for the first time undertaken to sweep its alleys. Much of the conversation concerned increased budgets and lots of it was devoted to cleaning up. What could be more basic? One of the Mayors said that his budget for trash collection and cleaning had tripled in the last two years.

One Mayor said forthrightly that if you had declared five years ago that any Mayor knew or cared anything about beautification you would have been crazy, but now a good many of them were finding out that it is good business and good politics. Mayor Lee of New Haven said the word "design" had become part of city administration. Actually, the word "design" threaded through the whole evening, dealing with street furniture, overall planning, freeways, greenbelts for the future. The vocabulary and the horizons seem to be changing on the anvil of necessity.

Then, preceded by a slight ripple of noise, Lyndon came striding in, took a seat and listened until the last one finished, and then he began to talk. That was the best part of the day. He was blunt and tough. He said if the cities had problems, if they needed massive help, it was up to the Mayors to help get the votes in Congress to obtain it. "I do not have enough horsepower. I can get just three votes in the Texas delegation. If your constituencies want model cities, they must express themselves." He told about how the bill passed last year, just by an eyelash, yet with all of the steam behind it that he and the whole Administration could muster. Nobody needs to be told about the different climate of this year's Congress, but if it is the Mayors' problem, if they think the cities need work on air pollution and water pollution and open spaces and helping the ghettos, they had better get busy with the only people who can make it happen—the members of Congress.

I wish we had a tape recorder. It was wonderful and I felt very proud, because, in a way, he was doing it for me. What had started out to be "tea and thank you" by a timid First Lady had turned out to be a fairly substantive meeting.

The big event of today was the signing of the Space Treaty in the East Room. Its purpose is to keep weapons of mass destruction from being used in outer space—no bombs riding on satellites. It was a spine-tingling affair, one of those times when you think you hear the drums of history beating in these corridors.

We walked into the East Room, Lyndon and I, a little past 5 and there was an unusually large battery of television cameras and cameramen and lights. The table from the Treaty Room, President Grant's Cabinet table, had been brought down. At it sat Dean Rusk and Ambassador Arthur Goldberg for the United States, Ambassador Patrick Dean for the United Kingdom, and Ambassador Anatoly Dobrynin for the USSR, with Disarmament Chief William C. Foster standing behind them. Lined up on each side in chairs were the Ambassadors of sixty nations, and a broad spectrum of those who had worked with Space—from the Hill, in Defense, in NASA itself. From the Leadership, Mike Mansfield and Carl Albert and the Vice President and that old space hand, Clint Anderson. From NASA, Jim Webb and Dr. Robert Seamans and Dr. Welsh, Astronauts Neil Armstrong, Scott Carpenter, Gordon Cooper, Richard Gordon, and James Lovell. I saw General John P. McConnell, the Air Force Chief of Staff; Donald Hornig, Lyndon's Special Adviser on Science, and a goodly representation from State besides Rusk—Katzenbach, Harriman, and Foy Kohler—and from the National Security Council, the National Academy of Science, and quite a few from the UN.

Lyndon went to the podium and said: "This is an inspiring moment in the history of the human race. . . . This treaty means that our moon and sister planets will serve only the purposes of peace . . . astronaut and cosmonaut will meet someday on the surface of the moon as brothers and not as warriors."

It was less than a year ago when Lyndon proposed this treaty, and it was written at the United Nations in spite of all the antagonisms that have been stirred up and exacerbated by the Vietnam war. This is proof that man can aspire mightily, and achieve greatly, and I was feeling a rich glow of exaltation because we had taken a step forward. Sir Patrick Dean spoke, and Arthur Goldberg, and Russian Ambassador Dobrynin in very clear English and very clear words and with dramatic effect. Then the four at the table signed the document. Lyndon and I continued on to the Blue Room where we stood in line to meet the sixty Ambassadors as they filed past. They were slow in coming because each one of them had to sign the treaty. We had a picture made with each, including several from Iron Curtain countries—Czechoslovakia, Poland, Romania, Yugoslavia, Bulgaria.

When we finished with the receiving line I went into the State Dining Room. I talked to the Dobrynins quite a while. Mrs. Dobrynin asked me how it was when we returned home to Texas. Could we really be just at ease with our neighbors? Did they look on us as different? She said when they were at home in Russia, their old-time neighbors kept on giving Dobrynin advice as Ambassador, just as though he were still the boy next door. Mrs. Dobrynin was vivacious and her English was perfect. She has mastered the language in ten years, she told me. I found them an attractive couple.

The wife of the Luxembourg Ambassador told me how she watched her husband signing the treaty and suddenly realized that he was using a pen she had given him twenty years ago. That inanimate little object is twice as old as the space age and today it had played a role in the history of this age. She said she was going to keep it always.

A little before 7 I left to go upstairs to the farewell party for Secretary of Commerce John Connor. All of the Cabinet were present—a few staff members, the Rostows, Kintners, Watsons, and many of the Connors' kinfolks, principally Mary's, their teen-age daughter, Lisa, who has really grown up the last two years, their son Jeffrey up from Williams College, and their son John and his wife, who are still at school in Cambridge.

During John Connor's toast someone handed Lyndon a folded note and I watched his expression as he read it. His face sagged and my heart lurched. I knew the news was something bad and something close. When the applause for the toast had died down, he said, "I have to make a sad announcement. We have lost three astronauts—Ed White and Virgil Grissom and Roger Chaffee at Cape Kennedy. There was a fire in the spaceship." He said a brief farewell to the Connors and left for the Situation Room.

I thought of those young astronauts I had seen only an hour ago and of Jim Webb's happy face.

Lyndon did not come home for a long time. I read and worked and waited. Today has run the gamut from exaltation to grief, from a major success to a major tragedy in the space story.

Tuesday, January 31

WEST POINT AND THE WHITE HOUSE

Today encompassed the whole scale of emotions. Lyndon had decided to go to the funerals of Grissom and Chaffee and he asked me if I would go to West Point to the funeral of Ed White. Congressman "Tiger" Teague's wife, Freddie, and I rode out together to National Airport where we met Hubert and Patsy Webb and Air Force Chief of Staff General John McConnell. The day was bitter cold.

We were met at the West Point airstrip by attractive young General Donald Bennett and I rode with him up the lovely winding Hudson Valley to West Point, past Storm King Mountain, and the Palisades of the Hudson. As the road hugged its way along the mountainside there were great cascades of icicles, like frozen stalactites. These will be flowing springs in warm weather. Then we entered West Point and my spine tingled. It is the very home of military tradition, a great name in American history.

We went to the old Cadet Chapel on the grounds of the Academy cemetery, a small quiet place. Hubert and Freddie and I were seated close to the front. In the first pews there were Ed White's fellow astronauts—honorary pallbearers—Charles Conrad, Thomas Stafford, and Neil Armstrong, who had been at the White House so short a time before under such happy circumstances, and James Lovell and Frank Borman. And then six soldiers, enlisted men.

There was a long wait before the family came in. Mrs. White, so very young—her beautiful blonde hair covered with a black mantilla—and Colonel James McDivitt, the command pilot of the space flight in which White had performed America's first space walk, gently protective as he guided her in, the Whites' two children, Bonnie Lynn and Edward, and his parents, General and Mrs. Edward White, the General big and solid and strong. I remember them all from that happy visit to the White House when the Whites and the McDivitts spent the night before they set off for Paris.

There was the astronaut's younger brother, James White—himself a Lieutenant in the Army—pale and solicitous. He looked so like Ed that it was heartbreaking as he leaned over Mrs. White. The funeral service was brief and personal, conducted by Ed White's own minister from the little Texas town of Seabrook where he lived. The West Point Choir in the loft sang their "Alma Mater" and then the song of "The Corps" and I was caught up in the beauty of the voices and the words. Later I was told that Ed White had a record of these songs and that he always played them in times of stress. Mrs. White had asked that they be sung. We walked to the graveside and stood with several hundred people—a beautiful view of the Hudson just below us. The astronauts stood together closest to the coffin. At a time like this the value of discipline and tradition becomes apparent—strength to lean on, to support. These things had been important in Ed White's life—the Corps, the Church, the other astronauts. There is a special brotherhood between these men.

There was an element of strength and beauty in this cruel day. Mrs. White wept softly as they presented her the folded flag from Ed White's coffin and then General Bennett nodded to me and I moved forward and leaned over to express our sympathy. She looked up at me and quite clearly and almost urgently she said, "Please tell the President that Ed loved him. Now will you remember to tell him that?" Holding on tight—it was almost too much—I went down the line and murmured words to all the family. To Bonnie Lynn and Edward I said, "I have a good picture of you all in a happy time and I am going to send it to you." One of the best pictures in *The Living White House* is of Ed White, young and strong, his arms aloft, poised on the edge of the White House swimming pool. He had just tossed Bonnie high into the air. On the way back to the airport, General Bennett told me how Ed had brought his twelve-year-old son to West Point last summer to see it through his eyes. He had loved West Point.

One of the difficult things about this job—and one of the interesting things—is the rapidity with which one must shift gears, mentally, physically, and emotionally, and go on to the next appointment. I have had to learn to do this. I knew we were unveiling Madame Shoumatoff's portrait of President Franklin Roosevelt this afternoon, and a number of people had been invited to share this event. So when we put down, I pulled myself together and shifted gears.

This occasion was something I had looked forward to for months. We had asked Margaret Truman and Clif Daniel to come up ahead of time and Lyndon and I had a few minutes to visit with them, during which Margaret told me, no indeed, her mother was not going to give her portrait, which hangs in the Truman home in Independence, to the White House. Margaret said she had her own name on the back of it! I asked how we had best proceed, as I certainly would like this house to have a portrait of Mrs. Truman. Margaret thought the same artist might make a copy. If it was a good one, Margaret might take the copy and release the original.

Look magazine had been doing a story of reminiscences on Margaret. She had spent the morning in the White House, visiting her old bedroom and sitting room, now our family dining room and kitchen. She told us she had had two pianos in her room—she often played piano duets with a friend—and one night when they had come in late, she and her father had noticed that both the pianos were sitting at crazy angles, one end hiked up several inches more than the other. Sure enough, the floor was sinking beneath them. They had called a couple of Secret Service men and lifted the heavy pianos to a more solid portion of the floor. The very next morning President Truman called in architects and engineers to go over the place.

Downstairs I went straight to the podium to welcome this roomful of President Roosevelt's family, friends, and fellow workers of those vivid years. There were three children, Anna Roosevelt Halsted, John, and Franklin, a dozen grandchildren, three great-grandchildren, and I asked them all to stand while the TV cameras swung in their direction. Aside from the family, there were so many whose names threaded the whole Roosevelt period—Mrs. Henry Wallace, Francis Biddle, Grace Tully, Tommy Corcoran, Jim and Libby Rowe, Averell Harriman—and so many newsmen and women who had covered FDR. I gave a brief explanation of how, when we first moved in, we had begun to search for a portrait of Franklin Roosevelt for Lyndon's office. For two years the search had been fruitless and then Charles Palmer, of the Warm Springs Foundation, had brought Madame Shoumatoff to me and the portrait turned from dream into reality. I introduced her, and Madame Shoumatoff pulled the cord. That was one of the great moments of the day and I think I sensed almost an audible wave of approval from this very special audience.

Lyndon spoke briefly and very much in the mood of the Roosevelt era: "Times of trial can bring out the best in men and in nations. His face and his voice became symbols in that other time of bitter testing of man's power to overcome . . . Like every one of our great Presidents, he was also a great politician. He proved again and again that politics, scorned by so many, is an honorable calling."

Then we had a scene from Dore Schary's play *Sunrise at Campobello*, without benefit of stage, props, or costumes. Charlton Heston took the part of FDR; Mary Fickett, who had played the role on the stage as Eleanor Roosevelt, appeared in that role; and Ann Seymour was both FDR's mother and Missy LeHand. Dore Schary was the narrator and also played Louis Howe. They told me they had been nervous beforehand. They needn't have been. It was marvelous! I was caught up in admiration and so proud to be offering it to this audience.

Afterward we went into the Blue Room and the mood was as nostalgic as you would expect. As Marie Smith of the *Washington Post* said, the White House is filled with memories, both spoken and silent. There was a long roster of members of FDR's Administration—Thurman Arnold, old but full of ginger, Ed Foley and Abe Fortas and Tex Goldschmidt. There were the Leon Keyserlings, both of them in FDR's Administration, and Gladys Tillett, Vice Chairman of the Democratic National Committee during FDR's time, and well-known White House figures Roberta Barrows and Toi Bachelder.

I was especially glad to see members of the press who had covered those yeasty years—May Craig, looking remarkably sprightly in a bright pink dress and hat, her trademark, and Bess Furman, whose book about the White House is still a classic, and Doris Fleeson and Merriman Smith, the dean of the press corps, who had begun with FDR.

There were some widows of FDR's officials—Mrs. Oscar Cox, very lovely but sad, and Jane Ickes, remarkably durable, and Mrs. Emma Guffey Miller, age ninety-two, long-time friend of Mrs. Roosevelt and National Committee woman from Pennsylvania. Mr. Justice Reed, retired, was going around saying that he was the only one who had been there from the very first of the Roosevelt era. Lyndon corrected him and said, "No, I was here, too, although I was just a clerk in a Congressman's office." Bob Kintner had been a newsman in his time writing a column with FDR's cousin, Joe Alsop, and since then his career has led him back to the White House as Lyndon's Special Assistant.

I had asked Mary Lasker, Anna Hoffman, and Mrs. Sidney Hillman— a few would remember that old phrase "Clear it with Sidney"—and I was very pleased to have Dr. Wayne Grover, U.S. archivist, who is invaluable on the Library, and the Melville Bell Grosvenors of the White House Historical Association. There were also the Armand Hammers, my friends from Campobello.

As in any gathering where she is present, Alice Roosevelt Longworth was one of the stars of the occasion, a natural magnet for everybody hoping to hear something spicy, and there was another Roosevelt from that side of the family, Mrs. Kermit Roosevelt, who goes to St. Mark's with me. And a real old-timer, Mrs. Nellie Tayloe Ross, Director of the Mint in FDR's time and one of the first women Governors. But it was by no means a bunch of old folks only, because of grandchildren and great-grand-children. Anna soon had a group of about twenty of them on a second- and third-floor tour at my suggestion. It was a replay of the New Deal, full of "Remember when?"

Wednesday, February 22

NEW YORK

Today, George Washington's birthday, was an offbeat day for me, spent in New York. I caught the 9 A.M. shuttle and arrived at the Carlyle at 10:15. Lynda Bird was there, sleeping very late. Thank goodness I remembered that it was a holiday. She had been out with John Loeb, Jr., the night before, and when she finally woke up she was full of gay chatter.

Mollie Parnis came in time for lunch, and Sally Victor. We had fittings of clothes and I made a few more tentative choices, being very parsimonious, according to Bess' way of thinking. She and Helen both look at me with mild reproval and assure me that I will, indeed, need everything that I am getting, and several more in addition that I maintain I cannot afford. We lunched in front of the big picture window giving out onto the park— an unforgettably thrilling view. I have all these scenes locked in my heart for the time when life is quieter. In this life there are at least two days, maybe more, usually in February and August, that are devoted entirely to clothes. Today was a partial one. And there are several women from the world of fashion that I've come to think of as my real friends, especially Mollie Parnis and Adele Simpson.

Tonight we were to attend a dinner party at Mary Lasker's. When Lynda came in, we went over the guest list that Mary's secretary had thoughtfully provided for us. Lynda knows more of the guests and more about them than I do. I had my hair combed, piled on top of my head, and wore my pale yellow dress with the jacket. A little before 8 we left for Mary's. From the moment we entered it was perfection—the flowers, the food, the setting, the guests. Everything in Mary's house is so exquisitely done. Here living is an art, and planning, imagination, and great taste have gone into making it so.

There were about thirty guests for dinner, memorable among them the Marc Chagalls. He looks rather like an aging faun with his sprightly, mobile face, his bushy eyebrows, and a smile that lights up. He spoke only French, with a few halting words of English. But he said charmingly, "The face talks." His does. Everyone was talking about the sets he had painted for *The Magic Flute*. Chagall loomed larger in the production than Mozart! The James Hesters were there. (He is President of New York University.) He said yes, they were having their share of protestors and placard carriers.

The distinguished and interesting Raymond Loewys were among the guests, and I thanked him again for his help in giving design planning for items for the handicapped to make. Mrs. Danny Kaye came without her husband, who is taping a show. Handsome Hugh O'Brian slipped in a bit late, and was sitting by Lynda at dinner. I sat between Richard Rodgers, the composer, and Lynda's boss, Bob Stein of *McCall's*, whom I found very easy to talk to. He seemed to take Lynda pleasantly as a matter of course and assured me that everybody at *McCall's* did too, though it certainly had posed problems at first. He had taken her around to meet every individual, he said, so they wouldn't gawk at her in the halls.

Here was I, great lover of the theater, sitting next to one of the biggest figures in it—over how many decades? three? four?—Richard Rodgers. And I couldn't think of anything terribly bright to say to him, so I asked him which of his musicals he had really loved the most. He thought a minute and said, "Carousel." Fortunately I remembered that *Carousel* came from *Liliom* and was one of the very first plays I had ever seen, when I was fifteen—part of a seed that yielded my long harvest of joy in the theater.

There were two outstanding toasts—an unusual one by John Gunther, a toast to this room and all the interesting company it had housed over the many years he has known it, for the good talk here, for the beautiful paintings that lined the wall, to the whole exquisite setting—very apt and bright. And then there was a toast by Lynda that caught us all unaware. "Because this is such an official occasion," she said, "I want to propose a toast to the President—George, that is." It took several seconds before somebody began to laugh, and then everybody around the table followed suit as they realized it was President George Washington! After all, it was his birthday.

Then we dispersed into the other rooms, and gradually the after-dinner guests began to drift in—Leonard Lyons, whom I have been seeing for much more than thirty years and who doesn't seem a bit older than the first time I saw him, the John D. Rockefellers, with whom I managed to have a few minutes to talk about Jay's wedding.

Mary had told me about the new method of smoke control that Major Alexander de Seversky had invented, and when she brought him over to introduce him I told her that I remembered his name well from the early 1950's when Lyndon and Stu Symington were so interested in increased air power. He is the very apostle of it—author of *Victory Through Air Power*. And he said, "Yes, I spent more than fifty years of my life working on airplanes and now I am a 'chimney sweep.' "

Lauren Bacall was one of the most charming women there. I looked at her and tried to analyze her magnetism. It's more than looks. I think it's a full, lusty interest in life. There were lots of "the beautiful people"— Kitty Carlisle, Marietta Tree, Susan Stein. I found it hard to talk to any one individual. The room was so full. I danced a little. But I was really more pleased when John Loeb said, "Come on," and took me to a quiet end of the room where we could look out on the river and the lights and talk with a few people. This was the happiest time of the evening for me.

It was a star-studded group! Richard Kiley of *The Man from La Mancha*, the best show of the season, was there, as well as David Merrick, dress designers, museum directors, and investment bankers. A marvelous cross section of a marvelous city, gathered together for me by the dearest friend— a sort of a feast. And so it was. The only person I was really disappointed in was me. And one I was particularly proud of was Lynda, who was taking it all in like a sponge—bright and beautiful. A little before one I said good night to a few around the room, and dearest thanks to Mary and good-by to Lynda. A few vagrant flakes of snow were sifting down. When I was back in the Carlyle in bed I could hear the wind roaring around that tower.

Spring 1967

Today I welcomed as houseguests members of the intimate family circles of former Presidents—Charles Taft, whose father, William Howard Taft, became President in 1909; Mrs. Van Seagraves, FDR's granddaughter ("Sistie" Dahl) who lived here a while with her mother, Anna Roosevelt, and visited often during the thirteen Roosevelt years; Barbara Eisenhower, so fresh and wholesome and pretty; and Margaret Truman who arrived late, because she had taken the train—she doesn't like airplanes. Her quietly sophisticated husband, Clifton Daniel, had arrived before.

We all sat around in the West Hall with a cup of tea and talked about their life and times here—a sort of preview of the reminiscences they will give the Congressional wives tonight. They all seemed excited, but not as excited as I was. Charles Taft handed me an envelope with pictures of where his father grew up, the old Taft home. The family wishes to turn the house over to the National Park Service.

490

I went to dress for the eighth and last reception for the Congress. I wore my pink dress and felt quite gala. We began to get word that it might be one of those nights—a late vote. The House members might not get here until 6:30 or maybe even 7.

By 6, twenty or more guests had arrived. I went to the Green Room to receive them without Lyndon, who was tackling his desk while they gathered. Lyndon joined us a little before 7, when there were still a dozen or more Congressmen to come. A little past 7 he took them off to the East Room and I asked the ladies to follow me to the Queen's Room.

Each time I have awaited these programs with trepidation and uncertainty. Tonight I felt that it was going to be good, and it was smashing! Lynda Bird was the moderator. The White House memories of those present spanned sixty-two years, beginning with Charles Taft, the first speaker, whose recollections actually went back five years before his father became President. He was a member of the so-called White House Gang, as a young school friend of Quentin Roosevelt in 1904. He recalled how his family had brought the first motorcar—a white Pierce Arrow—into White House life, and how he and Quentin Roosevelt had ridden up and down in the elevator—one in the cab and one underneath where the luggage was supposed to go—one pushing the "up" and the other pushing the "down" button, probably shortening the life of the elevator, and certainly its efficiency.

One fascinating fact Charles Taft mentioned was that the entire content of his father's papers for his four years in office numbered about five hundred thousand pieces. And for the first year of President Kennedy's, there were a million five hundred thousand. We are devoured by communications in today's world.

Mrs. Seagraves I thought quite shy, and I felt that her times in the White House had not been, perhaps, as carefree as the public thought. Next, Barbara Eisenhower said that living in the White House had given her a "pinch me" feeling—I know just how she felt! I loved her story about the three children putting on a Christmas pageant in the East Hall for their grandparents—the three of them playing nine parts and rushing into the Queen's Room and the Lincoln Room to change costumes and then out again to appear as wise men or angels or the Virgin Mary, whatever the script called for.

Margaret Truman Daniel, who is as matter of fact as her father, very assured, quite good-looking, told about playing ping-pong on the third floor with her mother, who was a whiz, and her father's well-known attempt to frighten her and two of her girl friends who were spending the night in the Lincoln bed. He had planned to send in a servant, wearing his (President Truman's) own tall Inaugural hat and a beard. The first three seemed to remember the White House with a certain awe and reverence and happy nostalgia, Margaret with more detachment—she could take it or leave it.

Last to speak was Lynda Bird, who told of her own times here—the costume party where there had been three "Teddy Roosevelts," and playing in the snow on the South Lawn with Warrie Lynn.

There was for me the gay feeling in the air of holiday . . . We had entertained the entire Congress in groups of seventy couples or so in a series of eight receptions! Now they were over, and we were leaving for Texas tonight.

As we flew homeward, I remembered those evenings and laughed to myself at one of the most delightful stories that was related. It was told by Mrs. Frank Karsten of Missouri—and it was typical of the kind of malapropism that occurs in politics. Her husband was making a speech during a campaign. When it was over, a large bustling woman, a strong supporter, came up to him gushing and said, "Your speech was just wonderful! It was absolutely superfluous!" Congressman Karsten, a little bit taken aback, said, "Thank you. I guess I will have to have it published—posthumously." Thereupon the lady answered, "That's fine. I hope it will be soon!" . . . He declares it really happened.

Thursday, March 9

This was one of those rat-a-tat days. It began early with breakfast with Lyndon. And then to Spanish class. Two hours in a capsule, two hours of application to only one thing; it is a relaxation and indulgence. Maybe I don't learn much, but I like the class. Then a session with Liz about the eight speeches which I will be doing on the trip to West Virginia, North Carolina, and Tennessee. Actually, they are rolling off so easily I am worried for fear there is something wrong with them.

Then fittings of the last three of my spring outfits, I hope. I can't get over the feeling that it's slightly ridiculous that clothes should take up so much time. I have a sort of a schizophrenic feeling that I'm cast in a role that I was never meant for and that it is probably not right to spend so much time and money on clothes. And on the other hand a sort of vain, feminine, increasingly delighted feeling that I do look rather well in them, a bit younger and slimmer than I used to.

I joined Lyndon at the elevator as he went down to his press conference, to be televised in the East Room. I wore my mint-green silk and sat in a lone chair on his right, and the ordeal began.

It was a very interesting press conference to me. Knowing the strain that Lyndon had been under, I marveled that he could be so restrained—so bland, dignified, calm, even perhaps a little bit *too* slow. He began with a surprise, asking Congress to restore the investment credit and the use of accelerated depreciation for buildings.

Then a reporter asked the inevitable question about a pause in the Vietnam bombing. Then followed the other inevitable question, "Would you end all the speculation first and tell us if you intend to run in 1968? And if Hubert Humphrey will be your running mate?"

It was like a play. This was a climax and the audience was very quiet. Lyndon rose to it like a good actor. "I am not ready to make a decision about my future after January 1969 at this time. I think that down the road . . . ," etc. And then glowing words about Hubert.

Lyndon was very much in charge throughout. His control never showed more than when they began to question him about his critics on Vietnam, hoping, I am sure, for some expression of bitterness or hostility. They got soft answers. "I'm just not in a position to know how much information each critic of my policy in Vietnam happens to have at the time he makes his criticism. I might say that it seems obvious to me that some of them do need more information sometimes." A mild laugh rippled across the room.

And then it was over and he took my arm. I threw him a congratulatory look with my eyes, which I meant to be all balm and velvet. We rushed out between the massed lines of reporters, with Joe Califano, Jack Valenti, Jake Jacobsen, and George Christian in our wake. Upstairs we held the post mortem—always one of the most interesting half-hours. We all felt pretty elated.

Tuesday, March 14

ASHEVILLE, NORTH CAROLINA

Today was the fullest, most dramatic day of our three-day trip through Appalachia to see Lyndon's programs on education translated into people. John Gardner, Secretary of Health, Education and Welfare, accompanied us. We woke early in the lovely mountain resort residence of the Governor of North Carolina where Governor and Mrs. Dan Moore were our hosts. Mrs. Moore had suggested that we have breakfast at the dining room table. I was down a bit late for delicious ham and grits and hot biscuits, and could with clear conscience throw caution to the wind because I was going to need all the strength I could get today.

Then into Trailways buses—two busloads—including Dick Graham, Director of the Teachers Corps, school officials, and more than forty press members. It was a two-hour drive, and they briefed us as we went along on the history, purpose, and operation of the Teachers Corps. The heart of it seems to be to put really good teachers in direct contact with the most needy students, such as you would find at Rio Grande City, Texas, or in Harlem or in the landlocked hills of western North Carolina.

Youngsters with a certain amount of rearing and family background can get along with a teacher on a thirty-to-one ratio. But where the school is the principal resource of the children, the only hope is for more teachers, and in that treadworn phrase, for more dedicated ones, to give each child personal attention. One teacher said that since the Teachers Corps had come, for the first time in his life "I've been teaching—not just policing a schoolroom full."

Mrs. Moore bravely went every mile. People were lined up along the street, waving and smiling, and a great number of flags were out. Always, always, that gives me a lift of the heart.

We stopped first at the Sylva-Webster High School—a consolidated school—actually out in the country. The entire student body was lined up along the highway and we couldn't bear just to pass them by, so we stopped, got out, and greeted them.

The road wound up and up into the Appalachian Mountains—breathtakingly beautiful, still in the grip of winter, thickly wooded with balsam and other evergreens, hickory and hardwoods, and whole masses of rhododendron and laurel. Rushing mountain streams came tumbling down in cascade, and then flowed down the valley in swift, clear little rivers, sometimes spanned by walking bridges leading over to a house across the hollow. The maples were just budding in the valleys and halfway up the mountains, making a red tracery, a promise of spring.

At Canada Township the paved road ended and we got into three smaller schoolbuses for the winding, narrow dirt road to the Mathises' house. This was the family we were going to visit to see just what effect the Teachers

Corps had on individuals, to show the raw material the Teachers Corps students had to work with—the background from which they came.

At first I had flinched at the idea. It sounded like an insensitive exposure of their poverty, a crass use of them. Liz had visited Canada Township and talked with Gertie Moss, the principal. She had come back convinced, and had convinced me, that if we were really to show what the Teachers Corps did, this was the best way. As for the Mathises, and all those like them in the hills and hollows, they were, for all their poverty, proud, hospitable, deeply interested, not in the least overwhelmed at the thought of our visit.

So there we were, walking down the little trail among the hemlock and rhododendron—Gertie Moss and I leading the crowd—hopping on stepping stones over Needy Creek (well-named), bending over to go through a rail fence into the yard where the Mathis family was lined up to meet us. Mr. Mathis, a grizzled wood cutter in his forties, and Mrs. Mathis greeted me with lively interest. Their seven children, from about six to nineteen, lined up around them in front of their two-room wooden shack in the hollow. A hound dog lounged in the yard, a few chickens scratched. There was one lone apple tree and some discarded rubber tires in which flowers had grown last summer.

They had a ten-acre farm and they made less than two thousand dollars a year, from that part-time work, wood cutting. But they had kept the seven children in school most of the time. All of them were small for their ages, and all of them had bad teeth. Every time a mouth opened, you knew that to go out into the world and get a job, they would have to have not only training, a skill, but also a dentist.

Mrs. Mathis asked us in, very brightly and comfortably. They really were glad to see us and apparently did not feel invaded by the army of fifty or more television and newspaper reporters in the front yard. Inside we met her elderly mother in her eighties, Mrs. Minnie Alexander. There were several sofas covered with throws, all with the springs nearly out, a potbellied stove and a curtain that led to the back bedroom where, presumably, there were beds, although I am sure four or five of the family must have slept on those sofas.

I had feared the conversation would be strained, but it wasn't. I asked if there were fish in these beautiful mountain streams. Mr. Mathis said, "Yes, mountain trout." There was a TV set. We talked about each other's favorite program. And Mr. Mathis said hospitably, "When the President comes on, we just kept him right on, listen to him just like it was a program."

Mrs. Mathis told us what a job it was to get the children off to school in the morning. And then, most important of all, she talked about the Teachers Corps. "It's grand. The children like the ones at school. We met them when we were up there at a meeting one night." Then she asked, "Do you have a garden on your ranch?" And I talked about our corn and tomatoes, and she about their corn, cabbage, and beans.

There were John Gardner and Liz and I and a pool reporter and all the Mathises in the tiny room. I gave her packages of preserves and honey from the LBJ Ranch, wrapped incongruously in the elegant embossed paper of the White House. Mrs. Mathis told me, with a lively spirit, that I ought to see the country in the springtime when the apple tree was in bloom and later when the rhododendron was out.

What keeps these people in the hills? It's beautiful country, but is it love of the land, or fear of the outside?

We all walked up to the schoolbus and the Mathises piled in with us, and we rode back to the long, low, brick structure that is the result of consolidating six one-room schoolhouses in as many hollows, bringing together 105 students where all eight grades are taught by four teachers.

As we came up the hill, we saw floating above the school the Stars and Stripes and beside it the flag of North Carolina. I felt a sudden, fierce elation. The school was the hope of the community—probably the only hope these mountain people had to acquire a skill that would enable them to go out into the world and make a living. And if you acquired a skill and wanted to stay here in these beautiful hills, what was there to do? School teaching, but what else? It was a grim, wracking problem. You looked at the people and the houses, and you felt the place was a dead end, that several generations of living here had had a self-defeating, brutalizing effect.

There was a ceremony in front of the school underneath the flags. The Glee Club sang "America, the Beautiful" and naturally, "Nothing Could Be Finer than to Be in Carolina." And then the children did a square dance, and I greeted the Head Start students.

The high point of the day was introducing the Job Corps Teachers—three men and a plump, sweet-faced woman, Mrs. Ramsey, who was their leader. Gertie Moss made a welcoming talk, and I answered, haltingly but earnestly, trying to look into the eyes of first one youngster on the right and then another one on the left or some bearded father in overalls out front. I tried to tell them how important it was that they stay in school.

"There is no more important journey you can take than your daily journey into the classroom." One of the children, I had heard, walks two and a half miles before he catches the schoolbus at 7. Often he leaves home by lantern light and has to use the lantern before he reaches home in the evening.

With only about twelve hundred members of the Teachers Corps in all the far-flung places like Canada Township, it's a mighty little David for a mighty big Goliath and the legislation is coming up soon. Unless Congress votes the $12 million appropriation, the Teachers Corps will expire in June. I hope we can "walk it across the stage" to expose it to the public and hopefully win support for it.

We went inside the school and watched the Teachers Corps in operation. In one room they were using visual-aid machines for faster reading. In another room Mr. Whitmire was cutting the hair of eight-year-old Bobby Carroll Owen. After-hours he cut their hair—"We're a long ways away up here." Gertie Moss had told me the nearest telephone is eleven miles away and nobody in Canada Township gets a newspaper. One intern was giving remedial reading. Another was working with cards with the primer class. I heard they'd put on a Christmas play—the first time ever. And they'd started teaching basketball.

Mrs. Moss led me into the cafeteria, and I had a full plate of tasty chicken casserole and green beans, salad, a roll, and dessert. The children also had milk. Mrs. Moss said to me, as though the food were coming to her or her very own family, "Oh, yes, that is one of the things the government has done. We give them a good hot lunch here. And then we serve oatmeal and milk to about thirty of the children who don't have anything at home before they come."

By 1:30 we were in cars leaving Canada Township. All that marks it on the main highway is the Mountain Ridge Baptist Church, Brown's General Store, and its heart—the school. I felt as if I understood my country better and also had made a real friend when I shook Gertie Moss' hand. Then we were off down the mountain to Western Carolina College at Cullowhee (an Indian name which means valley of the lilies).

We stopped in front of Hunter Library where the President, Dr. Paul Reid, met us, and went inside to meet the staff of this thirty-six-hundred-student college. A few years ago there were only six hundred students. Everywhere you looked a new building was going up. Now 65 percent of the teachers in the mountain schools of North Carolina are from Western Carolina College.

The reason for this trip was to bring public exposure to the eighteen major measures that Lyndon and the Congress have been able to pass to advance education. At the dedication of the Library, Ruth Graham (Mrs. Billy Graham) gave the invocation. John Gardner made an excellent short speech. Then I made a brief reference to the fact that federal participation in education is not exactly new, going back as far as 1785 in the Land Ordinance, the land grant colleges of the 1860's, and the GI Bill of Rights of our own day. "So that these things that we are seeing—the Teachers Corps, federal funds for Hunter Library, and new student loan programs, all these programs—are in an old and honored American tradition." I told how Lyndon, whenever he is asked which of his accomplishments he is proudest of, always answers what he's been able to do for education. I ended with a quote from Thomas Wolfe: "To every man his chance—to every man, regardless of his birth, his shining, golden opportunity—to every man the right to live, to work, to be himself, and to become whatever thing his manhood and his vision can combine to make him—this, seeker, is the promise of America."

We left for Asheville and were back at the Governor's beautiful western residence a little past 5. I had a real rest—more than an hour. And then up and dressed and ready to go with Secretary John Gardner and Mrs. Moore to Lee Edwards High School for a visit to an adult education class sponsored by the Asheville-Buncombe Technical Institute. Buncombe is a well-known name around here. That talkative, old-time politician was a native of this area, and he added a word to our language.

I walked into a class in basic English—thirty or more students, mostly white. The principal had told me that they ranged in age from eighteen to eighty-two and that in the last two years fifty-five hundred Asheville citizens had enrolled! Here the teacher was Mrs. Mildred Smith, a Negro, bright, unruffled, who kept drawing diagrams on the board and getting her class to parse sentences while the battery of cameras and writers moved in. After about ten minutes Mrs. Smith asked me to come up and say a word to the class. It was easy to salute their determination, their get-up-and-go, their drive to go back to school, to make a richer life for themselves and obtain a better job. One of their members stood and responded. He asked me to take back their thanks to the President for this program.

Out in the hall where all the other classes had gathered, I saw a great many Negroes, the majority middle-aged, some old. The women outnumbered the men. Liz asked one of them what she did. She said, "I'm a domestic, and I need to know how to read to do my job better." In its different way, this had been one of the most stirring things of the whole trip.

From the high school we went to the airport. I walked along the fence shaking hands, and then with a last good-by to Mrs. Moore, I was in the plane that brought us to Nashville and our old and dear friends, Buford and Catherine Ellington, Governor of Tennessee.

At last gratefully to bed in the beautiful Tennessee Governor's Mansion. What a day this had been! I wondered about the Mathises and where those seven children would be thirty years from now. Sadly, you are inclined to think the only solution is to get educated and get out, but you wonder why man has managed so ineptly. It's beautiful country and yet on those who live there, generation in and generation out, inter-marrying, the isolation has had a stultifying effect.

I hoped it had been good for the newspaper people—their seeing the face of America. It certainly had for me. A young journalism student at North Carolina College had asked me the inevitable question, "What is it like to be First Lady?" A day like today is the essence of what it is like! One gets to know one's country better. It's a cram course in geography, sociology, and people.

Wednesday, March 15

NASHVILLE, TENNESSEE

This was one of those marvelous days that I owe to the White House and that I will always cherish. I woke early in the bedroom of the Governor's Mansion in Nashville and left at 8 with Governor Ellington and Catherine for the airport to meet Lyndon. He was a little late. He had received a call the night before about 10 P.M. informing him that the grave of President Kennedy would be moved during the night and that there would be a 7 A.M. ceremony at the gravesite. He decided that he should attend. So he stood in the rain, sharing an umbrella with Bobby Kennedy, with only Mrs. Kennedy and the members of the family present on the gray, misty slope of Arlington while Cardinal Cushing prayed. Then Lyndon dashed as fast as he could to the airport. He was only a half-hour late, but I was fearful that the good ladies at the Hermitage (where we were bound for breakfast) and their grits soufflé would be inconvenienced by his not being on the dot. How often one cannot understand, simply because one doesn't know the facts.

There were several thousand people along the roadway and so many American flags. All day long through Tennessee I saw flags. And never without a lift of the heart.

For the first time in many years—I believe it's a gesture made only for Presidents—when we alighted there was an old-fashioned horse-drawn black carriage (it must have been very elegant in its day) with a dignified old Negro in livery and silk top hat sitting up front with the reins. And at the horses' heads stood an equerry in a gorgeous scarlet suit. I would have been crushed not to ride in that carriage and so I rode, but Lyndon chose to walk up the block-long cedar-lined avenue that leads to the white-pillared portico of the Hermitage.

Pretty, white-haired Mrs. Horatio Buntin, the Regent of the Ladies Hermitage Association, and a distant kinswoman of Lyndon, greeted us on the front porch. Assistant Postmaster General William McMillan, who was with us, had brought the first issues of the stamp honoring the two-hundredth birthday of President Andrew Jackson.

In the course of my little talk I said: "One senses a great presence in this stately mansion. It bears the mark of a unique man and his times. Of all the Presidents of the United States, there are only a few, I believe, whose image remains strongly with us today. Men we can visualize as having once been flesh and blood and not vague shadows on the pages of history. For me, Andrew Jackson was one of those men. A rugged man from the West. It was a proud day for the mass of the people. General Jackson was their own President. The people were touched by him. He was one of them."

If anybody thought there was any allusion to a similarity between President Jackson and the present President, in my mind, he was entirely right! But most of the speech was about education—beginning with the fact that the battle was fought and won for the principle of free, compulsory public schools during Andrew Jackson's time and going on till now with the eighteen new laws under which we are attacking old problems with new methods. I drew word pictures from my trip.

Governor Ellington introduced Lyndon. I felt I could see the pleasure it gave Lyndon, and certainly me, to have that good friend introducing him. Lyndon's speech, of course, was the high point of the morning to all of the several thousand gathered out under the cedar trees in front of us. (Why were there always cedar trees at the homes of the old great ones of the South? There must be a reason.)

After Lyndon's speech we walked down into the garden which I remember so well and affectionately and to the gravesite of the General and his Rachel. We placed a large wreath, standing for a solemn moment. This man was my almost favorite President, excepting only Thomas Jefferson and probably FDR, and, of course, my own. I loved his house and grounds. His home was the home of a gentleman.

Everything had been thought of at the breakfast. We were seated at the long table in the great dining room—about twenty of us—and we began with sugared strawberries, followed by grits soufflé (there is nothing better), Tennessee ham (I could not leave Tennessee without ham), fried apples, beaten biscuit, turkey hash. It was a feast!

Breakfast was served on Jackson's family china. The flowers, they told me, were Rachel's favorites. And there drifted in to us from the sitting room the music of the harpsichord, charming, sad, the perfect touch in the perfect setting.

We motorcaded into downtown Nashville to the Capitol, through streets lined with people four or five deep and lots of bands, lots of flags. Buford told us that the Tennessee Legislature had passed a Resolution supporting Lyndon's stand in Vietnam. A little before 12 we filed into the Chamber for Lyndon's address to a joint session of the House and Senate.

It was an impressive setting—a sober and expectant audience. The burden of Lyndon's speech was Vietnam, as it has been over and over and over. He gave a clear exposition of the historical background of the conflict and then the news that Ellsworth Bunker would replace Henry Cabot Lodge as Ambassador with Gene Locke to back him up and Bob Komer to work on pacification. At the last, he gave a salute to General Westmoreland, who had been stationed near Nashville and is remembered with warmest admiration.

As we walked out of the Capitol, there was a band playing and an enthusiastic crowd, though I had heard there would be demonstrators. I saw no sign of any. We got into the back seat of the car and started around a tablelike pedestal on which the Capitol sits. Just as we rounded the corner, something happened. It was all so fast we could hardly believe it. A youth broke from the thinning crowd and flung himself right in front of the car. The driver slammed on the brakes. Immediately there were officers at his side pulling him back, but suddenly a young girl threw herself more successfully flat to the ground, practically under the wheels. They were both picked up bodily and moved, and we drove on slowly— it took only a split second and it would have been quite possible to have missed the whole episode. I looked back and saw the young girl's naked legs—her dress around her hips, her feet held by one officer, her shoulders by another—being lifted from the road. I wonder what would have happened legally, psychologically, in every other way, if our driver hadn't been so quick and the officers so alert—if the young people actually had been hit by the car.

We drove on to Columbia, Tennessee, to Columbia State Community College. The new college is rising from a bare field. You could see a new foundation here and there as we went under the cold and dripping sky to the bunting-draped platform, led by the youngish college President-to-be.

I seldom make a speech in Lyndon's presence. Today I found myself doing it over and over, for he was joining up with my long-planned trip. My theme was that new colleges like this one are being established at the rate of one a week across our country, mounting from eight junior colleges at the turn of the century to 680 now!

Lyndon made a speech I loved. Into a good text he interpolated a deep passion, lines straight from the heart, saying, "My own college education meant everything to me at a time when my future hung in the balance. I hope somehow, someway, someday, in the time allotted to me, I may repay the debt I owe. And I shall try." A good many times I have heard him repeat the phrase "while I am President" or "in the time allotted to me"—and there is always, deep down, a tolling of the bell in my thoughts.

We next drove to the home of President James K. Polk, an indulgence planned for me. Sometime I hope to visit the home of every one of the thirty-five other Presidents. I have seen at least twelve. The house was impressive with handsome furniture, much of it original. Some of the furniture had been in the White House with Polk. The Polks did so many of the "right things." Both of them had their portraits painted by G. P. A. Healy. And Mrs. Polk's dress was designed by Worth.

Back at the Mansion in Nashville we attended a reception and a seminar for educators invited from the region—Tennessee, West Virginia, Alabama—college presidents and superintendents of high schools and social workers pioneering new phases of education. There was a round-table discussion moderated by Doug Cater with Dr. Frank Rose of the University of Alabama, Governor Hulett Smith of West Virginia, a striking, beautifully articulate Negro woman named Elizabeth Burgess, head of the Foreign Language Department of all the schools of Nashville, and a sweet-faced woman who teaches a classroom-on-wheels for crippled and handicapped children in the Appalachian area. It was moving, thrilling, exciting, to hear what is happening in education in this decade, in this country.

Lyndon spoke for about fifty minutes, a deeply stirring talk. Nevertheless, it was too long and I was writing out a note saying: "Close soon." Lyndon, with eyes in the back of his head, observed it and told the audience so—lightening the mood and making them laugh—and kept right on talking. Though it was too long, people went away, I believe, feeling that they knew this human being, Lyndon Johnson, better. And I think he left a lot of them with some inspiration—that rare gift.

Another high point of the evening for me was John Gardner's short speech. He said, simply, that normally he's reserved but because he was so affected by the trip, for the first time in his twenty months in the Cabinet, he wanted to pay respects to the President in public. "It has been a privilege to see the generative power of one man's deep conviction." That for me was the gift of the trip.

Saturday, March 18

THE WHITE HOUSE

This morning I went into the Yellow Oval Room to meet a student group from Texas, brought here by the Texas State Society for their annual brunch. Horace Busby was the entrepreneur and the purpose was to honor "the campus generation" in Texas and especially the University of Texas. This provided an opportunity to show another face of our young people and another face of Texas.

The honor guests were the members of the University of Texas College Bowl Team, which has just won the championship on television in a contest of academic knowledge against teams from other major colleges. The competition was a cliff-hanging thriller. Dr. Harry Ransom, Chancellor of the University of Texas, ordered the lights on the Main Building tower turned orange when they won, just as for a triumphant football team.

There was also Betty Ann Buckley who sang musical-comedy songs, and Mary Louise Summers of Baylor with a good operatic voice. She had twice been regional finalist in the Metropolitan Opera tryouts. Larry Farrar, from Lyndon's own San Marcos, was a handsome operatic baritone. And last, the North Texas Lab Band, which experiments in jazz and contemporary music—winners of numerous jazz festivals. They are very popular with "mod" young people.

Lyndon came in, breaking away from the Governors' briefing for a few minutes, and talked quietly and earnestly with them. I was grateful and proud. Much of the time he uses his minutes so skillfully—not always. He was in and out in a flick of time, leaving them, I believe, pleased, impressed, more understanding.

Meanwhile, the Governors' wives were congregating on the ground floor in preparation for our "beautification" bus ride and tree-planting ceremony. My staff was busy putting on that civilized aid to today's social gathering—name tags.

I felt a flurry of excitement about meeting certain Governors' wives. What would Mrs. Lester Maddox be like? (She was very nice.) And pleasure, as always, in seeing Happy Rockefeller, who is one of the warmest and friendliest of all the Governors' wives. She told me she was anxious to come to the coffee session and would surely be at the luncheon, but that the doctor wouldn't let her go on the long bus ride. Her baby is still very young. To be able to say "no" graciously and make people think you want to say "yes" is a prime social asset. I looked forward to seeing laughing, exuberant Betty Hughes. And I had the keenest interest in meeting Mrs. Winthrop Rockefeller—she and her husband were the only Rockefellers I had not met.

We boarded the buses, which were decorated with the pink paper flowers that were left over from Luci's wedding and used again at Lynda Bird's party for Princess Irene. I told the Governors' wives this, saying I hoped they realized they had a thrifty Administration.

Our destination was Gravelly Point—an empty stretch of land along the Potomac on the Virginia side on the way in from National Airport. We had fifty-four white flowering dogwoods ready for the last spadeful of dirt—one for each state and territory. We had planned for all of the Governors' wives to throw in their spadefuls of dirt simultaneously, followed by a fanfare from the Navy band—with state flags flying, smiling ladies planting against the blue sky with the Potomac beyond and in the background the Capitol dome. Alas for "the best laid plans"! The trees were located as much as two blocks apart. We walked through mud to the shoe tops, and the temperature was at a freezing 29 degrees, with a biting wind and white caps on the Potomac!

With chattering teeth and varying degrees of good humor, the ladies planted their trees—anything but simultaneously and with not many cameras clicking. For the press the big news was that there was no one to plant Alabama's dogwood, since Mrs. Wallace, naturally, was in conference with the other Governors.

I bus-hopped to ride with all the Governors' wives to show them what my Beautification Committee had accomplished in two years—cherry trees and willows around Hains Point, the double alley of pink magnolias on Pennsylvania headed toward Anacostia, freeway planting, the sophisticated brick paving and the crepe myrtle of New York Avenue, one of the schools, several of the small triangles and circles where the streets meet.

We arrived at the State Department muddy and hungry at one, and all of us made a beeline for the bathrooms and availed ourselves of stacks of paper towels. The real picture of the day would have been in the ladies' room with twelve lavatories in a row and twelve Governors' wives washing mud off their shoes!

The State Department offered a superb setting, for the furniture in the dining room is really beautiful. The seating had been very sensibly arranged by drawing numbers out of the hat. I found myself beside Mrs. Paul Johnson of Mississippi. We talked of their lovely Governor's Mansion there. Mrs. Paiewonsky of the Virgin Islands, who was at my table, reminisced about Caneel Bay and I expressed my joy in going there again tomorrow. Mrs. Robert McNair of South Carolina had the most forthright, hearty appreciation and approval of their predecessors, the Donald Russells. Mrs. Russell had "done such wonderful things with the grounds and the house was decorated in beautiful taste." I was amazed and bowled over, and warmly pleased. This is a "first" for me. Usually the incoming wife's description of the condition in which the Mansion, or Government House, was left by her predecessor is a fearsome recital!

Meanwhile, all day long, Lyndon and the members of the Cabinet had labored with the Governors in briefings and with give-and-take questions. At 7 we met for dinner. As the Governors and their ladies went down the line I felt a little sad—so few of them left that we had known well through the years. John Connally, of course, the handsomest man in the room, staunch Buford Ellington and Catherine, and Jack Burns who looks like a poet. (Mrs. Burns had insisted on going out in her wheelchair across the mud today to plant her tree, which was one of the farthest ones out on the point.) And Hulett and Mary Alice Smith of West Virginia. The room was full of new faces and, of course, the magnets for all eyes were the George Romneys of Michigan and the Ronald Reagans of California —both men sleekly handsome—and the George Wallaces of Alabama. (My conversation with the Wallaces leaned rather heavily on my Alabama heritage.)

Winthrop Rockefeller was on my left at dinner. He likes his job—and I like that. On my right was Governor William Guy of North Dakota, young, handsome, and thoroughly likable. Governor Claude Kirk of Florida had been present for the men's luncheon and the briefings, but left in the afternoon, Bess told me, to go and get his new bride who was still in Florida. They made it back for dinner, very much the center of attention.

A Republican Governor, James Rhodes of Ohio, gave a rousing endorsement of Lyndon at the end of the evening. After coffee and liqueurs we went in for one of the gayest entertainments I can remember, *Guys and Dolls* produced by Jean Dalrymple of the New York City Center Light Opera Company. As soon as the entertainment was over, the helicopter whirled in on the lawn. Lyndon said good-by to all of the guests, who crowded to windows and out on the porch to watch his departure. I kissed Lyndon good-by for his long trip to Guam, and he was off on what should have been the end of a valiant day's work, for an eighteen-hour flight, to begin work on another set of problems.

Tomorrow I am leaving for the Virgin Islands. I feel that special sense of relief you experience at the beginning of a vacation. And it is delicious, in spite of a guilty knowledge that my husband is still locked into an endurance contest.

Saturday, April 22

Shortly after lunch I started to Betty Talmadge's to play bridge. I went the long way around, by Watts Branch—that dismal, forlorn area on the outskirts of southeast Washington into which Laurance Rockefeller had poured about seventy-five thousand dollars through the National Park Service two years ago. I went with misgivings because I thought I would find the place trashy and unused.

But it was a thoroughly gratifying experience. There's a little stream that meanders through a rather dull part of town—not a slum, just drab. The banks had been planted and here and there was a little park area with benches. The stepping stones across the stream were inviting, and up the hill in the shade camellias were blooming and azaleas would soon be coming out. A man was sleeping on one bench and four children were running around and around. There were two "tot lots" and they were in use, though the day was chilly. Under the trees were three or four busy little boys. One of them hollered out, "Is that Lady Bird Johnson?" I said "yes," and waved to them. He turned around to his comrades, pointing and jabbering, and they all exploded in giggles.

What a happy thing to do—take three hours off on Saturday afternoon and play bridge with friends! Mary Ellen Monroney, Mrs. Maxwell Taylor, and Betty are all good players. They played just right for me—better than I play, so that I had to strive, and not so much better that my gaffes made me uncomfortable. It was a real women's bridge party, delightfully offbeat for me.

Tonight I wore my brown lace and joined our dinner guests in the Yellow Oval Room about 7. They included Eric Sevareid, the Max Frankels, Senator Gale McGee and Loraine, the Thomas McIntyres from New Hampshire, and Hubert and Muriel.

When Lyndon arrives in a room, the talk begins to revolve around him. The conversation becomes one circle and he is in the middle of it. So I used the time before his arrival to ask people what they thought of the Punta del Este Conference. Max Frankel was enthusiastic. He said if you don't have a character like Gomez Arosemena at a conference, you ought to invent one. He said this lone President arose to protest, oppose the United States, and it was up to his fellow Latin American Presidents to put him down, to speak for the other side, and to expose the inadequacies of his arguments. He thought Lyndon had conducted the conference quite skillfully, it appeared.

I asked Hubert about his trip to Europe. He spoke of the evening they had had dinner with Queen Elizabeth at Windsor. When the dinner was over, Prime Minister Wilson escorted Muriel and Hubert to their quarters. At the door Hubert said, "Would you come in and have a nightcap?" They went in and didn't find any whisky handy. Wilson gave an order and presently whisky appeared. The two men put up their feet comfortably, sipped their drinks, and settled down for a quiet conversation which Wilson began with the philosophical comment, "Pretty good for the son of an elementary school teacher and a small town pharmacist, drinking the Queen's whisky in Windsor."

A little after 8 Lyndon came and we went in to dinner shortly. I placed Hubert on my right and Senator McGee on my left. Zephyr had fixed a delicious dinner—sliced sirloin and mushrooms, asparagus with Hollandaise, ending with strawberry meringue. I have yet to find a great chef whose desserts I like as well as Zephyr's.

The evening launched into a series of stories about the great figures in the Senate. Lyndon was a gay, amusing host, a wonderful raconteur. He told about Senator Clyde Hoey of North Carolina, with his flower in his lapel and his clawhammer coat, and his way of calling people he really liked "beloved." There was a choice tale about the time he had been persuaded by Senator Russell of Georgia that he must change a vote he had given his commitment to cast. Senator Hoey said, "You must give me a few days—I've got to go back and rub out some tracks." Every story sparked another. Hubert would relate a tale about Senator Bob Kerr of Oklahoma, which would remind Lyndon of something about Tom Connally of Texas. The conversation had the real flavor of two decades of the U.S. Senate.

Tomorrow morning Lyndon leaves for Chancellor Konrad Adenauer's funeral. It will be a hard trip, so I am glad he had some relaxation and fun this evening. The thing I liked most of all tonight was one phrase he used. I wish I could quote it exactly, but the gist of it was this: What will concern the next generations, what will make or break the world in the decade just around the corner, are the population explosion and the food supply—those two things and their interplay.

This will be an interesting evening for us to remember someday in the rocking chair down on the front porch as we watch the Pedernales flow slowly by.

Sunday, April 23

We were awake early. Lyndon said he had slept hardly at all, a tough beginning for this trip to Germany—demanding as it is—as every day is. But I am living with the feeling that there is a slight lifting of the clouds, an occasional ray of sunshine. Things *are* getting better. Lyndon went down in the elevator about 8:45. I wasn't dressed, so I just rode down with him and kissed him good-by. I had planned a series, greedily, of all the things I like best, making the day chock full.

My first adventure was to go to Mrs. George Maurice Morris' house, The Lindens, a little past 10. She had dismantled an old house that had stood in Connecticut before the Revolutionary War. In fact, its front door has a bullet hole that was meant for the last Colonial Governor. She had brought it down, board by board, and reerected it lovingly, creating one of the most complete and beautiful and authentic homes of that period in the United States.

My hostess met me in the front yard and opened the door to the spacious halls, dimly lit, lined with a scenic French wallpaper, familiar to me here at the White House, a magnificent staircase rising at the other end past the Palladian window. There followed two absolutely enchanting hours. There were stenciled floors, Queen Anne and Chippendale furniture worth a King's ransom, handsomely paneled walls. And a secret panel that led to a narrow, winding staircase! There were fabrics dating back to the seventeenth century, bearing the handiwork—lifetimes of it, eyesights of it—of ladies long dead. Much of it was crewel work. There was a pair of gloves dating from 1625. Mrs. Morris' own great-grandfather's cradle from the early 1700's. And King George's own tobacco box! (She quoted King James, I believe it was, on the subject of tobacco. He said it was very dangerous to the lungs.)

We had coffee and I said good-by and rushed back to the White House to have lunch with Marny Clifford. Then at 1:30, Marny and I left, heading out across the beautiful Virginia countryside to Fredericksburg, to visit the James Monroe law office and to talk to Mr. Laurence Gouverneur Hoes, descendant of both Monroe and Madison, who, I earnestly hope, will give or sell to the White House an excellent portrait of Madison by Vanderlyn. One of my main goals in this house is to replace the poor posthumous portraits of John Adams and James Madison with good ones.

The first thing that greeted me in Monroe's law office were two old friends—the secretary desk that stands in the White House East Hall by the entrance to the Lincoln Room and the chest on the opposite wall—or so it seemed. Actually, these pieces had belonged to President Monroe. Mrs. Hoover, when she was First Lady, had had beautiful reproductions made for the White House. Mr. Hoes showed me a secret drawer in the secretary desk that he had jarred loose as a seven-year-old boy when he was climbing around over it and there had spilled forth marvelous letters to Monroe from George Washington, Alexander Hamilton, Thomas Jefferson, and George Mason—a whole roster of founding fathers.

Monroe's Presidential papers are stored in this office, Mr. Hoes told me, so this is the antecedent of all the Presidential libraries. And there was a marvelous portrait of Monroe hanging here. But I got no nearer to my goal—the portrait of Madison was not there. It was being repaired, I was told, after it had been injured in an exhibition. Mr. Hoes talked enthusiastically. He said, "I'm very interested in seeing that you get what you want." But I cannot say that he promised anything.

It was nearly 5 when we left Fredericksburg.

I had invited Jane and Orville Freeman to go with me to the Arena to see *Look Back in Anger*. It was an early curtain—7:30—with no time to eat. I settled into my seat with that eager anticipation that I bring to any play. Lynda had described this one, by John Osborne, as a sort of progenitor of the modern way-out plays—the Albee type. It took me only a few minutes to realize that I was alien. I found myself and I think a great deal of the rest of the audience doing the same—looking at each other with a puzzled frown, and wondering, how are you taking this? Were we hoping for a cue from each other? Disapproval perhaps? The characters, to me, seemed tortured, bitter, lost, not at home in the world, and making a wretched mess of life. But the acting was splendid, and no matter how much I disapproved, I must say I enjoyed watching it.

Orville and Jane, I was rather relieved to find, felt the same way about it as I did. I am searching, perhaps, to find whether it is really I or the theater that has changed. I liked Eugene O'Neill in his day, and some of the early Tennessee Williams' plays, and they raised the same sort of outraged protest that Osborne and Albee do now.

When it was over we came back to the White House, where I had had a platter of sandwiches put in the refrigerator—roast beef and pimento cheese. There was not a servant in sight. We went into the kitchen and fixed our own drinks and loaded sandwiches on a plate and we put up our feet and had a delightful hour, during which time Orville told me about his trip to several farm states, and meetings in which he had had a dialogue with farmers on the Administration and its policies. It's a rather gloomy picture. The only good part to me is that I believe he can express the Administration's activities ably and enthusiastically.

It was cozy, informal—real companionship of just three people—and was a perfect ending to what had been a marvelously varied and full day —a taste of many of the things I love most.

Tuesday, April 25

This was a full, busy day in the White House. With my coffee, I watched part of Chancellor Adenauer's funeral on television via satellite, hoping I would get a glimpse of Lyndon in the great old cathedral. But I only saw the grandeur and the chanting mourners.

Then I scurried about getting ready for our annual meeting of the Committee on the Preservation of the White House, one of the most important things that I am associated with here in this house. I had the carpenter climb up on a stepladder, hoisting above him the pasteboard mock-up of the chandelier of Waterford crystal that Oveta Culp Hobby is thinking of giving to the White House. She has been our guest in the Queen's Room, and I would particularly like it to be hung there, if it is in harmony with the room.

The Committee met in the Yellow Oval Room at 10 and we spent about two hours conferring. We only do this once a year, and it is most serious and dedicated business. I welcomed them over coffee and hot rolls, and then George Hartzog took over, reporting on the visitors' services —our tryout of the visitor orientation tape along the fence where sometimes in the spring big crowds wait for two hours to get in the White House.

I reported on the new dining room curtains and the chair upholstery. The fabric for the curtains is being especially woven for us by Scalamandre from a design that had been used in eighteenth-century Georgian houses in England. There will be new ones in the Great Hall and up the stairway. All together they will cost about thirty-seven thousand dollars, and we hope to have them ready in the early summer. Mr. West reported on other household matters—the Blue Room rug reproduction, and the big problem of the East Room mantels (and also the baseboards). They are marble, but dull red, ugly. So we painted them, a sort of an off-white camouflage to harmonize with the gold and white room. The paint comes off and they have to be repainted very often—almost every two weeks in peak tourist seasons—so that it is a real household chore. Could we get the marble industry to give us four new mantels? Well, we could try. Or could we buy them?

John Walker gave us a cheerful report from the White House Historical Association. Last year, the Association had allotted fifty thousand dollars for the White House, and the expected thirty-seven-thousand-dollar expenditure would not entirely deplete that. John said we could count on another fifty thousand dollars for the coming year. So we can breathe more easily. We can even afford to look for some new art object. Best of all, he told us that *The Living White House* had sold over one hundred thousand copies since November 28! And the White House guide book is in its seventh edition.

Jim Ketchum passed out a list of all our important acquisitions since our last meeting a year ago. Most prominently the Eakins painting and a tea service given to the Tafts on their twenty-fifth wedding anniversary in the White House and the FDR portrait by Madame Shouma-toff.

Then I talked about the desired acquisitions, at the top of the list, the portraits of Adams and Madison. I told them that we were nearer to acquiring one of Madison—though nothing was promised—and I proudly showed them the provenance on it which John Walker had gotten together for me.

Jim Fosburgh discussed the other paintings we might want to acquire. I put forward John Singleton Copley and George Caleb Bingham as two we most wanted—and perhaps Eastman Johnson. It all depends on what direction we want to go. I felt—and the others agreed—that we should concentrate on top American artists and that we could relax the criterion of the artist having been dead for fifty years and bring the date a little closer to today. We agreed that if the artists were dead or had stopped painting for twenty years, that would be enough time for judgment.

I told them about the offer to start a collection of Presidential letters and First Lady letters. We all decided that the criterion would be whether the letters shed a special light on their years in the White House or on their characters and that, in a limited way, this would be a very nice collection to use in our display cases or perhaps framed on the walls of certain rooms.

The meeting proceeded with lively interest, I thought, and some accomplishment. I felt good about it. I love it! My respect for this great old house grows every day, and I want to leave it a little richer than I found it.

Afterward I dressed for the Senate Ladies Luncheon. The day was chilly, though the flowers were beautiful in the South grounds. The lilac at the gate welcomes me every time I come in these days, and the circle around the fountain is a great blaze of color—yellow and red and orange tulips, white trumpeters and a border of white pansies, with the spray flying in between as the wind shifts it. All over town the tulips are glorious, and every visitor I have tells me about them.

At the entrance to the old Senate Office Building, I was met by Muriel and Mrs. Claiborne Pell and Mrs. Clifford Case, the Chairman and the co-Chairman of the luncheon this year. The luncheon was in the Senate Caucus Room—where the first one I attended in 1949 was, I believe—decorated with palms, with round tables on which there were green and yellow floral tablecloths—a salute to beauty—and white flowers.

It was a familiar, happy scene to me. All of the Cabinet wives lined up, with Muriel and me at the head. And the Senate Ladies in their Red Cross uniforms filed past with many an embrace and laughter and memories of the things we had done in the past. And then we went to our tables.

It was an absolutely delicious luncheon, beginning with crab au gratin, courtesy of the Maryland Senators. I talked to Mrs. Charles Percy about Sharon's wedding and to Ethel Kennedy about the new baby—he's beautiful. But most of my thoughts were on the old-timers.

At the end of the luncheon there were the reports on the work, the number of bandages rolled, the sewing, the knitting, and a warm, sweet speech by Muriel for the presentation to me of a vermeil picture frame "to be used sometime in June." (That is when Luci's child will be born.) Then I responded. It's much easier to say something if you have something to say. And to these ladies—so many of whom I have known for eighteen or more years—I do have something to say—shared memories, a common role in our husbands' lives.

This evening we were having the reception for Mr. Justice Hugo Black, celebrating the thirtieth anniversary of his appointment to the Court. In Lyndon's absence I asked the Chief Justice to stand in as my host. A little before 6 I went down to the Green Room to greet Mr. Justice Black and Elizabeth, the Chief Justice and Mrs. Warren, and their immediate families. In the Blue Room we stepped in line, the Chief Justice in the spot that would have been Lyndon's, and then I and Justice Black and the other ladies.

And by they came—a roster of those who loved Hugo Black. His family— his daughter Josephine and his sons, Hugo Black, Jr., and Sterling, with their families, and several nephews and nieces. All of his fellow Justices on the Supreme Court came to do him honor and forty of his law clerks from a roster beginning in 1937.

Each of them he greeted by name in a very personal manner, and usually kissed their wives, explaining to me that they were also his "family." There were former Justices of the Supreme Court, including Arthur Goldberg, the widows of Justices, and one son, Fred Vinson, Jr., and a sprinkling of eminent jurists and his special friends from around the country; both Alabama Senators, Lister Hill and John Sparkman; and then that delightful, perfect Hugo Black touch, his messenger, Spencer Campbell, and his cook, Elizabeth Howie. I never went to dinner at the Justice's home but that when dinner was over and with a certain ceremony he didn't escort us to the kitchen so we could tell "Lizzie Mae" how good the corn bread or the turnip greens or the dessert was, and I would be saying to myself, "only a Southerner . . ."

We went into the State Dining Room where everybody else was drinking and eating and talking all at once. What decades of things they had to talk about! It must have been a reunion for so many of them. Tom Corcoran and Ben Cohen were there, and Tom's daughter Margaret Josephine, who is the Justice's latest law clerk.

Then the toasts began. The Vice President, so much in tune with the philosophy of this Southern Senator and Justice, so warm of heart and quick of wit, gave the first toast but tonight he was outdistanced, because there was so much to say by those who had shared these years. One of the Justice's law clerks announced the establishment of a Chair of Law in his honor at the University of Alabama. And another former law clerk, now the Dean of the University of Alabama Law School, accepted it for the school. Then the Justice responded. Never did I wish more ardently that we'd had a tape recording.

It was one of those times when you get caught up in a stream of listening and feeling and you think you are living your life over, remembering events and people. He talked about the years he had spent in Washington—and they go back far beyond his thirty years on the Court, to the time when he was a Senator for twelve years. He talked about his feeling for his fellow Senators and Justices on the Court, and the changes of the Roosevelt years . . . the time when President Roosevelt called him down to the White House to announce that he was going to put him on the Court, and all the changes since. There was a web of silence in the State Dining Room and a communion between all of the guests. It was a long speech but we would have all liked more.

When it was over, Elizabeth invited the entire crowd out to the Blacks' house to continue the party. I said good night to them all with the happy emotions of a hostess who feels she has given a good and memorable evening to her guests, and who has most emphatically enjoyed it herself.

Never had there been so many Alabamians joined under the roof since I've been here!

NEW YORK

This was a tremendous day. With Liz and Simone Poulain, I caught the shuttle to New York and about 1:30 we left the Carlyle for Carnegie Hall. Only in the life of a politician could a day like today happen— two events aimed at opposite poles of life's spectrum. The first, a concert for retired members of the International Ladies Garment Workers' Union, and the second, a reception honoring the Head Start program, which involves youngsters four and five years old from culturally deprived families.

A full-page ad in the *New York Times* described the first event, "from sweat shops to Stokowski," telling of the progress of labor from lofts and long hours to leisure and Stokowski and "even the presence of the First Lady." Under the aegis of David Dubinsky, the retired membership had inaugurated a program for leisure hours which involves educational and cultural projects and this concert was one of a series.

As I stepped out of the car at Carnegie Hall I thought I heard a slight hissing noise behind me but I did not turn around. If there were angry faces and placards, I did not want to add to the attention that they were getting. If they were in front of me I thought I would simply walk through with a smile, saying, "Hello." But instead, there on the sidewalk was David Dubinsky—the retired President of the Union. To me he is a fascinating man—a passionate advocate of his people, great showman, great friend. Beside him was Mr. Louis Stulberg, the present President of the Union, who must have a difficult role following in Dubinsky's shoes.

Then began two wonderful hours. Carnegie Hall was packed, the balconies rising row on row, full, even to the "peanut gallery." Down below, a few determined old ladies were marching down the aisles searching for their seats, berating the ushers and grumbling, and all but getting into a fight with the persons they thought had their seats. Then Leopold Stokowski came on in a swallowtail coat and a great big striped cravat, his white hair flowing—every inch the showman himself. But for me, he met his match in David Dubinsky!

Stokowski waited, his delicate hands poised in the air like fluttering birds. Almost five minutes passed. Finally Stokowski said, "A painter paints his pictures on canvas, but musicians paint their pictures on silence. We provide the music and you provide the silence."

The program was made up of favorites—Wagner, Tschaikovsky . . . then the wild romantic music of gypsies—"The Romanian Rhapsody" by Enesco.

Then came the intermission. David Dubinsky was the first speaker, and it was his audience and his moment. (As the *New York Times* reported, "The gold-and-white splendor of Carnegie Hall sounded more like a Union hall.") He reminded the audience of the fifty-year struggle of the labor unions, the times when they worked twelve, fifteen, eighteen hours a day. He talked about a strike of 1912 or 1913, and I could see old gray heads bobbing through the audience in memory.

It was a great show and I was glad I was there to watch it, though I had the feeling that these battles are already won, this day is over, this is the last hurrah. David Dubinsky introduced me. I gave a plug to the Great Society, to Lyndon's work, the Medicare law and the Older Americans Act, saying that our goal was not merely to prolong our citizens' lives but to enrich them. I praised their Union for starting cultural and educational projects.

When I finished, one of the retirees of the ILGWU, dressed in her best, came up to me with a big bouquet of yellow roses which she gave to me with a wonderful little speech—that she and all of them loved my husband, were his strong supporters, and were going to work hard for him in 1968.

Then Stokowski took over for the last number—the great rolling music of Dvořák's *New World Symphony* which keeps repeating two themes, one of them so similar to that spiritual: "Going home, Going home." It was familiar—I loved it—I was exhilarated.

Just before the concert was over I heard a brief exchange between David and Mr. Stulberg behind me. I found out later that this was a debate as to whether the orchestra was going to finish within the allotted time or whether the Union was going to have to start paying the musicians "time and a half" by Union law! They finished with three minutes to spare.

In the evening I went to the Hotel Pierre for reception and dinner given by the Citizens' Committee for the Children of N.Y. Mrs. Milton Gordon, head of the organization, met me and we went into the reception where I met many old friends—a whole spectrum of people interested in children and their welfare—social workers, philanthropists, opinion makers, judges and politicians and educators. What a society we are. I wonder if, in all the world, there is anybody quite like us? We organize and work on such a wide spectrum of the world's problems and needs.

Mayor John Lindsay and his wife had come to pay their respects to the

Committee and to welcome me. But Lindsay was also on his way to the "Salute for the Seasons." So after one course he rose, greeted me in a warm and cordial way, and then went off for his second course elsewhere. My last choice for a job in politics would be as Mayor of New York. One of the chief qualifications must be a good digestion. He must eat dinner at four different gatherings many nights.

Mrs. Gordon made the introduction without a single note, with great presence and grace. I tried to make my few words personal, recalling the scene in the Red Room in the White House only two years ago when Head Start actually came to birth and how it has already touched the lives of one million four hundred thousand children. Trudy Lash, who had been Mrs. Roosevelt's last secretary, then introduced the real speaker of the evening—Thurgood Marshall. I had not heard him before. He began in a quiet manner but soon I realized I was in the presence of an orator. I was proud that he was in the Administration.

All during the evening, especially at the reception, several people had come up to me, shaking their heads and saying, "I don't see how you stand it, it's too bad . . ." Apologetic remarks that made me know that there were picketers outside, but I did not see them. (In the morning papers I learned they had been chanting their anti-war slogans on the street. This group called themselves "The Women's Strike for Peace.") During dinner Liz brought me a folded note which said, *The Secret Service says that there is one woman in the audience who may arise and say "Stop the War in Vietnam." You had better be thinking about what you will answer.* But this did not happen.

In the midst of the most affluence, opportunity, and hope that the world has ever known, there is turmoil and frustration and anger. We live in the shadow of danger.

Saturday, May 13

THE WHITE HOUSE

If my life can be said to have pattern it is that, as we go into spring and summer, the crescendo of work mounts. We pack as many engagements as we can into Tuesday and Wednesday and Thursday, and often Monday and Friday are full. On the weekends we go to Camp David or to Texas. If we are here, Saturday morning is a time to think and plan. Saturday is *my* day—a blank day on the calendar—a creative day. There must be some days like this to feed the rest of the week, to build on.

I spent this Saturday morning with book work. At a little past 3 Abe Fortas came over, and in the Queen's Sitting Room, my own special little fortress—it has only one door and I can be private there—we talked for an hour and a half on the subject that has engaged so much of my thinking ever since Lyndon got into this job—how to get out and when.

Many months ago I set March 1968 in my own mind as the time when Lyndon can make a statement that he will not be a candidate for reelection. I was following the pattern of President Truman, and I have counted first the years and then the months until that time. Now it is ten months away. For the first time in my life I have felt lately that Lyndon would be a happy man retired. I feel that there is enough at the Ranch to hold him, keep him busy, and that he can pour himself into some sort of teaching work at the University of Texas—in the Johnson School of Public Service, perhaps, with maybe an occasional lecture at his alma mater in San Marcos.

I find myself enjoying every return to the Ranch more and more. And I do not know whether we can endure another four-year term in the Presidency. I use that word "endure" in Webster's own meaning, "to last, remain, continue in the same state without perishing." I face the prospect of another campaign like an open-ended stay in a concentration camp.

I have thought that Lyndon was of the same mind—that he would at some proper time announce that he would not be a candidate for re-election—but I do not know. All these months I have felt that circumstances might keep him from it, that events might trigger him into running. If the polls became so bad that it looked as if he could not be elected, that might force him to try. Or if the Vietnam war were over, there would be the wonderful beckoning hope that the enormous economic muscle of this country, which in the past six or seven years has grown so vastly, could be thrown into high gear to achieve the goals of the Great Society—rebuilding the cities, redoubling the work on health and education and conservation. That could really be a siren song.

Over a cup of coffee Abe and I talked about it. There is almost nobody in the world that I can talk to. To Abe, I feel I can. He was quiet and a little sad, but very understanding. The gist of what he said at the end was that he thought Lyndon had done enough—had worked enough in his life—so that about next March he could make that announcement if the war situation had improved. If it had not—if things were as bad with the war as now or worse—Abe thought Lyndon simply could not withdraw—that he

1967

A grandchild comes to the White House. LBJ Library Photo by Robert Knudsen, C6157-6a.

Celebrating the Fourth Anniversary of Hello Dolly! with the cast following its White House performance, January 17. *LBJ Library Photo by Robert Knudsen, C4295-18.*

Camp David in the Catoctin Mountain of Maryland.
LBJ Library Photo by Yoichi Okamoto, C5738-26.

LEFT, TOP: *Head Starters at Montevideo, Minnesota. LBJ Library Photo by Robert Knudsen, C6696-36a.* MIDDLE: *Appalachia trip March 13–15. LBJ Library Photo by Robert Knudsen, C4715-28a.* BOTTOM, *Seeing handiwork of girls participating in Trailblazers summer program. LBJ Library Photo by Frank Wolfe, C6339-36.*

FACING: *Lunch in the Family Dining Room at the White House with the first grandchild, Patrick Lyndon Nugent. LBJ Library Photo by Frank Wolfe, 6220-6.*

must try for the nomination, which he might or might not win, and then try for the election, which he might or might not win.

It was a solemn, rather gloomy talk. Abe was insistent that Lyndon must not make a decision, and certainly not an announcement, before next March. He thought that any such decision or announcement would hamstring—almost immobilize—the war effort and Lyndon's domestic program, his leadership of the country.

I wonder if I have assessed myself correctly? I think I have. I admit cheerfully that I shall miss very much the bright, sharp conversation with highly placed people, fresh flowers in the room every day, an indoor swimming pool—all this I shall miss on the level of enjoyment. And on another much more significant level I will miss the feeling that I have accomplished something. I remember when the director of the school in Asheville, North Carolina, wrote me that after my visit there and the newspaper coverage ten people called up the next day to say they wanted to get into the adult education class. The school director squeezed them in, though the class was full—this could mean a difference in the lives, the jobs, of ten people.

At any rate, Lyndon's decision is never far from my thoughts. I cannot control the outcome, though I will have some effect on it. And it will not, I hope, be decided until next March.

Lyndon had called guests to go with us to Camp David. And at 5 on a helicopter we left with Margy and Bob McNamara, Jake and Beryl Pickle, Jack and Mary Margaret and Courtenay Valenti, with that delicious sense of relief, escape, of holiday, that always goes with us to Camp David though it was a rainy, foggy weekend as it has been all spring here.

What will I remember about Camp David? The two "Martians" in their silver suits and helmets, stiff and silent, who startle you when you first step off the helicopter (they are firefighters on hand for any emergency) . . . the cool, green tunnel that leads through the woods to Aspen, the main lodge . . . the drifts of snow, still there in late March . . . and the great valley below where a battle of the Civil War was fought . . . ham and grits and hot cakes, all for breakfast. Mamie and Dwight Eisenhower's bold signatures in the guestbook and those of many other famous guests. Hours of bridge, and bowling and good talk. But mostly just the carefree mood of being there—a spirit of release and relaxation—quite unattainable, somehow, in the White House, and usually in *any* house I am supposed to run, even the Ranch.

Summer 1967

This day began with that most dread and frightening sound that can happen in this house—the sudden ringing of the telephone in the middle of the night. It can never be good news. The insistent ring jarred me from the soft web of sleep.

I heard Lyndon's quick reaction, "Yes." Then a long silence, interrupted on his part by a few crisp questions. He finally hung up and fell back on the pillow. With an almost unbearable wave of sympathy, I asked him what it was. He said: "We have a war on our hands—in the Middle East." I looked at the clock. It was about 4:30. An hour later the phone crashed the silence again. Once more there was talk with a few clipped questions on his side and then long silences. When it was over, I leaned over and kissed him.

I cannot say I slept anymore. Rather there was a long period of continuing nightmares in which I was lost and wandering, though sometimes the places were familiar. Finally I got up. Lyndon had been gone a long time. Not since that day in October 1962 (during the Cuban missile crisis) had I felt so tense and strained, known such a feeling of foreboding . . . I remember that other day, when I stood in the bedroom at The Elms—a beautiful, clear, golden day—and looked out at the sunlight shimmering on the leaves of golds and crimsons and reds and wondered: "Is this the last beautiful October day we shall see?" But there is nothing I can do about the great clash of powers—nothing at all, except be quiet and sympathetic and cheerful when Lyndon is home. And when he's not I might as well go on about my little business of the day. Today it was work on the speeches for the upcoming trip to New England, lunching with Lynda, and planning the program for the award winners in beautification. Always, always, I feel that I would give a special prize to whoever would give us a better word than "beautification"! It sounds institutional, clinical; it doesn't have any of the joy of the work in it.

Then I went back to work with Ashton at my desk and turned on the TV. The news of the Middle East conflict was everywhere, but totally conflicting. The Israelis said the Egyptians started the fighting—the Egyptians said the Israelis had invaded their territory with planes and troops. The Israelis gave the numbers of enemy planes—vast numbers— that they had knocked down. And the Egyptians claimed victories over the Israelis, citing the number of planes downed, though not as many as the Israelis had claimed, with very little loss to themselves. Then there was the news that a State Department official had used the phrase "neutral in thought, word, and deed" to define the United States' position in the Mideast conflict. Rusk hastened onto TV to try to clarify the word "neutral."

The UN was struggling, with its major action arm, the Security Council, going into session for five or six hours, going out presumably for private talks among its members, and then promising to go back into session any minute. Like millions of others I strained with hope toward the UN and what it might produce. But I remembered with dismay the expressions of no confidence that I have heard applied to it these last months by many observers.

I turned off the TV and went over to the bowling lanes, where I used up my energy in three games, hurling a heavier ball than usual and running up scores in the 150's—all by myself. Not much fun, but exercise, and while I'm doing it I don't think much about anything else.

Then back to my little room where I worked, with the great white lights of television behind Lyndon's office glaring at the side of the White

House and into the room. In this place there are thermometers of trouble somewhere in the world . . . the presence of TV vans by the West Wing is always one, and in the space outside the press lobby a commentator with a mike standing in the spotlight's glare. Another is the sudden arrival of a fleet of limousines, some bringing Congressional leadership, and some Chiefs of Staff, to Lyndon's office.

It was a little after 10 when Lyndon came home to dinner. He looked burdened and the lines in his face deeper, and I felt it would be the greatest cruelty for me to ask him to talk about the war in the Middle East. I tried some brisk, bright reports on what I had been doing today, and they sounded hollow.

At 12 his light was out. I prayed that he slept because last night he had had only about four hours.

The evening paper headlines were, "WAR RAGES IN MIDEAST," "UN ATTEMPTS TO GET TRUCE IN ISRAEL BATTLE," "JOHNSON PUSHES UN EFFORT."

And so the anxious day came to an end.

Friday, June 9

NEW ENGLAND

I kissed Lyndon good-by a little past 9 this morning and was off for my four-day trip to New England. I would visit Massachusetts, New Hampshire, Vermont, and Maine, seeing Presidential homes of the two Adamses and Coolidge and looking at recreation facilities and crafts of the people.

A little before 11 we landed in South Weymouth, Massachusetts, and were met by Mayor and Mrs. James McIntyre of Quincy and the Republican Governor of the state, John Volpe with Mrs. Volpe. On the way in, in the car, the Mayor's daughter, Elizabeth Ann, recited her prepared speech for me, the text of which unfortunately had gotten lost in the confusion of the arrival.

We rolled down Adams Street—so properly named—and up in front of "The Old House" where four generations of Adamses had lived, beginning in 1787 with John Adams, followed by John Quincy Adams, Charles Francis Adams, and Brooks Adams, who had moved out in 1927. It was a long, low, white clapboard house with shutters and a brick wall, and a walk lined with huge lilacs. Mr. Charles Francis Adams met us—a courtly dignified man who, I'd been told, had been head of the Republicans-for-Johnson in New England in 1964.

Mrs. Wilamina Harris conducted the tour through the house. She had been social secretary to the Brooks Adamses, the last members of the family to live in the house. She was that marvelous mixture of someone who loved the house and was steeped in its history and anecdotes—a jewel of a tour conductor.

Stew and Lee, George Hartzog and I, with Mr. Charles Francis Adams accompanying us, walked slowly through this 236-year-old house, absorbing all that we could. The Adamses knew they were living right in the main current of history and they saved the physical evidence. During the Revolutionary War they gave their pewter spoons to be melted into bullets, and they saved the molds. And John Adams, when he signed the Treaty of Paris ending our War for Independence, used a personal seal which was handed down to the eldest son, generation after generation. There it was in a case. Dorothy Territo (our archivist) would have loved them.

In such a house, what catches a visitor's eye? For one thing, John Adams' traveling case, which looked like a medium-sized chest of drawers and accompanied him on his travels between Quincy and Washington and to Paris and London. The top drawer was virtually a desk, with an ink bottle and a place for stationery and pens. The next drawer was divided between a lavatory, with a place for shaving mug and brushes, and a medicine chest. Below, amazingly, was a toilet seat. John Adams went first-class!

Spread out in a long bureau drawer was a brown silk dress, beruffled in lace, that Abigail Adams had worn to have her portrait painted by Gilbert Stuart, and a scent bouquet that she had once clutched at parties in Paris. And, most impressive of all, there was a suit that John Quincy Adams had ordered made for his presentation to Queen Victoria when he was Ambassador—resplendent with gold braid showing the oak leaf and acorn pattern that appears in the Adams crest. The suit had cost three or four hundred pounds in that day, but he undoubtedly upheld the dignity of the United States.

What did I really love the most—what did my heart go out to? The huge lilacs—almost trees now, bending with fragrant purple blooms, that Abigail Adams herself had planted. They go on blossoming, a living link with the second First Lady.

The most interesting room was the Gentlemen's Room, with a desk used by four generations of Adamses—the one at which John Adams had conducted his long correspondence with Thomas Jefferson, which ended not long before they both died on July 4, 1826. There was the wing chair in the corner used when John Quincy Adams had posed for a portrait when he was ninety years old. This was the room where I wished the walls could talk. Many of the country's great men had visited the Adams house in those days, and many of the events that molded our lives must have been discussed and decided on in this room. But I was told that no First Lady had visited the house since Mrs. John Quincy Adams returned in 1829.

A number of members of the Adams family were present today, including Mrs. Abigail Adams Homans—the great-great-granddaughter of the second American President. She was a sprightly and erect eighty-eight-year-old Back Bay Boston grandame, who wore a hearing aid, talked in a foghorn voice, and brandished a cane with alarming abandon in a house so filled with historic objects. In fact we hadn't been in the Long Room but a minute—drinking our sherry, mine in a red glass that had belonged to the first Abigail, several others in green glasses that had belonged to President John Adams—when suddenly there was a crash and a splatter and Mrs. Homans' voice saying: "Hell and damnation! I hope it wasn't historic!" . . . I am *sure* it was.

We went into the dining room and were seated around a table beneath portraits of both the Adams Presidents for a luncheon of consommé, lobster, tomatoes stuffed with chopped peppers and celery, cranberry ice and ginger wafers—all recipes that were favorites of the Adams family through the years. We ate at John Adams' dining table on the Meissen china with the cornflower design and the Bourbon spray border that had belonged to John Quincy Adams. Abigail Adams herself had hemmed our forty-inch luncheon napkins, and we drank from wine glasses that Charles Francis Adams had owned. The coffee cups had belonged to the latest occupants of the house, the Brooks Adamses.

I was conscious every minute that this family, as they bought and handed down, must have been exceedingly aware of and prepared for history. I don't mean that they were pompous or self-important, but they seemed to have a sense of destiny, to be aware of the importance of the events that they helped shape.

I remarked on the taste and care of Abigail Adams in selecting the beautiful china and silver. Mrs. Homans replied she was a very extravagant woman. She also pointed out the portrait of one of the later Mrs. Adamses who she said "brought all of the loot." That is, she had brought some money into the family, apparently, which had enabled them to enlarge the house and purchase elegant things.

One of the most memorable moments came when I discovered two of the chairs—the original ones Monroe had ordered in Paris, whose companions once again grace the Blue Room at the White House. These chairs had been in use at the White House during Monroe's day and until the time of some later President (I think it was Chester Arthur) who had sold them at auction on the White House grounds, along with about twenty-six wagonloads of furnishings. The current members of the Adams family had very properly come down from Massachusetts and bought them, so discerning were they. Mrs. Kennedy, I was told quietly, had made an earnest attempt to obtain these chairs for the White House. The Adamses had declined. But Mr. Charles Francis Adams had paid a generous sum to have them handsomely copied to add to those already in the White House.

Mrs. Homans asked me if I was a college woman. And when I told her I was, she said it was the loss of her life that she hadn't been able to go off to college. She had been educated by her two uncles, and had just written a book entitled *Educated by Uncles*. Henry Adams, the writer, was one of them. Could she send me her book? I was delighted and look forward to it.

As lunch ended I rose and proposed a toast to the memory of the second and sixth Presidents of the United States—"our gratitude that in their roots of strength and character, Heaven bestowed the best of blessings on this country"—a play on the words of John Adams' inscription above the mantelpiece in the State Dining Room of the White House.

Charles Francis Adams replied with a toast to the President of the United States. Then we went out into the garden where the bridal wreath, day lilies and the purple iris, and the lilacs were everywhere. They presented me with a cutting from the Yorkshire rose which Abigail herself had planted and which had come across the ocean in a three-month voyage. And I gave them a seedling from the John Quincy Adams Elm, which grows on the White House lawn. He had planted it in 1826, the first historic tree of record on the White House grounds.

We then went into the Library for coffee—and this was truly the *first* Presidential library—an imposing room lined to its high ceilings with books in eleven languages that John Adams and all succeeding members of the family had owned and read. Most of them had beautiful tooled leather bindings—quite a few were made in this country in Nashville,

Tennessee. In describing this family I thought that one must truly use that overworked word "intellectuals."

We were back at South Weymouth by 2:30 and into the plane. We arrived at the Burlington Airport and there at the foot of the ramp were Joan and Phil Hoff, the Governor of Vermont. We got into the car for the motorcade to Mt. Mansfield. It was an hour's trip across country as beautiful as ever I will see, along a highway that should have won an award for design, for aesthetic consideration of the countryside through which it winds. We drove through the most verdant land—gentle mountains rising on each side, open meadows with cows grazing, swift rushing streams and white birches with ferns carpeting the ground below them, lilacs in the farmyards. And the most beautiful barns. I had the feeling that the men who had built those barns must have loved them. They were good craftsmen—their designs were varied and the structures settled into the hillsides most companionably, in artistic relationship with the land.

Around 4:30 we arrived at the ski lift at the foot of Mt. Mansfield to see New England crafts, old and new, at a show this evening, and there were Governor and Mrs. John W. King of New Hampshire, Governor and Mrs. Kenneth Curtis of Maine—a very young, attractive couple—and Bill Youngman and Tom Corcoran. Jerry Kivett got into the ski lift with me, and I docilely took the blanket they handed me. I must learn to say "No!" We slowly began our ascent to the four-thousand-foot top. It's like riding an open basket through the sky! But with a brace in front of me I felt safe. I had heard that from the top you could see three states and on a clear day even Canada. But a haze hung over the mountains in spite of the warm sunshine, and they assured me the view was not at its most spectacular best.

We tasted "sugar and snow"—hot maple syrup poured over a trough full of snow—saved, I was told, from the winter. The syrup hardens into little chewy strings which you pick up like spaghetti. It was delicious.

Back at the foot of the mountain, we went straight to our lodge—an attractive private cottage. As soon as I opened the door, I came face to face with an original Grandma Moses above the mantel. After a brief rest we went to the arts and crafts show. The weather was as hot as the blacksmith's forge. The camera lights were bright and the crowds thick. Imagine being in New England and suffering from the heat! Making my way through the sweltering room, I suddenly came upon Erich and Anne Leinsdorf. He was just back from conducting a symphony in Tel Aviv. He had left just hours before the shooting began.

We had dinner at Spruce House—I sitting between Governor Hoff and Governor King, who proved a most amusing dinner companion. Watching Liz bustling around tending to the press, he said, "There goes Liz like an Israeli General leading her troops." The hundred or more guests from New Hampshire, Maine, and Vermont were all conservationists or interested in arts and crafts.

The menu was pure New England—Maine lobster cocktail. (Except for breakfast, I don't think there was a meal without lobster during these four days! But I could never get enough.) And then New England clam chowder and roast Vermont turkey, ending with something I've never had —New Hampshire Indian pudding, as primitive as it sounds, but good.

During dinner Governor King told me that he was a solid Administration man in favor of Lyndon's policies—that he thought the much-publicized wave of unpopularity was more smoke than fire. He has a rather bland exterior, but surprising humor and freshness as you get to talking to him.

After dinner I met the craftsmen and gave certificates to each of them. And then there was a program—unavoidably too long, since there were three Governors present and each made a speech—and there was also music by Skitch Henderson. So it was nearly 12 when I returned to the lodge— weary and full of the emotions and scenes of the day.

Sunday, June 11

I was up early at the Rockefeller house in Woodstock, Vermont, and downstairs for breakfast by 8, coming upon Mary Rockefeller in a small room of the Victorian mansion that she had pointed out to me the night before as the Prayer Room, where her mother and the family had gathered to read the Bible and pray. There she was sitting quietly at a table, her Bible in her hand.

We went in to breakfast and it was hearty and delicious, including blueberry pancakes, and, naturally, Vermont maple syrup—hot, with melted butter. I thought of Lynda's maxim, "If you're going to be a bear— be a grizzly," and ate as though I were going to spend the day plowing those rocky hills.

We rode to Plymouth to the home of President Coolidge, following a swift and rushing stream through a little valley—part of the watershed that's going to be cleaned up by the project we are celebrating this afternoon. The city of Woodstock has voted a bond issue which, in collaboration with state and federal funds and planning, will result in some thirty-six miles of clear and unpolluted scenic waterways in the years to come.

It was so fresh and green that you could understand how the State of Vermont got its name—"Green Mountain"—almost a literal translation. I never had thought of it until this trip. Part of its charm to me was that not even Johnson City, Texas, was more rural, more off the beaten path, than this little green valley. And here I was going to the home of the thirtieth President of the United States—Calvin Coolidge. We arrived about 9:30 in the tiny hamlet with white clapboard houses and a store and post office. It had all jelled in time—and I imagine it had not grown by five citizens in the last fifty years.

A crowd of possibly two hundred—many children—was gathered in front of the Calvin Coolidge homestead—white clapboard with shutters and a front porch whose Victorian turned columns might have come from the same design as Lyndon's house in Johnson City. It was, in fact, so reminiscent that it went straight to my heart, although I had thought of no parallel before between Lyndon and Calvin Coolidge.

John Coolidge, the President's son, dignified and impressive, was there to meet us. We went up on the porch and there was a brief, pleasant ceremony, John Coolidge presiding and Stew Udall and Phil Hoff making short speeches and then my words—no notes, just a natural response to this situation of visiting the home of a President, where the land had made its mark on a man, had molded his devotion to duty, his capacity for hard work, his dislike of ostentation, and his ability to express himself in terse phrases. At the end I gave a National Park Service plaque, designating the Calvin Coolidge homestead as a registered National Historic Landmark —Nash Castro and I placed it, and it was quite heavy, on the cement foundation that had been prepared.

Then we went through the house. I was interested in the woodshed indoors; chopping the wood for the kitchen stove had been one of Calvin Coolidge's jobs as a young boy. And there was little progress between the kitchen stove of his day and of Lyndon's mother's. There was a buggy and a sled for winter in the carriage house. All are attached to the main house because of the heavy snows of Vermont winters. The sparseness, the frugality of the furnishings, impressed me, knowing that this was the home of a leading citizen of this little community in that day.

There was a kerosene lamp on the table at which Calvin Coolidge took his oath of office, a stereopticon, a horsehair sofa, a yellowed Boston newspaper of 1924 with the headline "KEEP DOWN EXPENSES IS COOLIDGE'S EXHORTATION." Stew read one of his campaign promises from the paper —"*Waste no time, words, nor public funds.*" And I was intrigued by the familiarity of a phrase from one of his political pamphlets, "*. . . a man who practices what he preaches—a square deal to all.*"

I told John Coolidge I knew my daughter Lynda would love to hear him talk about what it had been like in his day in the White House. He said, to my surprise, that he had the Secret Service with him then too. He had been off in college most of the time and they accompanied him there.

Then a little past 10 we were driving back over the lovely valley roads to Woodstock, arriving at the First Congregational Church which might have come off a postcard—so pure and white it was, its slim steeple rising against the green hills at the end of the street. The church bell had been cast by Paul Revere. And it was here that Laurance and Mary Rockefeller married thirty-three years ago. I sat in the pew with them. One of the most delightful things during this whole visit is the way that they move around as townspeople and wave and speak to neighbors, calling them by their first names: "Hello there, John. Where is Laura?" And people answer back with the same familiarity.

The music was lovely. There were familiar hymns—"Beneath the Cross of Jesus." It was a charming service, and we were out before noon. When I spoke to the minister, he told me that his eight-year-old son had said, "Why don't we invite Mrs. Johnson home for lunch?"

It would have been an easy little town to fall in love with. We walked down the street to the Woodstock Historical Association—a typical white clapboard house, green shutters, lilac-bordered walk. The Curator took us through, showing us their two-hundred-year accumulation of colonial furniture, and very much the touch of the Rockefellers, though they would be the last to say it. In the basement there was a small theater, given by Mary's mother for community gatherings. Behind the house a beautifully landscaped lawn led down to the river.

It was a little past 12 when we went out front for the most picturesque adventure of the day—a ride in a Stanley Steamer—vintage 1911, owned by a young boy who was working his way through college by taking tourists for a drive around Woodstock. Before we walked out of the Woodstock Historical Association we donned our "duster bonnets"—mine a dream of a hat with pink roses and a wide brim and pink chiffon that tied under the chin. Each of us had a vintage hat that was extraordinarily becoming,

Mary's so quaint and demure it seemed to have been made for her, and Lee's—perky and saucy.

The brass of the car was shiny, the running boards high, and the seats higher, and the horn let off a blast just like a train—no wonder, it was steam. The Rockefellers and Udalls and Hoffs were in the two back seats, and Curtis Bourdon, the driver, and I in the front where I could see the panel. The figures on the speedometer went up to "60 miles per hour." Yes, he had driven it that fast on the highway. But it didn't register unless you were driving at least fifteen miles per hour.

To emphasize the spirit of the day there were several horses and buggies around the village green. I flinched as we approached them at a merry clip, a flotilla of three Stanley Steamers. Curtis eased by without blowing his horn. The horses stood still, and we breathed a sigh of relief. Mary Rockefeller told us how, when her mother got her first car, she had asked all the folks who worked for her and the neighboring farmers to come up with their horses to her house and then showed the car to them, driving it quietly around so they could get used to it.

We circled the green, past the rambling white Woodstock Inn with its long veranda—it looked like the grandfather of all summer resort hotels. We passed the Woodstock Historical Association and the White Cupboard and the DAR house and museum—both built in 1807—all the little white steepled churches with their Paul Revere bells, the Town Hall where we had been welcomed the afternoon before, the little circle where the places of business are bright with pink and red petunias, and along elm-bordered streets where the houses range between pre-Revolutionary and pre-Civil War. We drove past the site of the railroad depot, built by Mary Rockefeller's grandfather, Frederick Billings, who had brought the little branch line railroad up here when he had bought his home about the time of the Civil War. (It was Frederick Billings who built the Northern Pacific Railroad and for whom Billings, Montana, is named.)

We drove back to Laurance and Mary's home which is called the "Mansion." So ended one of the most colorful rides of my career as First Lady—"Whistlestop," rubber raft, ski lift, and now a Stanley Steamer!

After lunch I had a few minutes' rest and was dressed by 3. I walked out on the long gallery that encircles the house and looked down across the expanse of green that descends to the rushing Ottauquechee River and is bordered by tall beautiful trees. There were several hundred of the Rockefeller neighbors—the selectmen of Woodstock and neighboring communities, state officials, conservationists, personal friends.

Laurance presided with his most remarkable brand of crisp businesslike efficiency and humor. My speech was twofold—first, a salute to George Perkins Marsh, whose home this had been for many years, and who was in fact a sort of a father of conservation in the United States, writing a hundred years ago about man and nature, the effect of man on his environment, erosion, many things that concern us today; and second, a salute to the present inhabitants of this house, describing Laurance Rockefeller as "America's leading citizen-conservationist today. From the Grand Tetons to the Virgin Islands—and here in your valley—he has made conservation and recreation his life work."

But the real thrust of the speech was to applaud local initiative, because in this watershed that is what has brought progress. Hopefully, in a couple of decades, they will have achieved their goal of unpolluted, beautiful streams, an invitation for tourists and for light, science-oriented industries, bringing with them their sizable payrolls as a bulwark for the state's economy.

At the end I unveiled the plaque designating the house as a National Landmark. On the chimney, high above, was the date 1806, and close by was a window of colored Tiffany glass picturing one hand passing a torch to another hand. Laurance had told me that they liked to think that that was the older generation passing on the torch of learning, culture, conservation, whatever wisdom they had, to the younger generation.

Wednesday, June 21

AUSTIN, TEXAS

The equinox—it was indeed the longest day of the year—the day I became a grandmother. I awoke dazedly to the noise of people moving around in Luci and Pat's house and hushed talk, with an occasional laugh. I thought, "This certainly has been a short night," and reached for the phone. I asked the operator what time it was, and he said 12:13! Something must be wrong. I had thought it was morning, then realized I had only been asleep an hour.

About that time Dr. Billy Bailey stuck his head in the door, grinning cheerfully, and said, "It looks like we're in business." And stupidly, I inquired, "Do you mean it's time to go to the hospital?" "Yes," he said. "I think so."

I got up and went into the kitchen to see if there was anything I could do. Joe Batson had gone through the ritual of putting on the coffee pot. Luci was in her room putting on her makeup. So there was plenty of time to dress. I had a cup of Joe's coffee. Luci was laughing and Pat was not. Yes, her suitcase was ready. I had seen it sitting on a table, packed, for days. Billy Bailey actually looked elated. He and Dr. Thompson, the obstetrician, had formed the habit of taking turns each morning calling, rather anxiously: "How do you feel this morning?" Luci said they sounded disappointed when she always said, "I feel fine."

It was a little past one A.M. when Luci and Pat left in one car for Seton Hospital and I followed right behind. We went straight to the fourth floor where Luci was taken to a labor room. Mary Love (Dr. Bailey's wife and our longtime friend) was there already. Billy Bailey called Dr. Philip Thompson and the other members of the team, our old friend Dr. Morgan, and the young pediatrician who will take care of the baby, Dr. Philip Kocen, and the anesthetist.

Later, I read a hilarious story about what the night looked like from a reporter's standpoint. The press had begun to gather at the hospital shortly after one. At first the hospital security guards insisted they didn't know anything about it, but added, "The nurses have been saying all day a baby was coming because of the full moon." Then they began to see the Secret Service everywhere and then Simone Poulain from our press office rushing in. She went up to the fourth floor. Then Stormy Davis with phones under one arm and phone books under the other—he'd saved both a pink phone and a blue phone for Luci's room. Soon the phones began to ring—Los Angeles wanted to know what was happening—followed by a radio station in Ohio . . . And the *Washington Post* was holding its 3 o'clock deadline waiting on word. Joe Batson appeared, bringing mints and gum . . . Columbia, South Carolina, called for news. The reporters saw a lot of sisters scurrying down the hall, and they thought that meant something. No, the nurses were just going to Mass . . . But they would pray for the baby and Luci!

I had telephoned Lyndon just before we left the house. As soon as Luci was settled in the labor room I went down to the room that had been assigned to me on the third floor and called Mrs. Nugent, waking her up as I had Lyndon. Then I called Lynda, whom I did not wake up . . . She was out dancing, her agent said, and I left word for her to call me, no matter what time.

My chief memory of the night is the respect for and the pride I felt in Luci. She approached this with such strength, such character. She really walks hand in hand with life, and she is supported by happiness. When I went into the labor room everybody was all smiles, the nurses, the doctors. They looked up at me and said, "She's cooperating beautifully. Everything is going fine." Finally the smile faded from Luci's face. She looked stern—earnest—and finally weary. But never frightened or in great pain. Her hair lay like black wings along her pale cheeks.

Sometime after 4, when Luci was partially under anesthesia, I went down to my room to get some rest and actually went to sleep, leaving word with Jerry Kivett to call me whenever the doctors had news. It must have been about 6:30 when Jerry knocked on my door and I slipped into my clothes and started back up to the fourth floor. I must have climbed these stairs two dozen times tonight. Just as I went through the swinging doors on the fourth floor a nurse said, "It's a boy!"

Once more, rather ridiculously, I said: "Do you mean *ours*? Has it already been born?" The nurses gathered around and confirmed the fact. In a moment Billy came out of the delivery room, all smiles, and said, "Luci has a boy. She's fine. She'll be out in a few minutes. And the baby's fine."

Without waiting for any more details, I went straight downstairs and phoned Lyndon, waking him up again. He laughed and said, "A boy? That's fine." Then he said something joking about me being Grandma. I phoned Mrs. Nugent, who was very warm and happy and sweet. Lynda had called me back only a few hours before at the end of an evening of partying and dancing with George Hamilton in New York. But I wanted her to hear it from me and not the newspapers. So I woke her up. All of her inquiries were about Luci. Was I sure she was all right?

A sister came in and brought me some coffee. Pat went down to see the reporters with cigars and candy, looking tired and happy and in need of a shave. Reporters are not his favorite people. He is not as easy with them as Luci is, but this time he met them with good grace and told them that Luci and the baby were both fine and that the baby weighed, surprisingly, eight pounds ten ounces. The most weight any doctor had forecast had been seven pounds, and Luci had only gained twelve pounds during her pregnancy. The baby was twenty-one inches long and had slate-gray eyes and blond hair. Then the hall was full of doctors coming and going, and nurses . . . and smiles and congratulations.

Simone had asked me to meet with the reporters for a minute. They all rushed out as excited and jubilant as any of us, for they had watched Luci grow up. Dorothy McCardle actually threw her arms around me with congratulations. There was a shower of excited questions, and I gave answers that will win no Nobel Prize for originality—"Happy and relieved," "Glad for Luci and Pat," "No, no, no, I can't go on television." "You all know where *I'm* going—to the beauty parlor!" Someone asked me how it felt to be a grandmother. I told them, "I like the status better than the title."

I drove out to the Ranch, tended to a day full of household chores, and returned to the hospital around 6.

Early in the morning shortly after the baby was born Luci had been groggy and she had known she was groggy. She had turned her head on the pillow and said to me, "Hi, Mother." And then she began to babble on and interrupted herself to say, "I don't know what I'm saying." Now, in the evening, she looked quite herself—beautiful, happy, bubbling with talk. I do not actually remember when it was—sometime in the morning— that I first went into the room next door and looked at the baby. I had asked Pat that morning if they had named him. He said, "We've decided on a name. But we haven't announced it yet." I said, "Well, don't tell me then, because I don't want to let it slip until you've said it." All day long I hadn't known what the baby's name was. In the middle of the afternoon Pat had called me at the Ranch and told me: "It's Patrick Lyndon."

Sunday, June 25

GLASSBORO, NEW JERSEY

Today was one of the strangest days I've spent as First Lady. It began at 6:30 A.M. at the Ranch, but it was the day scheduled for Lyndon's second meeting with Chairman Alexei Kosygin, at Glassboro, New Jersey. Yesterday Lyndon had asked me very casually, "Don't you think it would be a good idea if we asked Kosygin's daughter to come with him and you took her to lunch?"

I made numerous calls during the evening—to Liz about how to handle the press, to Betty Hughes who was to be our actual hostess as the wife of the Governor of New Jersey (I was depending on her completely to arrange the lunch and three or four interesting hours), and to McGeorge Bundy. He reported to me on the evening he had spent with Kosygin's daughter, Mrs. Ludmilla Gvishiana. They'd attended a small dinner party. He pronounced her "the easiest possible girl to get along with—intelligent, well educated in political science and history, excellent English—you couldn't pick a better companion to spend four hours with."

Betty Hughes, with perception, had suggested a delightful day for us— lunch at the Governor's beach home in a New Jersey State Park on the Atlantic seashore. The plans all hinged on whether Mrs. Gvishiana would ride in a helicopter. Just before we were aboard ourselves we got the word that she would. Among many other calls before leaving, I telephoned Bess about gifts and getting word to Mrs. Gvishiana that our entertainment would be a beach party—quite informal dress—and rehearsing the scenario. I never felt so uncertain and ill at ease about a State visitor before, I suppose because of the confusion, and the fact that it was in an unfamiliar setting. We had the stern admonition that the Russians must pass on and agree to everything that concerned press coverage. This was something that I had never faced before.

Mrs. Burg came at 8 and combed my hair—an absolute lifesaver after several wind-blown days. Then we were in the *Jetstar* to San Antonio and into *Air Force One* to Philadelphia—talking to Arthur Krim about his trips to Russia, searching for possible topics of conversation with Ludmilla, reading the papers, and then changing into my brown suit. One cheery note was seeing Lynda and Warrie Lynn. Warrie, as always, was all smiles and happiness.

We reached Philadelphia a little before 12:30 and helicoptered to Glassboro, a little college town, no more remarkable than San Marcos. The college campus was shaded by enormous oaks and had the aura of age, and "Hollybush," the home of the President, Dr. Thomas Robinson, and Mrs. Robinson, was Victorian red brick, turreted, old-fashioned, almost a prototype of the college president's house of half a century ago.

It was later I found out about the preparation that had gone on in that house in the hectic hours of Thursday night and Friday morning. Something like fourteen window air conditioners had been put in, and telephones with White House lines installed in every room. The Robinsons' very beds had been moved out, but the sofas and chairs, vintage about 1908, and tables with carved curlicues, the old family pictures of weddings, christenings and graduations, were still in place around the rooms. It was absolutely delightful and could not have been faked—the real McCoy—a part of America. (But, oh, such an earthquake for the Robinsons!) I thought it was somehow peculiarly appropriate to have the meeting in such a place rather than in the elegant glass-and-aluminum UN conference room or Waldorf suite.

We arrived only a few minutes before it was time to meet Chairman Kosygin and his party. We emerged onto the steps of the old Victorian house and up they drove, the hammer-and-sickle flag flying from the front of the black limousine. Across the drive, lined up under the oak trees behind a rope, were more cameras and newspaper people than I've ever seen for any meeting; most were standing on the ground, some on raised platforms. Then out stepped Chairman Kosygin, a very solid and strong-featured man, in his sixties I should think, unbending and tough-looking, but pleasant enough, and his daughter, Mrs. Ludmilla Gvishiana—a very young-looking thirty-eight—slim, almost no makeup, casual hairdo, completely at ease, in a simple navy-blue, white-trimmed dress. She could have been a professor's wife on any campus in thousands of American towns.

Lynda Bird was with us every second. She stays as close to her father as she can. From the very first moment I could see she was absorbing every detail. There was a great roar of cheers from the crowd as we met the Kosygins. At some moment we walked out to the roped-off edge of the hill. Down below us, over the drop, were massed the students of the college. There were only about twenty-eight hundred in the student body as it was summer time, but there must have been great numbers of Glassboro citizens and others with them, because it looked like many thousands of people. There were lots of homemade signs—a large one in Russian, one that just said simply, "PEACE," and all of them—all of them—in friendly, eager, hopeful mood—a tone of real friendship! It was a moving moment.

We went into the house and I took Mrs. Gvishiana upstairs to give her an opportunity to powder her nose. I smiled to myself at the thought of any legend she might have heard about the luxury of American bathrooms, because this one wasn't like that at all, although it was certainly adequate. And then the thoughtful Robinsons offered us iced tea.

Lyndon asked us if we would like to come and see the room where the group would meet. There was a long, plain table, and present, in addition to Chairman Kosygin and the stern Andrei Gromyko, were the Russian interpreter, who I think was very capable, and our interpreter, Secretary Rusk, Walt Rostow, the affable Dobrynin, and patient and philosophical Llewellyn Thompson, our Ambassador to Russia, along with a few others whom I did not know. They would all sit down to lunch together, I was told—about sixteen. That would crowd the room. Then Lyndon took us into the room where he and Chairman Kosygin had met alone on

Friday—just the two of them with the two interpreters. They would meet again there in about an hour.

I had that chilly, spine-tingling feeling that I was face to face with a historic event. Then suddenly I looked at the chair that Lyndon would sit in and it was the very twin of the one that sits in his boyhood home in the parlor—the one that Mrs. Johnson's mother had given her to start housekeeping with—Victorian, already well-aged in 1907. This one was upholstered in green velvet, and behind it was a sofa to match, almost identical with Mrs. Johnson's.

What a day! This possibly very momentous, certainly dramatic confrontation, held in a setting so quaint and homey—authentic Americana. We said good-by to the men, and to one of them I said, "God Bless," and then had a quick thought—that's a strange thing to say to a Russian!

Mrs. Hughes and Mrs. Gvishiana, Lynda, Liz, and I departed Hollybush, got into the helicopter, and set out over the New Jersey countryside. Betty Hughes was the tour guide—no better one could have been found in all the land. She pointed out the acres of vegetables below. Her state is called the "Garden State," and they have many truck farmers. There are hills of low, thick scrub pine, cranberry bogs, and once we flew over a race track. And always throughout the trip, we could see the long double line of the great highway that brings thousands of tourists from big metropolitan centers to Atlantic City. I pointed this out to Mrs. Gvishiana and told her how our American highways are such an important part of our economic and social life and how recently we have begun to try to add to them aesthetic values as well as functional ones. I wanted her to take home a sense of the rising desire of American people for beauty in their lives.

We flew over Atlantic City and I pointed out the big convention hall where Lyndon was nominated in 1964. As we flew along the Atlantic coast Betty showed her a public beach where anybody could come for twenty-five cents, with bath houses for changing clothes . . . and the long stretch of the Atlantic and the endless sandy beach. There were thousands of people sunning and swimming. It was a great sight. We could see the boardwalk and the big hotels, and I was every bit as interested as Mrs. Gvishiana.

It was apparent from the beginning that Lynda Bird took to her and she, I believe, to Lynda. They talked mostly to each other. Betty Hughes, our official hostess, was an excellent, highly amusing talker. I was rather quiet and so was Liz. There was never any need for an interpreter. Our guest of honor was indeed unpretentious and easy to be with.

Then the weathered, gray clapboard house right on the shore of the Atlantic came into view. This house had been the New Jersey Governor's summer residence for a number of years and at present it housed Governor and Mrs. Hughes and about seven of their ten children, not to mention the numerous visitors that are always in tow with children.

With weeks of preparation we could not have provided a better presentation of the American home than this. We were met by all seven children in residence, ranging from Tommy, aged six, who was wearing a shirt with "Peanuts" characters on it (this was one of the few things that stumped Mrs. Gvishiana), to the eighteen-year-old son (who had his surfboard handy and was ready to give a demonstration with his friends), to Betty's mother who was spending the summer with them, along with three neighbors who had dropped in for cocktails last night and had been roped into cooking lunch since the cook had left the day before. I was more and more aghast at the demands we had made on Betty Hughes.

Well, the neighbors were all smiles and the lunch was delicious—chicken cooked with wild rice and wine sauce, tossed salad and fresh New Jersey strawberries served with powdered sugar and whipped cream. The talk ranged over such themes as an American supermarket, which Betty said our guest ought to see. But Mrs. Gvishiana said she was afraid she couldn't get in one and really enjoy it without being swamped by a crowd. She had tried to go to Macy's because she had heard it was our biggest department store and she really wanted to see it. But the reporters and photographers and the crowd had become so overwhelming that she had bought the first pair of black shoes she could find and fled.

We talked about education in Russia. Mrs. Gvishiana told us that everyone started school at age seven and attended classes for ten years. That, I gathered, was similar to our elementary and high school put together. After that they were at college level, and the competition was very keen, she said, to go on into what would be considered our university education.

I spoke of the area we were in being a State Park and described some of our National Parks to her. I found her quite conversant with the names, at least such as Yellowstone, which she said she would so much love to see. I asked her about parks in her country and she said they had no system of National Parks as such. But as industry increases and as the great industrial cities grow and expand they are feeling the need to maintain some green wilderness, as she put it, and I believe she said that parks are in their planning for the future.

I said to her, suppose a stranger went to Russia and had only a few days—such a person as myself—what should I try to see? There was the usual nebulous answer to that very nebulous question—so varied, so diverse was her country (just as ours is), with so much to see, it was difficult to say. But of course a stranger would want to see Moscow. One can always learn from the capital of a country. She thought perhaps Leningrad would be the next most interesting. Leningrad was like Venice, built on the water by Peter the Great. She spoke of the monarch with great ease, although I have assimilated the legend that Russians don't look back to their past on the other side of the revolution.

She was easy, talkative, and at times quite animated, and I couldn't help but salute her for being willing to come here all alone. She was so outnumbered by Americans—no counterpart from her country, although we had asked her if she would like to bring a friend. She and Lynda chatted merrily.

She seemed impressed with the kitchen when we took her through. Betty gave her the full treatment about the washer and dryer and disposal and all the electric gadgets and the relative ease of keeping house.

After lunch I presented Mrs. Gvishiana with several books—*The Living White House* and the book on the art treasures of our National Gallery— telling her I hoped she could come again to see some of our treasures. She and Lynda had been excitedly discussing the Hermitage. We also gave her an antique mirror—a modest antique, circa 1780—in a Chippendale mahogany frame, the sort of thing a bridal couple would have received as a gift about the time of our Revolutionary War. (She had been discussing American history at lunch and was well versed in it—mentioning the dates of our Revolution and the peace treaty and names of founding fathers.) We also gave her a wrist watch. She graciously removed her own and put it on.

Presently Liz said in her eagerly polite way that almost always gets results, "Wouldn't you like to walk out on the beach so that they can get a picture of you looking at the sea?" So out we trooped—Betty and Mrs. Gvishiana and Lynda and I—to face the Atlantic with the wind whipping our hair, and sand up to our ankles. And the dozens and dozens of photographers jockeying for positions almost into the waves, and the pencils flying over the pads while we turned to each other with whatever innocuous conversation one can conjure up at a moment like this.

The reporters asked her if New Jersey reminded her of anything in her country. She said, "Yes, of two parts of it. The sand is like the Baltic and the hot weather is like the Black Sea area—in Georgia." Throughout it Mrs. Gvishiana's manner was good-humored and very friendly, but I did notice each time that it was always she who said, "We can go now, don't you think?" or "That's enough, yes?" When I tried to think back about any comment she had made, there was absolutely nothing that couldn't have been repeated anywhere. Her remarks were interested, friendly, animated, and could have come from a guidebook.

Back in the house we sat down in the family room and shook the sand out of our shoes, about a half teacup each. How I would have liked to have been on that beach barefooted. She had consulted her new watch several times and reminded us that her father had said she should be back by 5. We reassured her each time, and Jim Jones ushered us into the car, then into the helicopter, and this time we flew straight back with much less conversation.

We were back at Hollybush a few minutes before the appointed hour. The rows and rows of newspaper people had not budged an inch. They were still under the oak trees in the wilting heat. It was a humid sweltering day, and the storm clouds were piling up above us. Down below we could hear the murmur of the crowd—the students, the citizens of Glassboro, the curious. They apparently had not budged either. I heard later that people had gone through the crowds selling hot dogs and cold drinks just as if they were at a country fair.

We went into a room that had been set aside for us, actually the Robinsons' bedroom with the beds removed. Dr. Robinson and his wife joined us and we talked about their college. I told them about Lyndon's days at a very similar school in San Marcos, Texas, nearly forty years ago. Dr. Robinson smiled and said, yes, it is well known to everybody that the President attended a Teacher's College. And still the conference went on—minutes, then an hour passed. Reaching for good fortune, we all took this as a hopeful sign.

I do not know exactly when they emerged. It was well after 6. They called us out, and Governor and Mrs. Hughes, the Robinsons, Lynda and I, and Mrs. Gvishiana went out on the front steps to join Lyndon and Chairman Kosygin. The great battery of cameramen went wild—pictures of the whole group—pictures of the two principals—pictures of the four or five of us. There was a very brief statement by Lyndon, and a somewhat longer one by Chairman Kosygin, largely a repetition of thanks to the city of Glassboro, to the college, to the Robinsons, to the President. I cannot remember their exact words, but there was implicit in what they both said an admission that they had made no great progress but that each felt better for knowing the man who would be on the other end of the Hot Line.

Then, in response to the roars of the crowd, we went over to the embankment once more—the Chairman and his daughter, Lyndon and I and Lynda Bird. Lyndon always reaches out an arm and brings in other principals, this time Betty and Governor Hughes. We all leaned over and shouted greetings and waved to the students and townspeople below.

Kosygin seemed firm, tough, pleasant, courteous—all at the same time. I could not take the temperature of what had gone on in those hours of meeting except to know that there was no great advance or else I could have read it on my husband's face. Gromyko was impassive throughout and Dobrynin beamed. Then we were all saying farewells with special invitations to "come again" to Mrs. Gvishiana, and they were on their way—down to the open field and into their helicopter. We were behind them in a following car. We said good-by to the Hugheses and mounted our helicopter, though we sat on the ground until our guests were aloft and away.

The ride home seemed short. The first words I remember Lyndon saying were: "Well, I'd say we didn't move ahead far today." Most of the time was consumed with when and where he should make his televised report to the American people. The conclusion was that he should speak as soon as he hit the White House lawn. There were TV crews there ready, with a microphone poised a few feet from where he would emerge from the helicopter. He worked on getting his statement ready, and a little past 7:30 we were on the ground.

Lyndon made a quiet speech. He conceded we were a long way from agreement, but there was a hopeful air. He said he thought their ten hours of talks had made the world a smaller and a little less dangerous place, that we had improved understanding of each other's views . . . that out of their discussions might come the beginnings of future agreements.

By 8 we were upstairs, almost at the end of what must have been one of the most tiring days in my husband's life. The evening consisted of innumerable telephone calls on Lyndon's part, notably, I remember, to Senators Mansfield and Dirksen and Fulbright, to report to them his feelings about the day's talks. Then we watched on television Chairman

Kosygin holding a press conference at the United Nations. This lasted nearly an hour and a half. What an endurance contest—because he too had shared this grueling day.

I thought he acquitted himself quite well, though gone, alas, was all the cordiality that had marked the outward manifestations of our meeting at Glassboro. He was very tough in reaffirming the hard-line positions on both the Middle East and Vietnam. He did give a ray of light and hope on one issue—that he and the President had made some headway on a treaty to ban the spread of nuclear weapons—not headway, but hope, a glimmer of light. They both had the same philosophy and aim, and they would work to make something come out of it.

What a forum the United Nations was for a press conference—he was face to face with all the representatives of 120 or so countries, with the Arab nations particularly hanging on every word. And the questions were tough.

In the telephone calls that followed, I gathered something of the feeling of the four hours of talks today: that Kosygin unrelentingly thought of Israel as a perpetrator of aggression, drunk with power and intoxicated with success, and it was Lyndon's opinion that Kosygin had come here for one purpose—to talk about Israel's withdrawal of troops. That was what he had hammered on over and over and over.

McGeorge Bundy said, "Do you think Kosygin got notice that his first reports or recommendations were too soft?" That meant, I presumed, whether he'd been called to task between the first meeting Friday night and the second on Sunday morning by his colleagues in Moscow, worrying about the Chinese and the Arabs. In answer to his repeated insistence that Israel had started the war, Lyndon answered with what I expect was considerable forcefulness, clothed in mild words, that maybe the closing of the Gulf of Aqaba, the massing of Egyptian troops, and statements that they are going to run Israel into the sea could possibly have been considered an act of aggression.

Well, the day was one great try! And even if little headway was made, the thirst of the country for a meeting, a face-to-face confrontation, was somewhat assuaged. I am so glad that Lyndon and Kosygin met twice. I am very proud of Lyndon and somehow relieved, and he is very tired.

This was an offbeat day for life at the Ranch. I took a trip—a miniature version of one of my big, well-planned trips—mostly through the old Tenth Congressional District Lyndon had represented in Congress for twelve years. The purpose was to see grass-roots beautification and restoration under way in Lockhart, Round Top, and La Grange, Texas. This was the least "advanced" trip I have ever made, with just a quick "drive-through" by Liz the day before. The idea had been in the back of my mind ever since I had first heard of Round Top, and Congressman Jake Pickle had been the catalytic agent who had brought it to life today.

Jake and Beryl briefed me enthusiastically all the way to Lockhart. There we stepped out of the car into the baking, bright sun with the temperature in the upper nineties, and the Mayor greeted me with an armful of bluebells, which got the day off to a wonderful start.

The whole visit to Lockhart filled me with pride, that this little Texas town of six thousand population had the spark and the get-up-and-get to make the most of its Court House square. The focal point of the square is the old white limestone Victorian-style Court House, described by Mr. Zisman, the restoration architect, as "a structure ugly enough to be beautiful." There must be at least one hundred Court Houses in Texas of this vintage, built in the 1890's—unbelievable accumulations of turrets, towers, domes, gingerbread, columns, and carvings. And the Court House is always the hub of the town. Lockhart's Court House has been augmented by artistic lighting, and they were all chagrined that I couldn't be there at night so that I could see the lighting effects. In the square itself the merchants are striving to keep the original character of the turn-of-the-century buildings and still be modern.

A young University of Texas architectural student in community and regional planning, Garland Anderson, spearheaded the idea along with Mr. Zisman, and had made an impressive model of the town square in which all the old buildings, circa 1890–1910, with their elaborately decorated false fronts, were freshly painted in attractive colors—buff and warm beige, Indian red and a gray green—many of them with brightly striped awnings out front.

Some of the merchants have bought the idea and have gone to work painting. There are about six restored buildings around the square. A row of live oaks on each street forming the four sides of the square is planned for this fall. Some planting has already been done on the Court House square itself, and a series of tall flag poles, flying the United States flag and the Texas flag, are planned—one or two are already up. We raised a flag in front of an attractive old building—Westy's Drug Store—which has been in operation for nearly one hundred years. This store had a handsome new coat of beige paint, and appropriately on top of the false front the decoration featured an apothecary jar. The red-and-white striped awning out front practically said: "Ice cream parlor—come in!"

Congressman Jake Pickle was everywhere at once wanting me to meet "my old friend so and so," "this good Democrat," and the like. Countless people told me about campaigning with Lyndon in 1937 and 1946.

The important aspect of the restoration is that the local people themselves raised the six thousand dollars for the lighting project of the Court House and that they are determined to go on. They are proud of their town. Several of them told me how many City Managers and Mayors from other cities had come to observe and hear about what they have accomplished.

Then we were back in the car and headed for Praha—an old Czech community. We left the main highway and went down a narrow winding country road until suddenly before us we saw the two graceful spires of a large imposing church—standing alone in a serene pastoral setting. Praha, which is named for Prague, the capital of Czechoslovakia, was settled entirely by Czechs between 1850 and 1870, and at one time was a community of seven hundred families who worshiped in this church. The church was built in 1890. Now all that remains of Praha is a general store, the Post Office at the crossroads, two or three neat white farm houses, and the beautiful church—St. Mary's—to which thousands of Czechs return for an annual summer celebration. St. Mary's is the mother church of all the Czechs in Texas.

The landscape had become increasingly lush and pretty—rolling, verdant. Several times we had passed beautiful stands of bluebells in the meadows and clumps of live oaks. But the country was sparsely populated and it was surprising to come upon such an enormous church, out in nowhere, and to see several hundred people, many of them in bright-colored Czech costumes, clustered around it. In front stood the tall, imposing pastor— Reverend Marcus Anthony Valenta—about six feet four, a handsome, strong face, a commanding figure of a man. He had been on active battlefield duty as a chaplain from Pearl Harbor to Okinawa. Alas, the poor priest was dressed proudly in his chaplain's uniform, which must have been made for the coldest post he ever held. As we walked around in the baking sun—it must have been 98 degrees by now—there was sweat dripping off his nose and off his chin, which in no way detracted from his dignity.

Father Valenta took me into the church, and once more there was a surprise. Its vaulted ceiling, made of narrow strips of wood, was painted a delicate pastel blue, and around all four sides was an exotic garland of flowers and trees in delicate soft colors, not a single flower native to Central Texas. An itinerant artist, long since gone and forgotten, had painted them with considerable charm and skill—in a design drawn from his past or his imagination. There were also large portraits of saints, executed with varying degrees of skill—one by a former pastor; and another painted by a communicant who had been a soldier in World War I and had returned to record his impressions of it on the walls of the church.

Little vignettes that I remember: a line of Head Start youngsters (they were everywhere today), a scrubbed-faced little Boy Scout who pressed something in my hand as I moved on through the surging crowd— I looked down—it was a dollar bill folded dozens of times (he had said, "This is for your beautification project."), and the cemetery itself. Not a name could I read! All were Czech, with many x's and z's, the earliest date—1855.

It was a little past 12:30 when we got to Monument Hill Park. Along the banks of the Colorado River the local people had put up tables covered with red-checkered tablecloths, and a fish fry was going on. The live oaks in this region are hung with long Spanish moss, which imparted an impression of coolness helped along by great mugs of icy beer. The tables were loaded with fried catfish and black-eyed peas, fried chicken and thick slabs of homemade bread, and for dessert a typical specialty of the area—"kolaches," a rich pastry that has a center of dried apricots or prunes. There was a German band going "oom-pah" down on the banks of the Colorado. Jake and Judge Petris introduced me to everybody. I think the Court House must have been deserted that day, because every Commissioner, Judge, and official of any sort was there, and everybody interested in historical restorations. The woods are full of them these days in Texas. We're having a renaissance of interest in our past.

Monument Hill Park was dedicated by Sam Houston himself and was the first Texas State Park. It was so named because the bodies of the men from the Dawson expedition and the fatal Mier expedition were buried here—both those who as prisoners of Mexico had drawn the black beans in the lottery and had been shot and buried in Salado, Mexico, and those who had returned to live out their lives in this area. Their graves are marked by a tall obelisk, similar in design but much smaller than the Washington Monument. On one side have been painted—I don't know the medium—the faces of the pioneers who are memorialized here.

We pressed on to another Court House square. In La Grange, the Victorian Court House, already graced with handsome live oak and pecan trees, has been landscaped with rather impressive plantings, to which I added a pine tree. I chose one of the "lost pines"—of great interest to the botanists—which begin around Bastrop, Texas, and continue south, separated by many miles and also by the variety from any other strands of pine.

Here there was a sizable crowd and numerous officials and another group of Head Start children. There was a brief speech under a treaty oak, and I remember the photographers kept on looking at the thermometer on a building (which reported 98 degrees) and trying to work that into the background. I spent a part of the day urging all the men in sight to take off their coats.

The next stop was in Warrenton. Mrs. Faith Bybee (one of Texas' leading restoration enthusiasts) met me in front of the William Neece home, abandoned, dilapidated, but still with an air of gracious elegance, two stories high, with a veranda running the full length of the second floor. The whole second floor was a ballroom. The ceiling was elaborately painted and stenciled by Mathias Melchior, a German craftsman of the 1860's, with representations of the four seasons, delicate and beautiful. It was interesting to imagine the life lived here by the William Neeces and their neighbors on the frontier—what the ladies wore as they danced under the candle-lit chandelier, what they talked about and what they did for a living.

We drove on a few miles to Winedale. Here Miss Ima Hogg met me complete with hat and gloves—eighty-five years old and very active. "Miss Ima," as she is familiarly called, the daughter of Governor James Hogg, one of Texas' great men, is an outstanding authority on Early American furniture and household arts. Winedale is a restored stagecoach inn—a stopping place for travelers as far back as one hundred thirty years ago. It's a long, two-story building with verandas running the full length and columns—soft beige in color—with brown trim. Miss Ima bought Winedale, supervised the restoration, and presented it to the University of Texas as a center for study of architectural history—particularly that of the German settlers in Texas and their intellectual and social impact on the area.

Here Wayne Bell, the restoration adviser of the University, took over.

But it was Miss Ima whom I followed through the house as she pointed out the exceedingly wide boards of cedar used for the walls. (Cedar trees don't grow that big anymore.) There was Biedermeier furniture—much of it made locally—some brought from Pennsylvania; and bright, elaborate quilts on the beds. One of them she called the "Yankee quilt." It was made during the Civil War and was full of patriotic figures, eagles, Stars and Stripes, and similar insignia.

Here too there was stenciling and painting on the interior walls—evidence of the work of the same Melchior family. The inn is part of what will become a small complex. There is another restored home, air-conditioned, available for students in residence doing research on German architecture and early settlers. This settlement was named Winedale because the Germans had grown grapes and made wine in sizable quantity in their early days here, though the industry has long since disappeared. But they've even started growing grapes once more. The most interesting experience of all to me was observing Miss Ima herself, savoring her knowledge and devotion.

Then at last came one of the main destinations of this Central Texas odyssey—Round Top. In the center of this little community there is a town hall, where—complete with flag and Boy Scouts and bands—we had yet another welcoming ceremony with a few words from the Mayor. We embarked on a walking tour. There was one complex already restored by Mrs. Hazel Ledbetter which included three buildings, one of which was a charming antique shop where I could have lingered. There was the old volunteer fire department, with the ancient equipment out front, and a house in the process of being restored, again Mrs. Bybee's handiwork. In one room the walls were entirely covered with stenciling. Craftsmen Mrs. Bybee has trained were doing the work in the manner of mid-nineteenth-century craftsmen. They go to the woods, cut down trees that fit their specifications, haul them in, and do the work on the site, just as the Melchiors did in 1850. Mrs. Bybee is establishing a scholarship in John Ben Shepperd's name to train young men in this restoration work.

Our last stop was at the community's social hall, where the ladies had set out big bowls of punch and pots of hot coffee and all sorts of delicious German cookies, coffee cakes, and pastries. Everything in Round Top was as German as it had been Czech at Praha. Once again I was famished and had some of everything.

And then we made our last good-bys and John Ben Shepperd, who had helped out as tour guide, because of his knowledge of Texas history, and I got into the car and drove straight to Bergstrom Air Force Base and went by helicopter to the Ranch, arriving a little after 7. What a full and marvelous day it had been! One vignette that remains in my mind is that of the painters up on ladders busily painting away at the store fronts in Lockhart. We waved at every one of them, but most of them didn't even wave back, they were so busy.

Monday, July 31

THE WHITE HOUSE

This month that gives me so many days of my own has slipped away. But in it I have gotten a lot of personal things done and happy things when I have been able to save periods of three or four days, back to back, to be in Texas with Luci or with our house project. Today was an intensely family day. Luci, Pat, and little Lyn arrived on Sunday afternoon from Austin, and Lynda Bird returned from London Thursday.

In the afternoon something I had looked forward to very much took place—my tea for the ladies of the Texas delegation—the group with whom I have met for lunch once a month since 1937—the wives of the members of the House and the Senate, and wives of former members. Because summertime is the time to visit, and I thought there might be daughters and daughters-in-law in town, and even mothers, I had particularly included them in the invitation. And they came! There were four Kazens and three Caseys, and Mrs. Tom Connally, still remarkably impervious to the years, had brought her two daughters. Helen Mahon had Daphne with her, talking about what fun their children had had in the White House swimming pool. Mrs. Ralph Yarborough had brought her very elderly mother. Almost everybody had at least one daughter. And the de la Garzas numbered four. Jake Pickle's young daughter, Peggy—Mrs. Norris—could have been on a poster for "the bright young girl of 1967." And Mollie Thornberry, looking absolutely delicious, said that she had been wanting to "get out of the nest" all her life, and now that she was out—a government girl in Washington—she is realizing how good it would be to get back.

I stood at the door and welcomed everybody. Pretty soon Lynda came in, looking elegant. And Warrie Lynn, bless her heart, moving around sweetly. I introduced her everywhere as "my third daughter."

During a tour of the family quarters, little Lyn made his appearance. That broke up the sightseeing! They all crowded around him in a circle. He blinked unconcernedly and was as good as could be. Now, half a century hence when some future First Lady has a party for descendants of former Presidents, he can come here and say that he received in the Yellow Room in 1967 in the arms of his mother, just as the granddaughter of President Grant said to me! There were pictures on the balcony and then the party was over about 5:30.

I went to my room for desk work and telephone calls. At 8 Abe and Carol arrived and, joined by Oveta Hobby, we went out on the Truman Balcony. Lyndon finally came and the five of us had a good time. Everybody joined vigorously in the conversation. At one time there was a lengthy exploration of the riots in Detroit: Governor Romney's statements and telegrams and later his press conference . . . Lyndon's action—his speech of Thursday night . . . Cyrus Vance's presence . . . the Constitutional ramifications . . . the "1, 2, 3" process of how a Governor gets help from the federal government in a time of riot, and the fourteen or more times during our nation's history when federal assistance has been asked for or sometimes refused. I remembered something a friend had said about this country's whole handling of racial inequality and injustices, and the monumental attempt we have made in the last few years to even things up. I gathered from what he'd said that the very fact that we have tried so hard and done so much in the last few years might be the forerunner— even the cause—of this rioting now. I had tried to probe that aspect. He said, "Yes, it's like steam accumulating in a boiling pot. If you lift the lid, it comes out in a great 'whoosh' that may be destructive before the pressure dissipates. The only other way to handle it is the way they do in South Africa where they don't even lift the lid at all."

One of the things I've enjoyed most, living here in Washington, and here in the White House, is good conversation, interesting assessments. It's one of the fruits of the job. It was nearly 10 when we went in for dinner. I succeeded valorously in limiting myself to meat only and a little green salad and felt very self-righteous.

A subject that had been much on my mind over the weekend was our "coming down off the mountain"—our departure from this place. On Sunday there was a poll that showed a distinct downward trend in the number of people who approved Lyndon's handling of the war in Vietnam. Our own decision, our hope, our determination, is to leave when this term ends. But how to tell it to the world and when—in the fall, as John Connally suggested? Or not until March 1968—my own idea? Nevertheless, it does seem the leaves of autumn are falling rather early, since there are eighteen months left of this term.

Tuesday, August 1

The morning was a full session of work on the LBJ Library with Max Brooks, Gordon Bunshaft, Horace Busby, Arthur Drexler, and Dorothy Territo. We sat in my "Board of Directors Room"—where, beginning with President Andrew Johnson, the Cabinet of the United States had met for about thirty-seven years—using President Grant's Cabinet table on which the Space Treaty had been signed, putting out our cigarettes in Mrs. Rutherford B. Hayes' funny china dishes, and I was sitting in Grover Cleveland's big presiding chair—an interesting midwifery for our Presidential library!

The afternoon was desk work, broken briefly by a swim with Lyndon. It was nearly 8:30 when Lyndon came home, and I was in my dressing gown and all ready for a quiet dinner at home. But he said, "What do you say let's pick up some chili and go out to Bill White's and have dinner?" It is hard to say no to him when he is enthusiastic about something. So I changed into a dress, shouting over my shoulder my objections to taking Luci's baby with us, for we are baby-sitting grandparents this week. They were not heeded, but I did take out the insurance of asking the nurse, Miss Gfeller, to come along in another car behind us. And out we set— Lyndon carrying little Lyn—to go visiting at a quarter to 9 at night!

We walked in with Lyn—the best ice breaker in the world—and Bill and June and their girls, Vicky and Cia, were lined up to greet us. Somebody took the chili out of our hands and went to heat it up. They had already eaten dinner. Somewhere at some comma or period in the story we all kissed Lyn good night and sent him home with Miss Gfeller. Later we went into the dining room and had our chili with crackers while the four Whites sat around. Lyndon said, "I just wanted to come out and see you, because this is one of the few houses in town I can invite myself to at 9 at night and bring my own supper." And we all laughed.

It was 11 when we got back to the White House, and Lyndon wanted me to go into his office with him to take that last look at the news ticker. He is never separated from the events of the day. The news rolls out at him in great white sheets, and he absorbs it all—while I happily know only what intrudes upon me with irresistible demands.

Luci and Pat are staying at Mary Lasker's house, going out to dinner and the theater in New York. They will go on to the Bahamas sometime this week, just when I really don't want to know. I understand Luci's reasoning for not wanting to give out this information. In the climate of today, with bitterness and riots, as carefree a little soul as she is, she does not want to advertise the time when both she and Pat will be on a plane.

Thursday, August 3

NEW YORK

I spent the day in New York in interminable shopping and was grateful to be headed back to Washington. We were in good time and boarded the shuttle. The day had been stormy by fits and starts, with thunder and lightning that reverberated through the canyons of New York, and then just a gray and overcast sky, but finally the sun had begun to come out. I was relaxing a bit, though not too comfortable yet about flying. We had considered up until the last thirty minutes going on the train. At any rate, in good spirits, we got on the shuttle, taxied out to the end of the runway, delayed, delayed, and presently the pilot came on saying that because of bad weather between New York and Washington there would be a few minutes' delay while they decided how to go around it. Not exactly reassuring! Suddenly a couple of police cars and the black car I had ridden in rolled up at the foot of the plane, the steps went down, and my agent said, "All right, let's go!"

With a mounting question I descended the steps, got in the car and then asked my agent, Woody Taylor, "What's up?" He said, "That's what we're going inside to find out." The questions in my mind on the way in were the only aspect of the whole experience that approached being frightening. Of course, the questions were: "Has something happened to a member of my family?"—"to Luci?" "or the baby?" "or Lynda?" "or Lyndon?" You don't ask and you strive to appear quiet. In times of strain the only decent thing you can do is not to add to it.

The agent who had met us at the foot of the steps then said there had been an anonymous telephone call to Eastern Airlines that there was a bomb on the 5 o'clock shuttle that I would be riding on. And, of course, the agents couldn't take the chance. We drove up to an entrance and went quickly into a small VIP lounge where they shut the door. They told me the rest of the people on the plane were getting off too. The agents came and went. There was talk about which plane to take now. I felt curiously impartial about the whole thing. It's too incredible to imagine that a bomb was ever meant for me . . . We were airborne a little past 6. But it was a bad flight and a slow one. One gets mighty used to jets.

It was 7:30 P.M. when we reached Washington—a two-and-a-half-hour trip all told. I worked at my desk. It was 11 before Lyndon came for dinner, and then straight to his night reading, which went on until 2.

Thursday, August 10

THE WHITE HOUSE AND LBJ RANCH

Today began in the strangest way. Sometime in the very early morning hours I came awake as I do at the slightest sound or movement, and I thought I could hear a creaking of the boards or of the walls in this old house. I thought of all the White House ghost stories—completely undisturbed by them, however. And then I just knew there was somebody in the room—somebody coming toward the bed. With no sense of fright, I reached out my hand over the side of the bed and a hand closed upon it. I said, "Who is this?" Lynda's voice answered: "Mama, I want to talk to you."

She sat down on the side of the bed, and I whispered, "Let's go to your room." But it was too late. Lyndon was awake. Sleepily he rose on his elbow, reached for the light and said, "What's going on?"

I felt I knew what it was. Some lift of excitement in Lynda's voice, some feeling that she was trying to talk to me, but was not quite ready when I had watched her get dressed to go out for the date the evening before, had made me think it was about Chuck Robb—that she was getting more interested in him—just how interested I wasn't sure. She said, "Mother, Daddy, I am in love. I want to get married."

Lyndon was at once wide-awake. "Tell us about it," he said. So she told us about him. He is a Marine with six years of service. We've seen him in and out of the house for several months now. He's a Military Aide. In fact he looks as if he ought to be on a poster for the Marines. He has a degree from the University of Wisconsin—Business Administration, she said. She told us how many brothers and sisters he has and what his father does—he works for American Airlines. And about how much fun they have together. They like doing the same things. And this from Lynda, whose interests have been turning more and more these last two years to people on the stage and screen, café society people, people who are very rich or very talented or very social. Chuck Robb, on the other hand, looks like the "All-American boy," wholesome, handsome, masculine. Actually, I know very little about him, except that he plays a good game of bridge. There will be so much to talk about—a wedding date, the lists—very important, Vietnam, for Chuck has requested duty there and that time lies not very far away.

Lynda couldn't wait until morning. That's typical of her. After a while she went back to her own bed, wrapped in her aura of excitement, and Lyndon, thank God, went back to sleep. I lay stiff as a board, reaching for the beneficence of sleep and not finding it. Finally the telephone rang at 7:15 to waken me. Lyndon and I talked a little more about Lynda and Chuck while we had breakfast. Then, before 9, I had kissed Lyndon and Lynda good-by, waved to a group of early-morning tourists in the Diplomatic Reception Room, and was on my way to Dulles Airport where I took a plane for Texas.

I must work with Roy White on the new addition at the Ranch—our "rest-of-our-lives rooms." I had told Roy my recipe for my own bedroom was plenty of bookshelves, a fireplace, and a beautiful view. Decisions, decisions, decisions—mantel design, wallpapers, hardware, light fixtures. But hard as it is at long distance, it's better than living with the mess of doing it in 1969. I will move my own furniture from my White House bedroom down and search in the warehouse for some elegant old pieces to use in my White House bedroom. Maybe I can find a canopied bed there.

This weekend, I am going to get an interesting look at the problems I'll face when our tenure of the Presidency ends and we are back at the Ranch with minimum help. Everyone is off this week. If I want something done I lug that chair or ottoman or suitcase myself. I want to get used to it.

Sometime during the evening Lyndon called, and I could sense the loneliness in his voice and the desire just to talk to me. I try to keep that loneliness at bay and I felt torn between doing what I was doing, which must be done, and being with him. The "Mary" and the "Martha" in my life have an eternal war.

We spent the day on the *Sequoia*, one of the quietest Sundays I can remember. A cool front had blown in and there was a promise of fall in the air. It was a beautiful day—a bit overcast at first and then the sun came out sparkling and it was a joy just to be alive. This emotion played out against that steady counterpoint, that underbeat, of all the troubles in the world—riots and escalation and inflation and taxes—that keep closing in. You sense it, you feel it these last few weeks, more, I think, than ever. But in the circle of our own family and close friends, it has been a wonderful summer. Luci and Pat and little Lyn have been with us a lot—and Lynda Bird coming and going with her friends.

Today was a good day for talking. Lyndon discussed columnists who spoke of how decisions were arrived at in the Presidential office, and how some of them complained that decisions weren't made more quickly. He said, "The important thing is not to get problems off your desk—it's to make a decision that my grandchild and yours can live with." He spoke about how occasionally he has asked some of the most experienced people he knows (he mentioned a few names, George Ball is one I remember) to come in and be the "devil's advocate," to take the other side of a question, to give him a picture of all the bad things that could flow from a certain course of action.

At 12:30 we watched Clark Clifford and General Maxwell Taylor on television, and that was thirty minutes of sheer admiration. I was so proud of them. They looked so trustworthy and strong. They are both superior men. There was one period of several moments when General Taylor gave a résumé of the economy, the politics, and the military situation in Vietnam since 1954—swift, flowing, effective. Clark's answer to questions on the coming elections in Vietnam and the President's feelings about them as transmitted to Ky and Thieu was great. The most interesting thing of all was at the end when the three commentators just fell silent—out of steam, for once undone.

Luci and Pat were arriving from Nassau at 4:30, and I was anxious to see them. When we docked a little past 5 there Luci was, but I practically had to hold on to the sides of the boat. She had on bright green stockings, a very short dress—shocking pink with a floral design—huge earrings dangling. She and Pat explained that this is what you wear in the Bahamas.

Joe Batson was with them—quiet but beaming. He's become a sort of brother to all my children. First, Lynda. And then, Luci and Pat. And now, very much little Lyn.

We went straight to church—St. Dominick's—which Lyndon calls "Luci's Little Monks' Church." One of the priests leaned over and said to Luci, "Have you taught those nuns how to water ski yet?" The nuns who have a place right next to Capricorn, Rebekah Harkness' house, had become Luci's and Pat's friends on their honeymoon. They had taken the nuns boat riding and swimming.

St. Dominick's was a very simple Catholic church with many parishioners, black and white, of obviously modest means. Little notice was taken of us. There were smiles as we walked out. We were back on the White House grounds by 6, to be met by a tumbling army of dogs who flew upon Luci, jumping all over her. She was hugging and kissing them, and Lyndon was saying in his grave, earnest manner, "We've decided to keep Yuki and Lyn." Luci, silent for a half-second, came back with the perfect reply, "Oh, Daddy, I am so glad they have been able to give you a little happiness!" She used to respond with firecracker anger to his teasing when she was a little girl.

Lyndon went back to the office to read the ticker and to do a little work. Back upstairs with Luci and Pat and Joe, I was awash in a fountain of talk—all in exclamation points—and mostly from Luci, about Capricorn, and water skiing and scuba diving and what you see forty feet under the water, the fish and the coral.

Later we went down to the pool, where Lyndon met us, and I did thirty laps and Luci and Marie watched from the bank while Lyndon talked to Joe about ranching in Amarillo and to Pat about his work at KTBC . . . Then upstairs for as close to a family dinner as we ever get— Pat and Luci—Lynda Bird is at the beach with Chuck and won't be back until tomorrow—and Joe Batson, Marie Fehmer, and Jim Jones, who are very close indeed.

It's strange. You feel soothed and happy by the companionship of your daughter and your son-in-law, and the fine young people who are their friends and the members of your staff. And the cool, brisk, shiny beauty of the day. But simultaneously, you are way down and grieved, emotionally wearied by the troubles that you must try to solve—the growing virus of the riots, the rising list of Vietnam casualties, criticism from your own friends, or former friends, in Congress—and most of the complaining is coming from the Democrats.

There seems to be a sort of miasma spreading across the country, and you think that nobody outside can ever beat us—we, the American people— and we can solve all our problems here at home too. But maybe there are enough right in our midst—whiners, self-doubters, gloom spreaders, who *can* beat us. I think the most frustrated I've been lately is reading a speech that Senator Fulbright made in which he indicated that the country is damned because we are spending so much in Vietnam instead of spending it here to take care of the poor and underprivileged—this from a man who has never voted for any Civil Rights measure and who even voted against Medicare in 1964. It will be sheer luxury someday to *talk* instead of to *act*.

Today's poll has Lyndon down to thirty-nine percent—the lowest he has ever been. My instinct tells me the only reaction to it should be to work harder, be staunch, and keep smiling. But it is hard.

Wednesday, August 16

THE WHITE HOUSE

This was another one of those early mornings. How weary and depleted only six hours' sleep leaves me for the day. Lyndon and I watched Senator John Tower for the Republicans and Senator Joe Clark for the Democrats on television—the *Today* show—talking about Vietnam. What a twist of fate it is to see the Administration—indeed us—being explained, backed —yes, even defended—by John Tower, while that red-hot Democrat Joe Clark slashes at the Administration's policy with rancor and emotion. The wheel does turn.

We brought Lyn in. This will be the last time for quite a while. He lay on the bed and kicked and gurgled. As Lyndon read his innumerable papers and talked on the phone and read those reports, Lyn boxed the air with his little fists and eyed both of us curiously. Lynda came down and sat beside us. She is so good with little Lyn, and she loves him dearly.

I had a 10 o'clock date with Mayor Harry Akin of Austin. We drove around Washington—to our first little park at Third and Independence and Syphax School where, praise the Lord, they have taken out the dead trees. There were three or four teen-agers weeding the plots. And down the double avenue of magnolia soulangiana on Pennsylvania, S.E.—and Rawlins Park and Walt Whitman Park—while I gave Harry an explanation of what our Committee has tried to do in the two years and eight months of its life. And what I hope for the city of Austin in the years ahead.

When I got back I went into Luci's room and there was all the confusion of packing—open suitcases, Luci rushing around madly asking the maids if they had seen this dress or those shoes. The staff here all love Luci. They call her "Baby"—and it has no relation to the present slang use of the word "Baby."

The nicest time of all, in Luci and Pat and Lyn's visit, was Sunday night when we were all sitting around the dinner table and Luci made some careless, very positive assertion about the passage of a sales tax in Austin which she favored and thought anybody who didn't favor was pretty dumb. Her daddy calmly said, "Now honey, you must remember this. You and I and Gene Williams and Helen can only wear so much and eat so much. And in a sales tax everything you wear or eat is taxed. Now which one of us do you think is more capable of paying taxes? You and I or Gene and Helen? A sales tax really helps the rich people at the expense of the poor people." I wish I could remember that and explain it as exactly, as cogently, as simply as he did.

Then we simply sat and listened, with the children interjecting every now and then, and Lyndon talked about his college years, when there were three terms and in each one the tuition would cost seventeen dollars and every time a new term approached he thought surely he would have to drop out because he couldn't raise the seventeen dollars. Once Ben Crider had loaned him eighty dollars—all that he had in the bank—and that meant the difference between Lyndon staying another term or dropping out. Another time Lyndon had heard about a scholarship the Masons offered for two hundred dollars. He had written and applied for it, although his father was not a Mason, and they had granted it to him. He never knew quite why. He had left school before he graduated to teach a term to make the money to pay it back.

There was another time when he didn't see how he could possibly pay the tuition and Aunt Lucy had come to him with $3.60 and said, "I've been saving my egg money and I want you to have it." And Dr. Evans, whose pay as President of the school was a mere pittance, had told him he just *had* to stay in and he would personally find the money somewhere. Our children listened enthralled. Every now and then they asked questions and Joe Batson, who knows little, I am sure, of poverty or need, was soaking it up. Luci said, "Daddy, we needed to hear something like this." And indeed she does, because she lives in a soft cocoon in Austin with children of well-to-do people, on a lovely street where ease and security prevail. And, of course, as her mother, I am glad, but I recognize that it is also dangerous in its own way.

Luci and Pat were leaving at 2:30, and Lynda and Chuck went to the Queen's Room a little before to tell them their plans . . . I was proud of the foursome as I stood looking through the door watching them. Warrie and Lynda and I went down to the South grounds to see them off with much kissing and last farewells.

Then back upstairs in the Queen's Sitting Room, Lynda and Chuck and I discussed their plans. His present period of duty at the Marine Barracks in Washington will end around the first of the year and he has asked to go to Vietnam. So he will probably leave in February or March. There is usually a short lapse of time allowed for a man to get his affairs in shape, called "Procedural Leave" I believe. So their big decisions are when should the wedding date be? And when should they announce it? They are considering December 9 for the wedding date. That is a Saturday and nicely spaced between Thanksgiving and Christmas, which would give them, hopefully, a little more than two months for a honeymoon and some life together in a rented apartment in Washington.

And there's always the big problem, the list of guests—where to start, where to stop. And who should be the minister? This much Lynda Bird knows: She wants to be married in the White House in a military wedding with all the beauty and grace that a wedding can have. We got as far on bridesmaids as Luci and Warrie and Carolyn Curtis. Chuck has decided to have Doug Davidson as his best man. One of the big problems will be to announce the engagement before it gets announced in somebody's column.

Two thoughts threaded through my mind—one amusing, one sweetly sad. At the elevator when I had run into George Christian and Tom Johnson, Tom had said, "Oh, we sure are going to miss that boy—that little Lyn. He was a good story every day with all the riots and the war— he was a big help. About the only thing we can do now is to get Lynda Bird married off." I had smiled innocently. The sweetly sad thought came to me when I went into Lynda's room. I noticed something different and for several moments I couldn't decide what it was. And then I knew— gone, gone were all the pictures of George Hamilton—the romantic-devilish one on the chest of drawers, the patrician-handsome one, and lots of other little mementos—a faded telegram pasted on the mirror. She hadn't said a word about it. They had simply been removed.

Her father had promised to talk to them about their plans. He was having a business lunch and finished about 3:30. He came in the Queen's Sitting Room, looking ghost-tired, and sat down heavily. Chuck told him in very quick, straightforward fashion what their aims and hopes were—the old-fashioned expression is what "his intentions" were, I believe—and not a bad word. When Chuck used the phrase "your permission," Lyndon quickly said, "You have it, and my love." . . . But it wasn't the long, getting-to-know-you talk that I hope he and Chuck can have sometime soon.

Early in the day I had been to a ceremony in the East Room—a Vietnam Civilian Service Awards Ceremony—that was very moving. Former Ambassador Lodge was with us on the stage. A small group of civilians, workers in AID and members of a church group, received citations for their bravery and their dedication and their long hours in constructive work in Saigon hospitals and schools—a gigantic effort quite apart from the war. Were there ever such people as Americans?

Tuesday, August 22

Today began sluggishly, for me that is, but turned into a crescendo day at the White House. Lyndon was awake by 7, and I sleepwalked back into my own room and fitfully and unsuccessfully courted sleep. I gave up a little past 9, and then bathed and dressed rapidly, because I got the word that Walter Washington was still in Lyndon's office and it would be a good idea if I came over. I walked in to find Walter with a big smile, just saying good-by to Lyndon, and I had the feeling that things had gone well and that maybe it would work out for him to be our next Mayor. I hope so. We had a brief, warm exchange—for me, full of the work we've done together on our Committee.

I spent the rest of the morning working with Bess and with Ashton. Then I read about Iran, off and on casting a prayer skyward for good weather because we'd hoped to have the ballet outside for the Shah's dinner tonight. The changing weather predictions for the last two days have kept us on knife's edge.

It was almost on the dot of 5 when we went out on the South Lawn for the arrival of the Shah. The sky was gray and lowering, but the scene was bright as always, with flags and the stiff lines of military men, the trumpets circling the balcony above, and the eager expectant people lining the driveway as we walked past. A little ripple of applause crested with us as we walked along the driveway. There was Secretary Rusk, calm and smiling as always. I never cease to marvel at the personal peace he has attained in the midst of the turmoil of his job. Dean remarked that Lyndon had received sixty-six foreign Chiefs of State in the last twelve months, and though a good many of these had been at Guam and Manila, or just working visits, a great many indeed had been State guests. The color, the trumpets, the ritual, never fail to thrill me anew.

Then the Shah drove up. He is a romantic figure with a look of rapport in his face. He looks at each person as though he were really seeing him, listening to him with interest. It's a great compliment. I hope I can learn from it. Lyndon, in his speech of welcome, spoke of our several meetings with the Shah and of Iran's economy which has been growing at about 10 percent a year and its gains against illiteracy: "You are winning progress without violence and without any bloodshed—a lesson that others have still to learn." Then the Shah, speaking without notes, in perfect English but rather hesitantly, made a brief, earnest talk, disarming in its simplicity and its complete difference from the trite lines that are often read in a monotone voice at an arrival ceremony.

After the brief receiving line in the Diplomatic Reception Room, Lyndon took him over to the office to talk and I went back upstairs.

For the State Dinner I put on my ivory Stavropoulos dress. How much we miss the Empress! When a visiting Chief of State has a wife as beautiful as she is, there is that hushed moment of excitement after he's appeared when you wait for her to emerge from the big black car, eager to see how she is dressed, how she has her hair done, what jewels she is wearing. The Empress is an ornament and a great asset, I think, to her husband and to her country.

We had the exchange of gifts, and once more I have to remark in my mind that it is an art to receive gifts, to express appreciation—an art well worth cultivating because it gives so much pleasure to the giver. The Shah made us feel very pleased, although our own gifts were scarcely remarkable. And as for theirs—their gifts were indeed breathtaking: a bronze figure of a horse about fifteen inches high—a museum treasure. It was over two thousand years old. My mind hurtled forward to the time when someday we will put together an exhibit of artifacts—my very own and State gifts—in the Lyndon Johnson Library. And there were two handsome Persian rugs.

Lynda came in looking breathtaking—her hair piled high and curls falling over her shoulder, wearing a blue-and-silver dress with a peacock feather motif, a symbol of the throne of Iran. She had bought it especially for the dinner for the Shah when she had first heard he was coming.

Among the guests were my beautification benefactors, the Ralph Beckers—he is also President of the Iran-American Society. Two of the loveliest ladies there were Mrs. Lloyd Bentsen of Texas and Mrs. Francis Lawrence, Iranian born, absolutely stunning, who swooped in a deep curtsy when she met the Shah. And there were the Julius Holmeses, the Ambassador who was in Iran when we were there, and a perfect prototype of an Ambassador. Lynda had Philip Johnson, the architect, at her table and thought him one of the most interesting men at the party.

I had put young Mrs. Roy Hofheinz, Jr., at my table. Roy I had found to be almost a replica of his father—the dynamic young Roy Hofheinz who had managed Lyndon's campaign for the Senate in 1941 in Houston. His father had proudly told me that Roy, Jr., spoke eleven languages, had gotten his Ph.D. when he was nineteen, and was now teaching at Harvard. I asked his wife about him, and she said rather deprecatingly that it was really just seven languages. And what did he teach? It was Chinese politics! What a great American story. I remember meeting his grandmother in that campaign in 1941—a woman of very simple and modest origins—her German accent so thick that I could hardly understand her English.

The dinner began with striped bass "Isfahan"—named after one of the Shah's cities—and ended with a really glorious dessert—"August Basket"— the first dessert that Ferdinand has concocted since he got back from the hospital. Lyndon's toast was eloquent and had a touch of humor. He spoke of how much the company missed the Empress. "This Administration champions beauty in all its forms." And about the Shah's approaching coronation, which will take place in October after he has reigned for twenty-six years. Lyndon said, "I must add special congratulations on Your Majesty's superb sense of timing. You have had the foresight to schedule your coronation when your polls are up."

Once more the Shah made his response without notes—slowly, rather hesitantly, but with a very winning quality. He spoke of why the Empress has remained at home. "She has a lot to do, because, for the first time, I think, a woman will be crowned in our country. Lately women have attained many rights—first, franchise, then equality with men, and now even equality in wearing a crown." His voice faded off in a very amusing manner. I have the feeling he's becoming more used to power, more at home with humor. And there is a wonderful quality of humility in him.

Lyndon has worked so hard these last days and weeks, and he was weary and was ready to get the entertainment on the road. The American Ballet Theater directed by Lucia Chase staged a ballet called "Rodeo," introduced by its own choreographer, Agnes de Mille, with her remarkable sparkle and wit. There were the cowgirls and square dancers, the ranch owner's daughter and her Eastern friends in their old-fashioned costumes, the wrangler and the roper and the cowboys in their blue jeans and big hats and the kind of boots you can dance ballet in. It was so light and lively—so much fun—delightfully incongruous under the East Room chandeliers.

We took the Shah up on the stage with us after it was over and met and thanked all the young people. And there were lots of pictures to be treasured later. Then we walked with him to the North Portico for a rather early good-by.

It wasn't 12 yet. Lyndon went straight upstairs. I stayed, talking to Agnes de Mille especially, and to Armand Hammer who told me the marvelous news that he wanted to give the White House a Charles Russell bronze. He knew we had a Remington. I struggled with myself one moment and then said, "You are testing my loyalty." And he said, "What do you mean?" And I said, "You know, there will be a Lyndon Johnson Library within two or three years, and the artists of the Southwest are among my husband's favorites. But it will be marvelous for the White House to have it." But I got no further. He said, "I'll give one to the Lyndon Johnson Library, too." What a great addition those would be! I am always pleased to see him because I remember his generosity and forethought, his lasting love of a man in buying and preserving FDR's old summer home, Campobello, and then giving it to the National Park Service.

I saw David Lilienthal in the hall and said, "Come with me." I wanted to talk to him about his time in Iran. I started into the Red Room and, lo and behold, when I looked over my shoulder he was not there. I felt exactly like the little cowgirl in the ballet who couldn't get a man for the first two acts. It was really funny. Later in the evening, I got a second chance. I met him face to face and straightaway said, "I had wanted to talk to you. What happened to you?" He said something quite graceful about "I really couldn't believe I had heard you right." We went in the Green Room and had the kind of conversation that makes an evening memorable. Yes, he was full of hope about the work that he had done in Iran and about their future and about their ability to handle it. We talked of Korea's progress. Then I said, "What are you doing now?" He looked at me rather wryly and said something like this: "A very persuasive man has put me to work on Vietnam." Then I remembered Lyndon enlisting his expertise on plans for the agriculture, for the economy of Vietnam. He sounded full of hope based on knowledge and experience and he sounded as if he liked my husband.

It was one when I went to bed, and I chalked it up as a good day— a successful State visit with one of the most fascinating and likable monarchs I'll ever meet, and "A-plus" entertainment.

Saturday, August 26

LBJ RANCH AND WASHINGTON

It was a day of such breadth as I will only know during these White House years. The dedication of the beautiful Butt-Holdsworth Library in Kerrville (happy event for the Hill Country!), a session with architect, decorators, and painters at the Ranch, and an arrival at Mt. Vernon at the witching hour of 4:30 A.M.!

It was nearly one when I left Kerrville and was back at the Ranch by 1:30 for a quick lunch, and then worked with Roy White and Herbert Wells, the decorator, on the infinite details of building and furnishing these two rooms.

Sometime before 7 we were simply too tired to make any more sensible decisions. So I called Jessie Hunter and we drove and talked until night fell. It was 10 in the evening when I left for Washington, changed planes in Dallas and tried to doze as we flew, landing at Friendship at the ridiculous hour of 3:20 in the morning. It's Lyndon's birthday. And of course I wouldn't miss it!

There followed the most ghostly, unreal arrival that I can remember. I drove to Mt. Vernon in the big black car, a waning half-moon riding the shifting clouds. We pulled up at the guard gate, and one lonely guard came out, looked at us carefully, and then unlocked the gate and we drove through. We drove right up past George Washington's house and down the hill, winding close to his grave and on to the boat landing. Everything was so quiet, hushed, unreal. I thought of all the hundreds of times I had been to Mt. Vernon with constituents, making my way among the thousands of people . . . and I thought of the early, fresh, dewy mornings when I have been out on the lawn in front doing that television show on beautification. What a strange montage!

Far out on the river I could see two blinking lights—the *Sequoia*—anchored. We went out and I climbed on and carefully went downstairs, hoping I wouldn't wake up Lyndon—fruitless hope. Later he described my arrival as "preceded by two Filipinos carrying suitcases and followed by another two." And with a few muffled words of greeting, I sank wearily into bed. It was 4:30 A.M., and it was the morning of Lyndon's fifty-ninth birthday.

Fall 1967

The second of our four days at the Ranch . . . I was up and back at work at 8:30 with Herbert Wells. I spent the morning decorating in the new addition here at the Ranch, putting albums and books into the new bookcases. The first object I put on the shelf was Madame Shoumatoff's painting of FDR—my favorite of Lyndon's birthday presents of 1967. There are so many hundreds of details in working on a house! I relish each success, revel in the pleasure of lovely colors put together and find more abrasive all the things that are wrong.

A little before noon today, John Connally came up by plane for a visit with Lyndon. I knew this conference would be an important one. They were riding around together, and I told Mary to change from soufflé to shrimp curry for lunch. Lunch would have to be one of those meals that is served when the people want it and not when the food is ready.

We were a big lunch table full—the five Nugents, Mr.

565

Wells, Roy White, Lynda and Chuck, Lyndon and John and the staff and I. Lyndon took a look at little Lyn, placid and roly-poly in his mother's arms, and said, "He looks like Alvin Sultemier!" naming the most portly man in our acquaintance. That is the last straw! That baby is going to have to go on Metrecal.

After lunch Lyndon and John continued their talk, with Jake Pickle joining them. They rode and rode, and I wished I could be with them. I was struggling toward making decoration decisions for my bedroom. It was nearly 7 when I put myself into the hands of Mrs. Frederick Burg for a shampoo and set in my bathroom. This was the wrong thing to do! I soon got a message from Lyndon on the business telephone that he had "been waiting for me all afternoon" and when could I join them? Sometimes I have to make a guess on timing and sometimes I guess wrong. So I got out from under the dryer—not a moment for a comb-out—and put on my yellow robe, the fabric a gift from Madame Chiang Kai-shek; and with my hair all in little sausages I went down to join the President, the Governor, and the Congressman for what turned out to be a most serious and lengthy conversation of great import.

Lyndon and John, later joined by Jake Pickle, had had an eight-hour session, riding and talking about Lyndon's big decision—when and how to announce that he is not going to run again for the Presidency. Jake's attitude, I think, was simply not to believe it—not to face up to it. He spoke of the other folks who were running on the Democratic ticket, including himself. It would be hard on them, he said. I found that rather flattering. John did believe it. We had convinced him earlier in the summer. Lyndon asked John to explain to me how he would write the announcement. It went something like this: First, you must do it early to take it out of politics, to keep it from looking as if you were running out, to make it fairer, to give more chance to the other possible Democratic contenders. He spoke of the Democratic Dinner, October 7, or soon thereafter. And the reasons—just what they were—because he, the President, wanted to devote all his time, his brains, his energy, in the coming fifteen or sixteen months to bringing the war in Vietnam to a successful conclusion, to attacking the problems of the cities—in short, to working on the major difficulties that face this country. A campaign would necessarily siphon off hours and days of time and energy and brain power. He wanted to be free to do his best in the time he had. It was good reasoning. It was appealing.

I took the floor and talked about my feelings—that I simply did not want to face another campaign, to ask anybody for anything. Mainly the fear that haunts me is that if Lyndon were back in office for a four-year stretch—beginning when he was sixty years old—bad health might overtake him, an attack, though something not completely incapacitating, and he might find himself straining to be the sort of a President he wanted to be —to put in the eighteen hours a day—and unable to draw enough vitality from the once bottomless well of his energy. A physical or mental incapacitation would be unbearably painful for him to recognize, and for me to watch. And who—who—can tell? His Aunt Frank lived to be ninety, and Aunt Jessie is still going strong in her late eighties—and his father and his Uncle George died at sixty. He has had the most roaring energy and will of anybody I have ever observed. But these are not inexhaustible. I said, "If we ever get sick, I want to be sick on our own time." That broke the tension and everybody laughed. Somewhere in the course of it, I ordered in dinner on trays, and there I sat in my sausage curlers, eating and trying to help my husband and two good friends decide his future. I think we all knew that we would only really know what was going to happen when we heard it happen.

Thursday, September 12

THE WHITE HOUSE

This afternoon I went to the South grounds for the most unusual party that has ever been held here in my time or in all the times I've read about— a "Country Fair"! The guests were the children of Congressmen and Cabinet members and government officials between the ages of six and eighteen. There was a ferris wheel and a merry-go-round and a pony ring around the fountain and stands dispensing hot dogs, Coca Cola, taffy apples, popcorn, and cotton candy. The view from the top of the ferris wheel of the White House grounds, dotted with red striped tents and about five hundred children, milling, running, laughing, was one I will never forget.

In part, this had begun in my mind because I remembered what Lynda and Luci used to say when they were little. We would start out for dinner and they didn't want us to go. "Why are you always going out, Mama?" And then once Lynda said, forlornly, "Mama, Washington is sure meant for the Congressmen and their wives, but it is not meant for their children."

I remember saying once myself, when we first came to Washington, that a politician ought to be born a foundling and remain a bachelor. I wanted to have one great party meant for the children.

Lynda Bird was there dressed in a marvelous costume—camel-colored culottes with a Western cowboy hat. I wore a navy blue dress with a red-and-white scarf, and all of the many hostesses were in red, white, and blue. The men helpers wore red striped barker vests and straw hats. Everybody had been roped in on a job. Les Carpenter was in charge of the "test-your-strength" contraption. Tyler Abell, handsome and laughing, was running the ferris wheel. Jane Freeman was a fortune teller and so was Scooter Miller—dressed up in about thirty strands of beads, a sequin blouse, her pepper-and-salt hair augmented by a gray wig. Most fun to me were the antique cars. There were about ten of them lined up on the White House drive with their owners, who were the chauffeurs. There was a 1909 Mitchell and a 1915 Ford. The youngest of the lot was a 1932 Ford with a rumble seat. I am sure I must have dated in its contemporary at the University of Texas thirty-five years ago, and thought it very snazzy. I sent to the Archives for my old-fashioned pink picture hat from Woodstock, Vermont, and took a spin around the South grounds at least three times. The brass on the cars was gleaming, but not as bright as the owners' smiles. Hubert came out. He said he had an identical car at home in Waverly, and offered to give me a ride. The owner trustingly assented and off we put—chug, chug, chug.

Lyndon came out with Yuki and immediately became a sort of a Pied Piper, with the children following behind him, wanting autographs and taking pictures. And to my dismay, he picked up Yuki and they put on "*their* act," in which Yuki talks to him. (I could have done without that!) Yuki ended with kissing his cheek. I think everybody was having a good time, unless it was poor Chuck Robb, whom the newspaperwomen were besieging so persistently that Liz got him to be my "escort." He was everywhere at my elbow.

I was wild about the sack races! A lot of determined children, mostly between six and fourteen, climbed into sacks which they clutched around their waists, and at the signal, set off in a race for the finish line about a half a block down the White House lawn. There were many tumbles on the grassy slopes, and prizes for the winners. One persistent little girl with blonde curls and a red-and-white checked dress entered every race, time after time, no matter what age the children, and won a lot of them. All in all, it was a hilarious afternoon. I gave up completely on diet discipline and had something of everything—popcorn, and at great peril to my teeth a taffy apple. At last I went whole hog with a hot dog.

Well, it was the most fun. I was surprised when I asked the time and found it was 5:30. I didn't think I had been there more than thirty minutes, and I didn't want to go in even then.

Tonight we had the third of a series of small upstairs parties, gathering on the Truman Balcony or the Yellow Room and having dinner at round tables in the family dining room. The guest list usually included one or two members of the Cabinet, the Senate, and the House, along with some friends from the business world or the arts. Tonight there were Senator and Mrs. John McClellan—Norma is always lovely and so very feminine—and Betty Talmadge and Herman (I dare say one of the first times this year he has stayed up past 8). And the third Senatorial couple, from quite another part of our country, the Gale McGees—I find both of them charming and highly intelligent—and businessman Cyril Magnin and the Leonard McCollums.

At dinner, I had George Smathers on my right and Frank Church on my left. I liked Frank's description of his wife Bethine, and I think it is right. He said she can walk right through a picnic or a Country Fair and come out the other side and "she'll have more friends than I could have made if I had stayed there two hours."

The population explosion and birth control occupied much of the conversation for the evening. I repeated what I've often thought, that if I was destined to spend my life in politics I was glad I wasn't born in India where the problems one faces would be so nearly insoluble. It would be total frustration. What of the problems of the next generation, or somewhere down the line, of American politicians, or politicians anywhere? Suppose we learn how to control the weather? And think a minute of the economic, legal, and spiritual fallout of all the population-control measures. How is somebody going to cope with them fifty or one hundred years down the road? . . . So I guess we ought to live in perspective with today's problems.

With George, the talk was warm and easy—about our mutual friend BeBe Rebozo and our younger days. And my own keenly expressed regret that George—or so it's rumored—is getting out of politics when he finishes this term. He wisely did not affirm or deny. But his tone implied that he is. You know, if you are ever going to make a change there comes a time when you have to do it or else you're hooked for the rest of your life.

Last night was one of those bleak nights when the shadows take over. We both woke up about 3:30 A.M. and talked and talked and talked about when and how to make the statement that Lyndon is not going to be a candidate again. We discussed October 7, the date for the big Democratic Dinner. Perhaps we have already passed up two possibilities—Lyndon's birthday and the election in Vietnam—certainly a successful highpoint after Labor Day. I do not feel the announcement can be made on October 7 because the people who attend this dinner are the ones who love us enough, who believe in us enough, to have paid a thousand dollars to hear a speech composed of tough assurance and good cheer with some humor. In these discussions I feel that Lyndon reaches out to me more than ever, and yet I do not have the wisdom or the foresight for the answer. The only gift I have to give is the assurance that I will be content and happy saying good-by to all this, much as I have loved it—deeply immersed as I have been in it every day—even the painful days.

My first appointment of the day was with the Tiffany people and Bess down in the State Dining Room. Some time ago we'd decided we must choose a china design for the Johnson Administration and we'd been working on it since January. I very much want to have the wildflowers of our country as decoration. Tiffany is doing the design and Castleton will make it. The rooms are free of tourists on Monday mornings. A table was set up, complete with gold flatware and the Truman china and a beautiful flower arrangement—all ready for a State Dinner. Bess was presiding calmly and there they were—the Tiffany people, with the sketches of wildflowers. The designs are much better—freer, looser than the first drawings. We are almost "there," in design at least. The service plates are elegant. They have changed the eagle, now patterned after the Monroe eagle. I loved nearly everything—especially the big bowls for fruit or just used as decorations. I suggested very few changes. We congratulated each other all around with that glowing feeling of accomplishment and I went back upstairs for some desk work before I dressed for the luncheon.

Lyndon was entertaining Sir Robert Menzies and Dame Patty and Ambassador and Mrs. Keith Waller of Australia for lunch. Sir Robert, for twenty years Prime Minister of Australia, is a legendary character to me. Lyndon has talked so much about him, and I found him as delightful as his billing. Lyndon thinks he is just a notch below Winston Churchill in wisdom and eloquence. He was portly and enormously dignified, but quite humorous and very easygoing, too. Lyndon was obviously having a good time. They reminisced a bit, but mostly Sir Robert talked about how much he approved of what Lyndon was doing internationally, and how difficult he knew it was. And then he said what everybody is saying in chorus these days, "You've got to keep telling the people—go on TV." Only he said it better, with a delightful story. In a campaign in Australia, someone accused a candidate of making the same speech seventy times. The candidate answered, "Yes, that's true. But I made it to seventy different audiences." So, said Sir Robert, must Lyndon—over and over and over. We keep on hoping for a suggestion that somebody *else* can do.

Saturday, September 30

We were due to have a family picture made at 11 A.M. today—an event I always approach as an ordeal because it falls to my lot to try to get everybody in the humor. To corral them all at the same time, with the three women in dresses that have a harmony of color and line, is a job for a General. This time everything seemed to be going for me. The one and only dress Luci wanted to wear arrived, by a miracle of transportation, from New York in the early morning. In fact, the colors for all three of us were the best I remember for a family picture—Luci's, yellow and simple; Lynda's, bright coral red; and mine, a fresh green. Pat and Chuck were obligingly ready ahead of time. And so to a considerable degree was little Lyn—all dressed up in a new suit. He had smiled and gurgled and performed for us. Time passed. About 11:15 Lyndon asked me to go with him out to the airstrip to meet the plane from Washington bringing Ramsey Clark, Barefoot Sanders, Ed Weisl, Jr., Dean Erwin Griswold of Harvard Law School and Steve Pollak. We got them settled in the front yard with coffee and sent Jim Jones to take care of them. After 11:30 we all went into the living room for our family pictures. Alas, time had run out for little Lyn! He was getting sleepier and sleepier and hungrier and hungrier.

We took our seats on the orange sofa in the den—Lyndon and I in the middle with the baby on his lap, Luci next to me and Pat leaning over her on the arm of the sofa, and Lynda Bird by Lyndon with Chuck on the arm of the sofa by her. Patrick Lyndon screwed up his face and let out a yell. Everybody went into gyrations trying to amuse him. Luci went for a bottle of milk, and then there followed one of the most hilarious scenes of my lifetime. Lyndon gave Okie instructions on how to shoot the picture, then he stuck the bottle of milk in Lyn's mouth for a long suck, snatched it out and put it quickly behind my back while we all composed our faces into a hopefully appropriate expression and Okie snapped. This went on time after time, with little Lyn getting madder and madder, hollering louder and louder, and I melting into laughter between snaps until the tears rolled down my cheeks. Luci looked a graven image. Of course she cared most of all that her child behave well. Pat looked resigned. Lynda and Chuck, above it all, handsome and oblivious in their own circle of happiness. And Lyndon looked like the frustrated captain who can't make his team play right. We repeated the performance on the hearth in front of the big fireplace with no better results.

It was 12:30 when Lyndon gathered up his front-yard visitors and all of the family and we went out to the hangar, where the press was assembled, to announce the appointments that were being made, including the appointment of Dean Griswold as Solicitor General to replace Thurgood Marshall.

When the announcement of appointments was finished, the occasion turned into a real press conference, with Lyndon at his skillful best, I thought. Yuki did his part, moving around in front of the TV cameras, going from one pair of legs to another, smelling and inspecting and trotting on. Back inside we had a delicious, complete Mexican dinner—much relished by all us Southwesterners, but I flinched a bit for our friend from Harvard.

After lunch we took our five guests out to the plane. There followed an agony of indecision about another family picture session. This would be the last time we would all be together again until Thanksgiving. The children were all leaving now to go to a football game; Lyndon was asleep; Okie wanted to try it down by the river—quite informally. "But Mother, I didn't bring a casual outdoor dress. You didn't *tell* me," cried Luci. Finally, it all fell into place. Lyndon woke up, the children agreed to be late for their dinner date before the ball game. We all got dressed somehow, and once more Yuki led the way and sat happily in front of us while we all lived through it again. I am sure the pictures of Yuki will be great.

Today really began a little after midnight when I flew into Andrews Air Force Base and there in my waiting car was Dr. Hurst. He had been in Washington for his Committee work, and when Lynda Bird had phoned me the afternoon before, he had come on the phone. There was a note of concern in his voice that I have not heard in over ten years. He said Lyndon had a bad cold and seemed spent, depleted, low in spirits. Dr. Hurst wished he could talk to me. I told him I would be in around midnight—could he meet me at the plane? He was catching an earlier plane out to Atlanta, but he said he would rearrange it and be there. So I stepped into the warm circle of his smile just after midnight.

We got into the back seat and rolled up the glass and talked the forty-five minutes' drive to the White House. His feeling of anxiety had not abated. He did not see the bounce, the laughter, the teasing quality in Lyndon that he has watched over these twelve years. He thought he was running on marginal energy—that he was bone tired. He repeated, "You know, Bird, this is the first time I have said this to you." And he kept on saying that he expected a part of it must be a psychological result of seeing four papers every morning and three screens of television that kept on shouting all of the troubles of the world and all the things that were going wrong.

I asked Dr. Hurst point-blank if he thought, as Lyndon's doctor, that he ought not to run again because of his health. And here he came to a dead stop. He said it was beyond medical knowledge to determine what results this might have.

I wanted so much to tell him of our thinking, but as yet I did not feel free to do so. The more people who know it, the more chance there is to have the story looking back at us from the printed page some morning, and I think the announcement should come from us. I asked Dr. Hurst what he thought I should do. He said, "I think you ought not to travel so much. I think it matters to him for you to be with him. Stay home." I told him I was going to, after I finished this one trip to the colleges on October 8 and 9. Then he said, "And when have *you* had a thorough medical exam lately? For his sake you ought to get one every six months." I couldn't even remember when I had had a checkup. That much I can do—those two things—and I will.

It was comforting to see how much he cared even though neither of us knows the answer. I tried to make one thing clear to him, that is, that I wouldn't be leaving a thing behind that I yearned for whenever we left the White House. Also, that I thought Lyndon, approaching sixty, could be quite busy and happy out of public office. Here I ran into a complete blank wall. He looked at me in astonishment. "No, I don't think he can quit."

"Why?"

"Because he hasn't done everything that he wants to."

And so we left it on a sad but affectionate note at the Diplomatic entrance. He had to catch a 5 o'clock plane in the morning.

As it turned out it was a short night for me too. Lyndon was still awake when I went up—reading. His cold was very bad. He looked sick. We turned out the light and slept, but not long. It was a little past 6 when he was up and working again. We had a long talk, going over and over the same old ground—when could he make his announcement that he was not going to run again—when and how? Our mood was bleak and dispirited, and no answers came.

I began my day with a meeting with Liz and Sharon and Elspeth Rostow about my trip to Williams College and Yale. In three days we must hammer out, and I must practice, two good speeches.

About dark I went over to the bowling lanes and bowled two quick games, doing rather well—136 and 138. I came back in time to dress and greet Lyndon's dinner guests—thirty Senators—another in a series of his stag dinners. Since he was late, I welcomed the opportunity to go in and see them.

Lyndon came in about a quarter past 8, and I was amazed at the change in him since 9 o'clock this morning. His cold seemed better, his spirits vastly higher, and he looked jovial, full of controlled energy, cool and tough. I would not want to put it to the test, but it was a remarkable feat—a metamorphosis since morning. I know a part of it was because of the necessity to rise up and work. But I also remembered what Willis Hurst had told me about working on marginal energy.

Later I watched a TV program—Lyndon and Walter Washington and Tom Fletcher in the Rose Garden talking about the new government for the District of Columbia. I liked what Lyndon said. This has gone pretty well up to now—it's not full self-government but it's a sizable step toward something nobody else has been able to solve since 1789—an independent government for the District.

This day which I have looked forward to with a rising ripple of apprehension just below the surface and prepared for with hard work dawned clear and bright. In hours and energy spent it was one of the more civilized days, but in the sheer battering of emotions it was pretty wearing. I was going to Williams College to speak at the opening of a new Center for Environmental Studies, and then on to Yale at the invitation of the Yale Political Union to talk on environment.

Liz and I arrived a little past 10 at National Airport, where we met the James Linens with their son, got into their plane, and flew to an airport in North Adams, Massachusetts. The Mayor greeted us and gave me a key. We drove to Williamstown—a picture-postcard New England city— the streets elm-lined, a white spired church, the surrounding mountains turning gold and crimson with autumn.

The residence of the President of Williams College—Dr. John E. Sawyer —was a lovely white house built about 1801. The Sawyers themselves were pleasant, a bit restrained, completely suited to the college and to the environment. They were hosting a luncheon for sixty people—the degree recipients, the trustees, several members of the faculty. I was on President Sawyer's right and next to a very interesting man—Hugh Bullock, trustee of Williams College and a New York financier. He was quite outspoken in his approval of Lyndon, and that was one of the last words of approval I was to hear this day.

A little past 2 I put on my black robe with the white velvet-trimmed hood that the University of Texas had given me and out under the trees we waited for the procession to start. These processions are always thrilling but I feel utterly foreign to them no matter how many times I participate. There were the crimson hoods of Harvard, the deep blue of Yale, and the deep-gold crushed velvet cap that, I believe, comes from an English school.

We marched in dignified double file, I walking beside President Sawyer, down the quiet streets to Chapin Hall. Within a few steps I began to size up the crowd. The pickets were there as promised, but in no great number. Printed signs that said "CONFRONT THE WAR MAKERS IN WASHINGTON, OCTOBER 21." And some others I couldn't read. (They lose so much on me because of my eyesight.) But there were three big homemade ones that were close by. One was held by a small boy, and it said, "I AM 7 YEARS

OLD. WILL I BE FIGHTING TO PROTECT THESE PRESENT-DAY PACIFISTS?" And another, a big one, "MAY GOD GIVE LBJ STRENGTH TO CONTINUE HIS COURAGEOUS STAND ON THE PRESERVATION OF PEACE." Another, held by a silent, stern, youngish man, "I FOUGHT IN VIETNAM AND I BELIEVE OUR CAUSE IS JUST."

All of them, anti and pro, walked with us as we maintained our dignified pace to Chapin Hall. Most of the crowd were townspeople—bright, smiling children and their parents—eager to get a look—a wave of excitement going with us as we passed. They seemed completely oblivious to the escort of sign carriers walking behind them, rather like the furies in a Greek play.

We took our seats on the stage. As we sang "America," I looked out into the audience. The first several dozen rows were the graduating class in their black robes. As I saw a white arm band on the first one, I was not quite prepared for it, and I felt a quick pulse of emotion in my throat. I counted another and another. These were a symbol of mourning for the war in Vietnam. (The local paper said there were sixty-three in all.)

There were five of us who received honorary degrees. Besides myself, Stanley Cain, Assistant Secretary of the Interior, President Fairfield Osborn of the New York Zoological Society, Roger Revelle of the Center for Population Studies at Harvard, and Fraser Darling, Vice President of the Conservation Foundation—all very eminent, lifetime conservationists, masters in their field, and I a very new-comer.

When I was introduced, everybody rose, and it was at this point that some of the graduating class walked out. (The local Massachusetts paper said thirty-five.) This I had been forewarned about. But the college had its own rebuttal. This took the form of everybody standing so long and cheering so loudly that their departure was scarcely noticed and they must have felt rather flat.

I was both touched and humbled by President Sawyer's citation. It will be something to look back on in years ahead. He spoke of "quiet leadership and powerful moral support for deeply humane causes, ranging from project Head Start to the quality of the total environment in which we live."

Then began the thing I had come for—my salute to the new Williams College Center for Environmental Studies. I tried to look straight into the eyes of the students in front of me, and from one to another as the speech progressed, and I certainly spoke with passion if not expertise.

I began with real praise for a college of Williams' caliber setting up a

Center for Environmental Studies, and I said: "There is no time for annotated studies to gather dust on library shelves. While eleven thousand city planning positions must be filled in the next five years, planning schools are producing only four hundred and fifty graduates a year." What I hope, *hope*, HOPE, is that such a school will bridge the gap between the theorizing city planner and the Mayor, between the professor and the budget officer. I never tried harder. For that, in part, I can thank the pickets.

It was a very quiet attentive audience, and there was very loud applause when I sat down. Was it partly prompted by the pickets themselves? The last moment of the convocation was by all odds the most touching. Everybody rose and we sang "The Mountains." I did not know the song, but I read the words and loved them, and so, I felt, did all the students there. Then we filed out. The pickets were still there, but louder now. A strange thing happened then—as we turned and started on up the hill, with the pickets behind us, the ugly murmur rose in volume. I heard calls of "Shame, Shame!"

There is something weird and animal about mass psychology, and I wondered what would have happened if I had suddenly broken into a run. But of course we maintained our dignified gait and our smiles and walked under the elms up to the front of the house, where the procession broke up and I said good-by to several of the faculty members and to the "High Sheriff." He was one of the most colorful figures of the day, a tall, impressive man dressed in swallowtail coat and high silk hat. Carrying a huge staff, he had led the procession, and to begin the march he had banged on the floor and said, "In the name of the Commonwealth of Massachusetts, pray have silence!" The presence of the Sheriff is a custom begun around 1783, early in Williams' history.

I changed into flat-heeled shoes and my brown tweed coat. Professor James MacGregor Burns joined me to show me through Mt. Hope Farm which will be the site for the environmental planning center—a sort of a "think tank" for city-planning experts, students, and professors. There couldn't have been a more complete change of mood—of atmosphere. It was the most peaceful, quiet, beautiful New England landscape you could imagine—open meadows rolling away, woods turning scarlet and gold, a ring of blue mountains in the distance—a very Heaven of a place to walk, and we walked for about an hour and a half.

Back at the Sawyers' house, we walked in to the warm welcome of a fire. The crisp chill of the outside heightened our pleasure in it. This was another charming side of New England and I loved it. It was, indeed, "far from the madding crowd."

I changed again into another quiet understated outfit, and we went to the Sterling and Francine Clark Art Institute—a museum of white marble which to me seemed quite European and surprising in this New England setting. There we saw the most marvelous collection of French Impressionist paintings which had been left by a wealthy collector, Sterling Clark, to this little New England town of seven thousand. It was fabulous. Thirty-two Renoirs . . . sad, amusing, Toulouse-Lautrecs . . . a Mary Cassatt that I would never have recognized . . . many Degas, Matisses, and Winslow Homers . . . a wealth of bronzes and much old English silver.

It was nearly 8 when we got back to the Sawyers' residence. The house was quietly impressive, with quality and grace but nothing lavish. Then we sat down to dinner, with their attractive daughter Katherine—home for the weekend from her teaching job (she is just out of college)—and a small group.

How would I evaluate a day spent like this? Probably a mistake on balance, because what I had really done was to provide a vehicle for the dissenters, who were a minority, to mount a platform, to get inches in the paper and minutes on the television screen that they would not have gotten without me. So I was their bait—their creature—for the day. And what I had set out to do was to praise Williams for establishing its Center for Environmental Studies. This I think I had done. But the louder voices of hate and anger shouted it down. How did I personally feel as I walked among the picketers? Cool and firm and determined to maintain dignity. But through every pore, you sense a sort of an animal passion right below the surface.

All in all, I guess I lost this round. Lyndon called—distressed—"I just hate for you to have to take that sort of thing."

Monday, October 9

NEW HAVEN, CONNECTICUT

The second day of my journey into Academia began crisp and bright. About 10 we left with a big basket of lunch which Mrs. Sawyer had packed for us to drive through the back roads of New England—an indulgence I had allowed myself. We went from Williamstown to Pittsfield, Stockbridge, New Canaan, Litchfield, and Goshen. It was an enchanting journey—maples turning crimson and gold against the backdrop of green pines, white-trunked birches, graceful and shimmering, and asters and goldenrod all along the roadside, and sumac—its foliage, especially closer to the ground—turning those wonderful variegated shades of orange and red.

One thing along the road intrigued me—a firm-looking sign that said, "Minimum $50.00 Fine for Trash Disposal." Nowhere else have I seen that word "minimum" in such a sign.

There were pumpkins and apples and cornstalks at roadside stands. In Great Barrington, a pleasant little village, crab apple trees lined the streets, apparently set out within the last few years as an answer to the dying elms. We arrived at the Shaker village and Mrs. Lawrence Miller took us through, with a sizable crowd of press and members of her restoration committees. In this unique settlement, members of the Shaker religious cult had lived and worked and worshiped for about 170 years. The last of them, a few elderly women, had sold the land and buildings in 1960 to a restoration group and now they are open to the public. The Shakers lived apart from the world, got up before daylight, worked hard as farmers and as craftsmen of fine, plain furniture, and lived a life of celibacy. Members of this sect were early gatherers, packagers, and sellers of seeds—vegetables and flowers. (The latter they used, alas, only for medicinal purposes.) They had sold seeds as far afield as every state in the Union, and to London, and even Australia.

About 3 we arrived in New Haven at the residence of the Kingman Brewsters—he is President of Yale. There was a sizable crowd of picketers in front of the house. (The newspapers described the crowd as numbering more than one hundred.) They were carrying the usual signs.

I got out of the car with what I hope was a calm and natural expression and walked with a measured slowness to meet Dr. Brewster who was waiting for me at the gate. We exchanged a few words and went inside. We sat down on their back porch, and I asked him what we might expect of the evening. Quite soon the feeling came across to me that my presence here was really an imposition on him. His manner was absolutely correct, but if I have any antennae at all I sensed that he wished he had no part of it.

About 6 I put on my bright chartreuse dress and went down to join the Brewsters and John J. O'Leary, President of the Yale Political Union, who had invited me. We emerged from the house into a larger and more vigorous group of picketers and drove to Freshman Commons—also aptly named War Memorial Hall. On the way I could glimpse, as we passed street intersections, youngsters running pell-mell, as if on the football field, with their signs up high and their hair flying. I wondered if any one of them would dare speak out on the other side for fear of ostracism by his fellows. I wondered especially about my friend, John J. O'Leary, and how he would fare the next day. There was a car that raced along in front of us with two bareheaded girls in it. Later I heard that they too were sporting a placard—this one in favor of the President's stand. So I guess, even in that atmosphere, there were dissenters.

We went into a very impressive hall—high-ceilinged, cathedral-like, dark-paneled, the wall lined with portraits of long-dead Presidents of Yale, covering the more than two hundred and fifty years of its existence. In front of me at round tables sat the eight hundred or more members of the Yale Political Union, including a few of their dates who had stayed over from their weekend activities, a few members of the faculty—and, amazingly, Jack Valenti, who was there to make a speech to a lawyers' group. We laughed over getting our "bookings" on the same night. He said, "Just to clear my schedule with you, I am going to be in Topeka next week."

I sat between President Brewster and John J. O'Leary. Mrs. Richard Lee was also at the table, filling in for her husband, the Mayor, who was sick with laryngitis, she said. The number of picketers outside was about eight hundred (which was the same as the audience inside). They held a silent vigil, and then they broke into chants of "Peace now" and "Hell no, we won't go," which came through as a sort of a murmur inside the hall. If anything, it only added to the stir of adrenalin in my blood and the determination to do the best I was capable of.

I looked around me with intense interest, trying to pick up the mood of the crowd. When President Brewster rose to introduce me, I came with a jar to a more complete understanding of the situation. His introduction was generous, even eloquent. He compared me to Mrs. Roosevelt, which I did not deserve. But he was careful to say that in his own young days he had been opposed to another war in the time of another President (FDR), and added that as he had grown older he had come to understand more about the difficulties of those conducting foreign policy.

I wish I had a copy of his speech. At any rate, the impression I received was that he was disassociating himself from President Johnson, from this Administration, letting his own constituency—that is, the students and faculty of Yale—know that he was with them in heart, but at the same time maintaining a gentlemanly and correct stance of hospitality to the First Lady.

I received a standing ovation when I rose to speak, and I have never tried harder in my life—not even at Williams the day before. In all the days of working on this speech—and we really battled it out—everyone had insisted that I must have some humor in it. Humor is not my forte, but I tried. Only the reference to the coming of Vassar brought a real laugh. But they were a very quiet, very attentive audience.

I spoke as directly as I could, seeking the eyes of one young man and then the next and the next as I said to them, "If you are in the sciences, I hope you will apply their order to the environment. If you are in business or economics, I hope you will include beauty as part of the cost of doing business. If you are in the arts, I hope you will express their insight in the environment around you. For the environment after all is where we all meet; where we all have a mutual interest; it is one thing that all of us share. It is not only a mirror of ourselves, but a focusing lens on what we can become." In conclusion, I said, "Can a great democratic society generate the energy to plan and build projects of order and beauty? Or does democracy after all mean the lowest common denominator? Most of the great cities in history—most of the great works of beauty—were the creation of autocratic societies. The Caesars built Rome. Paris was shaped by the kings of France and the Empire. Vienna was the handiwork of the Hapsburgs; and Florence of the Medici. Our wealth surpasses theirs combined. Will our taste and intelligence and foresight be as great? The answer we give will reveal our quality as a civilization. A better answer will unfold, I think, in the next two decades—and they are yours."

I got a standing ovation again—long and loud and clear—and I hope they heard it outside. Not even the Secret Service was gladder, I am sure, than I was when the speech was ended and the evening nearly over.

We went upstairs to the President's room, and I stood in line with President Brewster to meet a few faculty members and the officers and a number of the leaders in the Yale Political Union. And then came the dessert of the day—the Whiffenpoof Chorus sang for us, enchantingly, ending with their most nostalgic song about the "tables down at Mory's" and "the poor little lambs, who had lost their way."

The reception was soon over and we left for the Brewsters' residence where they had a small gathering of close friends and faculty. A drink was very welcome and I settled on a sofa, but not for long. I remembered that President Brewster had to get up at 5 to leave for Paris. He had courteously postponed his departure for one day because of my presence, and I was more and more aware of the difficulty this has cost him.

If I had to capsule these two days in Academia, how would I? For one thing, both campuses seemed set apart from the world—insulated, encased in gelatin, with the window open on only one issue—Vietnam. There was also the feeling of a society where everybody thinks the same thing and does the same thing and anybody who dares not to has to be pretty brave—a sort of McCarthyism in reverse. There was also a lesson in it for me. I must not live only in the White House, insulated against life. I want to know what's going on—even if to know is to suffer.

Friday, October 20

THE WHITE HOUSE

This was a many-faceted day—beautiful golden Indian summer. I was up early for my daffodil planting. In my bright green jacket-dress with the white lapels—veteran of many plantings—I left the White House in a mini-bus with a number of members of our Beautification Committee. We drove to Columbia Island. Mary Lasker has given eight hundred thousand daffodil bulbs to be planted there in natural drifts along the banks of the Potomac under the willow trees and on up to Memorial Bridge, so that when you drive in from the airport in the spring, or come in from Arlington to work, or from the West as a tourist, they'll welcome you, year after year. This is the major gateway to the city—166,000 people a day see it. It will be glorious next spring.

Mary's gift had already been purchased before Congress clamped down on the Park Service funds for planting new material. So Nash Castro enlisted the efforts of all the garden clubs of Washington to plant the bulbs. Dozens and dozens of garden club ladies have been planting daffodils on Columbia Island for days. This morning I joined them—some wore slacks, some were in tweeds, some with their children along—everybody with a smile. We used a special tool from Holland, and I got down on my knees along with Mayor Walter Washington and a whole coterie of garden club ladies, and we planted and planted. There were autographs and jokes and general good will. I went up and down thanking every lady. I think we will all look at this display next spring with a more proprietary, more special feeling, because it's a little bit "ours."

About noon Lynda and I slipped into her little black car and went off together for lunch. We do this two or three times a year, just the two of us. It's our special self-indulgence. She took me to the Jockey Club. Lynda looks on this as a kind of therapy for me. We can get "housebound" in the White House. It *is* fun to get out.

Today we had an interesting experience. The manager greeted us with his big smile and took us to an inconspicuous table in the back. The place is so dark you can scarcely see, but the low lights do create an atmosphere of intimacy. At the table in front of us there were about six men who must have been having their second martinis. One of them talked very loudly and continuously. I paid no attention to what he was saying, but his tone was contentious. A middle-aged lady sitting at a corner table with a gentleman smiled at me in a deprecating, apologetic manner, as though deploring the noisy man. Presently she took him a note. He looked up and said in a very loud voice, "Thank you. I didn't realize I was talking so loud," and proceeded to talk just as loudly as they ordered a round of Irish coffees to taper off lunch.

A man came over, introduced himself, and asked if he might give us a letter. I accepted it with a smile and a nod and laid it beside my plate, uncertain whether it was a get-out-of-Vietnam or a we-believe-in-you letter. Later, as the middle-aged lady started to leave, she came by our table and leaned over and said, "Tell the President to have courage." That was a sweet thing to do, but more clearly than anything, it showed the depth of the wave that is sweeping the country—an avalanche—a tidal wave of stories, murmurs, whispers, that create distrust, frustration, and uncertainty. If you could chart it, I wonder when you would have seen it begin? Certainly it has had a great upsurge in the last six weeks and has borne pernicious fruit.

For Lynda, these lunch times are as much fun as for me. She loves to give, and I hated for this occasion to be flawed. Just before we left, the man who had given me the letter came over to say a word about what was in it. It sounded quite innocuous. I explained to him that I was sorry but I simply couldn't read in that darkness, that I was saving it until we got to the daylight. Having explained it, he took his letter back. Then Lynda and I walked out, greeting the Ambassador from Peru on the way. It had not been a gay, carefree lunch . . . but I do not want to be ignorant. I want to know what is happening.

Jim Cain arrived about 7 this evening to be our houseguest while he is in Washington for one of his innumerable committee meetings. We sat down in the West Hall and had a long talk about Lyndon. I told him my feelings—that I did not want to go through the grueling six months of another campaign, and that even more, if we should win I did not want to face another four years as devouring as these last four have been. I could stand defeat easily, I believe. I could stand retiring. There are so many things I want us to do! My list is a mile long. And for the first time in my life I believe that Lyndon, too, could be happy. But what I do not know is whether I could endure having Lyndon face the sort of trial that President Wilson did—that is, to be in office, to be incapacitated, or reduced to half his mental and physical abilities while still being President. I think that would be the most unbearable tragedy that could happen to him. I asked Jim frankly, as a medical man, what advice he could give me. He said, "Obviously he has aged. The last four years have taken a lot out of him . . . but I cannot say, as I think the doctors should have said to FDR when he ran for his fourth term, that he won't live out this next term, that he won't be able to serve as he should. No man can say what will happen." . . . And so the dilemma continues.

At 8 the Jack Brookses and the George Mahons came for dinner. Later Lyndon, Marie, and Joe Califano drifted in from the office, and we had a pleasant family dinner—George openly deploring the Congress' inability to act, and Jack with his pungent cutting phrases scoring both the House of Representatives and the Senate.

Lyndon said, as he often has, that he would give a piece of his life if Speaker Sam Rayburn could be back with the gavel and he (Lyndon himself) were over in the Senate for just one week. In discussing President Eisenhower, he said: "He has paid me back one hundred percent for what I did for him when I was Majority Leader by just trying to be decent." There is no way to understand a former President like being one . . . It will be interesting to see whether that carries forward into the years when we are out of here.

At dinner there was much talk of tomorrow—the day of the big gathering in Washington of dissenters on Vietnam—a great many of them from colleges, coming in by bus, plane, and car. There is a ripple of grim excitement in the air, almost a feeling of being under siege. I plan to stay home all day. Maybe for once I'll get a clear desk.

Thursday, October 26

Today is the day the Mexicans came to Washington—President and Mrs. Diaz Ordaz. It was one of the star State visits of our time here.

At noon, in my bright red coat and dress from Marquise, I went to Lyndon's office for the arrival ceremony. It was a brilliant Indian summer day, and the grounds were full of people. The big black limousine used by the heads of State rolled up for the thirty-seventh time this year and President Gustavo Diaz Ordaz emerged with Mrs. Diaz Ordaz. She was beautifully dressed in a pastel suit trimmed in fur and a fur-trimmed hat. I never see President Diaz Ordaz without remembering the charming story he told on himself at dinner in Mexico. He said that during his campaign his opponent was accusing him of being two-faced. "Now I ask you," Diaz Ordaz answered, "If I had two faces, would I wear this one?"

Several things set this State visit apart from others. One, there is a very real warmth between our family and Mexico. Second, the First Family of Mexico brought all their children—their handsome bachelor son, Gustavo, Jr., their pretty daughter and her Lebanese husband—the Salim Nastas (they are Lynda's favorites)—and young Alfredo who is just sixteen. And our Lynda and Chuck—he was a guest for the first time at a State Dinner—were very much a part of the day. So it was more than a State visit, with the warmth of two families.

After the welcoming speeches and the brief greetings in the Diplomatic Reception Room, we drove with them to Blair House—a very abbreviated parade, with the flags snapping briskly, large pictures of the two Presidents on lamp posts, a moderate-size crowd of the curious waving and clapping. It simply isn't possible for this town, so satiated with Chiefs of State, to turn out en masse for a parade. I remembered our triumphant progress through the hundreds of thousands in Mexico City in April 1966. We can't match them, so it is wiser not to try.

This old house was bursting at the seams! The Perry Basses and the Don Thomases and Larry Temple will share the third floor with the Tony Taylors and the Billy Baileys who have been here for several nights. Sometime during the afternoon we got word that Lyndon had invited his good friend Cantinflas (Mario Moreno) Reyes to be our houseguest—just saying, "You've got to make room." So we moved the Warren Woodwards (who are so close, we could) down to Luci's room and put Cantinflas in the newly decorated bedroom.

When there is a State Dinner, I try to ask some friends, either as houseguests or to come for tea in the afternoon or coffee the next morning. I want the visit to mean something to them and to me. A little past 3 I had invited the Jake Hersheys (my friends of the Mississippi River boat ride during my Midwest trip) to tea, and the Fleetwood Richards who had conducted that one-day tour through the old Tenth District to see grass-roots urban renewal and Texas restorations. And I also invited Dr. and Mrs. E. T. Ximenes of San Antonio. He's a new Regent on the Board of the University of Texas.

The Lincoln Sitting Room, which used to be the makeshift press room until Theodore Roosevelt's time, is getting to be my favorite place for these small teas—cozy and intimate. Its warm colors and Victorian furniture have been a happy setting for some good talks.

A little bit past 8 we were on the North Portico greeting the President and Mrs. Diaz Ordaz who wore a beautiful pink chiffon, glittering with beads. I found myself watching for each new outfit she wore—all of them extremely feminine and pretty. She said they were all made in Mexico. They might not be *Women's Wear Daily*'s cup of tea, but they were very womanly and would certainly please husbands.

We went upstairs with the family—the Nastas and Gustavo and Alfredo all smiles. Hubert and Muriel were there and Virginia and Dean Rusk—Virginia looking very pretty. There was a big *abrazo* when Tony Carrillo Flores came in with Fanny—one of the most popular Ambassadors ever to be in this town, I think. Their replacements, the Margains, I like a great deal also in their very different way—he is quiet and intellectual, does not have Tony's ebullience that embraces the world. But he is very high caliber.

Our Ambassador to Mexico and Mrs. Fulton Freeman were telling me about the ruins at Chichén Itzá where some special excavations are going on between now and December 15. Couldn't I come? How I would love to! Lynda and Chuck came in. I was aglow to be introducing them around. With Mrs. Diaz Ordaz our conversation is mostly family. And there was plenty to talk about—the weddings and grandchildren.

When we had greeted the 190 guests, I took the President of Mexico into the Blue Room where Aida Gardner sat on his right. Next was one of the most attractive stage figures ever to entertain us in the White House—José Limón—who danced the "Moor's Pavane" for the King of Morocco. Katherine Anne Porter, author of *Ship of Fools*, looking really frail, was at our table—white hair, very white skin, very pastel evening gown—and Honey Berlin, who looks no older than when I first met her—one of the most warm, feminine, glowing people I know. Tony Carrillo Flores sat on my left, which always makes my evening. It was a good table, a lively evening—a brilliant guest list, glamorous women, and later loud, lively, and successful entertainment.

Lyndon's toast was humorous and full of warmth. He spoke of something that is one of the real pluses of this decade to me—the development in Mexico in the agricultural experimental station of Chapingo of a remarkable new strain of wheat, which can produce more than twice the crop from the same amount of land and which, best of all, the Mexicans are exporting to underdeveloped countries—Pakistan and India—and which is now being tested for Turkey, Iran, and Afghanistan. Chapingo is partly financed by the Rockefeller and Ford foundations. They've concluded some of the largest international sales of seed wheat ever in any country. Plagued as this era is with wars and frustrations, we do take some steps forward.

We had coffee and liqueurs in the Red Room and then went in to hear Herb Alpert and the Tijuana Brass. Lynda introduced them with a delightful girlish speech. I could tell this band was an especial favorite with our guest of honor, and I think it was one of the most popular entertainments we have ever had. When the evening was over, we asked our houseguests to meet us on the second floor for a nightcap.

We talked of the dinner, of Texas, of things serious and light. I remember at one point Lyndon was explaining something about the bombing in North Vietnam, and he said, "We keep 600,000 men [the enemy] busy repairing what our four hundred bombers have taken out. That is a good trade."

He has a talent for putting complicated things into a simple sentence. I only wish he could reach two hundred million Americans with those simple, vivid pictures. We do so many things in this Administration, but as communicators I can't give us the highest rating.

Presently we said good night to our houseguests, but it was a quarter of 3 before Lyndon laid down the last of his night reading and turned off the light.

Sunday, November 12

The day began in Williamsburg at the Bassett House, which belongs to John D. Rockefeller III. This house has great colonial charm, surrounded by spacious grounds and approached along an avenue of live oaks. The floors of wide boards, laid down before the Revolutionary War, gleam softly and are scattered with bright needlepoint or hooked rugs. And on the walls are samplers and "mourning pieces" and quaint American primitive portraits.

This morning we went to the old Bruton Parish Episcopal Church—Lyndon and I and Lynda Bird and Chuck and Beryl and Jake. It's a venerable building, and in the past I've spent hours with Lyndon's mother in the graveyard and walking through the interior where the names of so many signers of the Declaration of Independence adorn the walls. We sat in George Washington's own pew in the front row. The choir was absolutely lovely. And then came the sermon.

The Reverend Cotesworth Pinckney Lewis gave short shrift to any Biblical text and launched into a general discussion of the state of the Union and of the world— touching on Civil Rights, disorder in the streets, and the general upheaval in the nation. And then I froze in my seat as I heard him say, "And then there is the question of Vietnam. But there is a rather general consensus that something is wrong in Vietnam—a conviction voiced by leaders of nations traditionally our friends, leading military experts and the rank and file of American citizens—we wonder if some logical, straightforward explanation might be given?". . . and on and on. "It is particularly regrettable that to most nations of the world the struggle's purpose appears as neocolonialism." He then veered 180 degrees. "We are mystified," he said, "by news accounts suggesting that our brave fighting units are inhibited by directives and inadequate equipment from using their capacities to terminate the conflict successfully. While pledging our loyalty, we ask humbly: "Why?"

I turned to stone on the outside and boiled on the inside. I thought of Lyndon's asking for equal time and rising to the pulpit to explain to him "why." But no, if I thought *he* shouldn't use the pulpit for what he is doing, how much less would it become a visiting worshiper to rise and answer? Lyndon had just spent two days and traveled thousands of miles across the country answering exactly his questions—why are we there?

I thought of the headlines of all the papers I had seen—three or four while we had had our coffee this morning. And they had recounted Lyndon's answers to all the minister's questions. Meanwhile, it was almost amusing to watch his expression—so unctuous it was.

All things end. Finally the beautiful choir raised its great voice, and then we were walking stiffly out the door. There, of course, was that inevitable melee—the flashing cameras, the crowds of casual tourists and visitors lining the streets, smiling, cheering, reaching out their hands. Off in the distance to the left, I noticed a very small group of protesters with banners. I could only see the word "PEACE." And there was Reverend Cotesworth Pinckney Lewis—hand extended. Be it said for my husband that he shook hands briefly with a smile while I said, "The choir was beautiful." We stepped into the waiting car with a wave to the crowd.

Later Lyndon looked at me with a wry smile and said, "Greater love hath no man than that he goes to the Episcopal Church with his wife!"

I felt very sorry for him and very angry—two days of hard work, a great evening at the Gridiron—all of it ending on this painful note. I must say it was a great coup for the other side. Somehow I felt even sorrier for Chuck than I did for Lyndon. He looked so peculiarly vulnerable, hurt, questioning, uncertain what a young man who is about to go out and fight this war should think or do about that sort of performance by a minister at home.

The minister was ready with plenty of mimeographed copies which he distributed to the press afterward, we heard, along with a rather amazing statement. "Criticism," he said, "was the farthest thing from my mind. I intended none, and I gather that the President took no offense, but understood it in the spirit of honest, reasonable exploration of an idea. One isn't privileged to tell the President of the United States what he thinks very often."

Back at Bassett House Lyndon changed into leisure clothes and took Chuck and Jake to play golf at the Golden Horseshoe Golf Club. I could not bear to waste my one day in Williamsburg, so I called up my friends, the Carlisle Humelsines. We spent the next few hours driving around the streets of Williamsburg seeing the new restorations under way or planned, and driving out to Carter's Grove to visit what has been called the most beautiful house in America, begun in 1740. The Tidewater Plantation house faces on the James River—a magnificent view—framed by great tulip poplars.

It was after 3 when we had our lunch—Lyndon in from a good game of golf—and me ravenous. We had ham—my visit to Williamsburg would not have been complete without Virginia ham. Throughout our stay in Williamsburg a sizable crowd remained around the gates of the Rockefeller house, waiting to see Lyndon. Every time we went in or out they would cheer and smile and wave. This visit was the oddest mixture of affectionate welcome and an unexpected slap in the face. But for me, at least, it was a day of low ebb—of being unable to shake loose from the paralyzing effects of the morning in spite of the picturesque historic setting and what ought to have been a relaxing time with dear friends.

Thursday, November 23

LBJ RANCH

Thanksgiving Day was a day of sheer contentment, satisfying to remember, soft as velvet or cream. The weather was bright blue and gold, and I had coffee in bed and did a couple of hours' work, knowing that Lyndon was content with little Patrick Lyn on the bed beside him—his feet straight up in the air, batting the newspaper, and Helen handy to take him if he squealed.

Later Lyndon and I drove around, with the top down, over the Martin and the Danz and the Reagan pastures. The last color of fall is almost gone . . . here and there a sumac or a red oak with the last leaves coppery red, and the frost has gotten even the cowpen daisies.

Luci and Pat and Lynda and Chuck had flown down to the big football game at College Station. After lunch, we all took a nap and then about 4:30 with Jesse Kellam and the A. W. Moursunds we drove around aimlessly—happy, looking, but not very hard, for red oaks or sumac to dig up and transplant to our Ranch. We found nothing perfect except views—the most glorious views. We stopped at one of them, the top of a mesa—so flat it looked as if it had been chopped off by some giant knife—a perfect 360-degree view. There was a long dead campfire with some smooth rocks beside it that someone had evidently dragged up as seats. Mariallen said, "Well, they had a wiener roast here." It's a delightful country to raise children in, if they love the outdoors and roam it and learn about it.

Dark comes early now. No more the long twilights of summer.

At 6 the Thanksgiving company began arriving. I had invited the Nugents who are visiting Luci—her father- and mother-in-law, and her aunt, Mrs. Landers, and Pat's brother and his wife. And I had invited friends who no longer have families—Jesse Kellam, Jessie Hunter, Cousin Lela, and Cousin Oriole. The cook brought in the great big turkey, fat and golden, weighing about twenty-five pounds, on the biggest platter in the house, and our anticipation rose.

There were nineteen of us at the two tables. Luci gave us a long and eloquent blessing, full of her pleasure in life and family. And then we all set to on the turkeys, both domestic and wild, dressing and cranberry sauce and hot rolls, luscious sweet potatoes with marshmallows on top, green beans, lima beans, and cranberry salad, crunchy with nuts and celery. And finally, mince pie and coffee. There are occasions when it is pleasant to stuff, and Thanksgiving the best of these.

When dinner was over, I went to the bridge table with unseemly haste, taking the first three who had volunteered to play—Mr. and Mrs. Nugent and Lela.

Finally someone rose to go, and presently we had said good-by to everyone. Only Luci and Pat and Lynda and Chuck remained. And we paused for a last good night and instead settled into our chairs, as one after another thought of a story he wanted to tell. I sat quietly savoring their talk . . . Lynda's bright and sometimes brittle vignettes of the people she meets and the events of her life, and Luci's bubbling flow occasionally interspersed with philosophic insights sage beyond her years. Then I realized that this was really Thanksgiving . . . and this is what I have to be thankful for. I am reasonably satisfied with the way both of these children have turned out . . . I truly like their two young men . . . and today has been perfect and full. I shall remember this evening; I hope they will. There was more to it than many I've crowded with excitement and big names and important events.

Wednesday, November 29

THE WHITE HOUSE

Today was a strange day. To begin with, I woke up at 10:20 in the morning—the best night's sleep I've had in ages. I had been in bed with a cold the day before. (Thank Heavens, I've hardly lost four days from illness in these four years in the White House.) Today my cold wasn't any better, but I was rested. I spent a long, quiet day working in bed, interminably autographing Christmas presents—family pictures, engravings of the White House, copies of *The Living White House*, sometimes more personal pictures. The work began to seem dull and stupid. And then I thought of that one picture that Lyndon has of FDR, autographed to him, and how much it has meant to us for thirty years. And if just three of these three hundred or more that I am signing mean that much to somebody, it will be worth the effort.

Over the whole day hung a pall—the departure of Bob McNamara from the office of Secretary of Defense to become the head of the World Bank.

The 106 member countries will vote today, though that decision is almost foregone. But we are tied—he is tied—until they decide and make a selection known. Meanwhile, for two days now, the press has been having a field day speculating that his departure means that the hawks will take over, that there's a rift between him and Lyndon, that the whole Cabinet is crumbling, rumors of so and so and so and so who will leave next. A sort of poison is being generated that could go by osmosis through the body of the government, spreading suspicion and distrust and paralyzing vigorous, constructive action. I feel lonesome when I think of Bob going. When things have been at their worst, I have always taken comfort in knowing that he was there, one of the troops—and a very small band we get to be sometimes, or so we feel. I have confidence in his ability and heart. He's looked worn and thin and running on sheer spirit for a long time now, and I know it will be good for him and for Margy, which does not minimize our crucial loss . . . and then ironically, his very departure is being maneuvered, manipulated, into a weapon to flay Lyndon.

It was about 10:20 when Lyndon's office called. He was on his way home to dinner. I joined him quickly at the table with George Christian and Tom Johnson. To my surprise and great relief, he was in high spirits, full of good stories and laughter. The member nations had made their decision on McNamara, and a statement had been issued. He showed me a copy of his statement and of McNamara's. Both were excellent. If the papers and the columnists read them and use them, the ugly mood created in the last two days will be dispersed.

Before we had finished, I got word that Governor and Mrs. Connally had arrived. We took our second cups of coffee into the West Hall and settled down with them for what turned out to be a session that lasted until nearly 2 A.M.

Lyndon talked of McNamara's leaving, relayed the sequence of events from the beginning—in August, I think it was, when McNamara stayed behind after a meeting and said, "I want to talk to you about a personal, personnel matter." And then he told him that in the years he had been here he had had many offers of jobs—some of them for fabulous salaries. Bob had told all of them that he was going to continue to serve the President as long as he wanted him, but that now the Presidency of the World Bank was going to become vacant, and he wanted Lyndon to know that that was one job he was interested in. Bob also thought that it might well be that in the job of Defense, the Administration would benefit from a fresh person.

Lyndon had listened and said nothing.

He went on through it all until his last conversation with Bob just an hour ago. Bob was at home. He wanted Lyndon to know how horrid all the furor had been. Lyndon said he sounded as if he were almost in tears. And then Lyndon told us, "Except for one, this is the hardest day I have spent in this job."

I have seldom felt as sorry for him. The sense of loneliness and separation is deep.

Monday, December 4

The wedding week begins! And I have that good feeling of being rested and wanting to get things done. The first big event today was a bill signing in the East Room—the Mental Retardation Amendments. I walked in with Lyndon at 11:30, and there was a whole front row of drama. There sat the members of Lyndon's Mental Retardation Committee, behind each one a story of involvement—Muriel Humphrey, Eunice Shriver, Bess Harris Jones, along with the doctors and the scientists. When the signing was over, the Congressmen went up and stood behind Lyndon, led by Senator Lister Hill, father of so many good things in medical legislation. Lyndon bestowed pens.

Then I went to the swimming pool for thirty laps . . . It's odd how I could have swum here for four years without ever, until a few days ago, noticing the initials "J. F. K." and then a date in March 1962, painted into the mural of the Virgin Islands on the door. This is the third such reminder I have found in the house. There is that plaque above the fireplace in my bedroom and an inscription in the side of the marble mantel in the President's room.

I went up to the Solarium for lunch—the first day of our protracted house party. I had written out a long list of cold meats, salads, hot casseroles, and sent a copy to each of the numerous cooks, asking them to put together menus for lunch, which would be served buffet from 12:30 to 2:30 in the Solarium, and dinner, from 7:30 to 9:30, buffet also. I listed the approximate number of guests, and the nights when they would be eating out. I thanked the staff for what I knew was really a great drain on them and a challenge to their ingenuity. Also, I asked them to fill the refrigerator with milk and Cokes and Frescas and beer and to set up a supply of cookies and Fritos, and to keep a centerpiece of fruit on the table, so that all the houseguests can have snacks whenever they feel hungry. It's going to be one long house party, and I plan to enjoy it more than anybody.

The first sizable crisis to develop is that Zephyr has had to leave for California to attend the funeral of her nephew. She will be gone at least three days. She's hard to get along without anytime, and especially this week.

Tonight was the night of the Harrimans' party to introduce Lynda and Chuck to the Diplomatic Corps. I wore my pink lace, sprinkled with silver, far too short I thought. I was waiting for Lyndon on the second floor when I got the frantic news to come quickly. He was in the car waiting for *me*. I did run, but not fast enough. This had been a bad day for him and I could feel his tenseness. There is too much to do, too fast. From this party he would go on to an important appointment with William Randolph Hearst, and then on a dead run to a National Foreign Policy Conference at the State Department. But he is attacking his battalion of troubles with vigor and determination.

This afternoon he was in the swimming pool with the Chief Justice and Abe. Every day now, for more than a week, he's taken exercise on that exercycle thing in his bedroom. He's done without desserts and bread and drinks—all except Saturday night—and he has lost eight or ten pounds. Hooray!

Averell and Marie were at the front door waiting for us. Lynda looked lovely with her hair piled high, wearing a pale ice-blue heavy silk dress embroidered with bright jewels, with earrings of the same color. On the table was the magnificent gift from the Diplomatic Corps—a five-piece silver tea service, including the tray, in Lynda's pattern, Chantilly—an encore of their gift to Luci.

Lyndon made a swift tour of the room with Jimmy Symington, greeting as many as he could and leaving in about twenty minutes. Everyone was telling Mrs. Nehru good-by. (There has been such a series of farewell parties for them that they will surely leave exhausted!) A large tent covered the top terrace of the Harrimans' garden, decorated with long red velvet streamers with big silk roses—the same red as Lynda's bridesmaids will wear. Through the plastic walls of the tent I could see the glistening green of their great magnolia trees in the descending levels of the garden, where in the summer, August 1966, they had had the wonderful party for Luci.

I completed the circuit, saying "hello" to Sir Patrick and Lady Dean. And to an extraordinarily interesting man—an Arab, I suppose—who wore a creamy white tunic, embroidered from head to toe. Almost entirely the members of the Corps wear dark Western suits now. Only the African women wear *boubous* and occasionally a Ghanian appears in a brilliantly striped blanket.

Luci was having the most fun of anybody—candid, quotable, liked by the press. She was scotching rumors that she was expecting again, surveying the crowd, saying, "This looks like old home week!" greeting her daddy, "Hello, Handsome!" and then leaving quickly like Cinderella. "I have to be back at the White House by 7, because my baby sitter leaves then." The wedding party were all present—and how generous it was of Marie and Averell to have them.

I stayed a full hour and left about 6:30.

At home, I autographed and recorded. Lyndon came in at 9:30 from addressing the National Foreign Policy Conference—the Business Executives—at the State Department. He's in a fighting mood. I admire him fiercely. I want to see him spend himself, give whatever it takes, against this miasma of despondency, this ugly virus that is infecting our country. And yet it would be so easy, so tempting, to—as I have heard him say— let the armchair critics save each other, announce now he is not going to be a candidate, draw a circle for our energies, our brains, our hours, around our family, our business, our personal friends, and have fun in what is left to us of life . . . But there is so much still to be done.

Tuesday, December 5

Today began early for Lyndon with a Leadership Breakfast. He bounced out of bed at 8:20 and was ready to go into the dining room at 8:30. It annoys me because he can get showered, bathed, and dressed so fast! At 9 I got a summons from Paul: "The President says will you please come into the dining room." I said, "He knows how I look?" "Yes, ma'am." And so, in my dressing gown, I went in to see the assembled Leadership gathered around the breakfast table . . . Senators Mansfield and Long, the Speaker, Carl Albert—a table full. Russell Long rose and brought forward a big box accompanied by a big smile. "We wanted to give Lynda Bird something—the Democratic Leadership did. Will you please take this to her?" In it were two "Blue Birds of Happiness" by Edward M. Boehm, resting on a branch of magnolias—a gift to treasure, and especially because they gave it. Shortly after I made my exit, Lyn made his entrance, propelled by himself in his walker, completely undaunted by the power structure in front of him.

In the afternoon I went with Lynda down into the basement of the White House to the gift room. Warrie Lynn had spent hours arranging everything on the shelves. Lynda showed me her presents with delight. There were silver spoons from a Robb relative dated 1802, a lovely silver bowl—an ice cream basket—from Chuck's eighty-three-year-old grandmother which had been given to her as a wedding present. There was a very splendid-looking picture—a copy of a portrait of Chuck's great-grandfather Trenholm (he was Secretary of the Treasury of the Confederacy) —and a lovely old ruby-red wine decanter with prisms which make it look like a kaleidoscope from some member of the Robb family.

There was a practical and very necessary silver chest from Willie Day and Mildred Stegall, and all of Lynda's everyday china from Jesse Kellam, bless him. There were a few lonely pieces of crystal, and a dear and touching number of crocheted, tatted, or embroidered handkerchiefs from the general public. And blue garters and pot holders of every description, known and unknown. These general public gifts are to me among the sweetest ones received.

Joe Batson had had a breakfast service designed with all the characters of Winnie the Pooh romping around the plates and cups and saucers. Marny and Clark Clifford had given Lynda a bridge table with chairs. Angie and Robin Duke—a bright, gay, modern picture of houses climbing a hillside in Spain. And Bill and Mavis Heath had sent an elegant piece of silver that will make an heirloom for her great-granddaughter. Going over the presents was such fun!

We spent a happy hour, and then I went upstairs to the Lincoln Sitting Room where Stew Udall was joining me for a cup of tea and thirty minutes' talk. I asked Stew to give me a thumbnail sketch of what the Administration had achieved in the field of conservation, because I want to be as knowledgeable as possible when I summarize it. He's a very articulate man. He speaks well for a cause on which he feels deeply. First, he said, we have raised our sights. We have set our national goals to have a clean country. And we have passed the basic legislation to prevent air pollution and water pollution, though it may take years to implement it. Second, the Wilderness Bill—we have set aside between 2 and 3 percent of the acreage of this great country to be left in its natural state for all the generations to come to enjoy . . . for recreation, for breathing room. Third, a new concept of parks—a necklace of National Seashore Parks, such as Padre Island

and Assateague. Fourth—and here he gave a graceful compliment to me—a concept of beautification along the highways of the country and in the hearts of the cities—the real urban areas.

Then we launched into what our Committee could do—our Committee for a More Beautiful Capital—this coming year. One, he thought, we would have to face up to the fact that we couldn't get much more federal expansion, moneywise. Far from expanding what the Park Service was doing, we would do well if we could obtain maintenance for what they had already done. And so we would have to enlist the vigorous interest and activity of the business community, for one thing. And two, to try to activate the young folks—work with schools—make them a part of conservation and beautification.

Then it was time to get ready for the Boggs' party for Lynda and Chuck. Lynda Bird looked elegant and alluring, in black velvet with white collar and cuffs, her hair piled very high.

Luci, now living on a modest housewife's budget, had on last year's velvet costume with a fringy white blouse, and in her eyes I could see the yearning and the awareness of the difference between her looks and Lynda's. I am not sorry. I think it is good for her. She has so much that is wonderful, rich, and valuable.

I put on my white satin with the brilliants and the red velvet coat and sat with folded hands in Lyndon's office while he read the ticker and signed a big stack of mail. About 8:30 we left for the Boggs', giving each other a résumé along the way of everything we had done today. He seemed tired. McNamara's departure is taking its toll, along with everything else.

How many times we have walked through that maze of boxwood at the Boggs' house! We've seen it grow from ankle high to knee high, and now it's waist high on me. This is a warm, loving, family-type house—always crowded to the limit with the Boggs children and their friends, members of Congress, Louisianians. An easy, casual, happy place. Some of my best times in this town have been spent here. Hale and Lindy met us out front. And then we were inside, and no more press. There were the Boggs children, Tommy and his wife, Barbara and her husband, Cokie and her husband, and Hale's brother, Archy, and his wife, and between thirty and forty people.

In the dining room there were four tables. We were just as crowded, and just as happy, as we could be.

I sat between Hale and Mr. Robb and divided my time between genealogy and inquiring about the heirloom wedding gifts from the Robb side of the family, and hearing through my right ear the progress of legislation, the state of affairs on the Hill, while Lindy and Mrs. Robb—in the manner typical of Southerners—dug up some mutual kinfolk from South Carolina.

Dinner began with New Orleans shrimp remoulade—Lyndon couldn't wait. And then Louisiana wild roast duck with artichokes, Texas rice casserole, District of Columbia green beans, and all-American apple pie with Wisconsin cheese.

The toasts were the high point of the evening. Hale led off nostalgically, graciously. Amusingly, Lyndon and Chuck tried to rise at the same time. Chuck's toast was very manly, poised. You felt, "This is somebody." Lyndon's toast brought tears to my eyes. It contained all the sweetness of a real father. Mr. Robb made a toast that ended in a delightful rhyme.

Lyndon was really tired so we left early and on the way home in the car Lyndon went sound asleep.

Saturday, December 9

Today, Lynda's wedding day, began overcast and gray, though with the promise of the sun breaking through. I went to Lyndon's room early. It begins to sound more likely that he will be leaving for Texas right after the wedding. With the house still full of guests, I will stay on.

Jean Louis had set up a shop in the East Hall and there were several dryers and a screen and dressing table. He and two assistants were combing hair from 9 on. Sometime during this bedlam I had lunch in the Solarium —the last lunch of our busy house party! I went downstairs, calling on all reserves of calm, for a final look at the preparations for the wedding. The cake was gorgeous, and the flowers in the tent a bright profusion of pinks and reds and pale oranges. And on the tables, the most beautiful bouquets —an absolute triumph from the flower room—ranging from tenderest pink to deepest velvet red.

We called Chuck. Lyndon told him he wanted to give them their wedding present. Chuck came about 2 and I loved what he said to Lynda: "How is my little girl feeling?"

Lyndon and I and Chuck and Lynda went into the Queen's Room, past the gauntlet of bridesmaids—the last ones getting their hair combed—and quietly shut the door. Lyndon was full of tenderness and understanding. We gave them a U.S. Savings Bond as our wedding present.

And then the great wheels of order and convention began to roll. I went to get dressed and Lyndon went to get dressed. And a few minutes before 4, I took my place at the head of the stairs. Bess, still calm in all the tumult, was the major-domo, and at her signal I took White House Aide Brian Lamb's arm and walked down the stairs past the throngs of wedding guests in the entrance foyer and down the hall, to the masses in the East Room, my eyes locking for a moment in a message of love to this good friend and that kin-person, and some childhood friend of Lynda's.

I took my place behind the rope, close to Aunt Ellen who was seated, seeing Tony in the background behind me. I glimpsed Lyndon's sister, Rebekah—tall and handsome, her hat a mass of ostrich plumes—Sam Houston, Becky, and David. And across the way Chuck's grandmother, looking elegant and frail and sweet, was seated on the bench that we had provided.

I was glad that sometime in the unbelievable hours before the wedding I had gone up to the Robbs' room for a few minutes. I found Mrs. Sims, Chuck's grandmother, surrounded by daughters, grandchildren, and great-grandchildren and well taken care of. I wanted her to know that it was quite special for us to have her here—four generations of Robbs sharing in Chuck's wedding day.

The ceremony began on time, they tell me, with Pat Nugent and Joe Batson coming in first, and then the other groomsmen, and the velvet-clad bridesmaids. Lynda had been right all along—red was a stunning color! Each one looked perfectly beautiful. Luci, looking ethereal and very solemn, was the last to come in, taking her place in the semicircle in front of the altar. And all the time, Chuck, facing forward toward the door, looked firm, strong, and happy.

Then the Marine Band struck up the march from Lohengrin, "Here Comes the Bride." Every heart in the place lifted, I am sure, and there was a hushed expectant moment. And there at the door was Lynda on her daddy's arm. Beautiful as she was, it was Lyndon I watched all the way— such a mixture of tenderness and farewell in his look. His hair looked whiter than I have ever seen it, and I was full of tenderness for him.

How would one describe the bride? With a mother's license—queenly, radiant, stunningly beautiful—and the whole setting was in the grand manner. I have never seen a lovelier ceremony. My heart was a roaring tumult of pride, of desire to wring from this wonderful time every second of pleasure, living to the fullest this milestone of their lives.

The altar was a raised platform on which Canon McAllister, from our little St. Barnabas Church in Fredericksburg, stood, and behind him, the window blanked out, were the great masses of greens on which tiny white "bee" lights sparkled. A tall white cross gave the final symbolism of a religious ceremony.

Chuck's responses were firm and clearly spoken. Lynda's were much softer. When Canon McAllister asked, "Who gives this woman in marriage?" Lyndon answered, "Her mother and I," and a ripple of emotion, I thought, went through the crowd. And then he stepped back—I was grateful that he was careful of her train—and joined me behind the velvet rope.

I had been rather startled when I saw some tiny slits in the white fabric behind the altar, and two sets of eyes looking out on the room, and then what was obviously the business end of a camera! Actually, it was a great job of camouflage. And I remember how solicitous Luci was in arranging Lynda Bird's train, taking her flowers at the proper moment, offering the ring to Lynda for her to put on Chuck's finger.

In just twenty minutes, Reverend McAllister said, "You may kiss the bride now." Chuck leaned over with a big smile and kissed Lynda on the cheek, the Marine orchestra broke into Mendelssohn's "Wedding March," and she was on his arm, headed across the East Room and out under the arc of swords. But I never saw it. So I'm glad I had a chance to view the exit yesterday at the rehearsal.

Each red-velvet-clad bridesmaid on the arm of a groomsman went out. And finally, I followed, escorted by Brian Lamb again. Then taking Lyndon's arm, we went through the halls, this time relaxed and ready to be joyous. And up the stairs. It had all been glorious—perfect!

Lynda's wedding dress, designed by Geoffrey Beene, fulfilled every expectation. Long-sleeved, high-collared, white silk-satin, its front panel outlined in embroidered silk flowers with seed pearls, it was, indeed, regal. There was a Renaissance feeling about it, and I hope I live to see a granddaughter wear it! I am sure it will be just as beautiful then.

Lynda's wedding dress, of course, had been the "something new," and the little bow-knot pin that had been worn to a party where General Lafayette was the guest of honor, given to Lynda by Mrs. Hudspeth, was the "something old." (It had been sewn carefully inside.) Great-grandmother Ruth Ament Huffman's handmade handkerchief was the "something borrowed." And inside the hem of the dress, "Lynda Bird Johnson, December 9, 1967, The White House," was embroidered in blue.

As we mounted the stairs, I gave a fleeting thought to what must be the controlled pandemonium below. As soon as the aides could deferentially urge the wedding guests out of the East Room toward the State Dining Room and the pink tent, where champagne and the big buffet tables awaited them, they would lock the doors, open the windows onto the terrace, and carry out the altar. The Marine Band would melt away and Peter Duchin's orchestra would replace it; the screen would come down from in front of the cake; and tables for champagne and refreshments would blossom in the corners. What a job!

Upstairs, the wedding party assembled in the Yellow Room, from which all the furniture had been removed. There was a press pool and a vast array of cameras. They took pictures of every conceivable grouping—four of us, then six of us, and then all the party—twenty-one in all. In that last shot we stretched entirely across the Yellow Room—Lynda and Chuck underneath the portrait of George Washington, and next to him, his mother and his father, Lyndon standing beside Lynda, then I came and then Luci.

Bess, for the first time, was looking a little nervous. "No, you can't go down yet," she said. And I remembered what a jungle the Blue Room had been—with massed equipment for TV, and furniture waiting to be conveyed into the East Room. Now it was being readied for the receiving line. Finally Bess came and said, "They're ready." Down the six of us went to the Blue Room, Lyndon first in line, with Lynda beside him, and then Chuck, Chuck's mother and father, and I bringing up the end of the line— and the 640 or more guests began filing by.

A sizable number of VIP's were present, led off by the Vice President and Muriel, the Chief Justice and Mrs. Warren, Secretary of State and Virginia Rusk. Alice Roosevelt Longworth was among the first, and Lyndon gave her a big hug. She said, to my relief, very warm things about how beautiful the wedding had been. General Lewis Walt and General Wallace Greene and General Leonard Chapman were all there, along with every member of the Cabinet. Only fourteen Senators and their wives—especially close—had been invited. Senator Dirksen embraced every one of us and planted a large kiss on the ladies. The amazing thing was how many Ambassadors had come from afar: the Dukes from Spain, the Heaths from Sweden, the Eugene Lockes from Vietnam, and the George McGhees from Germany.

There was a sizable number of Robb relatives. I got a thumbnail sketch of each from Mr. Robb as they came down the line. And I in turn gave him a sketch of the Bobbitts and the Tony Taylors, Elaine Fischesser and Aunt Ellen. I could feel the press' antennae rise whenever any of Lynda's movie friends came along—elegant Merle Oberon and her interesting husband

Bruno Pagliai, Carol Channing, wearing outrageous yellow mini-bloomers that came to mid-thigh, with her nice husband Charles Lowe. And the Henry Fords and Charlotte Ford Niarchos were there, causing almost as much of a flurry.

There were plenty of old beaus: Mike Phenner and Dave Lefeve, John Loeb, Jr., and Paul Dresser, and George Hamilton who had rearranged a performance to come. And there were members of "The Four"—Lynda's crowd who had been friends at O'Henry Junior High in Austin—Julie Valentine, now Mrs. Carlos Puentes, and Kristine von Krisler, finishing up her Master's in California, and Pam Ward, now Mrs. Brian Maedger, a housewife and mother. There were friends from NCS, Jane Taylor and Jennifer Urquhart, Jill McKelvie and Jan Nichols, and a host of NCS teachers, beginning with Miss Lee.

And the tallest man in the room, John D. Rockefeller IV, with Sharon, demure and dainty at his side. Our old neighbors, Dr. and Mrs. O. E. Reed from Thirtieth Place, were beaming.

About 7:15 the last guest went down the line. Then the six of us went into the East Room where Lyndon and I and Chuck and Lynda walked up on the platform where the cake was enthroned. Chuck's sword was brought and with their two hands on the handle, they cut the first piece. This Lynda shared with Chuck. Then Lynda took the sword and cut another big slice, and I had a bite of it—absolutely delicious pound cake with white raisins and a trace of rum and luscious white icing.

Then in a swirl, so that I do not remember who danced with whom first, there was Lynda and Chuck, and Lynda and her daddy, and I with Mr. Robb. Lyndon cut in on me, and with a big smile he said, "You sure have made progress from that purple dress." (He was referring to our wedding—at least three times today, and always laughingly, he has spoken of our own so-different ceremony.)

The bridesmaids and groomsmen were dancing and then it was no time until I heard a flurry of excitement, and people were saying, "She's about to throw her bouquet!" I was in the Green Room, and I couldn't possibly make my way to where I could really see her—standing on the landing of the great stairs. Behind a sea of backs, I heard the rising ripple of excitement as Lynda threw her bouquet and Warrie Lynn caught it.

Then she was off upstairs, and that was the last that the wedding guests saw of her. I found Mrs. Hudspeth and sat with her on the sofa in the Green Room—Daniel Webster's own sofa—and we had a loving talk about Lynda, who is as dear as a daughter to her. I asked Diana to take charge of getting the kinfolks up on the second floor after the crowd began to thin out. And I circled through the Red Room, the State Dining Room, the Blue Room, the Main Hall, visiting with everybody and trying to absorb every minute of it to remember. Somehow I never got to the tent.

There were two guests whom I had studiously tried to prevent from coming to this wedding. Yuki, I didn't want to come at all. But he made his appearance when we had gathered in the Yellow Room upstairs to have our pictures made, wearing a bright red blanket on which "Congratulations" was spelled out in sequins. (Liz has often said that Mr. Bryant ought to be an assistant press man. He gets Yuki ready and in on every occasion.) The other guest was an unwitting one—little Patrick Lyn. We had conspired—Luci and Pat and I—to see that he did not make his appearance until after Lynda had tossed her bouquet and gone. Both of them came to me frantically and separately, immediately after the cake cutting, to say that the President was asking for Lyn. I advised them to go in another direction and make no answer. But, alas, Lyndon won, and Patrick Lyndon came down for a brief visit, during which, I am told, he stood on the piano and walked, with some assistance. He was promptly whisked away by Luci, but returned again, brought back by his grandfather after the bride had thrown her bouquet. This time he visited around with everyone, looking very proper in his black suit with the little white stripe in the pants, until he went to sleep with his head on his grandfather's shoulder.

At a quarter of 9 Lyndon left from the South grounds, taking Luci and Pat and Lyn and a helicopter full of guests. Others had gone on ahead to *Air Force One* at Andrews and headed for Texas.

Downstairs the young folks were taking over. It was 9 and everybody was dancing. Back upstairs where the kinfolks were gathered, I saw Lynda coming down the hall, calm and contained, in a beautiful geranium red coat-dress with a striped scarf. Patsy slipped some rice in my hand. I gave Lynda and Chuck one loving farewell kiss. She spoke a word or two to the relatives and we showered them with rice. Then the elevator swallowed them up and they were gone.

She had looked pensive, as if she were already far away from us.

It was 11:30 when I said good-by to the last of the kinfolks and was almost alone in the house. And so this great day in my life slipped into history.

Today was a romantic, offbeat day. I woke a little before 9, asked for all the papers and a big pot of coffee, and leisurely read and read and read— reliving every moment of the wedding day.

And then I went to the little cupboard in my office-sitting room, and from the green metal box I took out the packet of letters tied with a red ribbon, Lyndon's letters to me beginning in early September 1934 and on up to about eight days before our wedding on November 17, 1934. There were a few letters on top as late as 1939. In roughly chronological order I began to read them until I felt immersed in those autumn days of 1934 when I had been doing over the Brick House, with all of my days and half of my mind, and with the other half trying to decide whether to marry Lyndon, while we wrote and he telephoned and we headed toward marriage. It was a strangely sweet experience, and the young Lyndon and the young Lady Bird were quite real and very close.

I did not get up until 3 in the afternoon! Then I dressed to go to Diana's party. Tony and Matiana came, and we went downstairs with Willie Day to see the wedding gifts. Tony had brought Lynda Bird a silver bowl with a grape pattern around the border. It had belonged to Mother and had been at the Brick House in my childhood.

It was nearly 5 before we left, and I had meant to be at Diana Mac-Arthur's party for the kinfolks at the stroke of 4. It was going full blast, and was one of the most relaxed and satisfying parties I've been to in a long time, partly because I was still glowing from that sensation of obligation finished—job accomplished.

I had told the White House staff that no one would be home for supper, so I heartily partook of Diana's refreshments, and went home alone a little past 7 to walk slowly through the first floor of the White House. Already, the wedding was relegated to history. A sixteen-foot spruce Christmas tree—beautifully shaped—was in place—Dan Arje will be decorating it all day tomorrow. And the crèche was beginning to be set up.

There was a strange addendum to this peculiar, tender day. I came wide awake about 4 in the morning and decided I was hungry. I went to the refrigerator and found some sandwiches and a bowl of Waldorf salad left over from our family dinner after the wedding, and some cookies and a glass of milk. These I took back to bed and got out the other packet of letters—those that I had written to Lyndon. I do not remember how they came into my possession. I suppose after we had married he said, "I've saved these—you keep them," or something like that. But there they were in the metal box, tied with a blue ribbon. I read them all, every one, ate my strange, middle-of-the-night meal, felt the sense of the lonely White House around me. I felt that I was slipping back in time to the fall of 1934. I remembered everything about the Brick House and what I had been doing—refinishing furniture, re-covering it, working with an architect in Shreveport, refinishing the floors, painting, planning for the planting of trees and shrubs later in the fall. I have never lived in any house as long as I lived in the Brick House—twenty-one years. And it was easy to feel that I was back there. A few outside activities—visiting with Dorris Powell, going to the Little Theater in Shreveport, the trip to Dallas to a football game, to see Gene Lasseter or Emily Crow, and the excitement of Lyndon mounting with every letter.

I closed the box—all finished—about 6 A.M. and drifted off to a half-sleep, ending one of the strangest, most off-key, but most satisfying days I've lived here in the White House.

Sunday, December 24

Christmas Eve 1967! Certainly there will never in my life be another Christmas Eve like this. I had asked the operator to wake me about 4:15 A.M. I phoned to see if Lyndon was on schedule. He was due about 4:45.

I slipped downstairs at 4:30. Lynda was already there. She had let Chuck sleep because he had a cold. Luci and Patrick were also there. We had been told when the plane touched down at Andrews and about 5 the helicopters settled to the ground on the White House lawn. The fastest, longest, hardest trip any President of the United States had ever taken was at an end.

We all rushed out and took turns hugging and kissing him. He was buoyed up on a wave of excitement. A few hours later, when I read the Sunday paper, there was the map of the world, his path in arrows, and headlines from around the world. "Lyndon B. Johnson has become the first American President ever to travel around the world while in office." He circumnavigated the globe in four and one-half days!

The trip had begun on Tuesday noon as a mission to attend memorial services for his friend and supporter, the late Prime Minister Harold Holt of Australia, but he went on to visit Thailand and South Vietnam, to a conference in Karachi with Pakistan's President Mohamed Ayub Khan, and ended with the late-night meetings in Rome. He had been in the air sixty and one-half hours and had covered twenty-seven thousand three hundred miles. There were two hundred members of the party (two of them had had heart attacks), and the last long day had begun in Thailand before sunup and ended over the Atlantic on the way to Washington.

We went up to Lyndon's room, but it was impossible to go to bed so we sat around and talked and talked about the trip for nearly two hours while Lyndon had his tea. We discussed the family of Harold Holt, who would succeed him, Ambassador Ed Clark, the stop in Vietnam, the surprise—at least to me—visit with Ayub Khan, our old friend, and much, much about the Pope, partly because of Luci's and Pat's presence and partly because the Pope interested Lyndon. (It always intrigues me—this unlikely affinity of interest in many successive Popes on the part of this Protestant Texas politician.)

Lyndon was riding high. The trip satisfied a deep inbred desire to show his respect and friendship for a dead friend, Harold Holt, and he hoped by his presence in Vietnam to give evidence of his special feeling as Commander-in-Chief for those troops, and he had made one further effort toward peace by meeting with the Pope.

He had brought us all presents. We looked at some of them and then just a few minutes before 7, Luci and Pat said they were going to Mass and he said, "I'll go with you." I was not about to get dressed, so in the reverse order of what seemed fitting, he went out to church with the children and I went back to bed. I woke up about 10 and Lyndon had gone to his office.

In the afternoon Harry McPherson, the Valentis, and Secretary Rusk came in. Lyndon worked on the résumé of his trip, combined with a Christmas message to the nation, which was televised in the theater, and then all of the photographers trouped up to the second floor. We had Christmas pictures in front of our Christmas tree in the Yellow Oval Room, with Patrick Lyndon and Yuki, and standing by our red velvet Christmas stockings that hang on the mantel below George Washington's portrait.

The feeling that pervaded the whole day was that familiar one that always happens—no matter how much the preparation or organization or planning—during the twenty-four hours before the Christmas tree, only this time it was all concentrated into even fewer hours—that overpowering feeling on Lyndon's part that he must remember *everybody*—gifts, gifts, and more gifts! He was sending Marie scurrying in all directions to wrap additional packages. Ashton had come down, and Lyndon was checking out the clothes with her that he had bought for "his girls"—me, Lynda, Luci, Marie, Juanita, Mary Slater. And no sooner does he present one than he has to see it modeled at once, and he is absolutely delighted if it looks pretty and the recipient likes it. We decided to have the Christmas tree just before dinner, and all was in readiness, packages piled high.

About 6 o'clock we were gathered—the family and Marie Fehmer, solicitously watching over Lyndon's pile of gifts with her pad and pencil, to make notes on proper "thank-you's." Lyndon always appoints himself Santa Claus, but he likes to see the work go fast so he called on Patrick to help him. (More and more Patrick just naturally moves as his companion and helper and I watch this with pleasure.) Of course, all eyes were on Lyn to see how he would like the tree and the toys. As a matter of fact, he liked anything he could get in his mouth and he was not particularly interested in the tree.

Lyndon gave me a yellow wool dress and jacket which fit beautifully, and Lynda and Chuck gave us a beautiful album of their wedding pictures, and Luci with a funny verse told me that their gift couldn't possibly be brought to Washington and I would have to wait until I got to the Ranch to see it and if it didn't turn out to be a cherished gift, she hoped it would at least be a family joke! (Luci and Pat's gift turned out to be a corner of a pasture at the Ranch, seeded with wildflowers, marked by a large granite stone with a sentimental thought engraved on it.)

There was an envelope of Savings Bonds from Lyndon, but, alas, the many good things that we get to eat year after year from old friends—the pecans, dates, candy and smoked turkey and grapefruit—some friends have been doing this for twenty years—we no longer receive. We just get the notice that edibles have been received and we write a nice thank-you letter. The Secret Service, in performance of duty, destroys the food. I cannot blame them. I can only bewail the waste. Occasionally something is sent to Ashton Gonella and she brings it in her own hands to the kitchen and we do get to eat it.

We unwrapped presents, and exclaimed, and showed, and thanked and kissed and sank knee deep in tissue paper and bright colored wrappings and ribbons. It was after 8 o'clock when everybody was finished, though I still had a bench piled high with gifts. We went in to dinner, all the family including Sam Houston and Marie. Luci gave a full and beautiful blessing and our Christmas reached its peak.

BOOK FIVE
1968-1969

Winter 1968

The world is shrouded in a gray cloak—weather fit only to "sit by the fire and tell tales." We spent nearly all day in the Austin office, Lyndon on staff talks with Sarge Shriver, Charlie Schultze, and Charles Zwick. At this season of the year it is especially difficult. The head of every department, who naturally is an advocate for his own work and programs, puts his needs before the President. But Lyndon—alas—has the hard job of finding where the money is to come from and evaluating each program with everything else. The budget must be slashed, and saying "No" is an exhausting, draining business. I am going to miss Charlie Schultze—he's both capable and fun—when he leaves the heavy, tough job with the budget. It looks as if Charles Zwick will take his place.

We drove back to the Ranch, with John and Nellie, through pea soup fog. After dinner we went back to Lyndon's bedroom—the four of us—and talked without interruption for nearly three hours. John said, "You ought to run only if you look forward to being President again—only if you *want* to do it." I think he meant Lyndon ought to run if he could find an element of joy in the work, but he ought not to run if the frustrations, the pain, the backbreaking work made him dread it. "You also ought not to run just to keep somebody else from being President."

One of the most lucid and interesting observations was made by Nellie who said, "You will probably find, after you've made the decision—if you decide not to run—that there is sort of an ephemeral period when you feel as if everything has stopped. You are sad. You almost feel like you are dead. And then when that time passes there is a great wave of relief." Looking at John, I could see no hint, no likelihood that he will reconsider his decision and run again for Governor, as some of the columnists in Texas are saying.

Lyndon spoke of the simple fact that he feels older and more tired than he did ten years ago, or five years ago. And what of the next five years? Suppose he runs and wins? Would he be able to carry the load in a way that he would be proud of and that the country deserves? For all of those years, always in the background there is the lowering shadow of nuclear power. Sometime, somewhere, will he have to make a decision about nuclear warfare? Yet, if he chooses to withdraw, what will history say of him? What will his friends and those close to him who believe in him say of him? What will the soldiers in Vietnam say of him? We spoke of the possibility of announcing the decision at the end of the State of the Union Message. But that, of course, would negate the whole message. John made one grim statement that went something like this: "The only way to answer all of those arguments is to die in office."

I got some insight into the reactions of the very strong and good couple who have faced a similar problem and made their own decision. Theirs was to get out. And I, as a citizen, cannot help feeling sad and regretful that they did. But for them there is certainly a measure of personal happiness in it. Who knows, who knows—and so we went round and round on the same hot griddle, finding no cool oasis, no definite time for an acceptable exit.

The day of the Israeli visit dawned cloudy and cold. We had a fairly early lunch today, after which Luci and Pat were supposed to leave. Lyndon simply couldn't bear to see them go, so I said, "Move the baby's bed down to my room and you can make it your headquarters," which would permit them to drive home after they had greeted Prime Minister Levi Eshkol and his wife.

A little past 3, dressed as warmly as I could in a bright red ensemble with an extra sweater, I flew in with Lyndon and Dean Rusk in the *Jetstar* to San Antonio. A sizable crowd had braved the bitter cold. There were the platform and long red carpet and a welcoming line, in which I saw Mayor McAllister, his son, Reverend McAllister (who had married Lynda and Chuck), Congressman Henry B. Gonzalez, Congressman Abraham Kazen, and quite a group of city officials, including Dan Quill, the Postmaster.

The great plane rolled up in front of us and we stood at the foot and down came short, stocky, craggy-faced Prime Minister Eshkol and his young chipper wife. I remember distinctly when I had first met her on the platform at the arrival ceremonies in Washington, and we had both flinched at the noise of the twenty-one-gun salute, she had told me she had been a sergeant in the Israeli Army. She had confided that she had been more afraid of her gun at the time than of the Arabs! It's not often that you meet a First Lady who has been a sergeant. She is thirty-four years younger than Prime Minister Eshkol, she told me a little later. She is very solicitous and tender with him.

Lyndon made a brief welcoming speech, flowers were presented to each of us, and the Prime Minister responded. There were a few signs in Hebrew, a small but eager crowd surged around him, and there, inevitably, was our old friend, Jim Novy. And then it was over and we were off, Lyndon taking the Prime Minister in the *Jetstar* and I convoying Mrs. Eshkol and Mrs. Avraham Harman, wife of the Israeli Ambassador, Mrs. Ephraim Evron, and two or three more Israelis in the helicopter.

We arrived at the Ranch about 4:30. Lyndon already had the Prime Minister out in the car showing him the deer. I settled them in their rooms and then we decided to ride around. I drove—just the four of us in the car alone—which seemed to impress them. They found many points of comparison between our terrain and Israel's. The live oaks reminded them of olive trees; the goats and the sheep were very familiar sights. I asked them about the reforestation of Israel. I had heard so much about it. (I think Lyndon has a forest named after him in Israel!) What sort of trees did they grow? Were they used for timber crop? They told me the trees were used principally for soil conservation—to keep the earth from blowing away. They had begun by planting eucalyptus; now mostly they plant a species of pine that can survive the lack of rain. The next day one of the gentlemen added another reason for planting trees—"to make the land green," to make it look pleasing instead of like a wasteland. I had thought of them as so intensely practical. Now this is a poet's reason.

We went to Lyndon's boyhood home where Jessie Hunter met us at the back door and we went through the house with many explanations and eager interest expressed. They were delightful guests. Dark overtook us before we started back to the Ranch. The fog that had been with us for the last six days returned.

When we got home, lo and behold, there were Luci and Pat and the baby. They explained that they had left for Austin and had just driven across the dam when Lyndon called and invited them back. He said, "Why don't you sleep in your mother's room and she can move in with me?" That is what we arranged, and Lyn got to eat his first State Dinner! Of course, at six and one-half months he had been present at other State Dinners, but this was the first one he *ate*. He was not with us at the table but had the same menu—breast of pheasant and vegetables.

We had found a chef Mary knew and could vouch for as a cook of kosher food, but I had gone to the kitchen one moment before dinner to see a luscious fruit plate being concocted by Mary. One of the gentlemen, we had discovered, didn't eat meat at all!

The Prime Minister was amiable, but the dinner conversation was weighty and I was grateful to have Luke Battle, the Assistant Secretary for Near Eastern and South Asian Affairs, on his other side. He was a great help. After all these years in Washington this was the smallest and most informal visit of a Chief of State we have ever had and, for that reason, unusually pleasant. I am sure for the men the meetings must have been heavy work because of the problems in the Middle East . . . planes, refugees, boundaries . . . It's so much easier being a woman!

I asked the Prime Minister to sign my menu, which he did in both Hebrew and English. Their gifts were absolutely thrilling! They had brought me a collection of artifacts, two of them dating back a thousand years before Christ, and some attractive jewelry—made, Mrs. Eshkol told me, from polished pebbles found on the beaches. Most delightful of all

1968–1969

President and Mrs. Johnson walking along the White House driveway. LBJ Library Photo by Mike Geissinger, B2305-8.

ABOVE: *Lucinda Desha Robb and her mother. LBJ Library Photo by Yoichi Okamoto, A7530-18a.*
RIGHT: *The First Family opens gifts on Christmas Eve in the Yellow Oval Room. LBJ Library Photo by Jack Kightlinger, B2899-15.*

RIGHT: *As Lyn boards the Presidential helicopter, a sergeant stands at attention.* LBJ Library Photo by Yoichi Okamoto, D2336-10a.
BELOW: *Inside Air Force One with some proud kinfolks.* LBJ Library Photo by Yoichi Okamoto, A5720-9.

The Cabinet wives gather for a formal portrait in the Yellow Oval Room,
January 10, l. to r.: Mrs. Alan Boyd, Mrs. Stewart Udall, Mrs. Willard
Wirtz, Mrs. Orville Freeman, Mrs. Dean Rusk, Mrs. Johnson,
Mrs. Hubert Humphrey, Mrs. Marvin Watson, Mrs. Clark Clifford,
Mrs. Wilbur Cohen (standing), Mrs. Ramsey Clark, Mrs. Henry Fowler.
LBJ Library Photo by Yoichi Okamoto, D3026-3.

FACING: *Austin, Texas, January 20. LBJ Library
Photo by Frank Wolfe, B3121-31.*

OVERLEAF: *The Redwoods. LBJ Library
Photo by Robert Knudsen, D2624-7a.*

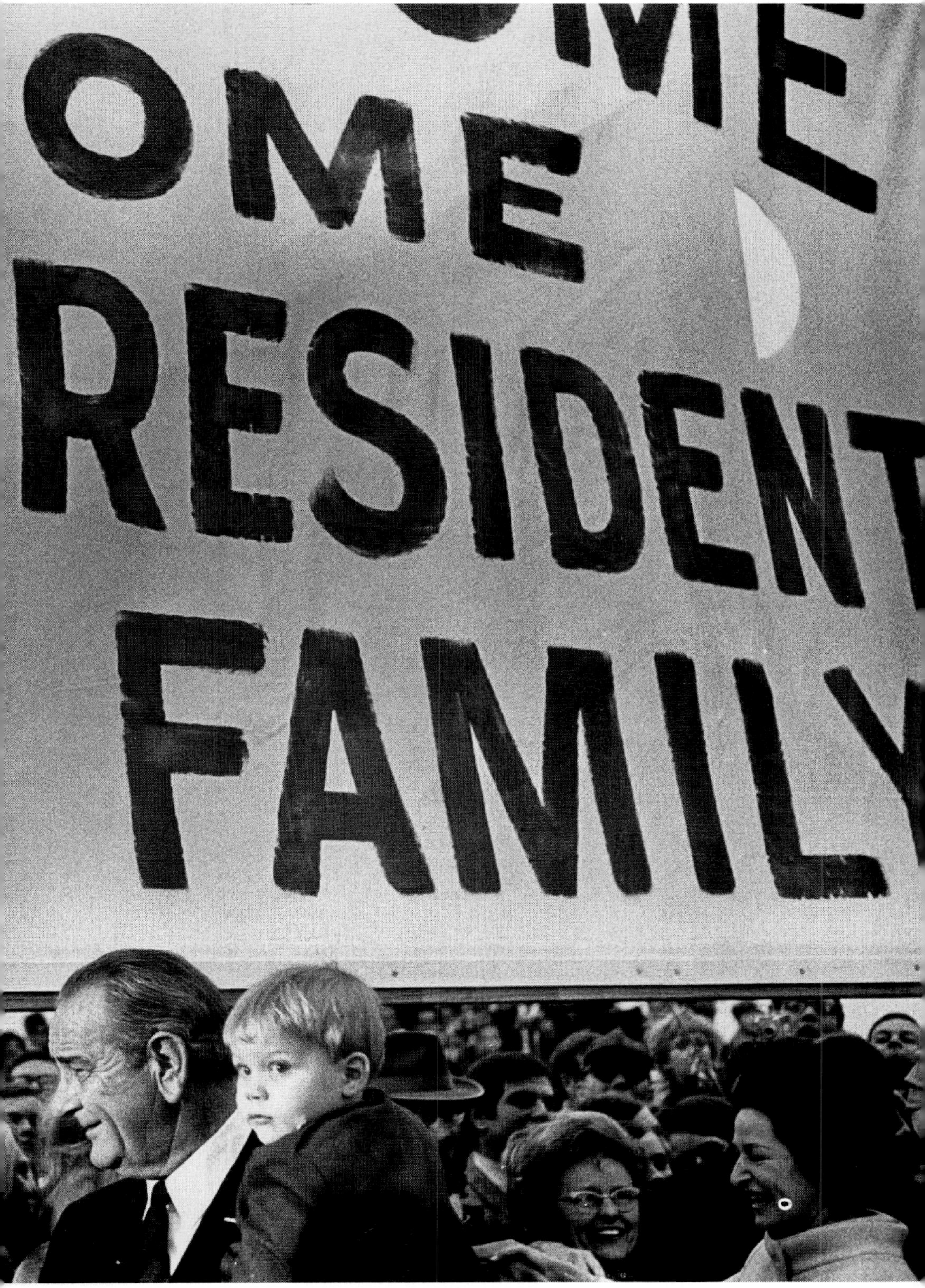
OME
RESIDEN
FAMIL

was a Noah's Ark for Patrick Lyndon—a large, hand-carved ark, with a droll Noah whose expression seemed to say, "Why did I ever get into this?" and a lion, tiger, elephant, crocodile, sticking their heads out of the portholes and other animals, two by two, arranged across the deck.

Shortly after dinner I stood up in front of the fireplace—the fire was now a cheery mass of coals—and introduced Jimmy Symington, who played a mixture of Jewish songs and American folk songs for us. This music was just right, I thought, a low-key, personal, warm sort of entertainment that maintained the intimate atmosphere of the day.

Monday, January 15

THE WHITE HOUSE

I spent this morning with Liz and Bess and Ashton, going over innumerable invitations, reading a proposal Liz had provided about the best trips to take, what groups to see, how to best spend my time. I signed an enormous stack of mail.

At 3:30 Lyndon was having lunch with George Christian and I joined them. I mildly reproached him for such a late lunch hour and he said something rather plaintive. "I have been in a hurry all of my life. I have never had time to stay in one place as long as I like. I've always been fighting an uphill fight." I could understand his mood so well, because I knew that his mind was lashed, as though to a Siamese twin, to that inescapable problem of: "How and when do I face up to running again or getting out?"

At 5 John Walker came to see me and we had tea in the Lincoln Sitting Room, in front of the fire. We talked about ways to make my interview with Barbara Walters on TV on art in the White House mean more. Simone was with us. I talked about the feeling I had for all of the paintings, the direction I thought the show should take to let the country know that acquiring works of art was an ongoing program and would last, like the White House, as long as this country and this Mansion lasts.

I went to the swimming pool for thirty laps. It was 10 o'clock when Lyndon came home for dinner, and thus typical of our Washington nights.

The day of the State of the Union address is always one of such tenseness for me, out of proportion to any responsibility that I have for it. Lyndon spent much of the morning reading the supposedly final draft—I think it was the eleventh version—of his State of the Union speech.

Lyndon had asked George Christian to draft a statement based on what Lyndon had said to him, announcing that he would not run. I believe it was around noon when George brought his draft of it in, his face calm, unrevealing, as it always is. He had written a good statement, very well said. My own draft, which Lyndon had asked me to produce, seemed feeble to me. And if there was ever anything we ought to say with clarity and strength—with words that have wings and fire—this was it.

I had the statement I wrote in August 1964 when Lyndon was facing going to Atlantic City and did not want to go. It was still in the right-hand drawer of my desk in my bedroom. I brought that out and we reread what I had said then and George read it. It sounded better now!

The announcement was not to be included in the text of the State of the Union Message. If Lyndon decided to make it, the statement would come at the end, beginning with a line something like this: "And now I want to speak to you about a personal matter . . ." He keeps looking from one to the other of us—those close to him—for an answer. But there isn't any answer . . . there is nobody who can decide but him.

This afternoon Laurance Rockefeller, Brooke Astor, and I made a quick call at Buchanan School, which the Astor Foundation is converting into a combination school playground and community center. Then back to the White House and upstairs to take off our galoshes and go to the Red Room for the first meeting of 1968, beginning our fourth year of the work of the Beautification Committee.

I suggested that it was a time to look back on what we had done for the last three years and forward to what we ought to do this year. What did each of them think ought to be our aim? Where should we put our energies . . . our usefulness . . . our money? I gave them the happy news that Mrs. Merriweather Post, since our last meeting, had sent us a check for street trees. I asked Stew to report on Larry Halprin's suggestions for Washington. The report was full of the opportunities and potentials, but all costing money.

We discussed trying to use Arbor Day as a vehicle to increase interest in tree projects and to spread contributions over a wider base—to reach people who might be able to contribute five dollars but couldn't afford to give five thousand, appealing to Washington citizens who love their tree-shaded streets. We came out loud and strong for one more trash pickup a week, if the budget could bear it, and for more trash containers. I felt cruel even mentioning this subject, because when I looked at Walter Washington, he looked practically pale. We talked about our work with the schools, especially Buchanan. We talked for two solid hours and it was a good meeting.

I knew that today Lyndon was meeting the Democratic leaders and the Republican leaders by turn. I seldom interrupt such meetings, but I had the statement in my keeping and I held it like a coal of fire—the draft by George Christian announcing that Lyndon was not going to run again. I wanted to get it back into Lyndon's pocket, so I took it over.

It was about 6:30 P.M. He was rushed. Standing in the door between the big oval office and his little one, he said, "Well, what do you think? What shall I do?"

I looked at him with that helpless feeling and said: "Luci hopes you won't run. She wants you for herself and for Lyn and all of us. She does not want to give you up. Lynda hopes you *will* run. She told me so this afternoon, with a sort of terrible earnestness, because her husband is going to war and she thinks there will be a better chance of getting him back alive and the war settled if you are President. Me—I don't know. I have said it all before. I can't tell you what to do."

This could hardly be called a conversation . . . just a few phrases with the knowledge always that the Fish Room, a few feet away, was full of important Congressional leaders waiting for him; and with the Secret Service and the staff just—I hope—out of earshot through the door. I had said it so often before—I had not the will and it was not the place to say it again. "One, either you make a conscious decision to run, in the same state of mind of a man who is becoming a monk, or some such vocation, giving up your life and saying: 'Here it is, I will take whatever comes. I will try to pace the stretch and keep my sense of humor for the next five years.' Or, two, you simply make the announcement that you won't run at a time and in words only you can choose, but as strong and as beautiful as you are capable of."

Lyndon handed me a piece of paper, a letter from John Connally with his recommendations that he go with the statement tonight, because he would never have a bigger audience, and John thought making the statement before a live audience would be better than announcing it only on

TV or in the papers. John felt this would remove the decision from a political context, as we all know things are on a bit of an upward slope now. I think what John really meant was that the occasion of the State of the Union was a noble time to make the announcement. Lyndon had to weigh this against the fact that the whole 1968 program of action would thereby be diluted, if not completely ignored.

I went back to the second floor and put on my red suit with the navy trim. Lynda was wearing the lovely navy blue dress with the white buttons her daddy had given her for Christmas. I studied the description of my guests for the evening for the last time and went over the seating chart. A few minutes past 8 I went down to the library.

Choosing the guests for the State of the Union is always important. This year I had decided to honor some of the people who had implemented the programs of Lyndon's Administration. This turned out to be a thrilling experience. They were all in the library—Sarabeth Walker, a twenty-four-year-old Oklahomian—a VISTA worker; Susan Helmuth, from a small town in New York, who is a member of the Teachers Corps in the Washington schools, teaching remedial reading; Paul Millner, seventeen, from the Job Corps in Washington, whose high IQ has resulted in his being selected as college potential; Specialist Lawrence Joel, a stocky, middle-aged, smiling Negro from Fort Bragg, North Carolina, who had received the Medal of Honor from Lyndon in one of the most touching citations I had ever read. He was a Medic and, although twice wounded, he had gone on and on and on to save life after life, crawling across the battlefield with his plasma and his medicines. They were all so full of enthusiasm and easy to talk to.

I tried to describe, on the way to the Capitol, what a dramatic evening this was, how the House and Senate would already be in their seats and then, after a stentorian announcement by Fishbait Miller, the Diplomatic Corps would walk in, and then the President's Cabinet, and finally the President. My guests were escorted two by two to their seats, including Walter and Bennetta Washington and some staff wives, and then Lynda and Chuck and I walked in. I paused and stood for a moment as Senators and Congressmen rose from their seats with a swelling roar of applause— I know it is just part of the drama, part of the excitement of being back on the Hill, but I savored it.

When Fishbait Miller announced, "The President of the United States!" Lyndon came in to a thundering applause which lasted three minutes. There was a different atmosphere from last year. He looked wonderful.

The fifteen pounds he has lost are all to the good, and I like his hair a little bit longer and not slicked down. The speech—and there were changes even in the eleventh draft—lasted forty-nine minutes. There were about fifty applauses. By all odds the most spontaneous and loudest one came when he said, "The American people have had enough of rising crime and lawlessness." One of the changes was an insertion on conservation about continuing to work for highway beautification. I would not have sought it for the world but I appreciated it.

Somewhere in the speech the teleprompter failed. I could tell, though I am not sure that many people in the audience could. I could see him leafing through three or four pages of the text in front of him while he interpolated—I thought it was gracefully done. A time or two he added a few adjectives that I would have left off. I liked the spare bones better.

As he approached the end, I tightened up in my seat. Would he end with his statement? Did I want him to? Would I be relieved if he did, or if he didn't? He ended on a strong high note and there was a great roar of applause. He turned and walked down the steps. In a moment or two I rose to follow, and joined him for the ritual visit to the Speaker's office— and here was where I began to wonder if I had been off the beam.

I had felt a surge of optimism in the Chamber, had listened to a roar of applause, but here, with the Cabinet members, with the Congressional Leadership, there was no rush forward to say, "That was a great speech, Mr. President. We'll get to work on the agenda. It is going to be hard, but we'll make it a good year." The first maggots of doubt began to gnaw at the good feeling I had.

Then we were back in the car and headed for the White House—as many of us as could pile in. I rode with Lyndon. Upstairs on the second floor, we began to assemble. I had asked close friends and the staff to drop by for drinks and a buffet, the TV show, and a general rehash which always takes place after a State of the Union Message.

There was a good buffet in the dining room. I settled down with a drink in my bedroom, because it was the only place we could get the NET show, and it was a lively one. The room was full. There were about fifteen of us in there watching it and there was support from an unexpected quarter, panelists Edwin Reischauer and Patrick Moynihan, and the most amusing remarks by William Buckley. I heard Bill Moyers for just a moment, speaking rather well I thought. Arthur Schlesinger was so bitter I found him funny. The new Mayor of Cleveland, Carl Stokes, was reasonable and articulate and mostly fair, but of course there is never enough money for urban affairs for the Mayors who need it and that accounts for criticism. All in all, it was an amusing and entertaining program and I thought we won more than we lost.

Lyndon, in his bedroom, was busy looking at other networks with a few of the guests. The hall was full and people drifted into the dining room. We had a fire lighted in the Yellow Room for anyone who wanted comfort and quiet conversation. There was an air of elation, good will, relief—a bright, short draught of the wine of success which we had tasted in 1964 and 1965—or so I evaluated it.

Thursday, January 18

If we tasted the wine of success last night, it was indeed a brief draught. As we looked over the press reports on the State of the Union Message—at least in the Eastern metropolitan papers—they were largely negative or unenthusiastic. This was like working very hard, putting out all you've got, settling back to hear the verdict, and then finding your efforts were not good enough.

This morning I went over my guest list for the first Women Doers' Luncheon of the year—our subject, "Crime in the Streets." The idea has been itching in the back of my mind for a long time, and recently I accepted the invitation to be a member of the National Emergency Committee of the National Council on Crime and Delinquency. Our guest list was a very good one, with many women leaders concerned with anticrime efforts—quite a few presidents of influential organizations.

At a quarter of one I went down to the Green Room for photographs with the panel of three speakers. After the receiving line, we assembled in the Blue Room where sherry and orange juice were passed. A few of the guests had been late and some of the staff ushered them up to speak to me—Eartha Kitt among them—there was a picture of her and Miss Katherine Peden with me. We went into the family dining room for lunch, quite a delicious lunch, I thought, a little on the sumptuous side—seafood bisque, chicken, and peppermint ice cream. But alas, I couldn't enjoy it, because I don't ever like to be the one who has the chief burden of the speaking.

I welcomed the guests by saying that crime was a grim subject for a pleasant meeting such as this, but I believed every thinking citizen was increasingly determined to come to grips with it. None of us who read or hear the news can escape the shock of the headlines. I said, "The most shocking fact to me is the incredible number of cases where cries for help go unheeded. The myriad of crimes know no safe neighborhood nor income level. The existence of crime and the fear of it have eroded the quality of all of our lives."

Then I got to the gist of the meeting—why we were there. "Within the limits of each of us, there is something constructive that we can do, and there are things responsible citizens *are* doing in crime control and prevention and legislation. Three women are here to tell us the way they see the problems, from where they live and work and what they are doing about it." First, I introduced Margaret Moore who, six years ago, had started a crusade in Indianapolis beginning with just thirty friends and now involving fifty thousand women. She talked rapidly, at ease, with zeal, and advanced many fresh ideas. She recommended a lighting survey of the city streets. In her city, over a period of six years, they had obtained nine thousand new lights on the darkest streets in town. They had been active in bringing the youngest and most articulate policemen into the schoolrooms—not to the auditorium for a big lecture, but into the classrooms—to talk to groups of thirty or forty junior high or senior high school students, in an effort to bridge the gap between them and the law. The ladies sat in on Court sessions and accompanied the police on their beats, and they were supporting higher wages and better training and pensions for the police. They had undertaken a campaign of helping dropouts, one by one, finding Saturday or Sunday jobs for them, rounding up clothes. That was their approach. I liked the hopeful "can-do" tone of it.

The second speaker was Martha Coe, a VISTA worker in the slums of Atlanta, who recruited volunteers for nine Head Start centers. She looked young and fresh, well scrubbed and enthusiastic. To me the remarkable thing about her and many like her is that they walk out of their comfortable lives and barge head first—unafraid apparently—into the problems of the ghettos, learning about them firsthand by working with the people.

A few minutes earlier, when Mrs. Moore was speaking, suddenly Liz had risen and said, "Mrs. Moore, will you yield to another speaker?" And in had walked Lyndon. He spoke briefly, calling for greater support of police and saying the place to start combating crime was in the home. And then he gave a salute to the power of women and assured them they *could* do something about crime. He closed by saying that when he thinks of tenacity he thinks of women.

As Lyndon turned to leave Miss Eartha Kitt, who had been seated at a table close to the podium, rose in his path and said, "Mr. President, what do you do about delinquent parents—those who have to work and are too busy to look after their children?" Lyndon told her, "We have just passed a Social Security Bill that allots millions of dollars for day-care centers." She moved, I think, a step more in front of him. "But what are we going to do?" she said. "That's something for you women to discuss here," Lyndon replied; then turned and walked briskly out.

Miss Kitt sat down, stubbed out a cigarette, tossing her long hair, and from then on I watched her, expecting something—I didn't know what. Apparently she did not eat, nor did she applaud any of the speakers. She smoldered and smoked. The last speaker was Katherine Peden, one of the eleven members of the Advisory Commission on Civil Disorders who had listened to numerous witnesses on the subject of what to do about crime, from the militants to the authorities. She was a good speaker.

When she finished I asked the guests for their observations and discussions, and Judge Caroline Simon, who had been on my right, was the first up. There were several more. I noticed Miss Kitt's hand go up and I knew I must, in turn, get to her. I did not know what to expect—only I sensed that she had come to say something and that it would not be good. When some speaker finished I nodded to her. She arose and began to talk, swiftly and passionately, beginning with an angry accusation that welfare checks were so small—just four dollars. "What can you get for four dollars?" And then, oddly, an attack on high taxes. "The young people are angry. Their parents are angry, because they are being so highly taxed." Mounting to a crescendo, she came to her real destination— to denounce the war in Vietnam. "Boys I know across the nation feel it doesn't pay to be a good guy. They figure with a record they don't have to go off to Vietnam." Then, advancing a step toward me and looking with intense directness at me (she is a good actress), she said, "We send the best of this country off to be shot and maimed. They rebel in the streets. They take pot and they will get high. They don't want to go to school, because they are going to be snatched off from their mothers to be shot in Vietnam."

I am glad to say that I looked back just as directly, stare for stare. She continued, pointing her finger at me, the papers later reported. She said: "You are a mother, too, although you have had daughters and not sons. I am a mother and I know the feeling of having a baby come out of my guts. I have a baby and then you send him off to war. No wonder the kids rebel and take pot. And, Mrs. Johnson, in case you don't understand the lingo that's marijuana!"

What do you feel in a situation like this? First, a wave of mounting disbelief. Can this be true? Is this a nightmare? Then a sort of surge of adrenalin into the blood, knowing that you are going to answer, that you've *got* to answer, that you *want* to answer, and at the same time somewhere in the back of your mind a voice that says, "Be calm, be dignified." Somewhere along the way—I think between the words "gut" and "pot"—I had a sense that maybe she was undoing her point. Miss Kitt stopped for breath to a stunned silence in the room and for a second I waited to see whether it was a comma or a period.

Then Mrs. Hughes of New Jersey rose to her feet and said, "I feel morally obligated. May I speak in defense of the war? My first husband," she said, "was killed in World War II, and I have eight sons. One of them is now in the Air Force. None of them wants to go to Vietnam. All will go. They and their friends. I think that anybody who takes pot because there is a war on is a kook. These young people are still juniors. They have to be regulated. I hope we adults are still in control." The room thundered with applause.

I am not sure whether I spoke next or Bennetta Washington. I felt a surge of gratitude that a Negro in a very responsible position, well-grounded in experience, answered. "I understand that Miss Kitt said she knew about anger. I know a little about it too, but we are here to release these energies in constructive rather than destructive channels."

One paper said that I was pale and that my voice trembled slightly as I replied to Miss Kitt. I think that is correct. I did not have tears in my eyes, as another paper reported. "Because there is a war on," I said, "and I pray that there will be a just and honest peace—that still doesn't give us a free ticket not to try to work for better things—against crime in the streets, and for better education and better health for our people. I cannot identify as much as I should. I have not lived the background that you have, nor can I speak as passionately or as well, but we must keep our eyes and our hearts and our energies fixed on constructive areas and try to do something that will make this a happier, better-educated land."

Once more there was thunderous applause. I felt that I must not let the meeting end there. I had seen the pencils racing across the pads of all the press ladies—several more had come in as the program started—and I didn't want the occasion to seem like a riot. Several hands went up. There were three or four more observations. One came from a Negro woman who said there was a double standard of justice and that we would not be done with juvenile delinquency until that was changed. She meant that if a Negro kills a Negro the crime is not pursued as diligently and with the full force of the law as when a white person is concerned. I believe there is truth in that.

It was about five minutes of four. The luncheon had gone on over three hours. I said something about how busy the guests were and moved to the door, with the intention of saying good-by to every guest, including Miss Kitt. It took me several moments to get to the door, as people stopped me on the way. I stood—very composed, I think—and said good-by to everyone who came along. Many said, "We were never so proud of you. You were magnificent." Some, I think, were embarrassed and anxious to get out at any cost. Norma McClellan was very warm in her admiration and I was comforted by it . . . I never lose that feeling of belonging with the Senate wives. I went back upstairs.

My next two hours were a succession of small duties, a few moments with Bess Myerson about a TV program, a photo for the March of Dimes in the Red Room with Anna Roosevelt Halsted beneath FDR's picture, a photo in the library for the *Evening Star* garden book, working at my desk and on my mail. Then about 6 o'clock I went down to the State Dining Room where there was a reception for the Commission on Federal Crime Law.

The genial Chief Justice was already there when I arrived, with Tom Clark and Governor Pat Brown, the Chairman of the Commission, Ramsey Clark and Senator Sam Ervin among others. But Lyndon was delayed. It grew later and later. The waiting was awkward. Chairs were arranged in the State Dining Room, and a podium. I slipped out and telephoned to hurry Lyndon, but I realized from his tone of voice that it was a cruel thing to do. I had interrupted him in the middle of some vital train of thought.

He came over at once, practically in a gallop. He covered his lateness with the apology that was due, made a brief, terse speech, thanked them for their work, and then we went into the Red Room where we shook hands with all of them.

I lingered a while talking to several guests. Apparently news of the luncheon had not gotten around yet, because one man asked me in an innocent voice, "How did the luncheon go?" And I said, "Explosively, although I am afraid the really useful things will receive short shrift." I left him probably mystified.

The city is in a state of tension that has been mounting since Monday, when North Korea seized the *Pueblo*. Sometime in the morning the news came to me that Lyndon had called up the Reservists, Air Force and Navy—about fourteen thousand of them—for active duty, a partial answer to the North Koreans seizing our ship.

Liz came over, looking as if the sky had fallen. Secretary John Gardner's resignation had been announced and the Viet Cong were attacking at Khe Sanh in what looked like a major offensive. We were badly outnumbered there. What a day! Of course, I had already had five days to absorb my sadness at Gardner's resignation.

When we finished with letters and invitations and answers to questions, I went over to the EOB for two fast, hard games of bowling. They do help. Back upstairs, I put on a gold lamé dress and fared forth to the first big dinner of 1968—the party honoring the Vice President, the Speaker, and the Chief Justice, with, I hope, a brave front—though with a sinking heart—on as inauspicious an evening as could possibly be.

I went into the Yellow Room to meet the honor guests, Hubert and Muriel, the Speaker and Miss Harriet, and the Chief Justice and Mrs. Warren. I always think of this as a sort of family party and how easy it is to forget that the Chief Justice is a member of the other political party! This dinner has a very different mood from one honoring a Chief of State.

I found myself talking too fast and too much, an attempt to combat the gloom that the troubles of the day brought down. When the Honor Guard came in—this is the first time I can remember that it has not been led by Chuck—I missed him and imagined it moved less skillfully with something less than the usual ballet precision. We followed them downstairs, I walking with my husband this time, with the Speaker and Miss Harriet using the elevator, but joining us at the foot of the stairs. We marched in and just as we reached the door an unprecedented thing happened. The room burst into spontaneous applause. Never before that I can remember has this happened either for us or for any other President.

As the 190 guests came down the receiving line, I sensed something of what may be the feeling of the whole country. One pressed my hand. Another murmured, "We are praying for you." Others, I think, tried to convey sympathy and understanding with a look. I do not believe their solicitude had any particular reference to Lyndon and Lady Bird Johnson.

I think it simply meant: "You are the President, and we know it is tough and we are in it with you."

I found myself pushing against the wall of gloom, hoping that I could help make it a good evening. I was lucky at my table. The Vice President always sits at my right at this dinner and he has that golden gift of happiness and of making those around him happy. Mrs. John King, the wife of the Governor of New Hampshire, was next and then the Chief Justice, Helen Hayes, the violinist Alexander Schneider, and then Mrs. William Randolph Hearst, Jr., very slim and elegantly dressed, Jim Rowe and Mrs. McCormack and the Speaker. It was a good table for talk.

Stars though they were—Helen Hayes and Mr. Schneider—they really had to bow to Hubert this evening! Tales of the stage had begun on their side of the table and then Hubert began telling about his father in the little town of Huron, South Dakota, where he was born and reared. His father used to buy time on the radio to read poetry. His wife would fuss at him for wasting the family's money, which wasn't plentiful, and he would say, "But the people need it!" Hubert told tales of how his father would go once a year to Chicago or New York to hear grand opera or concerts, and of how the whole family would be called on at the table to give their opinions on some public issue. We all mourned the passing of real conversation—was it television that killed it?—or what happened to family life?

Lyndon made the first toast, paying tribute to the American system of checks and balances. He said there have been times in our history when check and balance really meant "stop and freeze" and then went on to say that after the strong opinions have been aired, people want progress. They want checks and balances and then they want forward movement. Hubert's toast, delivered completely without notes, was the warmest and most personal one. He ended by asking us to raise our glasses in tribute "to a man who is firm and resolute, strong and kind, and governs with compassion." Then the Speaker rose, and from that frail and aging body, the hollow-eyed, gray-thatched head, there emerged the strong, powerful, sure voice. He is truly a professional and he generously included all of Lyndon's family in his toast. The Chief Justice's theme was unity in perilous times.

I had already received two looks from Lyndon that said, "Hurry." So I hastened to introduce the entertainment for the evening, rather lamely, and we launched into about thirty minutes of I Do, I Do with Gordon MacRae and Carol Lawrence. It was a good antidote for the day, a far cry from all the worries that these men had brought into that room.

The Speaker and Miss Harriet began the exodus as soon as the entertainment was over and Lyndon went upstairs a little before 12. I think
everybody could understand, because he did look gray and weary. He had
had hardly any sleep for two nights before. But there was one light touch
to the evening. Abe Fortas and Alexander Schneider took two violins from
the Marine Corps Orchestra and began to play a bit of Mozart. Lyndon,
about to depart, leaned over to George Meany and said, "Do you reckon
Abe has a Union card?"

Wednesday, February 7

For some time we've been wanting to do something to entertain
servicemen, to include them in White House entertainments—the wounded
veterans at Walter Reed and Bethesda. But we didn't want such a party
to get into the papers. Lynda Bird had given us the distinct feeling that
they are trotted out and put on review, and, in a way, used. She has been
going to the hospitals and for the first several times her visits had been
absolutely quiet. She liked going and the men had liked talking freely
with her. Then her visits had surfaced—maybe through some over-eager
public relations man—and she hadn't gone anymore.

We thought we had found a good recipe when we decided on showing
brand-new movies, but we found that movies were standard fare at the
hospitals. Bess came up with the idea of a cabaretlike setting in the theater,
little round tables with cokes and pizza, peanuts and pretzels, a group
of attractive, friendly girls moving around from table to table, just
chatting with the men, and lively music by some portion of one of the
service bands.

So here I was, standing in the corridor that approaches the theater.
The hall was lined with shrubs, bright geraniums, and they came down—
about thirty servicemen, three or four in wheelchairs, several on crutches;
a pinned-up sleeve, an empty trouser leg. With each new face, I felt
uncertainty as to whether I should stick out my hand or not. If you're
new to crutches, can you take one hand away with ease, to shake hands?

Lynda Bird slipped in beside me and she was terrific. Carol Channing
could hardly have been better. She made the afternoon glow and come
to life. At the end of the line, we joined the veterans in the theater,
where Tony Matarrese's band was already playing. I'd known him since
The Elms. He said, "I want to welcome you to Tony's Pizza Parlor!" Then

he was off into loud, brash music that changed to sentimental, and then he began to ask for requests.

I sat at a table about ten minutes and then moved on. It was not easy to make conversation. One opening always was, "Where are you from?" and the very first person I asked was from Austin! There were a lot of Southerners and three were West Virginians. The worst case of all was only half a man. He sat upright in his wheelchair, and his legs were amputated at the hips. He and two others were silent, unmoving, sort of stunned looking. Another was lively and smiled, and he and I talked animatedly but when I asked the others a question, they answered in monosyllables. I sat at about half the tables, I think, and never with Lynda, so I hope we covered the whole room. One table asked me for my autograph and I wrote it for them on White House matchbooks.

About 3 o'clock Lynda went to the microphone and said that she would like to take them around to see the house. And then tactfully added, "Anybody who wants to can take the stairs, or they can follow me. I'm going to take the elevator."

My 3 o'clock appointment, Mrs. Harman, had already arrived and was in the Yellow Room. I apologized without telling her why I was late. She'd come to say good-by—after nine years as Ambassador from Israel to the United States, they are leaving. It's quite the wrong way around that I get to know diplomats' wives much better in their farewell call, because this is the only time we really sit and talk for thirty minutes or an hour, just the two of us.

Mrs. Harman is one of the most interesting and, I think, intelligent women I have known among the members of the Diplomatic Corps; very quiet-voiced and very forceful. Some interesting excerpts: Between 60 and 65 percent of the people of Israel are "Oriental" Jews; this phrase rather startled me. She used it, I think, as opposed to "Occidental." I asked her where they were from. She said, "Yemen, India, Ethiopia, Iraq." She said, "Many people think that the people of Israel are highly skilled, literate, European Jews. This is not so. Many of these Oriental Jews have never eaten with a fork or sat on a chair, or seen a flush toilet. The people of Yemen were absolutely cut off from civilization about two thousand years ago, and they have remained in that same culture and economy. All that we have in common is Hebrew, and the customs of our religion." Nevertheless, she said, the people of Yemen are very quiet and gentle and teachable, and are making great strides. When they return to Israel, her husband will become head of the Hebrew University there.

She spoke of the press, in the very words I might have used. The press is absolutely free in Israel, she said, and gives poor Prime Minister Eshkol a great deal of trouble—in fact, all of the government, any government. I believe she said there are sixty newspapers in little Israel.

Then I went in and succumbed to the luxury of a nap, nearly two hours, and it was a great balm. These night I am not sleeping much and I dream, sometimes nightmares, sometimes just a long, long dream in which I'm lost and going from room to room and can't find my way. But poor Lyndon—he turns out his lights so late and wakes up so early. Sometimes I think the greatest courage is just to get up in the morning and start tackling the job again.

Thursday, February 8

This afternoon I saw Liz and heard the last round, I hope, of what is, without a doubt, the most ridiculous international furor so far. We had deliberately tried to plan entertainment for the dinner for Prime Minister Harold Wilson tonight that was pleasant and low-keyed. With the grave situation in the world today, this is not a time for dancing or even for the glitter and display of musical comedy or ballet. So we had invited our dear, reliable, and obliging Robert Merrill of the Metropolitan Opera to sing. Well, the songs he had chosen were: "On the Road to Mandalay" and "Oh, I Got Plenty O' Nuttin' " from *Porgy and Bess*. The press claimed this program was an insult to the British Empire which had just pulled its troops out of the Suez and devalued the pound.

Walt Rostow winced, I'm told. Should we change the program? It was all so ridiculous! The Prime Minister had read of the furor in the paper and sent word that these songs were his special favorites, and he hoped we would keep them. And so, at rest.

I dressed for the dinner in the champagne satin dress that goes under my beautiful gold coat. Flanked by the familiar lights and cameras, we met the Prime Minister and Mrs. Wilson at the North Portico. There too, was Lady Dean, and I made apologies to her. I don't know what happened at lunch at the British Embassy today. No doubt they had planned something for the Prime Minister there, and Lyndon, who had had a conference with Mr. Wilson which was supposed to last from 11:30 to one, had simply abducted him and brought him and his total party, about fourteen, to lunch on our second floor. I have no idea how many minutes' notice he had given poor Zephyr. Lyndon had knocked on my door a few minutes past one and said, "Come out and meet one of your favorite Prime Ministers." And there they all were, talking and working until past 3:30.

In the East Room we stood in line to meet the guests, who had grown in number to 150. For the last three or four days Bess and I had almost been praying for a snow storm or a flu epidemic! The usual percentage of regrets had not come in. The law of averages indicated the number of acceptances from those we'd invited would be below 140. It didn't happen this time. There we were, straight up with 150 people for dinner and only two staff members we could afford to ask to eat in the Navy mess, as we have done in a pinch before. John Fickland, invaluable veteran of the White House staff, saved the day by figuring out a way to squeeze in one extra table, although it was a little too crowded to be gracious.

We squeezed our way into the crowded State Dining Room. The Prime Minister was on my right. He told me that he loved appearing on TV, and conversely, did *not* like making a "public speech." I suppose that means the English version of the courthouse square. The toast he made in the State Dining Room he called a "private speech." We talked of young Winston Churchill who, I gathered, had run for Parliament and lost. I got the impression young Churchill is considered to have somewhat more ability than his father and a good deal less than his grandfather. At one point Prime Minister Wilson looked across at his wife and raised his glass, and a very nice look passed between them. He turned to me and said, "She was working for five dollars a week as a stenotypist, and I was doing" (and I forget what he was doing), "and we never thought we would someday be dining in the White House."

He was very interested in the house, and asked a lot of questions about the various rooms. And of the U.S. Army Strings he said, "I would fly across the Atlantic just to hear them. Whenever plans are being made to come over here and the date is set, then I start looking forward to this part of the dinner."

He spoke of Lyndon as Lyndon, and he called me Lady Bird. The only other Chief of State that I remember using first names was Prime Minister Harold Holt from Australia. Mr. Wilson warned me that his toast was going to be quite long and quite serious, and that Bill Fulbright wouldn't like it.

Sir Patrick Dean was on my left and there the conversation was interesting, too. I was discussing the imprint of Great Britain I had seen in our travels . . . in New Zealand, Australia, Malaysia . . . many places. And Sir Patrick said, "On the whole, perhaps, it would have been better for the world if we could have stayed around a little longer."

I spoke of some of the good things England had left behind—the beginning of Civil Service, the establishment of a common language. He said, "But there's no gratitude in international affairs." I find it impressive and admirable the way the Britishers I know look with a cool clarity, a lack of bitterness, a sort of detachment, at the breakup of the British Empire.

Lyndon's toast was long, too long, I thought, but it was a beautiful toast. He said: "The American and British peoples are not short-distance crusaders. We are veteran campaigners, not amateurs, and we have never been quitters. I have enormous confidence in the character of my own people in their ability to understand and master trial." There was one light moment. Speaking of the entertainment, and referring to the ridiculous "flap" over the choice of songs, Lyndon said, "Mr. Prime Minister, we could compromise and sing a duet. You sing 'God Save the Queen' and I'll sing 'God Bless America.'"

Harold Wilson's toast was indeed long and grave. He backed Lyndon's San Antonio formula for starting peace talks on Vietnam and told how in Moscow last month he'd explained Britain's stand to the Russian leaders, promising that once there's a move toward peace, the British will play their full part, both in negotiations and reconstruction in Vietnam. He told Lyndon that his restraint in handling the *Pueblo* incident will earn tribute from reasoning men everywhere, and indeed, from history. He's an excellent public speaker, I think, although he insisted on calling this a "private speech."

In a snatch of conversation I had with Mrs. Wilson, she described campaigning in England. She said that once they were in a car that was being rocked by angry students who were beating on the windows and the sides of the car with sticks, and that she was actually afraid. Well, we've had almost everything in this country, but not quite that yet.

When Bob Merrill had come down the receiving line before dinner, we had laughed simultaneously and I had said, "You and I have a penchant for crises!" Now, after dinner when his great, thrilling voice filled the East Room with the Gershwin songs and the "Road to Mandalay," I was moved to wonder why anybody could take exception to those old classics, but Bob added a witty disclaimer for the Empire by singing, "It Ain't Necessarily So." Veronica Tyler sang some songs from Puccini, Schubert and

Menotti, and then they sang a duet from Rodgers and Hammerstein's *Carousel*, "You'll Never Walk Alone."

We escorted the Prime Minister and Mrs. Wilson out to the hall; champagne was passed and there was a brief conversation, before I said good night at the door, as Lyndon saw them to their car. He went upstairs quickly to get the latest reports from Vietnam, saying to the few around him, "I've got to get back to Khe Sanh."

Spring 1968

I had been happy last night, when I had seen Lyndon's light
out at 11, and had read myself to sleep on *Nicholas and
Alexandra*. But this morning when I went in, I found that he
had waked up about 2 A.M., worked steadily all through the
night until 6, then turned out the light and slept fitfully
until 7:30. Nevertheless, he was in a good humor, with a sort
of serenity that has settled on him these last few days.
Things are just as bad as they can possibly be, and yet he is
calm, cheerful, and inspires confidence in those around him.

After lunch I dressed in my chiffon and went down to the
Lincoln Sitting Room to meet Madame Shoumatoff. I had
approached the painting of my portrait with fear and trem-
bling, but I must say I've enjoyed it. My sittings have
actually been a pleasure. Madame Shoumatoff is an entertaining talker, and she keeps right on painting and talking
at the same time. Today she told me about her life in Russia.
She showed me a picture of her home in the Ukraine. It

might have been my Uncle Harry's house in Selma, Alabama . . . stately white columns, a Greek façade, beautiful trees and shrubbery. She said Russian country life then was very like it is here now in Virginia. She had left Russia as a young woman with her husband, who was on a Diplomatic mission to this country for the Kerensky government. When they arrived here, they found that there was no longer a Kerensky government; the real holocaust had begun. Then she said the most delightful thing. "Mrs. Johnson, it is a great privilege to be suddenly deprived of all your worldly goods"—and added in an aside, "that is, if you're twenty and in good health." The two hours passed swiftly. Tomorrow will be the last sitting.

Ashton and I cleared my desk, a monumental job, and we both went downstairs to join Lynda's party in the Blue Room. She had shown the movie of her wedding to a small group of friends and staff people who had worked so hard on it. It was, in a way, sort of a good-by party to Washington, though nobody mentioned it, for Chuck will soon be shipping out to Vietnam.

Lyndon came home at a fairly reasonable hour. He was courteous and kindly, although I could tell his mind was far away from the dinner-table conversation with Lynda and her guests, the Flemings. He had had one victory. The Senate had voted cloture on the Civil Rights debate, and it looks now as if we might get a bill, including Open Housing. My heart goes out to him; he's working so hard, and the prospect is cruel every way we turn.

Wednesday, March 6

The first event of the day was the swearing in of C. R. Smith as Secretary of Commerce in the East Room at one. The changing of the guard is rather frequent these days—coming in and going out. This swearing in had a nice feeling, casual, good-humored. Congress was fully represented, and for the moment, cordial. And business was there in full force—and there were some members of the Smith family, C. R.'s son, and his sister. We stood in line in the Blue Room.

The guests filed by to wish C. R. good luck in his new job as Secretary of Commerce. It gives me a quiet satisfaction to have him join us, though I'm sad that young Sandy Trowbridge had to leave because of the heart attack. Lyndon has so many good men, and they give so much, though apparently nothing is enough. The whole world around us seems to be in a state of turmoil. Teachers are walking out on strike, here in Washington and in many other places. Students nearly everywhere are raising voices of anger.

Upstairs I found that André Meyer, who had come down for the swearing in, was staying for lunch with Lyndon. Lyndon was tied up for a moment, and so I sat in the Yellow Room and talked to André. I find him enormously interesting, though his life as an international banker is a far distance from mine.

Then I went in for my final sitting with Madame Shoumatoff. After about thirty minutes she said, "You know, I wish that we could show this portrait to someone. I need some help. Mrs. Johnson, there comes a time when you need to get an outside opinion." I said that my husband was having lunch right down the hall with a gentleman who knew a great deal about art. She said, "Let's ask them to come in." So I went to the dining room, and to my delight Lyndon and André Meyer were still there. I said, "Will you do something for me that will take five minutes?" They said yes. "Then come down in a few minutes, to the Lincoln Sitting Room."

Presently they walked in. I felt as if I would burst, for about thirty seconds, and then both of them simultaneously said, "I like it. I like it very much!" Lyndon went on to say that he liked the hair and the eyes, but that something needed to be done about the neck. Madame Shoumatoff said, "You have a good eye. It is not finished. I am going to take the portrait with me and work on it for a week or two. What you see below the face represents only the beginning, just a sketch."

André was lavish in his approval, and I don't know who was the more relieved, Madame Shoumatoff or I. When they left, we heaved a great sigh of relief. I ordered tea, and we sat and congratulated each other. Madame Shoumatoff will take the portrait with her. By Easter it will be finished, varnished, and can be shown to the members of the White House Historical Association, who have ordered it for the White House. They will say then whether it suits *them* or not.

Just as he left the room, Lyndon had looked back over his shoulder and said, "Tell her she can sign up to start painting me right away." Neither she nor I carried this matter any further but that is what I have been hoping for. After Easter, when we see the final version of my portrait, perhaps we can raise the subject of his.

In the afternoon we had a reception for Democratic State Chairmen, and after greeting them, and feeling terribly self-indulgent, I went out to the David Lloyd Kreegers' for a special treat—seeing their house which Philip Johnson designed, where their wonderful art collection is displayed. Philip Johnson was there to give a guided tour of the house, and John Walker, to discuss the collection. We wandered through the halls, the living room, the vast dining room, and out onto the most beautiful porch, with a superb view of the city spread out below.

The house is made of travertine marble, and there are arches and areas of openness, great expanses of glass, with a little interior courtyard, full of lush, tropical plants. It's a beautiful setting for the paintings, and the Bonnard, which I have fallen in love with, is right at the front door. They have two other Bonnards; a Monet of the same scene depicted in the Monet painting at the White House, but painted in a different light— morning light, John Walker said; and another enormous Monet of water lilies. There are Van Goghs, Gauguins, a Matisse—many that I didn't recognize—several Degas, and quite a few pieces of sculpture, among them some Moores, Rodins, a Giacometti, and a Lipchitz—and in the corner, a pre-Columbian piece. Then there was a whole room of bright abstracts, which I make no pretense of understanding.

We went downstairs to a room full of Picassos, several of them paintings of the women the artist had lived with. I do not like women with four eyes, or two mouths, or no mouth. I must say, though, I could see the characterization coming through. One of the women was totally serene and acceptant in spite of her scrambled features, and another totally sharp and angry.

Much too quickly, I had to say good-by, and I drove to the Gonella residence, having checked on the telephone and found that Lynda and Chuck were out there. I had never seen Ashton's new house. Her adorable little boy was seated solemnly at the head of the stairs, surveying everybody who came. Everybody there was an old friend! Presently Lyndon arrived— he loves to express his appreciation to dear friends like Ashton by sharing their celebrations but he was bone weary and we left soon. To my pleasure, Lynda and Chuck were waiting for us at the White House. The four of us sat down to dinner, and we talked about their plans. They're going to his parents tomorrow, and to Texas the next day, and on to Mexico Saturday.

Lyndon, in his patriarchal way, wanted to help them at every turn— with the flight to Mexico and back, any little gift. He suffers from the approaching departure of Chuck and Patrick, but he's so proud of them both. They have really become a part of our family. Lyndon wants to spend time with them, and he is a little hurt if they have plans to go out and spend it with friends their own age. Looking dead tired, he leaned back in the executive chair that he uses for a dining-table chair, closed his eyes, and reaching over to take Lynda's hand, he said, "I wish I could bear your burdens." Lynda leaned over and kissed him. I knew that right below the surface there were tears.

Sunday, March 10

This was a day of deep gloom—that is to say, gloom was purveyed in the newspapers and on TV. It weighted the air around me, and I felt it in my very bones, though it was not apparent in Lyndon. His voice was hearty; he had lively stories to tell when he stopped to talk with us. His work on the phone, and reading reports, ground on and on. I never took off my hat to him more, or felt more tender toward him.

We were awake early, and waded through pounds of newsprint. Then I said, "Let's go to Dr. Davis' church." When I returned to the room, dressed, about a quarter of 11, there was Lyndon, still on the phone. But he can break an Olympic record for getting dressed, so once more he did. We were out the door in about eight minutes and walked into church just in front of the choir. Dr. Davis was preaching on a topic I thought was comfortably safe—"The Old-Time Religion."

Secretary Rusk came by right after church. Tomorrow he goes up on the Hill to testify before TV. I admire him with all my heart. He is a great bulwark of strength, but even he looked weary. Afterward Lyndon told me something very touching that Dean had said to him. "Your courage keeps me going. These days are an exercise of sheer spirit."

It was well after 2 when Lyndon phoned to say he was hungry. We had a delicious lunch of crabmeat crepes and salad, hardly calculated to be reducing, but he's been so good so long, I really wanted him to break over. Afterward Lyndon said, "Let's walk around the South grounds." He took a golf club and hit some balls over toward Eisenhower's green, and we walked around in the beautiful sunshine. There are a few crocus out and the buds are beginning to swell. In the West Garden one of the magnolia soulangianas has a single pink bud opening.

Then we went over to the bowling lanes, but Lyndon left after the first game, to try to get a nap. I stayed and played another game, and overwhelmed myself by making 188, the best score I've ever made! About 5 o'clock I went back upstairs and did enough work at my desk to satisfy my Calvinist conscience and to leave me free for the rest of the day.

Lyndon sent word for me to come in. No, he hadn't really slept—he'd read and talked on the phone. Earlier, I had asked him: "Suppose someone else were elected President, what could 'Mr. X' do that you could not do?" He said, "He could unite the country and start getting some things done. That would last about a year, maybe two years." I think that is what weighs heaviest on Lyndon's mind. Can he unite the country, or is there simply too much built-up antagonism, division, a general malaise, which may have the Presidency—or this President—irrevocably as its focal point?

Lyndon called Hubert. There's still laughter in Hubert, but Muriel said that even this most happy and philosophical man has been weary and shaken the last few days. I thought there was hurt in his voice when he described some of the actions of certain Senators on the Hill. Hubert said, "It's bad, and it's going to keep on being bad, through the Primaries. I think we might as well brace ourselves for more of the same until the middle of June."

Those sties are coming back on Lyndon's eyes. First one and then the other, red and swollen and painful. I thought, wryly, that his life sounded more and more like the tribulations of Job; nevertheless, he is remaining calm, even-tempered, serenely philosophic about politics. But about the war itself, he is deeply worried.

So ended this melancholy day, about 11 P.M.

Thursday, March 14

This was one of those terrific, pummeling White House days that can stretch and grind and use you—even I, who only live on the periphery. So what must it be like for Lyndon!

We were up early. The headlines ran: "JOHNSON URGES HILL TO ACT ON D.C. PROBLEMS" . . . "FOWLER URGES CONGRESS TO ACT ON FISCAL PROBLEMS, CITES GOLD RUSH, WAR, INFLATION, PLEADS FOR TAX RISE" . . . "KENNEDY IS CONSIDERING RACE AGAINST JOHNSON" . . . "MAD RUSH IN EUROPE" . . . "GOLD BUYING SKYROCKETS."

This morning I put on my green ensemble for the arrival ceremony of Prime Minister Mohamed Haji Ibrahim Egal of Somalia and we marched out onto the South grounds, Lyndon and I. There was a sizable crowd of people and a ripple of applause greeted us as we appeared, but I, at least, moved in what I have come to think of through the years as the "riding in the tumbrel" attitude—shoulders just a bit squarer, and head just a lift higher. It was chilly and bright and beautiful, with the flags whipping in the wind, and the call of the trumpets making your blood leap.

Dean Rusk stepped forward and I said: "You are my hero." And then the big black car rolled up and out stepped the Prime Minister of Somalia, a youngish, round-faced, pleasant, and able-looking man wearing a white embroidered Muslim cap, and accompanied by a delicate, pretty wife, whose soft-spoken English was excellent. I was impressed with the simplicity and straightforwardness of the Prime Minister's speech.

At one I went into the Cabinet Room for the awards that Lyndon was presenting to the Federal Career Women. The seven of them were an interesting group, including a wildlife biologist with the Department of Interior, a statistician with the Economic Advisers, an attractive young woman with the Office of Civil Rights, and an air traffic control specialist with the FAA. Lyndon spoke, half-humor and half-earnestness, lauded them, shook hands, and was gone within moments. I stayed a little longer to talk with them about their work.

Then I made my third change of clothes for the day. Sometimes, living in the White House requires a ridiculous number of changes per day, to appear in outfits suitable for each occasion. And in my nearly favorite red suit with the navy trim, I left for the circus. This benefit for underprivileged children is an annual event with me and one that I have always liked.

It was nearly 8 when I heard that Lyndon had gone over to the State Department for a good-by reception for Sandy Trowbridge. My heart sank. How could he possibly get back and not be late for the State Dinner? But he could, and did. He had stayed seven minutes, kissed Nancy, thanked Sandy, made an amusing speech. He said that Trowbridge had promised him one thing—he wasn't going to run for President, and then he paused and said—"I ought to point out that that was a week ago." He was back at the White House and into a black tie and we were actually downstairs at the North Portico a few minutes past 8. For a great deal of his day, time is Lyndon's servant, not his master. He wrings from it every action, every achievement, every human contact that he can.

Simone had reminded me that we were on TV tonight, so we tried to take an extra moment in the greetings on the North Portico with the

Prime Minister and Mrs. Egal. Then we took them upstairs to the Yellow Room, where Hubert and his trip to Africa was much the topic of discussion.

Among our gifts to the Prime Minister and Mrs. Egal were a bamboo bowl, in vermeil, which is used on all the White House tables when we have a State Dinner—and thirty boxes of toys for her to distribute among her favorite orphanages. The selection of gifts created a slightly uncertain situation, because Prime Minister Egal has two wives, and I didn't know what to do about the one left at home. But anyway, the bowl will do for the house. Their gifts to us were an ivory desk set, quite complete and very attractive, including an ivory pencil holder, which we can put to use right away. The Prime Minister laughingly remarked: "Mr. President, I can assure your Congress that this didn't cost more than fifty dollars," which shows he'd done some research!

Behind the flags, we marched down the steps, to the tune of "Hail to the Chief." There's not a day here, no matter how battered we are with problems, that my heart won't rise when I hear it. Then we stood in line in the East Room to meet our 140 guests.

It was a pleasant, light dinner, as far as conversation went. The Prime Minister and I talked about the search for oil in his country, which has been going on for about fifteen years, unsuccessfully so far. My knowledge of Somalia is limited to frankincense and myrrh and leopard skins, which didn't lead to any extensive conversational gambits, but he was a pleasant, easy companion.

Lyndon's toast at dinner praised the Prime Minister for doing so much to lessen the tensions which have threatened East Africa with the waste of war. The horn of Africa had long been a powder keg, between Somalia, Kenya, and Ethiopia. Somehow this man, or fate, has brought about a period of peace. When the Prime Minister rose and made his toast to Lyndon, I almost thought he was quoting from Jack Valenti. He said he rested well knowing the great power of this country was in the hands of the man now at the helm.

Anita Bryant, star of stage and TV and our friend, sang "The Impossible Dream" which always makes my heart take wing, and closed with the "Battle Hymn of the Republic," with Lyndon leading the standing ovation for her.

During dinner, I had asked the Prime Minister what time it was in his country, and he had said, as I remember, 2:30 A.M.! (It was about 9:30 when I asked him.) So I thought it fitting for him (and for my husband) when shortly after the entertainment was over and the champagne was passed, with a little lingering and talking in the hall, that he and Mrs. Egal made their departure.

Sunday, March 17

LBJ RANCH

The four of us drove in to St. Barnabas—Lynda and Chuck, Lyndon and I, for the 11 o'clock service. Chuck will be leaving very soon. On the way in, Lyndon said something I will remember for its perception. We were talking about the rising tide of isolationism in this country, and I was saying how strong it was becoming in me—not thought, just pure emotion, fed by the actions of such countries as Sweden hosting a "trial" of the United States as "a war criminal" and France manipulating the gold market. I made a hotheaded statement about when we got the Vietnam war finally settled I didn't want to have another thing to do with any foreign country. Lyndon looked at me very calmly and said, "That's like saying James Davis' children have the smallpox, and I'm not going to do anything about it." James and his children live about a block from us. If they had the smallpox, my first thought would be, I've got to be sure they've got the best doctor and care. And my next thought would be for our *own* safety. Or, maybe those thoughts would be reversed. At any rate, we couldn't separate ourselves from them, no matter how much we wished it.

Back at home after the services, we watched the last part of a TV show— Hubert Humphrey was absolutely magnificent. He and Rusk are about the only two who are out speaking for the Administration now. I have a growing feeling of Prometheus Bound, just as though we were lying there on the rock, exposed to the vultures, and restrained from fighting back.

But the day was too precious to lose—the weather was glorious, with that anticipation of spring in the air! When that fails to excite me, I will be ninety years old and as good as dead.

Luci and Pat arrived at long last, with deliriously happy stories of their trip to Laredo. Luci is convinced that she has more of the best friends in the world, the nicest house in the world, the best husband, and the best baby! This is a typical greeting from her on the phone: "Hello, Daddy! I just wanted to make sure you hear a cheerful voice today. I haven't got any problems." Pat has received his orders, is returning to his old unit in Washington, and will probably be going overseas in a few weeks or months. Whatever problem it may be to them, this is something they can take.

Dinner consisted of all Lynda Bird's favorites—steak, and spinach, homemade peach ice cream, and a great big cake with one single candle on it, though her birthday is still two days away. We all sang "Happy Birthday" while she blew it out.

I observed the headline in the paper that read: "LBJ SEEKS AUSTERITY VICTORY—KENNEDY VOWS NEW POLICIES," but I can only stand immobile and watch.

Sunday, March 31

THE WHITE HOUSE

This day began early because Lynda was coming in on "the red-eye special" from California, about 7 A.M., having kissed Chuck good-by at Camp Pendleton last night as he departed for Vietnam.

I wanted to be right there at the door with open arms to meet her, but I begged Lyndon not to get up. "No, I want to," he insisted. So the operator called us in what seemed the gray early morning and both of us were downstairs at the entrance to the Diplomatic Reception Room at 7 when she stepped out of the car. She looked like a ghost—pale, tall, and drooping. We both hugged her and then we all went upstairs. I took her into her room, helped get her clothes off, and put her to bed. She'd had a sedative on the plane, slept a little, not much—and it was, I think, partly emotion and partly the sedative that made her look so detached, like a wraith from another world.

She said, "Mother, they were awful—they kept on pushing and shoving to get to us, and they almost ran over a child. And there were lots of other wives there, saying good-by to their husbands!" She meant the press.

When I went back into Lyndon's room, his face was sagging and there was such pain in his eyes as I had not seen since his mother died. But he didn't have time for grief. Today was a crescendo of a day. At 9 in the evening, Lyndon was to make his talk to the nation about the war. The speech was not yet firm. There were still revisions to be made and people to see. But he began to put on his clothes and got ready to go to church with Luci and Pat, something he does more and more often.

And I, exhausted, went back to bed, where I half-slept for a couple of hours.

On the way home from church, Lyndon stopped to see the Vice President at his apartment. Hubert and Muriel are leaving for Mexico, for a ceremony, sometime during the day. It was a day of coming and going—and it's hard to remember when what happened. Sometime during the morning Buzz came in, took up his place in the Treaty Room, and began to work on the speech. I had spent a good part of Saturday and part of Friday making suggestions on it myself. I read it over again for what was the umpteenth time, and then (I believe it was in his bedroom), Lyndon said to Arthur and Mathilde Krim and me, "What do you think about this? This is what I'm going to put at the end of the speech." And he read a very beautifully written statement which ended, "Accordingly, I shall not seek and I will not accept the nomination of my party for another term as your President."

The four of us had talked about this over and over, and hour after hour, but somehow we all acted and felt stunned. Maybe it was the calm finality in Lyndon's voice, and maybe we believed him for the first time. Arthur said something like, "You can't mean this!" And Mathilde exclaimed in an excited way, "Oh no, no!" Then we all began to discuss the reasons why, and why not, over and over again.

Buzz came in now and again with another page for the main part of the speech. Finally, a little after 2 o'clock Lyndon and I, and Luci and Pat, and Mathilde and Arthur went to the table for lunch. It was Lyndon who thought to call Buzz in from the Treaty Room to have something to eat.

Mathilde's eyes were full of tears, and Luci had obviously been crying forthrightly. Lyndon seemed to be congealing into a calm, quiet state of mind, out of our reach. And I, what did I feel? . . . so uncertain of the future that I would not dare to try to persuade him one way or the other. There was much in me that cried out to go on, to call on every friend we have, to give and work, to spend and fight, right up to the last. And if we lost, well and good—we were free! But if we didn't run, we could be free without all this draining of our friends. I think what was uppermost—what was going over and over in Lyndon's mind—was what I've heard him say increasingly these last months: "I do not believe I can unite this country."

Buzz made a poetic little explanation of the statement saying Lyndon would not run. Lyndon, indeed, was the architect and the planner, but I think it was Buzz who had cloaked it in its final words.

Sometime during the afternoon—the time is very hazy on this day— I think it was around 3 o'clock, Lyndon went to his office, and I talked to Lynda and to Luci. Both of them were emotional, crying and distraught. What does this do to the servicemen? They will think—What have I been sent out here for?—Was it all wrong?—Can I believe in what I've been fighting for? Lynda and Luci seemed to feel that Lyndon has been the champion of the soldiers, and that his getting out would be a blow to them. Lynda said, with an edge of bitterness, "Chuck will hear this on his way to Vietnam."

Later in the afternoon, I talked to Lyndon about what the girls had said. He said, "I called in General Westmoreland last year about that, about how it would affect the morale of the men. He thinks it will not matter appreciably." I felt that Lynda and Luci were looking at it from closer range as the wives of two young soldiers, and pointed that out to him. He looked at me rather distantly and said, "I think General Westmoreland knows more about it than they do."

He was still in the office and it was near 6 o'clock when Walt Rostow, looking gray and weary, arrived on the second floor, with Averell Harriman, who did not look at all weary, and Ambassador Dobrynin. Ambassador Dobrynin was called in because we wanted to make absolutely sure that Hanoi and its friends knew that we were halting the bombing and why we were doing it. Lyndon had told me this morning they were coming to talk about the speech. I took them into the Yellow Room and asked them what they would like to drink. Everyone, I noticed, cautiously took a Coke, in spite of what I've heard about the Russians drinking vodka and trying to toast their opposite numbers under the table. Dobrynin was affable and talkative—I equally so—our subject, safely, the possibility that the Bolshoi Ballet might come to the Hemisfair in San Antonio. Then Lyndon came in with that jaunty step that I've seen him rev up under the most intense tension.

It was a strange afternoon and evening. We would meet in the West Hall by twos or threes, or all of us—Mathilde, Arthur, Buzz, Lynda, Luci, Pat, and I—and look at each other, helplessly, silent, or exploding with talk. I felt as if I ought to do *something*. I must *do* something—but what? And how did I dare do anything, with the decision so momentous, one I could by no means implement, or take the responsibility for making turn out right. I remember that I kept on looking at the hands of the clock, and counting the hours until 9 P.M. and the broadcast.

Just before 7, I went over to Lyndon's office with him. He was looking at the news ticker. I told the kitchen we would have some light sandwiches, or snacks, from 8 o'clock on, but that we wouldn't really want to eat until after the speech was over—9:30 or 10.

Marvin came in around 8. Lyndon always speaks of him affectionately as "that tough Marine," and so he is. We've shared so much, we've been so close—that I can say about many people here, and that's been the great reward, second only to the sense of achievement. Clark and Marny Clifford came a little past 8. Lyndon had asked me to call them because he especially wanted them with us. And Walt and Elspeth Rostow.

And then about a quarter of 9, Lyndon, Marvin, Walt, and Jim Jones went to Lyndon's office—followed shortly by Luci and Pat. Luci clings to her father these days. It's wonderful to see. She's going to give him every comfort she can.

I went over with Clark and Buzz a few minutes before 9 and Lynda joined us. And there we were in the familiar oval office of the President, the floor a jungle of cables, under the brilliant glare of TV lights. What a stage setting!

Lyndon, very quiet, sat at his desk. The lines in his face were deep, but there was a marvelous sort of repose over-all. And the seconds ticked away.

I went to him and said quietly, "Remember—pacing and drama." It was a great speech and I wanted him to get the greatest out of it—and I did not know what the end would be.

The speech was magnificently delivered. He's best, I think, in the worst of times, calm and strong—those who love him must have loved him more. And those who hate him must at least have thought: "Here is a man."

Then came the end of the speech.

"What we won when all our people united just must not now be lost in suspicion, distrust, selfishness, and politics among any of our people. Believing this as I do, I have concluded that I should not permit the Presidency to become involved in the partisan divisions that are developing in this political year"—and so on . . .

"I do not believe that I should devote an hour or a day of my time to any personal partisan causes or to any duties other than the awesome duties of this office—the Presidency of your country. Accordingly, I shall not seek, and I will not accept, the nomination of my party for another term as your President."

Lynda and I had been sitting down, behind us Luci and Pat standing. Luci threw her arms around Lyndon. She was obviously holding back the tears, but just barely. Lynda kissed him, and Pat shook hands.

Then there was a great blur of confusion, and we walked out of the President's office and went back to the second floor, with Secretary Clifford, who stood outside the door a little behind us. I looked back at him, and there he was standing, holding his hands behind his back, his head tilted up, with the oddest, most faraway expression on his face.

We gathered on the second floor—Marny and Clark, and the George Christians; Leonard Marks came up, and so did Doug Cater; and Secretary and Mrs. Wilbur Cohen; and Juanita and a few others. Marny had tears in her eyes. Nearly everybody just looked staggered and struck silent—and then the phones began to ring.

I went immediately and called Liz, who was in a state of near shock. I was going to call Bess, when I was called to the phone by Abigail McCarthy, who said, "Bird, Bird, you know what I've always thought of you." And then she said, "When he made the announcement, I could only think of you standing in front of the Wilson portrait . . ." And she didn't have to go on. I know what I always think in front of the Wilson portrait. In that face you see the toll the office and the times extracted. Its message to me is: "A President should have his portrait painted reasonably early in the office."

Dean Rusk called Lyndon, and I got to say a word. And then I talked to Bess. Then Bill Moyers called him, and once more Lyndon put me on the phone . . . I talked to John and Ivo Sparkman; and to Alice and George Brown, who had Oveta with them, and they seemed stunned but satisfied with his decision. Mary Lasker called and it sounded as if she were crying, but she said, "I know it must be the right thing to do, since the President did it."

About 11, Tom Johnson came over, bringing thirty-five reporters, and Lyndon went into the Yellow Room with them, looking as if a great load had been taken off his shoulders. I believe he made it quite clear to them that his decision was final, and that any talk of a draft was foolishness.

Liz' request to me from the reporters had been, "How would I sum it up?"—what kind of a statement—and I told her, "We have done a lot; there's a lot left to do in the remaining months; maybe this is the only way to get it done."

It must have been one o'clock or later when the last guest left and Lyndon went to bed. And I, too, feeling immeasurably lighter. At last the decision had been irrevocably stated, and as well as any human can, we knew our future!

Lyndon's speech had been, I believe, nobly done, and in its way almost as dramatic as our entrance into this job—although the actual exit is still nine months away, if the Lord lets us live. And to these nine months I'm going to bring the best I possibly can.

I went to sleep planning.

Thursday, April 4

I was back at the White House by 3 o'clock from my brief visit to that beautiful never-never land—Mrs. Merriweather Post's home in Palm Beach. The headlines of the Washington papers today were so hopeful—"HANOI OFFERS TALKS ON BOMBING HALT" . . . "U.S. ACCEPTS, WILL ESTABLISH CONTACT" . . . "JOHNSON OFF TODAY FOR HAWAII PARLEY ON VIETNAM POLICY." And another headline—"RFK–HHH SEE LBJ."

I worked with Liz on my Texas trip. Seldom have I looked forward to a trip more than the one I begin tomorrow—Trails of Texas. It would give me a chance to do something for the "Discover America" program. There would be a large group of foreign writers along, brought by TWA. I have a passion for showing foreigners our country, not so much its major metropolitan areas such as New York and Washington, which they usually see anyway, but its countryside and little towns, and out-of-the-way gems, and this was just what I was going to do.

One of the flaws in the day was that it seemed to me Lyndon was going at an even faster pace than before he made known his decision Sunday night. Marie said he had had hardly any rest, and was very tired. He was leaving for Hawaii tonight. And there was a Democratic Fund Raising Dinner this evening. I got the word that we were going to that, which meant evening dress and up-hairdo.

While Mr. Per was fixing my hair, Lynda Bird, who had been watching TV, came flying into my room crying: "Dr. King's been shot!" Quieting down a little, she told us that Martin Luther King, about to lead a march in Memphis tomorrow, had been shot on a motel balcony, and was on his way to the hospital.

From that moment on the evening assumed a nightmare quality. A few moments later Lynda came in and said, "Mama, he's dead!" Everybody's mind began racing off in its own direction, as to what this would mean—to racial violence in our country, to the work of so many who were trying to bring us together—how far would it set us back?

There I sat with an elaborate hairdo, in my elegant, festive, flame-colored chiffon, ready for the Democratic Dinner, which was already in progress. But the hands of the clock had stopped, and we were in a strange sort of suspended state, for the next hour or two—Lynda and Luci and I.

Lyndon was in his office—I knew he was working on a statement. He delivered it on TV from the White House: "America is shocked and saddened by the brutal slaying tonight of Dr. Martin Luther King. I ask every citizen to reject the blind violence that has struck down Dr. King, who lived by nonviolence. I pray that his family can find comfort in the memory of all he tried to do for the land he loved so well. I have just conveyed the sympathy of Mrs. Johnson and myself to his widow, Mrs. King."

The line that cried out to me was, "I hope that all Americans tonight will search their hearts as they ponder this most tragic incident . . ." And then was the line that settled our personal, immediate questions—"I have canceled my plans for the evening. I am postponing my trip to Hawaii."

So I took off my flame-colored chiffon dress and put on a hostess gown. Sometime after 10 Lyndon came in with Clark and Marny Clifford, and Marie, and Arthur Krim, and Mary Rather. How fitting that Mary should be here with us at the ending of our years in Washington—she had been with us close to the beginning, and in so many of the moments of high crisis.

Dinner was a strange, quiet meal. I thought, and maybe everybody else did, that we had been pummeled by such an avalanche of emotions the last four days that we couldn't feel anymore, and here we were, poised on the edge of another abyss, the bottom of which we could in no way see.

If we were silent, the TV was not; it blared constantly—statements from everybody, speculations on what would happen in various cities . . . fearfulness, speculations and tensions. I do not remember when the first word came of crowds gathering here in Washington. I consulted with Clark Clifford as to whether I should continue on my own trip to Texas tomorrow morning. Clark, as always cautious, said: "Let's wait until morning and see what the situation is and decide then."

FREDERICKSBURG AND LBJ RANCH

I was up early after a restless night. I went into Lyndon's room for coffee. He was still firm in his feeling that I should go. Liz called and I told her the trip was still on. We both recognized we would have to make some changes in the speeches. The world had changed overnight.

I told Luci good-by and headed for Dulles Airport with Stewart Udall. We stopped under the nose of the plane for pictures—how many times we've done that! Inside the plane I went down the aisle, put out my hand right and left, and met all the foreign correspondents—thirty-eight from thirteen European countries, plus a sizable contingent of Washington press.

I was aware of a feeling of uncertainty and tension in the air. As soon as we were aloft, I went to the PA system, and in a quiet, serious voice I said, "We travel with heavy hearts today, because of the tragedy of Dr. King's death. Every man must look into his own heart, and ask himself if his every word, every act, leads toward peace and healing in our country. This lays a demand on all Americans, for understanding, self-control, and steady, determined work to attack the problems that made possible such violence. The greatest tribute we could pay to Dr. King is to bring forth from this cruel tragedy some good action on our problems."

Having said all I could, I put it behind me and welcomed them on a journey to the part of the country that I know best. The jolly air that is usually present when these trips begin was absent, but I thought the tension lessened. In a way, we were encapsulated, sealed off from the world in the plane.

For the next few days I would be tour guide, showing my own state—its historic towns, its blooming fields of wildflowers in April, the queen of seasons in Texas, trying really to say to those foreign writers that there *are* places in this country which are not aflame with hatred and riots.

At Fredericksburg, we piled into gaily decorated orchard wagons, each pulled by a tractor, about twelve of us in each with a guide in the lead seat. Mr. Bill Petmecky, looking like a burgomaster on his wagon, was telling the history and the sights of Fredericksburg in German. Mrs. Art Kowert was our guide, giving the interesting story of the old Nimitz Hotel, built in 1847 in the shape of a ship. She told how a young son of that home, Chester Nimitz, had become Commander in Chief of the Pacific Fleet in World War II. The building with the white elephant above the door had been the White Elephant Saloon! And she pointed out the statue of John O. Meusebach, who had led the settlers here, discarding his title of Baron. He had negotiated a treaty with the Indians in 1847, had started trade between them and the pioneers.

She told about the custom of the early pioneer, having his business place fronting the street—his saddle shop, or general store, or barber shop—and then building his home behind it. Old St. Mary's Catholic Church, built in 1861, with its stone steeple, added a touch of old-world charm to the landscape. We passed one of those Sunday Houses just as Mrs. Kowert was describing the use of the houses—how the pioneers would come in from their farms over the weekend to do their "trading," attend parties and civic meetings, and go to church. And there was a couple dressed in the costumes of the day, rocking on the front porch, and some children also in the clothes of 1850 playing out front.

Mrs. Kowert showed us Cross Mountain where the early pioneers had found the remnants of a cross left by the Spanish missionaries sometime in the 1700's, and described the Easter fires.

There was lots of German spoken, and all along the street were ladies in the costumes of the 1840's and 1850's. Some of the costumes were authentic-looking and you felt sure that they had retrieved them from old trunks at home. We stopped at the old Kammlah House, now the Pioneer Museum. Because this part of the building was the Kammlahs' old general store, I pointed out to them some of the articles that the pioneers had bought and sold—corn meal, ground at a local grist mill, sulphur matches sold in bulk from a big tin container, an ancient bottle of liniment, and other remedies for the ills of man and beast. Everybody looked at what interested him most—a handsome deerskin jacket elaborately beaded and fringed that had been worn to Baron von Meusebach's peace parley with Indian Chief Santana, a tiny-waisted white satin wedding dress, and an engraving made in some town in Bavaria of the weeping local citizenry saying good-by to the adventurous pioneers who were setting off for faraway Texas.

Sometime during the day I took my compact out to powder my nose. It crashed to the floor. I picked it up and opened it and the glass was shattered into a hundred tiny fragments. An involuntary chill went through me. Somehow, it was part of the dark undercurrent of the day. Underneath the sunshine and bright excitement and genuine interest there was a sense of expectancy of we knew not what, almost foreboding.

In the backyard of the museum there was a tent, with German pastries and hot steaming coffee, served by anxious hostesses. It had been a long time since brunch on the plane and I was ravenous, as I always am on these trips. But there were hands to shake, and thanks to bestow, and greetings to familiar faces across the crowd, and I knew that I was about to go home by car for a fifteen-minute advance before the press arrived at the Ranch on the bus.

In the car I asked Jerry, "How is everything in Washington?" His voice came back, heavily for him, "Not good . . . Fires and rioting, trouble on Fourteenth Street, supposed to have been three persons killed."

We hurried home and I changed into my blue denim skirt and red plaid blouse and was out by the side gate when the first of the press buses rolled up. For the next three hours I was their Number One Tour Guide around the LBJ Ranch, and this may have been the most memorable part of the trip for them, for the wrong reason. Later I heard that the Europeans kept on exclaiming, "How surprising. She did it herself! Can you ever imagine Queen Elizabeth doing this, or Mrs. De Gaulle?" It appeared that a London editor had bet one of the young women reporters he had sent that she would never even meet me.

Such affairs as a tour of the Ranch house are always disorganized and haphazard; even so, it was relatively good. I don't think I ever had a more interested audience. Mostly I talked about our personal feeling for the country and our home.

Then we boarded the schoolbuses borrowed from Johnson City for a ride through the pastures. To corral a crowd you really need a bull horn and a commanding presence, and neither one suits me! A microphone on a bus, bouncing over pasture roads, is not ideal either, but it had to do.

I tried to point out the deer, turkey gobblers, family cemetery, the house where Lyndon was born. Questions from the foreign press were frequent and showed a genuine interest that made me feel pleased we had come on.

It was 6 o'clock and growing remarkably chilly when we got back to the house. A long table, spread with a red-checkered tablecloth and laden with ribs, fried chicken legs, chili con queso with Fritos, was set up in the yard. Beer, soft drinks, and hot coffee were being passed and we were all hungry. I divided myself between gulping food and trying to answer questions enthusiastically. Tamales were the hit of the day.

After my guests had left for San Antonio, where I would join them later, I telephoned Lynda. She said the White House was like a fortress. Security was tightened on everybody who came in or went out. There was rioting and looting and fires on Fourteenth Street and down toward the Capitol. Fire hoses were being slashed by the rioters. There was a report that seven people had been killed and three hundred people were in the District of Columbia hospitals.

I remember that I asked her a number of questions and she finally said to me wearily, "Mother, I don't know. It would take the dropping of the hydrogen bomb to get my attention today." Of course, I wondered how this would affect our plans for tomorrow. Should I go to Hemisfair? I called Liz and we hammered and worked on and changed my speeches to make them pertinent to the riots, until I was relatively satisfied with them. I talked to John Connally and then I had a conference call with John and Liz. John felt that there might be disturbances at Hemisfair, probably three demonstrations. One peace-loving, and two militant, a Mexican-American group and about fifteen hundred SDS members. He and Nellie were emphatically going right on with their plans to be there, and he hoped that I would come—very much hoped so.

I talked to my agents. They suggested two changes. One, that I arrive a little late. Second, that I go from building to building in one of the mini-buses rather than walk. I agreed. I talked to Lyndon . . . he sounded tired and a little remote. It must have been a shattering day for him. He said he thought I should go on to Hemisfair. There was no flicker of uncertainty in his voice.

I finally got to bed around one o'clock after a day that ran the full gamut of emotions, against the background of mounting turbulence, while the whole nation seemed to be straining at its seams. And yet, I had a queer sense of ambivalence. Though I was right in the middle of it, because of my husband's job and the presence in Washington of all my family, I, myself, seemed removed and encased in a different world. Here we were just hearing about events and reading about them as though they were happening on the moon.

Monday, April 8

PADRE ISLAND, TEXAS

Today began early. When I spoke to Ashton in Washington, she told me that Patrick might be leaving Thursday for Vietnam. His mother and father were there and it sounded like good-by.

I joined the press on the big plane at the airport for the flight to Corpus

Christi. We fought the weather every inch of the way every day of this trip and we won the whole round, just by the skin of our teeth.

We drove toward Padre Island and a park naturalist told us that this was one of the great fly-overs, with hundreds of varieties of birds—whooping cranes, roseate spoonbills, white geese—settling at the close-by bird refuges at Anahuac and Aransas. We drove over the long causeway and at last reached Padre Island—the 113-mile-long finger of sand that parallels the shores of Texas, eighty miles of which now belong to the Park Service as a National Seashore.

About 11 o'clock we reached the dedication site and what met my eyes I shall always remember with warmth. There was a crowd of at least ten thousand people. Our buses rolled up and disgorged eighty U.S. and foreign journalists as six high school bands boomed out "The Eyes of Texas." The crowd cheered and I walked up onto one of the most picturesque platforms I have ever stood on. It was made of driftwood, bleached and worn and gnarled, festooned with ropes the size of a man's arm which had obviously seen service—perhaps on some fishing boat. I raised a silent little salute to whoever had put it together—and to so many things all during the day! Senator Yarborough came up to greet me, for Padre Island is his love.

We stood on the platform, facing the sand dunes fringed with grasses that bent in the light breeze, and behind us the waves rolling in. The day was still overcast but the sun broke out just as the proceedings began. The Bishop of Corpus Christi, His Excellency Thomas Drury, gave a poetic invocation and then Stew Udall introduced the guests—George Hartzog, the Director of the National Park Service, who spoke briefly; Kika de la Garza, who spoke at more length with Latin fervor. Padre Island has just become part of his District. Turning to me he said, "I ask your permission to say we love you, Lady Bird."

Yarborough described the history of Padre Island. He is deeply versed in history and folklore, and speaks his devotion well. And then the high school bands played "America the Beautiful," with a vast symphonic effect. Three of the bands were on one side of us and three on the other and they were speaking back and forth to each other. This was a moment to put a lump in your throat. On this high note, it came my turn to speak. I looked down into a sea of faces—eager, smiling, expectant—the sort of scene that would always have a special fascination to one who has lived the life I have. A bunch of Girl Scouts seated cross-legged on the sand, Brownies and Campfire Girls and Boy Scouts, each with a job to do to help in this crowd . . . kinfolks—I saw Tommy and Chris Taylor and their two little girls . . . and friends of thirty years—Carroll Keach and Bob Jackson.

I told them how delighted I was to be here on this important day in the life of Padre Island. "Its dedication into the National Park System means it will forever belong to the people, the generations of campers, scout troops, fishermen, birdwatchers, and sunbathers, the travelers from near and far." I spoke of the National Park Service and its 133,000,000 visitors each year to these national treasures. "What does it take to make a National Park? There are many here on this stand who could answer that. It takes a dream . . . help from newspapers like the *Corpus Christi Caller-Times*, surveys and legislation," and here I spoke of Congressmen John Young and Kika de la Garza. "And, if I may be forgiven for pointing it out, it also takes a President who recognizes the value of this kind of project. In his years in the White House, the President has secured thirty-five new additions to the National Park System, one million acres—the equivalent of Grand Canyon National Park and Grand Teton combined."

I went on to describe a family vacation we had had twenty years ago along one of these ribbons of sand on the Texas Gulf Coast. My mind turned back to it . . . how we walked the beach and felt that sense of timelessness that envelops one like the rolling waves. "There is always an ineffable tranquility when you are face to face with sea and sky, forces which put one's own problems into perspective. I remember the delicious sense of discovery, coming upon a treasure in the sand—a blue glass ball that had floated to these shores, maybe from a Portuguese fisherman's net. It has been my talisman ever since."

Then I said what I hope they will remember, if anything. "It takes not only the dreamers, the believers, the legislators—it will take also the keepers, the watchful stewards for national belongings such as Padre Island. So I would urge those who are charged with the facilities which will doubtless be built, not only in the seashore areas, but on its commercial fringes, to make man's structures in harmony with nature's"—a plea that the roads, buildings, parking lots, signs, and markers should be tasteful; an assertion that if they were, they would reap dividends over the decades.

I ended with a quote that Liz had found from the records of the Spaniard Diego Parrilla's own survey party, who first occupied Padre Island. "Her treasure is the gold of her sun, the silver of her moonlight, and the sapphire of her pearl-crested waves. This treasure requires no iron strong box. It is safe from the greedy hands of man, for it belongs to God."

George Hartzog and I then stepped down from the speaker's stand. There was a huge stump of driftwood with the dedication plaque bolted to it. Its veiling?—what else but a fish net! As I lifted it back with a flourish, I thought I had never enjoyed an unveiling more.

We drove down the beach, then, to the site of the fish fry. It was a perfect stage setting. Shrimpers were sailing out in the gulf, surfers with their boards were lined up on the sand and some were riding a long wave in. Under a gaily colored tent, tables were laid with blue and red cloths. Sea shells and bottles formed the centerpieces, and there were sand dollars as souvenirs, and on all sides netting with seafronds and shells. The buffet tables were laden with an incredible array, mostly of good things that come out of the sea—crab claws, shrimp—barbecued, boiled and fried—stuffed crab, fried filet of red snapper, fried oysters, vegetable trays and relishes, shrimp tacos (I had never seen them before), French fried potatoes, cole slaw, and the hit of the day aside from the fish—hush puppies! (These took a bit of explaining to the foreign press.)

When we finished I couldn't wait to get out on the beach. Alas, there were some blue jellyfish and Portuguese men-of-war around, but nevertheless I walked and walked, barefooted. It was the softest sand I ever felt and there are eighty miles of it, all free! That is what I kept on pointing out, over and over, to the foreign newspapermen when I was with one or two of them at a time. Some of the reporters stretched out on the sand and dozed in the sun or swam. A group gathered on the dunes with Brownie McNeil and Joe Frantz and listened to tales of Padre Island, of lost treasures and ghostly galleons.

It was after 5 when we got back to the Driscoll Hotel in Corpus Christi and I lay down gratefully for a few minutes of rest. Bess called from the White House. Obviously she was very much upset. She did not think we should go on with the State Dinner on Wednesday night. The curfew was still in force. She described the incessant barrage of TV coverage . . . of looting and fires . . . of seeing policemen stand by while people knocked the windows out of stores, grabbed TV sets and loaded them into their cars . . . a little child permitted to walk off with a teddy bear and toys, while a woman loaded up everything she could carry, ignored by the policeman standing by. It was as though I were talking to an inhabitant of another planet.

THE TEXAS COUNTRYSIDE

I awoke to a gray and foggy world and my heart sank. Our wildflower day! Well, no need to worry about something I couldn't change. I talked to Lyndon, who is at Camp David and about to go into a series of meetings. His voice was calm, the least flurried of any I've heard from Washington.

About 9 o'clock I boarded our bus headed for Goliad. It was a two-hour ride, with the rain misting the windshield. And a part of everybody's mind, I am sure (certainly mine), was in Atlanta at Dr. King's funeral. I had heard bits and pieces of what was going on. It sounded as if a quorum of the Senate had gone there. Every Presidential candidate was attending except Wallace, including Nixon, with Hubert to represent the Administration. There was a vast throng, numbering about fifty thousand people.

South Texas was low and flat and dotted with live oaks, and great splashes of wildflowers began to appear along the road and in the pastures . . . pale pink buttercups, wild verbena, coral paint brush, Indian blanket. Soon the skies began to lift. The bus stopped so we could see a herd of cattle driven close to the fence. It was a huge herd, about five hundred head, part Brahma, part Hereford, a motley lot—gray, white, spotted, red. There were a dozen cowboys herding them. I noticed that several of them wore chaps that looked as if they had seen real use. The foreign correspondents piled out of the bus and went up to the fence, eagerly taking pictures. It looked as if this bunch of steers was one of their favorite subjects of the trip. Several asked me to stand by the fence. Zac Lentz, a cattleman, rode on with us. He was asked about his twenty years as one of Lyndon's "lieutenants." He said how sorry he was politically, how glad personally, that Lyndon wasn't going to run again. He said to me, "Now you-all will have to come down and shoot birds with us and see our ranch!"

I had read about La Bahia and the four years of restoration invested in it, but I was not prepared for the sight. Suddenly in this flat expanse of land we came up over a slight rise and there, across a solid blanket of paint brush and gaillardia and wild phlox, rose the old, mellowed, stone walls of the Presidio and the church. It was breathtaking in its perfection. Not the least of its charm was the sense of discovery, so far was it off the beaten path.

As we approached the walls, the church bells began to peal—you could see the little sentry post at the corner of the Presidio, from which the

Spanish soldiers must have looked out for hostile Indians. The outpost was built in 1749 but had fallen into a mass of ruins and now had been faithfully restored by Mrs. Kathryn Stoner O'Connor, a lover of Texas history, now in her eighties, who had paid for the restoration and participated in it.

The ceremony took place in front of the Presidio, the six flags of Texas flying behind us, the sun at last really breaking through the clouds. We looked out over the rolling pasture land, spotted with the unbelievable green of early mesquite and great splashes of wildflowers, and sensed behind us the two hundred years of Texas history in this old fort. The name of Goliad is branded on the memory of Texans—it was here in 1836 that Colonel Fannin and his 342 men were massacred during our war with Mexico.

The ceremony was brief. Bishop Drury gave the prayer. (I doubt if these foreign newsmen had ever been prayed over so much as in these five days!) And then the Master of Ceremonies, Father Kircher, introduced Congressman Abraham Kazen, who spoke with rousing warmth of Lyndon. Stewart Udall was introduced. He always speaks eloquently and earnestly of the things he loves—recreation, wilderness, restorations. And I made my short speech, the theme of which combined so many of the things I loved —history, restorations, homefolk, and the most beautiful spring I have ever seen in Texas! Then we unveiled the National Historic Landmark plaque, and at that moment a cannon from the bastion in front of the chapel boomed out.

The architect responsible for the restoration, Raiford Stripling, took us through La Bahia, showed us the artifacts that had been dug up during the four years—cannon balls, shoe buckles, spoons, a part of a pistol, and an exhibit of seven levels of habitation, from early Indian tribes to the present. He showed us the room where Fannin and his little band of Texans were imprisoned, packed so tightly there was no room to sit down or lie down, before they were taken out and shot.

We walked over to the Chapel of Our Lady of Loretto where Mass has been held every year since before the Declaration of Independence of the Thirteen Colonies. On the altar there was a doll-sized statue of the Virgin Mary—the oldest image of the Virgin in any church in Texas, dressed incongruously in a peach-colored taffeta of the 1960's! And then our guide told me the story. Old as she was, the Virgin got a new dress many times a year. Every bride who was married in this chapel, by tradition, was entitled to have a small replica of her wedding dress made and to dress Our Lady of Loretto in it—and so she was appareled until the next bride came along.

We walked out of the chapel, loaded onto the bus, and drove on to Gonzales. There were huge yuccas lining both sides of the road, creamy white blossoms covering the four-foot stalks. As we looked down the highway, the right of way was an unbelievable expanse of red phlox, fading into deep pink phlox or paint brush that finally became mixed with bluebonnets, Indian blankets, coreopsis, and wine cups much taller than those in the Hill Country.

On a little-traveled stretch of road we made a stop. Everybody got out and there on our left in a pasture dotted with live oaks was the most solid blanket of bluebonnets, paint brush—the whole wide palette of wildflower colors! We took pictures of all the Germans with me, all the Italians with me, group after group, sitting in the bluebonnets. Every now and then somebody would warn, "Watch out for rattlesnakes!"

It was 2 o'clock when we reached Gonzales, the "Lexington of Texas," Joe Frantz having briefed us beforehand on the "Come and Take It" story of Gonzales; on Travis' letter from the Alamo, and how the only men who responded were the little band from Gonzales, who had actually fought their way *into* the jaws of death at the Alamo. Here on the courthouse square at Gonzales was the wrap-up scene, an official good-by for our five-day adventure.

I have had a long love affair with courthouse squares! To a Texas politician of our time they are what the agora must have been to the Greeks. On the courthouse square you stand before the public and state your views and look your people in the eyes. They look you over and decide whether you are the man they want to represent them.

We stepped off the buses to a familiar scene, the ornate old Courthouse —part Gothic, part Victorian. Six little Brownies were lined up to present me with a wildflower bouquet—Boy Scouts, Girl Scouts, FHA girls, the Gonzales High School Band, Liz' brother-in-law (County Judge John Romberg), the Mayor, and all the officials. We mounted the platform. There was an invocation and the band played "America the Beautiful" (what else?) and we all joined in singing; then came the welcomes and introductions.

When it was my turn, I aimed my speech at our thirty-eight foreign editors and our own press, too, especially those from Washington and the East. "There are, across this land," I said, "seventeen thousand towns about the size of this one. To discover America, you have to know them, as well as cities like New York, San Francisco, and Washington. Our visitors have come at a time of anguish and turmoil in our country. They have seen our frictions laid bare, but I believe they have also seen that the crashing headlines that shook us, as much as they did the world, are not the whole story of this country. They do not blot out the progress that has been made across this great democracy. Behind the smoke of our troubled cities there is a great wide land of strength and confidence and warmth and many cities where work continues and there is fellowship and understanding. Our tears for our country's troubles are deep, but deeper still is our confidence in the future, and our ability to meet and master man's basic problem—to live in peace.''

Well, I was topped! The star of that day was Hector Legge, of Dublin, Ireland, "Dean" of the traveling journalists, a towering figure about six feet five with a Lincolnesque face, who rose to deliver a farewell on behalf of all of his colleagues. He ended by making a better foreign policy speech than I have heard any American make in a long time. He said, "I think all countries owe a great duty to the American nation and the American people. They tax themselves, they endure, they suffer in the cause of freedom—in Vietnam or wherever else it may be. They made a stand to stop the onslaught of communism, that evil thing that is trying to destroy the souls of men all over the world." He went on to say that in his view many in this country and in Europe are forgetting events that happened not very long ago, ". . . but I suppose eaten bread is soon forgotten" (excellent line!). He noted that Australia and New Zealand are supporting the U.S. effort in Vietnam. "Because they are close to this peril, they know that this peril is there and it would annihilate them and their people but for the power of the United States of America." He had said all of this to me earlier and privately. I had not thought he would say it publicly and I was absolutely glowing.

On the courthouse square the three garden clubs of Gonzales had inaugurated a landscaping program and, together, we planted a Spanish oak. Then we were off for the last stop of the day and finally lunch.

Choosing a dress for such a day as this is an important part of the planning. I had worn my yellow ottoman cotton with an easy skirt and a coat and it proved just right—coat off when it was hot and a white mantilla for my head when we went into the chapel at La Bahia. I had stuck flat-heeled shoes in my straw bag for excursions into the fields of wildflowers.

We went to the rustic community building in nearby Palmetto State Park and there was a sight to behold—a long table loaded with a huge tub of fried chicken, potato salads of a dozen different kinds, fruit salads, pickles of every description, homemade breads! I told the foreign correspondents this spread was like "all-day singing and dinner on the grounds," which meant nothing to them until I explained that it was a typical church meeting of my youth in rural America. The Home Demonstration Club of Ottine, population one hundred, had furnished this wonderful meal, together with the officials of Gonzales and the "Wolf Hunters Club" (yes, they are still in business and need to be, I was told).

Everybody loaded his plate and we sat down without any formality and ate like the starving travelers that we were. When at last we had had our fill, there was a brief ceremony. This time it was the foreign journalists who took the lead. They thanked everybody. One delegation after another gave me a present from their own country as a memento of the trip. By this time even the most sophisticated French and somewhat frozen Swedes had warmed up. The Italians had long ago become completely convivial. At last the foreign journalists piled onto their bus. We said good-by all around and then they struck up, of all things, "Auld Lang Syne" and that was the last thing I heard as they drove away.

On the plane flying back to Washington, I had my only real talk of the trip with Stew. He had spent a good deal of time with his son and had a faraway look in his eyes. Now he sat down beside me, and I felt that he wanted to talk. He asked me if the reception for McNamara, Gardner, and Trowbridge was still on. I said certainly, but I was not sure what day it was. He seemed a little surprised. He said he and Postmaster General Lawrence O'Brien had talked about the election. He had said he hoped he could stay out of it and continue to work for the things in conservation in which the President believed and which he had spent his time trying to push forward. And then he said something about another Cabinet member who had, he knew, reservations about supporting Senator Kennedy, which he did not share.

Stew is a very articulate man, but I sensed that he could not quite get out all that he wanted to say to me. I can imagine how he feels these days, pummeled by conflicting loyalties. But I felt there was a withdrawal of his enthusiasm for the Johnsons. I would not be surprised if he got out of the Cabinet. But there is still a real dedication in him for all the work of conservation and I think he gives credit to Lyndon for his effectiveness in that field. He talked about the things that might be done in the next months to nail down further the conservation program. I was very, very tired. And it was, somehow, a sad conversation that left much unsaid.

When we reached Washington, near 11 o'clock, I could only think that this was one of the best trips I'll ever have. My homeland, my home people, had lived up to every hope!

I drove from Dulles to the White House with that sense of expectancy that you might have on a battlefield looking for trenches and gutted buildings and, of course, saw nothing except very silent and deserted streets. The curfew was still on.

Thursday, April 11

THE WHITE HOUSE

I went into Lyndon's room early to have breakfast with him and there in earnest conversation was Ambassador Ellsworth Bunker—gentle, patrician, experienced. I think he must command the respect of people of most diverse beliefs. He was speaking of countries or people who have a vested interest in our country's failure. They were talking about the peace negotiations and Lyndon said, "This is the most important thing in the world to me." They discussed the location for the talks. I caught phrases . . . "I am not going into any Communist capital. I am not going to run or bend or stretch." This was Lyndon. "They have got to learn that they are negotiating with the United States, Fulbright notwithstanding, and I do not appreciate their conducting negotiations in the press." Lyndon was speaking of the sort of countries that could be sites for peace talks. "They should be neutral, telephones untapped, good communications. I am not going to let them use me."

At one point the Ambassador drew from his pocket a letter from his wife, Carol Laise—also an Ambassador—written just after Lyndon had announced that he would not run again. It was so sweet. She had quoted a verse from the Bible. So many of these letters quote from the Bible. Well, if we can earn the respect of people like Ellsworth Bunker and his wife, I am proud. At one point he said wryly in his understated way that the TET offensive had had more effect here than it did in Vietnam. The South Vietnamese stood up to it.

Sometime during the course of the day I got word that there would be the signing of the Civil Rights Bill, passed yesterday by the House, in the East Room at 5. Lyndon and I entered the East Room, to prolonged clapping, to find an unusually large group from Congress, the Cabinet, Civil Rights leaders, and an enormous number from the press. Over in one corner were the Foxcroft girls who had had tea with me earlier. To see these girls from an elegant school steeped in Southern tradition at this ceremony was, somehow, a sign of the changing times.

This was the signing of the third major Civil Rights Act of Lyndon's Presidency, and his speech was rallying. He said that all America was outraged by the assassination of Martin Luther King. It was also outraged by the looting and burning that defiles our democracy. We must put our shoulders together and put a stop to both. The time is here. Action must be now. "Violence cannot redress a solitary wrong or remedy a single unfairness." Then Lyndon appealed to Congress to enact twenty programs that he had recommended this year that deal with social justice.

We went into the Blue Room for the receiving line and I was back upstairs before 6 with minutes to change into my brown lace dress for the mass departure of Cabinet officers, the farewell party that had been planned for the McNamaras, the Gardners, and the Trowbridges. Only yesterday Larry O'Brien had resigned and Bess had come to me rather grimly and said, "Would you like to include the Larry O'Briens among the honorees in the party tomorrow?" I said, "Sure. We will just give him a blank silver tray and engrave it later." These parties have always had a nostalgic quality, saying good-by to people you have worked with closely and well and hard and formed the sort of bonds of friendship with that are forged in no other way, except possibly in battle. This party was already an emotional tour de force with the three of them, and adding Larry O'Brien gave it still another dimension.

But underlying all of the events, all of the emotions of the day, was the one I kept returning to—Patrick was leaving sometime this evening for Vietnam. Just as I started into the party Luci called me and said, "Mother, will you come in our room a minute?" I went in. Her face was so small and white and the baby, who is always so happy, was restless and fussy. I think he sensed all day that something unusual was going on. Luci said, "Mother, Pat is leaving in about thirty minutes." I said, "I will be back in just a minute."

I went to the door of the Yellow Room and the first person in was Larry O'Brien who said, "Mrs. Johnson, I want you to know that nobody has ever been nicer to me than your husband." There was no need of the receiving line. We had all known each other a long time, the honor guests and members of their families and their closest friends. I hugged Margy and Bob. They both looked brown and rested and so did the Trowbridges, both so young and handsome. It is cruel that he has been snatched out of the front line by a heart attack at the age of thirty-seven. John and Aida Gardner were there—handsome, patrician, and—as they always have been —a little removed from it all—from the world of politics, I mean.

As soon as I had greeted everybody, I slipped out and went back to Luci's room, and there was a tableau that I shall always remember— Patrick in uniform, with a huge round can under one arm. I asked what it was—cookies made by Luci! He scooped up his son in the other arm. I hugged them all together and said rather foolishly, "Are you going right now?" And Luci said, "No, Mother, Patrick is going upstairs to sign his will." Larry Temple had prepared the document and was waiting for them in the Solarium, where most of their courtship had taken place. So they went down the hall—Patrick and Luci and the baby and their friends, the Alden Smiths. Later Luci told me that when they got to the airport and Patrick said good-by, the baby cried and cried and beat on the window of the car with the palms of his little hands crying, "Daddy, Daddy!" Even at ten months, he knew something was happening.

I went back in the Yellow Room. Lyndon was late (he had been telling Pat good-by). He circled the room greeting all the guests and got down to the business of his speech with a certain dispatch. I stood by him to present the trays. I remember his words as sort of a eulogy to the quality of the men who leave more comfortable and more remunerative posts to work for their government in the offices of the Cabinet. I remember with a rising of the heart one particular reference to a Cabinet member who was not there. He spoke of Rusk as "the noblest Roman of them all."

Then he began to hand me the trays, first the McNamaras' and I gave it to Margy. Bob came forward beginning his little talk amusingly: "Once before I tried to express myself about this Administration, with disastrous results." It was a dear speech and I think his feeling for Lyndon came through. Then we gave the tray for Secretary Gardner to Aida, and in his cool, elegant way, John spoke of his gratitude for working in this Administration. I felt good about the things he said about us both. And then Sandy Trowbridge spoke. Much the junior here, his speech was forthright, fresh, and charming and it endeared them to me as I have increasingly felt through these brief months. Then Larry O'Brien spoke about leaving us to work for Bobby. It was a hard spot. He tried to be humorous.

I talked with the close friends of the honor guests and, as always, to the Arthur Goldbergs whom I like tremendously. Most of the guests left about 8. Lyndon had long ago gone back to the office. A little past 9 Lyndon returned. Luci, looking small and white and silent, for her, and protectively flanked by the Alden Smiths and Lynda, had come back from the airport and we all sat down for dinner. What a day it had been!

The picture of Patrick was what I would remember. It's been repeated all across this land over a span of two centuries. I was so proud of him and so proud of the country that produced young men like him and Chuck.

The guests left about 10 but pieces of the day kept drifting through my mind. I was glad that I had lived it—every moment of it—but I felt beaten, exhausted at the end of it—and what, then, must Lyndon feel?

Saturday, April 13

LBJ RANCH

Today was as near idyllic as a day can be. Some of the headlines were easing up—"D.C. CURFEW OFF, GRADUAL PULL-OUT OF GI's STARTS." One jolting story—"RFK LAUDED BY McNAMARA IN TV TAPES." After the strenuous, demanding thirteen days—or was it two lifetimes?—this weekend was an island of peace and rest.

After lunch we began one of those long, open-end trips over the beautiful spring countryside—to the Green Mountain Ranch and the Davis Ranch and finally to the lake.

A little past 8 we landed at the West Ranch to see a strange, blood-red moon rising, ominous, foreboding, and across the sky a long white trail of a jet. It was dark and a curious sight, a dramatic combination.

The men settled at once into one of their domino games where Lyndon and A. W. play together and there is a great deal of bluffing and teasing, and as much talk as skill. Then we had one of Neva's delicious dinners. For longer than twenty years I have enjoyed the hospitality of this house. In country fashion we left very soon after dinner, and we were back at the home ranch before 11. What a good way to spend a day—that is, in contrast to those that have gone before.

And here I am back counting again! It is two down and fifty-four to go, that is—counting the weeks for Chuck. I had begun counting for Lyndon's term of office, just when I don't know, but I know it was before he was half-way through, because I was counting for the half-way point and thereafter counting the time he would make the announcement that he wasn't going to run again. But except for the boys, this was the sort of day when time stood still and I was satisfied with the present and didn't reach for anything else.

Oddly, when I had told Lyndon that Lynda Bird was not going to come with us to Texas this time, he had been a little irritated and asked, "Why?" and I explained that she was really just bone tired, physically and emotionally tired, and had to get some rest. He had said, "She is not pregnant, is she?" and I said, "Yes! Don't you remember?" She had told me on February 29—she and Chuck—sitting beside the bed in my room, quite simply. Not as a for-sure fact, but as almost sure, and since then she has hardly mentioned it at all. If it were Luci, she would be delighted to give you a progress report every day! Yes, her daddy said, she *had* told him that they had "hoped," but nobody had come back to tell him that it was absolutely sure. He seemed a little hurt and when I told him she wasn't feeling very well, he said, "You've got to get the best doctor. I want to be sure they know what they are doing. You call Jim Cain and you talk to that doctor yourself and you make sure that she is doing everything right."

Wednesday, April 17

THE WHITE HOUSE

It seems to me this April that I face every day as a mountain to be climbed. The headlines were relatively good this morning—"LAST GI's PULL OUT OF CITY," "COMMAND IN PACIFIC BRIEFS LBJ," and one funny one in the light of the whole thing, "LBJ's POPULARITY RISES 13 POINTS."

Sometime during the morning I talked to Lyndon in Honolulu. He sounded very tired. It was a very early hour out there—I think around 6 o'clock and he said he had been awake since 2:30 A.M. His eyes had been giving him a lot of trouble and he had not slept well. He said he would probably return to Texas Thursday night. I jumped at the chance to meet him there.

A little before 11, I put on my prettiest spring outfit, a white dress with a deep pink-red coat, and went down into the Rose Garden for coffee. It was a glorious, golden day and we deserve it after having done our beautification tour twice in the rain. The garden was beautiful and the almost two hundred guests—donors, members of my Beautification Committee or of the Society for a More Beautiful Capital, our Speakers' Committee and press ladies—were gathering there. A little past 11 we got into five buses, with Jane Freeman, Katie Louchheim, Nash, Sharon, and me as tour guides. This year, my last, nothing could have stopped me from being one of the tour guides! (And if there was anyone to whom the day meant as much as to me—it was Sharon Francis, who has handled our beautification mail.)

For more than an hour our buses rolled throughout the city, the guides pointing out the plantings of Mary Lasker's ten thousand azaleas on Pennsylvania Avenue, our first planting at Independence and Third—one of those hundreds of triangles that donors have transformed from a few scraggly wild onions to bursts of color and tree-shaded park benches. Off the Southwest Freeway, I pointed out the delightful Mexican playground equipment—some of the five thousand pieces sent up by Mrs. Diaz Ordaz, and then, Buchanan School, where Brooke Astor's generosity is making an "outdoor living room" for people of that low-income neighborhood. On Columbia Island we recalled that we had planted eight hundred thousand daffodil bulbs and twenty-four hundred dogwood trees—what a flowering gateway that will be to this great city!

So many hands—so many enthusiastic can-do people—so many generous gifts have sown the seeds. I couldn't say enough thank-yous. But back at the White House luncheon, I tried. I have three years of this subject in my heart and head, and a lifetime of interest behind that, and I was keenly aware that this was the last time that I would see many of these people, and I wanted them to know, very much, how grateful I was to them.

"Over the past three years, the people in this room have produced nearly two and a half million dollars to take steps toward making this nation's capital more livable and more beautiful. Not only is your handiwork enjoyed by the three million people who live and work in this city, it can be seen also by seventeen million visitors who come here each year, and our work here has inspired other cities across the country. This has been one of the most lovely springs I can remember in Washington's history. It has also been one of the most poignant and grave. That fact underscores the urgency of improving our environment for all people."

As always, I tried to get in my philosophy. My criteria for a project are that it receive the fullest use, that it can be maintained easily, and that the desire for it emanate from the neighborhood and its people.

I introduced Walter Washington, the main speaker. "In the most recent anxious hours for this city, he proved to all what many of us already knew —that he is a wise, compassionate, understanding leader. He epitomizes what I think makes a great public servant; for him no task is too big or too small. Threaded through everything he undertakes are zest and enthusiasm, and a belief that you can wrest from troubles constructive, forward action."

The Mayor looked so tired when he began that my heart ached for him. He spoke well, almost in a poetic strain. His thrust was that we, on our Committee, "make open spaces and recreation facilities a part of the daily living and the daily environment of people." And then he said so many kind, warm, generous things about me that I began to shrink down and look at my plate, but it was a great climax to three years of hard work together.

The luncheon was over at 3. And I had that mixed feeling of relaxation and "job well done," with an undertone of sadness, because this was, in a way, an end.

Tuesday, April 30

April is always the busiest month of the year. And this year it has been the most dramatic, the fullest, I have ever known. I find myself very tired. It is hard to get up in the morning. It was around 8:30 today when I went into Lyndon's room. Eric Hoffer was with him, his bulk filling the old wing chair, wearing as always when I have seen him a sort of workman's jacket—a man out of another age, cut to no pattern—intelligent, fresh, unique. He and Lyndon enjoy each other hugely and understand each other.

I read the newspaper headlines—"POOR PEOPLE'S CAMPAIGN BEGINNING PEACEFULLY" . . . "GROUPS CALLING ON CABINET OFFICERS" . . . "STILL NO AGREEMENT ON SITE FOR PEACE TALKS" . . . "COLUMBIA UNIVERSITY BEING TORN APART BY STUDENT REVOLT." But mostly I drank my coffee and listened. Hoffer said, "Why doesn't the middle stand up? We are so scared of the young." About the Negroes—"More doors are open than ever were before. There are more opportunities."

Lyndon asked him about his job—just what he taught, how many hours, and similar questions. He said, " I call myself a conversationalist in residence. Every Thursday afternoon I talk and people come in—they may be freshmen or Ph.D.'s, or a cab driver or a waitress from a beer joint."

For me, the big event of the day was a Senate Ladies Luncheon honoring me at the Capitol at one. It was held in the familiar old Senate Caucus Room—high-ceilinged, handsome—the scene of many explosive gatherings, including the Joe McCarthy years. But this one was a very happy gathering, nearly one hundred of the Senate wives, including many wives of the former Senators. Everybody, I think—I most of all—was conscious that this would be my last time with them as First Lady. I took my seat beside Muriel, who looked terribly weary. On the other side was Betty Talmadge who, they said, "had drawn a lucky number" placing her there.

The whole theme was Hawaiian and the entertainment was Hawaiian string music. But the substance of the meal for me was the people, people, people—Mrs. Tobey and old-timers such as Evie Symington and Mary Ellen Monroney. I was delighted to see Henrietta Hill. And a sprinkling of the young ones. Neither of the Mrs. Kennedys was present—and no surprise there—they were both out campaigning. When it was time for the speech, Muriel gave me a diagram and a note that said the ladies of the Senate had planted a white Chinese dogwood in my honor on the Senate side of the Capitol grounds, with a little plaque. I shall love that!

It was distressing to watch Muriel speak. She was so weary, I was afraid she was going to faint. She stumbled over words and could hardly get through a sentence. But she had told me during lunch that she had made a flight—I think it was to Chicago—to one of those innumerable charity events for retarded children that she so valiantly attends—this one at the urging of the Kennedys. She had not arrived home until 4:30 this morning, and she was going into the hospital for an operation right after the luncheon. I held my breath for her. I could see it was an endurance contest.

Then it was my turn to speak. During the luncheon they had passed out fortune cookies, and in mine there had been a slip that said, "Be most affectionate today." The right words came and the feeling was certainly there. I reminisced briefly about attending this luncheon for twelve years as a Senator's wife, and then as President of the group for the three years that Lyndon was Vice President, and then this, the fifth and last time, as honored guest. And I assured them that I would be coming back on my cane as a former member in years to come.

It was a sweet and pleasant time, and I left hugging all around, thanking all around, clutching my maple sugar candy in the shape of a leaf from Mrs. Flanders, who has given us maple sugar candy for lo! these many years, looking at the layettes and the afghans which the Senate ladies make for service families.

Then I went back to the White House, weary, for a short nap, recording, working at the desk. About 7:30 the Joe Alsops arrived for dinner. There would be just the four of us; Lyndon was about an hour late. I enjoyed talking to them. Joe is a rare man. He belongs to another age. Where in time to place him I do not quite know—wide-ranging interests—from archaeology (he had written a book on it), to antique furniture, to gardening, to gourmet cooking.

Lyndon came and we had a good dinner with wide-ranging talk of international affairs and of this unbelievable spring we are living through. It was easy to see that Lyndon was exhausted. Joe made a move to go at 10:30, and Lyndon didn't stop him.

And now it has been a month since Lyndon made his momentous decision. How do we feel? Nellie Connally had said something like this: "At first you will feel depressed, like the world had stopped. And then after a while enormously relaxed, relieved, happy." Well, certainly as yet there is no depression, no "valley of the black pig," no slough of despondency. At first there were those four or five days of almost euphoric relief, with thousands of letters pouring in from all over the nation—mostly admiring, grateful, understanding, and some urging us to reconsider—good editorials from places you would never expect to get them—a sort of a preview of your obituary perhaps. Then the whole nation had been convulsed by the hideous assassination of Martin Luther King and the ensuing riotings and killings in the cities. It is as though some beast abroad in the land has not been sated yet, his blood lust not yet satisfied. What a time to live through! If Lyndon had hoped to lance the boil, to unite the country, we have just made an offering—made a start—and the future will have to tell how it works out. But as for us personally, our main feeling is of growing relief and satisfaction that Lyndon made his decision when he did.

I think of what Trudye Fowler said when I went to a lunch given by Jane Wirtz for all of the Cabinet wives last Wednesday. Trudye looked at me solemnly and said (of Lyndon's March 31 announcement), "I think it was providential."

Another feeling I have is that the clock is ticking—a sense of urgency. There are so many things I want to do in the remaining eight months—so many people I want to have here to share this beautiful house, so many conservation measures—to push forward or nail down—highway beautification, our own Committee here in Washington.

The words of Professor Richard Neustadt ring in my ear. "It's a lot easier to get things done when you are President." And I want to use this time—each day of it—as fully, glowingly, happily, usefully, as I can.

And what of Lyndon? He has accelerated his activity if anything. No backward look, but a determination to push with every power he has toward peace abroad and toward furthering his programs here at home . . . the most philosophic and detached I've ever seen him.

What a day! As we advance farther into May I feel more and more like a pitcher that is poured completely full of some precious liquid until it cannot hold any more and it simply overflows at the top. What a series of emotions, of events, wonderful things that I would like to participate in vigorously and remember fully in detail! These last six weeks have been about the busiest in my life, and I am at the point where I yearn for a few days of *nothing.*

About 11 I went down to the library to meet some young students from the Moravian Seminary. A class from this same Moravian Seminary had presented to Mrs. John Quincy Adams a needlepoint sampler so popular in that day, and this class wanted to present a similar one to me! They were darling girls—bright-faced, excited at being in the White House. I couldn't imagine one of them walking in a picket line or throwing rocks at their Dean. We had iced tea and cookies and they gave me the sampler in a warm little ceremony. We had arranged a tour of the house for them and also made it possible for them to watch the ceremony of Habib Ben Ali Bourguiba's arrival from Tunisia.

Fortunately for me, custom does not stale these arrival ceremonies. They are done with great pomp and circumstance. When the trumpets blow, my heart soars. This time I was especially looking forward to seeing the visiting Chief of State, Bourguiba. He is an outspoken, volatile man, who has managed to remain the strongest friend of the United States in the Arab world. My impression, as he emerged from the big black car, was of a short, stocky, assured man, with a big smile, darkish skin, and white hair —the look of one who is used to wielding power. With him was a tall, elegant woman, his daughter-in-law.

While Lyndon and President Bourguiba were reviewing the troops, I turned to chat with Dean Rusk and met Habib Bourguiba, Jr.—a very handsome, suave man, with a French patina over the Arab. There was a brief receiving line in the Diplomatic Reception Room. A little past 12 I was back on the second floor for lunch and a long siege at my desk. And then tea in the Queen's Room with Bishop McKinstry, who about a third of a century ago had performed the marriage ceremony for Lyndon and me at St. Mark's in San Antonio. We've kept up with him through the years, inviting him to the Inaugurations.

It turned out to be a delightful half-hour visit. I was happy to see that somebody well-advanced in his eighties can have so much fun. He loves horse racing! He had brought Mrs. Richard duPont, an ardent horse racer and one of his close friends, and Reverend Reynolds. He told me a hilarious story of how he was considered "the Chaplain of the Horses." The Bishop and I reminisced about San Antonio. Together we knew all the politicians. He also told me—and this I shivered to hear—that he is always being asked to write his memoirs or to give interviews about our wedding!

I went down to the West Hall for my third tea of the day with some of the dinner guests for tonight—with whom I very much wanted to spend more than a "how-do-you-do" in the receiving line. Among them were the Ralph McGills of Atlanta, and he was a most interesting guest. I wanted to explore the reasons for, and express my admiration of, Atlanta's rather remarkable success among Southern cities in solving the problems of race. My brother Tony is in town for three days and he joined us. I was delighted when I had found there was a nook for an extra guest at this dinner. It means a lot to me to share this house—these opportunities—with the people who are a part of the mosaic of our lives, who have been a very strong thread in my thinking and in my days.

On the North Portico we greeted President Bourguiba and the handsome pair, his son, who is his Secretary of Foreign Affairs, and his daughter-in-law; then we went up to the Yellow Room. They gave us a handsome saddle, ornately encrusted with gold tooling, a huge hat worn by a desert horseman, and a lovely long cloak, which President Bourguiba draped around my shoulders. Already late, we hastened downstairs to the East Room for the receiving line—just the three of us, this time standing in front of the stage.

A very special guest was Dr. Thomas Mattingly, the heart surgeon at Bethesda, whom Lyndon had flown over to take care of President Bourguiba when he had had a heart attack last year. They greeted each other warmly. I had an interesting table, with President Bourguiba on my right and his son on my left, with Mrs. Paul Nitze taking lively care of the President on the other side, Cecil Carusi, Dean Acheson, Mrs. Dillon Ripley next to the Secretary of Foreign Affairs, and Rawleigh Warner of Socony-Mobil whom I especially wanted to thank for pioneering work in good design for filling stations.

With the President, alas, I needed a translator, but his son's English was excellent. I asked what a tourist would want to see in Tunisia. The beaches probably. They are wonderful—white sand. The Roman and Phoenician ruins? Were they doing much work on archaeological research? He smiled and said, "We have to work on the living before we can work on the dead." True, they were a source of tourist interest. But there were "so many places to put the dollars"—a philosophic observation that government is a series of choices of assigning priorities.

It was a good dinner—Coquille St. Jacques, roast sirloin of beef with Yorkshire pudding—always reliable. And the dessert named in honor of our guests. Both the President and his son signed my menu—quite legibly, in contrast with most Chiefs of State.

After the toasts I led President Bourguiba into the Red Room for coffee and liqueurs and everyone soon took his place in the East Room to watch a short entertainment—Carmen deLavallade and Geoffrey Holder in three dance numbers. When there is a language barrier with our guests, music or dance are always to me delightful translators.

Saturday, May 18

TARRYTOWN, NEW YORK

I had breakfast in bed this morning in Mary and Laurance Rockefeller's charming house. This trip up the Hudson is the most leisurely, civilized trip I've taken—no 7 A.M. departures. A little before 11, Laurance, Mary, Liz and I left for Van Cortlandt Manor—one of the Hudson River Valley Sleepy Hollow restorations.

The Manor house was an impressive, two-story building of native fieldstone and timber—much at home on its ground, and built, I was told, in successive stages, beginning about 1680. For more than two centuries a baronial estate flourished here but by 1941 whatever descendants of the Van Cortlandts remained sold it to the only viable owner—a Conservation Society. The interior of the Manor house appeared to be faithfully and effectively restored. There was handsome silver, beautiful furniture, mostly Chippendale, crewel work, fine old fabrics, and forbidding kitchens that make me so glad I live in the twentieth century.

Outside, the grounds were beautifully restored . . . a vegetable garden, a flower garden, a path that led down to the river. The family neglected nothing—they had run a ferry because they were on the post road from Albany to New York. And they had put up a small inn by the banks of the river, which had accommodated up to thirty people. As we went through the small, low-ceilinged rooms, I wondered how the thirty slept. We were told that often three slept in a bed! One room accommodated several beds for women, another, several beds for men. You simply took your chances on whoever your sleeping partners might be.

Of course, life on such a Manor was a self-contained society—they raised and processed nearly everything they ate or wore. There was a carpenter, a cobbler, a cabinet maker, and a blacksmith somewhere on the place. We saw a vignette of the life of that day, called "From Sheep to Shawl." In the backyard behind the big Manor house there was a big fat sheep lying placidly on his side while a man with a very Dutch accent in a Revolutionary-period costume sheared him! A group of little boys sat on the grass cross-legged. Everybody was in costume. The first little boy was pulling burrs out of the wool. Each little boy had some job as the process went along. Others were carding the fleece with a big flat board full of sharp points. Little girls were working too, and seven ladies plied spinning wheels.

We drove from Van Cortlandt Manor to Sunnyside—the home of Washington Irving. I have seen few houses on which the character of the owner was so clearly imprinted as Sunnyside—Monticello, certainly, but few others. This was a small, modest house, a sort of witty copy of a great baronial estate. Washington Irving himself described it as "being as full of angles and corners as an old cocked hat." And so it was—all peaks and gables, small rooms and low ceilings, but inviting, quaint, and charming.

The house is situated on the bank of the Hudson, or so you think, until you look below along the shore line and observe the railroad. About every thirty minutes during our lunch in a tent on the grounds the conversation and the entertainment were punctuated by the shrill whistle and the passage of a train. I believe the railroad was built in 1846—so even in Irving's day the lovers of a sylvan retreat had to deal with the inroads of progress— especially transportation. We saw the stump of an old tree to which boats tied up when visitors came up the Hudson to see Irving. There were many visitors to Sunnyside—diplomats, writers, artists, neighbors. He ran a sort of salon.

Above the entrance was a huge wisteria vine that covered the roof of the porch, drooping great garlands of lavender blossoms. Inside, the first little room was his study, a small, cozy room full of books, with a fireplace and a sofa which doubled as a bed for him at night—so crowded was his home with relatives and friends. And on it was spread his cloak with his hat—as though he had just come in. Much of the furniture in the house had belonged to Irving or members of his family. And there was the inevitable engraving of him as a small child, being taken to see General Washington, for whom he was named.

The life re-created at such restorations as Van Cortlandt Manor and Sunnyside provides a vivid picture of how our ancestors lived. To thousands of tourists, to busloads of schoolchildren, they tell a part of the American story. I am glad such houses are being restored all over our country. Why, at this particular time, I wonder? Are we becoming mature enough to look back to our roots and value them, even when, simultaneously, we seem to be tearing everything into shreds, descending into chaos? Interesting dichotomy.

It was nearly 4 when we finally left Sunnyside and headed back to the Rockefeller estate in Tarrytown. A little before 5 we drove up to the huge Rockefeller mansion for tea. We had planned to walk over—that beautiful, rolling, green countryside, the woods dappled with dogwood, invite you to walk—but it was drizzling.

The great stone house, where Nelson Rockefeller now lives, belonged to his parents. The house commands a hilltop and is forbidding, imposing, but softened with a frieze of beautiful American elms. You wind up a driveway past statuary, some of it wildly modern. There are two great torchères at the entrance of the house and at night the Tiffany amber glass must look like twin flames when you drive under the porte-cochère. As I mounted the steps I could see down the length of the hall a graceful, elegant statue—ancient Eastern art—and there was the Governor, smiling and genial, taking us in out of the rain and mist. And Happy, warm and friendly, with their little son, and later we were joined by her attractive young daughters.

I stood in awe of the house—the vast expanses of halls, high ceilings, ornate moldings—and here and there, surprisingly, a bright, wild smash of modern art. The Governor and Happy could not have been kinder hosts. Nelson took us all over the house, pointing out the pictures, sculptures, objects he had bought—many of them years ago. He buys such things constantly, changes them constantly. Art is one of his real enthusiasms.

Downstairs there was a whole room cleared to hold his purchases—a sort of art gallery, full of the way-out modern things. One was a shadowbox full of lights and clanging metal that went absolutely mad when you turned the switch. Others resembled the insides of old cars. There was a piece in bronze that I could approach with understanding and excitement—armies of little bronze figures which you could imagine were men on horseback, marching men with spears. Nelson spoke of his feelings for modern art with such enthusiasm, but to me it was as though he were speaking in a foreign tongue. I felt dissatisfied with myself for being unable to comprehend.

We went into the big dining room dominated by a portrait of John D. Rockefeller, Sr., by John Singer Sargent, and gathered around the baronial dining room table. Happy served tea with big slices of delicious cake.

Back at Laurance and Mary's, I changed into my pink evening dress with the beaded jacket and we set out for Lyndhurst, the restored Jay Gould mansion, for cocktails. This house is now owned by the National Trust for Historic Preservation and is open to the public. It looks like the grandfather of all great mansions—a huge Gothic structure with a superb view of the Hudson. The architects of that day must have imagined themselves building castles on the Rhine.

We had a tour through the house, saw a collection of paintings of the Hudson River School. There were such familiar names as Kensett, Thomas Cole, Frederick Church, Cropsey, Thomas Moran, Eastman Johnson, and George Inness. I met the officials of the National Trust and was presented with a scroll. But what I remember most poignantly in all that vast, forbidding, uncomfortable house was the room of the last daughter of the Goulds. She apparently felt guilty about her wealth, because her room was full of pictures of train wrecks!

As we departed, we saw the glass-roofed greenhouse which stretched on and on, for what looked like about four city blocks, incredible evidence of great wealth. The whole way of life represented here is a page from America's history that will never return—glittering, impressive, but—I thought—burdensome.

We went on to Brooke Astor's, a lovely house also overlooking the Hudson, but here was a totally different picture. The house exuded all the grace and charm and beauty that wealth could offer, but was on a human scale, with warmth and simplicity compared to Lyndhurst.

Brooke was at the door, utterly enchanting. She bubbles, she glows, she defies years. She led us inside, and we made our way leisurely from room to room meeting her guests, a group mostly of Hudson River folk interested in the arts or restorations—including the Carl Carmers (author of *Stars Fell on Alabama* and a history of the Hudson River), the Leland Haywards (theatrical producer and entrepreneur), and Robert Massies (author of *Nicholas and Alexandra*).

The star of the evening, as always when she is present, was Helen Hayes, a close neighbor. When she walks in, she takes over the room for me.

Brooke lives in the Hudson Valley on weekends and a large part of the summer. She told me once that "a widow has to have roots," and in that spirit she has lined the walls of the house with many family pictures. I think she has very strong roots in life. She works, and she loves her work.

Dark had fallen and there was mist and rain. The open fires were a magnet. We had dinner at round tables in a garden room, where I sat next to Louis Auchincloss, who wrote *The Rector of Justin* and many other novels. He was very good company and easy to talk to—polished, very Eastern. I couldn't imagine him living or writing about life west of the Mississippi River.

There were toasts to the President, to me, to Brooke. At a fairly early hour the Rockefellers gathered me up solicitously, because it had been a long day, and we drove home, retracing this Hudson Valley of some of America's roots.

This will be a day to remember in the life of Lady Bird Taylor of Karnack, and Mrs. Lyndon Johnson of Johnson City—a day with the Rockefellers and the Astors and the Goulds—seeing the Hudson River Valley—about three hundred years of it!

Thursday, May 23

THE WHITE HOUSE

Today was a busy, significant day for me, the date for the last of one of the dearest events of my days here—the First Lady's annual luncheon for the Senate Ladies. Mrs. Eisenhower was coming again. I had called her myself a week or so ago to tell her how much it would mean if she could come, but was not really expecting her since the General is in the hospital. And so it was a good sign about him that she came.

Mrs. Eisenhower and I stood in line to greet the 101 guests . . . nearly all the Cabinet wives . . . old-timers from the Senate . . . and the young and beautiful—Marvella Bayh and Mrs. Scoop Jackson, and Mrs. Charles Percy, looking about Lynda Bird's age in a very short, very pretty white dress . . . dear Betty Talmadge and Loraine McGee . . . so many memories of work and trips together.

There was so much hugging with nearly every guest that I soon lost my pearls! And nearly everybody was on a first-name basis. And then there were the wives of former Senators—glamorous Baroness Silvercruys who was married to Senator O'Brien McMahon . . . Mrs. Harold Burton whose husband had been both Senator and member of the Supreme Court —she is my nominee for having attended more Washington parties than anybody, always with both her earrings on one ear and always very friendly and nice—and Mrs. Frances Parkinson Keyes in a wheelchair. She is celebrating this week the publication of her latest book. In my mind's eye I kept on seeing *me* coming back sometime in the future!

I had Mrs. Eisenhower on my right at lunch. And next, Henrietta Hill, then Maureen Mansfield and Gladys Johnston (Mrs. Olin Johnston). Here I had used my prerogative, which I so seldom do in this house, of adding to the established list several of my own choice. It is a custom to invite wives of former Senate members who still have a Washington address or live nearby, but this time I had asked Mrs. Johnston, Mrs. Harold Burton, and two or three others from a long way away. Gladys had come and she enjoyed it very much, I think. I certainly did enjoy her presence. Next at the table came La Donna Harris, Mrs. Hugh Scott, Mrs. Charles Tobey, and Mrs. Aiken of Vermont who had been the Chairman of the luncheon given for me this year, and on my left, Muriel.

The conversation was far better than the lunch, which was not particularly distinguished. Mrs. Eisenhower and I talked about the General, of course. She had been telling everybody that he was doing well. Her very presence at the party attested to that. She said, "When our beaus"— she always uses this expression about husbands—"get to be a certain age, they are all we have." She was explaining that she stayed with General Eisenhower all the time and felt that she could come away for just a few hours now, because he was feeling better. In the course of the conversation she said, "You know, I never knew in this group who was Democrat and who was Republican." That is the way we have all felt in the Senate Ladies Red Cross. It's been a very special relationship—one of the strongest and the most cherished of my years in Washington.

Gladys Johnston asked, "How is Mrs. Nixon?" And I was glad she did. Pat Nixon had been a good presiding officer in her years with the Senate Ladies Red Cross, and it's my omission that I haven't made a special effort to urge her to come to some of these luncheons, though, of course, as a former Vice President's wife, she is invited. But everywhere one looks, there is a lack, a failure, an omission. One can only try to fill the days as full as one can and not worry about the rest.

One of the big excitements of the day was the use of the new White House china—ours! There were many compliments. Then Lyndon dropped in on us and said a few warm, affectionate words to the ladies.

Presently the last of my White House luncheons for the Senate Ladies was over. I went to stand at the door to bid farewell to each of the guests. There was a moment of wrenching. If, this spring, I have gone through a great deal of emotion, of saying good-bys, of awareness of a change in our lives, my feelings, I think, have always been well under control. But this was a particularly poignant farewell. I felt it deeply and came close to showing it. The interesting thing was that it had next to nothing to do with our leaving the White House—it was the last vestige of the *Senate* I was saying good-by to.

I relished the last moment of the party, and went upstairs to rejoin my houseguests—my three college roommates from my youthful days at St. Mary's and the University of Texas—Helen Bird Falley, Emily Crow Selden, and Cecille Marshall. What a happy visit we have had these last two days—everybody talking at once and so much to tell! Their being here is a personal indulgence I'd looked forward to and enjoyed to the fullest.

Summer 1968

It was a short night. The phone jarred me awake from a deep sleep. Lyndon was saying tersely, "Will you come in here?" I did not see how it could be morning. I was too tired. And sure enough, I saw that the hands of the clock stood at 4:20.

He was propped up against the pillows, looking as though he had never been asleep, and all of the TV sets were turned on. He was listening intently, and I realized at once that something serious was happening. I am not sure whether I heard it first from the TV set or from Lyndon. Senator Kennedy had been shot. All three faces of the three TV sets were on and the scene was total confusion. Bobby had been at his headquarters in Los Angeles with Ethel, celebrating his victory in the California Primaries. Every few minutes the tabulation of the voting would come on the screens. The vote was about 44 or 45 percent for Kennedy and 41 or 42 percent for McCarthy.

679

The whole terrible event had taken place under the eye of the television cameras, and we saw, over and over, the film of the shooting itself and heard the light crack of the gun. We saw Senator Kennedy lying on the floor, a pool of blood under his head, and heard that he had been taken to one hospital, where he was briefly treated, and then dispatched to another—the Good Samaritan. There was an air of unreality about the whole thing—a nightmare quality. It couldn't be true. We must have dreamed it. It had all happened before.

Every few minutes the flashbacks would come on the screen—the smiling face of Senator Kennedy, tasting the wine of victory, making little jokes with Ethel by his side. And then the whole nightmare would start over again.

Lyndon was using the telephone almost from the first moment I went in, giving instructions about putting Secret Service guards on all the candidates, listing them: Kennedy and McCarthy and Humphrey and Nixon and Rockefeller and Stassen. If there weren't enough Secret Service men they could borrow from the FBI or from the Marines. But get them, he said—assign them now.

At 5:30, Lyndon was calling Attorney General Ramsey Clark.

Very early in the morning—I can't remember exactly when, I think it was around 7 o'clock—Senator Mansfield came in. I got him a cup of coffee. He had a staring look in his eyes. He said, "What is happening to our country?" The feeling of being a sleepwalker in a dream persisted. But Lyndon was functioning. He talked to Senator Mansfield about how they could get legislation moving on a Gun Law, about how to protect the candidates, how to carry these safeguards through the maze of legislative action, and about how or whether we could get further action on a Crime Bill.

The three faces of the television kept repeating the hideous story. Senator Kennedy was going in for brain surgery. It had been determined that the bullet had lodged somewhere behind his ear. Those hours all melt into a montage, and I do not remember times exactly. At one point I went back in my room and tried to sleep a little more. But it was hopeless, and after about an hour I returned to Lyndon's room. And all the time the three-faced television screens went on. The Senator was in surgery. Doctors were interviewed; men in the streets.

Finally I began to relate this whole hideous unreality to my own day. It was clear that nothing could be the same, that we were in a state of suspension, waiting for the hand of fate. Liz came in—the whole story written on her face—and said, "Don't you think you had better cancel that 3:30 appointment?" Yes. As soon as people were in their offices, we began to cancel all appointments. And so there stretched in front of me a long, empty day. But I was tired. Everybody was exhausted from the impact of the news.

Liz and I put together a wire for Mrs. Rose Kennedy and one for Ethel. Lyndon had been able to do one thing to help. He made planes available to carry various members of the family to California—several of the children—and, I believe, later the Kennedy family doctor.

Luci called, distressed. She had not been to sleep at all. I had left word with the kitchen that I wanted to know when Lynda awakened. I went into her room and her first thought was of Ethel and the baby she was going to have and of all the other children. She said, "Mother, is there anything we can do for them?"—the same words her younger sister had just used. I told her about her daddy sending the planes.

The minutes had lengthened into hours. The day flowed along like a dark river—work at the desk, a few hushed telephone calls—everybody with stricken faces—the air of unreality. This can't be happening here. And underneath it all, a deep, racking sob—my country, my country—remembering Martin Luther King, murdered just two months ago today, and President Kennedy. There was a hideous story in the papers about two Marines being shot in a Georgetown café by, the reports said, some of the marchers from the Poor People's Demonstration.

Lyndon had gone to his office for an 11 o'clock meeting, and he did not come back for lunch. Very late in the afternoon, he came over for what hopefully would have been a nap but turned out to be only telephone calls. He went back to his office at 6. About 6:30 I took a short break and went on the Truman Balcony with Lynda. We felt oddly self-conscious that we were so clearly visible from the dining terrace on the roof of the Washington Hotel. Not that I ever feel any fear for myself at all. Fear of physical harm is absolutely foreign to me or even to Lyndon. But maybe neither of the Kennedys had felt fear either.

I had told the kitchen that dinner might be very late and that Lyndon might have some of his staff with him. At 10:07, Lyndon went on TV. He must have had at most two hours of sleep last night. He did look tired, but strong, commanding, and reassuring. All day long I had heard this cacophony over and over—the reactions of people questioned. What is our country coming to? What is happening to us? Are we a sick society?

I welcomed what Lyndon said, after a condemnation of this assassination attempt on Senator Kennedy and of the spirit of violence that made such things possible, that "two hundred million people did not strike down Robert Kennedy . . ." We have to cling to the belief that the fabric of American life is still strong; that people are still good; that it's not the fault of every last one of the two hundred million of us; that there is enough virtue and courage and discipline and hard work in Americans to solve our problems.

I had been running the intelligence between Lyndon's office and the kitchen—making educated guesses about when he would arrive for dinner. Finally about 10:30 I gave up and had dinner with Lynda and we looked at an interminably long TV summary of this dreadful day.

It was a little past one A.M. when we heard the three rings that signal Lyndon's elevator, and he came in with Joe Califano and Harry McPherson, Larry Temple, Jim Jones, and George Christian. They all sat down for dinner while Lynda and I sat with them in our robes. Dinner was interrupted by constant telephone calls. The conversation was about how to get through the Gun Bill, the chances for crime legislation, and then a report from the Secret Service that Senator Kennedy was sinking and it would be a matter of hours.

Saturday, June 8

NEW YORK AND
ARLINGTON NATIONAL CEMETERY

This was a day completely detached from the normal, a capsule of time suspended in unreality—the day of the burial of Senator Robert Kennedy. We left about 8:20 from the White House lawn in the helicopter, and then from Andrews we flew in a small jet. Lyndon and Marie—always a comfort—Joe Califano, Jim Jones, and I.

New York was a strange sight. The streets were lined with people who stood silent, motionless. For three days the television had been invoking the phrase "like a Greek tragedy," and indeed, there was much of a Greek drama about this, these mute crowds, the voiceless chorus.

We were escorted into St. Patrick's Cathedral—that magnificent setting —equal to any sorrow or any joy. I knew that all around us, in the throng of twenty-three hundred, there was a great outpouring from the government, most of the Cabinet, a quorum of the Senate probably, and many members of the House—Governor Rockefeller and Mayor Lindsay—stars of the entertainment world—the famous and the unknown. I did not look to right or left. The only face I saw was that of Pierre Salinger, who met us and led us down the aisle. He looked absolutely drained.

As we approached the dark, shiny coffin covered with a flag with tall candles burning at each side, Lyndon paused briefly and so did I, and then we turned to the left and took the seats to which we were directed in the front row.

I had noticed, just as we settled into our seats, that the congregation, silently and without signal, had risen. When we had been seated for only a few seconds, Lyndon had looked over to the left and seen Mrs. Jacqueline Kennedy in black and veiled, with her two children, entering. He swiftly rose, followed by the rest of the congregation. She passed in front of us and sat in a front-row seat on the right-hand side with the numerous Kennedy family. Somehow, Ethel and her children slipped in quietly to the front seat on the right side.

The ceremony was one of staggering drama and beauty. The whole altar area was filled with high officials of the Catholic Church in robes of varying shades of red—the deep purple red and the bright orange red—Cardinal Cushing on his throne—the most commanding figure there, I thought. And Terence Cooke, the new Cardinal. And Cardinal O'Boyle, who had helped to preside at Luci's wedding.

One of the most beautiful moments occurred when eight young children of the Kennedy family—the girls dressed in white or navy, their long blonde hair caught back with ribbons and hanging down their backs, the little boys in dark suits—walked up to the altar in pairs, carrying an offertory, while an orchestra of violins was playing a beautiful melody. I could see only the back of the director, which was, in itself, a study—an expression of the utmost passion, of torment and talent—a magnificent element in this whole tragic mosaic. It dawned on me that the conductor was Leonard Bernstein.

There was one lone mike standing in front of all the robed priests and archbishops, and to it went Senator Teddy Kennedy, who delivered a most beautiful eulogy of his brother. He was strong and composed, though his eyes were red-rimmed. Part of the way through his voice began to quaver, but then came under control, and he ended calmly. He asked that his brother be remembered simply as "a good and decent man, who saw wrong and tried to right it, saw suffering and tried to heal it, saw war and tried to stop it." He quoted one passage from Robert Kennedy that was sheer poetry, "Some men see things as they are and say, why? I dream things that never were and say, why not?"

I was aware of Secretary Rusk behind me, and the bleak faces of Dorothy and Arthur Goldberg. During the Communion, when all of the Kennedy family went to the altar rail first, followed by the public, I saw Senator McCarthy. Always the mind was riveted on the flag-draped coffin in the middle of the aisle with its incredible burden. This has been the most shocking, the most unbelievable, event in the nation's life as I have shared it, intensified, made all the more tragic, by President Kennedy's assassination nearly five years ago.

Cardinal Cooke made a strong, good statement, I thought. He quoted Lyndon's remark that two hundred million people did not kill Senator Kennedy, and he went on to say that the act of one man must not demoralize and incapacitate two hundred million others. "For, to permit this to happen would be to fail utterly to grasp the message of hope and optimism in Senator Kennedy's life."

Then at last it was over.

One of the Catholic dignitaries came and leaned over to tell Lyndon that he should leave first. Senator Ted Kennedy came and put out his hand, and they exchanged a few words. I simply grasped his hand.

We walked to the right, past the front row where all of the Kennedy family were seated, and stopped to speak first to Ethel, whose face was beautiful, sad, composed. She said very simply, "You have been so kind," to Lyndon. We spoke to several of the children and then to Mrs. Rose Kennedy.

Then I found myself in front of Mrs. Jacqueline Kennedy. I called her name and put out my hand. She looked at me as if from a great distance, as though I were an apparition. I murmured some word of sorrow and walked on . . . It was somehow bewildering.

We got into the car silently and made our way among the crowds that were still silent, but now occasionally a hand went up in greeting or there was a slight smile. We went back to the plane and returned to Washington to await the arrival of the funeral train. There was a delay of hours. The train carrying Senator Kennedy's body and several hundred mourners was two hours behind schedule. I could not bring myself to work. There was so much to be done—so much piled on my desk and in my little sitting-room office that required concentration and the best thinking I could give it. But in this interval of time, between the funeral ceremony and the burial, with everyone in a sort of emotional trance, I could not detach myself and work.

So I gave up and looked at TV endlessly—the train plowing on and on. And there were more awful things happening. Two of the mourners standing by the track watching the train were suddenly struck down and killed by another train. One young man who was watching from some high vantage point had reached up and touched a hot wire and been badly burned. There were reruns, over and over, of Senator Kennedy's eulogy of his dead brother in the Cathedral, reruns of everything—constant coverage by all three networks, with the commentators hard put to fill the time as the hours wore on.

There was one break. Angier Duke called and said he had Princess Grace and her brother with him. Could he bring them by for tea? I said yes. I visited with them in the Yellow Oval Room for nearly an hour. Princess Grace is pretty, gentle, very much a lady. Her brother has apparently inherited his father's political interests along with his business. Luci came in and brightened up the conversation. All in all, the shadows were a bit lifted.

A little past 7, Lyndon came in with Billy Graham, who had been in his office. I was glad to see him. They like each other, and it has been a long time since he's visited us. We had dinner. Finally, at about 8:45, it was time to go to Union Station to meet the Kennedy train arriving from New York and to join the funeral cortege to Arlington Cemetery.

As I walked into the great vaulted concourse of Union Station, I thought of the last time I had been in there as part of a funeral. It was the State funeral of General MacArthur, and for a while I had stood beside Bobby Kennedy. The train had not arrived. We saw Hubert and Muriel and asked them to come and sit in the car with us. Hubert, the ever ebullient, looked drained and empty. He said, "Eric Sevareid sure had it right for once when he said, 'Whoever gets the Democratic nomination, it will be a tarnished shield.'" For reasons more emotional than rational, it seems to me, this whole tragedy turns the nation toward the Republican Party.

One good thing had happened—one thing on the side of law and order, made more dramatic because it happened at this time—the accused slayer of Martin Luther King, James Earl Ray, was seized at London Airport. And somehow this event seemed to say: "This government will not be mocked."

There was a flurry when someone came to Lyndon and said, "Cardinal Cushing had an attack on the train, and they need to get him to a doctor. Could they have a plane to fly him straight back?" Lyndon said yes, and gave instructions to have the plane standing by, and a doctor to fly back with him. Lyndon instructed his own doctor to give the Cardinal every help possible.

Then we got the signal to get out of the car. As I made my way through the crowd to stand by Lyndon, suddenly they were passing . . . all the family in black, silent . . . all the little children . . . and then the coffin. We followed, several cars behind the coffin, and drove the appointed route —past the Capitol and the Senate Office Building and the Department of Justice where there was a brief stop, and then past the Lincoln Memorial.

There were crowds everywhere, and a larger one here—many from Resurrection City. Here we paused while a choir sang. As in New York, the crowds were strangely silent and immobile. Some of them must have been standing there for many hours, since the burial had been expected to take place about 4:30 in the afternoon. Now it was after 9.

There was one curious, touching thing that carried its own message. Every now and then in the crowd you could see a small light. Sometimes it was just a lighted match or a cigarette lighter that the person was holding up. Sometimes a rolled-up bit of newspaper that had been set afire. And sometimes a candle. After we crossed Memorial Bridge and began our ascent up the hill into Arlington Cemetery, the glow of the candles increased.

I had read that Mrs. Paul Mellon had selected the gravesite. It was on a gently sloping mound with two lovely magnolia soulangiana trees shading it, close to President Kennedy's grave.

Lyndon and I walked up the hill, behind the family, who took their places along the side and at the foot of the casket in a group, and we stood a little behind. Ethel and the children went up and knelt and kissed the coffin, and so did Bobby's sisters. And then a stream of young Kennedys— quickly, no tears, no outcries. Then Mrs. Jacqueline Kennedy, alone, followed by her two children, knelt and kissed it. The children put on floral offerings, and then Ethel and the children knelt and so did we.

When she rose, we said good-by. There was nothing to say to her except how brave she is and how wonderful all the children are. Several of them had participated as altar boys. Some of the older boys had stood as honor guards beside the casket—young Joe Kennedy, looking so much like his father that it took your breath to suddenly see him.

We walked ahead down the slope. There was a great white moon riding high in the sky—a beautiful night. This is the only night funeral I ever remember. But then this is the only such time in the memory of our country—an incredible, unbelievable, cruel, and wrenching time.

Friday, June 21

THE WHITE HOUSE

Today is Lyn's first birthday. I woke up early and went to work. The return from a trip always staggers me, so high is the desk piled. Ashton needs to see me—Bess and I must get to work on the social side of the house—and Liz has to have some decisions on speeches and travel.

I went to the pool for thirty quick laps. And then back upstairs to get dressed for Lyn's birthday, putting on my wet hair an unaccustomed "fall," which looked frankly like what it was. Then I went down with Luci and Lyn to the Rose Garden to what Luci had laughingly called "Lyn's press conference." There were an amazing number of cameras and press lined up in the Rose Garden. Lyndon came out of the Cabinet Room.

There was a little tiny table and a chair, and a modest-sized white cake trimmed with red roses and one blue candle and lots of American flags— all for a one-year-old boy in a red, white, and blue jumper. A ridiculous note—around his neck hung his White House pass—with his picture and the information that cleared him to come and go in the White House. We did not tell the press that the pass had been accompanied by a letter from J. Edgar Hoover himself, saying that "nothing derogatory was found in the files of the FBI against Patrick Lyndon Nugent"!

Luci, who is never at a loss with the press, had plenty to say in answer to their questions. But Lyn had practically nothing to say. In fact, a usually gay, laughing, funny little boy was silent—even solemn—I think maybe because he had slept so late. If Lyn was noncommittal and I was just an onlooker, both his grandfather and his mother made up for it. He has twelve teeth, Luci said. And he speaks about six words: momma, dada, by-by, more, want. And he wears a size toddler three. Lyndon said, "You've got the platform. Anything you want to tell them?" And then, "Lyn says, 'No comment.' "

Then Lyndon took out his little pocket knife and cut a big chunk of cake for Lyn, who preferred a red rose off the top and tried to take a bite out of the candle. Luci looked adorable—all peaches and cream in a pink dress, her black hair shining and so proud of her son.

Lyn's real family birthday party took place a little past 5 in the Yellow Oval Room with an extraordinary guest list. A Catholic priest, Father Kaifer; a Jewish doctor and his wife, the Kraskins; a family, Mr. and Mrs. Lindow and Helene—with all of whom, of varying ages, Luci has the same degree of compatibility. No generation gap in her life! There was our twice-bridesmaid, and good-friend-of-all-four-of-us, Warrie Lynn Smith. From the staff, Ashton and Willie Day, and to my pleasure Simone, who had handled the press when the baby was born and whom Luci included with a delightful remark, "Simone just might as well have had him."

I am sure the Yellow Oval Room has seldom been the stage for such a party! A black-and-yellow-striped tiger, five feet tall, standing by the mantel was the first thing that I saw. And then a great pile of packages, and Lyn sitting on the floor near them with all of the guests ringed around him in chairs. His mother came in bringing a cake she had made—chocolate all the way through. When she put it down in front of Lyn, I ran for a sheet out of respect for the White House furnishings.

Patrick Lyndon eyed the cake for a few moments and then he raised one foot and brought it down "ka-plop," right in the middle of the cake, while we all fell out of our chairs with laughter. His poise was in no way shaken and he kept on taking a lot of interest in us and in the gifts and everything while his foot stayed right there in the cake.

His favorites among the presents were the all-day suckers and the gift wrappings, or maybe the rubber canoe that said *"Heap Big Indian Lyn,"* which Warrie Lynn had given him.

I, alas, kept on acting the villain by attacking him every few minutes with a wet wash rag to get the chocolate off his grubby little hands and the sticky sugar off his face, thinking of my stewardship for the lovely yellow sofas and the apricot chairs. Luci had a tape recorder which she kept passing around to the crowd so that everybody could record a word to Pat, in between times describing for him the scene around us.

When all the guests had left, Father Kaifer held a special mass in the Queen's Sitting Room for Patrick Lyn, with only Luci, Lyn, Warrie Lynn, and me present. We covered the center table with a white cloth and put up a portable altar and went through the service with those two pretty girls kneeling on the floor and Patrick Lyn toddling around and all of our hearts several thousands of miles away with Patrick . . . quite possibly another first within the walls of this old house.

It was 10 when Lyndon came over for dinner, bringing with him Houston Harte who is going to be our houseguest. Houston presides over his newspaper empire with considerable will and activity and withal a graceful acceptance of the years. He travels, he fishes, he writes some—a pleasant life. I am glad we have shared a part of it, and I am particularly glad that here in the White House between us, Lyndon and me, we have managed to write a postscript to many long-time friendships, such as his, with a pleasant interlude in this wonderful place.

What a year this has been—the first year of Lyn's life—one of the most tumultuous and often painful in the public life and yet, in the small circle of our family life, one of happiness and fulfillment . . . curious dichotomy.

Wednesday, June 26

OREGON

Today was remarkable for three reasons, at least to me. I made my last planned trip and speech—certainly the last for a long, long time. I saw a part of America that I knew the least of all—Oregon—the far Northwest. And third, Lyndon nominated Abe Fortas for Chief Justice and Homer Thornberry for Associate Justice.

It was a fresh, clear, beautiful day, and everywhere you looked you saw roses, roses, roses. Portland lived up to its billing as "The City of Roses." Orville Freeman and I drove to the Civic Center where the American Institute of Architects was having its annual convention. Mr. and Mrs. Robert Lewis Durham—he's outgoing President of the AIA—met me and escorted me to the stage. A familiar sight—an audience of several thousand and a standing ovation. You would have to be dead not to get a lift of the spirit!

Orville introduced me, and I delivered the B. Y. Morrison lecture on nature and architecture. I've hardly ever worked as hard on a speech and it was the longest one I've ever delivered. I spoke of "the new conservation," which means first a concern for the total environment, attention to the human scale, and a new emphasis on the areas of natural beauty. I spoke of some of the places made for delight and intimacy that I enjoyed most: Ghiradelli Square in San Francisco; San Antonio with its little river winding through the center of town; Georgetown, so attractively restored, showing how the past can serve the present. And a few sentences that I particularly liked occurred when I spoke of the enormous housing developments that were so dull and all alike that—in the words of Gertrude Stein—"There's no there there." I likened some shopping centers to a sort of "urban strip mine"—and ended on a call to city planners and architects to work on the problems of monotonous housing developments, unsightly shopping centers, and on ugly, ragged city fringes. At the end Orville announced that an azalea, pure white and very lovely, was being named for me—the "Mrs. LBJ"—and this was another one of those times when I wished I hadn't acquired a nickname but had just been Claudia all of my life.

Our entourage then left and drove across the beautiful Oregon country-side toward Timberline Lodge, stopping for lunch at Toll Gate Camp-ground, with everybody famished. Two huge salmon split open, broiling over a fire (giving forth a delicious aroma), made a most enticing sight. I could hardly notice the beautiful setting for looking at those fish! Enormous trees towered skyward on all sides of us and ferns made a carpet as far as you could see.

We set to immediately on the lunch—a long table was spread with roasting ears, cole slaw and Oregon fruit—a distinctly "fruit-of-the-lands" sort of lunch that brought back so many pictures to me—a clam bake on the rocky coast of Maine—a fish fry with the surf breaking on Padre Island—barbecues on the banks of the Pedernales!

We drove through beautiful farm land, very green. Luscious berries were one of the principal crops and the roadsides were lined with purple vetch and a tall-stemmed purple flower. Then we came to the forest—Douglas fir and hemlock, enormous trees that soared skyward, two hundred feet or more, straight, magnificent trunks, hardly any limbs until way up high. Every now and then we would come over a rise and there would be Mt. Hood, gloriously framed by these giant trees. A zigzag river ran along beside us. It flowed off a glacier and was icy cold and there were many little rapid streams that tumbled into it.

Soon I noticed moss on the trees that looked rather like a gray beard, downy and soft. The forester told me that the deer loved it for food, but that it was very bad for forest fires. A fire would just race through it. He pointed out the bear grass, which was a cone-shaped mass of tiny white flowers, delicate, and beautiful.

When we came into a clearing there would be a great line of mountains against the sky—spectacular country! We were gradually rising—climbing a mountain. About 3:30 we pulled up to Timberline Lodge—a fantastic building that looked like the biggest chalet in all of Switzerland, built of weathered timbers—as much at home on the mountainside as the rocks and trees. The lodge had been built in the depths of the Depression by the WPA to put to work all sorts of craftsmen who were unemployed. It was a superb monument to the daring dreamers of those days. FDR himself had dedicated it in 1937. He and Mrs. Roosevelt had spent the night in the suite that I was to use.

I went straight to the suite—a charming bed-sitting room with a fireplace, handmade furniture, a big sofa, a bouquet of wildflowers which one of the foresters had thoughtfully put there. I changed into a beige pants suit and then, with the clouds already gathering over the mountaintops, we got into a strange vehicle called a "Sno-Cat," a long cab on caterpillar treads.

We crunched along through snow, heading for the magnificent views of the higher range. Clouds were settling on top of Mt. Hood, and very soon we were enveloped in a soft white blanket. And so, admitting defeat, we turned around and came back down the mountain. In the evening I put on my white "Discover America" dress with a bright scarf and went in to dinner. We had cocktails in the lounge—a balcony that surrounded a great, six-sided lobby, a vast high-ceilinged room that looked like the baronial hall of some ancient Viking. The guests were foresters, a few Oregon state officials, and a bunch of young skiers who were practicing for the Olympics—long-haired, earnest-faced—different from the young folks I've known, but attractive.

The main attraction was Timberline Lodge itself, made of the stone and wood of Oregon, its pictures and carvings all showing the Cascade Mountain environment in three themes: pioneers, Indians, and plants and wildlife. The stairway treads were made of old railroad ties and the newel posts of telephone poles, topped with hand-carved animals of the region, made by some down-and-out, anonymous artist of the Depression days—a little bear curled up, a duck, an eagle, a raccoon. And the massive light fixtures that hung from the ceiling were made like Indian storage baskets. Everywhere there was the handwork of artisans—in wrought iron, carpentry, carving, painting—a wonderful legacy of the artistry of the 1930's!

On the registration desk I saw the signatures of FDR and Mrs. FDR and all of those accompanying them.

But what I liked best of all, I think, were the carvings throughout

Timberline Lodge of the Indian symbols of the months—the snow moon of January, and the hunger moon of February, the planting moon of May, the green corn moon of August, the leaf-falling moon of October, and delightfully, the long night moon of December.

We went into the Cascade Dining Room for dinner, where a big fire was burning in the fireplace. We had beef fondue, good homemade bread, a red wine, and local strawberries for dessert. Seated next to me was a former state official who was very interested in Lyndon's appointments of the day—Abe Fortas and Homer Thornberry. Indeed, everyone came up to me with questions or expressions of interest, but I was unable to assess the color of their thinking, approval or disapproval, surprise or whatever. Actually there is a tremendous difference in the whole thinking of the rest of the country outside of Washington. Political events are important, yes, but they are not the whole universe. Washington sinks into perspective when you are twenty-five hundred miles away. I love Washington, but it *is* a self-important town.

Monday, July 1

THE WHITE HOUSE

Some days have their harvest of hope. This one did, with the signing of a very special Treaty in the East Room at 11:30. The room was jammed full of participants and spectators. The table from the Treaty Room had been brought down, and behind it sat the Soviet Ambassador Dobrynin; Britain's Sir Patrick Dean; William C. Foster, United States Director of Arms Control and Disarmament; Dean Rusk; and then Lyndon took his seat and a full battery of cameras was upon them. All across the east wall of the East Room were representatives of other nations.

Dean Rusk spoke, followed by Sir Patrick Dean and then Dobrynin. There is always a little rustle of excitement when he rises. Lyndon said this Treaty was the most important international agreement since the beginning of the nuclear age. The gist of it was that the United States, Great Britain, and the Soviet Union, as well as fifty-eight non-nuclear nations, signed the Treaty to prohibit the spread of nuclear weapons. The Treaty has been in negotiation for six years. Next it goes to the Senate for ratification. Dramatically, the same sort of ceremony was going on at the same time in Moscow and in London.

At the end came the most momentous statement. Lyndon announced that the United States and the Soviet Union had agreed to begin talks "in the nearest future" on the limitation and reduction of offensive nuclear missiles and antimissile systems. He had first broached the subject in a private letter to Khrushchev in January 1964. There has been an exchange ever since. And now, finally, a breakthrough. When and where the talks would start, we do not know. They are being referred to as Strategic Arms Limitation Talks (SALT). At least a beginning has been made; maybe in years to come we'll look back on this day as the turning point in the nuclear decades.

Lyndon took out some insurance. "Discussion of this most complex subject will not be easy. We have no illusions that it will be. I know the stubborn, patient persistence it has required to come this far. We do not underestimate the difficulties that lie ahead. I know the fears, suspicions, and the anxieties we shall have to overcome." But still, it was a moment of hope.

When it was over we went into the Blue Room for a receiving line, and all of the Ambassadors filed by first, with congratulations and a feeling of warmth and accomplishment. As Arthur and Dorothy Goldberg came by, she said, "Today was worth leaving the Court for." And I felt a pang.

I went upstairs and ate a hamburger on a tray in my room. Then once more I went down to the Blue Room (how quickly this house has to change its face for different meetings!) to receive the International Consumers Committee—representatives from many countries—gathered here to discuss consumer problems. Betty Furness is their Washington hostess.

I always try to put myself into a receiving line with all of the vivacity and outgoing warmth and interest I can muster but there comes a time when you are almost a robot. There were so many guests today whose languages I could not speak, whose problems I did not know, that I found myself being mechanical and left with a dissatisfied feeling.

I changed into my beige lace to go to Perle Mesta's for a brief drop-in before a dinner party she was having in honor of Tom and Mary Clark. When I stopped by Lyndon's office he had a stack of work and didn't see how he could possibly leave, so I went alone. It was a small gathering in Perle's apartment. I circled the room, engaged in some light and pleasant talk, and left before I thought it was time for them to go in to dinner.

The second most important news of the day was that Lynda heard from Chuck—her first letter in two weeks—a short one. He said he had returned from a mission and had found a big stack of mail. He had only time to read two or three letters, write her this short one, stuff a few more into his pocket, and leave on another mission!

Tuesday, July 16

This was stamp day. About 1:30 Mary Lasker came, and she and Marvin Watson and Nash Castro and I met in the Yellow Oval Room to talk about a new series of stamps boosting beautification. Mary's list of projects, her suggestions of how government can help do good things, is endless! Her ammunition today was a stamp album—her own—which displays beautiful stamps of other countries. Several small countries in Africa or islands in the Pacific make a sizable part of their government income from stamps, beautifully designed, printed, and sold to experts who collect them. An additional exhibit was a group of photographs and drawings of a beautifully designed and planted highway—lupines and poppies along a California road and bluebonnets on a stretch of farm-to-market road in Texas —a picture that I had sent Mary.

She hoped three things. First, that we could make some of our stamps larger. Second, that we might try having some of them photographic rather than engraved. Third, that we could emphasize beautification, environment, conservation, in one or two more stamps before this Administration says good-by.

In Washington it seems you are always trying to convince somebody of something or trying to sell an idea. Today we had the novel experience of finding that the man we wanted to sell was not an opponent but an ally— the new Postmaster General Marvin Watson met us more than half-way. He had already planned a series of stamps on conservation. There could be one stamp on urban conservation, some beautification project in a big city. And there could be one on highway beautification.

Mary accepted his invitation to become a member of the Stamp Advisory Committee. This stamp project is a relatively small matter, but as I look back on our four and a half years, I think it would have been better if Lyndon had appointed more of his own men to strategic positions— Cabinet positions—not too long after he assumed office and certainly a great many more after he was inaugurated in January 1965. He kept many Kennedy appointees, in some departments practically the whole flock. I could not name all the reasons why. I think he did this partly out of respect for President Kennedy and a desire to treat him, even in death, as he (Lyndon) would have wanted a Vice President to treat him and his men under similar circumstances. And partly out of respect for the ability and liking of the men that Kennedy had appointed. In many cases it worked fine. But there is a certain quality of direct relationship between you and the people you personally have chosen and put into jobs that results in a teamwork that does not always come from someone who inherited the job from another President. In retrospect, the considered course of action might have been changed to advantage. It is only at the very end of the Administration that we arrive with our own appointees in certain strategic positions.

This evening I changed into a gay summer dress. We had invited for dinner Bob McNamara, who was back in town, though Margy was still in Europe. I went to the Truman Balcony. Cy Vance, our houseguest, came down and Bob arrived, looking wonderful and very happy. It was a half-hour before Lyndon came and I greedily used the time to ask questions because I knew I would have to yield to a more important questioner during the rest of the evening.

Bob described their trip to Egypt and going to dinner at the home of one of Nasser's ministers, from the terrace of whose house you could look straight onto one of the major pyramids, beautifully lighted. As Bob and Margy held their breath at the fantastic view, one of the guests laughingly asked, "How do you like the way a Socialist Minister lives?"

I gathered the McNamaras had found Nasser interesting and personally attractive. Bob had been to the Aswan Dam, and he said the whole course of current history might have been changed if we had gone on with the loan to build the Aswan Dam. He cited the amount that the Russians had invested in it and it was a very small sum, in terms of international finance. Meanwhile the Suez Canal is closed as the result of the Israeli-Arab War, and that part of the world heats up like a tinder box.

Lyndon came; we lit the candles on the table and had dinner. The setting (as I looked at the Washington Monument and the Jefferson Memorial, I could appreciate the Socialist Minister's view), the companions, the significance of the things we talked about, made it a starry evening for me . . . There have been many such, and I know it, and I am thankful.

I spent most of this day with Park Service men making plans for the park across the river. In the afternoon I came home for two hours of lying in bed and recording my diary and making telephone calls. While I watched out the window, a beautiful storm came up—great rolling black clouds, thunder and lightning—a magnificent show. Finally a lashing of rain, but brief . . . The corn is tall and green beyond the fence—it's a beautiful prospect right outside one's bedroom window!

The pink crepe myrtle—our own, which we planted fourteen or fifteen years ago—is full of pink blooms. The white crepe myrtle, alas, has not had a single blossom. The day lilies, which were so beautiful in June—every shade of yellow and orange into bronze—are just about spent. I am more and more satisfied with the view from my bedroom window.

About 6 I went for a drive around in the Martin, with the Park Service men and the deer raced along beside us and all the little dappled fawns. It was one of those glorious summer evenings. The storm was spent, and the air itself a caress. The scissor-tailed flycatchers swooped and dipped in their twilight ballet. Then I got word that Lyndon was calling me, and I went back to the Ranch and took the call. It was Jim Jones on *Air Force One* saying that they were en route home from the meeting in Honolulu and would be here a little before 10. We had a real midsummer dinner—much of it from the garden—roast and Mary's delicious corn bread, fresh corn and green beans—and I enjoyed that pleasure peculiar to the landsman who says, "These came off the place."

The men left a little before 10, and I went out to the airport to meet Lyndon. Odd, the way I live insulated from the world here, when he is not here. I never turn on the TV, I do not have a newspaper. But with him the world returns, TV and the newspapers.

He came swinging down off the plane, always glad to get back. It had been a good trip, he said, and he seemed reasonably satisfied. Thieu was as cooperative as he could be, caught in all the tides of demands of his own country, his allies, the enemy.

We went swimming. The water was a marvelous temperature, soft and relaxing. And we lay there floating and looking up at the stars and talked and rested. It was about 11 o'clock Saturday night. Lyndon had left for Honolulu at 11 Thursday morning, traveled thousands of miles, lived through hours of conferences and sensitive, demanding decisions. And here, so quickly, he was back!

What will it be like when January comes and there is a surcease from all of this?

I thought of the stories the Park Service men had told us at dinner about the Indian pictographs on the cliffs down in the Amistad Dam area. For over two years I have tried to get down there to see them! They talked of their trip to the Cascade Mountains—the most magnificent part of this country, they say—and I thought of my last phone call from Tony, telling about his camping trip in the mountains with his two grandchildren. All of those things for me have allure!

Thursday, August 1

THE WHITE HOUSE

At noon I found Lyndon having lunch with Mayor Richard Daley. He asked Lynda and me to sit down with them. The Mayor was giving Lyndon a sales talk about coming to Chicago. The Democrats wanted to give him a rousing welcome; they wanted to show their appreciation. Lyndon gave him little encouragement. He stopped just short of a positive "No." And what of me? I said I would do whatever Lyndon wanted me to do, but I have no enthusiasm for going. This Convention belongs to others, and I am delighted to let them have it.

There was a tape machine on the table, and they had been listening to the tape Chuck had sent Lynda from Vietnam. Lyndon played it again, and I listened with a strange mixture of awe and compassion and pride, too. He is such a man—Chuck. And Lyndon is so proud of him. I could see Lynda Bird did not like having us listen to the tape, and later I heard about this very belligerently. Her daddy simply does not understand.

Lyndon and Mayor Daley talked about the war. It was easy to see that Mayor Daley doubted our presence in Asia. Lyndon cited the example of Korea—when we had been there it had seemed to us a strong, capable, "on-its-own" nation. In the course of time, couldn't Vietnam develop into the same? But the Mayor simply wants out. Lyndon tried to explain to him what he faced. While he, the President, speaking officially for the United States, was trying to bargain for peace, the would-be candidates for President were busy making unofficial offers of their own. He said, "Just suppose

I was trading with you, to sell you a house. And I said, 'Mr. Mayor, I'll sell you and Mrs. Daley this house for twenty thousand dollars and not a dollar less.' And you started to leave and Lady Bird followed you to the door and said, 'Mr. Mayor, if you don't buy it for twenty thousand dollars, I'll sell it to you next week for eighteen thousand dollars.' And Lynda Bird followed you on out to the gate and said, 'If you don't buy it from them I'll let you have it for sixteen thousand dollars.' What would you do?"

It was an effective story. The President and the Administration are being badgered and undermined every foot of the way to the peace table by the candidates. The whole thing makes me gladder and gladder we are not one among them! But the Mayor's attitude spoke eloquently of the growing concern in the country.

I dressed and went into the Yellow Room to receive the five new Ambassadors' wives—from Burma, Indonesia, Mauritius, Paraguay, and the Ivory Coast.

I took my seat on the big yellow sofa next to the fireplace between two of them. They turned out to be the most talkative ones, from Burma and Indonesia, and very attractive ladies they were—excellent English. We had a delicious tea, or rather tea was offered. On occasions like this everybody is as delicate as a bird about eating. Then I moved to the other sofa and chatted with the wife of the Ambassador from Paraguay. We talked of General Stroessner's visit. And with difficulty I endeavored to talk to the new Ambassador's wife from the Ivory Coast who speaks only French. And the nearly silent little lady from Mauritius.

Doing battle against yesterday's slump, I was energetic and did everything that I could to make them have an interesting time and feel at home.

At 5 I went back to the Yellow Room for the second reception of the day, this time for the college interns. We had another delicious tea, and this time the guests enjoyed it. The number of cookies and tea sandwiches consumed goes up markedly when the guests are high school and college students. There were forty-five young people who work on the Hill in Congressmen's or Senators' offices and in various Cabinet departments, at OEO and AID, and our half-dozen who work here at the White House. I had added some of our personal friends here for the summer.

After they had gone, I changed clothes again into something gala and festive—my brown lace. We were going to the Monroneys' for dinner. I arrived at Mary Ellen's charming house to find Marny Clifford, the Bill Whites, Trudye and Joe Fowler—he was just "on leave" from the hospital where he had checked in for the operation and was wearing a pair of wild strawberry-pink pants in defiance of his condition—and Hale and Lindy Boggs.

Mary Ellen is one of the best hostesses I know. The conversation always seems to be exciting at her house. And after all, that to me is the best thing about a party—to "bring out" the guests—their talent for communion, for amusement. At one time I found myself saying that I had always planned to go on a river boat down the Mississippi. I had hardly gotten the words out of my mouth before I was joined by Bill White who said he wanted to sign up to go along if I ever did. And Trudye and Joe Fowler said they had always wanted to go too! It turned out that Hale and Lindy Boggs even knew where you got on the boat—Minneapolis—it took eight days to get to New Orleans, and the only boat remaining on that run was called the *Delta Queen*. So we practically signed up a party for some day in the spring or Indian summer of another year.

Lyndon was very late joining us. I kept saying to Mary Ellen that she must take us in to dinner. Lyndon finally arrived at a quarter of 10 and he was worth waiting for. He was aglow—full of good stories, laughing, looking tanned and fine, enjoying everybody, and making them enjoy the evening more. He had just been addressing the National Bar Association, and he said this organization of Negro lawyers had given him a wonderful ovation.

It was all very relaxed and lots of fun and thoroughly spicy. And Lyndon was the most entertaining person there. I am concerned about Mike. He has a difficult race.

Friday, August 2

EN ROUTE TO TEXAS

The helicopter rose from the South Lawn a little before noon today and we went directly to Walter Reed Hospital before leaving for Texas. Lyndon wanted to visit President Eisenhower, who is in the hospital. That is one of the things that I love about Lyndon—his regard for former Presidents.

Cheering groups of people waved us into Walter Reed. The military met and escorted us up to the suite. Lyndon went directly in to see the General. Mrs. Eisenhower said to Lyndon, in the most graceful manner, "You'll leave your girl out here to talk to me, won't you?" So I had about an hour's visit with another First Lady—the longest I've ever had. Mrs. Eisenhower was wearing a light, fluttery, green-and-blue summer dress. She was vivacious, cheerful, pretty—all good qualities in a woman. What a lucky man he is to have her constantly at his side! She said she stayed right with him all the time. "I know the General would worry so about me if I were out at the farm." She showed me her room. It was tiny, almost like a monk's cell, the only touch of luxury a soft, delicate, velvet coverlet. She said airily, "I brought my own comfort."

During our conversation she expressed several times her desire to get free from "things." She said she used to care about clothes. She doesn't anymore. And she keeps all of her jewelry locked up and wears only costume jewelry. It was very much on her mind ultimately to dispose usefully of so many accumulated things. Once before at the White House she had mentioned the vast array of gifts that a President accumulates. I spoke up for any items of real family closeness for use in the little house in Denison where President Eisenhower was born, now a museum. And I told her how wonderful it was to me that they had turned over, in their lifetime, their home in Gettysburg to the National Park Service.

She spoke of how crowds continued to come and look at the farm. She said they had had their fence wired but once someone had managed to get in anyway and had walked right into their yard. She said, "You'll have all this too!" Then we talked of grandchildren, of movies—a thoroughly easy, pleasant, delightful hour.

Friday, August 9

LBJ RANCH

Today was a busy day with almost as much air traffic as Dulles. The first plane brought the Vice President and Muriel. Hubert was his lively, happy self. He looked fit and healthy, and so did Muriel. She told me about her plans for the campaign. She will travel mostly with Hubert. When she goes off by herself she will try, in each town, to attend a lunch or reception with Democratic women and to give talks on the subject that she knows best—child health, with special emphasis on retarded children— to some appropriate group. She said she would have a press meeting, which she is loath to call a press conference. We are somewhat alike—she and I. Neither of us feel we have anything important enough to say to call a press conference—but a discussion, now that's different.

I made one forthright request of Hubert laughingly, saying that whoever was the next President of the United States I had one favor to ask and now was my chance to ask him. If he wound up in that big house, would he please keep Blanco? Blanco is a patrician. The White House lawn is the perfect setting for him. At the Ranch, he is scared of the cattle. He is scared of the peacocks. He is scared of everything that is unfamiliar. And he beats a retreat for the house, the President's room, and finally gets under the President's bed.

We then discussed, with happy frankness, our opinions of Senator George McGovern and Senator Eugene McCarthy. Hubert and Muriel left about 3 in a flurry of new arrivals. The "Washington shuttle," bringing Secretary Robert Weaver and Joe Califano, and also Edgar Kaiser and his son and an assistant, was due.

We then got a message that Senator James Eastland's plane was circling and about to land. I thought I could be useful by meeting Senator Eastland and entertaining his party, driving them around the place, while Lyndon conducted his business with the Secretary and the Kaiser group.

I was just in time to be at the foot of the ramp as the Senator descended. He was accompanied by two Deep South friends—D. A. Biglane and W. O. Schurden. I made apologies for Lyndon, asked them to get in with me and see something of the Ranch while Lyndon attended to some pressing business. We drove down by the family graveyard—no unfamiliar sight for Mississippians, and the house where Lyndon was born and around the Ranch, looking at the cattle. I proudly displayed the "coastal Bermuda." Yes, they had "coastal Bermuda" in Mississippi—plenty of it. This they thought was mighty fine. They were exceedingly complimentary of our registered cattle.

Senator Eastland was determined to talk politics. He said, "You know your husband is going to be nominated, don't you?" I said, "No, sir, not at all. There is not going to be any movement of that sort—that is, not with any force behind it. And if he were, he wouldn't accept." The Senator seemed, somehow, taken aback—a little disbelieving—as though I had hoped it would happen that way, but relatively unshaken in his conviction. As little as they see eye to eye, as much as lies between them, I believe he would rather see Lyndon nominated than anybody now being considered by the Democratic Party.

Finally I drove them back to the main house and saw Lyndon's convertible just going around the barn, conveying Secretary Weaver, Joe Califano, and the Kaisers to the plane. It was only later that I learned the tremendously exciting nature of their visit—an effort to get started some inexpensive housing. For all of his five years in office, Lyndon has been talking to housing people, architects, everybody throughout the framework of government, trying to get a prototype of small houses built that could sell for five thousand dollars or less. Now in his last few months, he has just challenged Kaiser and about ten builders to produce such a prototype. They are going to do it in Austin, Texas, and before Lyndon is out of office! It is an exciting prospect, and—who knows—maybe a step up in putting home ownership within the reach of very poor people.

In a moment Lyndon was back greeting the Senator and his friends warmly. I think Lyndon was trying to blunt Eastland's hostility to Abe Fortas, if not to win him over—and that may not be possible. The Senator is a very determined man, a positive man. At least Lyndon tried to draw off any venom he may have, to explain Fortas as we know him.

It was an interesting hour. The raillery, reminiscences, play of their two personalities—rather like two boxers dancing around in the ring exchanging blows, but good-natured. Mr. Biglane and Mr. Schurden were typically old-school Southerners. I felt a kinship with them, engendered by having been born and raised in very much the same region. But I shiver to think what an Eastern writer would have done with their words, their political and social views, their wonderful accents. Somewhat to my surprise they were ardent LBJ supporters, and for all the right reasons, I thought. They saw in him just the same sort of champion of the poor folks that I do—a practical, earthy, determined, sometimes skeptical man but always hopeful and believing that you can do something about man and his troubles. All three of them were insisting that Lyndon was the only man for the Democratic Party in the coming election. How surprising that was, coming from three staunch Mississippians!

Finally we had seen every cow and bull on the place and almost every blade of grass—even the auction barn to which Lyndon had taken them as a last show of what was happening in this country. And at long last we put them on the plane, with good-bys just before dark came.

Saturday, August 10

Secretary Rusk, Dick Helms, and Cy Vance came down by plane early this morning for the briefing with the new Republican candidates and sat on the lawn with Lyndon and talked. About noon Mr. Nixon arrived, cordial and confident, with Spiro Agnew descending the plane behind him.

I had called Pat Nixon when I'd heard the men were coming, to invite her and Mrs. Agnew to come to lunch. Pat said she had better not, because one of the girls had a sore throat and fever, and she should stay in the hotel room with her. But she did say: "I've always wanted to see your Ranch." We would have had a lot to talk about with all our mutual years in the Senate Ladies and I was sorry she didn't come.

Lyndon was courteous and affable—even warm—and both Nixon and Agnew were the same way. I could see that Lyndon had considerable sympathy for Agnew, augmented, I am sure, as was mine, by the cruel treatment the press has been giving him. In our case I find that it is quite easy to be around former adversaries. There is no barrier of venom or rancor—no abrasiveness, for we both know a bit of what it's like. Alas, it is much easier to let your temperature rise when you are dealing with sometime friends, members of the same party or even members of the same Administration!

The men worked for about an hour and a half; then I took them in to lunch, with Dean Rusk on my right, and Spiro Agnew on my left, and Mr. Nixon on Lyndon's right. We had planned a delicious lunch—steak and fresh corn. We wanted to put our best foot forward. It was impossible not to wonder whether we were looking at the next President of the United States today, or if we had been looking at him yesterday. I asked them to sign the guest book on the page with Hubert's and Muriel's names.

Tuesday, August 20

THE WHITE HOUSE

This was a day of excitement and upsets. I had expected to be back in Washington all week by myself. But instead Lyndon had arrived late last night after a speech in Detroit to the Veterans of Foreign Wars. We were filming the family floor of the White House—the West Hall, our personal living room, and I was considerably upset because Lyndon's presence meant that we wouldn't have the freedom of the place—which must always serve his uses. As it turned out, his uses were to sleep briefly, telephone at length, and go straight to his office.

There was an air of excitement in the White House, more than usual staff coming and going, a feeling of tenseness, of something about to happen. There was talk of a press conference scheduled for Wednesday morning. Then, when I was asking Walt Rostow about some future dates for visiting Chiefs of State, I said, "Is there anything good going to happen in the next day or two?" In his quiet but humorous fashion he said, "It looks as if the Russians have emptied their out-basket to us. They have answered *all* of the President's correspondence." It looked as though all the roadblocks to our nuclear weapons talks with the Soviet Union had been overcome.

In an atmosphere charged with hope and expectation, I managed to get a good deal of work done—autographing, reading memos, consuming the "Read and File." I had lunch alone in my room. Then more filming. Just before 4 I broke loose, dressed up in a gay summer print, met Jane Freeman and her daughter, Connie, and stood with them at the door of the Yellow Room for a tea in Connie's honor. She is to be married on Saturday. Her parents are among my favorite members of Lyndon's Cabinet.

Most of the Cabinet wives were there—nine of them, and Muriel, looking lovely. The members of Connie's wedding party—bridesmaids, school friends, fellow Peace Corps members. One of the signs of the time was two young girls chatting together in the Yellow Room of the White House —one a Peace Corps friend of Connie's, very black, very bright, very outgoing, the other the very blonde daughter of Marvin Watson from deep East Texas.

Late that evening, with some dinner guests, I was listening to Dean Rusk on TV when Lyndon came in. Dean was testifying before the Platform Committee of the Democratic Convention, when there was a dramatic turn of events. Rusk was making a statement on Vietnam, a strong, clear, effective statement, when someone came up to him and handed him a note. He asked the Committee's pardon and turned to go—it was about the invasion of Czechoslovakia by the Russians! There was a churning air of expectancy and excitement in the room.

I gathered that Lyndon had learned about this only a short while before, although he and his advisers had concluded at lunch that it might well happen. And what events would follow in its train? There would be a National Security Council meeting which Lyndon had already called. Lyndon ate hurriedly and went back to his office.

And so our high hopes of this morning were dashed. For a few hours it had looked as though we were making a step forward with Russia. And then suddenly, catastrophically, the word had come that the Soviet forces were moving into Czechoslovakia.

I, at least, felt a little like Moses, glimpsing the promised land from the mountaintop—and then suddenly having it disappear like a mirage. I was in bed by midnight, knowing that this day would shape many of the days to come, but not knowing how.

Tuesday, August 27

Today, Lyndon's sixtieth birthday, was probably as strange and dramatic and, in a way, sad a birthday as any he will ever have. For me this whole week has been a sort of suspended-in-space time. The decision not to run had been made irrevocably on March 31, but there was a special saying good-by this week to our whole political life. The Convention would be choosing from among others, and for us it was really over—no matter that it was over by choice. Some time ago there had been talk about Lyndon's going to the Convention to make a valedictory speech, to receive good wishes on his birthday. As the days passed, my betting odds were more and more that we would not go. When the Convention virtually erupted on Monday, the likelihood of our making the trip seemed to me to dwindle to almost nothing.

The Convention had grown so exciting Monday night that I had stayed up until 3—I, who love to go to bed early! When some contingents had had the presumption to contest the seating of the Texas delegation, I couldn't possibly go to bed until John Connally had won that fight!

And so on Lyndon's sixtieth birthday I woke to a sense of void and yet excitement. I called Mrs. Dick Daley to thank her for her invitation to a luncheon and to say that we had no plans to be there.

I walked down to the birthplace house for exercise and to be alone. I came back to find that the press was intent on getting a birthday picture of Lyndon and that he thought we would fly into Austin, go by Luci's house, and let them take their pictures there with the four of us cutting the birthday cake. With all vestige of a possible trip to Chicago ruled out, I began to call some close friends, all of whom were standing by, to come on over and celebrate Lyndon's birthday tonight.

Liz called from Chicago to report that there had been a wonderful women's luncheon and style show with Abigail, Muriel, and Mrs. McGovern all seated at the head table, and Bess Abell looking darling in the role of Dolley Madison. Even Liz sounded glad that we were not in Chicago, however. From afar the Convention seemed like a seething cauldron of emotions and striving cliques—of every stripe of Democrat—and hippies and yippies and police standing by. If I could have been there without being *me*, I would have liked very much to see what was looming up as one of the spectacles of our time!

We left for Austin about 5 by helicopter, landed at Camp Mabry, and drove in to Luci's house. Like magic, Luci's friends had converged on the house, spread the table with a beautiful array of cakes and punch, polished candle sticks, newly shined silver, wedding present china. The press arrived in sizable numbers, considering that the big news was more than a thousand miles away. Lyndon sat on the sofa and Luci brought in his cake with one candle on it. He took Lyn on his lap and cut his cake and gave a piece to Lyn, who promptly began making a mess. Yuki helped to clean it up.

The press, rather subdued, asked Lyndon a few questions. He talked at length and in mild good humor. But it was all very low-key and, somehow, this added to the sad atmosphere.

We choppered back and were at the Ranch by 7. In the long twilight, Lyndon set out at once for a ride, and I to get ready for the birthday party. Then the Convention news started and with all three TV sets going in the living room we stopped to greet all our good friends and then to turn our faces back to television—to the wildness of the scene in Chicago. More than twenty of us congregated in the living room and we simply couldn't break it up for dinner. Finally I had Mary put the dinner out on the buffet in the dining room and, as we could tear ourselves away, we filed in, filled our plates, rushed back and took our seats and watched the spectacle.

It was a three-ring circus! There was a Stop Humphrey movement by McCarthy and McGovern and a Draft Teddy Kennedy movement, with the TV commentators running in a circle from one Kennedy supporter to another, trying to stoke the fires under it. You would have thought there were no delegations to the Convention except those from New York, California, and Wisconsin. Finally the forces of the South moved in and favorite son delegations began releasing their delegates for Humphrey . . . first Texas, then South Carolina, and then Tennessee. The Convention moved on toward the bitterest fight of all, the crucial Vietnam plank in the platform. And so, in spite of all the hell raised on the floor and in the city, the work of the Convention did go forward. Thus this strange day came to an end. In fact the whole strange week was characterized by Luci as the "longest wake I ever attended."

This August we have spent more time at the Ranch than any month I can remember. Luci lets me read her letters from Patrick and listen to her tapes. He seems so young and vulnerable and good. But I am afraid for him, oddly, more than I am for Chuck who is in more danger, but who has the backlog of his Marine training. Less often, Lynda lets us read her letters or listen to her tapes from Chuck. She holds her personal life close to herself. She flinches when her daddy quotes Chuck.

And so we go on through this strange year. Personally, it is a happy year in the close circle of our family, because I think we are each proud of what each one of us is doing. How strange that might sound to somebody on the outside who is looking in at us! But it is true—the world is in convulsions all around us—our party, our country—the whole world. Lyndon is plowing right on, working as hard as he can every day on those things he can control and assaulting those things vigorously that he has even a little hope of controlling. I know that it is a wracking year for Lyndon physically, and it must be mentally and spiritually as well.

Fall 1968

THE
WHITE HOUSE
Monday,
September 9,
1968 This was a day tailored to my liking. Much work, some exercise, and a gay convivial ending to look forward to—the "Country Fair" on the South Lawn for White House staff and their spouses!

This afternoon I had an interview with James Egan for *Good Housekeeping* on my future plans. We sat in the Lincoln Sitting Room drinking spiced tea, and I spent an hour trying to maintain a course between guarded and candid. There are so many things I want to do! Follow autumn from the tip of Vermont—or would it be Maine?—down through gold and crimson New England and past familiar Washington and Maryland and Virginia and on down to the South to home. And, in reverse, follow spring—beginning maybe with the historic homes and gardens of Natchez, Mississippi, and going on up through South Carolina and once again to New England. I'd love to walk the Appalachian Trail and I want to go down ever so many rivers! The Snake

River and the Rio Grande have just been a taste. One thing I shall do is go to the homes of all the Presidents. By now I have seen at least twelve and often you find that there are two or three homes to commemorate each President. (When it comes to Lyndon, the homes of his lifetime will all be a package, from birth to death, right there in our little river valley.)

And I want to pay for the boon of living in this wonderful country. I want to know and work at what's going on in my community, in my area, in my state—for the good things. Always, always, I will be working on parks and conservation. And I shall pursue more luxuriously the pleasures of the local theater. The Palo Duro Canyon Pageant and the Albany Fandangle have just been tastes to whet the appetite. I would like to explore the Trinity Theater in San Antonio. Why, I have never even been to the Jefferson Museum!

Compellingly, there is the call of all the faraway places that I want to go to see—the snorkeling in the clear waters off Mexico, Cozumel, and the archaeological digs in the Yucatán Peninsula, the Tigris-Euphrates area—or Greece. It's a family joke—my "going away to the Isles of Greece" on a boat to get away from everything. When I do go, I shall try to take some of my family along—there's nobody that I find more fun.

But all this would sound so naked in print, before any of it has been done. So I talked to Mr. Egan a good deal about the prosaic and necessary things—months that must be spent unpacking possessions of thirty years' accumulations and helping get a daughter, whose husband is overseas, temporarily settled with her baby in our home until he returns.

Tuesday, September 24

Today was one of those full, back-to-back Washington days. Actually, I enjoy them. Though I find after nearly five years that I am much more physically and mentally wearied. And what of Lyndon? There is the relief, the joy, the insurance, that in a little less than four months we will not have to have this endurance!

About one today I left the White House with Ashton, Liz, Jane Freeman, and Lynda, bound for an annual occurrence—the "Louisiana Gumbo" luncheon, cooked by Senator Ellender of Louisiana himself and served to a group of favored ladies in his little hideaway in the Capitol. We entered through the hall adorned with the Thomas Jefferson columns, with ears of corn as a decorative motif. The walls still bear the scars of British bullets when the British set fire to the Capitol in the War of 1812. A host of memories walked with me. As presiding officer of the Senate wives I had gone to meet Mrs. Kennedy here when she, as First Lady, was our guest of honor at the annual Senate Ladies Luncheon. I remembered pointing out these things to her.

Upstairs there were seventeen congenial ladies—from the Senate and the House, one Ambassador's wife, a couple of newswomen—and one lone man, Senator Ellender. The Louisiana gumbo was as good as ever and the description of the ritual of its cooking eagerly listened to. It was the Senator's birthday, and I presented him with a cake made by the White House chef, inscribed, "*Happy Birthday to a Great Chef.*" The Senator wears his years philosophically, even gaily. He talked of his thirteen grandchildren, his trips to Africa—where some slavery still exists, he says, at least in the case of women. He talked about the Fortas nomination—foreboding, painful estimate that he did not think a cloture vote could be obtained to stop a filibuster . . . and that would mean dooming the appointment of Abe.

The star of the occasion, to my in no way impartial eyes, was Lynda Bird, who is expecting her baby next month with her husband so far away. I am practically in awe of her these days. She is so full of common sense and undramatic courage. She's humorous, calls herself "Agnes Gooch" (from the character in *Auntie Mame*), gives imitations of her own waddling ungainliness, and is unremittingly disciplined about diet and exercise. Today she was very funny, telling her end of the table about our family. (She—that most private of people!) Actually they were keen but humorous assessments—that Luci should have been on the stage and there would have been no middle ground for her in roles—she would always be playing either Little Mary Sunshine or Ophelia! That I, her mother, am like a character in Voltaire's *Candide*—whatever is going on it's "the best of all possible worlds." And regarding her father (so true): "He doesn't hear you at all unless you are saying something you don't want him to hear—then he somehow hears the whole thing!"

At 4 I went down to meet representatives of the American Association of Nurserymen on the front lawn. They brought a little booklet which they presented to me called, "Landscape Beauty Depends on People," which showed how to present a pretty face to the world with the landscaping at your front door, or how to have a more attractive place for recreating in your backyard, or heralding beauty as a community effort.

My next meeting was a tea for the three hundred members of JANGO—the daughters of Armed Service personnel, from fourteen to twenty-three, who volunteer their time at hospitals, in Soldiers' and Sailors' Homes and Service Clubs. What a country of effort we are! We *try*—innocently, hopefully, industriously, in every field—God help us. There were only a few I knew—Mrs. Lew Walt, wife of the General, little Susan Voss, the daughter of the White House physician, who has herself given two thousand hours of volunteer work in the past two summers, and Mrs. Robert Patterson, wife of the one-time Secretary of War.

I stood by the fireplace and they filed past—the beautiful and plain, the smartly dressed and simple—all bright, eager, a little excited. I tried to rise to the occasion and be just as warm as the visitors deserved. Every now and then I would pause to thank one of them for what they all did or to ask another where she worked. About 5:30 I went upstairs, with the feeling that the good work of the world goes on in spite of all the dire headlines in the paper—"MEXICO CITY BATTLE KILLS 15 AS ARMY TAKES OVER SCHOOL," "AGONY IN BIAFRA."

About 8 I went down to the pool to find Lyndon and Clark swimming. I always welcome that. He has been marvelous about getting exercise lately. I could tell that the men's conversation was purposeful, probing, and tense. Marny and I chatted about our day at "Winterthur" while the men swam and talked. And then we went upstairs.

We had dinner about 9:30, joined by some houseguests. I had a sense that the conversation between Clark and Lyndon was being temporarily halted. Lyndon relieved me of indecisions by suggesting that the ladies have coffee in the Yellow Room.

When our houseguests retired, Marny and I began to wait out Clark and Lyndon, who were talking earnestly on the green sofa in the West Hall. Their looks and their gestures did not invite us to join them. I thought of Clark's weariness, knowing that he likes to get to bed early and also that he has an important speech tomorrow. Why have I all that much confidence in Lyndon's indestructibility?

I knew that they had been talking earlier, from snatches that I had overheard, of all the portents of the Czechoslovakian tensions—of the situation in West Germany, of Russia's intentions, Moscow's possible moves into Yugoslavia or Romania.

Marny kept urging me to go to bed. By this time we were seated in the hall—having progressed that far and then realizing simultaneously that we should not enter their conversation.

At last they rose, and standing kept on talking, sounding grim and troubled, but coming our way. It was 12:30 by the time the Cliffords left—all of us looking and feeling very weary. Lyndon went to bed after one, with still the night reading to do, exhausted and burdened.

Saturday, September 28

It is a sad season. Troubles are crowding in on all sides. Luci is here, but for a cruel reason—the funeral of LeRoy Bates, who used to be her beau when he went to the Naval Academy and was one of the most wholesome, happy, "approved-by-family" of the young men who have filled this house in our time here. LeRoy was killed in a flight-training accident and Luci has asked his young widow, Melinda, who has been here many times with LeRoy, and her father and mother—the Venables—to stay at the White House while they are here for the funeral.

It is a joy to have Neva and Wesley West here. They came Thursday and will be leaving tonight. I had told them I wanted them to come to one more State Dinner, and Neva had said, "Wesley hopes you'll ask us up sometime when there is *not* a State Dinner." So we had, planning it around one of our small upstairs dinners for about twenty-six people on Friday night. We've had snatches of time for family talk and stories of home.

We had a walk around the grounds. Yuki, that perennial ham, made a beeline for the fence to make friends with all the tourists who soon congregated there. Patrick Lyndon waded right through the white petunias and pink geraniums trying to get into the fountain! Down at the fence there was much clicking of cameras and we waved at the people. They don't interfere anymore with my feeling of being at home here.

Lyndon asked Carol and Abe to come over for dinner. I was glad. I had been hungry to see them for days and weeks. But I hadn't asked them, for a curious reason. I wondered if they could stand to see us, the unwitting architects of all the agony they have been going through. Lyndon's only thought—months ago when he had nominated Abe to be Chief Justice—had been to find the best Chief Justice the country could provide and to accord Abe an honor he so magnificently deserves. Well, it hasn't turned out that way. So often through the years I have seen this drama played out but with a different set of characters. Somebody was being maligned, torn apart, his character and life questioned by the Congress and press, and finally, you suppose, by people in general. But there was always a wise, able, and compassionate guide for them to turn to—and that was Abe Fortas. Now when Abe is the man who is being pilloried, where is there an Abe Fortas for him to turn to? There isn't anybody. And so the sorry story is nearly played out—the end will probably come sometime next week.

When they came, Carol was bouncy and strong and expressed her observations in salty and, I thought, healthy language. I was reassured by her. She is quite sure it is all over—Abe has lost. Senator Dirksen's complete turnaround was the end. But she is philosophic about it. Abe was very quiet, contained, and dignified.

We explored the future of the country, the temper of the time, the campaigns of Nixon and of Humphrey—the likelihood that there might be a swing to strong conservatism. And we talked of the heritage of McCarthy the first and McCarthy the second. What days we have lived through here!

There have been this summer so many occasions for reflection. My mind goes back to that evening in July in San Salvador, a night I sat enthralled with a small group of staff as Lyndon reminisced and philosophized about the whole political and social spectrum of the day, about communism— what was its vitality around the world and in our country? What was the virus or the miasma that was infecting the universities and the communications media and the entertainment world? Lyndon said there were two conflicting emotions in him. He said something like this: there is a great tide running—a great pendulum swinging—in the country. In response to the permissiveness, the lawlessness of the day, there may be a great swing back toward authoritarianism and conservatism. He said there would be a part of him that would welcome it . . . think it necessary. But there is the other side of him that says if such a reaction happens it would set back all the things he stands for, that he has fought for, that he believes in and wants—the attacks on ignorance, poverty, and disease. It will set us back many decades.

He talked as though he were a long way off, looking back at this small planet, and I found it very interesting. I asked him if he didn't feel his enthusiasm blunted and his quest for more education for everybody in this country and for other countries diminished—because of the way our students are behaving—and the professors, too—with draft-card burning, flag burning, rioting. For myself I find it so easy to be passionate rather than thoughtful about such attacks on our institutions and symbols.

No, he was just as firm in his faith in education in the long run.

I did not understand his feeling entirely. He seemed to think: "This is just an episode, a phenomenon that will pass." As for the professors, he suggested they had come by their attitudes because, for so long, their salaries, their economic status, their prestige had been so low. They were now feeling power for the first time.

I was respectful of his attitude. Even in a way proud of it. But my own annoyance at the disruptions in the universities and colleges is not assuaged.

Wednesday, October 2

Today was a tumultuously full day at the White House—a mixture of pain and triumph. The pain was resoundingly described on the front page: "SENATE REJECTS FORTAS CLOTURE"—the vote, 45 to 43—almost the last page in this long agony in the nomination of Abe to be Chief Justice. The triumph was quietly reported on the inside pages, but was a source of warm satisfaction to me and a lot of conservationists. "Two new National Parks and a system of scenic rivers and trails were added to the nation's outdoor public preserve today." And one of them was the 58,000-acre Redwood National Park!

The first ceremonial event of the day was the arrival ceremony on the South grounds to meet President François Tombalbaye of Chad. At 11:30 Lyndon and I walked out of his office for this first of the State visits to be handled by Ambassador Abell—our fourth Chief of Protocol. President Tombalbaye was very black, his face a network of scars—the result of tribal initiation, I suppose—and he spoke only French, so it was difficult for me to have any real contact with him then or later.

A little past one I went down to the Usher's office with Ashton in tow, signing mail—handing letters to her, and making decisions until the last minute, when Lyndon emerged from the elevator and we walked together, and with a sense of triumph, into the East Room for the signing of the four landmark bills in the story of conservation in this country.

Besides the Redwood Park, which has trees in it that are a thousand years old and range up to 367 feet in height, there also came into being today the North Cascades National Park in the State of Washington—an area that's called the American Alps and is still very much frontier. Two other victories: a system of urban and rural trails, including the Pacific Coast Trail from Mexico to Canada; and the establishment of a National

Wild and Scenic Rivers System, reserving sections of eight rivers, with twenty-seven more under study. Afterward, when Lyndon signed the bills, he gave the first pen to Senator Hayden and then one to me.

A little before 2 I was back upstairs in the family dining room for one of the shortest but most entertaining luncheons I can remember in the White House. Laurance Rockefeller did most of the talking. He was as excited as a child about having enlisted new recruits for conservation—and what a list! One was Charles Lindbergh, who has shut the door on the world for thirty-five years, but now is opening it himself to talk to people and groups in the interest of conservation. Laurance described a luncheon in which three of the other guests were Colonel Lindbergh, Doris Duke, and Arthur Godfrey. Laurance is now trying to save an area in the Hawaiian Islands which he tells me is beautiful beyond belief.

We gulped our lunch, then went downstairs to meet the other members of the Beautification Committee and board the bus for the dedication of the Hobart Community Parks. Every time I see a bus, I shall think of our Beautification Committee—the places we've been in them . . . a long and happy roster. These two small parklets on Hobart Street in a low-income area were a gift to the city by David Lloyd Kreeger.

Back at the White House we had a Committee meeting in the library where Nash Castro and Walter Washington gave us a glowing description of the program, "Summer in the Parks." Their summary of the things they had done—community concerts, plays, bus trips, and cookouts—was humorous and full of hope.

Our State guest, President Tombalbaye, arrived under the North Portico a little past 8 p.m. We took him with his small party of Ministers up to the Yellow Room. He was wearing a beautiful blue flowing robe, handsomely embroidered, and a matching blue cap and carried a walking stick. Blue, I was told later, was a color limited to those of very highest rank in Chad. His Ministers wore similar robes in other colors. I think it is a good idea for representatives of foreign countries to wear their native dress. It imparts glamor to us and naturalness to them.

President Tombalbaye told me that there were parts of his country in which rain had never fallen! We discussed his coming trip to Lubbock, Texas—especially to Texas Tech there, where the problems of arid countries have been explored—and my trip to his neighboring Senegal. He inscribed my menu in French. Alas that I have no French. At least one foreign language would be such a helpful tool for a First Lady.

LOUISVILLE, KENTUCKY

Today was reminiscent of many, many campaign journeys in the past. This one was for Hubert Humphrey and the rest of the Democratic ticket. I was up early, read my speech over several times, talked to Lyndon about the trip, left with Liz about 9:30 for Kentucky, wearing my new shocking pink dress and feeling ready for the occasion.

At the airport there was a sizable crowd led by the Republican Mayor and Mrs. Schmied, a hospitable, totally correct greeting with an armful of flowers, along with Lieutenant Governor Wendell Ford who is running for Governor, and Katherine Peden who is running for the Senate. All along the airport fence, smiling faces and waving hands, Girl Scouts, Boy Scouts, Cubs, Brownies, friendly signs—"WELCOME PATRICK LYNDON'S GRANDMOTHER!"—a group of Job Corps men. I made a particular point of seeking them out, shaking hands with every one of them—"What are you taking?" "Brick masonry." "And you?" "Carpentry." "Good—our country needs your skills." Everybody had a big, friendly smile and there was not a single unfriendly gesture. I felt like Merlin, the magician in the legend of King Arthur, that I had been "taken backward in time!"—to a different political climate.

There was a sizable crowd in front of the Sheraton Hotel, nearly all adults. From a small platform, there was a welcoming ceremony by Lieutenant Governor Wendell Ford, who made me "an Admiral of all the Waterways of Kentucky." (I had been made a Kentucky Colonel once before.) Then began a series of presentations—so often a part of a political gathering—that tell so colorfully of the local crafts and produce. A silver mint-julep cup from the Kentucky Garden Clubs; two baseball bats from two cute Little Leaguers, one for Patrick Lyndon and one for somebody else who hasn't made his appearance yet (bats are a major industry in this town); a horseshoe of red roses from the pretty young Queen of the Kentucky Derby. Then the funniest thing of all, a couple who had a breeding farm presented me with a very small burro for Lyn! There was a complete feeling of good will and happiness in the crowd. Only one sign was hostile, and it fairly amusing. A young man held it up, and it said, "I AM IN FAVOR OF A SLIGHTLY DISHONORABLE PEACE!"

We went into the Sheraton Hotel ballroom and walked through a cheering crowd of nine hundred, the Kentucky Democratic Women's Club luncheon. Governor Edward Breathitt was on my right and had strong, warm things to say about Lyndon.

When it was my time, I invoked our Kentucky ancestors—the Buntins and the Deshas—and Kentucky greats I had known—Alben Barkley and Earl Clements. Then I launched into about a twelve-minute talk on the constructive work of the last eight years' and why I thought it ought to continue under Hubert Humphrey who had been so much a part of it all. His name from the very first has appeared on some of the most progressive legislation of our time—Medicare, Peace Corps, Nuclear Test Ban Treaty, Civil Rights Acts. Because I do not really believe it and because I wouldn't feel like myself doing it, I had no ugly things to say about the other candidates. I just described Hubert as he is: "He is without vindictiveness and bitter hatred, and God knows our country needs that today. He is a builder, a unifier, who does not try to set American against American. He does not pander to the fears in the souls of our people—he calls on the best that is in us—the affirming spirit of hope." In spite of the warmth of my welcome, I left feeling uneasy about Democratic chances in November.

I got back to the White House in the afternoon and we left in the helicopter about 6 for Camp David. I began to realize how tired I was. And the other side of that coin is how glad I am that we are not in this campaign!

As I was about to go to sleep, I thought of a funny thing that a lady had said to me as I shook hands in the crowds today in Kentucky. With the conspiratorial look of someone imparting exciting news, she said, "We had two chickens and I named one Lady Bird and one Lyndon." "I hope you didn't eat them," I said over my shoulder as I went on, shaking hands with the next group.

Tuesday, October 8

THE WHITE HOUSE

This morning I went to the Treaty Room where Dr. Grover, Gary Yarrington, Dr. Chester A. Newland, and Ralph E. Becker were already assembled. There, spread out on the table of the Treaty Room and displayed on easels around the walls, was Ralph Becker's gift to the Lyndon Johnson Library—a fabulous collection of political memorabilia, going all the way back to a George Washington medallion! There were clay pipes from Old

Hickory's time, watch fobs from several campaigns, women's suffrage banners (I can almost see Daisy Harriman carrying one), a torchlight from a torchlight parade, a mourning badge worn after Lincoln's assassination, and some original cartoons about Lincoln that made Herblock look like a kindly illustrator of children's books. There were gadgets galore, and it surprised me how far back many of our modern-day campaign ideas go.

I was excited and grateful to Mr. Becker and I was disappointed to see later how little press coverage there was of the gift, which represented the first big offering of exhibit material to the Library.

After bidding Mr. Becker good-by, I picked up my bowling bag, joined Muriel and Jane Muskie, and we walked over to the bowling alleys, preceded by enough press and photographers to record a "Summit Meeting." The photographers swarmed all up and down the lanes, clicking and flashing, leaving us barely room to roll. I got a spare the first time, and then did something I've hardly ever done—rolled two balls that went in the gutter for my second frame, causing me to come up, obligingly but unintentionally, a poor third. The remarkable thing was the widespread coverage our bowling received the next day—in columns, pictures, and news stories.

After conferring with Lyndon's office this evening—it looked as if he were going to be very late—I left with Luci for our dinner engagement with General and Mrs. Westmoreland. We drove up to Quarters One at Fort Myer, and looked down below, through the trees in the valley to the lights of Washington—a glorious view, with the Washington Monument as its chief jewel. At first there were only the four of us, and then General and Mrs. Earle Wheeler joined us. Both the Generals were in civilian clothes, looking curiously different and defenseless without those uniforms, which do have a charisma for me. Do I belong to a different age?

It was exactly the sort of evening that I had been hoping for—personal, warm, intimate talk. I've come to have a lot more understanding of what the military puts up with and especially the wives—moves, separations, hardship posts—and now the hostile mood of the country. But I remember Kitsy Westmoreland's words, "It's a very special fraternity."

Lyndon was extremely late. He came in at 9, looking as tired as I have ever seen him, as worn—the fight temporarily gone out of him. He was warm to the company he was in, even sentimental. We went in to dinner in a dining room that looked out over the Federal City and had dove and quail and a delicious rum pie. Conversation ranged all over the world and up and down several decades, from General MacArthur to today. One of the things that Lyndon said in describing the mood of the country concerned the great disservice that has, somehow, been done to the military. Their influence, prestige, place in society, are under attack. The glitter is off the stars.

The three men discussed the Paris peace talks. It was close to midnight when we left, and Lyndon slept all the way home. As we approached the White House I noticed that we were not going in the Southwest Gate as we always did. Instead we went through the closed-off street, past the EOB, and around onto Pennsylvania Avenue, and came in the front entrance. I asked the Secret Service agent Clint Hill why, and he said, "There has been a penetration." The alarm had gone off, because someone had gone over the fence, they believed. They were searching the South grounds.

I remembered a newspaper story a few days ago which stated that there had been six thousand threats against President Johnson and his family. I never think of such things with any personal reference at all. I have never had any fear of physical harm to Lyndon or to me. We went upstairs and heard no more of the intruder, if such there was.

Wednesday, October 9

This morning I went to Lyndon's office for the arrival on the South grounds of Prime Minister and Mrs. Keith Holyoake of New Zealand. The Prime Minister, stepping from the car, was as ruddy and as exuberant as I remembered him. And Mrs. Holyoake as sedate and motherly. It is pleasant to have a State guest who speaks English. One phrase of the Prime Minister's struck home particularly—"You have truly known the ordeal of power, Mr. President."

As we walked in, Lyndon stopped to scoop up Lyn, still clutching his New Zealand flag, and introduced him to the Prime Minister. The Prime Minister walked on into the Diplomatic Reception Room with Lyn holding on to his finger.

When the short receiving line was over, I went upstairs for what has come to be one of my favorite rituals about a State Dinner—that is, inviting a little group of guests that I especially want to visit with for coffee and talk upstairs in the Lincoln Sitting Room.

This time the small list included the Leon Urises; his books *Topaz* and *Exodus* I have enjoyed immensely. One of my personal self-indulgences in this house has been to arrange a quiet visit with authors, such as John

Steinbeck or Upton Sinclair, or businessmen who have made a special mark on our country's life, such as Tom Watson or Irwin Miller, to spend some personal time with especially bright people from the whole range of our country's society.

Mr. Uris was talkative and amusing. He said they lived in Aspen. There had been a heavy snowfall—they had come through a blizzard and snow drifts to attend this dinner! I was enormously flattered. He talked of his new book which will be about a libel suit in England.

How different the house is when Lyn is here. Passing the Treaty Room, I saw by that august door the engine of a little toy train. Down the hall I could see three small figures coming—the two little Mann boys (their mother is visiting Luci) holding "little guy Lyn" (as they call him) by the hand. Lyn just gets a big grin whenever he gets within sight of them, and off they go hand in hand, as companionable as can be. He's very independent since he's had that haircut. It's changed his entire personality. And in one of the lovely Hepplewhite chairs there was a little pink teddy bear . . . Well, it will be that way again, as it has been in the past. That's one of the wonderful things I love about this house.

Later Lynda and Luci and Lyn came in, climbed on the big canopy bed with me, and we had a happy long talk, dispensing with Lyn before too long. He is adorable but strenuous.

Lynda and Luci are having a very companionable time now. When I am with Lynda alone she will tell me how much Luci helps her and how she's going shopping and selecting everything that the baby will need and also sending Lynda lots of her own things from home. And when I am with Luci alone, she'll be bubbling with happiness about how she's enjoying Lynda. It has not always been so, as every parent knows. And I am getting any parent's pleasure from the sort of companionship they are now sharing.

But things are not so good elsewhere in the house. My office is literally falling apart. Liz is in the hospital following surgery for a ruptured appendix. Simone left this morning for something long-planned and unbreakable. Carol has a displaced disc and Marta is pregnant and so is Ashton. I think we will all just about make it to January 20!

This evening we greeted the Prime Minister and Mrs. Holyoake on the North Portico. Not even the director of the astronauts could time these arrivals perfectly, and there was just a moment there when Lyndon and I stood on the portico alone and leaned together and talked to each other.

New Zealand is extremely sports-minded, so we had asked Lieutenant

Arthur Ashe, the tennis champion, and seated him by Walt Rostow, our own "in-house" tennis champion. And the Stanley Dancers who own champion race horses from New Zealand. Another guest of especial interest to the New Zealanders was Lieutenant Commander Richard Byrd, Jr., the son of the Admiral. New Zealand was the jumping-off place for many of Admiral Byrd's explorations, and he is well remembered there.

The world of arts and entertainment was well represented this evening—including lovely Maria Tallchief who had danced for us on the lawn at one of the most beautiful dinners we ever gave, and the Otto Premingers—she wore a stunning white satin dress.

Mine was an interesting table tonight, with the Prime Minister on my right, and included Martha Graham, the dean of American choreographers, and Dr. Melville Grosvenor of *National Geographic*, to whom Lyndon referred with praise, adding that when we get out of the White House he is going to give me a *National Geographic* map and we will find some islands that Captain Cook overlooked!

The Prime Minister in his toast spoke in a straightforward manner about Vietnam. "[We] fought, because we felt deeply that if we did not fight and if we did not win, then the world we know would not be worth living in," he said.

But there was little else encouraging in today's news. The headlines read: "DISORDER—THE MAKING OF A RIOT ON 14TH STREET AFTER WHITE POLICEMAN KILLS A NEGRO" . . . Poor Mayor Washington. "McCARTHY WON'T BACK TICKET" . . . this I no longer consider bad—just ludicrous.

Tuesday, October 15

It was a grim day for Lyndon, but a satisfying, even fun day for me, so unfair is the division of labor and responsibility in this house. I woke up about 6:30, by no choice of my own. But tension does have a way of communicating itself by osmosis. All day yesterday I knew something was building up, was about to happen—I didn't know exactly when or how. A bombing halt was in the making, and about the steps that led up to it, I did not want to ask any questions, lest I speak when I should not.

I went down to view the dining room, set for the luncheon where I was gathering together a varied group interested in historic preservation. The very tables themselves were a show of history—the Lincoln china on one; the incredible Hayes china with the hand-painted flora and fauna on another, its centerpiece from Grant's Administration; the Harrison china, one of my favorites, at my table, the Thomas Jefferson tureen in the middle; the Theodore Roosevelt china at the table where Alice Roosevelt Longworth will sit; and the LBJ china at another. On each table a card identified the china so that my preservationist friends could savor it in full. We used the FDR crystal—very elegant and seldom used now. I worked with Bess on the seating—asking James Biddle, Laurance Rockefeller, Henry du Pont, and Alice Roosevelt Longworth to be hosts at tables.

This luncheon was one I had planned for my own special pleasure. True, the preservation of historic homes and sites is becoming an increasingly important part of our national life and culture—something to be fostered and worked at by the First Lady, but for this particular First Lady, it's no duty—it's a pleasure. And so a lot of planning had gone into choosing the guest list, but it was impossible to invite everyone I wanted because I did want the luncheon to be small enough so that I could talk to everybody, and so we could fit into the family dining room.

Among the guests were the Curator of Mt. Vernon, Mr. Charles Wall, who had fed me fresh strawberries from George Washington's own garden when I'd done the TV show out there; Mrs. Frances Anderson from the dusty, crowded, colorful Mark Twain Museum in Hannibal, Missouri— I'd loved my visit there last September; and Mrs. Robert Robinson who is fighting to keep the Vieux Carre in New Orleans from being destroyed by a freeway.

At lunch, Gordon Gray, Chairman of the National Trust for Historic Preservation, and I talked about the opening of the Woodrow Wilson home and about my trip last Sunday to see Oatlands, which is now in the keeping of the National Trust. Walter Beinecke of the Nantucket Historic Trust told me the fascinating story of Nantucket Island which reached its prime in the days of the whaling ships and is now coming back as a small, select tourist resort. I enjoyed the luncheon, but I look forward to the time when I shall be guest and not hostess. Being carefree is a condition much to be desired, and I think probably adds to one's interest as a dinner partner.

When the luncheon was over, Leopold Adler of Savannah told the exciting, daring story of how preservationists hope to save eleven hundred historic buildings in that lovely old Georgia town from the bulldozer and get them into the hands of private owners who will return them to their glory. Then John Ben Shepperd, having been warned by at least three people to be funny, was funny indeed! But nevertheless he conveyed the

flavor of the renaissance in preservation that is going on in Texas now—
so much of it implemented by him. Then Carlisle Humelsine, whom
Lyndon recently appointed Chairman of the American Revolution Bicentennial Commission, gave a thumbnail sketch of what we hope communities with historic sites everywhere will set as their targets for our country's
two hundredth birthday in 1976.

I was upstairs around 3:30, lying in bed in a posture of queenly ease,
when Lyndon stuck his head in the door along with Harry McPherson.
His looks rejoiced me—rested, confident. My spirits soared. He joked with
Harry about my leading a life of such ease, and then went back to the
office to begin the next chapter in whatever was unfolding in the bombing
halt. He has such remarkable powers of recuperation! Yesterday morning
and last night he had looked as near the end of his resources as I have
ever seen him. And so, sustained by just looking at him, I went in to my 6
o'clock meeting with those Texans who had come up for the historic
preservation luncheon, heading for a good time.

Mrs. Bybee said, "We are so glad you both are coming back now, and
not like Albert Thomas or Mr. Sam—in a box." I hadn't thought of it
quite that clearly, bluntly, before. But everybody, over and over, all the
Texans, expressed pleasure that we are coming home.

I could tell at once when Lyndon came in tonight about 10 P.M., bringing
Mary Rather with him, that whatever had happened had not been good.
He looked dead beat and very low. He put his arms around me and hugged
me and said quietly, "I almost hit a home run, but I struck out."

A strange aura has hung over this whole day—a divided one. Congress
adjourned without a quorum, ignominiously, and the Apollo spacecraft
performed gloriously. What is happening over there in the West Wing,
I do not know, but it is very grinding, to judge from the face of one man
who has participated in it.

Saturday, October 19

THE WHITE HOUSE AND CAMP DAVID

Mrs. Kennedy is going to marry Aristotle Socrates Onassis! And more
women are reading more lines in the newspaper about a wedding than at
practically any time I can remember—probably men, too.

In the middle of the morning I had a little visitor—Walter Jenkins' son,

Lyndon Jenkins, up from McDonald School spending the weekend with dear Mildred Stegall. He looked very young, very homesick. We had a good talk about all the family. I liked it when he said, with pride in his voice—we happened to be talking about high school—that his daddy had graduated from high school when he was thirteen years old. To my pleasure, Lyndon came out and joined us and brought some presents for little Lyndon—a bookmark, a pen, a handful of souvenirs.

After lunch I had one of the most interesting hours with regard to the Library that I have yet spent—a meeting on the exhibit of "Life in the White House." Bess brought over all the programs of the entertainments that we have had here in the nearly five years of our stay. What a beautiful, rich, varied, wonderful assortment it is! Ballet and opera, Indian dances and Country Fairs! Our hope is to translate the character of the life here, the flavor of it, into an exhibit. Somebody suggested including Carol Channing's big plumed hat from *Hello Dolly!* as one of the artifacts. It sounded smashing! From there we went on to other possible elements— a piece of sheet music autographed by Van Cliburn . . . how about a plumed war bonnet from the Indian dancers or Maria Tallchief's ballet slippers? Or the fringed buckskin jacket that Bob Merrill had worn when he sang "Tumbling Tumbleweed"? A collection of autographed programs would be great. Helen Hayes, Leontyne Price—the roster is endless!

A little past 3:30 we left by helicopter for Camp David—Mathilde, Arthur, Lyndon, the Harry Middletons, Jane and Charles Engelhard, C. R. Smith and Marie. We were at Camp David by 4 on a gray and cheerless autumn day. But the flight had been beautiful, and we had looked down on the Catoctin Mountains—a magnificent show of gold and bronze and green, and every now and then the scarlet of maples. To me Camp David is more a psychological journey than a physical one. I leave my troubles outside the gate.

We had dinner, incredibly, at 8 P.M.—a normal hour. Of course the conversation was very much of Mrs. Kennedy and her approaching marriage. Remembering her eyes when last I had seen her at the funeral of Bobby Kennedy, I thought this complete break with the past might be good for her. After the endless stories of school strikes in New York, the Czechs under the heel of Russia, the gray and murky maze of trying to find a breakthrough in the negotiations in Paris, it was a relief to read about a wedding.

The most interesting story of the evening was Jane's report about a friend she hadn't heard from in several years who called her and said that she knew how helpful Jane had been to Mrs. Kennedy in her restoration work on the White House and to Mrs. Johnson on her beautification project. She wondered if Jane couldn't find a "gimmick" for Pat Nixon? My face fell. Four years of enthusiastic hard work, and the lady calls it a "gimmick"! And the same applies to Mrs. Kennedy's efforts on the restoration of the White House.

Lynda Bird came in and she and I curled up on my bed and talked until after midnight. She and her agent had gone for a walk around the perimeter of Camp David. At one point, out of the dark, a Marine guard had reared up and cried: "Halt! Who goes there?" "Lynda," she said, and the Marine said, "Advance and be recognized." We both collapsed in laughter at her near disaster with the ever-vigilant Marine guards of the President.

I went to sleep satisfied and happy to be at Camp David. Now that the time grows short, I count the days that are left and I want to use them carefully and spend them lovingly. Churchill's words go over and over in my mind: "So little done, so much yet to do." And one of the oddest things is that as the result of the wedding which will happen tomorrow on a Greek island, I feel strangely freer. No shadow walks beside me down the halls of the White House or here at Camp David . . . I wonder what it would have been like if we had entered this life unaccompanied by that shadow?

Thursday, October 24

THE WHITE HOUSE

I was up early—about 7:30—and had breakfast with Lyndon, worked on my speech for today's luncheon, went to Mr. Per's shop with that Siamese twin, my straw bag, full of letters to sign, and the luncheon program of the American Association of Nurserymen. Next came a three-hour Library meeting. The most important event of the day began to take place about 6 P.M. I noticed Lynda wandering through the room as though she had something to say to me. Warrie Lynn was with her. As soon as my Library group left, I turned to Lynda and said, "Honey, what time is it?" She looked at something in her hand and gave me an answer, oddly, that was in seconds. Suddenly I realized that the thing that she held in her hand was a stopwatch and that she must be counting labor pains! I was flooded with guilt that I should have had my mind anywhere else. I said,

"Honey, have you called the doctor?" She had. I talked to Mike Howard, who would have the cars standing by. Lynda has had her suitcase packed for days.

Luci was everywhere at once—the most "in charge" of anybody, scintillating with excitement. Dr. Lonergan came a little past 6 with a calming influence. He's been just right for Lynda—a competent, professional, detached physician. And yet to him, Lynda has become an individual, not just a case. They are good friends now . . . no problem at all that she is the daughter of the President. I think humor has helped on both sides.

I took Lyn over to Lyndon's office, hoping to see Lyndon privately to explain to him that we would be going to the hospital and to warn him to be quiet about it until we got out there and called Liz. A quiet moment with him is hard to come by, and I gave him the message in shorthand talk, with his next appointment coming in the door. Then I went back over to the West Hall, where business had picked up! There was an air of departure. Yes, the doctor said, the time had come to go.

I called Lyndon and told him we were leaving. He said, "Wait just a minute." And truly, in just a minute he was there. Lynda, who was in considerable pain by this time, drew herself up proud and tall and very composed. He kissed her, and told her how proud he was of her and spoke of the day she was born.

Then we were off in a flurry of excitement in two small cars—the doctor and Lynda in the first one, Luci and I in the second one. At the last moment little Lyn seemed to know that something was happening that affected him and he didn't like it very much. He sensed that we were not looking at him or thinking about him, but about Lynda and something else.

Always when I drive over the George Washington Memorial Parkway, I take pleasure in it, exulting in the heavily wooded hills, the river below, and the city that stretches along the Potomac with the Capitol dome like a great white pearl in the middle. Tonight I didn't care. The ride seemed to last forever, and as the speedometer crept up above 50 to 60, the moments stretched endlessly. Actually, it wasn't quite 8:15 when we went up in the elevator to the Presidential suite and it looked so good to me.

A nurse came in and took Lynda, and the doctor disappeared. I tried to put in a call to Chuck, somewhere in Vietnam—receiving an answering one from Lyndon, who said we could get the message to him through General Walt, who was going out tomorrow. General Walt was in the process of making arrangements for his trip and would add the message to Chuck on his telephone call. I took out the added insurance of sending a cable to Chuck that Lynda had gone to the hospital and "more later." Then I called the Robbs—got Mr. Robb—he was delighted. He said that Mrs. Robb had just called him to say that she was going to stay at a campaign meeting with Mrs. Bruce Solomonson, Humphrey's daughter, and he "could get his supper out of the icebox." Before I could call Liz, she called me. I confirmed that we were at the hospital, and we had just gotten word to Chuck, or tried to.

Dr. Lonergan came back in. He was dressed in strawberry-pink pants and jacket! And in came the anesthetist in lime-green pants and jacket. The nurses, of course, were in white. The doctors saw my surprised face, laughed, and said, "We wear these colors so they won't get lost in the laundry"—a psychedelic note added to this exciting evening.

Luci, jumping up and down with excitement, practically knocked my coffee cup out of my hand when she threw her arms around me. She engaged the doctors in conversation, using professional terms, and she told Lynda about every two minutes how well she was doing.

Later when I did a tape to Chuck, I told him that he would have been proud of her. She would make a pretty good officer herself.

It was almost a quarter of 12 when the doctors put Lynda on the cart and rolled her up to the delivery room. I called Lyndon immediately. He said he would come. Liz hoped very much that he would be the one to make the announcement to the press and hand out the cigars.

Lynda had been fiercely anxious that I get word to Chuck and to Chuck's parents and to Lyndon before the press was informed. She clutches her privacy determinedly, if not always effectively. A few minutes past 12, in my room across the hall from Lynda's, the phone rang once, I snatched it up, and there was agent Mike Howard's voice, saying, "Mrs. Johnson, it's a little girl and Lynda's fine," and he hung up.

I put in a call to General Walt, told him the news—a little girl—they are both well—more details later—please get it to Chuck as soon as he could. I asked Luci to call the Robbs.

Then Lyndon himself walked in, having, by mistake, gone past the whole ranks of the press on the way up. We told him the good news, and together the three of us—Lyndon and Luci and I—went down to meet the assembled press, led by a beaming Marcia Maddox. Lo, there was Liz—her first appearance since her appendix operation.

Lyndon started passing out cigars—I don't know whether absentmindedly or with a sense of humor—to the wire service girls, Helen and Frances. Luci and I were following along behind with a box of candy for the ladies.

We went to the microphone and Lyndon announced in a few happy words that Lynda had had a little girl at 12:03—that the baby was healthy and vociferous, and "seems to know that she's here and has her work cut out for her—she is already expressing herself." It was the only press conference I remember in recent months where everybody was content with the news!

The whole night melts into a montage for me. The vignettes I remember best are Lynda gathering herself together with pride and strength to say good-by to her father as she left for the hospital. And once again, as she was wheeled in from the delivery room on that hospital cot, covered with a sheet, she managed a smile for him and said, "You and Mother wanted a girl, didn't you?"

As for Baby Robb, she was very pink, with lots of black hair, very vocal and active. She flailed her little fists and turned her little head from side to side. Her fingers were extremely long and delicate. I see no likeness to anybody—just a new little person in this world.

Lyndon and I went hand in hand down the hall back toward the Presidential suite and he stayed a few minutes longer, saying good night to Lynda, looking through the glass at the baby. And so, by just a few minutes, Baby Robb turns out, after all, to be Friday's child who "is loving and giving."

Tuesday, October 29

This was another demanding day in this long period of unremitting tension and strain. The mood had begun—or at least I had tuned in on it—when Lyndon returned from Texas on Monday, October 14, and since then it has followed a graph of soaring hopes and frustrating declines. It did not surface in the papers for two or three days—I believe last Thursday. Since then the papers have speculated, probed, made everything as difficult as possible.

Last night when we went to bed, Lyndon left a call for 2 A.M.—even for him, that is bizarre behavior. I said, "What is it, honey?" He said, "General Abrams is coming in." At 2 the phone shrilled and Lyndon jumped up, quick as a fireman, and was in his clothes and downstairs to meet General Creighton Abrams. Apparently there was a full-fledged meeting in the Cabinet Room which went on for several hours. General Abrams had been called secretly for final consultation on the bombing halt.

In the very early morning Lyndon and General Abrams came over with some staff members to the second floor. I had given instructions the night before to put the General in the Pineapple Bedroom, Room 327. (I still do not know whether he ever had any rest.) Lyndon went back to his office and stayed a while—came back over about 8 A.M., got into his pajamas, and went to bed just as I was getting up. I asked few questions.

Luci called. I had arranged for Madame Shoumatoff to paint a watercolor portrait of Luci for Lyndon's Christmas present. We had decided to use the Queen's Room and Luci would wear a dark blue evening dress with puffed sleeves and white lace front that Lynda says makes her look like a "sexy Puritan." Luci called to say that Madame Shoumatoff would like to use the Pineapple Room because of the light. Aghast, I said, "No," we had "a guest" in there, or might have a guest in there, who must not be disturbed. General Abrams' presence is a tightly held secret in a house that is full of secrets these days.

Back upstairs I went to bed, for though I had not shared the work of the night I had indeed shared the sleeplessness.

Lyndon's bed was loaded with the red tag folders that were labeled "Eyes Only," "Top Secret," and mine was loaded with pictures and books to be autographed for Christmas—again, the unfair division of labor! I worked for a while on them—no chance of real sleep.

Around 6, Lyndon sent for me to join him in the Cabinet Room, and there were all the White House Fellows assembled and Walter Humann, President of the White House Fellows Association, was reading a report to the President that they had all put together—their suggestions of things that ought to be done. Lyndon responded. They presented me with a vermeil bamboo bowl, charmingly inscribed from the White House Fellows. I was delighted. This was what I had meant to buy for *myself* as *my* going-away present from the White House! And the inscription made it dearer.

Then, still not knowing the burden of the day's decisions, with a suspended-in-time-and-uncertainty feeling I got in the limousine and drove to the hospital for a visit with Lynda, finding her in high good spirits, on a wave of euphoria that was a pleasure to watch.

Her room was full of roses—pink, red, white, yellow. She has had many letters and telegrams—about 350 yesterday. There was one that made tears come to her eyes—a sweet one from Ethel Kennedy. Her kindness stabs you anew with a sense of her own situation. But there were dear, funny, sweet things, and most especially from the general public, people she doesn't know at all—lots of them service wives. "GP" means "general public" in our mail room—I shall walk out of here with a warm feeling for those words!

I stayed about two hours, and then drove home . . . fall is really coming. It is chilly, and the leaves are falling. Lyndon came over for dinner about 9:30 with Mary Rather. He is getting a bad cold. At least up to now the press has not learned of General Abrams' presence in the White House and he has already left to return to Vietnam.

Thursday, October 31

Halloween Day, after a sleepless night. Lyndon was awake at 4 and again at 5. We gave up trying to sleep and had breakfast about 7:30, an ill beginning for a momentous day.

Lynda is coming home from the hospital. I went in her room which is waiting, warm with books and pictures and her record player. Luci's room is ready for the baby. There is the white wicker bassinet Jimmy Allred gave us nearly twenty-five years ago for Lynda herself (he was Governor of Texas then and Lyndon a young Congressman). The bassinet has served at least a dozen babies—our own and our friends', and now it is all fresh and dainty, with new ribbons and laces, and inside a little pillow that Lynda Bird used when she was a baby. There's a white chest, my gift, that Warrie Lynn has painted with figures from *Winnie the Pooh*.

During lunch I kept on getting messages from the Secret Service about Lynda's time of arrival. Lyndon had been alerted also. A little before 3, I went down to the South Portico, and there was Lyndon and enough press representatives to welcome a visiting Chief of State.

We were a little early. Lyndon put his arm over my shoulder and we walked over to the Rose Garden where quietly, away from the newsgatherers, he said, "It looks as if Ellsworth Bunker has done the impossible, in light of all that has gone before. He's gotten Thieu aboard for the bombing halt." And so the last piece in the mosaic is falling into place. Abrams' presence on Tuesday, so carefully kept secret, had laid the groundwork for the cessation of bombing tomorrow. It had been on again, off again, in the most nerve-wracking fashion for the last two days, at the very blade-edge of happening and then not quite. In fact this whole month of October has been one of the most unremitting strain, the most protracted tension that I ever remember in our five years here. George Christian and Tom Johnson came up and they discussed when to make the announcement. They decided on a time between 7 and 8 tonight.

The big black car rolled up the driveway and out stepped Luci, so at home holding the baby until Lynda could get out. Lynda was wearing her going-away costume for her wedding—the loveliest orange-red coat and dress with a bright scarf around her neck—her makeup beautifully done, her hair simple but elegant with a fall, looking absolutely radiant. The baby had on a dress that Lynda had worn as a baby and booties and a white blanket knitted by her grandmother Robb. In the wisp of dark hair there was a little yellow ribbon. All the news ladies clustered around happily.

In the mid-afternoon there was a surprise birthday party for Helene in the Solarium, planned by Luci. Because it also happened to be Halloween, that dear old room was decorated in witches and pumpkins. Orange ice cream with chocolate sauce was served for staff and Helene's mother. A party struck an odd note in this day and yet, somehow, it was all of a piece—the small and personal and the momentous are interwoven here.

About 7 I went first to the map room and then to Lyndon's office. There, a little past 7, we watched Lyndon on all three TV channels making the announcement of the bombing halt.

The next hour was a ludicrous mixture of grave and heavy, and warm and funny. Lyndon and I sat side by side and watched the story of the bombing halt unfold. Staff members came in and out—Rostow, Christian, Jones, Larry Levinson, Tom Johnson. And in the midst of it all, Lyn arrived dressed in his Halloween suit—a red-and-white costume that said, "SUPER PRESIDENT"—and in his fat little hand, a pumpkin. He and his mother had stopped by the office on their way to "trick or treating" at some friends' houses. Lyn kept trying to attract his grandfather's attention. Finally he went over and gave Lyndon's face on the TV screen a big kiss, first on one screen, then another, then another, looking up for our approval.

When the announcement was over, we watched the commentators. Most of them were good. What a change! But there were some acid calls from the public, calling the halt a political move, on one of the open telephone programs.

I thought Lyndon had made a good speech. I especially liked the lines: "I do not know who will be inaugurated as the thirty-seventh President of the United States next January. But I do know that I shall do all that I can in the next few months to try to lighten his burdens."

The day after the election was like a continuation of election night. I had gone to bed a little past midnight, with Hubert running neck and neck with Nixon—a surprising, pour-on-the-steam, magnificent race, with a come-from-behind climax to an outcome too close to be certain for hours and hours. Occasionally, during the night, I drifted to consciousness and could hear Lyndon's TV set still on.

The next morning, before 8, I went into Lyndon's room. He had been awake, off and on, all night, and the results now were fairly firm—victory for Nixon. That is, by the electoral college count; the popular vote was still neck and neck—43 point something for Nixon, 43 point something for Hubert, with Wallace's votes making the difference. Texas had gone for Hubert, and that was of primary concern to us.

Jim Cain called and told me that Luci's father-in-law, Mr. Nugent, had had a back operation for disc trouble which had been serious. My reflex reaction, barely restrained, was to say, "Did he vote absentee?" rather than, "How is he?" Jim assured me Mr. Nugent would be all right.

We called Muriel and Hubert. Lyndon talked to both of them, and I to both. I wished I could have poured across the wire the pride and respect and admiration I felt for them and the race they had run. Hubert's speech of concession was gallant and warm and looked to the future. It was a healing speech. And I thought Nixon's speech was also wise and hopeful.

To me, one of the good moments of the day occurred on a TV program in which Walter Cronkite and Teddy White were analyzing the vote in two of the decisive states, Illinois and Texas. Teddy White, in a provocative, amazing way, aided by Cronkite, was painting a picture of bossism, chicanery, and dishonest political control that he unmistakably ascribed to these two states. John Connally was on the phone to the program at once. In a courteous, masterful, dignified manner he called Mr. White's hand, answering his charges in a way that soon had the commentators backing off.

In the evening we gave a Mexican dinner in the hangar for all the military personnel who have been assigned to this Texas White House over the past five years and have been so helpful. Lyndon presented several citations and made a speech. There were lots of stories told and my favorite came from a soldier soon to retire. He said he was going to retire in Texas. Then he went on to say, "Mr. President, my daddy's been visiting me from Indiana. He's seventy-five years old and he never has been anywhere at all

—just worked in the coal mines all his life." At this point his wife interrupted and said, "He went into the mines when he was thirteen." The soldier said his father flew to Texas and they took him to the beach at Galveston and then one night, as luck would have it, *Air Force One* came in at Bergstrom. This man and his father were leaning over the fence watching as Lyndon got off the plane and started, as he so often does, over to the fence to shake hands. "I was praying, 'Dear Lord, make him come this way. Send him over here,'" the man said. "Hadn't nothing ever happened to my daddy." Lyndon did come that way and shake hands with his daddy. The man said he didn't even remember what Lyndon said, but it didn't make any difference. Later on that evening his father said, "Well, son, this has been the greatest time of my life. I rode on an airplane, I saw the ocean, and I shook hands with the President of the United States!"

Monday, November 11

THE WHITE HOUSE

This was a once-and-only day in the White House for us as hosts to the family who will succeed us here. I was up early and spent the morning at my desk, calling Jim Ketchum to be on hand in case Mrs. Nixon would like to meet him. I had already arranged for Mr. West to be present.

We went to the South Lawn to greet the President-elect and Pat. (Somehow, I could never call him "Dick," but it is easy to call her "Pat," because she was presiding officer of the Senate Ladies during eight years of my time there.) With the White House as a backdrop, we posed and posed and posed—all four of us—the two men together—smiling, talking, looking left and right and straight ahead. We took them upstairs to the family sitting room where Marvin Watson was waiting. Lyndon introduced him to the Nixons as sherry was passed. Mr. Nixon turned to Marvin and asked him if he was as good a man as Billy Graham said he was. Marvin made a modest, discreet reply. Lyndon told Mr. Nixon he could look to Marvin for any interim help.

Soon we went to lunch. It was a long visit, lasting nearly four hours, proper, circumspect and cordial throughout. Lyndon, I thought, was generous and rather fatherly. I thought, it was not so much Nixon the man he was talking to, but the next President of this country.

The men did most of the talking, and Pat and I were politely attentive. Mr. Nixon mentioned several government bureau heads of a non-partisan variety, including Helms of the CIA and J. Edgar Hoover, and asked Lyndon's opinion of them. He said Lyndon would be remembered for two things: his stand on Vietnam, which was the only thing he could have done—and right—and his achievements for Negroes. An accurate judgment as far as it went, I thought. We talked about the Nixons' close friend, Bebe Rebozo, whom we know and like. Lyndon's advice was paternal and quite earnest. "Don't take him to church too often with you or single him out or the press will attack him—they'll try to cut him up."

They discussed press relations in general, and I gathered they had a certain amount in common—particularly when I heard Mr. Nixon use the expression, "Georgetown dinner parties," with an inflection of voice reminiscent of Lyndon's. Lyndon talked about the School of Public Affairs and how he hoped to turn out two hundred "trained troops" a year, prepared to play a role in elective or appointive offices. Mr. Nixon told him to send all two hundred of them to him and he'd put them to work. The President-elect asked a number of questions, not just for the sake of politeness, I thought. One was a question that must have occurred to a whole army of people these last four years. He asked why it was that Lyndon had made so few changes, kept so many of the appointees of his predecessor.

Lyndon answered in a measured, thoughtful tone. "Well, there are several reasons. One, respect for President Kennedy. He had trusted me, and I tried to put myself in his shoes. How would I have felt if, as soon as I was gone, he had disposed of all my people? I wanted to be loyal to him. Two, I didn't know for a good while whether I had an excellent man or an incompetent. And three, I didn't always have all the troops I needed." Then Lyndon reflected, "Maybe I made a mistake . . . maybe after January 1965 I ought to have made some changes." Mr. Nixon said swiftly, "Yes, you won by—what was it, 61, 62 percent?—the biggest majority anyone ever won by. That would have been the time for you to clean house." I think Lyndon agreed but he didn't say so.

After lunch the men went over to the Cabinet Room. Pat and I went into the West Hall and there was John Ficklin, the head of the staff here. Of course he and Mrs. Nixon knew each other, but with a certain formality I reintroduced them. Mr. West came up and we went over the blueprints of the White House so that Pat could get an idea of the space in the family rooms and plan about her own furniture or things that she wants to bring.

She told me that Julie's wedding was to take place on December 22. I couldn't help but think what a lovely chance they were passing up. I have adored our two White House weddings, in spite of the headaches!

Then we went on an extensive tour. I told Pat that when our things were taken out there would be plenty of furniture to replace them from the White House storehouse—some antiques and a good deal of furniture that had come in with the Truman restoration. She said that she did not have much that she wanted to bring, because they had moved so often.

We went up to the third floor and I told her how useful I had found it to have an office there and introduced Ashton and Marilyn Taylor. In the two major guest suites and the smaller rooms we gave especial attention to the closets which are little gems—the gift of Hammacher Schlemmer to the President's house. They are perfection, making all of our female houseguests dissatisfied with whatever they've got at home. I'm sure I've caused a lot of complaining husbands!

I spent a good deal of time trying to reassure Pat about the efficiency, devotion, and impersonal professionalism of the staff here. I think they have liked us, but we come and go, we Presidents and First Ladies. That is as it should be. The first devotion of the staff must be to the White House and its workings.

When we said good-by at the Diplomatic entrance, Pat kissed me. I was touched. Then they were gone. And so that was a major encounter—gracefully completed, I thought.

Tuesday, November 12

If there have been days in this Administration that were a draught of vinegar, today was a diet of honey! It began with snowflakes settling lightly on the Andrew Jackson magnolia from a very gray sky. But the Herbert Hoover oak is still red, and there are even a few vagrant blooms on the crab apple trees. We had planned our beautification meeting for outdoors on Columbia Island, and it was lucky we had changed it to the Department of Interior Auditorium.

About 2:30, I went down to the Blue Room to receive a plaque from Laurance Rockefeller on behalf of the National Recreation and Park Association—with some lovely glowing words from them. I then went into the library to join the members of the Beautification Committee. At 3:30 we left by bus for the Department of Interior Auditorium. We began with a welcome from Stew Udall and then the presentation of the dogwoods from Dale Miller, Chairman of the 1965 Inaugural Committee—forty thousand dollars' worth of dogwoods, two hundred and twenty trees, already planted on Columbia Island where more thousands of tourists come into this great city from the National Airport and from the highways leading south and west than almost any other entrance. What a superb legacy for our Inaugural Committee to leave such a stamp of grace and beauty on the Capital City!

Carol Fortas, who is the Treasurer of the Society for a More Beautiful National Capital, then presented the gift from the Society—Mary Lasker's one million daffodils, and the twenty-five hundred dogwoods that came jointly from the Society and the National Park Service, along with one and two-tenths miles of "hike and bike" trails. Nash Castro accepted for the National Park Service, and then it was my turn.

I had practiced my speech and was able to "talk it" rather than read it. So I felt light and competent and satisfied with the effort. The audience even joined me in laughter when I said, "I shall return—some spring to see the blooms on Columbia Island!"

The next item on the little yellow program was described as: "*Special Announcement—Secretary Udall.*" Stew said that several times during these years, he and others had discussed with me the possibility of naming some park or spot after me. I had always said no. This time they had not discussed it with me, and Columbia Island was being named "Lady Bird Johnson Park"! I was stunned, but, it can't be denied, pleased that they would want to do this for me. Stew also announced my appointment to the Advisory Board of the National Park Service.

We unveiled the plaque, Stew, Carol, Dale, and I, to the music of the U.S. Marine Band, which has been more a part of my life and times here than nearly any other group. Finally, with that pleasantly overstuffed feeling of a surfeit of good things happening, similar to having eaten too much Thanksgiving dinner, we filed back and boarded our bus. It might be surprising to someone just entering the White House as First Lady to know that a bus plays such a big part in one's life.

We rode by Columbia Island, looked at the trees already planted, and those balled beside holes already dug, thought of how great a fountain would someday look in the circle, and drove on to the Rockefellers' home. Even the Rockefellers are subject to troubles with a dinner party! Last night a storm had blown down a tree across the power line. There were no lights, no electricity for the stove, the house was immobilized. Repairs had been made just a few hours before thirty of us arrived for the Committee meeting and dinner.

We settled down to the Committee meeting and at the end of it Laurance rose for another "special announcement." He brought in a big watercolor rendering, pulled back the veil, and there was pictured a spot on the grounds of the Lyndon B. Johnson Library in Austin, a high place under the live oak trees, beautifully landscaped, with benches for quiet contemplation. This was just a suggested sketch for "The Look Out," he said, and I was going to have to be the real architect for it. The landscaping was the gift of my Committee to me as we said good-by to each other. There couldn't have been anything more aptly chosen, more absolutely perfect for our future! To have this gift come from this Committee with which I have worked for four years is a dear and wonderful thing.

The whole evening was pervaded with a warm feeling of camaraderie and pleasure in the work we had done together. And there was a slightly mournful feeling that the end of our beautification effort—together, at least —was about to take place. Finally I rose to try to thank everybody— especially Mary and Laurance—and to say good-by.

Back at the White House, Lyndon and Mary Rather came in a little after 10:30 from the office. I sat with them while they had dinner, and we talked about the day and about this diary I am keeping. Lyndon is curiously proud of it and I am touched by that. He talks more about it than I ever would.

Thursday, November 21

Today began early—all of Lyndon's days do. I disappeared from his room rather soon to meet Jim Webb and Liz and talk about our visit to Cape Kennedy, only two days away. I am staggered by my lack of preparation! This is a last trip—cross-country from the Atlantic to the Pacific—from the Space capital to redwood forests—a sort of last hurrah for me.

Then I went to the Yellow Oval Room for coffee with some of our guests of the evening at the party for the National Council on the Arts. I knew I wouldn't have time to visit with them then . . . the Alexander Girards, whose wonderful collection of folk art had fascinated me at Hemisfair; Dr. John Crosby, Director of the Santa Fe Opera Company; the Paul Bakers, he's head of the Drama Department at Trinity University in San Antonio; and the Tom McCrummens from Austin. Jessica and Henry Catto joined us.

I had just an hour to go over the guest list for the party for the National

Council on the Arts, which was to begin at 6. Lynda had brought Lucinda in and put her down on my lovely canopied bed. She was having pictures made to take to Chuck on "R and R" leave in December. Lucinda is a delicate, adorable little girl with tiny hands like starfish and a perfectly shaped head. She is nearly a month old and growing in weight and height, and she is very strong. But she doesn't sleep much!

I put on my sparkly pink lace dress and went down a little past 6 for the party I have looked forward to—the gathering of our favorite people in the world of the arts and entertainment.

Lyndon was on time, thank goodness. We went into the East Room where all the chairs the room would hold were lined up in front of Rebekah Harkness' lovely stage. Roger Stevens went to the podium and praised Lyndon as having done more for the arts than any other President —words well-savored by me, especially because I have loved our participation in the Arts Council and enjoyed all the facets of the arts across this country.

The entertainment was presented by the Alvin Ailey Dance Theater, a beneficiary of a National Council of the Arts grant. If before I thought I had seen the whole gamut of entertainment in the White House, from Grand Opera to Broadway musicals to Indian dancers, I had not! This was a marvelous combination of spirituals and ballet, the numbers entitled "Pilgrim of Sorrow," "Take Me to the Water," and "Move, Members, Move." It was an absolutely stunning entertainment—exciting, moving, and beautiful. I don't remember a more spellbound audience—one more in tune with what we had to offer. I think it was Isaac Stern sitting next to me who kept murmuring about a certain dancer, "How beautiful she is— how beautiful!" The costumes were varied, but there seems to be a certain style in ballet today for the dull earth colors—beige and gray and black. Some of them actually looked like the gunny sacks of my youth. When the dancing was over there was thunderous applause, and I could hear Lyndon leading it.

It must have been past 7 when we went to the Blue Room and stood in line to meet our guests. I had worked happily on this guest list. In many ways it expressèd my own pleasures of the past five years in the field of arts and entertainment. Most of the members of the Arts Council in whose honor it was given were there—Marian Anderson, Duke Ellington, his long hair curling over his collar, O'Neil Ford, Larry Halprin, Bob Merrill, and gentle, kindly Rudolf Serkin.

We had invited a host of those who had performed for us in the White House or at Democratic galas—the David Brubecks, Theresa Coleman, Martha Graham, José Limón, Geoffrey Holder, Lucia Chase, Stephen Kates, Jean Dalrymple, Leontyne Price, Richard Tucker. Five years of wonderful evenings unfolded before us! And for many of these guests, I have a very personal feeling.

There were art critics, donors to the White House and to beautification, a few from government and from our staff, including the Ernie Goldsteins (she is an artist). There was Dr. John Hope Franklin, the historian, who is on the Board of Review of our oral history program, and Dr. Joe Frantz who is doing the program.

There was also David Merrick who has had more hits on Broadway, off and on, than practically anybody; Jo Mielziner who had designed our own lovely stage. And Lynda Bird Johnson Robb—very much at home with all of them. There was at least one representative from the world of fashion which I have discovered these last five years, George Stavropoulos, and two Johnsons whom I have enjoyed, in their different ways—Ruth Carter Johnson of the Amon Carter Museum in Fort Worth, and Philip Johnson, the architect.

Well, when the line was over I could only think how good it was, how much fun! But I wished I had crowded in "so and so" and "so and so" and "so and so"! Almost always for me the things that I *don't* do are the ones that I regret.

There had been a sudden informal change of plans just before the receiving line formed. Lyndon had said, "I am going upstairs to watch Luci and Patrick (in Hawaii on R and R) on television. It won't take but a few minutes." Actually, this was thoroughly in keeping with the tone of the evening. It was high time everybody had a drink. The line formed quite casually just a few minutes later, and there was a sumptuous buffet in the State Dining Room which I sought as soon as we'd greeted everyone.

I hardly remember a happier time in the White House, but as I went from group to group, there was a faint note of sadness as one after another told me good-by. Around 9 I followed Lyndon upstairs. I could hear the sounds of gaiety continuing on the State Floor.

It was not until the next day that I heard that Isaac Stern had coaxed Abe Fortas into playing a duet with him! He borrowed an antique violin from a member of the Marine Band, and Dr. Howard Mitchell accompanied them. Then Duke Ellington had played "Satin Doll," and the illustrious

Leopold Stokowski, for a few minutes, directed the Marine Band! So, I managed to miss some of the high moments of one of the best parties we ever held in the White House.

Saturday, November 23

CAPE KENNEDY

How to describe a day as gigantic as this, as packed with information and emotion, excitement and spine-tingling vistas of the future? It is not possible. I can only describe vignettes—little bits from the mosaic. It was a great privilege to have lived it, in that company and in that fullness.

It began in a low-key manner. Lynda and I walked out of the hotel in New Orleans at 9, and were soon in flight to the Cape. About noon we landed at Cape Kennedy, where we were met by the "big brass" of Space, Dr. and Mrs. Thomas Paine, Dr. and Mrs. Kurt Debus, Dr. George Miller, Dr. and Mrs. Ed Welch, and Jim Webb, without whom I would have been lonesome. In buses we started for the Visitors' Information Center. All day we rode in buses. I think there were about three of them, with wonderful briefing officers on each one. The landscape was low and flat, dotted with scrub palmettos and cabbage palms, often with the sand showing through. There were Australian pines imported for wind breakers. The white herons were everywhere. Sea gulls were dipping and circling and whole flocks of ducks landing on a lake or an inlet, and the pelicans, which to me are the clowns of the sky.

We went first to the Visitors' Information Center. One of the most remarkable things I found on this remarkable day was that Cape Kennedy is open to the public and that in the last three years there have been 1,750,000 visitors who just come in with no questions asked. TWA Tours provide a regular service to the Cape. There is a guest book. You may sign it or not, as you choose. Once the officials noticed that two of the names on the guest book were typical Russian names and the address Moscow.

The trip costs $2.50, and you are briefed by experts and transported by bus. And you begin the tour at the Visitors' Information Center, as we did. There was a group of school children going through. A little girl came up to me and pressed a note into my hand and said, "My mother used to know you at Billingsley." Suddenly the whole group broke out into "This Is My Country." I saw one young blonde woman in their midst, probably a teacher, who was having the same trouble I was, holding back the tears.

We met astronaut Walt Cunningham, whom I had met before at the Ranch, and were shown Gemini 9 and the Apollo command module and the Lunar module. The day rapidly became a montage as we went from building to building, but certain pictures stand out in my memory like whitecaps on the surface of the ocean. The one that stood out the most, of course (especially to the press), was the simulated landing on the moon.

Lynda and I, accompanied by Walt Cunningham, climbed a ramp into the Lunar module simulator, which looks like a big bug on tall legs. The module is the vehicle in which two astronauts will detach themselves from the mother ship and descend to the moon's surface, while the third astronaut remains in the parent ship as it orbits the moon. Inside, it was almost dark. There was a huge console of instruments, their round dials glowing in the semi-twilight. There was a big window out of which we looked at the simulated moving surface of the moon. We were to be given a make-believe moon landing.

I tried to think up sensible questions to ask Walt Cunningham. "When you first put your foot out on the surface of the moon, what will you be walking on? Something like sand, or pebbles or rock? . . . I've read that you are going to bring back eighty pounds of material from the surface of the moon. Will you just reach down and scoop it up with a shovel?" What ignorant questions they must have seemed to him.

Actually, the main thing I thought of when I looked around the interior of that tiny ship was the completely non-technical matter of being cooped up with two other human beings in this cramped space for two weeks or more, like Siamese triplets. How important to space exploration is the sheer social factor of being level-headed and good-natured! I dared to mention this and Cunningham said, "Oh well, by the time you have worked as closely with people as we have you know them pretty well." This must be a very special fraternity.

When we were in the briefing room, we were served a light lunch, including bites of the food that the astronauts will eat, similar to tiny cubes of bread and fruitcake. I sampled these, and they were very good. There followed briefings by one of the astronauts on the Apollo 8, and by Lee Scherer, the Apollo Lunar Exploration Director, who talked about the meaning to man of space exploration. I remember one exciting, spine-tingling sentence: "We stand now at a point in history comparable to 1492 when Columbus discovered America."

But not yet had I hit the paydirt I was looking for, the thing that would make the program come alive and be understandable to me. I followed up something that Wally Schirra had said once at the Ranch about a high-flying vehicle called an "earth resources satellite." Schirra had said that there may be vast pools of water somewhere under the surface of the earth which it might be possible for a high-flying satellite to locate and photograph. If we knew where these underground water resources were, we could dig deep wells, irrigate, and maybe feed the starving millions of India, for instance. He said nothing stood in the way of achieving this goal except knowledge and money.

I tried to explore the idea a little further with Walter Cunningham. He said that the satellite which could do that eventually—the "earth resources satellite"—is not actually in flight yet, probably won't be for about two years. But by piecing together information from similar satellites' flights, it was possible to obtain an idea of what such an earth resources satellite could accomplish. It could locate not only water supplies under the earth, but geologic domes which would indicate the presence of resources of oil and other minerals. Imagine, the inner earth treasures made known to man!

Some of the most interesting briefings took place on the bus. One of the officers told us that during the excavations for Cape Kennedy buildings they had unearthed numerous artifacts—many of them pre-Columbian, some of them probably pre-Christ. Another pointed out that Jules Verne, who wrote in the mid-nineteenth century about voyages under the sea in submarines and voyages to the moon in spaceships, had selected an island about one hundred miles from Cape Kennedy as the site from which his imaginary moonship was launched.

At one point we got out of the bus in an open space some distance from Pad A, where the fully assembled Saturn 5 rocket, taller than the Statue of Liberty, will take off. Rocco Petrone, the Launch Operations Director, took the microphone here and explained the rocket to us, describing all its components. The rocket itself was bright red, weighing about a half a million pounds without fuel, like some unbelievable thunderbolt of some imaginary Zeus, and housed in an enormous cocoon of steel. He showed us the "crawler transporter," the size of a baseball diamond, weighing five and one-half million pounds, which carried the rocket, at one mile an hour, over an eight-lane roadway made of the hardest rock they could find. This rock comes from the Alabama River beds.

Always, from the bus, we could see in the distance an enormous square building—very white on the landscape. Jim Webb told us it "had been called the largest building in the world," but then, his voice in parentheses, he said it is possible the Russians have built a larger one. It is 524 feet high, its main core hollow from top to bottom. This building is so vast that clouds could form in the top and send down snow or rain under certain conditions. There is one door, 456 feet high, through which, if you could jack up the United Nations building and put it on rollers, it could come rolling in!

In this structure the components of the three-stage Saturn 5 rocket and Apollo spacecraft will be assembled for the Apollo 8 mission. One component is the launching rocket, another is the ship in which the astronauts live for days and days and days, and the third is the buglike vehicle which detaches itself when they come within a certain distance of the moon.

We walked and walked, and listened and listened, and my mind staggered with all I was trying to take in. Two things I remember very well. One is that the general public, from all over the world, standing in this Vehicle Assembly Building in a glass-walled room was being briefed, just as I was. And second, this whole great work has been accomplished in about ten years. Certainly there were decades of experimenting and research before, but the vast complexes at Cape Kennedy, at Houston, and at Huntsville are the products of ten years' work, of just a portion of the muscle of this mighty country. What does this say to us with regard to other challenges?

At the end of the tour we went to the ground level of the Vehicle Assembly Building, where there was a small platform with rows of seats. With Dr. Paine, Dr. Kurt Debus, Jim Webb, and a small group, I sat on the platform and watched the award ceremony. Dr. Paine presented group achievement awards and exceptional service medals. I was aware that I was seeing a new type of hero on this earth. Finally it was time for my speech, which was personal and low-keyed. I went back to the night of October 4, 1957, which is, I think, one of the watersheds of time. It was the night we heard that the Soviet Sputnik had been launched. I told them where we came in. We were at the Ranch when we heard the news and Lyndon and I and a few friends walked down the road, saying nothing for what seemed ages. The sky was like velvet and the stars hung down close, like brilliant diamonds around us. Each of us was pondering what the future now held. We had lived with the sky all our lives, and suddenly it was as though we had never seen it before.

That was our "launching pad," and the Preparedness Subcommittee of the Senate Armed Services Committee was my husband's vehicle. I remember the excitement and the urgency that he brought home with him in those days, along with a heavy briefcase of work on the legislation which established the National Aeronautics and Space Administration. There were months of hammering out all those legislative steps that make up a program, and the bill was finally passed on July 29, 1958.

When this ceremony was over, the nicest thing happened. I was given for the Lyndon B. Johnson Library a model of the rocket and a scale model of the Lunar module in which the two men would descend to the moon, with the inscription on it that hailed *"Lyndon B. Johnson's vision and leadership at each crucial step forward from 1957 to 1969."*

En route to our quarters at Surfside Cottage, I engaged Dr. Debus in conversation about the "earth resources satellite." As he talked, my numbed ability to respond came to life again. He's one of the scientists from Peenemünde, whom we brought to the United States after the end of the war with Germany. He is an attractive, gentle-seeming, articulate, impressive man. He spoke of the relation of the earth resources satellite to the world's crops and weather and minerals—and the relation of all these things to earth population. Simone and I both said at once how much we wished the press could hear this too.

My hosts at Surfside Cottage were General and Mrs. David Jones (naturally called Davy Jones). It was a simple and informal place, right on the Atlantic. We arrived at 5:30 and I had a blissful rest. Later on, Dr. Paine discussed the earth resources satellite with an assemblage of American and foreign press. He described its staggering promise—the great possibilities and the great problems that it opens up. When he was discussing weather control, the possibility of regulating the gathering of humidity and therefore the falling of rain, I couldn't help saying: "Well, we on the Edwards Plateau are sure going to try to get our share. And what's that going to do to everybody else?" He smiled and said, "There is enough to go around up there."

Thursday, November 28

LBJ RANCH

Thanksgiving Day and much to be thankful for. We were up in time to leave about 8:30 for services at St. Barnabas in Fredericksburg. Lyndon has this stubborn thing about wanting everybody to ride together in the same car while he drives, no matter how many of us there are. This often results in nine or ten of us riding in one station wagon, with about three people in the back seat with their knees right under their chins.

Today there were nine. It was a cool, crisp, sunny day—just about perfect. The river was roaring over the dam after the rains. A restful Tuesday and Wednesday had made me a human being again after the trip. I was happy to walk into St. Barnabas for one of the last times in front of ranks and flanks of cameras, all the faces above them good-natured today, and greet a lot of familiar people and be a part of a service with which I am much more in tune than with the Catholic and Lutheran services, which I often attend these days with my very ecumenical husband.

All the Rostows were out surveying the countryside today. It will be so marvelous if they decide to come down and live in Austin and teach and have a part in the School of Public Affairs. They will make their decision this week about a house and an exact place in the university life.

After lunch Lyndon turned the music high and began to show Lyn how to dance, doing a sort of country jig, a "buck and wing." Little Lyn began to dance himself and to try to imitate Lyndon, mostly standing in one place and squatting up and down and shuffling his feet around.

Today was one of those glorious golden days when just to be alive is enough. There are green velvet patches of oats here and there, and the Spanish oak outside the picture window of the dining room is a blaze of red. On the hillsides the oaks are turning from red to russet—the sumac here and there more brilliant, but some of its leaves have fallen, for fall is advancing.

In the evening about twenty of us set to on Mary's delicious Thanksgiving dinner. And, indeed, every one of us at the table, I am sure, was thinking of how much he had to be thankful for: a year of good health; the Vietnamese war at last maybe on the long slow way toward peace; the Tax Bill passed, and thereby a rein—though a light one—put on inflation; our dollar—so threatened just a few months ago—relatively stable once more. And, in the personal realm, Chuck and Pat still all right, though far away.

There are just fifty-two days left until our time in this job is over. It seems like an eternity, and yet, only yesterday when it began.

THE WHITE HOUSE

All days begin early now and end late. The crowding rush of events grows ever more unmanageable as over and over we try to add "just one more thing." At the same time our staffs are eaten away at the edges by illness and departures.

This afternoon we had one of our parties—probably our last—for the Vietnam veterans who are hospitalized at Walter Reed or Bethesda. We talked of where they were from, when they were going home for Christmas, what they had seen on their White House tour. They were always interested in Chuck and Pat and Lynda and Luci and the children. I asked one man how long he had been in the hospital. He said eleven months and he was due for more surgery. Another told me he had been supposed to leave Vietnam to return home but was ordered elsewhere the very day before and was wounded there. But he quickly went on, "It's all right now. I've seen my wife and everything is fine." Fine, except that he is in a wheelchair—and I could not ask the reasons.

In some things they are very alike—these groups of servicemen—and I keep feeling over and over that they are so young and that there are not many of them who have had the chance to go to college. And there have been, I believe, more Negroes than their ratio of 12 percent of the population. But they are very varied too. Some so bright and inquisitive, sharp and eager and full of questions . . . some withdrawn and stolid. But almost all of them act as though it were a real pleasure and a real surprise to them that they are here at the White House and that it is like this, so informal.

I told Lyndon that I hoped he would make it by the Women's National Democratic Club Reception being given in our honor this evening. I was expected for sure, and he said he would come if his work permitted. So began two hilarious hours. The reception started in orderly enough fashion —gracious and leisurely. Paula Locker, the President of the Club, met me at the door, and I took my place in line with her, with Fishbait Miller doing the introducing. Some of the old pros, like Carrie Davis, handled the door, and for almost an hour we shook hands with about eight hundred guests. How much of my past filed in front of me! Faces back through five Administrations. I noticed sadly that many of us looked older.

Every few minutes somebody would lean over and ask me, "Is the

President coming? When is he coming?" And I would say, "I don't know. I am afraid he can't make it." Suddenly there was a flurry of noise and everybody rushed to the door and somebody said, "It's the President!" But it was Hubert, tanned and jaunty, with his sideburns growing a little longer, and wearing a marvelous striped shirt. An excited gathering followed him as he made his way across the floor. Then a Secret Service man leaned over and said, "The President is on his way." Almost within the moment, Lyndon walked in the door. What happened next I do not believe could have been prevented, by forethought or planning. It was pandemonium! Paula Locker and I made a dash to meet him but the crowd closed around him, and from then on it was like a football game. We flowed, pushed, surged our way through the entrance hall, the front parlor, the receiving line room, and on through the large hall. Hands reached up to him from right, left, front, and behind, with people clinging, clutching, calling. It was wild! It was gay! I got left way behind, but didn't mind, emerging in dignified enough manner, with good-bys over my shoulder. And then we collapsed in the car. I was in a state of near hysterical laughter, and not at anybody in particular. Just at people!

Lyndon said, "Why don't you call up the Vice President and Muriel and ask them to come over and eat dinner with us?" Happily a little past 8 they arrived. I lit the fire in the Yellow Room, and we had about twenty minutes before Lyndon joined us. They looked marvelous.

Before Lyndon came, Hubert said something that was so exactly like what I often think. He said, "You know, working as hard as we have keeps us from getting rusty—you and us—all of us." He said, "I kept looking at my schoolmates and the people I had grown up with, and I kept imagining that I looked younger and I know I felt younger. Work is good for us. We work hard but it sharpens us." Muriel added, "It challenges us every day."

Then Lyndon came and it was a good, good evening in front of the fire and grouped at one end of the table in the family dining room. Lyndon spoke of Senator Fulbright having come in this morning, and said, "I will have to admit, he was decent, considerate, and compassionate. He said we ought to get with the Soviets and table our papers." I believe they were talking about moving forward immediately with the SALT talks which we had worked so hard to bring about and which were postponed when the Soviets moved into Czechoslovakia. So much still hangs fire. There is so much that is almost done, and yet perhaps irretrievably beyond our reach.

Lyndon said, "One of the first letters I wrote as President was to Khrushchev." There was a great deal of talk about foreign affairs and how or whether we could work toward some better understanding with the Russians in the brief remaining weeks of this Administration. They spoke of Nixon and the next Administration. Hubert said that he had been offered the appointment to the UN but he had refused. I believe it was Lyndon who said that John Mitchell appears to be one of the most influential men in the Nixon entourage, and he is able.

This getting together—just the four of us—was something I'd hoped for since November 6—when Hubert was defeated.

Monday, December 9

My Lynda's first wedding anniversary! It was a day so full at the White House that I felt as if I were going through it on roller skates. Events and groups followed so fast on each other's heels that you could have almost made a musical comedy out of it, if you had had time to laugh. At one point I came upon the housekeeper, Mary Kaltman, busily applying the carpet sweeper herself at the head of the stairs, tidying up before the next event.

Bess and Carol and Marilyn and I met in the early morning on the Christmas list, which had proliferated from fourteen pages to thirty-five sometime last week, when I had called an SOS, and they were making suggestions. I asked Marilyn to allocate the items or pictures to be inscribed to me at twenty-five or fifty a day, because I want to savor Christmas this year. I want Christmas to be unhurried and deeply enjoyed, every moment of it.

At 5 in the Yellow Oval Room I met with Alan Boyd and thirty-five highway engineers. They were all young men completing an eighteen-month training program in federal construction project offices. They were scheduled to go out to work in different states where federal money is being spent, to make sure it is being used according to the philosophy of the Transportation Department. Under Alan Boyd that has meant building roads with some regard to aesthetics—to the social problems of the people it affects, and to landmarks and park lands.

I talked and they talked about how building roads was affecting the face of our country. Sharon and I had planned this meeting hopefully as a small shot-in-the-arm—a sort of a planting of a last seed on my part for beautification in years to come, because some responsibility for it would rest in the hands of these young engineers.

It was a pleasant exchange. Finally I said, "Does anybody want to ask any questions?" "Yes," said one young man. "Are you going to be sorry to leave here?" I laughed. It always gets back to what people are really interested in! "How does it feel to be First Lady? What do you do? Will you be sorry to see it end?" It is a very personal thing. How could it not be?

I put on my pink-gold Thailand dress and went into the Yellow Oval Room to greet our guests for the dinner honoring Jim Webb and saluting the space program. We had invited upstairs, besides Jim and Patsy Webb, six of the astronauts—the Cunninghams, Eiseles, and Schirras, who had flown the Apollo 7 in October, and the Anders, Bormans, and Lovells, who were to fly on the Apollo 8 later in the month. And Jim and Patsy's children, Sarah, an attractive young woman of college age, and James Webb, Jr., who is at Princeton, and Jim's brother and sister-in-law, the Gorham Webbs.

We had asked the Charles Lindberghs, of whom, I must admit, I stood in more awe than anybody there. But Colonel Lindbergh seemed to have a good time. I noticed him sort of rocking backward and forward on his heels, listening intently to a group of astronauts.

After Lyndon's circling the room to speak to everyone, we gathered up Jim Webb and the six astronauts and Hubert and went into the Treaty Room. I noticed Lindbergh rather hanging back, being ushered in. President Grant's table was placed crossways at the end of the room with six chairs for the astronauts. On the table, spread open, were the Space Treaties signed during Lyndon's tenure as President—the one that promises there will be no warheads on satellites in space, and the other that declares that signatory nations will attempt to give aid to astronauts downed in the wrong country.

Lyndon and I and Jim Webb and Hubert lined up behind the astronauts —Colonel Lindbergh standing a bit diffidently to the side. The astronauts signed the document which began, in Sandy Fox's elegant script, "On the occasion of a dinner given by President and Mrs. Johnson honoring James Webb and the Apollo astronauts." It will be hung on the walls of the Treaty Room to join one which Jacqueline Kennedy had placed there on May 21, 1963, when President Kennedy presented awards to the astronauts, signed by Gordon Cooper, Scott Carpenter, Wally Schirra, Alan Shepard, Gus Grissom, and Donald Slayton. I had put a second one there in June 1965, when the first American astronaut to walk in space, Edward White, and his fellow pilot, James McDivitt, received an award from Lyndon. And so this paper will add its bit of lore to those who come after us here.

Then, behind the color guard, we went down the stairs and into the East Room to receive our 140 guests, who were probably the most homogeneous group ever to assemble in the White House—certainly in our time—because all of them were connected with space. There were twenty-three astronauts and their wives, including four of the original astronauts— the Gordon Coopers, the Wally Schirras, the Alan Shepards, and the Donald Slaytons. The widows of the three astronauts who died in the tragic explosion were there—Mrs. Virgil Grissom, Mrs. William Canfield, who had been the wife of Roger Chaffee, and Mrs. Edward White. And there was the other member of the team who had walked in space, James McDivitt, and his wife.

The NASA "big brass" was there—from Washington and Huntsville and Cape Kennedy—and scientists, including James Van Allen, who had discovered the Radiation Belt out in the stars, and leaders from industry whose firms made the craft that the scientists designed and the astronauts flew, among them James S. McDonnell. Besides Charles Lindbergh, there were other legendary figures from the field of aviation—Jacqueline Cochran who is our good friend as well as an outstanding aviatrix, and Major Alexander de Seversky.

Dinner began with oyster bisque, and ended with Moon-shot Jubilee. One of the interesting moments came when Jim Webb told me that the first astronaut down the line, Colonel "Buzz" Aldrin, had written his thesis on the minimum amount of fuel it would take to fly from earth to rendezvous with a satellite in orbit. Years later, he had been the one who had done it!

The toasting period was probably the most unusual I remember. Lyndon loved the subject and the man he was toasting, so he was very good, I thought. In the end, Lyndon gave the Medal of Freedom—the nation's highest civilian honor—to Jim Webb, who seemed absolutely floored with surprise. He's a most remarkable man—with all his elasticity and all his versatility, having served in many capacities in the federal government, each very demanding, and this last certainly a pioneering one. Yet he still has some of the old manners, the old rules, some of the best of North Carolina left in him.

We had coffee and liqueurs in the parlors. It was touching and very nice to me to see that the astronauts and their wives were as wide-eyed in the White House and in the President's company as all of us were in theirs. Our entertainment was Jacques Offenbach's *Voyage to the Moon!* There is enough youth and sense of humor and acceptance of fantasy among these unusual people to be amused by this fairy story about Dr. Blastoff, the scientist, and the respective Kings of the Earth and the Moon—well done by Sarah Caldwell and her Boston Opera Company.

Champagne was passed and everybody took to the dance floor, the astronauts themselves and Hubert, of course, in the vanguard. It was one of the dancingest nights at the White House! I did not go up until one although Lyndon had left earlier. I probably wouldn't have gone then except that I thought I caught the Webbs with that uncertain look on their faces, wondering whether it was proper to take one's departure before the First Lady had left the floor! For a moment I paused by the great doorway of the White House, saying good-by to the guests, looking north toward Pennsylvania Avenue, where the Inaugural stands for the Nixon Administration are rising day by day.

Thursday, December 12

Events, emotions, duties, followed so fast on each other's heels today that there was no chance for real savoring or full enjoyment. Quite early I heard that the children of the Nixon Administration were going to be brought through the White House on a tour by Tricia. I called Luci, who is no hand to get up early, particularly after a State Dinner (last night the Amir of Kuwait had been our guest), but she rose magnificently to the occasion. While I was under the dryer at the beauty parlor, she was standing at the Diplomatic entrance saying "Welcome to the White House" to Tricia and the thirty-three children of the Nixon Cabinet appointees. She escorted them through the house, and while Jim Ketchum gave details of the history and art, she filled them in on all sorts of family happenings in each room, together with a dose of philosophy, "It can be the loneliest place in the world or the most rewarding. It can be as much as you put into it." Meanwhile, we got word that Chuck had joined Lynda in Bangkok for his leave—R and R. They had, as the papers expressed it, "gone into five days' seclusion."

At 11:30 I went into the Yellow Oval Room to greet for the last time the Committee for the Preservation of the White House—Mr. Henry du Pont, Alice Brown, Bill Benton, and the six official members.

The fire was crackling, the room was lovely, and I had a sense of well-being and accomplishment as I looked around the group. George Hartzog talked about the expansion in visitors' services. Mr. West reported on the new rugs in the State Dining Room and the family dining room. John Walker gave a report on the White House Historical Association which had given the White House fifty thousand dollars for 1968, and projected another fifty thousand dollars for 1969 from profits earned by the guidebooks—this in spite of the fact that visiting had fallen off in the White House because of the April riots.

Jim Ketchum reported on acquisitions in the field of art. The four Glackens paintings were the most important. We hung three of them in the second-floor hall, giving it a feeling of warmth and family.

Jim passed around photographs of two mantels by Latrobe, from a house called "Brentwood" Latrobe built in 1816 for an official of Washington, which have been given to the White House. Brentwood was built about the time Latrobe was restoring the White House after it was burned by the British. The long, long thread of history keeps winding through this house!

Jim provided a list of acquisitions from 1964 to the end of 1968. We had some recent acquisitions on view—two miniatures of President McKinley and his wife, and an oil painting of George Washington in an idyllic country setting.

I thanked them all informally and warmly for their work on the Committee. We had achieved that sort of feeling that is possible only with people who have worked together on a project they all love. I shall miss these people too, as well as my Beautification Committee!

Bill Benton said that our mistake as a Committee had been our failure to promote—to publicize our successes, our acquisitions and our goals—all the pictures that we wanted, a John Singleton Copley, a George Caleb Bingham, a Benjamin West, an Eastman Johnson. And he is so right! I came very late and timorously to the uses of power. I really turned aside from it, half-knowing what could be done with the leverage of the White House, an invitation here, a handwritten letter there, a story planted with a columnist about how much the White House wanted the John Singleton Copley, let us say. It would have been possible to create an atmosphere that it was "smart" and very, very patriotic to give a painting to the White House . . . But it comes more easily to me to thank than to ask. Would I do it differently if I had the chance?

We went in to lunch in the Treaty Room. We had used the china of the day when the Victorian Treaty Room was the very height of fashion. The table was covered with one of Mrs. Merriweather Post's elegant table-cloths. It was a pleasant time—full of talk of the house and what we hoped for its future. We agreed that we ought to ask great contemporary artists to will a painting to the White House. I said I would love to see an Andrew Wyeth hanging here someday. John Walker volunteered to write Wyeth and make the request. The whole meeting was permeated with the sense that this was the last time we would be together as a group.

It was virtually an all-day gathering for the members of the Committee, for they remained on to help me say thank you at a tea for donors to the White House. I had asked Jim Ketchum to point out the Charles Russell bronze to the guests, because I wanted Dr. Armand Hammer to know how much it is appreciated. I also wanted to make sure that everyone saw the four new Glackens pictures because the donor, Ira Glackens, son of the painter, would be coming.

Alas for such hostess plans! Later on at the reception one of the first ladies to come down the line in the Green Room cast a quick look around and then demanded: "Where are the armchairs I gave?" I could only feebly reply, "Oh, the lovely ones that always sit beside each of these sofas?" And then a helpful voice by my side, somebody on this wonderful White House staff, said, "We've moved them into the East Room during the reception."

Later, I invited all the guests to tour the second floor and see the new acquisitions in their settings. I hope their stay was not ungraciously brief, for shortly we shuttled them downstairs again to the State Dining Room for tea and to clear the second floor where Luci and I were scheduled to meet with Pat Nixon and Tricia.

I had gone over a possible agenda to discuss with Pat. Could I mention leaving Blanco here? As usual, I left the hard task to Lyndon!

As we settled down in the West Hall family living room, I described to Pat the makeup and the work of the Committee for the Preservation of the White House, and, once over lightly, the services of the elastic staff— the flower room, correspondence office, the smooth, continuing operation of the maids and the butlers, some of whom have been here through many Administrations under the general direction of the Head Usher, Mr. West (that very undescriptive title!), and the housekeeper. Pat and Tricia couldn't have been nicer. I have no idea what Pat's plans will be with regard to the Committee for the Preservation of the White House or what part of her husband's Administration she will be most active in. Why should I, or anybody else, at this point? Every First Lady must make her own way, find the things to which she responds with joy and excitement.

We walked around to show Tricia the rooms that might be hers, with special attention to Luci's and Lynda's rooms. I pointed out how wonderful the great bank of closet space was between those two rooms—by far the best closet space in the house.

Mrs. Nixon was interested in the warehouse, the sort of furniture available there, and the amount of budget she would have to do over the private portions of the house. She spoke jokingly of how her daughter Julie had taken a great deal of her furniture for the new apartment she and David will have. I assured her there was considerable furniture in the warehouse and that through the regular appropriation she would have a sufficient amount, or so I thought, to make their bedrooms and the West Hall seem like home. We went for the second time into my bedroom, which I think is so lovely.

Suddenly it dawned on me a little past 7 that we were due at the reception at the Kuwait Embassy given by the Amir. Lyndon and Mr. Nixon appeared and we left the Nixons with Luci with excuses and good-bys and started late to the Kuwait Embassy.

Here occurred one of those funny bits that once more says: "It's time to depart!" As we emerged from the Diplomatic Reception Room, there was a long line of big, black, chauffeured limousines. We started, as always, to get into the lead car. Suddenly we realized it was a strange automobile. So we tried the second. Finally the Secret Service ushered us into the fourth, which was ours. Naturally one would expect a guest to depart first, and so the President-elect's car was at the head of the group! We tore off down the driveway, and the President-elect's motorcycle escort unknowingly blared out in front of us! We called them off on the walkie-talkie and proceeded to the Kuwait Embassy—a lovely new building on a wooded street at the edge of the park.

The Amir himself was at the door, along with the Ambassador and their party, in long black Arab robes banded with gold embroidery and white headdresses also banded in gold and flowing over their shoulders. Lovely· Madame Talat Al-Ghoussein looked absolutely smashing in a gown that was similar to theirs but simultaneously very Western—short, black, sharp, with gold embroidery and fluffy white ruffles around the neck and wrists. She's a stunning woman.

The Amir led Lyndon, and I followed with Ambassador Talat Al-Ghoussein, into the most crowded room I have ever seen. Fortunately it was very high-ceilinged. All twelve hundred guests they had invited must have been in that one room. We made our way through, shaking hands to right and left. The only possible thing one can do at an Embassy Reception is to see and be seen.

Our hosts escorted us into a charming low-ceilinged room, where the walls were lined with low sofas and big fat cushions were on the floor and little tables of hammered brass, elaborately decorated. The place spoke of Kuwait—the tile, the grill work, the paneling, which had in fact come from an old house in their country.

The waiters brought in a whole roast lamb, brown and juicy, stuffed with rice, on an enormous platter. When they carved the lamb and began to serve plates, I discovered that there were all sorts of nuts and spices in the rice. It was a delicious dish. We had a feast sitting there on the little sofa. Madame Al-Ghoussein—who was managing everything, and very skillfully, considering the crowd—was giving directions with her eyes and hands and then turning back to me for gracious words. Lyndon and the Amir and the Ambassador and from time to time other men in long robes talked on one of the low sofas—no women around them. I think we broke a record for staying at an Embassy party. It was after 9 when we left.

On the way back I thought of George and Alice Brown at the White House as overnight guests! I asked the Secret Service to phone the Usher and get them some food immediately and walked in, full of apologies, confessing that we had had our dinner. The four of us sat in the West Hall for what will be the last time together there. But that is the refrain against which all our days are played now.

We had a long, happy talk, and then said good night. I went to bed reading over the big news of the day—the names and biographies of Nixon's Cabinet. One satisfaction was that Nixon has said he will reappoint Mayor Washington and Walter will accept. Next to the Ambassador to the UN, the Mayor of Washington has probably the roughest, most hopeless job. But in my opinion, Walter is absolutely the best man for it. I am so glad Nixon has left him there. And completely on the other side of the political spectrum, there was happy news about one of the Kennedys. Ethel's baby was born—the eleventh child—a daughter.

So a day that was full of "last times" came to an end around midnight— and so to bed.

Today brought another good-by—this one a farewell to the ladies of the press who have been so much a part of my days in this house.

I greeted them just inside the door of the Yellow Room. No announcer necessary here since I knew every one of them, from river rafts and forest trails and art galleries and White House parties! A fire burned merrily, and there were Christmas decorations everywhere. A bar was set up out in the hall. A small group of the Marine Band in their red coats were playing Christmas music down toward the east end of the hall. The family sitting room was opened up invitingly and a delicious spread was on the table in the dining room.

There were the regulars—some eighty-five or more. And all of us seemed to feel the kind of sentiment that only comes through sharing so many events—weddings, tree plantings, and miles of travel all over the United States. Everyone was saying, "Oh, we're going to miss you so." It was less than a month ago that we had had a smaller midnight session at the airport in San Antonio when they dropped me off from our "Last Hurrah" trip across the United States from Cape Kennedy to the redwood forest. I was deeply touched when standing there and waving me good-by they had burst into a chorus of "Auld Lang Syne," and then, "For She's a Jolly Good Fellow." I'll treasure that trip always, especially the redwoods, which somehow are an appropriate exclamation point for the companionship we have had over two hundred thousand miles of forty-seven trips in these five years. I think the newswomen and I have ridden every conceivable form of transportation—plane, bus, carriage, ski lift, rubber raft, snow plow, orchard wagon, Stanley steamer—and, of course, some of the most interesting adventures were by foot.

We laughed, joked, and talked and I thanked them again for the Eleanor Roosevelt Candlestick Award which the Women's National Press Club presented me at a dinner the other night with a beautiful inscription that I shall try to merit.

One thing marred it—Liz wasn't there to share it. A frightening telephone call had summoned her to the hospital where Les was seriously ill. Otherwise, wild horses could not have kept her from this party!

Perky Bonnie Angelo once told me, "We like our beat!" I've enjoyed it too. And, all in all, I like this crowd. I've gotten better from them than I deserve, by and large.

Last night was a short night. In the middle of the night, Lyndon awoke to chills, alternating with fever. The Medical Corpsman went in and out of the room. Finally, at 4 A.M., the doctor came and was quite insistent he go to the hospital. Lyndon said he would wait until 8 or 9 in the morning because of the furor it would cause to go in the night— the possible effect on the stock market, the next day's decisions and appointments, the rumor machine.

I rested only about an hour, unable to sleep, and was in the West Hall by 9:30 for my first appointment. At that moment Lyndon came out of his bedroom headed for the hospital, bundled up in his dark overcoat with his hat on, looking ill but very much in charge of things.

I worked all morning and made a dozen necessary phone calls and shortly after noon I left for Bethesda Naval Hospital. Lyndon was installed in the comfortable Presidential suite. He was just lying there. (In fact, that is what he did for a couple of days—not talking, not reacting, just lying still—a very untypical posture for Lyndon and the measure of his misery.)

A little past 4 I returned to the White House, put on my red wool Christmas dress, and went downstairs to the Children's Party in the East Room just in time to see the finale of *The Wizard of Oz*. The children were all sitting forward in their chairs, and many of them had moved down and were on the floor close to the stage or even on the steps mounting to the stage.

These Christmas parties for children from poor families—these were from Junior Village—are a White House tradition I will always cherish. There were the familiar little low tables and tiny chairs in the stately old room, with about ten guests at each table ranging from five to eleven years of age. They were as varied and different as any other group of children. From one I could barely elicit any response—just a shake of the head and a vacant stare. And another's eyes were sparkling and excited and sentences came tumbling out. Several of them asked about the President. "Where's Johnson?" asked one. I stayed until Sandy Fox, as Santa Claus, made his entry—the undeniable star of the occasion.

A little before 8 I left to go to the McNamaras' for the dinner that had been planned in honor of Lyndon, feeling sorry for him. This was supposed to be "his" night.

We drove down Tracy Place and the car came to a halt. I got out and went up to the door, thinking, "Isn't it funny, somehow it doesn't look as I remember it!" I knocked on the door, and presently a butler opened it. I went in and found myself in a hall I had never seen before. The butler and I stared at each other in growing confusion, until at last I blurted out: "Is this the McNamaras' house?" "No, Ma'am," he said "Please excuse me." And I hastened out the door. Well, it must have provided an interesting conversation piece for the guests, whoever they were, at that house that night.

We drove on down the street about half a block—my driver and agent much chagrined—and I walked in to be greeted by Margy and Bob and most of Lyndon's Cabinet, although the flu had taken its toll. The Rusks, Clark Clifford, and Henry Fowler were there, and tall Ramsey Clark, standing quietly in the background, one of the most interesting and difficult-to-understand members of the Cabinet. And those other two who have been members of the Cabinet along with Dean Rusk since it began in 1961—Stew Udall, with a bubbling Lee, and Orville and Jane Freeman to whom I naturally gravitate.

John Connor was back with Mary, Bill Wirtz and Jane, the Wilbur Cohens (every government should have some Wilbur Cohens in it), the John Gronouskis, for whom I have great respect and liking, and quietly philosophic John Gardner. Aida is ill, he said. Bob Weaver came without Ella. Bob seemed the most pleased man in the group. It was he, it turned out, who had had a sizable hand in planning the reception for Lyndon given by the high-ranking Negroes in his Administration. He was so happy that it had taken place, that Lyndon had gone and had so obviously enjoyed it. Despite his cold, Lyndon had returned from the reception elated and told me how thrilled he was when Supreme Court Justice Thurgood Marshall had made the group's presentation, a desk set. Thurgood Marshall said, "The people in this room have just one purpose—to say 'Thank you, Mr. President.' You didn't wait. You took the bull by the horns. You didn't wait for the times. You made them!"

Tonight, alas, the honoree was hospitalized.

Perhaps those I was happiest to see were Martha and Luther Hodges. Luther, full of his activities—on the board of this, traveling for that, helping to run the Research Triangle Foundation in North Carolina—a happy "retired" man. Hubert was grounded in Arizona with the flu, but Muriel was there—I think one of the most attractive and well-loved. Every day of the last four years it seems to me she has grown . . . and especially in the pressure cooker of a campaign.

They were all talking about the election. John Connor said he could sum up his feelings about the whole thing in one word: "Damn!"

The Katzenbachs were there and Lydia had on long, slinky evening pants. She looked as though she had always been meant to wear them, with her exotic eye makeup and piled-up hair. I always wondered how she managed to make 8 A.M. car pools or put on that first pot of coffee in the morning.

After a half-hour Bob asked Dean to say a few words. Dean was as ever, magnificent! After graceful remarks to the ladies of the Cabinet, he made a reference to having addressed all of those present as friends, saying how surprising it was, in the context of history, that after these tempestuous years they could honestly continue to think of each other as friends. One of the unusual features of this unusual Cabinet is that they have never had any knock-down, drag-out public quarrels, nor any private ones that I know of.

Dean said, "Years from now our children and their grandchildren will be proud to say of us: 'They served in the Cabinet of Lyndon Johnson.' " Oh, how I wished Lyndon had been there! I have *had* my nights. I have had so many nights. So many people have been so much too generous to me. This was supposed to be *his* night!

Then Dean handed me a package for Lyndon. Bob told me it was a silver tray with everybody's signature and an inscription. I responded briefly, but very affectionately.

At nearly 9, I said good-by to everybody and returned to the hospital to report to Lyndon all the details of "his" party.

Tuesday, December 24

Christmas Eve was the nicest day of the Christmas season to me. I decided just yesterday to ask some close friends for open house from 4 to 7 this afternoon.

I spent the morning winding up the endless lists of pictures, books, and engravings that I was autographing for friends and family and staff, and finally I opened up my heart to the Christmas spirit. The house was beautiful! This is a time of frost patterns on the windowpanes. I love to stop by the entrance to the Yellow Room and look through that great central window framing the nation's Christmas tree. And if you move a little bit to the side, there is the Washington Monument. The fragrance of evergreens filled the halls and holly was everywhere, throughout the house—all around the great light fixtures—and there were huge bowls of it on the tables.

And deep within me—and in millions of others, I think—there was a feeling that at the end of this most awful year, there had been some things that had come out right . . . unemployment was at a fifteen-year low; the *Pueblo* men were home at last. And there was the glory of achievement of our three astronauts flying around the moon. For me, quite personally, the word from Mayo's that my brother Tony was successfully over his brain surgery made me humbly grateful.

Never was a party at the White House put together so quickly and informally! I made most of the calls myself. By 4, all the fires were burning, and the spirit of Christmas and real joy was as strong as I have ever felt it. The guests were old friends from our long life in Washington, many bringing their children or grandchildren or visiting family—so that the ages ranged from over eighty to three months—as pleasant a picture as these State Rooms have seen, I think. And Lyndon's sister, Lucia, and Birge were spending Christmas with us, together with their daughter Becky and her husband and baby.

Lynda Bird came early and stayed late, bringing Miss Lucinda in her carriage, dressed like a princess in her Dior dress with a little white fox fur on her jacket. She "received" in the Red Room and the Blue Room at the Christmas tree and in the Green Room and up and down the Great Hall, giving us an impassive Buddhist stare, as Lynda describes it. Luci and Lyn soon made their appearance, with Lyn now the center of all our friends' exclamations and interest. It was 5 when Lyndon came down. He has not yet returned to robust strength. There was a table in the State Dining Room decorated with holly—coffee and fruitcake at one end, a great bowl of eggnog at the other, with punch for youngsters. Everybody enjoyed the decorations—the great Christmas tree in the Blue Room and the lovely crèche with seventeenth-century Neapolitan figures in the East Room. All the guests returned for more eggnog or sat by the fire with somebody they hadn't seen in a while.

When all except the family had left, we went upstairs to the Yellow Room, where the red velvet stockings—now eight—hung from the mantel. Given by Marietta Brooks, their decorations told the story of our lives. My sentimental Lynda had put small gifts for Christmas morning in all of them. Our own Christmas tree was covered with icicles and snowflakes and gingerbread men, toy drummers, strings of pop corn (real) and cranberries (not real) and topped with the star that had been on FDR's tree back in the early 1940's. It was beautiful! And I purred with a sense of completion.

The floor was soon knee-deep in wrappings which Patrick Lyn was enjoying as much as his toys. Lucinda watched us all from her baby carriage. The room was a pretty sight . . . Luci in her velvet lounging pajamas, and I feeling elegant in the blue caftan trimmed in gold, and Lynda Bird regal in the peach dress brocaded with silver that her father had just given her for Christmas. (As soon as he gives you something he can't wait for you to wear it!)

Predictably the character that put us all into hysterics was Patrick Lyn, who tried to climb up onto the baby buggy to look at Lucinda. Whenever Lucinda is sitting in somebody's lap, Lyn stares at her, big-eyed, and pokes her with his little finger. Now he began to climb on the underpinnings of the perambulator and was soon doing a trapeze act there, in and out and spinning above the floor, while we all collapsed in our chairs with laughter.

We had put in a call to Patrick and Chuck early and we reached them together right after our dinner, somewhere near Da Nang. Patrick had gone to the place Chuck is stationed to spend Christmas with him and they had just returned from church. Lynda and Luci and Lyndon and I took turns talking, and both the babies were put close to the mouthpiece and urged to make noises. It was happy nonsense, but their voices—the boys'— sounded reassuring, strong and natural. We had an early bedtime, wrapped in that warming sense of family and Christmas and the hope of better days to come.

Friday, January 10, 1969

This was one of the great days in the White House. It began early; breakfast at 8 and then desk work and then to the swimming pool—how I have loved and used that pool!

In the afternoon there were two groups for tea and then around 4 I went to the Lincoln Bedroom for a two-hour sitting with Robert Berks, the sculptor. Posing for him has been a thoroughly interesting experience and I've enjoyed getting to know him and his wife. He is a tall, craggy-looking man with bright, warm eyes and a beard chopped off square at the end that reminds me of Hammurabi. He is on very good terms with life and loves his house on the tip end of Long Island, an extraordinary, rural-sounding place to be so close to New York City. Mr. Berks has interesting things to say about people whose heads he has done—David Dubinsky and

Einstein, and Bobby Kennedy, whom he said he saw as a wounded eagle. His sculpture of Senator Kennedy will be dedicated in the courtyard of the Justice Department in a few weeks. He's made two heads of Lyndon, whose sittings were always in the West Hall, a place so much like Union Station that I withdrew for my sittings to the Lincoln Room.

Tonight we gave a farewell dinner for the Cabinet, honoring Hubert and Muriel. I was all dressed early and eager—for I care deeply about this group—and they were there, every one of them. For me it was an evening charged with emotion—with a desire to drink it all in, to remember it all. Every guest was special. Luci and Lynda feel close to our Cabinet, so it meant a great deal to me to have them present. Lucinda and Lyn made a brief appearance.

Dinner became a very snowfall of menu cards being passed around the tables for autographs and carried from one table to the other. Mine will remain one of my most precious possessions—these very special names on the stiff white card with the gold borders and the embossed seal at the top.

Everyone talked about his plans, where he would live next, work next, of vacation trips in between, and Jane Freeman set about getting everyone's address so she could "bring us all together" (no pun intended), when some of us were back in town.

At the end of dinner, Lyndon made the first toasts to Hubert, to Dean, to all the Cabinet. Dean responded with that marvelous flow of English, so eloquent and yet so simple. I know when Lyndon talks of Dean and his work his voice shifts into a deeper gear of admiration and enthusiasm.

Then Hubert spoke, cheerful, looking ahead. He was not cast for the role of tragedy. I could never find myself really feeling sorry for him. Even less than a week after the election, he was ready to embrace life again.

I wanted to speak and I used Dickens' words, "It was the best of times, it was the worst of times," and spoke of the comradeship forged in working together on tremendously important problems and feeling you've made some progress—"it's a rare, unequaled feeling, a once-in-a-lifetime thing, and we are fortunate to have known it, to have shared it with you, and we are grateful."

Then Luci, in her tentative, little-girl way, asked if she could make a toast. She spoke with freshness and truth. "You have been working so hard that people like me and Lynda, and even more Lyn and Lucinda, will reap the benefits of what you have done. So I want to say thank you for *our* generation and for those that are coming on."

To me, the mood of the evening was tenderness—every moment to be caught and remembered—separated from the stream of time. I think every one of us must have looked back over our shoulders for a parting glimpse of the Jefferson Memorial before we said good night.

Monday, January 13

THE WHITE HOUSE AND NEW YORK

We have spent our last weekend at Camp David, returning last night. I awoke this morning in my dear familiar room at the White House, but no, everything was already changed. The room had the impersonality of a hotel room. To get the house ready for the next family, I had had all of my things packed for Texas and moved out over the weekend. The smiling face of "Arturito" no longer looked down from the wall. Gone is the beautiful Guillaumin landscape, its pinks and lavenders and shadows I loved so much no longer above the mantelpiece. A strange piece of furniture stared back at me from the place where my own mahogany chest had been, and where my rose satin chair had invited guests to linger, there was just a vacant spot. Everything was gone, no pictures or pillows or books or loved little objects. I still get a thrill of sheer pleasure when I look at the canopy bed, rose and yellow and soft green flowered moiré taffeta. I hope it will be enjoyed, wherever it is in the White House, in the future. Then Helen raised the shades and the view from my window was magnificently the same, now and forever.

I was up early and spent some time alone at my desk, plowing deep into the middle drawer, carefully removing very private things, such as the letter I wrote Lyndon on that August afternoon in 1964, when Lyndon had looked at me and said he did not believe he should go to Atlantic City, that he should not accept the nomination. I had felt as convinced then that he should run as I had felt four years later that he shouldn't.

There were all sorts of small personal things tucked away in envelopes that I didn't want to file. I gathered them up carefully and turned them over to Dorothy Territo for safekeeping. And close to the top of the stack were the lines I had written last January when we were getting ready to go up to the State of the Union Message and Lyndon had asked me to write a statement saying that he would not be a candidate for reelection.

Emptying a desk is a bleak business. I thought about how the house had looked when I had visited Mrs. Kennedy five years and two months ago. With packing boxes and half-empty closets, it is assuming the same look. I was gripped by sadness then. Today I am not. It simply isn't sad. The time has come, the role has been filled to the best of our abilities and is finished except for one week. I want to absorb, live every moment, every emotion, but I cannot feel sad.

I had a sandwich at my desk, worked with Helene who will be going to Texas with me, dictated a memo to Marilyn about the division of household chores at the Ranch. Ah, how soon I shall go back to being a housekeeper! I loved it for twenty-nine years and then how happily I laid it down when I discovered Mr. West and this staff. Now I shall return to it. About 4, I went down to the Blue Room for a reception for the Democratic National Committee, actually just a receiving line followed by refreshments in the State Dining Room.

We left the grounds by helicopter before 5, arrived at Andrews, and boarded *Air Force One*. I never set foot on the bottom step without thinking affectionately, "What a wonderful plane and what great trips we have had on it." And on the last trip I must be sure to take off my blue robe that I keep on it and Patrick Lyn's porta-crib. Such household thoughts inevitably crowd into the memories of great moments. For the last time, I flew above the magnificent skyline of New York City in *Air Force One*. We landed at Kennedy Airport and motorcaded to the Pierre Hotel for the most smashing farewell party of all, given by Brooke Astor, the Engelhards, the Fords, the Krims, Mary Lasker, the John Loebs, the André Meyers, the Laurance Rockefellers, and the Ed Weisls.

Never was there such an outpouring of affection, and such ability on the part of the Johnsons to enjoy the whole evening with gay abandon. The group of hosts and hostesses had arranged it with perfection.

It was a glittering, golden evening, to be treasured always!

Tuesday, January 14

NEW YORK AND THE WHITE HOUSE

Tonight Lyndon gave his last State of the Union speech and made his last appearance in the historical House Chamber in an official position.

For me the day began in New York in the Pierre. I tried on my Inauguration Ceremony dress and coat, a less than exciting business. I wanted to look proud and elegant, but there was no great importance about my costume this year.

A little past 12, I left the Pierre Hotel with Bess. As we waited for the Secret Service car, the doorman looked at us with half-attention and said, "Does anybody want a taxi?" No flurry, no ripple of excitement as I passed by. Portent of things to come? Ah, well, I could settle into this anonymity easily! We went home on the shuttle.

Lyndon spent most of the afternoon working on his speech. He seemed very weary and has for the past month. Now that he's so near the finish perhaps he can afford to show it, at least to those close to him.

Every year our personal guests for the State of the Union are chosen with great care and have a very special meaning. This time I did not have to think at all about whom to ask. I knew I wanted, without a shadow of a doubt, my own staff and some of Lyndon's.

I was scheduled to leave for the Capitol about 8:30. Lyndon would follow in one of those split-second-timed tour de force arrivals that brings him into the Chamber at the exact moment he is expected to make his entrance. Years of experience have taught me that this split-second timing is hard on the nerves, and so I go earlier.

It was about 8:15 when the traumatic part of the evening began for me. Always, I think, and especially since last March 31, I have lived fully, deeply, the drama of our situation, the events that have buffeted our country, and the part we have shared in them. I have been tuned in on the tragedy and the glory, the warmth and color and pain, of these times. I have kept an impassive face, I hope, even a rather dignified face. I have said to myself that sometime I would cry, but it would probably be when some third-grade class in some little community broke into "America" and not at a great State occasion, not at any glittering event. Well, tonight I did cry, in public, on TV, and with an audience of several million, but for a ridiculous reason I never expected.

The hour was approaching 8:30 when Luci brought Patrick Lyn in to kiss his grandfather and tell him good night. He had on his pajamas. Lyndon looked at him surprised and said, "Isn't he going to the State of the Union?" Luci said, "No, Daddy, we thought it best—" and I broke in, horrified, and said, "No, dear, I don't think we had better take that little boy up there." Lyndon looked up at us with a pathetic expression and said, "Have I asked you to use any seat for anybody?" Well, he hadn't. I had disposed of every one myself. Luci said, "All right, Daddy," threw me a desperate glance, and went out with Patrick Lyn in her arms. I would as soon have taken a sack full of lighted firecrackers.

In about five minutes Luci had him dressed and together we started for the Capitol—Lynda, Luci, Lyn, and I in the back seat of the big black car. As it rapidly consumed the short distance to the Capitol, we looked at each other and said, "What are we going to do?" Lyn had been becoming increasingly rambunctious, and adorable as he is, I felt that he had been exposed a bit too much to cameras and crowds and newspaper stories and was inclined to wind up inappropriately on center stage. "What shall we do?" we all said, looking frantically at each other.

"Luci, we'd better phone back to the White House and get Olga (the nurse) to follow us within ten or fifteen minutes. She can stand outside the gallery and be ready to take him after he's been there a few minutes. His grandfather can see him as he walks in and then we'll just let him disappear. Can you work that out, Jerry?" Jerry said he could and would and got on the phone with instructions. Then we began to talk about how on earth we could, sitting in the first row, get Lyn back to the door of the Gallery, since every aisle seat would be filled with a live body. Jerry McKinney put in cheerfully, "We could pass him over our heads, hand over hand!" And on that delightful word picture, we drove up to the side door of the great old Capitol building.

There Luci's friend of school days, Don Anderson, who used to be a Senate Page, escorted us from the car down the aisles and into the elevator, and presently there was Fishbait Miller. As we were whisked down the halls, I could see crowds of people gathered behind the barriers all waving, some calling out. Then we were asked to wait in an upper hall for a few moments, because timing is important in this panoply and pageantry. When we got the signal, I led the way into the box, pausing to look down on the assembled House and Senate of the United States in that dear familiar Chamber. And then below me, they began to rise and applaud and broke out into cheering on both sides, Republican and Democrat. I acknowledged with warmth their standing ovation and then picked my way carefully down the steps between the wives of the members of the Supreme Court and our Cabinet, past my own guests, and took my seat in the front row, with Lynda on my right and Luci on the step beside me and Patrick Lyn on her lap. I leaned over him to speak to Muriel.

The hands of the clock stood at about ten to 9. From then on the evening began to disintegrate for me, hopelessly, irreparably. Lyn crawled over his mother's lap, over mine, waved his bottle of milk in one hand

and his book in the other, reached for the railing that separated him from the void below—there was a drop of about twenty feet to the floor of the Chamber. In the press box to our right I was aware of all the heads turning as though at a tennis match—eyes trained on our incredible situation. I could see the faces of Frances Lewine, Helen Thomas, Betty Beale, and then Mary McGrory—mouth open, incredulous. Lyn gave his milk bottle a particularly hefty swing. I thought, "Oh, Lord, what if he should drop it on one of the legislators below, perhaps H. R. Gross, or Senator John Williams! What an ignominious departure from this town!" Luci threw me another martyred look and Lynda Bird gave her attention elsewhere, as though she didn't belong to our group. Only Lyn remained blissfully, innocently unaware that he was causing a furor.

As he continued to climb over and around us and gurgle and respond to everybody's attention, I began to laugh—helplessly, irresistibly—holding my handkerchief in front of my mouth, trying in that extremely conspicuous spot to be inconspicuous. Tears were running down my face as I laughed and cried—partly from sheer nerves, partly from this hilarious situation. All dignity was in shambles! So much for cool assurance and high resolve!

My eyes were drawn irresistibly back to the press box. Mary McGrory's expression remained frozen.

Meanwhile, the pageantry unfolded below with scant attention from me. About five minutes of 9 Fishbait Miller's resonant voice announced the Diplomatic Corps and they marched in, Guillermo Sevilla-Sacasa at their head, followed by a full contingent who took their places below us on the right of the Chamber, and then the Supreme Court were escorted in and seated down front, and then Lyndon's Cabinet—and did I just imagine a special wave of applause as Dean Rusk came in? I think not, I think it was real, and warm. Whatever the rancors of these years, he goes out with the respect of this town, even—I think—its admiration, if sometimes grudging. Fishbait's voice rang out, "The Pres-ee-dent of the United States." The Chamber rose, the wave of applause washed across it, was sustained, and down the aisle came Lyndon, following the committee that led him in, turning to the right and left, smiling, waving, pausing to shake hands now and then. He went to the Speaker's stand and paused a full several moments to receive and absorb the ovation, the farewell of the members of the House and Senate, so many of whom had shared his working life for years or decades.

He made a good speech and I was increasingly glad that he had decided to come here and make it, and not just send up a farewell message. They liked it when he said it had been thirty-eight years since he had first stood in the House Chamber as a doorkeeper in the Gallery. I think we all liked it and felt it was fair and generous when he said: "President-elect Nixon in the days ahead will need your understanding, just as I did." There was a forthright statement that there have been some disappointments, some failures of achievement. I liked it best of all and I particularly relished looking at our two daughters when he said, "I cannot speak to you tonight about Vietnam without paying a very personal tribute to the men who have carried the battle out there for all of us. I have been honored to be their Commander in Chief." The applause swelled through the Chamber. About ten minutes after Lyndon had started to speak, Luci had scooped up Lyn and managed to make her way up the crowded aisle and give him to Olga outside the door, but she was back now.

As with all good speeches, the ending was the best. It went like this: "I hope it may be said, a hundred years from now, that by working together we helped to make our country more just, more just for all of its people, as well as to insure the blessings of liberty for all our posterity. . . . But I believe that at least it will be said that we tried."

Friday, January 17

THE WHITE HOUSE

The day began with headlines that said, "U.S. AND HANOI BREAK DEAD-LOCK—BEGIN TALKING TOMORROW"—a note of cautious satisfaction on which to leave this office. Diplomacy is like wading through hip-deep mud—slow, uncertain progress, but you become grateful for any inching forward.

The fitter came this morning and I tried on my Inaugural costume—a peach-pink wool coat and dress with a lovely fur helmet and muff. Alas, this costume has been plagued with bad luck from the beginning. First I decided to wear red, only to discover that Mrs. Nixon's costume would be red; then, because this should be *her* day, I switched to yellow—too late, the sample they had shown me was no longer available on the market.

At 12 there was a Medal of Science Awards Ceremony and shortly afterward Lyndon and I went to the National Press Club for a farewell to the press corps, which has been so much a part of our lives these five years, and indeed for the last thirty years. As we approached the Press Club I saw, to my amazement, a big crowd which seemed to have come from nowhere and on practically no notice. I myself didn't know we were going to the Press Club until a little while before we left.

People were pushing to get to Lyndon, holding out their hands over other heads, and a good many of the ladies crying, "Oh, Mr. President, God bless you, Mr. President, we'll never forget you." It was a strange outpouring of emotion. Lyndon reached over heads to shake hands, patting a child, occasionally scribbling an autograph—sort of rowing his way through the crowd with handshakes with both hands, reminiscent of innumerable campaign occasions.

Lyndon went directly to the podium and his remarks were delightful. First came a warm greeting to the press, and then he said, "I have never doubted your energy or your courage or your patriotism—that is why I asked General Hershey to get in touch immediately with each of you." The speech was about three-fourths laughter but toward the end turned sober and he told them that his greatest unhappiness on leaving office Monday noon would be "that peace has eluded me."

I looked out at the assembled faces of the press, who have held in their power so much of the success or failure of these last years, and felt oddly detached. Among them there are quite a few that I have a personal affection for. Mostly I was terribly proud of Lyndon who was behaving just to my liking with a mixture of dignity and grace and humor. Someone had asked if he had brought Lyn and he answered: "No, Lyn was confined to quarters for recent rambunctious behavior."

At 4 o'clock, Mrs. Alice Longworth came to tea with her granddaughter, Joanna Sturm. During these five years, visits with her have been sparkling events. Always before I have sought her. This time she had telephoned and said she wanted to pay a call and bring a present to the baby. I like her tremendously, although I always have the feeling that I must gird my armor, not so much to do battle, as to be ready, alert, at least. I always try to meet her downstairs at the door, a deference to age and position and to the way I really feel about her. I remembered the last time she came. It was last October, and she'd gotten out of the car with her big stiff-brimmed hat—her trademark—and come toward me, like a ship under full sail, exclaiming, "Isn't it delicious, isn't it delicious?" She was talking about Jackie Kennedy's remarriage and could barely wait to get within speaking range.

This time I met Mrs. Longworth a bit self-consciously, partly because the papers had reported in the last few weeks that she had said some tremendously nice things about me, and also because I thought this could very well be the last time I would see her. We had such a good time. Lyndon came in briefly and hugged her. She gave him a book about her father's life and she had brought Lucinda a silver cup and a pen. Lynda Bird, who is one of her greatest admirers, came in and hung on every word.

Mrs. Longworth told us an interesting story about her father's departure from office—in March 1909. There was no fanfare at all. They'd gotten on the train, carrying their own bags, with her father holding a jar of terrapin. Terrapin was one of his favorite things and some admirer had remembered how much he liked it and had presented him a jar as a departing gift. I thought of my Iranian caviar! One of my last acts must be to take it out of the refrigerator and perhaps I will leave with it under my arm!

Mrs. Longworth told us about filming a television interview for a British company in her own apartment, and said that in the course of the filming she had done her famous imitations of Eleanor Roosevelt and Mrs. William Howard Taft. We exclaimed at once, "We never have seen them—would you do them?" So she did, there in the Yellow Oval Room. The mimicry was astounding. It was as though she suddenly transposed herself into Eleanor—with an adjustment of her big hat, a certain rigidity in her posture, and her face assuming that expression so well remembered. What an actress, a really accomplished performance! Then she did a take-off on Mrs. Taft. The whole afternoon was one of remembering. She talked about Franklin and their youth and the amusing things they did and all the young folks did in those days.

Sunday, January 19

The golden coin is almost spent.

Today dawned gray and dreary with a light rain falling. I've lost my hope of having snow before I leave Washington. A few scattered flakes fell one afternoon but they didn't stay on the ground. Carrying an umbrella, I went down to the Children's Garden, which will be our departing gift to the White House. I've been watching the flagstones go in during the week and I know that Bess had imprints of Patrick Lyndon's foot and Lucinda Desha's hand made and then transferred to a bronze plaque, in what must have been the quickest job such artisans had ever accomplished.

Even in the gray day, the garden was a charming little spot, tucked away close to the tennis court on the South Lawn. Flagstones lead off between the holly bushes in what is almost a secret tunnel and then open up into a tiny garden, where there is a lovely apple tree. The tree will be so pretty in spring with pink blossoms and then in autumn with red apples. The land-scape designer, Edward Durrell Stone, Jr., told me that it is a winesap and that they had searched all over and found just the right size for the spot in an old orchard near Washington. There's a place for rustic furniture, child-size, which will make a nice area for six-year-olds to have tea parties, and there's a small goldfish pond. The little garden is a very secret, quiet place and will be a good place for some grandmother who's in the White House to roll out a baby carriage and enjoy being outdoors and private at the same time.

We had talked about a good-by gift for months and months, but as in so many things, I must give the credit for the action to Bess and Liz. When we had this idea, only ten days ago, I thought there couldn't possibly be time, but they, the eternal optimists, called in Ed Stone, Jr., who presented me with a sketch; we decided to go ahead and here it was.

Back in the White House, I went up to see Billy and Ruth Graham who had spent the night in the Pineapple Bedroom. We were bound for Dr. George Davis' church together. For once both Lynda and Luci were on time, Lyndon too, and we went off to the National City Christian Church.

The girls have been so considerate, even more so since last March, to give their daddy every support and cooperation and sense of family solidarity and presence. Dr. Davis, no surprise to anybody, had a bulletin in his church pamphlet which was, according to Luci, "the essence of Daddy." The article spoke of how hard Lyndon worked and how he wanted to make things better for all the poor people of the nation, and it took what, for Dr. Davis, was a restrained jab at the press, ending with praise of Lyndon's generous attitude toward Nixon. Dr. Davis called on Dr. Graham to give the benediction.

On the way back, Billy told us of Mr. Nixon's plans to hold religious services in the East Room, with a different minister each Sunday. Billy was going to conduct the first service next Sunday—a final interesting touch to the transition. Billy spoke of the fact that having the service in the house would provide the Nixons with an opportunity to invite many people to the White House who would, otherwise, perhaps never come.

There was one more small, but important, use of the day I wanted to make and that was to write a letter to Jim Ketchum, the Curator, which he could keep if he wanted to in the White House file. We have been making a collection of letters from First Ladies. We already have acquired several and promises or possibilities of more. So I wrote mine—the next to last on White House stationery that I would write—about our good-by gift, the Children's Garden, saying why we had chosen it and how I hoped it would be used and enjoyed in the future.

Lyndon had gone straight from church to his office. With less than twenty-four hours remaining, he still had some important decisions to make. One of these was what to do about setting aside seven million acres of land for National Parks that Stew Udall had recommended. The conservationist in Lyndon was excited by the idea, but the old Congressman of twenty-four years' tenure withdrew from it. He really doesn't believe in government by executive order, but in a mutual working together of the Congress and the President.

At 2 there was a very special ceremony. Last week General Chapman had said that the Marine Band would like to come over and serenade us, to say good-by. Lyndon's aide, Colonel Haywood Smith, brought General and Mrs. Chapman up to the Yellow Oval Room where Lyndon and I met them, and with Lynda and Luci we went out on the Truman Balcony and there on the South Lawn was given the last performance for the Johnsons. The Marine Band in their bright red uniforms lent a striking note of color to the gray day. They played the "Pedernales River March," which had been composed for and dedicated to Lyndon. When they played "The Marine Hymn," I looked at Lynda Bird—her face was quivering but strong. We leaned over the balcony and thanked them and waved a fond good-by.

At 4:30 I was dressed to go down to the library to meet our little group for the dedication of the Children's Garden. The stars of this event, Lyn and Lucinda, joined us with their mothers and off we started across the South Lawn, a straggling retinue led by Lucinda in her baby carriage, with Lyn, always glad to go *anywhere*, marching sturdily along.

Mr. Williams, the gardener, had told me that there would be crocuses coming up under the apple tree and between the flagstones in about two months. We talked about putting a little basket swing on the sturdiest limb of the apple tree. We took some pictures of Lyn with his feet planted firmly in his own bronze footprints. But once inside the enclosure where the fish pond was, we promptly lost one of our "stars"—Lyn walked right into the fish pond! Somebody turned loose of his hand for one split second. Curiosity led him on and he walked right in—sinking with an outraged expression into the chilling water up to his shoulders. Everybody jumped to the rescue and both Liz and Bess whipped off their coats, and in a flash the wet and howling little boy was wrapped up. Luci picked him up and dashed up the driveway to the White House with that big bundle in her arms. Lucinda took over then, and we wheeled her under the apple tree and sat down with her in the children's furniture, though she's not a member of the tea party set yet.

I ran on ahead of the rest to the White House and up to the third floor to make sure Luci had put Lyn into a hot tub and rubbed him good. There he was, all grins, none the worse for his experience.

The accident was useful, for Mr. Alexander told me later he would install a sturdy mesh wire about two inches below the surface of the pool, strong enough to support a child, without spoiling the visibility of the gold fish.

Back upstairs, I continued my final assault on the drawers. My beautiful room is a shambles. There are packing boxes all over the floor and an open foot locker to receive contents of drawers that have not been really properly sorted. When will they be properly sorted? I am afraid, somewhere, there will be left behind small hostages to the future. It was a rather sad note while I was turning things out, to open an unused cupboard door in the West Hall and come upon some of Mrs. John Fitzgerald Kennedy's notepaper. I turned it over to Mr. West.

For a brief hour we dropped by the F Street Club for a party given by the Henry Fords. The door to that most dignified club was lined with young people and I wondered briefly if they were some of the protestors who were planning their own counter-Inaugural march on the Mall. But they were smiling broadly and a cheer went up as we made our way between them up the steps. They called out, "Good luck, Mr. President," and hands went out from right and left. Lyndon stopped to shake a few and I kept on walking. One boy called out: "You sure did try, Lyndon." It was all sort of merry.

Inside that sedate and elegant old club, where I've had so many good times, were Henry and Christina and a large gathering, many of whom we didn't know. Already the town is filling up with new faces. Well, these old rooms will see a lot of new people and maybe some old, old people in the next four years. And that is the pattern of Washington. We said good-by to the Fords and went back to our own party at the White House.

Weeks ago when we had talked about what we wanted to do on this last night, I had said there was only one group of people I wanted to spend it with—Lyndon's top assistants, and mine. So there were sixty of our staff for buffet dinner. Those whom I think of as "the early morning boys," the speech writers, the girls from Lyndon's office, so many round-the-clock top aides, and from my own side of the house, Liz and Bess and Ashton.

The evening was long and strange but, to me, endearing. I wanted it to be a very special evening for these wonderful people.

Everybody signed the guest book, one of the most precious possessions I shall take out of this house, and eventually we had a delicious buffet supper which we ate on our laps. The evening melts into a montage and I cannot possibly remember it in sequence, but I recall vignettes—sitting with Joe Califano hunched over a card table in the West Hall while he told me how much these years had meant to him . . . stories about our funniest and most poignant or most-to-be-remembered moments in the White House—Liz, dependably, brought forth some very funny ones, and even George Christian, who has earned the nickname "Ole Blabber Mouth" because of his taciturnity, added his share. The atmosphere was charged with emotion, overflowing feelings, of keen awareness that this was the last good-by to so much, and so many. The orchestra played and we all sang "Auld Lang Syne" and we found ourselves standing in a circle in the hall. I reached out and took hands and everybody else did so. Everybody was really fighting back tears, for these had been years of high excitement and grinding work that had used us up—each of us—and that we would never experience again and never forget.

One special moment I remember is standing by the window, taking a last look from that spot at the greatest view in Washington out over the South Lawn to the Jefferson Memorial and the tall shaft of the Washington Monument.

The orchestra played "The Yellow Rose of Texas," and "Hello Lyndon," and once again "Hail to the Chief," and we all rode along on successive waves of emotion in our own separate ways. Harry McPherson offered a toast, a beautiful eloquent address to these last five years and to Lyndon. Then Lyndon began to talk, quietly, even gently, saying what they meant to him.

At last it *was* time to go home and everybody began to drift away. The mood of the party perceptibly changed. We had all come in at a high key, tense, emotional, but I felt that everybody, me included, was leaving with the feeling that we were played out, numb, all passion spent, ready for it to be over.

THE WHITE HOUSE AND LBJ RANCH

I was up early, the way it was when I was a child and it was the day to go to the County Fair and I didn't want to miss a thing. I had coffee at 7, a small private smile for the big canopied bed that I would not sleep in again, and for the courteous deferential White House butler who brought me the tray. I'm glad I had spent a lot of Saturday afternoon saying good-by and thank you, because there would not be time to do it today.

In my robe with a cup of coffee in my hand, I made a last pilgrimage of my own into all the rooms on the second floor. This was partly the house-wifely need to see whether any personal object had been left anywhere, but mostly just to stand still and absorb the feeling of the Yellow Room and the little Lincoln Sitting Room. I found a whole coffee table full of dirty dishes in the Lincoln Sitting Room which I reported to John. I asked him to please take down the portraits of Lyndon and me, still on the easels in the East Hall, and put them in the care of the Curator. I went into the Queen's Sitting Room and then into the lovely Queen's Room, whose flower arrangements I have loved most of all.

About 9:30 I went up to Ashton's office—one of the last to be dismantled and to stop functioning. It was pandemonium, knee-deep in boxes and files and papers. She said she would be out by noon. And then into Luci's room which looked absolutely hopeless, full of scattered bags, half-opened. We would dispatch Patrick Lyn and Lucinda to the Cliffords' with their nurses about the time we left for the ceremony at the Capitol. Thank Heaven, with one hour of the Secret Service left to Luci, I don't have to handle that!

I went into the Pineapple Bedroom where I found a guest book of the myriad guests who had stayed upstairs with us, and into the rest of the guest rooms and finally into the Solarium—its personality all stripped away and looking cold and clinical now, and what a gay, happy room it had been—the citadel of the young.

Finished, I went back down to my room and put on my peach-pink dress and went down to the Red Room. The floor was alive with butlers and cleaning people and there was a strong smell of ammonia in the air. What a surprising household smell for this place. John assured me that it would be gone in thirty minutes and the fires would be lighted and we would have some sweet rolls with coffee for the new family that will gather here before we ride to the Capitol for the Inauguration.

A couple of times I went into Lyndon's room. He had been on the phone constantly since 7 A.M., talking with aides, dictating, dispatching Jim or Larry for some last thing to be done. Once he showed me a couple of sheets of paper—citations for Mary Lasker and Laurance Rockefeller. He was giving them the Medal of Freedom and these were brief records of their accomplishments for their countrymen. There was a list of about twenty names that we had discussed over a period of months. I was glad he was doing it.

After a while it was time to put on my elegant mink hat—what an indulgence . . . how often will I wear it at Stonewall?—take up my muff, tell Lyndon I was ready and to come as soon as he could, and go down to the Red Room.

For me, in any time of crisis all the real emotions—the leave-takings or whatever-it-is—have already been lived through in a previous, quieter time. By now I was sort of anesthetized—in armor—and still I had the feeling of "going to the Fair" and wanting to absorb and take in everything, remember it, but not feel it.

The day blurs into a montage and I am not sure of sequence. I think Leonard Marks was there all the time and I believe Hubert and Muriel were the first to come. And then, as it so often had happened, we received the message, "They're two minutes away," and Lyndon and I walked out on the North Portico, lined heavily on both sides with cameramen. On the left was an incredible sight! Mr. Traphes Bryant, at his feet a bouncing Yuki, freshly washed and wearing a bright coat that Mrs. Bryant had made for him, and the dogs of the new family—a gray poodle, clipped and brushed and proud, and tucked into Mr. Bryant's coat a miniature of a dog, breed unknown, surveying the scene with bright, alert eyes. Until the human members of this drama arrived, these characters had been willingly filling in for the cameramen!

The big black car rolled up and out stepped the President-elect, growing momentarily more impressive, somehow, and then Pat in a smashing rosy-red outfit, belted, with lapels and a fur hat. Tricia was wearing a powder blue coat with touches of fur. She's tiny and very feminine. And there was Julie, taller, darker, and more vivacious, with David, lanky and smiling that famous Eisenhower smile.

We stopped on the Portico for pictures and then the funny business that so often happens about who should go in the door first happened, until

I took Pat's arm firmly and said, "Shall we go in?" Then we were all in the Red Room, the crowd enlarging to include Senator Dirksen, Speaker McCormack, the Vice President-elect and Mrs. Spiro Agnew and their son, who had been in Vietnam, along with his wife, the Agnews' two daughters, Senator Mansfield, Gerald Ford, Senator Jordan, and Carl Albert, and Lynda and Luci who gravitated at once to the young Nixons. I noticed Luci and Tricia in animated conversation in a corner and Lynda asking David if he really did leave all those notes under the rugs. I was asking John Marriott, the Inauguration Chairman, how he was managing with his thousands of friends who must suddenly have come from the far reaches of the United States, demanding a suite with a large living room.

I remember Leonard Marks saying, "It's time to get into the cars." And Pat and I and Speaker McCormack went out together and took our places in a car. Lyndon and Mr. Nixon were in the lead car and in between were the Secret Service and somewhere behind Lynda and Luci and Leonard.

While everybody was getting in, I looked up at the facade of the White House and there, glued to one of the windows, were the faces of John Fickland and Jerman, and another butler—was it Johnny? . . . And on the steps smiling and blowing kisses were many members of our staff. That was my last view as I drove away from the White House.

We started the parade down Pennsylvania Avenue. It was strange— there were very few people—a little knot here, a small group there. I waved busily and tried to lock eyes whenever I saw an animated face, but mostly they just stood. I did not see a familiar face the whole length of Pennsylvania Avenue. But there was considerable bunting and lots of banners.

Our conversation was desultory and trivial—we were glad it wasn't sleet-ing—we might even avoid rain although it was a gray brooding day—but it was cold. I said I felt sure that the stands were going to be full by the time they rode back. I felt vaguely sorry that they weren't. Every now and then a booming remark of substance emanated from the Speaker, all the more surprising coming from that gaunt, frail man. We saw a few children with flags and he said, from deep within the well of his thoughts, "I like to see them with flags," and we both looked at the Capitol, he and I. I talked about how, driving in from Virginia on summer afternoons with the other Speaker, Mr. Sam Rayburn, he used to say, "How do you like my Capitol?" And we all said together something like, "We *all* feel that it's ours!"

Then as we drove up under the portico at that great old building we were met and escorted, with minimum confusion, to the office of Senator Margaret Chase Smith. There was Mrs. Eisenhower in a dark dress with an off-the-face hat, as poised and friendly and lively as she has been in all the more vigorous years I have known her. I was glad to see her and I had one brief minute with her to tell her how much I had always appreciated her coming to the Senate Ladies Luncheons in my time in the White House. She in turn recalled how nice it had been that Mrs. Woodrow Wilson had come to these functions in her day.

Lyndon and Mr. Nixon went to an adjoining office. Presently the orchestrator of all this drama gave us a signal, and together Muriel and I walked out the door and down the great steps of the Capitol under the commanding, handsome, newly built portico—face to face with the great sea of faces that stretched off to the right to the House Office Buildings and to the left to the Senate Office Building and in front of us to the Supreme Court. We went in side by side, and it gave me a warm pleasure that we walked together. Later Muriel said the same. We took our seats in the front row and then turned our heads to watch the next entrance onto the stage of this great quadrennial American pageant. Try as I did to soak everything up, I cannot remember for sure but I think that when Lyndon walked in, they played "Hail to the Chief." And this time truly the last time. He looked very tall and handsome and impressive, and very relaxed too, I thought. Mrs. Nixon came in alone—her bright rose-red dress a dramatic success. And finally, the country's new President.

For all the preparation that had gone into it, it was a brief ceremony—only about forty-five minutes, I believe. And how to describe it? It was low-keyed, restrained, grave, it seemed to me. Perhaps the times set the mood. None of the youthful ebullience, the poetic brilliance of the Kennedy Inauguration, nor the robust, roaring Jacksonian quality of ours.

Bits and pieces stand out—a special smile between me and Mrs. Warren . . . among the five prayers, one by the head of the Greek Orthodox Church who had been my companion on our trip to the funeral of the King of Greece, along with President Truman . . . looking out into the sea of faces and finding so few familiar ones—Allen Drury, I did see—and the personal warm smiles from some of the newspaperwomen down front—Wauhilla La Hay, Betty Beale . . . a murmured remark now and then to Mrs. Agnew who was on my left—something like, "There's going to be so much that you'll enjoy," or "We wish you good luck in all the years ahead." And always, towering in front of us, the camera stand—it seems to get bigger every four years—the great eye of television trained down on us. I remember with corresponding appreciation and dismay that when there was a prayer, or the orchestra broke forth in the "Star-Spangled Banner," in one of the booths one of the commentators rose to his feet, unself-conscious, natural, and in the other booths the commentators sat sprawled around their tables. Perhaps handling their electronic gear required this.

And finally, finally, the Inaugural speech itself. The papers said it was seventeen minutes long and President Nixon delivered it rather quickly, in an even voice. There were no high trumpet calls to action, and probably that is just as well. God knows there's been plenty of striving in the last five, actually the last eight, years. Maybe the country is tired of striving—maybe we just want to hold still—absorb the deluges of change for a while. The address was interrupted by applause from time to time, but there was no great surge of emotion that swept the sea of people in front of us.

Well before one o'clock, President Nixon had finished and we all rose to take our departure. I said good-by to Muriel and to Tricia, in case I did not really get to make a formal good-by to Pat or the new President. As it happened, I didn't.

Then I was swallowed up in the great departing throng going up the stairs, trying to take in every face that I saw, so many of them unfamiliar. The Cabinet was behind President Nixon and over beyond, off the stand, a group of Senators, and then up the stairs on one side the Diplomatic Corps—I gave a last big smile to Sevilla-Sacasa.

Then we were in the big black car—Lyndon and I, and Lynda and Luci—driving with a motorcycle escort away from the Capitol and down the streets, now more filled with people, on toward the Cliffords'. Clark and Marny—foreseeing the situation of an outgoing President—had arranged a farewell luncheon before we left for Texas.

I was prepared for some press coverage outside their house, but not for what we found. It looked as if we had moved backward in time to some particularly homey campaign rally! The Cliffords' quiet front lawn, secluded from the highway by a hedge, was jam-packed with people—little boys up the apple trees, babies in arms, high school and college youngsters carrying signs—"WE'LL NEVER FORGET YOU, LBJ," "YOU DID A GOOD JOB," "WE STILL LOVE YOU, LYNDON," "LBJ, YOU WERE GOOD FOR THE U.S.A." Somebody had a Texas flag and there was a great big U.S. flag waving precariously in front of us across the sidewalk. Marny, without a coat, and Clark were standing at the end of the sidewalk to greet us. We made our way up the sidewalk shaking hands, trying to think of a courteous brief phrase for the microphones that were stuck in front of us, and finally pausing on the front stoop for a picture with the Cliffords. We lost Luci in the crowd, because, of course, her Secret Service agents had departed at the stroke of 12, but I really think she was reveling in it, rather than having difficulty.

Inside that warm and welcoming house there awaited us one of the most significant and dear parties we shall ever attend. Most of Lyndon's Cabinet were there. There were the Rusks and the Fowlers and the Freemans and the Alan Boyds and C. R. Smith and the Marvin Watsons, and from Lyndon's staff, Walt Rostow and the George Christians, and from mine, Liz and Bess and their husbands. Hubert and Muriel, of course, and from the House, the Hale Boggses, and Jake and Beryl Pickle; in all about sixty people. There were four Senators there—the Mike Monroneys and the Birch Bayhs, and the Scoop Jacksons and the Gale McGees. Out-of-towners Arthur Krim, and Jane and Charles Engelhard, who were asking about our plans to come to Florida. The Bill Whites, and from the Court, Abe and Carol Fortas. And from elsewhere in the government, the Leonard Markses, the Bill Deasons, and Averell Harriman.

Only one thing marred my sheer delight in the occasion and that was that we had to leave not later than 3 to get to Austin before the Inaugural proceedings there got under way. We did not want to conflict with our own State of Texas Inaugural, so time was our tyrant. One of the blessings of the future may be that this tyrant will fade into the wings!

I remember vignettes. There, right outside the open window, not eight feet away, was the whole yard full of people, the little boys up the apple trees, and a young man with a sign that said, "LBJ IN '72." I smiled and waved and then he turned it around and it said, "LYN IN 2004."

There was a moment when I received an imperious request to come upstairs at once. We converged on Clark and Marny's bedroom, along with Averell Harriman and Bill White and Lyndon. And Lyndon told us that early this morning he had conferred the Medal of Freedom on Clark and Averell and Bill White and seventeen others. He read Clark's citation and Harriman's and gave them to them. Bill's would be sent to him later. I think I saw tears in Marny's eyes. What Lyndon said was a personal, intimate talk in a low voice, very earnest, no speech at all. Bill White responded and this tough and seasoned man seemed close to tears. He described his feeling for Lyndon briefly, just about four words—one of them was "gallant."

The hands of the clock prodded us on. I went down and led the group in loading plates at the sumptuous luncheon table. Emotion and times of great significance do not spoil my appetite—they seem to fuel it. I divided my precious moments between food and the guests, every one of whom meant so much to me. Lucinda made an appearance now and then, regarding us all with solemn big eyes and occasionally a toothless granny grin. Patrick Lyndon, as usual, was weaving among legs while Luci or I retrieved Marny's treasures from the low tables at his approach.

And then, too soon, I got the signal: "Time to go!" I hugged Marny and Clark, not expecting to see them again, although they insisted they were going to race us to Andrews Air Force Base. We stopped on the porch briefly and Lyndon said a few words into Ray Scherer's microphone—how he had been a part of Washington for more than thirty years and loved it and he would come back to visit. And to waves and handshakes and calls of "God bless you, Mr. President," "We'll miss you, Lyndon," we made our way to the car and headed for the helicopter on the grounds of the Bethesda Naval Center. Only en route did I remember that I had left behind my elegant fur muff and my brand new gloves!

There was a small crowd at the helicopter pad. We flew in silence over Washington and landed at Andrews. And there was a big crowd, lining the fence and drawn up around *Air Force One*. Lyndon strode past the lined-up military and began to shake hands at the fence. The band played "Ruffles and Flourishes," and "Auld Lang Syne," and "Yellow Rose of Texas." And there was a salute of guns, I think twenty-one, but anyway, it was total confusion, and dear, and wonderful. Luci was crying—more from the impact of the day than sadness, and saying of Lyn, "He's just lost twenty-one of his best friends," meaning the Secret Service.

In the crowd I glimpsed many familiar and beloved faces. And to my amazement standing at the foot of the steps were none other than Clark and Marny and Dean and Virginia! They had, indeed, raced us and beaten us there, along with a group of the luncheon guests. We mounted the steps of *Air Force One*, Lyndon carrying his faithful companion, Lyn. We stopped at the top, the family, and turned and waved in a good-by tableau, I searching for the eyes of the most dear and most familiar—and there close to the foot of the steps stood Liz with a sign that was an invitation to laughter: "CULPEPER SAYS THANK YOU, MR. PRESIDENT." Shades of 1960! The door closed, the motors revved, and we were airborne in the plane.

It was a quiet flight down. One of the first things I saw in the plane was a big bunch of yellow roses with a card from the Nixons. What a thoughtful thing to do! And I saluted their efficiency, too, knowing something of the demands on them and their staff today.

About 5:30 we arrived at Bergstrom. Here five thousand people were packed along the fence—and a receiving party stood at the foot of the steps of the plane. Lieutenant Governor Ben Barnes in his dinner jacket, only moments away from one of his own Inaugural parties . . . Eloise and Homer, Chancellor Ransom and Hazel, Mayor Akin and his wife, who presented me with a beautiful bouquet of the first flowers of spring—iris, tulips, narcissus, violets—and Carolyn Curtis with both her children and the Deathes. The Longhorn Band was there in bright orange and they played "Ruffles and Flourishes," and then "The Eyes of Texas." There was a big sign above the Base Operations that said: "WELCOME HOME, MR. PRESIDENT AND FAMILY." Lyndon made a brief speech ending with the hope that the country would be understanding with Nixon. And at the very last, "Whether we are Democrats or Republicans, Texans or New Yorkers, we love our country, or we ought to love it."

And then once more, he took to the fence, with the wind blowing him in the face, grabbing for hands with both of his, and finally picking up Lyn and taking him along the fence while Lynda with Lucinda in her arms and I followed, smiling and waving.

With a last good-by to an airport fence and also good-by to Luci and Lyn who were going to their own house, Lyndon and Lynda and Lucinda and I got on the *Jetstar* and headed for the Ranch. I looked over my shoulder and there was a silver crescent of a new moon, bright and clear and full of promise.

But there was still one more reception committee. We got to the Ranch just as dark was falling. There around the hangar were about five hundred local folks, some who had known Lyndon all his life and his father before him. Lyndon invited everybody into the hangar and made them a rather long and glowing talk about how glad he was to be home.

We went into the house then. The fire was burning on the raised hearth in the living room, flickering on the familiar pictures and old books and the big comfortable chairs.

The luggage was piled up out by the kitchen door—a mountain. It would be some time before we got to the bottom of that stack. After a while Lynda went out to dig around in it, looking for something she needed for the baby. She came back in, lugging two suitcases, looking a little harassed and deserted. I smiled at her.

A little past 9 I went to bed, with a line of poetry reeling through my mind. I think it's from *India's Love Lyrics*. "I seek, to celebrate my glad release, the Tents of Silence and the Camp of Peace." And yet it's not quite the right exit line for me because I have loved almost every day of these five years.

Index of Proper Names

Abel, I. W., 315, 316
Abell, Elizabeth C. (Bess), 14, 15, 21, 31,
   53, 55, 59, 68, 105, 130, 140, 167, 194,
   214, 224, 256, 258, 259, 280, 287, 289,
   324, 355, 392, 395, 399, 407, 426, 455,
   461, 487, 506, 535, 559, 570, 599, 601,
   615, 627, 630, 655, 662, 687, 705, 724,
   748, 765, 770, 773, 774, 780
Abell, Tyler, 205, 568
Abidia, Fathi, 69
Abrams, Creighton, 371, 728–29, 730
Acheson, Mrs. David, 239, 389
Acheson, Dean, 144, 671
Ackeley, Gardner and Mrs., 472, 478
Adams, Brooks, 522, 524
Adams, Charles Francis, 135, 522–23, 524,
   525
Adams, Eva, 17
Adams, Henry, 525
Adams, John and Abigail, 36, 132, 134,
   151, 152, 153, 522, 523, 524, 525
Adams, John Quincy and Mrs., 151, 177,
   522, 523, 524, 670
Adams, Thomas Boylston, 151, 153

Addams, Jane, 95
Addonizio, Hugh, 309
Adenauer, Konrad, 23, 508, 510
Adler, Leopold, 722
Adler, Richard, 44, 47, 223
Aeschbacher, William, 314
Agnew, Spiro and Mrs., 702–03, 777, 778
Agong, King Yang di-Pertuan, 442, 444
Ah Cheu, 102
Ahmad, Bashir, 151
Ahmed, Aziz and Begum, 336–37
Aiken, George D., 49, 413
Aikman, Lonnelle, 417–18
Akin, Harry, 556, 782
Alam, Mr., 155
Albee, Edward, 461, 510
Albert, Carl B., 17, 75, 230, 258, 260,
   295, 368, 418, 454, 481, 595, 777
Aldana, Juan, 209
Aldrin, Edwin (Buzz), 250, 643–44, 645,
   750
Alexander, Becky, 20
Alexander, Birge, 20, 333, 760
Alexander, Lucia, 20, 333, 760

Bhutto, Zulfikar, 336, 337, 338–39
Biddle, Francis, 485
Biddle, James, 135, 722
Biemiller, Andrew J., 32
Biglane, D. A., 701, 702
Billings, Frederick, 530
Bingham, Barry, 114
Bippus, Mrs. Alvin, 373
Birdwell, Sherman, 194
Black, Hugo, Jr., 513
Black, Hugo L. and Elizabeth, 513–14
Black, Josephine, 513
Black, Sterling, 513
Blair, William, 299
Blake, Eugene Carson, 252
Bliss, Anthony, 56
Blough, Roger, 33, 127
Bobbitt, Rebecca, 20
Boehm, Edward Marshall, 595
Boggs, Hale and Lindy, 17, 96, 173, 174,
    196, 215, 230, 288, 361, 368, 408, 473,
    597, 598, 699, 780
Bonilla, José A., 69
Boozer, Yolanda, 404
Borman, Frank, 483, 749
Bortman, Mark and Mrs., 151, 152
Boudin, Stephane, 54
Bourdon, Curtis, 530
Bourguiba, Habib Ben Ali, 670, 671–72
Bourguiba, Habib, Jr., 670, 671–72
Boutin, Bernie, 241
Bowen, Catherine Drinker, 152, 287
Boyd, Alan, 474, 748, 780
Boyd, Forrest, 333
Boyd, Julian, 135
Brademas, John, 62, 82, 94
Bradley, Omar N., 124, 145
Braganza, Duke de, 88
Branigin, Roger, 396, 397
Brawley, William, 194
Breathitt, Edward and Mrs., 54, 118, 122,
    141, 144, 397, 717
Brennan, Walter, 367
Brennan, William Joseph, Jr., 149
Brewster, Mrs. Herbert, 85
Brewster, Kingman, Jr., 579, 580, 581
Brinkley, David, 116
Brooke, Edward W., 472
Brooks, Jack S., 4, 17, 247, 584
Brooks, R. Max and Marietta, 312, 313,
    314, 550, 760
Brown, Mrs. Archibald, 278–79
Brown, J. Carter, 370
Brown, George and Alice, 133, 137, 153,
    646, 751, 755
Brown, Lillian, 283

Brown, Edmund G. (Pat) and Bernice,
    190, 305, 423, 424, 425, 426, 624
Brown, Winthrop, 446
Brubeck, Dave, 111, 739
Bruce, David and Evangeline, 327
Bruce, Mrs. Mellon, 370
Bruce, Preston, 404
Brucker, Herbert, 114
Bruno, Joseph, 392
Bryant, Anita, 640
Bryant, Farris and Mrs., 68, 197
Bryant, Traphes L., 405, 603, 776
Bryce, Lord, 241
Buchwald, Art, 318
Buckley, Betty Ann, 503
Bullock, Hugh, 575
Bulow, Mrs. William, 131
Bunche, Ralph, 190
Bundy, McGeorge (Mac) and Mary, 21,
    44, 47, 157, 160, 167, 187, 188, 191,
    192, 220, 241, 261, 286, 304, 361, 362,
    458, 534, 542
Bunker, Carol Laise, 661
Bunker, Ellsworth, 154, 428, 501, 661,
    730
Bunshaft, Gordon, 550
Buntin, Mrs. Horatio, 500
Bunting, Mary, 159, 160
Bunton, Phil and Hazel, 207, 209
Bunton, Phoebe Ann Desha, 116
Burden, William, 146, 147, 148
Burg, Mrs. Frederick, 535, 566
Burgess, Elizabeth, 502
Burke, Mrs. Edward, 131
Burkley, George, 138, 317, 324, 405, 436,
    464
Burleson, Ruth, 128
Burnett, Carol, 223
Burns, Jack and Mrs., 505
Burns, James MacGregor, 577
Burns, Hayden, 197
Burris, Howard, 228, 229, 288
Burton, Mrs. Harold H., 677
Busby, Horace (Buzz) and Mary V., 230,
    243, 252, 367, 503, 550
Busch, Gussie, 127
Bush, Dorothy Vredenburgh, 130
Butler, Nellie, 31
Butterfield, Lyman, 135, 152
Butterfield, Victor L., 475
Butterworth, W. Walton, 58
Bybee, Faith, 546, 547, 723
Byrd, Gretchen, 195, 478
Byrd, Harry F., 35, 75, 145, 253
Byrd, Richard, Jr., 721
Byrd, Richard and Helen, 129, 195

Ford, Gerald, 17, 214, 777
Ford, Charlotte, 154, 171, 602
Ford, Henry, II and Christina, 127, 602, 764, 773
Ford, O'Neil, 738
Ford, Wendell, 716
Fore, Sam, 259
Foroughi, Mrs., 155
Fortas, Abe and Carol, 56, 148, 205, 275, 299–300, 304, 486, 518–19, 549, 594, 627, 689, 692, 702, 712–13, 714, 736, 739, 748, 780
Fosburgh, James, 55, 56, 61, 79, 134, 137, 240, 256, 512
Fosdick, Harry Emerson, 459
Foster, William C., 481, 692
Fowler, Henry H. (Joe) and Trudye, 108, 109, 311, 362, 454, 669, 698, 699, 758, 780
Fox, Robert, 405, 433
Fox, Sandy, 463, 749, 757
Frankel, Max, 507
Franklin, Benjamin, 46
Franklin, John Hope, 739
Frantz, Joseph, 379, 655, 658, 739
Frear, Esther, 131
Frederick IX, King, 90
Frederika, Queen, 61–63, 88, 89, 90, 93, 94
Freedman, Max, 153, 264
Freeman, Connie, 704
Freeman, Mrs. Fulton, 586
Freeman, Orville L. and Jane, 21, 22, 70, 109, 110, 111, 170, 197, 207, 208, 234, 241, 350, 355, 371, 510, 568, 665, 689, 690, 704, 709, 758, 762, 780
Freylinghuysen, Peter, 62
Fritchey, Clayton, 357
Frosch, Aaron, 284
Frost, Robert, 154
Fry, Elizabeth, 278, 389
Frye, Kimberly, 247
Fugazzi, Fred, 141
Fulbright, J. William and Betty, 50, 52, 62, 162, 185, 190, 191, 244, 260–61, 298, 360, 368, 472, 541, 556, 630, 747
Funston, Keith, 459
Furman, Bess, 486
Furness, Betty, 693

Galbraith, John Kenneth and Kitty, 148, 158, 160, 178, 235, 349
Gandhi, Indira, 125, 374–75
Gardner, John W. and Aida, 305, 326, 493, 496, 498, 503, 586, 625, 663, 758
Garza, Nick, 305

Gautier, Felisa de, 130
Gerstenfeld, Norman, 224
Getz, Stan, 442
Gfeller, Miss Mary, 550
Gibson, Gerald, 135
Gibson, Gwen, 36
Gilbert, Mrs. Carl, 158, 159
Gilstrap, Sam, 311
Girard, Alexander, 737
Glackens, Ira, 753
Glaser, Vera, 169
Glynn, Paul, 252
Godfrey, Arthur, 715
Goldberg, Arthur and Dorothy, 14, 170, 200, 299, 305, 322, 323–24, 328, 337, 338, 347, 463, 481, 482, 513, 663, 684, 693
Goldman, Eric, 151, 242, 267, 387
Goldner, Herman, 479
Goldschmidt, Arthur E. (Tex), 486
Goldstein, Ernie, 739
Goldwater, Barry M., 84, 167, 178, 183–84
Gonella, Ashton G., 31, 214, 232, 279, 289, 332, 389, 392, 453, 454, 521, 559, 607, 615, 634, 636, 652, 688, 709, 714, 720, 735, 774, 775
Gonzales, Henry B., 464, 613
Goodenough, James, 282, 283
Goodpaster, Andrew, 371
Gordon, John, 55
Gordon, Kermit, 27, 32, 33, 51, 214, 355
Gordon, Mrs. Milton, 516
Gordon, Richard, 481
Gould, Dr., 231
Govatos, John, 63
Grace, Princess, 685
Graham, Billy and Ruth, 67–68, 191, 229, 300–01, 303–04, 498, 685, 733, 771
Graham, Frank, 40
Graham, John, 135
Graham, Martha, 721, 739
Graham, Phil and Kay, 153, 205
Graham, Richard, 494
Grant, Julia, 456
Grant, Ulysses S., III, 242
Gray, Gordon, 722
Green, Charles, 112
Green, William, 19
Greene, Wallace, 601
Greenewalt, Crawford, 127
Griffin, Isabel, 36
Griffin, James, 349
Griffin, Robert, 477
Griffith, Mary, 3

Hoffman, Paul and Anna, 105, 299, 323, 489
Hofheinze, Roy, Jr., and Mrs., 561
Hogg, Ima, 546–47
Hogg, James, 546
Holder, Geoffrey, 739
Holifield, Mrs. Chet, 269
Holland, Spessard, 196
Hollings, Ernest, 477
Holmes, Julius, 561
Holmes, Mrs. Oliver Wendell, 159
Holt, Harold and Mrs., 393, 431, 432, 433, 434, 605, 606, 630
Holyoake, Keith and Mrs., 430–31, 434, 435, 719, 720–21
Homans, Abigail Adams, 524, 525
Hooten, William, 112
Hoover, J. Edgar, 111, 227, 252, 253, 687
Hoover, Herbert C., 182, 311
Horgan, Paul, 242
Horner, Jack, 333, 475
Hornig, Donald, 391–92, 481
Horsky, Charles, 240
Hotchner, A. E., 132
Houghton, Arthur, 357
Houston, Sam, 181
Howar, Bader, 407
Howard, Mrs. Howell, 340
Howard, Mike, 727
Howard, Rhea, 112
Howe, Charles M., 301
Howell, Trevor Louise, 144
Howie, Elizabeth, 513
Hruska, Roman L., 60
Hudson, Alex, III, 464
Hudspeth, Mrs., Frances, 600, 602
Huffman, Ruth Ament, 600
Hughes, Richard and Betty, 309, 311, 504, 534, 535, 537, 538, 539, 540, 541, 623
Hughes, Sarah T., 5, 222
Hume, Paul, 47
Humelsine, Carlisle, 589, 723
Humphrey, Hubert H. and Muriel, 52, 174, 178, 184, 193, 197, 215, 217, 223, 225, 226, 230, 231, 240, 256, 288, 291, 337, 341, 347, 355, 368, 370, 376, 454, 455, 460, 463, 470, 474, 475, 477, 483, 507, 508, 512, 513, 514, 568, 586, 593, 601, 625, 626, 638, 640, 641, 643, 656, 668, 685, 700–01, 705, 706, 713, 716, 717, 718, 732, 747, 748, 749, 751, 758, 762, 778, 779, 780
Humphrey, Walter, 112
Hunter, Jessie, 209, 316, 563, 590, 614

Hurd, Peter and Henriette, 273, 274, 330, 331–32, 469–70
Hurst, Willis, 138, 140, 191, 317, 319, 325, 362, 455, 573–74
Hussein, King, 109, 110–11
Hutchinson, Everett, 216
Hutton, Mrs. Edward, 251

Iakovos, Archbishop, 82, 94, 226
Ickes, Jane, 486
Ikard, Frank, 367
Ingrid, Queen, 88
Inonu, Ismet, 168
Irene, Princess, 61, 62, 89
Irving, Washington, 673
Ives, Mrs. Ernest R., 299
Izzard, Wesley, 112

Jackson, Andrew, 177, 181, 190, 500
Jackson, Henry (Scoop) and Mrs., 676, 780
Jackson, Robert, 112, 654
Jacobs, Jane, 169
Jacobsen, Jake, 351, 367, 369, 464, 493
Jacqueline, Sister, 305
Javits, Jacob K., 323
Jean, Grand-Duke, 87
Jean Louis, 400, 410, 460, 598
Jeffers, Robinson, 425
Jefferson, Thomas, 46, 170, 176, 181, 271, 364, 524
Jenkins, Beth, 37, 137, 280, 282, 285, 294, 405
Jenkins, Lyndon, 723–24
Jenkins, Walter W. and Marjorie, 16, 62, 74, 79, 158, 177, 204
Jennings, Pat, 272
Jensen, Oliver, 242
Jetton, Walter, 22
Jewell, Ingrid, 38
Joel, Lawrence, 618
John XXIII, Pope, 406
Johns, Lem, 4
Johnson, Luci Baines (Mrs. Patrick J. Nugent), 8, 10, 14, 15, 16, 18, 20, 32, 34, 35, 37–38, 44, 50, 51, 52, 54, 64, 68, 74, 76, 95, 107, 108, 113, 125–26, 129, 137, 139, 140, 146, 154, 161, 173, 174, 178, 184, 186, 192, 194, 197, 203, 205, 214, 217, 218, 222, 224, 225, 229, 232–33, 239, 244, 256, 260, 274, 276, 277–78, 279–80, 282–83, 285–86, 292, 293–94, 297, 298, 299, 300, 302, 305, 306, 321, 327–28, 329, 331, 333, 337, 338, 347, 348, 351, 354, 356, 359, 362, 375, 388, 389,

Mattingly, Thomas, 671
Mauldin, William, 325
Mauntel, Mrs. Fred, 318, 319, 320
Maury, Mrs. John M., 85
Max, Prince, 88
Mayborn, Frank, 112
Mazzei, Philip, 46
McAllister, Canon Gerald, 599, 600, 613
McAllister, Mayor Walter W., 613
McCabe, Thomas, 127
McCammon, Vicki, 175, 247, 404
McCardle, Dorothy, 36, 468, 369, 384, 463, 533
McCarthy, Eugene J. and Abigail, 50, 131, 185, 193, 260, 646, 680, 684, 701, 705, 706, 713, 721
McClellan, John and Norma, 253, 352, 474, 569, 624
McClendon, Sarah, 36
McCollum, Leonard F., 33, 569
McConaughy, Walter, 337
McCone, John, 51
McConnell, John P., 481, 483
McCormack, Edward, 473
McCormack, Harriet, 625, 627
McCormack, John W. and Mrs., 9, 34, 35, 75, 216, 225, 230, 323, 368, 389, 396, 473, 475, 476, 625, 626, 627, 777
McCrummen, Thomas, 737
McDade, Joe, 38
McDivitt, James and Pat., 288–92, 483, 750
McDivitt, Mike and Ann, 288
McDonald, David, 32, 119, 120
McDonnell, James S., 750
McElroy, Isaac Stuart, 403
McElroy, Neil, 33
McGee, Dean, 25
McGee, Gale and Loraine, 59, 507, 569, 676, 780
McGhee, George, 21, 114, 264, 601
McGill, Ralph E., 691
McGinley, Phyllis, 287
McGovern, George S. and Mrs., 701, 705, 706
McGowan, Carl, 298
McGregor, Louis, 349
McGrory, Mary, 133, 243, 287, 767
McGuirk, Patty, 217
McIntyre, Elizabeth Ann, 522
McIntyre, James, 522
McIntyre, Thomas, 507
McKeithen, Fox, 197
McKeithen, John J., 197
McKelvie, Allan, 111

McKelvie, Jill, 602
McKinney, Jerry, 766
McKinstry, Bishop, 670–71
McLendon, Winzola, 363
McMahon, O'Brien, 677
McMillan, William, 500
McNair, Mrs. Robert, 505
McNamara, Craig, 41
McNamara, Robert S. and Marjorie, 32, 33, 41–42, 44, 51, 66, 70, 104, 114, 167, 170, 184, 187, 190, 192, 197, 198, 214, 228, 234, 240, 244, 260, 264–65, 286, 394, 463, 465, 478, 519, 591–93, 597, 662, 663, 695, 757–58, 759
McNary, Mrs. Charles, 131
McNatt, Judge, 333
McNaughton, Andrew, 221
McNeel, Jess, 340
McNeil, Brownie, 380, 655
McPherson, Courtenay (Coco), 360, 361
McPherson, Harry C., Jr., and Clay, 361, 606, 682, 723, 774
Means, Marianne, 36
Meany, George, 32, 47, 475, 627
Melchior, Mathias, 546
Mellon, Andrew W., 97, 276, 374
Mellon, Mrs. Paul, 97, 98, 127, 137, 190, 373–74, 686
Meloy, Frank, 44
Menzies, Sir Robert and Dame Patty, 570–71
Merrick, David, 474, 475, 489, 739
Merrill, Robert, 44, 47, 342, 629, 631, 738
Messina, Mrs. Milton, 353
Mesta, Perle, 47, 57, 389, 693
Meusebach, Baron von, 24–25
Meyer, André, 635, 764
Michael, Prince, 84, 88
Middleton, Harry, 724
Mielziner, Jo, 285, 739
Miller, Arthur, 56–57
Miller, Dale and Virginia (Scooter), 47, 96, 194, 197, 205, 228, 229, 288, 735, 736
Miller, Emma Guffey, 486
Miller, William M. (Fishbait), 215, 252, 618, 746, 766, 767
Miller, George, 740
Miller, Hope Ridings, 36
Miller, Irwin, 720
Miller, Mrs. Lawrence, 579
Miller, Thomas, 27, 416
Miller, Thomas, Jr., 340
Miller, Uri, 252
Milligan, Norma, 363

Thomas, Helen, 15, 36, 111, 122, 167, 308, 361, 363, 400, 406, 454, 455, 465, 487, 590, 767
Thomas, Jean, 100
Thomas, Lucille Pattillo, 100
Thompson, Llewellyn E., 428, 536
Thompson, Philip, 532
Thornberry, Eloise, 25, 334
Thornberry, Homer, 4, 8, 17, 231, 257, 294, 295, 334, 689, 692
Thornberry, Mollie, 548
Thunberg, Penelope Harland, 296
Thurmond, Strom, 66, 195, 215, 368
Tillett, Gladys, 486
Tobey, Mrs. Charles, 110, 131, 668, 677
Tobriner, Walter, 240
Todd, Paul, 420
Tombalbaye, François, 714, 715
Touhy, Walter, 128
Tower, John, 215, 556
Travell, Janet, 138
Tree, Marietta, 57, 298, 489
Treyz, Clara, 58
Trout, Lawana, 162
Trowbridge, Alexander B., Jr., (Sandy) and Nancey, 634, 639, 663
Truman, Harry S, and Mrs., 82–84, 87, 88, 90, 91, 92, 93, 94, 95, 98, 123, 124, 180–83, 189, 248, 312–14, 389, 403, 485, 518
Tucker, Richard, 739
Tuckerman, Nancy, 73
Tully, Grace, 485
Turman, Solon, 33
Turner, Marie, 141, 143, 169
Tydings, Mrs. Millard, 131
Tyler, John, 83–84
Tyler, Veronica, 422, 631

Udall, Stewart L. and Lee, 107, 161, 166, 197, 217, 234, 238, 240, 242, 249, 325, 350, 379, 381–82, 424, 426, 427, 523, 528, 529, 530, 596, 649, 653, 657, 660, 736, 758, 772
Umberto, King, 88
Uris, Leon, 719–20
Urquhart, Jennifer, 602

Valenta, Marcus Anthony, 544–45
Valenti, Courtney, 519
Valenti, Jack J. and Mary Margaret, 77, 112, 125, 128, 130, 177, 188, 205, 226, 230, 231, 247, 252, 254, 305, 324, 351, 369, 493, 519, 580, 606, 640
Van Buren, Martin, 152, 248
Van D'Elden, Stephanie Cain, 222

Vanderbilt, Jeanne, 357
Van den Heuvel, Gerry, 287
Vandiver, Frank, 242
Van Doren, Mark, 242
Van Fleet, James, 94
Vance, Cyrus, 42, 549, 702
Van Roijen, Madame, 69
Van Tassel, Mr., 363
Vaughan, Harry, 82, 83, 94
Verdun, René, 11, 48
Vickland, Art, 289
Victor, Sally, 487
Victoria, Queen, 91, 523
Vinson, Fred and Roberta, 34, 121, 313
Vinson, Fred, Jr., 513
Volpe, John, 522
Von Braun, Wernher, 25, 98, 99, 100, 101
Voss, Susan, 711
Vreeland, Diana, 357

Waffen, Joyce, 247
Wagner, Duncan, 186
Wagner, Gerald, 284
Wagner, Robert F., 57, 186–87, 322, 323
Wagner, Robert F., Jr., 154, 186
Walker, John, 53, 78, 164, 239, 266, 370, 372, 374, 511, 512, 615, 636, 752, 753
Walker, Sarabeth, 618
Wall, Charles, 722
Wallace, George C. and Mrs., 197, 363, 365, 505, 656
Wallace, Mrs. Henry, 485
Waller, Keith and Mrs., 570
Walt, Lewis and Mrs., 601; 711, 726, 727
Walter, Hulda Saenger, 24
Walters, Barbara, 615
Walton, William, 53, 60, 78, 98, 241
Wan, Prince, 438
Warburg, Edward, 357
Ward, Barbara (Lady Jackson), 112–13, 236–37, 338
Warner, Rawleigh, 671
Warren, Earl and Mrs., 9, 46, 61, 69, 110, 162, 170, 226, 232, 473, 476, 513, 594, 601, 624, 625, 626, 778
Warren, Robert Penn, 164
Washington, John, 409
Washington, Walter and Bennetta, 240, 249, 278, 351, 352, 353, 559, 574, 582, 617, 618, 623, 666–67, 721, 755
Watson, Marvin and Marion, 252, 301, 303, 324, 325, 351, 369, 390, 392, 401, 454, 645, 694, 704, 733, 780
Watson, Thomas, 33, 200, 301, 303, 720
Watzek, Peter, 319